WORLD
WAR
TWO

NATION BY NATION

Peter G. Tsouras
24 November 1995
Alexandria, VA
A gift from Anna & Armour

WORLD WAR TWO

NATION BY NATION

J. LEE READY

ARMS AND
ARMOUR

Arms and Armour Press
An Imprint of the Cassell Group
Wellington House, 125 Strand, London WC2R 0BB

Distributed in the USA by Sterling Publishing Co. Inc.,
387 Park Avenue South, New York, NY 10016-8810.

Distributed in Australia by Capricorn Link (Australia) Pty. Ltd,
2/13 Carrington Road, Castle Hill, NSW 2154.

British Library Cataloguing-in-Publication Data:
a catalogue record for this book is available from the British Library

ISBN 1-85409-290-1

Cartography by the author

Printed and bound in Great Britain by
Hartnolls Limited, Bodmin, Cornwall

CONTENTS

HOW TO USE
THIS BOOK

This book covers the war in a unique manner. It respects national integrity as it exists at the time of writing, not at the time of occurrence, e.g. Kenyan soldiers are described as Kenyan, not as British, though they are so called in almost every other history of the war.

Some campaigns that are important to a nation may not be adequately covered in the national chapter, because they are covered in the chapter of the nation where they took place, e.g. the Italian campaign is covered under the chapter titled Italy. The battle of Guadalcanal is under the Solomon Islands – not a battlefield created for the Americans and Japanese by the God of War, but a country in which ordinary people lived and tried to survive during such a calamitous epoch. This is a challenge to historians who have been cemented in racist perceptions, such as those who describe the Battle of Cassino without once mentioning the townsfolk who lived in that city.

Each chapter begins with a list of useful information; names, status, government, population, ethnic make-up, religion, location. Refer to it often.

Each nation, e.g. Poland, has received a chapter, but for logical reasons some chapters narrate the story of a group of nations, whose experience was identical or tied to each other in some way, e.g. British East Africa. Some nations have different names. I have chosen the most common English language version.

The Jews-Gypsies and Russians have a chapter to themselves, because during the conflict they were treated as separate nations by the Germans. Russia has since gained international recognition as such, in any case.

The status is listed simply; thus if I believe a nation to have been under the thumb of another I give a simple description: colony, protected state etc., rather than confuse the reader with such things as semi-autonomous mandates.

Likewise the description of the government is solely my opinion: therefore if I think it was a dictatorship, I say so. Others may have a different opinion.

The population is my estimate. The size of ethnic populations is also my estimate. Groups such as Gypsies and Jews are mentioned if it is relevant to the narration.

The basic religious aspect of the nation is also mentioned as it was relevant to the nature of the conflict.

The location of the nation is given, as it is needed in cases like Tajikistan, less so for the USA, but helpful to young students.

At the end of each chapter will be pointers in other directions, e.g. at the end of Russia is the pointer 'see India'. Please use the index for more in-depth research on the activities of a particular general or politician or army, e.g. the German Army is mentioned in over half of the chapters. Refer to the glossary for explanations of such words as 'hiwis' and 'panzer'.

GLOSSARY

Airborne: a unit that is trained to enter the battlefield from the air via parachute, glider, helicopter, or transport aircraft. Of necessity contains lightly armed infantry.

Armoured: a unit that relies primarily on armoured fighting vehicles for its fighting power.

Armoured fighting vehicles: any vehicle which permanently carries a fixed weapon and armour-plating.

Armoured car: like a tank, but wheeled.

Army: the army = the nation's land forces. An army = two or more corps.

Army Group: two or more armies.

Automatic: firearms that shoot as long as the trigger is held down.

Battalion: about 600 to 1000 troops, unless stated. Part of a regiment or brigade, unless stated.

Battery: four to six artillery guns manned by 100 plus soldiers. Part of a battalion, unless stated.

Battleship: the biggest warship.

Brigade: three or four battalions, unless stated. Part of a division, unless stated.

Cavalry: a unit that relies primarily on horsemen for its fighting power; but mechanised = armour; unhorsed = infantry.

Company: about 100 to 200 troops, unless stated. Part of a battalion, unless stated.

Corps: two or more divisions; several brigades.

Cruiser: warship, next biggest to a battleship.

Destroyer: warship smaller than cruiser.

Division: a composite force of many types of soldiers, circa 10,000 to 15,000, unless stated, normally fronted by infantry.

Engineers: soldiers whose job is to build or destroy, often under fire.

Flak: anti-aircraft guns or automatic weapons.

Guns: artillery

Hiwas: Hilfeswacht-mannschaften: 'Watchman Unit Helpers' volunteers for sentry duty with the German police, raised in the USSR and Poland.

Hiwis: Hilfeswillige: 'Willing Helpers' volunteers for rear-echelon service in German military, paramilitary and police units, whose ethnic make-up originated in Poland and the USSR.

Infantry: a unit that relies primarily on infantry for its fighting power.

Marines: soldiers who permanently provide the navy with a land fighting unit.

Osttruppen: military units of citizens of the USSR used by the Germans.

Panzer: German word meaning armour, as in Panzer Division = Armoured Division.

Panzergrenadier: German

units of infantry heavily armed with automatic weapons, plenty of vehicles and usually self-propelled guns.

Partisans: guerrilla fighters.

Platoon: about 20 to 40 troops, unless stated. Part of a battery/company/squadron unless stated.

Regiment: two or three battalions, unless stated. Part of a division, unless stated.

Schumas: Schutzmann-schaften: 'Guard Man Units' German police battalions raised for anti-terrorist duty, recruited in Germany and throughout Eastern Europe.

Self-propelled guns and assault guns: resembling tanks, i.e. usually tracked rather than wheeled, but belonging to the artillery and used as such.

Squadron, air: ten to twenty aircraft.

Squadron, cavalry: equivalent to a company.

Squadron, tank: approximately sixteen tanks.

SS: Schutzstaffel: 'Guard Unit' A German catch-all organisation which began as Hitler's bodyguard and finished up controlling much of the police state apparatus. Most members belonged to its fighting branch, Waffen (i.e. weapon) SS.

INTRODUCTION

This is not the history of a war. It is the history of many wars, for World War II was a different war to each nation involved.

For the British it began on 3 September 1939 and lasted six years to the day. For the Norwegians it began in April 1940; for the Greeks in October 1940. For the United States it began on 7 December 1941, despite the fact that its armed forces had already been fighting for months. The Albanians claim it began in April 1939; and for the Chinese it began in 1931! To the USSR it began in June 1941, officially that is – the Soviets did not like to be reminded it had begun two years earlier and that they had then been a partner of Nazi Germany.

For the Belgians it ended in May 1945, but for the Dutch not until September. The Yugoslavs did not cease fighting until 1946 and the Ukrainian Army did not give up until 1957! This does not count individuals – one Japanese surrendered in 1974 – and for a child who lost a limb in 1945 the pain of the war might not end until the year 2045.

To the British the war had been so all-encompassing that they have never really been happy since. This may have something to do with the fact that they won. British veterans of defeats such as Dunkirk and Singapore are far more likely to be fêted than veterans of victories such as Imphal and Kohima. There is no doubt the British are embarrassed by victory.

The French are also embarrassed by the war, for they suffered the greatest humiliation – not the defeat in 1940, for that can happen to anyone – but the liberation of 1944. To be liberated by foreigners is the greatest humiliation a Frenchman can suffer.

The Germans are also embarrassed, for on the one hand they are ashamed they lost, and on the other hand 99% of all Germans are extremely glad Hitler and his madmen were destroyed.

The Japanese are also embarrassed, for the defeat was a great loss of face and the destruction of their religion. Hence they like to think that but for the atomic bomb the end would have been different – pure nonsense of course. As a result the Japanese since the war have pursued the exact same goals, but by commercial rather than military means.

For the United States it was really two wars: the 'people's' war in the Pacific; and 'Roosevelt's' war in Europe. Few Americans saw duty in both. For the Finns it was three wars.

For the Australians it was a betrayal, for in 1940 they saw it as their duty as 'Britons' to defend the motherland, an island under blockade and air attack, defenceless to the invader. However, one year later when Australia became an island under blockade and air attack, defenceless to the invader, the British refused to help them. The people of Australia began the war as Britons and finished it as Australians.

The Austrians claim the war was an occupation by despots, but fail to mention some of the despots were Austrians.

For the Italians the war was a comedy of errors dissolving into bloody civil war. They emerged victorious, to the chagrin of everyone else, who to this very day refuse to accept that the Italians won the war.

To the people of Yugoslavia, that powder keg state created by the French and British, the war was a genocidal conflict so brutal it took fifty years before the people were fit enough to wage another genocidal conflict.

1	Iceland	13	Sweden	25	Greece	37	Ukraine
2	Irish Free State	14	Finland	26	Crete	38	Russia
3	United Kingdom	15	Germany	27	Turkey	39	Caucasus
4	Spain	16	East Prussia	28	Bulgaria	40	Armenia
5	Gibraltar	17	Switzerland	29	Romania	41	Azerbaijan
6	France	18	Italy	30	Hungary	42	Georgia
7	Monaco	19	Malta	31	Czecho-Slovakia	43	Kazakhstan
8	Belgium	20	Sicily	32	Poland	44	Turkmenistan
9	Netherlands	21	San Marino	33	Lithuania	45	Uzbekistan
10	Luxemburg	22	Austria	34	Latvia		
11	Denmark	23	Yugoslavia	35	Estonia		
12	Norway	24	Albania	36	Byelorussia		

To the vast majority of Chinese the war was an enigmatic battle within a puzzling struggle within a confusing conflict. Only the Americans even attempted to ally with them, and for those Americans who were sent to China the enemy was the least of their problems.

For the civilised natives of New Guinea the war was a horror; for the uncivilised it was quite literally a religious experience.

In 1939 the British chose the name 'Second World War', thereby relegating the 1914-18 'Great War' to the new name 'First World War'. If, however, by world war one means a war fought on every continent, then the 1939 conflict was in fact the ninth such affair. Moreover, by this rule it really did not become a world war until December 1941.

The Americans named it 'World War II', as if they expected it to be one of a series. The Soviets named it the 'Great Patriotic War', hoping that by doing so the non-communists in the USSR, which was damn near everybody, would perceive the German incursion as an invasion rather than a liberation.

The Germans officially call it 'Zweites Weltkrieg' (Second World War), but the man in the strasse is just as likely to call it the 'Hitlerkrieg', perhaps in a sub-conscious attempt to lay the blame for it all on that Austrian immigrant.

Jews the world over cannot help but think Holocaust when reminded of the war, quite natural when the fate of Jews in some countries is considered. In the post-war era the Jews gained tremendous publicity for

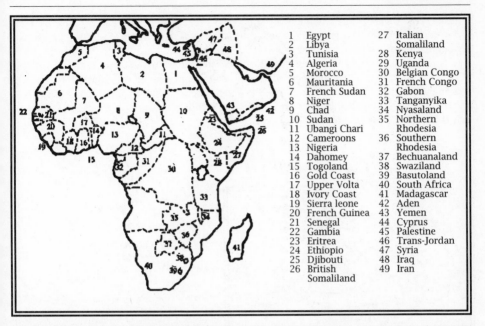

1	Egypt	27	Italian
2	Libya		Somaliland
3	Tunisia	28	Kenya
4	Algeria	29	Uganda
5	Morocco	30	Belgian Congo
6	Mauritania	31	French Congo
7	French Sudan	32	Gabon
8	Niger	33	Tanganyika
9	Chad	34	Nyasaland
10	Sudan	35	Northern
11	Ubangi Chari		Rhodesia
12	Cameroons	36	Southern
13	Nigeria		Rhodesia
14	Dahomey	37	Bechuanaland
15	Togoland	38	Swaziland
16	Gold Coast	39	Basutoland
17	Upper Volta	40	South Africa
18	Ivory Coast	41	Madagascar
19	Sierra leone	42	Aden
20	French Guinea	43	Yemen
21	Senegal	44	Cyprus
22	Gambia	45	Palestine
23	Eritrea	46	Trans-Jordan
24	Ethiopio	47	Syria
25	Djibouti	48	Iraq
26	British	49	Iran
	Somaliland		

1	Ceylon
2	Nepal
3	Burma
4	Thailand
5	Malaya
6	Singapore
7	Netherlands East Indies
8	North Borneo
9	Sarawak
10	Brunei
11	Cambodia
12	Laos
13	Vietnam
14	Hong Kong
15	Tajikistan
16	Kyrgyzstan
17	Uzbekistan
18	Turkmenistan
19	Russia
20	Afghanistan

their suffering as they had access to publishing, film, the press and broadcasting, and even their own government in the form of Israel. Contrast this with the Armenians, whose genocide during World War I is still little known, or the Ukrainians, whose genocide was ignored by the liberal left-wingers of the 1930s, or that of the Tasmanians, whose genocide at the hands of Britons in the 19th century was so successful that no one lived to tell the tale except the boastful killers. As a result of Jewish publicity a half-century after the Holocaust we non-Germans blame all Germans for allowing it to happen, while we hypocritically ignore the genocide that is taking place today.

Like the Crusades, the French Revolution of 1789, and the 19th century white-skinned scramble for dark-skinned continents, World War II is now embedded in our minds and will no doubt someday become part of our race memory and human heritage.

The war was unique in its progress, in that it began with sabre-wielding horse cavalry and ended with a raid by a dozen Americans, who in a matter of hours sneaked into a city, killed tens of thousands of men, women and children, and escaped without so much as one of their own wounded. On reflection, perhaps 'progress' is not the correct word.

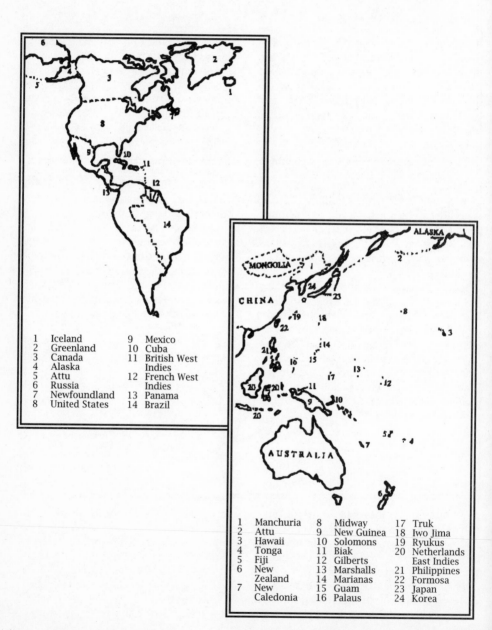

1	Iceland	9	Mexico
2	Greenland	10	Cuba
3	Canada	11	British West Indies
4	Alaska		
5	Attu	12	French West Indies
6	Russia		
7	Newfoundland	13	Panama
8	United States	14	Brazil

1	Manchuria	8	Midway	17	Truk
2	Attu	9	New Guinea	18	Iwo Jima
3	Hawaii	10	Solomons	19	Ryukus
4	Tonga	11	Biak	20	Netherlands East Indies
5	Fiji	12	Gilberts		
6	New Zealand	13	Marshalls	21	Philippines
		14	Marianas	22	Formosa
7	New Caledonia	15	Guam	23	Japan
		16	Palaus	24	Korea

ACKNOWLEDGEMENTS

It would be dishonest of me to claim sole credit for this work, though I do claim responsibility for errors and opinions. However, a list of all who have helped me would be a book in itself. They number elders, who told 'war stories' in the early years after the war; fellow-soldiers who experienced that conflict; veterans of ethnic armed forces that never appear on a map, such as Tatars; Lithuanians and Ukrainians of Cold War US Army labor battalions, who during World War II had worn German uniform; German Volksdeutsch, French, Americans, Britons, Yugoslavs, partisan veterans, police veterans, SS veterans, army veterans, navy sailors, merchant sailors, airmen, civilians – the list is endless.

Certain institutions have been exceedingly kind and professional: The Lithuanian Association of Great Britain; the Royal Draza Mihailovich Association of Great Britain; the Association of Ukrainian Former Combatants; the British Public Record Office, Kew; the Imperial War Museum, London; the National Army Museum, London; the Smithsonian, Washington D.C.; University of Lancaster Library, UK; University of Manchester Library, UK; University of London Library, UK; London School of Economics and Political Science Library, UK; University of Tulsa Library, USA; Oklahoma University Library, USA; Lancashire Library, UK; Merseyside Library, UK; Tulsa County Library, USA. Dennis Green deserves commendation for 'coming through'. I must also thank certain historians who have been influential by their encouragement, though they are totally unaware of it: John Ellis, Martin Gilbert, H. P. Willmott and David Cesarani.

There are also a few individuals who have made a tremendous impact on this work; my mother Constance T. Horan, father Jack A. Ready, mentor Marvin Lowe, fellow scholar and comrade Jerry Kirk, standard bearer Christopher V. Stafford, my daughter Louise, and above all my patient wife Kay.

J. Lee Ready

Preston, UK
Tulsa, USA

WORLD
WAR
TWO
THE NATIONS

ADEN AND YEMEN

Status in 1939:	Aden a British protected state; Yemen independent.
Government in 1939:	Aden, British administration; Yemen, monarchy.
Population in 1939:	4,500,000.
Make-up in 1939:	Arabs 3,150,000; Indians 500,000; Jews 450,000; Somalis 225,000; others 175,000;
Religion:	Moslem.
Location:	Near East.

Yemenis ignored the borders drawn by the British and Italians. The Italian Army regularly recruited Yemenis, for they proved to be good soldiers, and did not ask where they were born – Yemen, Aden, Eritrea or wherever. They served well in the Ethiopian War 1935-41 and against the British 1940-41.

The British recruited Aden residents as merchant seamen and a few into the Navy. Local workers were essential to keep the British naval base going, and the base was paramount to British strategy as it protected the approaches to the Red Sea and Suez Canal. The British Army recruited about 400 into a pioneer company to perform manual labour.

In June 1940 Aden was brought into the war with a jolt when Italian aircraft bombed the main port.

In March 1941 the pioneers accompanied a British invasion force to Berbera, an Italian-occupied town in British Somaliland. There was no opposition, but a pioneer was severely wounded clearing a minefield.

After this the British chose to disband the pioneers.
See Index

ALBANIA

Status in 1938:	independent.
Government in 1938:	Monarchy.
Population in 1938:	1,500,000.
Make-up in 1938:	Albanians 1,300,000; Greeks 100,000; Macedonians 100,000;
Religion:	About two-thirds Moslem and one third Christian.
Location:	South East Europe.

Albania's war began Good Friday, 7 April 1939 with an amphibious invasion by four Italian divisions. The Army resisted the 50,000 invaders over the weekend, but by Easter Monday the battle was over.

The Italians, led by dictator Benito Mussolini and his fascists, had supported the self-styled King Zog of Albania for years, but had grown tired of his corruption. Not every Albanian was a Zog fan, and therefore many saw the Italians as a modernising influence. The Italian soldiers were astonished how primitive this nation was. Albania was taken into the Italian Empire, but allowed an autonomous government, a new army and a fascist party of its own.

But invasion was invasion, and a few diehards refused to surrender, went into the mountains and began a low-key guerrilla war against the Albanian police.

On 28 October 1940 the Italians used Albanian soil as a springboard for their invasion of Greece. However, this was the worst possible place to do it – in snow-covered high mountains and narrow valleys – and the worst time – at the beginning of winter. As a result the Italians were confined to the valleys and then struck by Greek counter-attacks coming down from the mountain sides. By 22 November the Italians had been repelled all along the border. The Albanian Army, which had been allowed to take part in Mussolini's offensive, soon split into three parts – those who fought, those who ran and those who joined the Greeks.

By mid-December the front stretched across Albania, with its obvious impact on Albanian villagers. The nation was also under air attack by Greek and British planes, and at sea Albanian merchant ships were at the mercy of the British Royal Navy.

The Italians weeded the Albanian Army of unreliable elements and sent the remaining 3,000 into the snowy trenches. The Greeks formed an Albanian Legion from the defectors.

On 12 April the Italians launched a massive offensive which pushed back the Greeks, whose reserves were busy fighting a German invasion. After ten days the Greeks surrendered. In north Albania a Yugoslav invasion was easily held at the same time by

Italian troops, while the Italians and Germans conquered Yugoslavia.

Most Albanians were happy with the outcome for villages of Albanians in Greece and Yugoslavia were united with the motherland in a Greater Albania. The only drawback was that all had to toe the fascist party line.

Meantime the guerrillas in the mountains continued their small-scale operations. The guerrillas were also known as partisans, because each band followed a different political party and in September 1941 a secret meeting of the leaders was held in order to create harmony. The meeting was a disaster and the main factions – communists, Zogists, nationalists and Catholics began arguing. Within days they were shooting at each other.

With about 10,000 fighters, the communists quickly gained control of the most mountainous region in the south, while the rest with about 10,000 fighters in total ruled a similar roost in the north. The police controlled the valleys and towns.

At the end of 1942 the communists became a serious nuisance: Italian barracks were sniped at, sentries were stabbed, truck convoys were ambushed. Therefore on the second day of 1943 the Italian Army took the field. At Gjormi the communists defeated two battalions. The Italians also expanded the Albanian Army from 7,000 to 9,000, recruiting some men from the Albanian villages of Yugoslavia.

At the political level too the Italians made sweeping changes, shifting prime minister three times in 83 days.

The Italians were slowly sucked into the guerrilla war and at Permet communist partisans inflicted 500 casualties on them. In July and August partisans of all persuasions fought full-scale battles with the Italians and fascist Albanians.

On 8 September 1943 Italy exploded into civil war with fascists versus anti-fascists, and the pro-Italians were caught in a dilemma. They felt they had to side with the fascists, because the anti-fascists were going over to the partisans. The partisans were willing to accept Italians as men who had finally seen the light, but they were not willing to accept Albanians who had been wearing pro-Italian uniform for four years. When German troops flooded the nation the pro-Italian Albanians found a new home as pro-Germans.

The partisans had been taken totally by surprise by the Italian collapse and also by the German invasion. Their attempts to stop the Germans were futile.

The Germans set up a strict regime, but declared they had no territorial ambitions and allowed the police, army and fascist party to continue to operate. They also negotiated a truce with the partisans. Only the Zogists and communists refused to talk. The Germans and other partisans, therefore, had two mutual enemies, and they began to coordinate their actions against the Zogists and communists.

In November 1943 the Germans and partisans launched an attack on the communists. The combat was bitter, with neither faction giving quarter, and always innocent villagers were caught in the middle. Often illiterate they knew not the subtleties of fascism versus communism. They could not refuse to provide provisions to whoever entered their village on pain of death, but would be murdered by another faction if it was known they had done so.

The Zogists also attacked the communists. By early 1944 the communists were surrounded by three German divisions, several battalions of Albanian troops and 15,000 partisans, yet under Enver Hoxha the communists fought their way to Yugoslavia and linked up with communist Yugoslavs. Only in April did the fighting die down as all sides felt mutual frustration and exhaustion.

On 28 May the Germans and partisans began a new attack on the communists, soon using two German divisions, an Osttruppen division, and the 21st SS Skanderbeg Division recruited from Albanians. The combat was as fierce as had been expected, especially when some communists had to be rooted out of caves. This was no gangster shootout: the battle involved tanks, artillery and air strikes.

Yet again the communists escaped, leaving 2,500 dead and prisoners. The attackers had suffered 120 killed and 300 wounded by mid-June.

The Germans and Albanian Army pulled back now, leaving the various partisan groups to fight among themselves. They only became involved when called upon for help and then preferred to use Osttruppen or the Skanderbeg rather than actual Germans.

Suddenly the entire war picture changed as the armies of the USSR broke through as far as Yugoslavia and the Germans began an emergency evacuation of Greece. All Albanian partisans sniped at the truck columns making their way north.

On 30 October the communists felt strong enough to assault Tirana, the capital. The German/Albanian garrison fought ferociously, but a relief column coming from Elbrasin was ambushed. Therefore, the garrison retreated northwards. The last fascist hold out in the city died on 17 November.

Of the entire Skanderbeg Division only 537 remained with the Germans, the remainder having died or deserted.

By December Albania was free of invaders for the first time in almost five years, but this simply meant that the next battle would be fought to see who ruled the country. With Soviet and communist Yugoslav supplies the Albanian communists were able to win victories over the various partisan factions and by July 1945 Hoxha was firmly in power. The surviving partisans could be handled by Hoxha's police.

Albanian war casualties are impossible to calculate with even a modicum of accuracy. Certainly many thousands died, and in a nation of this size, that is a very high percentage.

See Index

ALGERIA

Status in 1939:	French colony.
Government in 1939:	French Administration.
Population in 1939:	8,000,000.
Make-up in 1939:	Arabs 5,400,000;Berbers 1,500,000; Europeans 900,000; (i.e. French, Italians, Spanish) Jews 120,000; plus desert tribes.
Religion:	Moslem, Europeans and some Arabs were Christian.
Location:	North Africa

The indigenous Algerians were never ecstatic that the French had chosen to rule over them, but by 1939 they had learned to live with it. When France declared war on Germany in 1939 almost all men in their twenties and thirties had to report for military duty. Algerians served in their own units, but some of the sergeants and all of the officers were European, predominantly French, though these Europeans had been born and bred in Algeria.

On 10 May 1940 the Germans attacked Belgium and at once French 1st Army Group, including the 4th North African Division of Algerians, was swiftly moved into Belgium to meet the enemy. Like other French divisions, the 4th contained around 17,500 men. On the 14th near Anthee the division saw their first action when they were forcefully attacked by German tanks, infantry, artillery and planes. With no air cover of their own, and soon without artillery as it was needed elsewhere, the division had no choice but to retreat, reaching Philippeville by the 19th. Roll call showed that whole platoons were missing. Two days later the men were informed that they were cut off from France by a German advance and would have to evacuate by sea.

Only a portion of the troops made it to the ships, and they had to leave behind their equipment.

The campaign had been a complete fiasco and when Marshal Pétain, the new French Prime Minister, asked for an armistice it seemed like the end of the world.

However, when the details of the armistice were announced the Algerians were pleasantly surprised. Algeria was not to be occupied by the Germans, would remain a French colony and was allowed a garrison of 55,000 troops, plus a French naval fleet and air units.

Then despair, which had turned to relief turned to bewilderment on 3 July 1940 when a British fleet arrived off the Algerian port of Mers-el-Kebir to demand the French fleet surrender, scuttle or sail to a neutral port. While negotiations were taking place by radio the British warships suddenly opened fire and carrier planes began dropping bombs. Within minutes three battleships and a destroyer were sunk or crippled, the port damaged and 1,297 French (and Algerians) killed and 351 wounded.

This despicable act began a war with Britain. The war was fought on the high seas, at Dakar, in Gabon, but not in Algeria, and life began to take on normalcy again. The most noticeable change was anti-Jewish legislation by Pétain's government: foreign-born Jews were arrested; Jewish property was confiscated; and Jewish soldiers were transferred to penal units to perform manual labour in the desert.

On 8 June 1941 French-controlled Syria was invaded by the British. Among the 33 battalions of defenders were six Algerian. They put up a good defence in places, but the territory was far too large to defend adequately and on 10 July the French commander surrendered. The Algerians were given the option of joining the British or going home: not surprisingly most chose the latter.

Also in June Germany had invaded the USSR and had asked for French volunteers – 200 idealistic young Algerians volunteered to fight on Germany's side in the struggle against the atheistic USSR. Thousands of Algerians went to France to work for the Germans, including 18,000 who were put to work building the Atlantic Wall to keep out the British. Later the Milice, an anti-terrorist police force, recruited 200 Algerians.

In November 1942 the French high command was warned that a massive armada of allied ships was coming through the Straits of Gibraltar. The Algerian coastal defences were alerted. On the night of the 7th a body of French and local Jews began arresting military commanders including Admiral Darlan, the French Commander in Chief, who just happened to be in Algiers.

This rebellion was poorly coordinated and by dawn most of the rebels were themselves under arrest and their prisoners freed.

Off Oran an allied fleet appeared and as landing craft began moving inland French (and Algerian) shore guns opened fire. Within minutes every shore position was under naval gunfire and air strikes. Two troopships entered the harbour, but one was driven off and the other badly damaged and her cargo of American troops killed or captured. However another landing put American troops as far inland as La Senia airfield.

That same day Algiers was attacked and at sunset Darlan ordered a cease-fire, but only in that city. On the 10th Darlan agreed to join the allies and he ordered all forces in North Africa to cease-fire.

The French-controlled forces had suffered 490 killed and 969 wounded in the three-day campaign and lost four warships and eight submarines. British and American losses were 2,300 killed and wounded.

In December the Algerian Algiers and Constantine Divisions marched into Tunisia alongside the allies. Almost at once they ran into German and Italian troops and battle commenced. Within days heavy rain turned Tunisia's dirt roads into mud and the allied advance came to a halt.

By 18 January 1943 the Constantine Division was holding a series of hills in the drier south of the country when they were assaulted by German tanks and infantry. With few anti-tank guns and no tanks of their own they fell back, but the Germans did not pursue. One Algerian unit was cut off for two days before escaping.

On the 31st another unit was trapped at Faid Pass, but escaped. Each time the Algerians' French commander, General Welvert, had asked for American help, but had received none.

On 14 February the Americans retreated under heavy pressure, forcing the Algerians on their northern flank to pull back too. Algerian rear echelon troops behind the Americans were also forced to fall back under air attack. This left an 80-mile gap in the line. On the 18th the Constantine was ordered to retreat all the way back to Tebessa in Algeria. This brought home to the Algerians the seriousness of the situation. However, by the 21st a scratch force of French, Algerians, Americans and British stopped the enemy at Kasserine Pass.

At Siliano the Algiers Division repelled an attack.

From now on the allies held the upper hand, but their task was difficult in the extreme. By 11 April the Constantine had only advanced a few miles and taken a few hilltops, but had received heavy losses including the commander General Welvert.

On the 19th the allies launched an all-out offensive and by the 26th the Algerians had taken Fkirin Mountain, which together with other allied success compressed the enemy into a tiny pocket with their backs to the sea. They included a battalion of Algerians, who had backed the wrong horse, i.e. were fighting alongside the Germans. The Americans asserted their overall control now by moving their troops to the north for the final victory, and the Algerians were squeezed out, being ordered to round up stragglers while the Americans and British captured the world press headlines.

On 12 May the axis forces in Tunisia surrendered. It had taken the allies six months to advance the last twelve miles!

French losses in Tunisia were 2,156 killed and 10,276 wounded, of which about half were Algerians. Thus about 10% of total allied killed and wounded were Algerian.

In January 1944 the 3rd North African Division of General Monsabert moved to the front in Italy. This Algerian division had been reinforced with a Tunisian regiment and stood at 20,000 strong, far more powerful than an American or British division. Silently the men struggled up the snow covered mountain slopes near the headwaters of the Rapido River. On the 25th, as part of the French Expeditionary Corps the division attacked and captured Colle Grosso and Monte Belvedere from the Germans within 48 hours.

From now on Algerian patrols kept the enemy on their toes.

Only in May did the allied armies advance. The Algerians did very well against tough opposition in the steep mountains – indeed the French corps outdistanced all other allied corps. After liberating the city of Siena in July the Algerians were informed that the corps was being withdrawn for a new mission: the liberation of France from German and Pétainist control.

The US Seventh Army invaded the south coast of France on 15 August 1944, and only when they were securely ashore did they allow the French forces to land. The Americans wanted the French to know who had begun the liberation.

The 3rd North African Division, its casualties replaced by fresh eager faces, assembled its vehicles and drove westwards towards the great port of Toulon, which was of vital importance to the allies for it and Marseilles would be the only major inlets through which they could supply their advance. The Algerians found the port defended by 30 forts and on the 22nd they began to battle the first of them.

Against orders Monsabert sent his 800-man reconnaissance battalion towards Marseilles, where they found the local anti-fascist resistance in open revolt and begging for assistance. The battalion commander responded and joined the fight. Two days later the heavily outnumbered battalion was relieved by the French 1st Division.

On the 27th the defenders of Toulon surrendered – 2000 had been killed and 17,000 gave up. Next day the defenders of Marseilles surrendered – 3000 had been killed and 37,000 gave up.

The Algerians now rushed north to join the rest of the French forces, renamed First Army, and advanced up the Rhône Valley, liberating town after town. The Germans were on the run and were chased past Lyon up the Saône Valley to the mountains of Alsace and Lorraine, where the allies finally stopped in mid-September having outrun their supplies.

On New Year's Day 1945 the 3rd Division and an American division were assaulted in Lorraine by Germans as part of Hitler's Operation Northwind. The two divisions held on in snow thigh deep in places and Northwind proved to be a gust rather than a blizzard. There were slight withdrawals, but within two weeks the allies went over to the offensive and by 10 February had driven the Germans east of the Rhine everywhere but the German Rhineland.

On 15 March the 3rd Division attacked into the Rhineland and within two weeks had reached the ancient regal city of Speyer on the Rhine.

The Americans and British did not wish the French to gain any laurels in central Germany. As in Tunisia they intended to squeeze them out again. Thus while the Americans and British had tremendous rear-echelon support to cross the Rhine in several places the French had nothing.

Not to be cheated of victory at this stage of the war, the 3rd Division launched its own invasion of central Germany at Speyer on 30 March – with one boat and ten men!

Finding more boats on the east bank the division put 200 men across by dawn. This day the division crossed at Germersheim with 200 men in 20 boats, but in daylight this was not a good idea. The Germans saw them and only 30 reached the far bank. The divisional artillery kept a wall of shrapnel between the 30 and the Germans, while, using just three boats, the divisional infantry put another 1,200 men across by next morning.

This day other French troops borrowed a bridge from a sympathetic American general and swung round to hit the Germans in their rear. The Germans had to pull back and the 3rd Division could now advance.

On 3 April the division fought for Bruchsal, and the next day began cutting a swathe across German fields, taking Bretten, Muehlacker and Pforzheim.

By 8 May, the day of the complete German surrender, the Algerians had reached the Swiss and Austrian borders.

Algerians had fought for France, defending the national soil and then liberating it. At no time were the Algerians considered inferior to actual French soldiers and they had been given some tough assignments at times.

To some Algerians this meant they had earned the right to be considered loyal Frenchmen. For others it meant they had earned independence. It would take another war to decide whose wish would come true.
See Index

ARMENIA

Status in 1939:	Member State of the USSR.
Government in 1939:	Communist, under Stalin dictatorship.
Population in 1939:	1,300,000.
Make-up in 1939:	Armenians; a few Russian colonists.
Religion:	Christian.
Location:	Central Asia.

Armenia, once the ally of the Roman Empire, is one of the oldest nations on earth. In the early 19th century it fell to a Russian invasion from the north and a Turkish one from the south. During World War I the Turks massacred their Armenians, killing about 800,000, but at the end of the war in 1918 Armenia became independent of both Russia and Turkey.

It was too good to last and in 1920 the Turks and Russians invaded again: but the traditional enemies of Armenia had changed faces, for the Turks were no longer killing Armenians and the Russians were no longer Christian, but communist. Life under the communists, soon called Soviets, was much harder than under the Turks, with a denial of the Armenians' culture and their religion.

In 1941 when the USSR was invaded by Germany the Soviet Red Army conscripted thousands of young Armenians and entrained them for the front, where the Red Army suffered mammoth defeats – whole divisions, corps even armies were ordered to lay down their arms.

German treatment of Red Army prisoners of war was at best negligent and at worse a brutal enslavement including death by torture and hanging. But hope soon arrived in the form of German recruiters. They asked for volunteers who would receive similar treatment to German soldiers, complete religious and cultural freedom, and a chance to fight communists. Is it any wonder that many Armenians volunteered?

Armenians served either as hiwis i.e. rear-echelon volunteers for German army, SS, police and other organisations as cooks, drivers, mechanics, etc. – or as Osttruppen i.e. companies and battalions of combat soldiers whose prime purpose was to hunt down communist partisans in the USSR behind German lines. Eventually about 7,000 Armenian Osttruppen were recruited.

The Armenians proved good soldiers and in spring 1943 some were honoured by formal induction as members of the SS. Already Armenian hiwis had followed their German parent unit to whatever country they were assigned, and by 1943 Armenian Osttruppen were serving in German-occupied USSR, Poland, Greece, Netherlands and France.

The war ended in May 1945 with Germany's complete defeat and those Armenian volunteers who were caught by the Red Army were either executed at once as traitors or sent to concentration camps and a slow death. Those taken by the British were handed to the Red Army. Only those who fell into French or American hands or who managed to hide among Germans stood a chance of survival.

Most Armenians served in the Red Army to the end of the war and had as much right as anyone to celebrate the victory over Germany.

See Index

AUSTRALIA

Status in 1939:	a dominion of the British Commonwealth, Australia was as independent as she wanted to be.
Government in 1939:	democratic monarchy
Population in 1939:	7,700,000.
Make-up in 1939:	Predominantly British and Irish stock; about 75,000 aboriginals.
Religion:	Christian.
Location:	South Pacific.

In 1914 Britain had plunged Australia into war with Germany and as 'Britons' the Australians had responded to the call from the motherland. When Britain declared war on Germany on 3 September 1939 Australia for the first time had the freedom to choose between war and peace. Her parliament chose war and most people were in full agreement with this, for they saw it as their patriotic duty to support the mother country.

The small reservist Royal Australian Air Force (RAAF) of 3,500 personnel asked for volunteers. Previously Australians who wanted to serve in a full-time air force had joined the British Royal Air Force (RAF). The Royal Australian Navy (RAN) was in better shape as it contained some very modern warships. The Army, a reservist force of 82,000 also asked for volunteers – either to serve in the Imperial Forces for overseas duty or in the Militia for home defence.

The first problem for the Australian government was how to wage war. They had never done it before. They soon sidestepped the issue by simply handing their armed forces to the British government.

In spring 1940 10 Squadron began flying Sunderland flying-boats around the coast of Britain searching for German submarines. In June 1940 3 Squadron began flying Gladiator biplane fighters over Egypt in search of Italian bombers. Both squadrons were under British orders and had been equipped by the British.

In the Mediterranean the RAN cruiser *Sydney* in company with smaller British warships encountered the Italian destroyer *Espero* on 28 June and quickly sank her. On 19 July the *Sydney* in company with the RAN destroyer *Stuart* and British destroyers met two Italian cruisers. They sank one and drove off the other. The exploits of the *Sydney* made her famous and a British admiral made her his flagship.

On 30 September the RAN *Stuart* sank an Italian submarine in the Indian Ocean.

In addition to these actions the Australian warships had to fight off constant attention from Italian planes.

In December 1940 the Australian 6th Division, about 14,000 men, was assigned to the British Western Desert Force in Libya. Riding in trucks in a cold wind the Australians took their first look at conquered enemy territory – sand, rock, scrub brush and near Bardia a few irrigated fields. They wondered why anyone would want to fight for this.

On 3 January 1941 they formed up for their first attack, moving awkwardly across the sand in long overcoats, rifles at the ready. Within a few hundred yards they heard firing. Startled, as green troops always are, they quickly realised the Italians were shooting at them, and then they hit the ground, taking cover behind tiny bushes, in gullies and depressions in the sand that seconds earlier they had not even noticed. British tanks charged the Italians, whereupon the Australian infantry and engineers got up and walked forward again, not at first realising that some of their pals would never get up again. The battle continued all night.

On the afternoon of the third day the Italians gave up. Bardia was a great victory – 35,000 Italians and Libyans were taken prisoner. Among the Australians about one man in twelve of the attacking infantry had become a casualty.

In a couple of days the men mounted trucks and began driving westwards – the terrain never altered. Reaching Tobruk they put out patrols for two weeks and then attacked on the 21st. Veterans now, they knew the mistakes to avoid. Yet, by the end of the day they had been brought to a halt by Italian fire, and when they were counter-attacked some nearby British officers began to worry. British officers always mistrusted the ability of Australians because they could not or would not march as elegantly as British troops. On the next day the Italians surrendered to the Australians and British 7th Armoured Division.

The Australians assigned a small guard to watch the 25,000 prisoners, while the division mounted trucks and drove westwards again. Reaching Derna they patrolled for three days, but the Italians pulled out. Days later the campaign was over.

Unfortunately the Australian press declared the campaign had been a piece of cake, because all Italians were 'cowards'. When this was expressed in letters from back home, the Australians in the desert were livid. This easy tour had cost them 800 killed and wounded.

A month later the division was sent to Greece and given a rest.

In the first week of April 1941 Greece was invaded by Germany. The Germans also launched an offensive in Libya. The 6th Division in Greece was ordered to halt the Germans at the Aliakmon Line and the fresh Australian 9th Division in Libya was ordered to keep the Germans out of Tobruk.

In Tobruk the 9th was joined by a brigade of the fresh 7th Division and a British tank brigade. On 11 April the Germans reached the perimeter and attacked at once. On the fourth day of battle 38 German tanks broke through, but a combination of Australian infantry and artillery and British tanks knocked out sixteen of them and repelled the rest. The next day Italian infantry failed to break in. Both sides now settled down to a siege.

In Greece the Australians were informed on the 9th that the Germans had outflanked their line and that the only choice open was to retreat southwards. As the troops walked along the narrow mountain roads, choked with dust, vehicle exhaust, hungry, thirsty and under air attack, rumours flew fast and furious about the various plans the generals had for getting them out of this scrape. Rearguards fought well, but by the 24th the division had reached the Athens area. The men found the coastal villages packed with thousands of civilian refugees and troops from a score of British, New Zealand and Australian battalions. Offshore ships were waiting to take off the troops, while German planes were trying to sink them. Black smoke from burning ships drifted across the beaches to block out the sun. Contradictory orders arrived – remain here, go there, move into the south of the country, evacuate at once, and so on.

At sea four RAN destroyers and a cruiser were part of the evacuation fleet. The *Waterhen* and *Vendetta* loaded up 420 soldiers and took them to Crete. At Nauplia the *Stuart* and the cruiser *Perth* waited until 4.30am before leaving, which was against navy orders for that was when the enemy planes arrived, because they wanted to squeeze in every last man. Reaching Crete they disgorged 2000 troops, an unbelievable number for warships not designed with surplus space. The Perth made a trip to Kalamata but was warned the Germans had overrun the beaches.

The 6th Division took roll call on Crete: 320 men were known killed, 494 of the evacuees were wounded and 2,030 were missing. Much of the equipment was lost. Perhaps the worst thing was the knowledge that Crete was not safe: German planes were bombing them. Four divisions of Australians, British, New Zealanders and Greeks were told to defend the island, for the generals expected the Germans to come.

They came alright, and from a flank that no one had really seriously considered: the air. On 20 May German paratroopers began jumping. This put the rear-echelon troops into action as they fought back with rifles. At Retimo one Australian unit could not believe their luck, for the Germans arrived in transport planes like tourists. The Australians sprayed them with machine-gun fire, inflicting terrible losses. However, the next day at Maleme airfield more Germans arrived and they spread out easily.

On the 28th the Australians were told to make their way to Heraklion or Sfakia to evacuate by sea. Offshore the RAN *Nizam* was damaged in an air raid, but took off scores of troops from Sfakia. The *Perth* was also damaged: seven crew and nine passengers were killed. The *Nizam* made another trip with the *Napier*, the two RAN vessels hoping to take 250 men off. Before dawn they had loaded 1,510!

The British Royal Navy called off the evacuation because of high losses to ships, but political pressure from Australia, New Zealand and Britain made them make one more run – they took off another 3,700.

In Egypt the Australian 6th Division took roll call again. The defenders of Retimo, who had thought themselves so lucky, had never learned of the evacuation and had been abandoned. The division was missing 2000 men. With 5,700 casualties (40%) in five months the 6th Division was destroyed as a fighting force.

Just one week after the Crete defenders reached Egypt, the British invaded Pétainist-French Syria with a British, a de Gaullist-French and the Australian 7th Division. The 7th Division, which still had a brigade in Tobruk, found opposition at the Litani River, but allied commandos outflanked the French and the Aussies could advance.

However, near Lake Merjuym another element of this fresh division dug in and was not disposed to do ought else. Many claimed they had volunteered to fight Germans (Dad's enemy) not the French (Dad's ally). On the 15th they withdrew when attacked by the French. Their officers talked to the men about honour, the political situation, that British generals knew what they were doing etc.

This poor morale reflected a growing problem among the Australian population. Wartime restrictions on the press meant the ordinary citizen in Melbourne or Sydney did not know which British units were where, but it was obvious that Australia was bearing the burden of the war: a division in Tobruk with its back to the sea, another

thrown into the sea twice, and now a third asked to fight Frenchmen. Where was the British Army, many asked? With seven times the population as Australia they should have had seven times the troops in action.

The Australian government was even more aware of the discrepancy, for they knew that not one British infantry division had been in action in the last twelve months. In fact in terms of full-scale battle not one British infantry division had yet been in action at all. In addition the British were asking for the Australian 8th Division to be sent to Malaya in case the Japanese declared war. The loss of the RAN *Waterhen* to air attack on 29 June only added to Australian grievances. The RAAF had four squadrons in action in Libya and Syria and five in Britain. With three squadrons going to Malaya, this left Australia with only training aircraft for defence!

In Syria the Australians advanced from the Litani and helped take Damascus, aiding the French to destroy the French – the war was becoming more complicated everyday, thought the Aussies. On 8 July the Australians took Damur on the coast. Two days later the French in Syria surrendered.

The Australians had performed in a mixed fashion. Some refused to fight, while others took on the French Foreign Legion and won. The division, fighting with only two-thirds of its infantry, suffered 236 killed, 1,049 wounded and 387 captured – about 28% of the combat echelon.

In August 1941 the Australians began to withdraw from Tobruk, being replaced by a British infantry division to the surprise of all, though the British asked some Australians to remain until December.

The RAN *Sydney* was on her way home for a refit when she sighted an unidentified ship off the west of Australia. At 4000 yards the ship opened fire: she was the German raider *Kormoran*. For one hour the two ships blasted away at each other, exploding metal superstructure into fragments, spreading slicing shrapnel and crumpling bridges and turrets like paper. The slaughter was horrific and it ended with the *Sydney* blowing up and the *Kormoran* sinking. The only evidence of what had happened to the *Sydney* and her 645 man crew was the story of German survivors who made it to the shore and two of *Sydney*'s lifeboats, which came ashore on a wave, empty.

On 7 December 1941 the Japanese went on the warpath, attacking American and British possessions in the Pacific and Asia. When news of a landing in northern Malaya reached the men of the 8th Division they were confident, for everyone said the Japanese would be easily beaten, and besides Malaya had almost 100,000 defenders, 150 aircraft and the British Far Eastern Fleet.

Two days later the Japanese defeated a British/Indian division and their planes sank the two largest warships in the 'fleet'. The Australians began to re-examine the situation and check their weapons. Days later the British command in Malaya ordered a complete retreat. It was the worst possible word any soldier can hear.

On 8 January 1942 British Field Marshal Wavell was given command of the region and there was a surprise: he called his command ABDA, which stood for American-British-Dutch-Australian. For the first time in history the Australians were being recognised as being other than British. It was obvious to the Australians the confidence of the British had been shaken.

The Australian government shipped troops to Java, Ambon, the Solomon Islands, Timor and New Britain. They intended to stop the Japanese in these islands rather than on the shore of Australia.

On the 13th the 8th Division dug in along the Gemas Line and the following day the Japanese came charging out of the jungle screaming like banshees, bayonets glistening in the sun. The Aussies stood their ground and stopped the enemy dead. It was a good performance for green troops. Then came orders to retreat. Disheartened, to say the least, the men obeyed, saying goodbye to the members of the rearguard, which was effectively suicide duty.

On the 23rd the 1,400 Australians on New Britain were attacked and quickly ordered to surrender.

A week later 800 Australians and a Dutch force resisted an invasion on Ambon, until their commander called it quits.

The following day the 8th Division marched across the causeway from Malaya to Singapore Island.

General Bennett of the 8th Division was now given command of the north stretch of the coast, a very swampy area. On the night of 8 February his men opened fire on scores of barges as the Japanese tried to land. They inflicted heavy losses, but the enemy just kept coming and after dawn Bennett authorised a withdrawal. For one week the division battled the Japanese in a cramped corner of the island until they were informed by radio that the British commander of the island had surrendered.

The division had suffered 1,789 killed and 15,395 taken prisoner. Bennett was not among them. With a few diehards he found a boat and sailed away, eventually reaching Australia. He was treated like a leper. Where was his division the people asked? A victim of the bankrupt British generals, he was nonetheless blamed. The Australians needed a punching bag and Bennett was available.

On 19 February the port of Darwin, Australia was bombed by 188 Japanese planes: seventeen ships were sunk, 22 defending fighters shot down and 240 sailors and civilians killed. This was the first real 'battle' in Australian history and the psychological effect was out of all proportion to the military effort expended by the Japanese. Over the next year further raids continued on Darwin, Wyndham, Broome, Katherine and Daly Waters.

The three air squadrons in Malaya were lost. Three others had saved their personnel, but not their planes. Only one fighter squadron could be spared to defend Port Moresby, a town of Australians in New Guinea. When they flew in the local flak gunners shot at them!

On Timor the Australian garrison went into the jungle to wage guerrilla war when the Japanese invaded.

On Java there was an allied army of Dutch, British, Americans and 2,200 Australians, but the four air forces could only supply 28 planes. At least there was an allied fleet. An Australian officer aboard the RAN *Perth* was allowed to take command of the

British contingent too – another sign of lost British confidence.

On 27 February the fleet tackled a Japanese task force: five cruisers and twelve destroyers against the Japanese four cruisers and fourteen destroyers. The allies, under Dutch command, were plainly outfought: two allied cruisers and three destroyers went down.

Next day the *Perth* led the charge in another battle. Only when half the *Perth*'s crew of 676 lay bleeding did they abandon ship: 317 survived to be taken prisoner.

On 4 March a lone Australian sloop the *Yarra* ran into the enemy: only thirteen of her 152 man crew lived to tell the tale of her last fight.

On the 9th the Dutch commander of Java surrendered. Only 400 Australians escaped to Australia.

The Australian government was numbed. Over 23,000 Australian men and women in uniform were missing. A provisional plan was drawn up to abandon Australia north of Brisbane. The government demanded the British release all troops, planes and ships at once to come home to defend Australia.

The British government refused! The Australians were astonished. The British had 25 divisions waiting in Britain in case the Germans invaded: but with the Germans locked in battle on the Russian front and American troops pouring into Britain that was surely a remote possibility. The Australian Army had seven divisions to defend Australia, a shortage of equipment, almost no veterans to rally morale, no fleet and no air force. The British told the Australians to ask the Americans for help and the historic link between the countries was stretched to breaking point until a compromise was reached.

The 9th Division would remain in Egypt. All air squadrons would remain in Egypt and Britain; indeed Australia would provide still more RAAF recruits. The RAN would come home as would the 6th and 7th Divisions, both of them crippled by casualties.

Though the Japanese Seventeenth Army had invaded New Guinea, that island was so large that this gave the Australians a breathing space. They conscripted all white male settlers on the island and evacuated as many white civilians as possible and altered the law so that the Australian militia could serve in New Guinea, under the guise that this could be considered home defence. There was one change the Australians did not like. In order to accept American help they had to agree to let the American General MacArthur, who had been defeated in the Philippines, take command of all air, sea and ground forces in the South West Pacific. An arrogant nationalist, he refused to have Australians on his staff. Diplomatic argument between Canberra and Washington DC forced him to put Australian General Blamey in command of all ground forces: there were no American combat troops in the region yet; but once done MacArthur ignored Blamey from then on.

One command of MacArthur's was liked. He said there would be no more talk of retreat.

MacArthur began instructing the veterans of Bardia, Tobruk, Crete and Syria how to fight. He really got up the noses of the Australians, who had to dig deep into their resources of humility and patience.

In May 1942 Australian commandos kept a close watch on Japanese progress in New Guinea, while a reconnaissance force edged along the Kokoda Trail across the almost impenetrable Owen Stanley Mountains towards the enemy's advance bases at Gona and Buna on the north coast of the island. In August the 7th Brigade protected US engineers who built an airstrip at Milne Bay in extreme eastern New Guinea.

To MacArthur's anger Americans not under his command launched the first counter-offensive against the Japanese. They invaded the islands of Tulagi and Guadalcanal, protected by a huge US naval fleet, which included some RAN vessels.

One night at 2.00am the RAN cruiser *Canberra* was suddenly caught in the glare of searchlights: seconds later shells began to strike her. A Japanese task force had sneaked into the US fleet. Within minutes uncontrollable fires raged throughout the cruiser and her crew abandoned ship: 729 dazed and shocked survivors were picked up; 85 were lost. The following day the Americans had to sink the blazing hulk.

Now began the real battle: in pubs and cafés in every Australian port American sailors accused Australian sailors of cowardice. The Australians claimed the Americans owed them a ship. Fist fights were commonplace. As the Australians and Americans were not getting along at top level either, Churchill the British Prime Minister stepped in to prevent a rift. He gave the RAN a British cruiser the *Shropshire* as a peace offering.

At Milne Bay the Americans and Australians were too busy to argue, for on 25 August Tobruk veterans, raw militia and green Americans were invaded by a Japanese task force. MacArthur demanded to know why the enemy was not thrown back into the sea at once.

In fact the defenders did exactly that, but it was a hard fight and took until 7 September. As the Americans on Guadalcanal were still in battle, and the Australians on Kokoda Trail were being pushed back by light enemy forces, the Battle of Milne Bay was the first allied land victory over the Japanese.

In Egypt the Australian 9th Division had been resting in the manner of soldiers since time immemorial. At Tobruk they and a brigade of the 7th Division had lost 832 killed, 2,177 wounded and 941 missing. Such casualties (almost 30% of the combat echelon) cripple a division.

But in June 1942 the division was alerted: the Germans and Italians had counter-attacked successfully. On 4 July the division settled alongside four other allied divisions at Alamein, a water-stop on a rail line. The Australians took the coastal flank.

On the 9th the Australians repelled Italian infantry, and again on the 14th. On the 16th they attacked, but were driven back the following day. On the 21st they attacked again, then waited for British tanks to take over. They arrived but were defeated, leaving many an Aussie high and dry and forced to surrender. On the 26th this was repeated, but this time the tanks never arrived at all. Despite this series of futile fights, the generals told the Aussies the month-long battle of Alamein had been a victory.

At the end of August the Australians were attacked again, but they held the Italians and after a couple of days the shooting died down. This was the victory of Alam al Halfa.

To the impatient Australians these were not real victories for the enemy had remained in his position. However, there seemed to be a different attitude in the division come October as they prepared for an all-out offensive to shove the enemy not just back, but out of Egypt. This attitude change was brought about by an influx of supplies, new vehicles, tanks, a burst of activity in the rear areas and a series of pep talks, one of them by the Eighth Army commander, General Montgomery.

At 9.40pm on the evening of 23 October 1942 a thousand allied guns opened fire. The Australians were impressed. Twenty minutes later they began to walk forward in the dark. They did not march like the British further down the line, but sort of sauntered, oblivious to the noise, shot and shell.

At dawn they were told to wait: flanking units had not done as well. The Australians now put into operation a plan to trap the German 164th Division on the coast by swerving their left flank troops to the right. It almost worked – on the 29th several hundred Germans were cut off, but then an enemy counter-attack by the 164th and 90th German and Trieste Italian Divisions broke through the Australians to rescue their comrades.

Evidently this was all part of Montgomery's plan, or so he later claimed, and he now launched his armour against another part of the line. By 4 November the enemy, Rommel's Armoured Army Afrika, was in full retreat.

In the twelve day affair the 9th Division lost 620 killed, 1,944 wounded and 130 missing. A third of the infantry were casualties.

If Second Alamein was a 'British' victory, New Guinea was an 'American' victory: MacArthur's press team would make sure of that. He sent Blamey to the Kokoda Trail to find out why General Pownall's men were falling back. Blamey saw for himself that conditions on the trail were ridiculous. In some areas not even primitive natives had ventured. A wounded or sick man had to be hand-carried by four men over as much as 200 miles of terrain that would exasperate a mountain goat. By September Australian casualties were 314 killed and 367 wounded, the high death rate caused by the long trip a wounded man had to make to receive adequate medical attention. Over a thousand were laid low with jungle illnesses. The casualty list was low, though, but not because of a lack of enemy opposition, but because usually only a dozen men could fight at the head of the trail at any one time.

MacArthur complained to Prime Minister Curtin that the Australians wouldn't fight. Curtin pressured Blamey: Blamey pressured Pownall, and he ordered the 25th Brigade to counter-attack on 26 September.

The attack succeeded, for after all the trail was just as tough on the Japanese. The Australians approached Kokoda village on 6 October, but it was the 17th before they had brought up enough supplies to attack the village and it took two weeks, 92 killed, 200 wounded and hundreds laid low with disease to capture the village and cross a 20-foot-wide stream.

MacArthur, who had never visited a battlefield since World War I, ordered the commander of the Australian 7th Division and General Pownall dismissed. Blamey gave the Syria veterans to General Vasey with orders to move quickly. This was all the more galling to the Australians when they learned MacArthur had told the press the Americans were winning in New Guinea. No one on the trail had seen an American.

As the Australians on the trail approached the coastal plain an American unit did land on the north coast and attack Buna. The green Americans were repulsed at once. Australian commandos with them were surprised to find they were state troops. MacArthur had been angered that he had not received any regular US Army combat troops. MacArthur dismissed the American general at once. At last, the Australians realised MacArthur was not anti-Australian. He simply disliked anyone who would not deliver him a newspaper headline.

On the trail the 16th Brigade asked for relief. Green Americans were sent to replace them and proceeded to mortar the Australians in error. Such was the ill-feeling

between Australians and Americans by this date that the Australians refused to leave and waited until relieved by an Australian unit, though that unit, the 30th Militia Brigade, was equally green. By now the 16th Brigade was down to 338 men – they had come to New Guinea with over 2000.

On 9 December the 30th and 21st Brigades fought their way into Gona and on 2 January the 18th Brigade and an American regiment (same size as an Australian brigade i.e. 3 battalions) captured Buna. This trapped a Japanese force at Sanananda. For this the allies attacked with six Australian and three American battalions – a paper strength of 8000, but now down to 3000. In a three-week battle they killed the 1,600 Japanese for a cost of 600 Australian and 270 American killed and wounded.

The 17th Brigade flew to Wau airstrip, held by commandos, and this attracted the Japanese in that area of New Guinea like flies to honey. The fight was fearsome. In one incident artillery was landed and opened fire point-blank within feet of the aircraft. The Japanese were repelled.

It was time for the Australians to take stock. Leaving only two divisions to protect Australia and one to garrison other islands, this gave them seven divisions to fight the enemy: the 9th, the victors of Alamein, were on their way home. The RAAF was flying seven squadrons from New Guinea airstrips and 24 from Australia, bombing the East Indies, patrolling the seas, training or transporting cargo. Cargo missions were among the most deadly for the enemy air force was still very active. Another eighteen squadrons were flying in the Mediterranean or from British bases. At sea the RAN was being used by a very grateful US Navy.

The next major move in New Guinea was a three pronged offensive to take the coastal base at Lae. It began on 23 August 1943 when the 15th and 17th Brigades charged the log bunkers of Salamaua, 150 miles further west along the north coast from Gona, and 30 miles from Lae. On 2 September the 7th Division flew to Nadzab airstrip 20 miles on the other side of Lae. On the 4th the 9th Division made an amphibious invasion of the coast 60 miles north of Lae on the Huon Peninsula. Obviously Lae was surrounded.

However, the Japanese retreated, something no one thought they would do, leaving behind 8000 corpses, mostly dead from disease and malnutrition. By the end of September the allies could claim an expanse of jungle won, but nothing else for their casualties of 477 Americans and 1,763 Australians killed and wounded. Naturally MacArthur claimed the victory for his Americans.

To sweeten the victory in October the 20th Brigade stopped cold an enemy counter-attack: and American and Australian rear-echelon troops repelled a Japanese attempt at an amphibious landing.

From November through to January the 7th and 9th Divisions and 54th Brigade chased the remnants of the Japanese, and when the 5th Division relieved them only starving stragglers were found. Some Japanese were actually surrendering. On 22 April 1944 major American forces landed on the north coast 400 miles ahead of the retreating Japanese.

Not only did MacArthur's Americans leave the starving ragged Japanese behind, but he left the Australians behind too. He presented his new plan: he would not use Australian troops to capture the islands that lay in his path leading to the Philippines and Japan. Those battles, and those newspaper headlines, would be reserved for the Americans. However, he ordered the Australians to mop up the thousands of Japanese left behind on New Guinea and take over guarding American bases on Bougainville and New Britain.

The Australian generals were flabbergasted! To be sent to worthless jungle to kill soldiers who had already been bypassed was utter insanity. Worse, it was murder. The murder of the Japanese and the murder of the Australians who would have to fight them. MacArthur was heading for the Philippines. It galled him that he couldn't liberate that nation single-handedly, John Wayne style, but had to use an army. Well, at least it was going to be an all-American army.

In August 1944 General Savige unloaded his Australian IIIrd Corps of the 3rd Division and 11th and 23rd Brigades on the 120- by 50-mile island of Bougainville, relieving

Americans who told him the Japanese had a division and a brigade, 13,400 men, but that they would not bother him if he did not bother them.

In October General Stevens moved his 6th Division to the front in New Guinea. The outgoing Americans told him the Japanese Eighteenth Army still had 60,000 men, but were too busy growing food to come out of the jungle highlands and fight.

This month General Ramsey led his 5th Division to the 300- by 50-mile island of New Britain, where the Americans estimated the Japanese had two divisions and two brigades, about 38,000 men.

Stevens ordered an advance to capture the food growing areas. Naturally the Japanese resisted, but Stevens used artillery and air strikes rather than infantry when possible.

Ramsey began his offensive in January 1945, but used only a couple of infantry battalions at a time. Savige's offensive was a two directional one, spreading out from the beachhead.

The US Navy, unlike MacArthur, was glad to have the Australians and used RAN warships at Manus, Los Negros, Wakde-Sarmi, Biak and the great battle of Leyte Gulf. It was at Leyte where the Americans were introduced to Japanese suicide pilots, the kamikazes. The RAN cruiser *Australia* was struck by one.

At the invasion of the Philippine island of Luzon at Lingayen the kamikazes were busy again. The RAN was here too, and the amount of respect earned by the Australians is evident in the fact that the US Navy allowed a task force including the battleship *Mississippi* to come under RAN command. In this invasion the *Australia* was rammed by a kamikaze, causing 30 killed and 46 wounded. Then another kamikaze struck the *Australia* killing fourteen and wounding 26, and three other kamikazes were shot down yards from her. She remained on station. Another kamikaze was shot down just yards from the *Arunta*: the explosion killed two sailors and wounded four.

The British had organised an international fleet to fight the Japanese, though they insisted on calling it the British Far

East/Pacific Fleet. They had regained their confidence since the retreat of 1942 and were no longer allowing others, e.g. the Australians, to have recognition. The RAN joined the fleet with 25 warships. The fleet sent carrier planes to attack the East Indies, bombarded shore positions with guns, fought off air raids and in 1945 joined the Americans in the Pacific, who promptly gave it the unromantic name of TF 57. The fleet took part in the terrible three-month battle of Okinawa.

Meanwhile the Australian Army had not given up searching for a worthwhile piece of real estate to die for, and in early 1945 they found it: Borneo, which provided Japan with many raw materials including oil.

MacArthur agreed, but only if Americans were in command. Blamey stood his ground as the Australian Commander in Chief , though he had no support from the dying Curtin. MacArthur compromised: overall American command, but Australia's General Morshead in charge on the ground and AVM Bostock in charge in the air.

During the planning there was a problem with the RAAF – mutiny. Crews making attacks on the East Indies including Borneo saw no profit in it, for they were taking casualties and the Yanks were getting the headlines. Commodore Cobby visited them and revealed as much as he dared about the invasion of Borneo. Once they realised there was a purpose to their sacrifices they went back to work. In the first week of April alone they sank 29 ships and damaged 32 off the Borneo coast.

On May Day the American fleet, with nine RAN warships, delivered the 9th Division's 26th Brigade to the fifteen-by-ten-mile island of Tarakan off Borneo. It took a full week of combat to capture the oilfield, then the Aussies drove the garrison into the swamps. On the 26th the Japanese obliged the Australians by charging out of the swamp: the Aussies mowed them down with rifle and machine-gun fire.

On 6 June the 9th Division landed its 24th Brigade on eight- by six-mile Labuan island and the 20th Brigade on Borneo itself at Brunei.

On 1 July the fleet delivered the 7th Division to Balikpapan on the opposite side of Borneo 450 miles from Brunei. With such an expanse of primitive jungle terrain between the Tarakan, Brunei-Labuan and Balikpapen landings these were really three separate battles.

On 16 August it was all over: Japan surrendered.

The landings on Borneo were spectacular for those who were there, but for the rest of the world they remain a footnote in history. The Australians had been used too much by the British and not enough by the Americans, and they had the misfortune to come under command of MacArthur – had they been in US Admiral Nimitz' command they would have been respected.

On Tarakan the Australians lost 225 killed and 669 wounded, killed 1,540 Japanese and took 300 prisoners. At Brunei-Labuan they lost 114 killed and 221 wounded, killed 1,234 and captured 20,000. At Balikpapan they suffered 229 killed and 634 wounded, killed 1,783 and captured 15,000. Upon learning how brutal the Japanese had treated local natives and Australian prisoners of war, the Australian guards allowed the natives to take their revenge on the unarmed Japanese. How many were killed will never be known.

On New Guinea Stevens suffered 442 killed and 1,141 wounded, counted 9000 dead enemy and captured 13,500. On Bougainville the IIIrd Corps lost 516 killed and 1,572 wounded, counted 18,000 Japanese dead and captured 23,750. On New Britain the Australians lost 52 killed, 150 wounded, and took the surrender of 70,000!

Australia had provided the Americans with a major base: her cattle alone were a priceless contribution to the allied war effort. Industrial production increased tremendously when the Australians realised they were orphaned from Britain: Australian-built planes, tanks, ships and guns were in allied hands by 1943.

Despite such a small population the nation put an incredible one million men and women into uniform. Against the Japanese they suffered 951 RAN, 1,331 RAAF and 9,541 Army killed, plus 7,964 prisoners – more than one in three – died in Japanese custody from air raids, submarine attack, neglect and murder. Against her other ene-

31

mies Australia lost 903 RAN, 3,631 army and 5,116 RAAF killed, and of 8,622 prisoners taken 264 died in custody. Together with 1,400 dead from disease and war-related accidents, 46,000 treated for wounds and 285,000 hospitalised with disease, this gave Australia a high casualty list. With 109 merchant service deaths it comes to 31,200 dead.

Unlike World War I in which Australia reaffirmed her Britishness, in this war she affirmed her independence. Betrayed by the British and patronised by the Americans, the Australians came to the conclusion that in the future they would have to stand alone as a great nation.

See Index

AUSTRIA

Status in 1937:	independent.
Government in 1937:	democracy.
Population in 1937:	7,000,000.
Make-up in 1937:	Germans (i.e. Germanic and Alpine Celtic); 185,000 Jews; a few Slovenes.
Religion:	Christian.
Location:	Central Europe.

At the end of World War I Austria was defeated and all her non-German-speaking provinces lost, plus some German-speaking districts. Yet ruling the remainder was no simple task and in 1934 following a series of riots and strikes the leader, Chancellor Dollfuss, sent in the Army to disarm the communists and socialists of Vienna. Dollfuss won this short civil war, but was then shot by Nazis who attempted to take over. They failed and were either imprisoned or they fled to Germany, a nazi state run by Adolf Hitler.

On 12 March 1938 Hitler's army invaded Austria, having bullied the Austrian government into surrendering. The German troops, met by cheering villagers who threw flowers at them, called this the Battle of Flowers.

Most Austrians believed that by unifying with Germany they could once again be part of a great empire. They certainly did not look upon this as disloyalty, for Hitler himself was an Austrian. In their minds they had simply traded an unpopular Austrian leader for a popular one and had achieved an age old dream: German-Austrian unity.

Only the communists, socialists and Jews did not cheer.

Within hours of the invasion the Gestapo (German political police) arrived in Vienna and gave the police an arrest list of potential troublemakers, including Germans who had fled Hitler's state. Concentration camps were set up to contain them. The Nazis, once outlawed and now top dog, behaved insufferably. Their attitude towards Jews convinced 58,000 to emigrate.

Throughout the remaining years of Hitler's reign the percentage of the Austrian population in nazi organisations: the party, SS, SA etc.; was far higher than the percentage of Germans.

The Austrian Army was absorbed en masse into the German Army and when the wars began in September 1939 Austrians were also conscripted as they were now German citizens. Many Austrians achieved prominence: General Rauss commander of Fourth Panzer Army; Walter Nowotny ace fighter pilot; Odilo Globocnik SS boss of Slovenia; Otto Skorzeny Hitler's commando chief; Franz Stangl founder of Sobibor extermination camp; General Loehr commander in Yugoslavia; and Artur Seyss-Inquart political boss of the Netherlands.

Austrian mountain infantry were most welcome and served brilliantly in Norway 1940. Austrian units served on all fronts but Libya.

In 1941 the police began rounding up the Jews and Gypsies to be sent to colonies in the east. The victims wondered where they were really going. The Christian Austrians wondered too, but to ask questions was dangerous: the Gestapo had big ears.

There was an anti-Nazi resistance, and though they spent most of their time putting out leaflets, there was a guerrilla force in the southern mountains which linked up with Yugoslavian partisans across the border after June 1941. Many anti-Nazis had fled and joined the allies: British Army as pioneers, commandos and saboteurs; the USSR as ordinary soldiers; the French as labour troops or Foreign Legion; the US Army, at one time in an all-Austrian battalion.

On 13 August 1943 allied bombers struck Austria, damaging the aircraft factories at Wiener-Neustadt. The air offensive gained in momentum as rail lines, factories, bridges, airfields, oil depots etc. were targeted. In Vienna, once the city of Mozart and Beethoven, the Opera House and other famous buildings were destroyed, as were the apartments of the workers, many of them communists and socialists and therefore anti-Nazis.

By April 1945 the armies of the USSR were at the eastern border and the German and the Hungarian armies made a fighting withdrawal towards Vienna. There the Nazi party bosses frantically grabbed everyone to defend them. The conscription age was already 15 to 60. Now boys as young as twelve were thrown into the line without training. Girls as young as fifteen manned flak guns against tanks. When adults tried to surrender, teenage boys called them traitors and shot them in the back. The children, mothers and elderly huddled in cellars praying for the slaughter to end. Only after ten days of battle was it over. Now Soviet soldiers marched through the streets, cheering and waving huge flags. Others got wildly drunk on looted liquor and raped and pillaged. Tens of thousands of women were treated for the effects of rape. Anyone who interfered was gunned down.

Elsewhere in Austria the combat lasted until mid-May.

Post-war Austrian politicians claimed that Austria was as much a victim of Hitler as, say Poland. In one sense they were right, but this does not take away the fact that millions of Austrians swallowed Hitler's promises hook, line and sinker.

About a million and half Austrians served Hitler in the armed forces, police or paramilitary units: of which about 380,000 died. About 40,000 civilians were killed in air raids or in cross-fire; a minimum of 10,000 were killed by drunken Soviet troops or arrested and sent to Soviet concentration camps to die; 71,000 were murdered by the Nazis because they were Jewish and 8,000 because they were Gypsies; plus another 40,000 died at the hands of the Nazis, because they spoke out against the madness (the resistance claim 28,880 of these). Total

deaths were, therefore, about 549,000. So much for an occupation that began as a battle of flowers.
See Index

AZERBAIJAN

Status in 1939:	member state of the USSR.
Government in 1939:	communist, under Stalin dictatorship.
Population in 1939:	2,500,000.
Make-up in 1939:	Azerbaijanis; some Russian colonists.
Religion:	Moslem.
Location:	Central Asia.

With the collapse of the Russian Empire in 1917 the Azerbaijanis declared independence but in 1921, following a war between Iran and the new Russian state, the Soviet Union, southern Azerbaijan fell to the Iranians and the north to the Soviets.

When the Soviet Union was invaded by Germany in 1941 the Soviet Red Army conscripted thousands of Azerbaijani men to repel the invader, but they were sent to the front just in time to be surrendered by inadequate Soviet generals. Bewildered, starving, sick, the prisoners were herded into giant fields without shelter or medical attention, where they sat waiting to die. Conditions were criminal.

Then hope arrived in the form of German recruiters, seeking volunteers for anti-communist units and offering treatment similar to that of German soldiers and complete religious and cultural freedom, something the Azerbaijanis had not seen for a generation.

Thousands signed up, becoming either hiwis, rear-echelon soldiers attached to German units, or Osttruppen, all-Azerbaijani anti-partisan battalions. At first their welfare was looked after by the Turkestani Legion, but in 1942 as a reward for their excellent service they received their own representation, the Azerbaijani Legion.

By 1943 there were 36,500 Azerbaijani Osttruppen serving as far afield as the Soviet Union, Poland, Italy and France.

One of their roughest fights took place in Warsaw, where on 1 August 1944 the local Polish resistance rose in revolt against the German garrison, including an Azerbaijani battalion. The Azerbaijani barracks was surrounded and the men ordered to come out with their hands up: they did; and the Poles slit their throats. Needless to say when other Azerbaijanis heard of the massacre they began to hunt down the Poles with a vengeance. The Germans required urgent reinforcement and among those who arrived were five Azerbaijani battalions.

After three weeks of butchery four of these battalions could be withdrawn, but the last Poles did not give up until 4 October.

In the second half of 1944 Azerbaijanis retreated alongside the Germans in France, Poland and Italy. In Italy a battalion was assigned to the 162nd Division which was battling the British on the front line.

In May 1945 with the collapse of the Germans any Azerbaijani who fell into Soviet hands was executed or sent to a concentration camp. Those who were captured by the British were handed to the Soviets. Only those who gave up to the Americans or French, or managed to hide among the Germans, stood a chance of survival.

Most Azerbaijani men served honourably in the Red Army and this included those who invaded Iran in 1941 and carved out a new state in Iranian Azerbaijan. In 1946 under Anglo-American pressure the Red Army withdrew, abandoning the new state, whereupon the Iranians invaded and crushed the state's small Army.

World War II was a bitter experience for Azerbaijanis who faced a no win situation, for even those who survived inside the Red Army returned to an oppressive life.
See Index

BASUTOLAND

Other names:	Lesotho
Status in 1939:	British colony.
Government in 1939:	British administration.
Population in 1939:	553,000.
Make-up in 1939:	Sesotho; Nguni; Smaller tribes
Religion:	tribal; Missionary Christians.
Location:	Southern Africa.

When Britain declared war on Germany in 1939 she asked her non-white imperial subjects to volunteer for military service. Basuto volunteers were placed in the Pioneer Corps, a force that performed duties no soldier wanted: digging trenches, filling in bomb craters, unloading trucks and ships, maintaining roads etc. The Basutos were formed into 52 oversize companies and ostensibly these 20,000 men were destined for non-combat i.e. rear-echelon duty. However, as the war went on they found themselves retrieving land mines, fighting fires caused by accident, sabotage and air raids, carrying provisions right up to the front line and often working under air attack and artillery fire.

Basutos served with the British Eighth Army in Egypt, Libya and Tunisia, finishing the latter with a tragic incident – on 1 May 1943 618 Basutos were lost when their troopship was torpedoed. On the first day of the allied landings in Sicily, 10 July 1943, Basutos were there, working on the beach under shellfire. Some took part in the invasions of Italy at the toe on 3 September and at Salerno, 9 September, a particularly rough battle, where they worked under air raids and artillery fire for two weeks. From September onwards Basutos supported British Eighth and US Fifth Armies in Italy until May 1945. Two companies were mentioned in dispatches for working continually under shellfire for six weeks.

About 500 Basutos were killed in the land battles and air raids.
See Index

BECHUANALAND

Other names:	Botswana
Status in 1939:	British colony.
Government in 1939:	British administration.
Population in 1939:	300,000.
Make-up in 1939:	Setswana.
Religion:	tribal; Missionary Christians.
Location:	Southern Africa.

When Britain declared war on Germany in 1939 she asked her non-white imperial subjects to volunteer for military service. Bechuana volunteers were placed in about 25 oversized companies, about 10,000 men, of the Pioneer Corps, a force that performed duties no soldier wanted: digging trenches, filling in bomb craters, unloading trucks and ships, maintaining roads etc.

Bechuanas served all over Africa and the Middle East, and as the war went on they found themselves retrieving land mines and carrying provisions for the British Eighth Army right up to the front line and often working under air attack and artillery fire.

Their record of calm composure under fire earned one company a place in the landings in Sicily, 10 July 1943, and the toe of Italy, 3 September. Eventually 4,400 Bechuanas were soldiering in Italy.

On 2 December 1943 one company was unloading ammunition from ships in Bari harbour when German planes attacked. Ships began to burn and ammunition began to explode. It was the most devastating air raid of the campaign. Despite casualties and the constant danger, the Bechuanas continued to unload the burning vessels.

Another Bechuana company was praised for bravery serving as ammunition carriers and stretcher bearers during the Battle of Frosinone in May 1944.
See Index

BELGIAN CONGO

Other names:	Zaire
Status in 1939:	Belgian colony.
Government in 1939:	Belgian administration.
Population in 1939:	11,000,000
Make-up in 1939:	Over 200 Tribes;
	48,000 Europeans, mostly
	Belgian.
Religion:	tribal;
	Missionary Christians.
Location:	Central Africa

Once known as the Heart of Darkest Africa, a phrase which referred to white man's ignorance about the area, this land of great variation was conquered by the Belgians in the late 19th century. The newcomers soon realised the land's immense natural resources and proceeded to exploit a wealth out of proportion to their investment. One reason for the profit was the virtual enslavement of the native people. Belgium may have appeared to be 'poor little Belgium' when invaded by Germany in 1914, but in the Congo the Belgians behaved with an arrogance far more inhumane than any British, German or French colonials in Africa.

As a result the military forces of the Congo, the askaris, i.e. native soldiers with white officers – a black clone of a white army – were primarily concerned with protecting the white colonists from tribal revolts.

When Belgium was conquered by Germany in 1940 the Belgian forces in exile would have loved to have drawn upon the vast population of the Congo to build up an army of liberation, but their fears for the colonists only allowed them to use some white volunteers.

Only in summer of 1941 did a Congo army take overt action. They marched across French territory to Ethiopia to engage the Italian enemy. Their mere presence helped trap an Italian force which surrendered
See Index

BELGIUM

Status in 1939:	independent.
Government in 1939:	Democratic Monarchy.
Population in 1939:	8,300,000.
Make-up in 1939:	Flemish 4,800,000;
	Walloons 3,200,000;
	Germans 300,000;
	Jews 7000;
	immigrant Jews 60,000.
Religion:	Christian.
Location:	Western Europe

When neighbouring France went to war against neighbouring Germany in September 1939 Belgium tried desperately to remain neutral. No serious protests were made when a dozen Belgian merchant ships were lost to German mines and submarines. The Belgians had expected a German invasion since 1935, since Hitler rearmed Germany in contravention of the Versailles Treaty. After all, Belgium had taken part of Germany in 1918 and invaded Germany in the 1920s. They knew Hitler wanted revenge. However, when the French built a concrete defence line, the Maginot Line, along the German border, the Belgians refused to extend it to the Belgian-German border, lest it provoke Hitler. They did, however, make an agreement that the

French and British could help them if Germany attacked.

On the morning of 10 May 1940 without warning lightning struck Belgium – lightning war, that is, blitzkrieg, as German planes bombed and German troops crossed the border, where the massive fort at Eben Emael and its 700 gunners dominated the countryside. On the 11th German troops landed on its top in gliders and captured the entire garrison for the loss of just six men!

Even for battle-hardened veterans the sudden onslaught of aircraft, tanks, artillery fire and infantry charges can be unnerving. For peacetime regulars taken by surprise it is positively paralysing.

On the 14th the large Belgian reserve, men called up over the previous three days, was ordered to hold the north end of the front line, while the British Army, just arriving, held the centre and the French held the south along the Meuse River. But within 24 hours the British were falling back and the French admitted the Germans had pierced the Meuse defences. The Belgian divisions, each only 10,000 men with no inherent artillery and anti-tank guns held at divisional headquarters, proved totally inadequate to face the German Sixth Army. The Belgians too began falling back. In fact Germans in trucks actually bypassed the Belgian infantry.

Civilians fled onto the open roads, mingling with soldiers, and both were constantly strafed by German planes.

On the 25th the British began evacuating by sea from Dunkirk, with the French retreating to the sea too. On the 28th King Leopold negotiated the best deal possible and surrendered his country and armed forces.

About 6,500 troops had been killed, 15,900 wounded and 200,000 overrun and captured. Upon the surrender another 430,000 marched into captivity including the king. Civilian deaths were about 13,000.

A few hundred soldiers had evacuated with the British, some airmen had flown to Britain and the navy and merchant service had sailed there. These 'Free Belgians' set up a government in exile in London.

Not everyone in Belgium recognised defeat: there were those who continued to resist, albeit by subterfuge, forming resistance cells; secondly there were those who believed they could work with the Germans: the Germans of eastern Belgium considered the invasion to be a liberation, until the evils of nazi rule became apparent. Their menfolk took off Belgian uniform and put on German uniform – to refuse meant imprisonment in a concentration camp.

The Germans retained several members of the government, the civil service and the police and the German SS arrived to recruit a battalion of Flemish combat soldiers. The fascist parties of Belgium believed this was a good sign, and one party organised its own SS in imitation of that German paramilitary unit. The fascist parties also had their own uniformed militias who now began to act as if they were in charge. However, Degrelle's catholic party, more religious than fascist, preached against helping the Germans militarily, though working for them. By 1941 82,000 Belgians were voluntarily working for the Germans in Belgium and 321,000 in Germany.

In June 1941 Germany invaded the USSR, and Degrelle had to rethink the situation. The Soviets were communist, the antithesis of Christianity, therefore he now authorised his members to help in that struggle. He formed an infantry legion and joined it as a private soldier. The Flemish fascists and devout Christians also formed a legion, and the German SS recruited a second battalion of Flemish.

By November all these formations were in bitter combat on the Russian front.

In Britain the Free Belgians were continuing their war: six warships escorted allied convoys, often containing Belgian ships, across the Atlantic in the teeth of German warships, submarines, aircraft and mines. There were more Belgian sailors than ships so the allies were building more for them.

Belgians were flying and maintaining planes from British airfields fighting German fighters and bombing German installations in Western Europe including Belgium. By 1943 there were over 400 pilots, several hundred other flight crew and well over a thousand ground crew.

The horror of the Russian front continued and in March 1943 Degrelle's legion barely managed to escape a trap by charging right through a Soviet tank unit. Shortly after this the 1,600 survivors were honoured with SS status, a dubious award to say the least, but one they could hardly refuse. Henceforth the legion would be known as SS Sturmbrigade Wallonie. At the same time the Flemish legion and all Flemish serving in the German SS were united into the SS Regiment Langemarck. Both formations were allowed home to recruit: they took in old men looking for a second youth, boys looking for adventure, and real idealists who thought this was God's will.

By the time it went back into action the Wallonie had 2,000 men. They passed a freezing dangerous winter, and in February their worst nightmare became a reality – they were suddenly trapped on the wrong side of the Gniloy Tikich River. Degrelle, in command now, chose to fight on, for the Soviets were not known for their kindness to prisoners. The men charged through a Soviet tank force and dived into the freezing river. The prudent Soviets did not follow. Degrelle had managed to save 632 of his troops, and many of those were wounded and suffering from frostbite.

Belgian troops were also in combat in Italy this winter: Free Belgian commandos who could not take the constant waiting in Britain any longer had lobbied Churchill, the British Prime Minister, to be allowed to fight alongside the British. He agreed and sent them to Italy. They performed well.

The allies had been planning the liberation of Belgium since 1940 and as part of this plan in 1944 they stepped up their air attacks on anything that could be of value to the Germans: rail lines, bridges, canal locks, factories, ports, and any vehicles found on the roads. Needless to say, not all bombs hit their intended target and casualties among Belgian civilians were extremely high.

The first step in the liberation of Belgium was the allied landing on the Normandy coast of France 6 June 1944. Belgian commandos hit the beaches, Belgian ships protected the troopships and Belgian planes attacked the defences. In late June a Belgian SAS (paratroopers) company parachuted into Brittany to aid the French Resistance in an open revolt against the Germans. They held their own until relieved by advancing Americans in August.

A Free Belgian unit, the White Brigade, now crossed the English Channel to join the allied infantry fighting their way from Normandy towards Belgium.

To defend Belgium the Germans had a mixed bag of flak gunners, rear echelon and exhausted survivors of the fighting in France. Additionally, there were those Belgians who for whatever reason had tied their fortunes to the Germans: 25,000 men in various types of fascist militia with glorious names like Brigade Volante Christus Rex; several hundred armed guards of Organisation Todt the body that had built the air-raid bunkers and gun positions on the coast; 3,000 NSKK, which supplied drivers and mechanics to whoever needed them; 60,000 armed harvest guards, who protected the farms from sabotage; and the Belgian police who had been hunting terrorists for four years. The Germans did not know how many of these they could really count on. They would soon learn.

On 2 September British tanks reached the Belgian border and 24 hours later they entered Brussels unopposed: the Germans and their Belgian supporters had run. A day later British tanks reached Antwerp. Here many of the Germans and fascists were cut off and they fought like trapped rats. It took several weeks for the Resistance, now openly rebelling, to hunt them down.

In northern Belgium resistance was stiffer as the White Brigade and other allied troops battled for every canal and stream. The White Brigade liberated Bourg Leopold after a 36-hour struggle.

By late September the allies had to call a halt, for liberating Belgium had used up their supplies. The people of Belgium had suffered grotesquely from air raids and cross-fire and now the inhabitants of Antwerp were subjected to a missile offensive by a wrathful Hitler throughout the winter. The population of the eastern towns, some of them German-speakers, lived within earshot of the front line for the next few months.

In December the Germans attempted a come back, advancing into the Ardennes Forest and heavy combat took place between the Americans and Germans at Stavelot, Malmedy, St Vith and Bastogne, where an American corps was surrounded for a week. The civilians dodged shells and fled. In some villages members of the Resistance, who had thought their war over, had to hide once gain. At the end of January the Germans were thrown back to Germany.

The fascists, men, women and children, who had escaped to Germany were put to use by the Germans, either as workers or soldiers. All able bodied Flemish men 16 to 60 were placed into the SS Langemarck Regiment, which with a strength of 8,000 was redesignated a division. The Wallonie took in all Walloon men and was also redesignated a division. Both were, however, sent to the Russian front rather than the Belgian border.

On 9 February 1945 the SS Wallonie Division attacked the Soviets in eastern Germany to knock them off balance, but the Soviet riposte was so fierce the Walloons almost cracked open. Hitler ordered another attack for the 16th. The Walloons did as ordered and within two days were in trouble in the village of Lindenburg. A nearby attack by the SS Langemarck Division also failed miserably and on the 20th Hitler had to agree to a cessation of the attack.

Four days later the long-awaited Soviet offensive came and at once everyone had to begin a fighting retreat. On the first day the Belgians suffered 10% casualties.

By early April SS Wallonie Division was down to 800 survivors. The Langemarck was not much better off, and by the end of the month they were pushed northwards with their backs to the sea. Degrelle then spoke to 35 men, all that he could gather, and said he was fleeing aboard ship to Denmark.

On 6 April 300 Belgian SAS parachuted into the Netherlands in order to cause havoc behind German lines. In north Germany Belgian commandos accompanied the British advance. On the 25th the White Brigade and a brigade recruited during the winter shot their way into southern Netherlands. Three days later the Germans in that nation asked for a truce.

Two days later Hitler was dead, and a week later Germany gave up.

Between King Leopold's surrender and the end of the war the Free Belgian forces lost 500 killed and wounded. The merchant service had lost twelve ships before May 1940, 6 during the invasion and 78 sailing with the 'Free' forces, and scores of ships were damaged: 832 sailors lost their lives.

The Resistance claimed 16,000 dead – a few killed in action, but most executed or slowly murdered in concentration camps. As well as the 6,500 troops killed in 1940 1,264 Belgian soldiers died in German custody.

Belgian fascist deaths are unknown, but must be in the area of 10,000 killed in action. Plus over a thousand German-speaking Belgian citizens died wearing German uniform. Officially, after the liberation 230 fascists were executed and 77,000 imprisoned, but how many were unofficially murdered by Resistance kangaroo courts is anyone's guess.

About 13,000 civilians were killed in air raids and crossfires during the 1940 invasion and 27,500 in this manner from then until May 1945.

Few Belgian Jews died at the hands of the Nazis, but 29,000 of the immigrant Jews were murdered.

All told at least 77,000 Belgian citizens died from war related causes.

See Index

BRAZIL

Status in 1942:	independent.
Government in 1942:	fragile democracy.
Population in 1942:	41,000,000
Make-up in 1942:	65% European Stock, mostly Portuguese, with some Spanish, French, German and Italian; 34% mulattos and negroes; a few thousand aboriginals.
Religion:	Christian.
Location:	South America.

When Europe exploded into war in 1939 the South Americans ignored the conflict, in the same way that the Europeans had ignored South American conflicts. Brazil warned the Germans not to antagonise them by sinking Brazilian ships, but in 1942 Brazilian ships did indeed become the target of German submarines. By July a dozen had been sunk.

On 15 August the Brazilian people were angered when a troopship was sunk with the loss of 300 lives. Over the next six days three more Brazilian ships were sunk. The people clamoured for a response from their leaders and on the 22nd Brazil declared war on Germany.

Mind you, the Germans were not exactly quaking in their boots when they heard this, for many Latin American nations had declared war on them as a diplomatic move to please the USA. However, the Germans were sorely mistaken if they thought the Brazilian declaration was just such a gesture, for at once Brazil allowed US planes and ships to use her soil to patrol against the submarines and Brazilian planes and warships did the same.

In the next six months Brazilian forces sank five submarines. Coupled with US victories in the South Atlantic this seriously hurt the German submarine fleet.

By October 1943 ten Brazilian merchant ships had been sunk by submarines since the war declaration and the Brazilians had sunk eleven submarines. This month a passenger ship was shelled by a submarine. The captain ran her aground and ordered the crew and passengers to climb onto the shore, while local villagers ran down to help them. The submarine shelled them, then submerged before Brazilian planes could arrive. There was no longer any doubt in the minds of the Brazilians as to what kind of enemy they were fighting.

Brazil prepared an army unit to take the war to the Germans and General Moraes visited US Fifth Army in Italy in December 1943 to find out how the unit could best be used.

On 12 April 1944 a Brazilian air component went into action in Italy, flying reconnaissance, fighter and bombing missions.

At sea in 1944 Brazilian and US warships together sank a German blockade runner – a Brazilian naval vessel was sunk by a submarine – and while hunting submarines a Brazilian corvette was lost in a storm. In the second half of the year Brazil took over all responsibility for anti-submarine warfare in the South Atlantic.

In August 1944 a few officers and sergeants of the Brazilian Expeditionary Division climbed into US foxholes in Italy to learn at first hand what they would be up against.

On 16 September the first battalion went into action at Massanosa, and at the end of the day proudly marched back their first German prisoners. By October the entire division was in action at Marano-Riolo. The US Fifth Army respected the Brazilians and Moraes was given command of some US units. On the 28th Fifth Army called a halt to all attacks, but the Brazilians were so confident by now they felt they could go on alone: at Pian de los Rios they received a bloody nose for this cockiness.

On 12 December the division was repulsed again at Monte Castello, where German artillery spotters could look down their throats. By the year's end the Brazilians had lost 1,300 killed and wounded.

In February 1945 the Brazilians were still staring up at Monte Castello, but Fifth Army came up with a plan: the Brazilians would make a frontal attack while the US 10th Division, the only US mountain unit, would infiltrate the German rear. The battle began on the 18th and, though the plan worked, the fighting was tough all the way, and only on the fourth day was the mountain peak captured. The Brazilians were ordered to make another attack. This was launched on 3 March, and the Brazilians covered five miles before sundown: an unheard of advance in Italy. This did, however, bring out the anger in the Germans, who counter-attacked for three days. The Brazilians desperately held on: attacked again on the fourth day, liberated three villages and took 1,200 prisoners.

The Brazilian soldiers did not know it, but this battle was one of Fifth Army's preliminary moves to enable it and the British Eighth Army to take the offensive in the spring and liberate the remainder of Italy.

On 14 April Fifth Army launched the spring offensive. The Brazilians aimed for the city of Parma: the advance was steady.

On the 30th the Brazilians took the surrender of the entire German 148th Division, having trapped it against the Po River, and two days later the campaign was over.

In Italy Brazil's air and ground forces suffered 448 killed and 2,760 wounded. The war at sea cost several hundred dead.

Brazil proved she was not a nation to be toyed with and as a result she became the first Latin American nation to send an army to fight in Europe. Though her efforts were small compared to her population, they must be seen in context with the response of the other Latin American nations that also lost ships at sea to German submarines.
See Index

BRITISH EAST AFRICA

Other names:	includes British Somaliland; Kenya; Northern Rhodesia (Zambia) Nyasaland (Malawi); Southern Rhodesia (Zimbabwe); Tanganyika-Zanzibar (Tanzania); Uganda.
Status in 1939:	British colonies.
Government in 1939:	British administration.
Population in 1939:	13,000,000
Make-up in 1939:	Somalis in Somalia; elsewhere hundreds of tribes; Arabs in ports; 145,000 British colonists, half in S. Rhodesia; 100,000 Indian colonists.
Religion:	Extremely diverse.
Location:	Eastern Africa.

It took several days for the news of Britain's declaration of war on Germany to reach the tribal villages, farms and plantations. The response among the whites was immediate. From all walks of life they volunteered: farmers, plantation owners, merchants, employees, itinerants, adventurers; choosing the Royal Navy, the Royal Air Force or the British Army. In the latter case Southern Rhodesian whites formed their own force of infantry and artillery, and white Kenyans formed an armoured car unit.

There was another option: to serve as officers and sergeants in native units, for the natives too were volunteering to fight for King George. The vast majority of the native volunteers were placed in the Pioneer Corps to perform duties no soldier liked: stringing barbed-wire, digging trenches, unloading ships and trucks, grading roads etc.

There were also native combat units. The Somaliland Camel Corps, which included an infantry company of Nyasalanders, the Northern Rhodesian Regiment and the (Southern) Rhodesian African Rifles. The elite force was the King's African Rifles (KAR). Like all British regiments, its size was open-ended, the number of battalions corresponding to the number of volunteers. The KAR recruited only the finest physical specimens from the more aggressive tribes of Kenya, Uganda and Nyasaland. A few natives from elsewhere, including non-British colonies, managed to get in.

The prospect of combat for these Africans seemed imminent when Italy declared war on Britain in June 1940, because Italian territory bordered on British Somaliland and Kenya.

The Italian advance came on 1 July 1940 near Fort Moyale on the Kenya-Ethiopian border and a battalion of the KAR fired upon them: a mere probe, the Italians fell back. The Italians were in fact African native units with Italian officers. The real attack came on the 14th and by nightfall the KAR withdrew from the fort under orders. At Dobel on the Kenya-Italian Somaliland border a KAR battalion was forced to fall back by camel-mounted Italian Somali troops.

The true goal of the Italians was not south into Kenya, but north into British Somaliland, which they invaded on 3 August with five columns. The Somaliland Camel Corps, in vehicles and on camels, sniped at the invaders, but the colony's garrison could not fight all five columns, so they chose to give one a black eye. The Somalis, a battalion of the KAR, and two battalions of the Indian Army waited at Tug Argan Pass.

On the 11th the pass defenders were attacked. A Northern Rhodesian and a British battalion now arrived – the British having come to corset the native troops, an ugly term meaning to stiffen their moral backbone. When charged by the Italians the British fled!

On the 17th the colony commander decided on a sea evacuation, and within a couple of days all had sailed away. They had lost 250 killed and wounded and had inflicted casualties on the Italians of 2000 killed and wounded.

British generals were already planning the conquest of Italian East Africa and to this end assembled in Kenya the 11th African Division of the 21st, 25th and 26th East African Brigades (each of three battalions of KAR); the 12th African Division comprising the 22nd East African Brigade, the 24th Gold Coast Brigade (West Africans), and the 1st Brigade of the (white) South African Army; and the 1st Division of the (white) South African Army. The 11th and 12th Divisions had British artillery, engineers and rear-echelon troops, and all were supported by East African pioneers.

The offensive began on 4 February 1941 as the 25th Brigade advanced into Ethiopia and the 22nd Brigade captured Beles Gugnani oasis in Italian Somaliland. In days the South Africans and Gold Coasters overcame enemy resistance on the Jaba River in Italian Somaliland.

In fact the biggest obstacle was the primitive terrain – the pioneers and engineers had to create and maintain roads, build countless bridges and constantly shift supply dumps across desert scrubland, wide gullies, goat tracks and rocky escarpments. By March all of Italian Somaliland was cleared, a separate amphibious invasion recaptured British Somaliland almost without a shot and the allies were soon poised to invade Ethiopia from the east – but not until they had brought up more supplies, for they had travelled 800 miles.

To date the three divisions had captured 10,350 actual Italians and 11,732 native troops, many of them sick and wounded. This naturally put a tremendous strain on allied medical teams and supply officers. Fortunately, an estimated 30,000 enemy native troops had deserted. Total casualties to the allies were 445 killed and wounded. This was the greatest allied victory in the war to date, and the East Africans could be proud they played an integral part in it.

Now came the invasion of Ethiopia. The 11th Division advanced towards Jijiga and the 12th Division for Neghelli. Opposition was negligible until the 12th Division reached Soddu and Jimma in May. Soddu only fell after a serious fight. At Jimma the Italians abandoned their sick and wounded to the 22nd Brigade and retreated westwards. The East Africans chased them, fought twice at Demli and Gimbi and then

took the surrender of the remaining 6,500 Italians on 6 July. The 25th and 26th Brigades aided thousands of Ethiopian guerrillas to besiege Chilga, Wolchefit Pass, Kulkaber and Gondar. Several assaults on the Italians were repelled. On 27 September Wolchefit Pass surrendered. In November the allies concentrated their attacks on Kulkaber and after a stiff battle over two weeks the enemy gave up on the 27th, surrendering all Italians in East Africa.

At last this unbelievable campaign was over. It was fought in terrain that would appear daunting to a peacetime explorers' expedition and it was fought primarily by native Africans on all sides. At no time did British officers report concern about the stamina, courage or loyalty of their native troops.

There did not seem to be any further need for East African combat units. The pioneers continued to work, some remaining to help civilise Ethiopia, others to serve at British bases all over Africa.

Then a new combat mission arrived. As part of Britain's war against Pétainist France, the 22nd East African Brigade was sent to Madagascar and on 11 September 1942 they began an advance down a long narrow jungle road. By rotating companies in the lead the brigade overcame small ineffective French rearguards until one day they were informed the French had surrendered. The little affair had taken 56 days and cost the brigade 33 killed and 96 hospitalised with wounds and sickness. A brigade of Northern Rhodesians had also participated in the campaign, but saw little action.

The white Rhodesians had placed an infantry company and an artillery battery with the British Eighth Army's 7th Armoured Division, which gained a reputation as the famed Desert Rats, and saw fierce action in North Africa at the relief of Tobruk November-December 1941, Gazala May 1942, Alamein July, Alam al Halfa September, Second Alamein October-November 1942, and Tunisia March-May 1943. The white Rhodesians also formed a Long Range Desert Group unit, fighting behind enemy lines in North Africa. Aditionally 1,500 white Rhodesians were attached to the 6th Armoured Division of the South African Army and saw combat in Sicily July-August 1943 and throughout the Italian campaign September 1943 to May 1945. In total 8,000 white Rhodesians served.

White Rhodesians also flew and maintained aircraft in British squadrons and in three all-Rhodesian squadrons, one flying heavy bomber missions over Europe, one flying reconnaissance/ground attack missions in the Mediterranean and one Typhoon ground attack squadron in Western Europe 1944-45.

In North Africa 30,000 East African pioneers supported the Eighth Army, on occasion coming under air raids and artillery salvoes. In one instance 400 unarmed East Africans were overrun by the Germans – 75 risked their lives to escape. By 1942 East African pioneers were doing all sorts of jobs: e.g. fighting fires caused by accident, sabotage and air attack, handling land mines and manning flak guns.

When the British lost Burma to a Japanese offensive in 1942 there was an overwhelming desire on the part of British generals, if not their government, to reconquer that British colony. They decided that Africans would be useful in such an enterprise.

To prepare for Burma the 11th African Division of the 21st, 25th and 26th Brigades (eight battalions of KAR and one North Rhodesian), with British and East African support troops, was put through intensive jungle training in Ceylon.

In 1944 the division sailed to India and moved up to the India-Burma border in July: the mission was to follow a retreating Japanese unit down the Kabaw Valley from Tamu to Kalemyo.

Almost at once they came upon stragglers, not tough little jungle experts as they had been led to expect, but sick and starving city boys from Osaka and Tokyo. Some wandered like zombies. The Africans were astonished to see the depths to which an army could sink. Nothing in Ethiopia had prepared them for this. Yet even while dying on their feet many Japanese fought back.

Only in August did the division run into real opposition at a hill they christened Jambo (Ki-Swahili for 'Hello'). For two killed and twelve wounded a Kenya company killed

seventeen Japanese and found thirteen dead from artillery fire. A week later they encountered another rearguard: they pulled back and let air and artillery pound the enemy for five days. The enemy retreated and the Africans followed. They continued day after day encountering enemy stragglers in twos and threes. By 31 August they had burned their 800th Japanese corpse.

The monsoon rains increased and soon the two tracks they were using could accommodate only mules, elephants and men.

On 28 September an Uganda battalion had a frightening night when they had to repel infiltrators and next day repulsed a bayonet charge. The enemy did not retreat and the division was brought to a halt.

On 10 October the Ugandans made three attacks, but failed. On the 22nd, reinforced by two battalions, they tried again. One company lost five of its six officers, but the Japanese had had enough and withdrew.

Near Mawlaik Nyasalanders and North Rhodesians captured a defended hill and on 9 November the division took Mawlaik despite enemy artillery fire and air strikes. On the 14th Kenyans took Kalemyo and held it against counter-attacks for several days.

By 8 December divisional artillery was firing across the mighty Chindwin River while the engineers built a bridge. On the 10th, spearheaded by Nyasalanders, the division crossed the bridge and captured Schwegyin by nightfall. The division was now informed the mission was over.

At the end of December the fresh 28th East African Brigade entered the Burma campaign by capturing Gangaw and attacking towards the Irrawaddy River. Its experience was similar to that of the 11th Division. It was February 1945 before they reached the river after an advance of 100 miles.

Throughout March the 28th Brigade resisted counter-assaults. On the 20th a company of about 150 Somalis was driven from their foxholes, but plucked up enough courage to recapture them. Later they counted 160 enemy dead in their positions. The brigade was relieved in April.

About 45,000 East Africans served in Ceylon, India and Burma. Their infantry echelon was eight brigades manning 14 KAR, six Southern Rhodesian and four Northern

Rhodesian battalions. Others served as engineers, pioneers, artillerymen and reconnaissance troops.

East Africans earned a fine war record: 1,924 paying the ultimate sacrifice in hopes that something good might be preserved and something better gained.

See Index

BRITISH WEST AFRICA

Other names:	includes British Cameroons; British Togoland; Gambia Gold Coast (Ghana); Nigeria; Sierra Leone.
Status in 1939:	British colonies.
Government in 1939:	British administration.
Population in 1939:	28,000,000
Make-up in 1939:	250 tribes; a few thousand British colonists.
Religion:	extremely diverse.
Location:	Western Africa.

When Britain declared war on Germany in 1939 she asked her white and indigenous colonial subjects in West Africa to volunteer. Some entered the merchant service; others joined the Royal Navy, Army or Royal Air Force.

The vast majority of the native volunteers were placed in the British Army Pioneer Corps, which performed labour duties: road and airstrip construction, unloading ships and trucks etc. Some combat infantry were raised for local defence.

As the German submarine menace became serious the British set up air and sea bases in West Africa and local pioneers provided a significant proportion of the labour. In 1941 the British asked for more volunteers and conscripted white males in West Africa aged 18-48. Soon 100,000 natives were in uniform. There were not enough West African white officers for them so East African whites and actual British were drafted. 18,400 West Africans pioneers went to North Africa to support the Eighth Army.

In 1940–41 the British government had a policy of using as few actual British troops in combat as possible, and as a result many hodge podge units were established. In order to invade Italian East Africa from Kenya two African divisions were created and a South African Army division was brought in. The 24th Gold Coast Brigade was created with three infantry battalions and attached to the 12th Division.

In February 1941 the invasion began and the Gold Coasters rode in bone-jarring trucks along rough tracks in desert scrubland. 100 miles into Italian Somaliland they jumped out and attacked the Jaba River defences. They met resistance from African soldiers with Italian officers who made several half-hearted attempts to kick them back across the river. After this the Italians retreated and the Gold Coasters remounted their trucks. On and on they drove, clearing out a pathetic handful of stragglers here and there and by March had covered 800 miles.

They rested and were reinforced by the 23rd Nigerian Brigade, who took the lead to enter Ethiopia. On the 18th the Nigerians ran into serious opposition at Marda Pass, the first since Jaba River. They found actual Italian infantry here. For 24 hours they were held up.

On the 24th the Nigerians met more opposition at Babile Pass, but the enemy fell back that night. Over the next two days they tried to cross the Bisidimo River and made it on the 27th.

From now on the advance was much quicker and the brigades fanned out. The Nigerians had a short fight at Abalti, two major fights at Demli and Gimbi and were withdrawn in early July.

The West Africans had performed admirably.

By 1942 the combat echelon of the West Africans might have been forgiven for thinking the British had forgotten about them, but their courage and discipline must have impressed somebody, for they were suddenly ordered to form two divisions for duty against the Japanese.

The 81st Division formed the 4th Nigerian and 5th Gold Coast Brigades and the 6th Brigade of a Nigerian, a Gambian and a Sierra Leone battalions. The 82nd Division had the 1st Nigerian, 2nd Gold Coast and 7th Gold Coast Brigades and an extra Sierra

Leone battalion. The 3rd Nigerian Brigade was independent. Most of the other elements of the divisions: artillery, engineers, reconnaissance, rear-echelon were West Africans too. The first stop was jungle warfare school in Ceylon.

The reconnaissance battalion of the 81st Division was detached and ordered to launch raids on the Burmese coast, while the division was ordered to begin walking down the Kaladan Valley, about 40 miles inland. The men were quite aware that as yet no British unit had been victorious against the Japanese.

They met the enemy and held their own. In January 1944 Gold Coasters on the coast became the first 'British' to capture a Japanese artillery.

In March the reconnaissance battalion rejoined the division with full credit, their commander being promoted to brigade commander.

The 3rd Nigerian Brigade was made Chindit – indeed an honour, because the trainer of the Chindits, General Wingate, was a shrewd chooser of men. In mid-March the brigade was given its orders: the 6th Battalion was to fly into Aberdeen airstrip inside Japanese-occupied Burma. Once there, though, they were despondent that the British just wanted them to guard the airstrip while they hunted Japanese.

In early April they were moved to guard another airstrip, White City, half hoping they would meet the enemy on the way. Once at White City, however, they were shelled by the enemy and that night they were ordered to assist a Gurkha patrol that had run into the enemy. In the pitch black night they stumbled through thick vegetation, shooting at gunflashes and at dawn allied aircraft chased away the enemy. The Nigerians had kept their nerve and had suffered just a half dozen losses.

This day the Nigerians came under air and artillery assault and after dark an infantry assault. The Nigerians and others defended the perimeter. This was repeated for three more days. The Nigerians now had all the action they had ever wished for.

On the 11th the 7th Battalion arrived and joined Gurkhas and Burmese in a sweep around the perimeter and next day held the rear while the Gurkhas fought. The 7th then moved out on their own and defeated a company of Japanese at Mawlu. On the 14th the 6th moved out and ran smack dab into a major Japanese assault: in minutes they were in hand to hand fighting. Allied aircraft bombing just 200 yards away caused the enemy to break off.

The 3rd Brigade now marched to a new airstrip at Hopin, code-named Blackpool: on the march the 7th Battalion killed 40 Japanese. They took up defences ten miles from Blackpool, feeling very vulnerable, especially as by now many men were low with dysentery, typhus and jungle sores. On 14 May Blackpool was assaulted and the brigade went to the rescue. This happened again on the 23rd.

In July allied doctors examined the Chindits and raised hell, declaring they were all far too sick to be in combat. Under this pressure the generals agreed to fly them out, except for the Nigerians and one British brigade, who were judged essential. The Nigerians finally flew out on 18 August.

In July the 81st Division had been withdrawn from front line duty. In the Kaladan Valley and on the coast the division suffered 431 killed and wounded and hundreds sick. They turned their mission over to the 82nd Division, who resumed the march despite the monsoon.

It was October before the 82nd encountered heavy opposition, at Mowdok from 2,000 Japanese. They beat them, but were held for a few days at Taung Bazaar, where they had to climb 3000 feet to outflank the enemy.

On the night of 15 December, near Buthidaung the division repelled a major enemy counter-attack: some broke through and Gold Coast infantry rescued an Indian artillery battery, which was fighting the Japanese hand to hand! The division captured Buthidaung on the 18th. Ahead of them lay more rearguards and almost impenetrable jungle for the next six months.

About 45,000 West Africans served in the Burma campaign and all units pulled their weight. They had met the feared Japanese and had bested them.

See Index

BRITISH WEST INDIES

Other names:	includes Bahamas; Barbados; Bermuda; British Guiana; British Honduras (Belize); Caymans; Jamaica; Leewards; Trinidad & Tobago; Turks & Caicos; Windwards.
Status in 1939:	British colonies.
Government in 1939:	British administration.
Population in 1939:	14,000,000
Make-up in 1939:	Mostly negroes; a few thousand aboriginals; a few thousand British, Indian and Chinese.
Religion:	Christian.
Location:	east of the Gulf of Mexico, coastal America.

When Britain declared war on Germany in 1939 individual West Indians were allowed to volunteer for the merchant service, Royal Navy, Royal Air Force and British Army, the latter for home defence.

The Army eventually established the following island defences: Bahamas, a few infantry companies; Barbados, an infantry battalion and a battery of shore guns; Bermuda, an artillery battalion, a battalion and a company of infantry, and an engineer company; Leewards, an infantry battalion; St Lucia, a battery of shore guns; Windwards, an infantry battalion. On Jamaica there were an artillery battalion, a battalion of shore guns, an infantry battalion and considerable rear-echelon forces, all Jamaican, and also a battery of shore guns manned by Turks Islanders.

The mainland colonies had: British Guiana, an infantry battalion, an anti-aircraft gun troop, and a battery of shore guns; British Honduras, an infantry battalion; and Trinidad-Tobago, three batteries of shore guns, two troops of anti-aircraft guns, a battalion and a company of infantry and rear-echelon forces. The officers were white and most of the rear-echelon personnel in the colonies were British.

Individually these island defences were sparse, but their purpose was not to deter invasion, but to handle such things as enemy commando raids – which never happened. Only in the war at sea were West Indians able to distinguish themselves in action.

In August 1940 as a result of a new treaty 50 US Navy destroyers were loaned to the Royal Navy in return for leases of bases on Antigua, Bahamas, Bermuda, Jamaica, St Lucia, Trinidad and in British Guiana. These populations were 'invaded' by thousands of Americans, bringing with them bulldozers, trucks, planes, ships – all the impedimenta of war. The purpose of these bases was to patrol against German submarines.

There was considerable submarine activity in these waters. For example, on 5 August 1944 a 64-ton ferry, the *Island Queen*, disappeared while making an overnight inter-island trip with a crew of ten and 55 passengers. Wreckage found near Grenada provided evidence that she was blown out of the water by a submarine.

As the war progressed the British needed manpower and they asked for more volunteers: 10,000 West Indians eventually served in the Royal Air Force as ground crew and flyers. Civilians were also asked to come to Britain to work: thousands did so, e.g. 1,200 to fell timber in Scotland and 1,000 to make munitions in Lancashire. They met no racism from the grateful British workers.

However, there was considerable racism in the corridors of power. The West Indians had constantly offered a combat ground unit. They were aware that black Africans were fighting and wondered why they were not. In 1944 Churchill, the British Prime Minister, ordered a composite battalion to be sent to fight in Italy. The British generals obeyed, but placed restrictions on the unit: no negroes could serve above the pay grade of corporal and only the fittest volunteers among the home defence units were chosen. As it was enough passed to overfill the battalion: 56 officers and 1,200 men.

The battalion reached Italy in August to be inspected by 15th Army Group, who reported the unit unfit for combat – which if true was a serious indictment of the British Army, for these fellows had been serving for five years or more! By 20 September the battalion had only received eight instructors and was woefully short of white sergeants. Obviously someone was dragging his heels. Now the generals decided that Italy was too cold for the West Indians and they should be sent to Egypt to train! If Scottish winters were not too cold for West Indian tree fellers, then an Italian autumn was not too cold for men in uniform, therefore, there must have been an ulterior motive. There were plenty of black Africans serving in 15th Army Group, so it is disappointing to discover this under-use of able-bodied fighting men.

The general in Egypt telegrammed 15th Army Group, hoping the battalion would at least have the equipment peculiar to 'Indians' – some British generals obviously did not bother to find out the nationality of their soldiers. This farce continued in Egypt, with Churchill urging use of the West Indians for political reasons.

On 6 May the generals in Egypt reported the battalion ready for action and suggested South East Asia, where the war was still on. However, now the British government decided to send the battalion home and ordered the generals not to tell the soldiers the truth until they were aboard ship. Thus while Churchill was telling the Americans the British Army was bankrupt of manpower and he could only supply a few thousand men for the five million strong American force preparing to invade Japan, he was sending an unused battalion home.

The British were also hurriedly repatriating the West Indian workers home.
See Index

BULGARIA

Status in 1939:	independent.
Government in 1939:	democratic monarchy.
Population in 1939:	6,200,000.
Make-up in 1939:	Bulgars 5,475,000;
	Turks 620,000;
	Jews 63,000;
	a few thousand Macedonians;
	a few thousand Gypsies;
	a few thousand Volksdeutsch;
Religion:	Christian.
Location:	South-East Europe.

Immediately after World War I Bulgaria lost territory to Romania and Greece, thus in the years before World War II the reclamation of Greater Bulgaria was a theme constantly heard in politics.

By 1939 Tsar Boris was being courted by Hitler, but Boris was playing hard to get. He was no fool. He knew Bulgaria had no friends except the USSR, and with the communists as friends who needs enemies?

At first this coy demeanour paid off: Hitler restrained Romania while Boris' army reoccupied the Dobrudja in 1940; and in April 1941 as payment for allowing German troops to cross Bulgaria the Bulgarian Ist Corps marched in to take over Thrace from Greece. The same month Fifth Army followed the Germans into Yugoslavia and grabbed most of Macedonia. Boris wanted it all, but Mussolini's Italians got to some villages first. Hitler stepped in and stopped the squabbling.

Greater Bulgaria had been reclaimed, and all it cost was a few air raids on Bulgaria, which upset the cows.

However, Boris refused Hitler's invitation to the next party: the invasion of the USSR. This angered Hitler, who saw Boris as an ingrate. To keep Hitler off his back, Boris declared war on the USA and Britain in December 1941, though he had no intention of actually fighting anyone.

This is not to say all was sweetness and light: in Thrace Bulgarians returned to their homes of twenty years earlier, found Greeks living in them and fighting broke out, whereupon the Greeks began waging guerrilla war; in Macedonia, where the Bulgarian Army was made up of reservists called to duty they took out their frustrations on the local peasants. The best Bulgarian soldiers were stationed on the Turkish border: Boris did not trust the Turks. As a result of their attitude in Macedonia local anti-Bulgarian guerrilla bands were created.

In spring 1942 Hitler asked for help controlling Serbia in Yugoslavia, and Boris let him have his First Army.

By 1943 the Bulgarians were having a hard time in Macedonia. In one raid at Skopje 32 soldiers were killed and 26 wounded. In retaliation the Bulgarians arrested 1,003 people at random, shot 228 and imprisoned the remainder. Hitler also badgered Boris about his Jewish citizens – surely Boris wanted to get rid of them. Boris did put many Jewish men into labour gangs. Hitler said they should be eradicated. Boris refused, but in a compromising mood he let Hitler have his new Jews, i.e. 7,800 in Macedonia and 4,000 in Thrace. The Bulgarian police put them onto trains and the Germans took them to oblivion – about 3% survived.

Though Boris had kept out of the war against the USSR, the USSR ordered Bulgarian communists to make waves. Strikes and sabotage became commonplace and by December 1942 the Bulgarian police had arrested about 4,000 communists and shot a few.

In September, 1943 after one of his trips to see Hitler Boris suddenly died. Foul play was suspected, though it was probably a genuine illness. His heir was an infant, so the politicians began arguing and the communists turned to guerrilla warfare. Over the next year 500 Bulgarians and 200 German guests were killed in gunfights or assassinated by the communists.

In November 1943 the Anglo-Americans began bombing raids. Bulgarian flak gunners and fighter pilots did their best, but the bombers kept coming. In one raid on Sofia in January 1944 1,400 civilians were killed.

The results of playing at war created deep divisions in the nation: Bulgarian generals no longer helped the Germans in Yugoslavia and the Jews were released from the labour gangs. Yet in Thrace Bulgarian generals loaned their troops to the Germans – in one action for a score of casualties they killed 254 Greek guerrillas and caught 400 and in another for seven dead they killed 96. In March the guerrillas became bolder: an outpost of 22 Bulgarians was overrun and in another action 84 Bulgarians were killed and 34 wounded.

In August 1944, Bulgarian soldiers began surrendering to guerrillas in Thrace and others began retreating! A rot had set in.

In early September the Soviet Army reached the northern Bulgarian border. On the 6th strikes broke out in the cities. Next day a new government was formed, which ordered all German guests out of the country – at once Bulgarian and German soldiers began shooting at each other – the government declared war on Germany. The next day the Soviets invaded and declared war on Bulgaria. A new government took over, communist, and surrendered to the USSR.

Events had happened so quickly it was unbelievable, yet real enough that soldiers had to make up their minds in seconds – should they fight the Germans or join them? About 2,000 joined the Germans. The remainder chose to fight and by the end of the month the First, Second and Fourth Armies (each comprising three 10,000 man divisions) was in full-scale combat against the Germans along the Bulgarian-Yugoslav border, with Yugoslav guerrillas on their left flank and a Soviet force on their right,

Meanwhile at home, with the communists in power backed by the Soviet Army, betrayals, revenge, denouncements were the order of the day. Thousands were arrested.

During the winter at the front the Bulgarian Army held the trenches in conditions of rough weather, poor rations, patrols, sniping, artillery barrages and communist commissars looking over everyone's shoulder. They made a short advance in January 1945 at the cost of high casualties and a major move forward in February.

On 19 March the Bulgarians launched their big push and against withering fire they advanced, regardless of losses, approaching Lake Balaton in Hungary by the 31st.

On 1 April they battled for Csurgo and Nagy Kanisza, taking 2,000 prisoners. Three days later they took 7,000 prisoners and reached the Austrian border.

During April they crossed Austria, finishing their combat at Wolfsberg when the Germans surrendered on 9 May.

In fighting guerrillas in Yugoslavia, Greece and Bulgaria the security authorities lost about a thousand killed. Several hundred Bulgarian guerrillas were killed. Air raids killed about 3,000. Of the 2,000 who sided with the Germans in September 1944 few survived. In the war against Germany the armed forces lost 9,000 killed and 23,000 wounded. It is believed that at least 40,000 people were murdered by the communists after they took power.

Thus the total losses in the conflict are in the area of 56,000 killed.
See Index

BURMA

Other names:	Myanmar.
Status in 1939:	dominion of the British Empire.
Government in 1939:	Autonomous British Administration.
Population in 1939:	16,800,000.
Make-up in 1939:	Burmese 10,080,000; Karens 1,680,000; Shans 1,180,000; Bengalis 1,000,000; 100 other tribes.
Religion:	Mostly Buddhist, Also Moslem, tribal.
Location:	South-East Asia.

By 1939 the British presence in Burma was reaching the third generation and on the face of it the British were grooming the colony for independence, but a Burmese attempt to gain their own kind of freedom in the early 1930s was bloodily put down. As a result the ethnic Burmese did not trust the British. Other ethnic groups in Burma trusted the British to an extent, but disliked the Burmese.

The colony was precious to Britain for two reasons: it had a wealth of natural resources - e.g. rubber, oil, tin, tungsten, rice; and it protected the eastern flank of India from land invasion. By 1941 it was also precious to China for a road leading through the northern provinces from India to China had recently become a lifeline for allied (primarily American) supplies to China which was locked in a deadly war with Japan.

When Britain declared war on Germany in 1939 Burmese natives had enlisted in the British merchant service and a tiny air force and a Burma Division had been recruited for home defence.

Training for these forces was low priority until December 1941 when Japan suddenly struck British Malaya without a declaration of war and conquered Thailand in days, putting a Japanese army on the eastern Burmese border.

The Burma Division consisted of native rear-echelon troops and two infantry brigades each of two native battalions. On loan were some British rear-echelon and artillery and the Indian 13th Brigade. Few of the natives were actually Burmese - most were Shans, Karens, Kachins, Gangaws, Chins, Lushais and so on. As if to emphasize the weakness of the division, the 1st Burma Brigade was at Mandalay and the 2nd at Moulmein 500 miles apart.

The 2nd Brigade was sent to the Thailand border at once, where it was reinforced by the Indian 16th Brigade. The Burmese Police (mostly Indians and Bengalis) was told to beware of a Burmese revolt. Tenasserim was abandoned to a Japanese incursion, but otherwise the Japanese only hit Burma with air raids: one on Rangoon killed 3,000 civilians and caused utter panic.

In January 1942 Burma was reinforced by the Indian 17th Division, but it came with only three infantry battalions. It was now that the Japanese advanced. The 16th Brigade fell back. The 2nd Brigade had to follow and within two weeks the entire Kra Isthmus was abandoned. Thousand of Burmese civilians fled with their pitiful belongings. Britain asked China for help.

By 9 February the newly arrived Indian 46th Brigade fell back to the Billin River to join with the new Indian 48th Brigade, where both hoped to cross a single bridge over the Sittang. However, British high command refused. None of the defenders had fought an actual battle yet and they were ordered to defend the bridge. The Japanese easily outflanked them and the bridge had to be blown - trapping both brigades on the wrong side of the river: they swam across abandoning their equipment and supplies.

British engineers were also blowing up installations in Rangoon, which naturally caused panic when the inhabitants realised they were to be abandoned. The recent arrival of the British 7th Armoured Brigade and Indian 63rd Brigade counted for nought and on 7 March high command ordered a complete retreat. Next day the terrified Burmese watched as Japanese scouts crept into Rangoon unopposed.

The Chinese, who had entered the north, now retreated as well, while the allies, eleven infantry battalions of British, eleven of Indian and four of Burmese, were on the run northwards towards India, chased by 4 Japanese divisions (double the size of British divisions). At Yenangyaung the Burmese Division, now assembled, was cut off, and only the return of a Chinese division, which distracted the Japanese, enabled the Burmese to escape.

The retreating allies were constantly harassed by 400 enemy planes: a raid on Mandalay killed 2,000 civilians.

By 30 April the allies were across the Irrawaddy and just as the monsoon began they crossed the Chindwin and walked into India. The Japanese did not follow: India was not on their shopping list.

The thousand-mile retreat was the longest in British history. Taking roll call they found they were 13,500 men short: 1,250 Britons and Indians and 249 Burmese were known dead.

Already Aung San, an ethnic Burmese politician, had been meeting with the Japanese. It was obvious to anyone that the days of the British Empire were gone: there was a new empire in Asia, and the Burmese had to make the best deal possible. With Japanese aid Aung San formed the Burmese National Army recruited from the Burmese ethnic group. At first the 7,000 men were given sentry duty. Later they helped the Japanese keep the other ethnic groups in line.

This was not easy for allied intelligence agents were among the Karens, Shans, Kachins, Chins, Lushais, Palaungs and others advising guerrilla bands. Only a few ethnic Burmese joined the guerrillas.

However, what the guerrillas and the 400,000 refugees who had fled to India did not realise was that the British had deserted them in more ways than one. An agreement between British Prime Minister Churchill and American President Roosevelt made Germany and her partners Italy and Pétainist France the number one enemy and Japan the number two enemy. Moreover, Churchill decided Japan was an American problem and the Americans were intent on liberating their colony the Philippines and then attacking Japan itself. Burma was important to them only in that China had been supplied across the Burma road. With that road lost to the Japanese, the Americans chose to fly supplies to China over the Himalayas until such time as the British reconquered the road. Therefore, Churchill had no urgent need to spend men and money in Burma. The

natives of Burma were, therefore, eagerly awaiting a liberation that was not even being planned.

The guerrillas fought a fearsome war, because the Japanese ruled with ignorance as their guide, kidnapping thousands of men to work on various projects and thousands of girls to work as prostitutes for their soldiers, and murdering anyone who objected. Their biggest project in South-East Asia was the railroad in Thailand, where the civilian workers and prisoners of war were both quite literally worked to death. When the railroad was finished in October 1943 the Japanese Army engineer officers celebrated with sake and songs with no thoughts of the 16,000 prisoners of war and 50,000 civilians, many of them Burmese, who had died building it.

According to the British press the British invaded Burma in January 1943. The Japanese were probably amused by this phantom invasion. It consisted solely of six infantry battalions creeping along the Arakan coast. The battalions were allowed to advance without opposition, then suddenly awoke to find the Japanese in their rear. By April they had fought their way out of the trap. The campaign had cost the lives of 221 Indian and 171 British soldiers and they managed to kill 400 Japanese. The Japanese were not worried for in Burma they still had their Fifteenth and Twenty-eighth Armies, and independent 18th and 56th Divisions and 24th Brigade, which with airmen and rear-echelon troops came to 316,700 men. At the current rate it would take the British 400 years to kill them all!

It did seem that the British invasion had been purely a ploy to convince the Americans that the British were going to help them fight Japan.

Of far greater effect was the first Chindit raid. The Chindits of General Wingate were a composite brigade of very light infantry who marched into Burma. The front line was so sparsely manned it was a week before the Japanese noticed them. The one British and one Gurkha battalion, Burmese company, and commando company of Britons and Burmese then split up into sabotage parties, raised hell for two months and walked back to India.

For the first two years following the fall of Rangoon the Japanese were far more concerned with Burmese guerrillas than any British invasion and believed, quite accurately, that if they gave the impression they wanted to conquer India in 1944 it would stop all British thought of liberating Burma. It is no wonder that the British troops assigned to the India-Burma border called themselves the 'Forgotten Army'.

Yet the British were truly assembling a liberation force. A combination of events made this necessary: the Indian Army generals were anxious for India and wanted revenge for their defeat in Burma; the Americans were crying 'Where are the British'; and the Chinese got tired of waiting for the British and launched their own liberation of Burma in late 1943 in order to embarrass the British into attacking. Additionally, Churchill was thinking about Asian attitudes to the British in the postwar world.

Wingate had convinced Churchill that a large-scale Chindit operation would greatly assist the invasion and despite protests from the generals he got the go-ahead to train seven brigades; three British, two Indian, one African and one American and his own 150-plane American air unit, though he soon lost the American brigade to General Stillwell and a British brigade to General Slim.

At the end of 1943 an African and two Indian divisions slipped into the Arakan, their first battle coming in January at Maungdaw. The Japanese repeated their previous year's manoeuvre and trapped the Indian divisions, but this time the Indians were supplied from the air and held their ground. Subsequently it was the Japanese who retreated. This was the first victory for the allies in Burma.

On the central front three Indian divisions had also advanced, but then halted for three months bringing up supplies. There was no serious combat. Then suddenly in March three Japanese divisions appeared in their rear and they reacted as the Japanese expected and retreated to India, dropping all pretence at invading Burma. Of course, this meant the Chindit brigades deep inside Burma, 12,000 men and 2,000 mules, who were waiting for the allied advance to reach them, were suddenly redundant.

Unfortunately, Wingate was killed in a plane crash, so the Chindits were up for grabs: the American General Stillwell commandeered them and ordered them to harass those Japanese who were facing the Chinese invasion. As the Chindits moved to their new area of operations their Burmese units negotiated with local guerrillas for assistance.

By May the Chinese invasion, led by Merrill's Marauders, the American unit trained by Wingate, had reached Myitkyina, where they met Kachin guerrillas and found them to be a well-organised, disciplined force of seven battalions. The Kachins were told to go back to their favourite activity, ambushing Japanese convoys on the Myitkyina-Bhamo road, while the Chinese and Americans captured Myitkyina.

A Chindit brigade, including Burmese troops, spent June besieging Mogaung at Stillwell's orders. Not only were Chindit casualties extraordinarily high by this date, but they all suffered from diseases. The victors of Mogaung were down to 350 survivors when they were flown home.

By August the allies had thoroughly defeated the Japanese 'invasion' of India and the Chinese, courtesy of the Marauders, other American troops, the Chindits and the Burmese guerrillas, were able to advance southwards. Burma was ripe for liberation.

British orders were to advance now, despite this being the monsoon season, leading with an African division in the Arakan and an African, an Indian and a British division in the centre. Everywhere local guerrillas gave valuable assistance. By December the centre forces had crossed the Irrawaddy.

A brigade of two Lushai and one Chin battalions joined the centre forces and made a frontal assault on Gangaw on 27 December. With an African brigade they soon captured the town. Gangaw was damaged in the battle, but fortunately few of the Burmese communities were damaged during their liberation as the Japanese rarely fought for them, preferring jungle ridges and rivers. Allied bombing caused most of the destruction, especially in Rangoon. In fact on 3 May when an allied fleet, including some Burmese-manned warships, sailed into Rangoon they found the enemy had fled towards Thailand.

Aung San had paraded his Burmese National Army in front of Japanese generals and given a moving speech how he was going to fight to the death, whereupon his army marched into the jungle, joined the guerrillas and began shooting at the Japanese. Aung San was no fool.

When the Japanese formally announced a surrender to the allies in August 1945 they still had thousands of troops in Burma, but most of them were lost stragglers, hunted by guerrillas. It took weeks for the allies, using Japanese prisoners as interpreters, to locate these stragglers and convince them the war was really over. Until they surrendered they were fair game for the guerrillas.

Burma suffered a devastating war. Their casualties in regular British units were low, a few hundred killed, as were Aung San's losses, but the guerrillas suffered a high loss. Air raid casualties were high, certainly over 10,000 dead caused by both sides, and the refugees in India were caught up in the famine caused by the war, suffering thousands of deaths. Japanese brutality accounted for about 100,000 civilian deaths.

See Index

BYELORUSSIA

Other names:	Belorus, White Russia.
Status in 1938:	member state of the USSR.
Government in 1938:	communist under Stalin dictatorship.
Population in 1938:	5,000,000
Make-up in 1938:	Byelorussians 4,400,000; Jews 407,000; some Russians.
Religion:	Christian
Location:	Eastern Europe.

Not allowed to express themselves as a nation by the Russian tsars or their Soviet successors Lenin and Stalin, the Byelorussians nonetheless were never troublesome, preferring a live and let live philosophy. However, in September 1939 Stalin's Red Army invaded Poland and conquered among others another 1,100,000 Byelorussians, who had been living in the freedom of the Polish state. Stalin mistrusted these people

for they had been allowed to think for themselves as managers, teachers, doctors, lawyers, priests, artists etc. Behind the Red Army came the NKVD, Stalin's political police, who arrested everyone in Polish Byelorussia (Byelorussians, Poles and Jews) who had shown the ability to 'think'. By June 1941 about one person in twelve had been arrested and sent to concentration camps or penal colonies or had been executed.

This all changed on 22 June 1941 when the Germans invaded. The Red Army defences collapsed at once and within a week almost all of Polish Byelorussia was overrun and the Germans entered Soviet Byelorussia. Most of the refugees who fled the Germans were Jews, for the Byelorussians welcomed the Christian Germans as liberators. Indeed many men and women asked to join them and some German units took on hiwis, rear-echelon volunteers. German officers also searched among their Red Army prisoners of war to recruit Byelorussians as hiwis and actual combat soldiers, called Osttruppen.

Not all Jews had been able to flee, such was the speed of the German advance, and a longstanding hatred of Jews emerged among the Byelorussians – increased in part by the knowledge that many of the communist oppressors, NKVD personnel and their informers, were Jews. Every community in the world has criminals and anti-socials and in Byelorussia they joined with anti-semitic fanatics to arrest Jews and communists and beat them to death. By order of Hitler, the German dictator, the Germans were not to interfere in this internal problem. He had in fact sent his own murder squads, about 750 men of the einsatzgruppe, into Byelorussia to kill Jews and communists, and they found enough local willing volunteers to enable them to do the job easily. Indeed on occasion they let the volunteers do the killing for them. Near Byalystok 700 Jews were killed in one day.

The Germans allowed the local Byelorussian police to continue to function and set up a defence militia, the Byelorussian Popular Self-Defence Corps (BNS), whose members were on standby in their villages to help repel raids by Soviet partisans, i.e. Red Army stragglers and trained guerrillas who had been inserted behind German lines by parachute. The German police recruited their own anti-partisan police, schumas, the German Army recruited a battalion of labour troops, and German civilian labour recruiters toured the towns offering jobs in Germany with good money, Sundays off and annual leave. Tens of thousands volunteered, some becoming armed Werkschutze – factory guards.

Schuma volunteers had not enrolled to kill Jews and when one company of schumas was ordered to surround Borisov and keep the Jews from fleeing while the einsatz-gruppe went in, there was much soulsearch-ing and discussion. The schumas were invited by the Germans to a pre-execution party, the object being to get as drunk as possible before attempting to carry out such an immoral order. The morning after, the schumas, no doubt still with hangovers, guarded the perimeter of the town while the einsatzgruppe and their Byelorussian volun-teers roamed the streets looking for Jews. Local Byelorussian townsfolk who tried to intervene were beaten senseless. That day over 6,000 Jewish men, women and children were butchered. Some of the schumas joined in the killing, but others allowed about 2,000 Jews to escape into the woods.

In spring 1942 the partisan problem became worse as Jews and some Christian Byelorussians joined them. The partisans raid-ed villages to conscript all men and childless females aged seventeen to 50 and a refusal was met with a bullet in the brain. Obviously this was a recipe for bitter civil war with no quarter. Conscripted partisans were sent unarmed into their first action to test their loyalty. The Soviets claimed they had 374,000 partisans in Byelorussia: if a true figure it included conscripts and many Russians.

The BNS was more necessary than ever and it quickly expanded to a strength of 55,000 men, including six battalions of full-time soldiers (BSK). The schumas increased to eleven battalions, the labour troops were sent on anti-partisan sweeps and more hiwis were recruited.

In early 1943 a major offensive was launched against the partisans based in the Pripet Marsh. Units of various types and nationalities, including Byelorussians, con-fiscated thousands of pigs, sheep and cattle,

killed 2,219 partisans, executed 7,378 vil-lagers for aiding the partisans and 3,300 Jews found in hiding. The German SS offi-cers in charge bragged they had destroyed a major partisan force, but embarrassingly had to admit to the German Army that they had captured only 186 weapons and their losses in the campaign were two Germans and 27 others killed.

In early 1944 the Byelorussians saw some German rear-echelon units move their base a few miles to the west. Then more did the same. Then everyone realised the truth: the Germans were retreating in the face of heavy Soviet attacks. The lucky ones were those hiwis, schumas and BSK ordered to duty elsewhere in Europe. They eagerly went as long as the Germans organised accommo-dation for their families. The NKVD were notorious for arresting families if they could not catch their intended victim.

The BNS was now called to full-time duty and organised into 60 battalions, which began to retreat with the Germans in the spring. Some Byelorussians joined the partisans now, hoping their three years of neutrality would be overlooked by the NKVD. Others fled, car-rying their household goods in hand carts.

The police and two schuma battalions were organised into the Siegling Brigade and sent to fight partisans in Poland. They were luckier than the BSK, who were put into the front line to help stem the Soviet tide: they suffered badly.

Heinrich Himmler, the SS chief, was ever on the lookout for new soldiers for his own army, the Waffen SS; espying the Byelorus-sian refugees he created the 30th SS Division, made up of the Siegling Brigade, Byelorus-sian hiwis, schumas and BNS members. To fill it to division size he took in Ukrainians and Russians, too. As members of the SS, these men were now on better pay and conditions and their families were looked after.

After training in Germany during 1944 the division was sent to France, where the Germans had also suffered a long retreat, and in November was ordered to counter-attack. The division was quickly shattered by French armoured troops, and the survivors were withdrawn to Germany.

In April 1945 the division was disbanded and its members allowed to join the axis Russian Army, not an ideal situation for Byelorussians, but at least there would be safety in numbers when the Red Army attacked.

Meanwhile the BNS and BSK had retreated all the way to Berlin where in April-May they died in the streets battling a million Red Army soldiers.

In May the axis Russian Army was ordered to fight the Red Army near Prague, but many of the Byelorussian members deserted and walked to the west, hoping to surrender to the Americans. On 9 May the war was over.

About 160,000 Byelorussians served the Germans in an armed capacity and many hundreds of thousands worked for them voluntarily. How many survived is anyone's guess. Those who managed to convince American or British troops they were citizens of pre-war Poland were accepted as prisoners. Those who did not ran the risk of being handed to the NKVD.

Some Byelorussians served in the Polish forces during the war and most served in the Red Army.

Civilian losses are impossible to verify: they were murdered by partisans, Germans and NKVD: they were kidnapped by the Germans for slave labour and imprisoned for anti-German activity and suffered the same at the hands of the NKVD; they were starved and wracked with disease; they were bombed and killed in crossfires. It has been alleged that three-quarters of the Jews resident in Soviet Byelorussia did not survive. *See Index*

CANADA

Other names:	does not include Newfoundland.
Status in 1939:	as Australia.
Government in 1939:	democratic monarchy.
Population in 1939:	11, 500,000.
Make-up in 1939:	8,000,000 British and Irish stock; 3,000,000 French stock; many thousands of aboriginal stock; Remainder of various immigrant stock.
Religion:	Christian.
Location:	North America.

When Britain declared war on Germany on 3 September 1939 some Canadians assumed the declaration spoke for them – it had done so in World War I – but in 1939 Canada had a new independence and had to make this decision for herself. Many did not want war, primarily the Isolationists and the French-speakers. The former because they wanted to isolate themselves from European squabbling, saying that World War I had solved nothing, and the latter because they saw this as Britain's war and they felt no obligation to Britain or Canada's English-speaking politicians, nor to France from which they had been cut off for almost 200 years.

Parliament debated the matter for a week and the 'British' faction won: Canada declared war on 10 September.

The next item on the agenda was how should the Canadian government wage war? They had never done it before. William Mackenzie King, the leader of the 'British' faction, gained acceptance for his policy: Canada would simply loan her armed forces in the same manner as she supplied Britain with timber or wheat, i.e. with no great control over their ultimate use.

In the forefront of the war was the Royal Canadian Navy (RCN), which with six destroyers, a handful of small craft and 4,000 sailors was expected to patrol the North Atlantic coast. Shipyards began churning out ships by the dozen and volunteers flocked to the RCN. Once at sea the RCN warships obeyed British orders and soon the Canadian merchant service did too as convoy sailing was enforced. The enemy was the German submarine fleet, in addition to normal bad weather, and convoying introduced a new danger, collision, e.g. the destroyer *Fraser* went down with 40 of her crew when accidentally rammed. Her replacement, the *Margaree*, went down with 140 of her 170 crew following a collision.

Canadians who had wanted to fly military aircraft full-time had had to join the British Royal Air Force (RAF), for the 3,100 strong Royal Canadian Air Force (RCAF) was only reservist. It was now expected to recruit volunteers to meet the war emergency.

The 55,000 man reservist Army naturally had to ask for volunteers. Eventually the government resorted to conscription, but gave conscripts the option of overseas service or domestic service. Many chose overseas service, because they were embarrassed into doing so by friends and relatives. Many French-speakers chose domestic service as the lesser of two evils in 'Britain's war.

Canada was, however, extremely fortunate in that she was given years to prepare her Army, for only one division reached France during that great campaign in 1940, only to be told to reboard their ships and go to Britain. Few nations are so lucky.

Apart from naval encounters with submarines, the first Canadians in real action were the RCAF squadrons who reached Britain in time to help defend that island nation in the 1940 Battle of Britain against the German Air Force. By 1941 seven squadrons were flying from British airfields. The RCAF also controlled its own squadrons flying anti-submarine patrols from eastern Canada, Newfoundland and Iceland. RCAF training facilities proved excellent and many allied nations sent their aircrew to train in Canada.

In June 1941 the RCN produced its own combat headquarters, the Newfoundland Escort Force of six destroyers and seventeen corvettes, with the mission of protecting all merchant ship convoys between Canada and Iceland. Additionally some RCN warships were still serving under British command and a motor torpedo boat flotilla was raiding Western European ports from a base in Britain.

The RCN had grown so much that in December 1941 the US Navy borrowed seven corvettes and 24 anti-submarine trawlers, minus crews.

That month saw the beginning of the Japanese offensive and in Hong Kong Canadians were suddenly at the sharp end, for two battalions and a brigade headquarters had been sent there two months earlier to endorse the British message to Tokyo to steer clear of the territory. In an eighteen day battle the 2000 Canadians suffered 786 killed and wounded and were then ordered to surrender by a British general. Such was one result of Mackenzie King's 'donation' of the poorly trained Canadian Army to Britain.

In Western Canada there was a small population of Canadians of the Japanese race. Their maltreatment by their own government was purely racist motivated. This same government consistently refused to accept Jewish refugees, even after learning of their fate at the hands of the Nazis in Europe.

One consequence of abdicating to the British all responsibility for waging war seriously was that the British never saw Japan as the major enemy. After all the two nations are on the opposite sides of the planet. Canada, however is a Pacific nation and in June 1942 Japanese troops occupied two US islands off the Alaskan coast: in Pacific Ocean terms they were close to Canada. Yet, even when Japanese planes bombed Alaska the Canadians only provided the Americans with the following assistance: three air squadrons and an infantry brigade. They shot down one plane, dropped some bombs and invaded a deserted island. Canada's government had felt unable to do more, though she had plenty of air squadrons available, 25 were now in Britain, and her five division Army had yet to fight the Germans, because it would have upset the British timetable.

At sea by summer 1942 there were 147 allied warships protecting North Atlantic convoys, of which half were RCN. The German submarine fleet was bolder than ever: e.g. the RCN destroyer *Charlottetown* was torpedoed and sunk in Canada's St Lawrence River, and after sinking the RCN destroyer *Ottawa* a submarine proceeded to sink eleven merchant ships in the convoy.

In Britain the Canadian troops were bored stiff and they often got into trouble. It didn't help that they were paid much higher than British soldiers and were often taller and healthier looking and as a result were more attractive to local girls. If a fight didn't start over a girl, it started because the British, who had sent their boys to war years earlier, wanted to know why the Canadians weren't fighting.

Churchill, the British Prime Minister, came to the rescue. The Americans had been clamouring for an invasion of France, but the British were loath to return there, where they had been slaughtered in 1914–18 and humiliated in 1940, so to prove to the Americans the German shore defences were too strong to invade Churchill authorised a one division raid, with the hopes that the troops would be defeated – it would have been very embarrassing for the British if the raiders found no defences. Churchill agreed to let the Canadian 2nd Division have the honours along with some British commandos and American rangers. It would satisfy the Canadians' craving for action and fulfil British policy, which at the time was to use as few British troops in combat as possible.

The raid on Dieppe in August 1942 was the massacre which culd surely be foreseen: British 45 killed and 87 missing; Canadian 907 killed and 1,946 missing. There would be no more American talk about invading France in the near future.

In 1943 the Canadian Army was at last given a real mission. The 1st Division (c17,500 men) sailed from Britain and invaded the south coast of Sicily on 10 July as part of British Eighth Army commanded by General Montgomery. The Canadians, many of whom had been training for almost four years, found the day anti-climactic in that the Italian shore defenders were too dazed by allied bombing and bombardment to offer a coherent defence. It was two days before they met their first real opposition, the 15th Panzergrenadier Division at Ragusa. There was also a short fight at Vizzini where they captured the headquarters of the Italian Napoli Division.

From then on it seemed that all roads in Sicily led upwards, never downwards, as they climbed into the mountains along roads that appeared primitive compared to the British roads they had trained on, and behind every bend there was an Italian or German rearguard. After three weeks the division was pulled out for a rest. Sicily cost the Canadians 400 killed, 1,200 wounded and 300 captured. At times it had been hard, but the nature of the fighting can be judged by comparing these casualties incurred over 24 days with those lost at Dieppe to a smaller force in a few hours. Because of the quality of the division General Simonds, the divisional commander, became Montgomery's protégé.

The Eighth Army's invasion of the toe of Italy on 3 September was all noise for the Italians welcomed the invaders. Five days later Italy divided into civil war, with the pro-allied faction definitely holding southern Italy. It was a marvellous opportunity for the Eighth Army to charge ahead and reach the US Fifth Army pinned down at Salerno. Instead Montgomery moved with such caution as to destroy all chances of victory. The Germans were astonished as were the soldiers of Eighth Army. A few war correspondents got tired of waiting for Montgomery and advanced by themselves to Fifth Army encountering no opposition.

After sixteen days in sunny Italy the Canadians encountered a fight at Potenza. Following advice from Montgomery Simonds pulled his men out and ordered a bombardment to destroy the town. Then the Canadians re-entered, finding no German bodies, but 2,000 dead civilians and countless wounded. The Germans, all 60 of them, had retreated.

It was 2 October before Eighth Army reached the German defence line along the Biferno River and on the 5th Canadian tanks arrived literally in the nick of time to repel a counter-attack. The Germans then suddenly withdrew.

Marching north through Italy the Canadians captured the 2,600-foot stronghold of Molise and in December attacked the fortress towns of Orsogna and Ortona. It took three weeks of bitter fighting to capture them and by year's end the division had lost in Italy 713 killed, 2,625 wounded and 195 captured. Since leaving Britain half the combat echelon had become a casualty.

By late 1943 134,000 RCAF personnel were maintaining and flying eleven fighter, eight bomber and eight patrol squadrons from British airfields, a fighter squadron in the Mediterranean and several squadrons of patrol aircraft from Eastern Canada, Newfoundland and Iceland. Canadians were also flying in British squadrons: e.g. in 617 Squadron, the famous Dambusters squadron of hand-picked airmen, 27 of the 130 flight crew were Canadian.

In Italy the Canadian 5th Armoured Division joined the 1st Division, which with some smaller units created Canadian Ist Corps, which Montgomery gave to Simonds, at 41 the youngest corps commander for the

Western Allies. However, early 1944 was not a time for back patting: the allies were stuck at Cassino and Anzio for the first five months of the year.

On 15 May 5th Armoured Division was alerted for the next breakthrough attempt and on the 22nd they repelled a counter-attack and on the 26th defeated German tanks. The offensive succeeded, Cassino fell, and on 4 June American troops entered Rome. In truth some of the first troops into Rome were Canadians of the US 1st Special Service Force. Canada had provided a battalion for this experimental two-nation unit and had then promptly forgotten about it: e.g. Canadian casualties were not replaced.

The Canadian, US and British governments were much more concerned about the invasion of France, which the Americans had finally convinced the British to undertake, hitting Normandy on 6 June 1944. The assault troops consisted of eight divisions, five US, three British and one Canadian, and seven British and one Canadian independent brigades all under the command of General Montgomery. Shelling the shore was the greatest invasion fleet of all time, including 120 RCN vessels of war. The great allied air force, which attacked the shore and fended off German planes, contained 39 RCAF squadrons.

It is always a nerve-wracking moment when green troops go into action for the first time, and an opposed amphibious invasion, which ensures everyone is sea-sick as well as tense, is probably the worst way of doing it, unless one counts dropping by parachute in the dark. This day Canadians did both: the 3rd Division hitting Juno Beach; and the parachute battalion jumping alongside the British 6th Airborne Division to capture bridges on the eastern flank in the dark to guard against German counter attacks.

The 3rd Division swiftly conquered the Atlantic Wall defences – swiftly but not without terrible cost in lives – the infantry and engineers then moving inland, oblivious of their flanks. The Canadians covered more territory than any other force this day, with divisional reconnaissance vehicles taking a peek at the town of Caen, but it cost the divi-

sion 355 killed and 600 wounded. The generals were well pleased.

The next day's orders were to finish taking Caen and press on, but at once the Canadians found a fresh SS panzer division in front of them. They got nowhere and lost 242 men and 21 attached tanks.

On the 12th the Canadian 2nd Armoured Brigade cautiously drove down a hedged lane until hidden enemy anti-tank guns took out the lead vehicle: the brigade backed away and called for infantry. Each day the Canadians and neighbouring British tried a different method of advancing, but gained no ground.

On the 19th the Americans took the port of Cherbourg. The folks at home wondered what was going on: the Canadians were still outside their first day objective! Montgomery later claimed this was all according to his plan: his left wing (British/Canadians) was to draw upon itself the bulk of the German armour, while the right wing (Americans) advanced and outflanked the enemy.

Be this as it may, Montgomery was under political pressure to break out with his left wing as well and on 4 July 21 battalions of British and Canadian artillery plus aircraft softened up the enemy defences, after which the Canadian 3rd Division attacked Carpiquet airfield: it took 30 hours of battle to cross the runway. Then on Montgomery's orders allied aircraft bombed Caen. It was Potenza all over again. Even Simonds was here to witness it, having been brought from Italy at Montgomery's request. Civilian losses were terribly high and again no German corpses were found. The Canadians now attacked and took Buron for a loss of 262 men and eleven tanks. Only on the 9th did British troops enter the rubble of Caen eight miles from the beach.

Simonds was given command of Canadian II Corps (2nd and 3rd Divisions, 2nd Armoured Brigade and smaller units) and in an offensive on the 18th advanced 2,000 yards in three days.

The Canadian public was right to question the strategy and tactics of the Normandy campaign, for despite Montgomery's sucker punch strategy on his left flank, there was something inherently wrong with the Canadian tactics: first their method of fighting was incomprehensible, especially to their German opponents. In a nutshell the Canadian 3rd Division had been sent into action with hardly any battlefield training, which considering its men had been waiting for action for over four years is indefensible. Secondly, the Canadian government acted like it had forgotten it had sent an army overseas, rather like an absent minded professor who misplaces his essential notes, and had made no adequate provision to replace their casualties with trained personnel. Replacements were arriving who had never fired a rifle and rear-echelon soldiers had to be sent into the line. That this should happen at the beginning of a campaign is a terrible indictment of the incompetence of the Canadian politicians and generals, and to a lesser extent of their British counterparts.

In August while the Americans charged across France, the Canadians were still in the Caen area. The paratroopers were still in their first day foxholes. Gaining more rear-echelon units the Canadians established First Army under General Crerar, but with only one corps it had to borrow a British corps headquarters and a Polish armoured division. Crerar put the Poles and the fresh Canadian 4th Armoured Division into the British corps, and on the 16th this corps was given orders to advance southwards and reach American units in order to cut off the enemy retreat from Normandy. This would be the most important mission allocated to either Canadian First or British Second Armies, and with hindsight it should not have been given to two green divisions, especially as the Americans were told not to advance and shorten the distance.

Not only did fanatic flank guards hold up the Canadians and Poles, but the narrow country lanes were choked with abandoned German trucks and horse-drawn carts. Eventually, the tanks drove over them! On the night of the 20th they reached the Americans and cut off thousands of Germans. However, Montgomery now realised that most of the Germans had escaped and not willing to accept the blame he looked for a scapegoat. The commander of the 4th Armoured Division was dismissed.

There was also considerable intrigue among the Canadian generals, but consider-

ing the lack of support from their government it is no wonder that incompetent leaders were kept on while others were sent home in disgrace.

First Army now advanced northwards along the coast, dropping off infantry to besiege ports. Dieppe fell on 31 August, Zeebrugge, Belgium on 9 September, Le Havre on the 12th, Cap Gris Nez not until the 29th and Calais a day later. Dunkirk still held out and was handed to Czech troops to besiege.

On 3 and 4 September the British had gained headlines with their liberation of Brussels and Antwerp, but the latter, the greatest port in allied hands, was useless as long as the German Fifteenth Army held the Scheldt River between the docks and the sea. The First Army was ordered to liberate this area, the Breskens Pocket, by attacking frontally from the south and by cutting off the north bank of the river with a drive west from Antwerp. This was done, but the combat was bitter – at one point Canadians were fighting their way along a 30-yard-wide causeway with sea on either side. Only after British and other allied troops helped the Canadians capture Walcheren Island on 7 November was the port usable. The First Army had killed 10,000 enemy in the two-month battle and took 12,707 prisoners, but 90,000 Germans had escaped, and all the time the allies desperately needed the supplies that a free Antwerp could have brought them. The Canadians were the victims of yet another Montgomery victory.

In Italy Canadian Ist Corps found that as they advanced up the Italian boot each village resembled the last one, each mountain road mirrored the one before. The war correspondents became bored, for their reports were copies of the previous day's. There was no glory here, just terror and death. It was with a sense of relief that the Ist Corps received orders in January 1945 to join First Army. Since its formation the corps had suffered 4,287 killed, 15,665 wounded and 505 captured.

First Army had been resting since Walcheren, but Simonds was eager to get to grips with the enemy and he convinced Montgomery to let his corps take part in a British operation to eliminate German forces west of the Rhine and north of the German town of Xanten. This little operation was a success, took fifteen days and cost his corps a thousand casualties and a high sick list.

Capturing a wood and a few farmhouses was all very nice, but if men have to risk their lives they want to do it for something they consider worthwhile. Since arriving in France the Canadians had not done that yet – holding down German armour so that the Americans could gain headlines liberating France, then mopping up ports while the British got headlines liberating Belgium was not the reason the Canadians had come to Europe. Then, at last, the Canadians received a mission worthy of Canada: the First Army was ordered to liberate the Netherlands.

On 23 March 1945 allied troops under Montgomery crossed the Rhine, aided by an airborne drop, including the Canadian Parachute Battalion, and charged eastwards, ostensibly towards Berlin, while Canadians used the bridgehead to follow the north bank of the Rhine as it curved into the Netherlands. Canadian engineers built two bridges, the shorter 1,350 feet, in 33 hours in the tidal part of the river under shellfire and attack by explosive rafts!

Crerar's army (1st, 2nd, 3rd, 4th Armoured, 5th Armoured, Polish 1st Armoured and British 49th Divisions, two Canadian, two Belgian, a Dutch and a mixed brigades) launched the liberation. One element followed the Netherlands-German border to the sea, a second element followed the Rhine into the Netherlands, taking Arnhem, Enschede, Zwolle, and Apeldoorn, and on 25 April the third element fought its way over the lower Maas and Rhine northwards into the Netherlands. The Germans asked for a truce, which came into effect on the 28th and a week later the war in Europe ended.

The liberation cost First Army 1,482 killed and 4,818 wounded. Since arriving in Normandy Canadian troops had suffered 10,740 killed, 30,910 wounded and 2,250 captured. In effect each infantry battalion had been wiped out twice.

Some Canadians were still at war, for RCN warships were at war with the Japanese in the Pacific. This had not come about because the Canadian government suddenly remembered the Japanese enemy, but because they had loaned a flotilla of ships to the British Royal Navy, who had placed them into their 'British Pacific Fleet'. The fleet shelled Japanese island installations and sent carrier planes to bomb the enemy including towns in Japan itself.

Once the truth of the casualties sustained in Europe became known to the Canadian public, the government agreed that no conscripts would serve overseas in future. Therefore, the warships were ordered to come home on 27 July 1945 to acquire all-volunteer crews. The Japanese surrendered three weeks later.

Canada's industrial output was monumental as she provided not only her own armed forces with material but the allies too, including such major projects as the building of aircraft carriers. Her military contribution to the war effort was significant and was almost equally balanced between ground, air and sea forces. Her losses of seventeen warships and 59 merchant ships do not accurately reflect the indebtedness of the allies to her sea contribution. However, her air losses do reflect her air contribution, for as many Canadians were killed in the air as on the ground.

Canada's armed forces suffered 39,219 killed and 53,174 wounded and 1,437 merchant service dead.

See Index

CAUCASUS REGION

Other names:	includes Chechen-Ingush; Daghestan; Kabardin-Balkar; and Ossetia.
Status in 1939:	the above were member states of the USSR.
Government in 1939:	communist under Stalin dictatorship.
Population in 1939:	10,000,000
Make-up in 1939:	Kabardins 700,000; Ossetians 600,000; Chechens 350,000; and over 30 other ethnic groups.
Religion:	Some Christians and Buddhists, mostly Moslem.
Location:	Central Asia

The Russians had colonised the Caucasus in the 19th century and when the empire collapsed into civil war in 1917 most of the peoples seized their independence: they were, after all, ancient nations with a history measured in millenia. However, by 1922 the communist Russian Red Army of the USSR had reconquered the region, nation by nation.

Thrown off their land, their crops and herds confiscated at gunpoint, their religious leaders imprisoned or forced into hiding, some survived by working their own land as employees, but many were reduced to starvation and thousands died. By 1935 they could take no more and they revolted. Stalin replied by reinforcing his political police (NKVD) with the Red Army and air units. Even then it took a year to pacify the region as concentration camps were filled with men, women and children whose only crime was to be hungry.

Five years later the USSR was invaded by Germany and this time the Red Army officers conscripted thousands of young Caucasians to fight the invader. Many wanted to surrender at the first opportunity, but most did not have to, for their incompetent generals handed them to the Germans. Conditions in the German camps were atrocious, as the men were herded together in open fields to face a coming Russian winter without shelter or clothing. Malnutrition and disease were rampant.

Hitler had been courting Turkey as a potential partner and he thought it might be a nice gesture if he recruited a Turkic Corps – Turkic being the language group to which Turkish and several other languages belong. So he sent his recruiters into the prison camps to ask for Turkic volunteers, offering similar treatment to that of German soldiers, complete religious and cultural freedom and a chance to fight communists – thousands stepped forward.

Not understanding whom they were dealing with the Germans created two legions: the Turkestani and the Moslem Caucasian. Few members of the latter spoke a Turkic language and not all were Moslems, but the Germans did at least understand the need for individual companies and battalions for each language, so

that a corporal would know what his sergeant was saying.

Once trained the Moslem Caucasian Legion sent battalions all over German-occupied USSR with the mission to hunt down communist partisans: i.e. Red Army stragglers and actual trained guerrillas infiltrated behind German lines usually by parachute.

The Germans continued to advance until in the autumn of 1942 they reached the northern Caucasus, though they left a gap between here and the German Fourth Panzer Army near Stalingrad. Patrolling this 200-mile gap was one German division and the local Kalmyks who hated communists. The Kalmyks formed a horse cavalry unit so competent that only three Germans needed to be assigned to it.

Recruitment in the north Caucasus went smoothly: the Chechens and Karachais had already revolted against the NKVD in anticipation of the German liberation.

In November a massive Soviet offensive trapped the Germans in Stalingrad and pushed troops of four axis nations hundreds of miles to the west coming close to cutting off the Caucasus. The Germans frantically retreated and their newly recruited Caucasian soldiers and families went with them. These included 5,000 Kalmyk horse cavalry.

Once safe at a new base at Lielau in Germany in early 1943 the Caucasians expanded their legion by accepting the male refugees as soldiers. This gave them a strength of 110,000 troops, mostly serving in independent battalions, but a Caucasian artillery regiment of three battalions was attached to a Cossack Division and sent to Yugoslavia, the 450th Regiment went to Byelorussia, the Kalmyk Cavalry Corps went to the Plavna Marsh in Ukrainia, and the Savage Division of Caucasians and Tatars and some Kalmyk cavalry squadrons went to Italy.

In 1944 as the German armies retreated into Poland, Caucasian and Kalmyk units protected their line of retreat from partisans, and when Warsaw rose in revolt a unit of 1,200 Caucasians was sent to reinforce the garrison. Having just been awarded SS status they were expected to prove worthy of the honour in this bloody no quarter battle.

In Greece a battalion of Ossetians learned that their partisan enemy were not communists, and in twos and threes they defected. Rather than risk a complete mutiny the Germans disbanded the battalion and sent them to prisoner of war camps.

When Germany surrendered in May 1945 the Caucasians and Kalmyks desperately sought to surrender to the Western Allies. Those who reached the Americans and French were usually released into the melting pot of displaced persons, but many who were taken by the British were handed to the NKVD.

In the Caucasus the NKVD had already been arresting suspected traitors and by 1944 over 300,000 Chechen men, women and children were held in open fields watched by trigger-happy guards. Every one was found guilty of treason and sentenced to life in penal colonies in the eastern wasteland. 100,000 Ingushis were similarly sentenced, leaving their nation a ghostland. Most of the Karachais were sent eastwards as were countless others. Russian colonists then arrived to fill the gap. Stalin played chess with nations.
See Index

CEYLON

Other Names:	Sri Lanka.
Status in 1939:	British Colony.
Government in 1939:	British Administration.
Population in 1939:	6,600,000.
Make-up in 1939:	Sinhalese 4,620,000; Tamils 1,320,000; plus various groups and a few thousand Britons.
Religion:	Buddhist, Hindu in Tamil Areas.
Location:	Indian Ocean.

A long-time British colony, Ceylon was known to the world for its tea. A large and beautiful expanse, it must have seemed like a fantastic idea to extend its home defences when Britain went to war against Germany, for how could the Germans ever reach the island? Ceylonese had to enter the British Royal Navy or merchant service to see action.

However, in December 1941 fantasy turned to stark reality when the Japanese attacked the British Asian empire. Each day there was more news of Japanese conquests and as these were naval in execution the Ceylonese suddenly felt very vulnerable stuck out in the ocean.

By now the defence force consisted of the Ceylonese Artillery with a battalion of flak guns and one of shore guns, the Ceylonese Light Infantry with five battalions, Ceylonese rear-echelon troops and a unit of white colonists the Ceylon Planters Rifles.

The arrival of a British fleet was most welcomed, especially as on 1 April 1942 British Intelligence got word of a Japanese task force aiming for Ceylon and the ships put to sea to intercept it. On the 4th, with no sign of the enemy, the fleet returned to port to refuel.

However, Intelligence had got it right and on the next day the port of Colombo was attacked by Japanese carrier planes. The flak gunners tried to remain calm and use their training to good effect, but the raid was a disaster: installations, warehouses, equipment were wrecked, defending fighter planes were shot down, and a destroyer and a merchant cruiser were sunk. The cruisers *Dorsetshire* and *Cornwall* were caught at sea by the enemy and quickly sunk.

The fleet was refuelled by the 6th and the Ceylonese troops steeled themselves to repel an invasion, but the Japanese turned their attention to the coast of India sinking 22 merchant vessels and an Indian sloop. Everyone in Ceylon breathed easier. Evidently this was all the war they were going to get.

They were wrong: on the 9th the city of Trincomalee was attacked by Japanese planes. Here too flak gunners fought a real action for the first time. The airfield was badly damaged and a merchant ship and a monitor were destroyed, while up the coast the British aircraft carrier *Hermes* and Australian destroyer *Vampire* were found by the Japanese. Within minutes both were sinking.

In the two air raids on the Ceylon ports 37 defending planes had been destroyed, four large warships and two smaller ones and a merchant ship sunk, and 85 civilians killed in addition to military losses, and much valuable stores and equipment were destroyed. The onshore and ship flak gunners shot down 36 Japanese planes. The real value of the raids to the Japanese was the

caring of the British fleet so that it withdrew from the Indian Ocean.

Despite being defenceless Ceylon was
not invaded and in 1943 became a major
Allied base with troops of many nationalities
undergoing jungle warfare school and at the
end of the year provided a home for the new
British Far Eastern Fleet.

See Index

CHINA

Status in 1931:	Independent.
Government in 1931:	a loose alliance of warlords.
Population in 1931:	450,000,000.
Make-up in 1931:	Chinese speaking the following languages: Cantonese; Fukien; Hakka; Kiangsi; Mandarin; Wu; also 3,000,000 Tibetans in Tibet; Manchus and Mongols in own areas.
Religion:	various.
Location:	Eastern Asia.

In the 19th century the feudal state of China
was open to aggression by any nation with
the military muscle to impose its will on a
warlord, or the money to buy him off, and in
the ports European businessmen protected
by European troops controlled the trade
between China and the outside world. In
1894 the Japanese imitated the Europeans
by warring against China, stealing Formosa
and joining the international enclaves in the
ports. The Americans arrived soon after.

In 1900 the Chinese attempted to throw
out the foreigners, but an army of Americans, Britons, Japanese, Germans and many
others defeated them in a brutal manner.

In 1911 revolutionaries overthrew the
child Emperor and attempted to deal with
the foreigners on a basis of mutual respect.
This failed and the Japanese gained the right
to station troops in Manchuria.

By 1931 two powerful rival forces had
emerged, the communists under Mao-Zhe-
ung, and the Kuomintang of Chiang-Kai-
shek. That year the Japanese tired of their
arrangement with local warlords in
Manchuria and attacked them, driving them

out by February 1932, and setting up a puppet state (Manchutukuo) with the former
Emperor Henry P'u-Yi as head of state. The
warlords had asked for help from Chiang,
but he had refused.

In 1933 the Japanese attacked out of
Manchuria and overran Jehol Province.
Again Chiang refused to help the local warlords. The communists did form guerrilla
bands in Jehol to fight the Japanese.

The Japanese continued in this manner,
digesting China a morsel at a time, until by
early 1937 they controlled all the land
between the Great Wall and the border of
Outer Mongolia.

The communists waged guerrilla war
against the Japanese, and local warlords
defended their particular acreage, but Chiang did not become involved. This was not
because he lacked the means: he had 300
divisions, on paper 10,900 men each, a small
navy and an air force of 200 obsolete aircraft. He was much more concerned with his
war against the communists. He had
launched five major offensives against them
between 1931 and 1934, the last one forcing
them to walk from Kiangsi and Fukien
Provinces to Shensi Province, a march which
took them a year to complete.

In December 1936 Chiang learned just
how fickle his own warlords could be when
the Manchurian Chang Hsueh-liang arrested
him. The price of his freedom was a truce
with the communists so that both they and
the Kuomintang could fight the Japanese.

On 7 July 1937 a shoot-out between Chiang's troops and some Japanese near Peking
(Peiping, Beijing) sparked open war between
Chiang and the Japanese. Chiang's propaganda made out that the Japanese had engi-
neered the whole incident, but if so it
certainly fell in with his own plans. The
Japanese were caught off guard and had to
bring in reinforcements from Japan. On 30
July Chiang's men lost Tientsin and nine
days later Peking to the Kwantung Army: a
combined force of Japanese, Manchus, Mongols and Chinese.

In mid-August the war took on a different complexion when two Japanese divisions, about 50,000 men, landed on the
coast near Shanghai, 700 miles south of the
front line. American and British troops in

Shanghai's international settlement remained neutral and had to fight off thousands of panicky civilians when Japanese planes bombed the city.

At the end of August Shensi Province was invaded by the Japanese First and Second Armies, where Chiang amassed 400,000 men to stop them, but the Chinese ran at the first sight of the enemy, losing Hopei Province by mid-October and North Shensi by November. The communists had put up a better show, but had also been forced to retreat. Not only was there no coordination between Chiang and Mao, but Chiang insisted on controlling all artillery himself, only loaning it out when he deemed necessary, which was rare.

On 23 October the Japanese created another puppet state (Suiyuan) in North China-Inner Mongolia.

The defenders of Shanghai did not give up easily, though by November they were under assault by seven enemy divisions, but now Chiang ordered a withdrawal lest they be cut off. The battle for the city had cost Chiang 270,000 killed and wounded and innumerable civilian lives.

Chiang was also fearful for his capital, Nanking 200 miles inland from Shanghai, but no amount of pleading, demands, dismissals and arrests could prevent his troops from retreating and Nanking fell on 13 December. The Japanese soldiers were ordered to teach the people of Nanking a lesson by rape, pillage and murder: they did their job well and it is estimated that at least 200,000 civilians and wounded soldiers died at the end of a bayonet.

On the same day as their troops were committing genocide in Nanking, Japanese generals in Peking were installing another puppet government made up of pliable warlords.

Huge areas of China had been lost, yet Chiang's 300 divisions had been up against only fifteen Japanese divisions (equivalent to 40 of his), plus thousands of his men were behind enemy lines waging guerrilla war and the communists had about 150,000 doing the same. What Chiang's army lacked was equipment. He had hoped Japanese air attacks on British and American vessels and installations and Japanese infiltration of the

USSR border would cause one of those nations to join him, but all three of those governments were much more worried about Berlin than Tokyo.

1938 saw a steady retreat southward from Hopei, with Chiang's troops here worried that the enemy in Nanking further south would suddenly advance into their rear. They defended the land between, Shantung and Kiangsi Provinces. Also further west in Honan Province other Chinese troops were falling back.

Meanwhile the butchers of Nanking set up another puppet state, which was a rival to the one in Peking: reflecting not animosity between Chinese warlords, but animosity between Japanese generals, who had been in China so long they had begun to act like independent warlords, a law unto themselves.

Chiang could not prevent the Japanese from reaching the Yellow River in March, nor his Shantung Military Region from retreating, as its commander General Han Fu-Chi knew that the enemy could outflank him on his right, i.e. seaward flank, as they controlled the seas. When Han lost the port of Tsingtao, Chiang had him executed! Resistance suddenly stiffened all along the line from general down to private. In fact in April on the Shantung-Kiangsi border the Chinese repelled the Japanese 5th Division and held the town of Tsowhsien for a month before withdrawing.

This new spirit in Chiang's army caused the Japanese to alter their plans: three divisions attacked north from Nanking meeting the northern forces on 18 May, thereby cutting off Kiangsi Province from the rest of China. However, the Japanese divisions were stretched thin and the Kiangsi defenders had no trouble breaking out into the interior of the nation.

Chiang now hit upon a new idea. He opened the dykes on the upper Yellow River thus creating a second river which forced its way southwards turning Kiangsi Province into a veritable island. Of course, the flood drowned tens of thousands of innocent villagers, ruined irrigation on the original Yellow and therefore disrupted farming and caused famine, but this did not concern Chiang, for the strategy worked: it was August before the enemy could attack again and then only due west from Nanking. Within a month the Chinese were fighting for Hupeh Province, while Chiang withdrew his government to Chungking in Szechuan Province.

The war continued into 1939, but it was obvious the Japanese were running out of steam. They had one gain – Wang Ching-wei, at one time Second in Command of the Kuomintang, defected to the Japanese. He was installed in a new government in April 1940 at Nanking, though he was denied authority over the other puppet states.

This was more evidence that the Japanese were their own worst enemy, for despite Chinese of all intellectual levels being willing to work for them as workers, civil servants and soldiers, the Japanese could not overcome their racism, which at senior level meant they never created a real alternative to Chiang's regime and at grassroots level meant they conscripted thousands of ordinary Chinese women into their army brothels, enslaved millions of men as coolies, and bullied, beat and murdered anyone who complained. The war was costing Japan $5million a day and holding down 500,000 troops and they could have won it by kindness in the first year.

Despite his incredibly high casualties manpower was the least of Chiang's concerns. What he needed was sophisticated equipment and trained men to operate it. By 1940 he was down to 65 planes. In early 1941 he received 250 aircraft from the USSR and in the autumn he got 100 P-40s from the USA. Most importantly, along with the American fighters came a hardy bunch of American adventurers to fly them, unofficially blessed by President Roosevelt. Commanded by Claire Chennault they painted shark's faces on the noses of their fighters and called themselves the Flying Tigers.

This was more like it, but Chiang's idea of having allies was for them to help him, not the other way around, yet that is exactly what happened. On 7 December 1941 the Japanese became frustrated with China so they attacked Britain and the USA who were supplying China. Within days they had invaded British Burma and the British asked Chiang for help.

Chiang responded with the Fifth Army of General Tu Lu Ming, the Sixth Army of General Kan and the Sixty-Sixth Army of General Chang Ching all under the command of American General Stillwell and his staff, loaned to Chiang by Roosevelt. This was not goodwill on Chiang's part, for he knew if Burma fell he would receive no further supplies over the route India-Burma-China.

Stillwell's army group reached Burma just in time to join the British in retreat. On 30 March 1942 the British 1st Burma Division was cut off, so the Chinese 38th Division reversed its steps and attacked an oilfield, causing the Japanese momentarily to take their eyes off the British, who then quietly slipped away. On 30 April as the British had almost reached India, Stillwell learned he was cut off too. He ordered his army group to walk back to China over jungle-clad mountains. He became something of a hero to the American press (who were desperate for heroes), because he chose to walk out with his troops rather than fly out: an incredible feat of stamina for the old man, called Vinegar Joe by his men, if not much of a feat of generalship.

Despite the fall of Burma the British and Americans decided to supply Chiang anyway, by flying provisions over the Himalayas and enemy-held terrain (over the Hump the flyers called it), though much of these supplies were destined for a fledgling American air force set up in China by Chennault, who could now wear US uniform officially. Chennault had convinced his superiors that a force of heavy bombers based in China could reach Japan and whip that nation. In April US twin-engine bombers took off from carriers in one of the great experiments of aviation and bombed Japan, before landing in China. Psychologically this was a victory and overly impressed the US government. However, the Chinese themselves did not want a US Air Force flying from their soil. They had come to accommodate the Japanese and in some parts of the front line not only was their no fighting, but both sides were trading entire trainloads and truck convoys of goods!

This put the onus of defending his airfields from a ground offensive on Chennault, which he could not do, so Chiang said he would do it if he received enough equipment and advisers to create a super corps of troops. Stillwell knew that Chiang had no intention of using his super corps against the Japanese: he would use them to keep his warlords in line and fight the communists. The Americans who were actually stationed in China with Stillwell wished Washington would find some other cause, so that they could leave this hotbed of corruption, intrigue and betrayal, but as soldiers and diplomats they obeyed orders.

When the monsoon ended in Burma in October 1943 Chiang expected the British to begin liberating Burma: they had wasted one year already. He never expressed sympathy with the allied flyers crossing over the Hump in volatile weather with no emergency landing strips and only Japanese fighter planes for company. He demanded more supplies.

To facilitate this he agreed to help liberate the Burma Road using elements of his super corps, and this month the First Army of General Sun Li-jen and the Sixth Army of General Liao Yao-hsiang advanced into the Hukawng Valley, both under Stillwell, who was glad to be away from the madness in Chungking. They forced back the enemy 18th Division and then the Chinese 22nd and 38th Divisions continued to advance, liberating the Maingkwan-Walawbaum area by March 1944.

Chiang kept his eye on this use of his super corps, but was distracted in April by a Japanese offensive. Chennault's 14th Air Force had 600 planes raising hell with the Japanese in China and Indo-China, and the 20th Air Force, also in China, was ready to begin launching B-29 heavy bomber raids on Japan. Knowing that even a B-29 had a maximum range the Japanese launched the offensive over the Yellow River and in east central China to capture the airfields. The Chinese fought bravely, but were hopelessly outclassed: Liuyand fell on 14 June, just hours before the first B-29 raid on Japan, the Fourth Army lost Changsha on the 18th and the Tenth Army lost Hengyang air base after a seven-week battle 8 August. The 14th Air Force spent most of its time trying to halt the enemy advance.

Economically speaking (and this is how a strategic bombing offensive must be judged)

the B-29 raids on Japan were not cost effective: not worth the tremendous effort getting supplies to China, not worth the losses of the 14th Air Force and Chinese lives lost defending the airfields, and not worth the lives of Chinese peasants lost after the Japanese occupation of these areas. In fact the Americans soon had much better airbases in the Pacific and began to fly B-29s from there. The entire effort had all been for nought.

Meanwhile in Burma three American battalions of Merrill's Marauders led the Chinese to Myitkyina and took the airfield on 17 May. Stillwell at once told the world that American troops had liberated the first town in British Burma – he had no love for the British. But the town had not been captured, so Stillwell threw the Marauders against the enemy, grabbed US engineers and sent them into battle, and when the enemy still resisted he personally went through the hospitals ordering sick and wounded back into the line. Every day the town resisted he ran the risk that the world would learn what a liar he had been. Yet here were several Chinese divisions, which refused to do more than make noise. The town fell on 3 August and the Chinese announced they had lost 4,344 casualties in the siege, but the Americans who had lost 2,207, could not understand how the Chinese who had not really fought could have lost so many. Obviously the Chinese report was written to give the impression they were carrying their weight.

Stillwell had also ordered British Chindits, commando style troops, to take Mogaung and promised them aid from the Chinese 38th Division. The Chinese arrived days late and then made only feints and a lot of noise. The British took the town in a rough battle, whereupon Stillwell announced to the world that American and Chinese troops had taken it: the Chindits were not amused.

To be fair to the Chinese soldiers, they were under Chiang's strict orders not to risk themselves as they were part of his super corps.

At the same time 75 miles east of Myitkyina along the upper Salween the 72,000-man Yunnan Expeditionary Force of General Wei Li-Huang advanced against the depleted

Japanese 56th Division from April onwards, taking Kufeng and Chiangchu by 20 June. Though the Japanese reinforced this front with a division taken away from the British front in western Burma, Wei's advance did not worry them.

In China, Chiang's armies could not prevent the enemy advancing southwards to take Lingling on 8 September, or the Japanese in the port of Canton from marching inland towards the US air bases at Liuchow and Kweilin.

Chiang demanded Roosevelt recall Stillwell on 6 October. He was replaced by General Wedemeyer. Just about everyone was happy to see Stillwell leave, for his morals appeared to be no better than a warlord's.

In November Kweilin and Liuchow were lost and Japanese forces advanced out of Indo-China to besiege Kunming, and on 8 December the northern forces, Canton forces and the Indo-China forces all met up, cutting off a large portion of China between them and the sea. On 29 January 1945 the airbase at Suichuan was lost.

In Burma the Chinese had advanced at the end of the monsoon season in November, spearheaded by a US formation, Mars Force. The Chinese Sixth Army's 14th, 22nd and 50th Divisions crossed the Irrawaddy at Shwegu on the 7th and First Army's 30th and 38th Divisions to the east moved on Bhamo, which was abandoned by the Japanese on 15 December. Now both Chinese armies and the Yunnan Expeditionary Force were aiming for Lashio.

Lashio was taken by the Yunnan troops on 7 March and by the end of the month Burma became solely a British problem.

In China the 14th Air Force abandoned their base at Laohokow on 25 March in the face of a Japanese advance. However, in May the Chinese were taken totally by surprise when the Japanese began withdrawing. This was the first sign to the Chinese that their enemy was weakening. At once the Chinese went over to the offensive and liberated Nanning on 27 May and Liuchow on 30 June. The eastern Chinese, cut off from China since December also attacked northwards towards Shanghai taking Wenchow.

Warlords took over factories, mines, warehouses, any place of value, often making agreements with the enemy not to attack if the Japanese promised not to wreck everything.

On 8 August the USSR's Red Army invaded Manchuria and a week later the Japanese Emperor announced the surrender. The war was over.

Now the warlords moved swiftly: not to round up Japanese; they were completely ignored and the Americans had to organise their imprisonment and later repatriation. The warlords wanted weapons, not prisoners, artillery especially, for the more weapons a warlord had, the more troops he could recruit or conscript, the larger his private army, therefore the better his chances of surviving the post-war period, for everyone knew that post-war China was going to be just as bloody and anarchic as wartime China.

China's dead in the 1931-45 struggle have been estimated at 13.5 million, including communist losses, those who fought alongside the Japanese and all civilians. Of these, Chiang's military dead are estimated at 1,400,000. The true figure of total dead will never be known, but these figures give an indication of the scale of the Chinese tragedy. Japanese deaths in China are more accurately known at 388,600.

Historians have hinted that after Japan brought the USA formally into the war in December 1941 the Chinese ceased to fight, allowing the USA to defeat Japan for them, and while this does seem to have been Chiang-Kai-Shek's policy, the above narrative has shown that as early as 1939 the Japanese had run out of ideas as to how to defeat China. At no time did the Chinese launch offensives against the Japanese, though Chiang did launch them against the communists. Against the Japanese the Chinese always fought a defensive war, so it was the Japanese, not the Chinese, who were responsible for the truce-like atmosphere after 1941.

It was the US Air Force, with their dreams of defeating Japan solely by air power, who rocked the boat in China and caused the Japanese to begin attacks in 1944 to capture the airfields.

It is noteworthy that over half of all Japanese losses in China came after December 1941, and while it is realised that some were owed to American air raids, nonetheless it does suggest that the Chinese did fight back whenever the Japanese attacked them.

There is one undeniable fact. Without Chinese resistance the Japanese would have been able to fight a different war against the Western Allies. They would have had comfortable access to all of China's natural resources and would have been able to increase their air units and supplies in the Pacific and in Burma. They would have had more manpower available, but as the Japanese never suffered from a shortage of troops, this is not a relevant issue.
See Index

CUBA

Status in 1941:	independent.
Government in 1941:	dictatorship.
Population in 1941:	4,700,000.
Make-up in 1941:	mostly Spanish stock; some negroes and many mulattos.
Religion:	Christian.
Location:	off South East USA.

Following Japan's attack on, and Germany's declaration of war on, the USA, in December 1941, most of the independent nations of Central America and the Caribbean declared war on Japan and Germany, because they felt obliged to do so, not least because of the USA's habit of propping up their dictatorships in return for trade concessions.

Though these declarations were purely a diplomatic gesture, Cuba did at least agree that her ships and planes should help the Americans patrol her coast. Four Cuban merchant ships were sunk by German submarines. On one occasion a Cuban vessel became the smallest warship to ever sink a German submarine.

Individually, many Cubans joined the US armed forces.
See Index

CYPRUS

Status in 1939:	British possession.
Government in 1939:	British administration.
Population in 1939:	300,000.
Make-up in 1939:	Greeks and Turks in own neighbourhoods.
Religion:	Greeks and some Turks were Christian; most Turks were Moslem.
Location:	Eastern Mediterranean.

Cypriots lived under British rule for the simple reason that the British Royal Navy required an eastern Mediterranean base. When Britain declared war on Germany in 1939 Cypriots were invited to join the British Merchant Service, Royal Navy, Royal Air Force or Army. Far from hating the British, many Cypriots were proud to serve and assumed they would be treated as equals.

In March 1941 2,500 Cypriot soldiers were put aboard ship for Greece. The men knew their mission would not be exciting, for the British had put them into the Pioneer Corps, which performed such inglorious duties as unloading ships and trucks, digging trenches and grading roads: though there was excitement when Italian planes tried to sink them before they reached Greece.

On 6 April a German army invaded Greece and in two days broke into the main allied port of Salonika. Now the fact that the British Army had never bothered to train the Cypriots how to survive in battle and had not armed them became a glaringly obvious deficiency. As German vehicles entered the streets some Cypriots could do nothing but throw up their hands.

The entire allied presence in Greece was forced to retreat southwards, and the Cypriots among them walked along curling dusty mountain roads under sporadic aerial attack for two weeks, until reaching the coast near Athens. They were told to wait until dark to board ships, for German planes could be easily seen waiting to pounce on anything that set sail.

Five of the Cypriot companies were taken to Crete and the rest to Egypt. In Crete in May the Cypriots were forced to evacuate a second time when the Germans overran the island.

When all the Cypriot companies were assembled in Egypt they took roll call and found that 2,100 men had been killed or abandoned – 84% of those who, so eager for adventure, had gleefully sailed from Cyprus in March.

The survivors were put to work in Egypt and joined by other Cypriot pioneers until by 1942 there were 5,600. Cypriots fulfilled their orders with dedication.

Cyprus remained a valuable British base and in 1945 provided camps for prisoners of war and European Jews who had attempted to reach Palestine against British orders. Cypriot troops and civilians provided assistance to the British at the naval and air bases and camps.

See Index

CZECHO-SLOVAKIA

Other names:	includes Czechia (Bohemia-Moravia); Ruthenia; Slovakia; Sudetenland.
Status in 1937:	independent.
Government in 1937:	democracy.
Population in 1937:	14,350,000.
Make-up in 1937:	Czechs 7,100,000;
	Sudeten Volksdeutsch 3,000,000;
	Slovaks 2,600,000;
	Hungarians 675,000;
	Jews 320,000;
	Ukrainians 290,000;
	Other Volksdeutsch 250,000;
	Poles 75,000;
	Gypsies 33,000.
Religion:	Christian.
Location:	Eastern Europe.

The Czechs emerged from World War I with an empire, courtesy of the British and French governments, though this was a democracy and thus ethnic unrest usually took the form of the ballot box: e.g. in 1935 the Sudeten Nazi Party took 62% of the vote in that region, a clear mandate for Hitler, the German nazi dictator, to interfere, as he saw it. His interference culminated in 1938 in a war scare, when he demanded the Sudetenland be handed to him.

Britain and France were alarmed, especially as France had an obligation to defend the Czechs, so Chamberlain, the British Prime Minister, negotiated with Hitler during the summer. At the final meeting Chamberlain and Daladier, the French Prime Minister, agreed that Hitler should have the Sudetenland. The Czechs were not even invited to discuss the matter, and feeling betrayed they did not resist when German troops marched into Sudetenland to be greeted by cheering Volksdeutsch.

Immediately, other nations with a grievance jumped in: Poland took Teschen, the home of 75,000 Poles, 20,000 Volksdeutsch and 133,000 Czechs; and the Hungarians marched in to take the homes of 500,000 Hungarians, 272,000 Slovaks, 67,000 Jews and 38,000 Ukrainians.

The world was too relieved that war had not broken out and too honest to deny the right of Poles, Hungarians and 'Germans' to have national self-determination to notice that a democratic state had been carved up by dictatorships.

Yet Hitler was not sated and throughout the winter he talked with Slovaks, Czech Nazis and Hungarians to seek the right method of eradicating the Czech state.

On 15 March 1939 he struck: without resistance his army took Bohemia-Moravia; Slovakia declared its independence; Ruthenia declared its independence; and the next day Hungary crushed the tiny army of day-old Ruthenia. Hitler made it possible for Ruthenia to be born and ensured it was still-born. Ruthenia contained 250,000 Ukrainians, 175,000 Hungarians and 75,000 Jews.

On the first day of Hitler's invasion German political police (Gestapo) entered the Czech capital Prague and issued the local police with a list of potential troublemakers, including Germans who had fled Hitler's regime. The police obeyed, arrested them, and a makeshift concentration camp was established.

Hitler renamed the Czech land the 'Protectorate of Bohemia and Moravia', reshaped a government of friendly Czechs, shrank the Czech Army to 7,000 unarmed soldiers, brought in German police to advise the Czech police and instituted a policy of rewarding Volksdeutsch at the expense of others. Over 100,000 Czech farmers were thrown off their land, which was given to Volksdeutsch and Germans. Added to the Czechs who had been kicked out of Sudetenland this put a severe burden on those Czechs who still had an income, who now had to help look after the refugees. As days went by thousands of Volksdeutsch took the best jobs and homes. Within months thousands of trade union activists, writers and politicians and 27,000 Jews emigrated.

From 1 September 1939 Germany was at war and the Protectorate fell under wartime restrictions, such as food rationing. A liveable ration went to Volksdeutsch, a poor ration to Czechs and a pittance to Jews. Indeed many Czechs signed up as Volksdeutsch, stating they were racially Germanic, Nordic or Alpine Celtic. Knowledge of the German language was not necessary: only proof that one had less than two Jewish grandparents. As these Czechs signed up in order to get better food rations for their families and keep a decent job, they were nicknamed Margarine Germans. There was one downside: as the war progressed Margarine German males were conscripted into the German armed forces – eventually the age was 15 to 60!

At least the war meant plenty of employment and soon 140,000 Czechs were voluntarily working in Germany.

Slovakia had become independent under the government of Josef Tiso a one-time Catholic priest. When the Germans invaded Poland on 1 September 1939 Tiso loaned them his 1st Division, which had trucked infantry and 79 Skoda tanks, and which fought through the Dukla Pass for a few days.

Meanwhile in France an anti-German Czech government in exile was created by President Benes, which established a new army and air force recruited primarily from Czechs and Jews. When France was invaded by the Germans in June 1940 the Czechs fought gallantly, but on the 17th when the French asked for surrender terms the Czechs made an attempt to reach Britain – only 5,000 made it.

Many of the Czech flyers had flown to Britain and by September they were in action again, flying two fighter squadrons against German attackers and a bomber squadron which hit German installations in Western Europe.

In June 1941 Hitler sent his armies against the USSR. Slovakia could hardly keep out of this: Tiso had sent troops to fight the Poles, who were fellow Roman Catholics, and the USSR was the capital of atheism, so he supplied an expeditionary force of the 1st and 2nd Divisions and a mobile brigade of 32 38t tanks and 21 Vz40 tanks, all under General Catlos. To remind everyone of their Christian ideals each vehicle was painted with a double armed cross.

By 7 August the Slovaks had achieved a modicum of respect from the Germans, though their light losses (106 killed, 30 missing and 188 wounded) suggested they had not yet been tested. The Germans loaned Catlos enough equipment to expand the brigade into a division and assigned it to their Ist Panzer Corps, while the other two divisions were given an anti-partisan (i.e. anti-guerrilla) mission.

The Mobile Division saw fierce action in the great encirclement of Soviet troops at Kiev in October. By December the division was just west of Rostov, where it went into winter quarters.

In North Africa other Czecho-Slovaks were gaining respect from the Germans, as their enemy. The Czech Army in Britain, though down to about 4,000 troops, had clamoured for action and finally the British agreed to send one battalion to the port of Tobruk in Libya, which was besieged on the landward side. Attached to a Polish brigade in October 1941 the Czechs spent each day in close proximity to the German and Italian lines and each night patrolled the flat cold desert.

In late November the Czechs were ordered to demonstrate as part of an allied plan to relieve Tobruk. The battle was successful and on 9 December the British Eighth Army reached the garrison. The Czechs and allies followed the retreating enemy and attacked them at the Gazala Line on the 13th. After a three-day fight the enemy withdrew and the Czechs were pulled back for a rest.

The Czechs had not won great glory, but they had fulfilled every mission assigned them. No one could ask for more.

In September 1941 Hitler dismissed his Protectorate protector, von Neurath, for being too soft on the Czechs, and replaced him with Reinhard Heydrich, Second in Command of the SS, chief of all SS security police, including the Gestapo, and organiser of Jewish genocide. At once Heydrich ordered executions of known spies, saboteurs and anti-nazi resistance members. However, the Czechs quickly noticed he also executed the criminals, black market gangsters and war profiteers who were making life doubly hard. Some of them were Volksdeutsch and Germans. By November the police had arrested 5,000 such people, including the Prime Minister Alois Elias. It did seem that Heydrich was unbiased in his judgement, though the arrests of Jews continued. He also instituted better policies, such as fairer rations, factory canteens for workers, pensions for the sick and widowed and other socialist programmes, going far further than any Czech government had gone.

On 18 December 1941 new forced labour regulations made work compulsory for all Czech males aged 16 to 65 and females aged 17 to 45. About 250,000 such Czechs were found to be employed in non-essential industries and they were soon entrained for factories in Germany, where they would be paid, have time off and annual leave if they kept their nose clean – if not they could be swiftly transferred to slave labour, which was practically a death sentence.

As a result of Heydrich's policies the Czech government in Britain was worried. Of sixteen of their agents parachuted into the Protectorate fourteen had been caught by May 1942. There were few safe houses for resistance members, because the general public seemed to believe German propaganda that they were all fanatics or gangsters.

These politicians, safe in London from any midnight knock on their door, came up with a plan: they would assassinate Heydrich, blame it on the Czech public, which would result in a heavy crackdown by the Germans, which would force ordinary citizens into the arms of the resistance.

On 25 May 1942, Heydrich was riding to work in Prague in an unescorted open-topped chauffeured car – such was the passivity of the Czechs by this date – when two agents of the government in exile threw a

grenade at the car, wounding Heydrich. Fleeing, the two agents gunned down a Czech policeman. A passing baker took Heydrich to hospital in his van.

At once the city was surrounded by Czech police, German police, SS Security Police, Volksdeutsch SA stormtroopers and German soldiers, who began a house-to-house search. Within a week hundreds of suspects had been arrested of which 157 were executed.

Benes played his part by fuelling the flames: broadcasting on London radio that the Czech people had risen in revolt.

Then on 4 June Heydrich died of his wounds. Czech and German police surrounded the village of Lidice and forcibly expelled all its women to concentration camps and its children to orphanages, while 23 SS Security Police shot all 196 men.

On 16 June an agent defected to the authorities and told them the assassins were hiding in a church in Prague. No less than 759 Waffen SS (combat troops) attacked the structure. All seven inside were killed or committed suicide, but they inflicted heavy losses on the Germans before succumbing.

The plan of the government in exile had worked. With every nazi atrocity the resistance gained new members. Even the last stand in the church played its part, for it instilled into the resistance movement a romanticism that it had hitherto lacked.

A company of allied Czech infantry found no romanticism in their new orders. They were ordered to help defend Tobruk, for the enemy had broken through again, and it looked like there would be another siege. Attacked on the afternoon of 20 June 1942 they held their own, but next morning were ordered to surrender by the garrison commander! They could not believe it, but obeyed orders and, somewhat bewildered, marched into an Italian prisoner of war camp.

On the Russian front the Slovak Mobile Division took part in the great 1942 offensive, which outflanked Rostov and poured into the Caucasus. Advancing hundreds of miles the Slovaks ran out of supplies and had to halt on the Chechen-Ingush border.

In November a mighty Soviet counter-offensive drove straight for Rostov, threatening to trap the axis forces in the Caucasus. The Slovaks and others retreated and on the road to Krasnodar the Slovaks were cut in twain by a Soviet thrust. The trapped men begged for assistance and the German Air Force flew them to the Crimea, but they had to leave their equipment. Many Slovaks took the bold step of surrendering to the Soviets, asking to join them!

In 1943 the division was reconstructed with German equipment and modern tanks and sent back into action.

On the Soviet side of the Russian front in March 1943 at Sokolovo Colonel Svoboda's Czecho-Slovak Brigade went into its first action. Consisting of about two thirds Jews and one third Czechs these fellows had fled the Nazis by one method or another. They did well in their first battle, earning 84 Soviet decorations for bravery. In November they fought in the great struggle to liberate Kiev.

In Britain the Czech flyers could by this date celebrate several hundred patrols, 1,000 bombing missions and the downing of 173 German planes.

In 1943 General Catlos, now Tiso's minister of war, reorganised his army. Casualties on the Russian front had been 8,000 and replacement personnel had to be trained to man the 1st, 2nd and 3rd Divisions, however because the Germans were not happy with the performance in the Caucasus the combat veterans were reassigned to the new 1st Construction Brigade to serve in Romania and the 2nd Construction Brigade to serve in Italy. The veterans had mixed feelings: they were glad to be out of the front line, but they were insulted.

Political intrigue and bad morale plagued the army all the way to the top. The anti-nazi resistance movement in Slovakia, originally a band of communists and Jews, had expanded to 27,000 members as rabble rousers influenced privates and generals alike. The Slovak police and the Hlinka Guard (a local version of the SA) were on the lookout for subversives and there were arrests, but even the most loyal Tisoists realised Germany was losing the war.

In May 1944 eleven battalions of the Protectorate Army were provided with weapons and sent to Italy to guard rail lines, but within three months 20% had defected to the partisans. Many of the 2nd Construction Brigade had also defected.

Realising Tiso could not control his country any more, Hitler chose to do it for him, and on 28 August 1944 the German 108th Panzer Division invaded from Hungary, the German 86th SS Regiment and Battle Group Schaeffer from Poland, and from the Protectorate German Tatra Panzer and Estonian 20th SS Divisions and Schill SS Panzer regiment. Within 24 hours the Tatra met resistance at Cadca and Zilina and the Estonians at Trencin and Povazska Bystrica, much earlier than expected. Total confusion reigned as conflicting orders came from Tiso in Bratislava and the generals of the Army. The Hlinka Guard, much of the police and about 9,000 troops remained loyal to Tiso, 24,000 refused to do so and were disarmed and imprisoned, 18,000 defected to the resistance and 42,000 simply went home.

The resistance council appointed General Rudolf Vierst to coordinate all activity against the invaders. He called upon all resistance members, male and female, to fight openly and radioed Moscow to ask for Soviet aid. In response Soviet planes struck the invaders.

Nonetheless by 6 September the partisans (resistance members and rebel Slovak Army soldiers) had been cut up into pockets, the largest around Strecno, just north of the Vah River, and in the Nitra Valley. Telegat was overrun, but the partisans pushed back the 108th Panzer upon Dobsina.

On the 17th a Soviet-trained Czecho-Slovak air unit landed on rebel-held airstrips and began flying close support missions and a few days later the Soviet-trained Czecho-Slovak 2nd Airborne Brigade flew in to join the battle: the 2,000 paratroopers were mostly Ukrainians and Jews from Ruthenia.

On 8 October the Soviets launched an offensive into Ruthenia with two armies and Svoboda's forces, now raised to corps status: he had his old brigade and a new brigade made up of Ukrainians and Jews from Ruthenia and the Slovaks who had defected the previous year. The paratroopers also came under his orders.

The fighting in the high cold mountains was rough and on the 25th the Soviets and Svoboda's men were brought to a halt.

Meanwhile the German generals were getting nasty messages from Hitler, so they brought in reinforcements: Battle Group Wildner of Ukrainian SS led by a Slovak Volksdeutsch attacking towards Brezno, Dirlewanger's SS Brigade of criminals of many nationalities entering the Ostrovo Mountains, and advancing towards Tisovec the 708th and 271st German Divisions and the 18th SS Division of Volksdeutsch from many lands.

Under this overwhelming onslaught Brezno fell on the 25th and Banska Bystrica on the 28th. Knowing it was all over, Vierst ordered all personnel to try to break through to the Soviets. About 10,000 made it to join Svoboda: Vierst and 15,000 were captured. Perhaps 4,500 rebels, resistance and paratroopers had been killed. The remaining 17,000 or so hid in the mountains.

In Italy an entire battalion of the Protectorate Army entered Switzerland to surrender, so the remainder of the Army was disarmed and turned into labour troops. They were reinforced by new Slovak conscripts who arrived not only without training but without uniforms. A large number defected to the Italian partisans.

In September 1944 General Misker's armoured brigade of the Czech Army in Britain arrived in France. Having sat out the war in Britain for four years they were eager to begin charging down country lanes, liberating villages and striking terror into the hearts of the enemy as they had been trained to do, but instead were told to surround the port of Dunkirk, where the German garrison had yet to give up. They spent the remainder of the war there.

On the Russian front, which was no longer in Russia, Svoboda's corps held the winter line in the Svidnik-Stropkov area.

In March 1945 the Soviets made a two-pronged effort to liberate Slovakia, the 2nd Ukrainian Front aiming up the Danube Val-ley for Bratislava and the 4th Ukrainian Front, including Svoboda's corps, rolling along northern Slovakia towards Moravska Ostrava, and a Romanian army cut into Slovakia to take Bansk Bystrica on the 26th.

The bully boys of the Hlinka Guard fled Bratislava leaving the defence of their capital to the Hungarian Third Army, some Germans and the new 31st SS Division of Protectorate Volksdeutsch, which included many teenage sons of Margarine Germans. The city fell on 4 April and everyone retreated towards Vienna and Prague.

On the 16th the US Third Army reached the border of the Sudetenland, but for political reasons was ordered to halt.

On the 28th the Czech Resistance movement contacted General Vlasov of the axis Russian Army to ask him to switch sides and liberate Prague. Two days later Hitler was dead and mass surrenders of Germans began taking place all over Europe. The US Third Army was at last allowed to enter Sudetenland, but halted again on the 7th.

Already in Prague the people had had enough – they could bear the wait no longer – they ran into the streets and began mobbing the police and the Germans. They did not take prisoners. The Resistance was forced to join them. Vlasov heard this and made up his mind: his Russians entered Prague and speedily captured the airport and radio station. Simultaneously, the German garrison had been negotiating with the Resistance and the Americans and a truce came into effect on the 8th. The Resistance, though not the populace, allowed the Germans and Vlasov's Russians to evacuate to the west. Few reached the Americans, as the Soviet 1st Ukrainian Front swept down on them and all surrendered on the 12th. The war was over.

The nation was free at last, but the nightmare was not over yet, for a terrible retribution loomed. The Czech government in Britain wanted the Sudetenland with its farms, munitions factories and breweries, but not the people who had lived there for centuries, the Sudetenlanders. Expulsion took many forms: some were marched by Czech Resistance soldiers without money or belongings to the German border and kicked across it; others left of their own accord after witnessing Czechs rape, beat and murder; others were imprisoned for months in cold warehouses. There seemed to be no formal method. The expulsion took a year and only proven anti-Nazis could remain.

It is impossible to count the human loss to the state of 1937. The Czechs sitting outside Dunkirk lost 184 killed and 406 wounded 'watching' the Germans. The forces in exile in France and North Africa had several hundred dead. The deaths of Sudetenlanders, other Volksdeutsch and Margarine Germans in German uniform was probably about 100,000. Slovak military losses were about 4,400 killed, half against the allies, half against the axis. The Resistance lost perhaps 3,000 in combat, but many more to executions and concentration camps. Svoboda's corps suffered very high losses, for the Russian front was a mincing machine.

The number who died wearing some other uniform, Hungarian, Ukrainian, British, Italian partisan is certainly a thousand or so.

Added to these are the deaths caused by poor diet, war-related illnesses, air raids including those killed while working in Germany, and those who died in slave labour and concentration camps or by firing squad or hangman's noose, as a result of breaking some rule. Of the 145,000 Jews who fell into Hungarian hands two-thirds did not survive the war. Of the 55,000 who lived in Tiso's nation 40,000 were murdered. Of the 93,000 who lived in the Protectorate 79,000 did not survive. The Nazis murdered 3,600 Gypsies.

According to post-war German records, 267,000 Sudetenlanders and Volksdeutsch disappeared after the 'liberation' in May 1945. It must be realised that some of these died in cross-fire, air raids or fighting the Soviet advance as Volksturm home defence, so the figure is only to be used as an indicator of their treatment at the hands of the Czechs.

The post-war Czecho-Slovak government reported 215,000 total civilian dead: obviously a figure plucked out of thin air to please some journalist. This author believes a more accurate assessment is 640,000 dead among the citizens (and their children) of the 1937 state from all war-related causes.
See Index

DENMARK

Status in 1939:	independent.
Government in 1939:	democratic monarchy.
Population in 1939:	4,100,000.
Make-up in 1939:	Danes;
	A few thousand Volksdeutsch
	along the border;
	the nation's 6,000 Jews were
	completely assimilated.
Religion:	Christian.
Location:	Northern Europe.

On the morning of 9 April 1940 paratroopers of Hitler's Nazi German state dropped onto neutral Denmark, tanks drove across the border and marines climbed ashore. The nation was taken totally by surprise: one fighter plane got off the ground, and was promptly shot down. Amidst a battle in Copenhagen King Christian ordered a ceasefire. Come midmorning he had agreed to welcome the Germans as guests.

The Danes, still in shock, buried their thirteen war dead and dressed the wounds of their 23 injured and sought spiritual guidance to come to terms with the traumatic event.

To Danish merchant seamen the reality of death and destruction this spring morning came as no surprise. In the previous seven months 35 Danish vessels had been sunk by one side or the other in the war between Britain and Germany that Denmark had so naively thought it could ignore.

Weeks earlier the Danes had been more concerned about Finland's war with the USSR, because 800 young Danes had gone off to fight for Finland. The Finns had surrendered in early March. And now the invasion – it was unreal – most Danes had seen and heard nothing.

The Germans did not at first behave like conquerors. Labour recruiters arrived and convinced 25,000 Danes to take jobs in Germany. Waffen SS recruiters took in 250 Danish volunteers. Eventually 363 Volksdeutsch joined the German Army and 1,393 joined the Waffen SS – the latter offered better conditions.

There were two political parties that felt betrayed: Frits Clausen's Danish Fascists and the Volksdeutsch Nationalists, as both had expected Hitler to put them in charge.

Clausen reacted by sending his Storm Afdel-ingr militia into the street to fight the police, hoping the Germans would intervene. The Germans stayed neutral and the police actually recruited more men.

In April 1940 the Danish merchant service had refused orders to return to German-occupied Denmark and had opted for allied ports. They gave good service to the allied cause and a small navy was created using allied-built warships.

In June 1941 Germany invaded the USSR. As a Christian country Denmark organised a unit, the Frikorps, to fight alongside the Germans in this struggle between God and atheism, though the government did not formally enter the axis until November.

In May-June 1942 the Frikorps fought in the Demiansk Pocket losing 40% casualties, including two commanders, and from 17-23 July they held off fanatic Soviet bayonet charges, but suffered 78% losses. The survivors were sent home to rest and recruit.

In November 1942 as snow fell on Kondrotovo in Russia the restored Frikorps dragged their frozen feet into the trenches, the multi-wounded veterans explaining to the new guys how to stay alive in a Russian winter.

On Christmas Day the atheist Soviets launched a major offensive, but the handful of Danes stood like a rock. When the Soviets withdrew, the Frikorps was moved to Moschino, where they held off another offensive on 25 February 1943. Their heroism was reported to Hitler and the Danish public. After a month of rough combat they were withdrawn for a rest.

By 1942 103,000 Danes were working in Germany and the SS recruited among them to establish a three-battalion regiment, which was sent to the Russian front and later to Yugoslavia to hunt communist partisans.

In May 1943 the Frikorps was given the dubious honour of SS status and merged with the Danish SS regiment, brought back from Yugoslavia, and the Danes and Volksdeutsch who had individually joined the Waffen SS. The new force was assigned to the 11th SS Division, the rest of which consisted of Norwegians.

Free elections were held in 1943 and the fascists won 2% of the vote. Typical of fanatics they began to blame each other for the embarrassing defeat and diverged into two parties and several paramilitary militias.

However, the German presence was no longer subtle and on 28 August, when they ordered the Danish government to crack down on the leaflet producing anti-German resistance, the ministers resigned in protest. The Germans reacted instantly, disarming the Danish Army, which they outnumbered fifty to one, and attempted to disarm the Navy, but the sailors fought back, some ships making it to neutral Sweden, others scuttling. The battleship *Niels Juel* was at sea and refused to come home, whereupon she was bombed by the Germans until she ran aground. The King's bodyguard fought so well that the Germans agreed to let them keep their weapons! The police were not disarmed.

A few days later some Germans tipped off the Danish resistance that Hitler had ordered the arrest of all Jews. Now it was the turn of the resistance to go into action like clockwork. Only 400 Jews were arrested: the remainder were spirited away to Sweden by the resistance.

In spring 1944 the 11th SS Division was assigned to the defence of Narva on the Russian-Estonian border. The men steeled themselves, for it was clear the next Soviet offensive might push them into the sea. When it came the division fought remarkably well, and only withdrew when German forces far to the south collapsed. The troops fell back towards the coast.

In Denmark the fascists realised they had chosen the losing side in this war and became more brutal in their frustration, even creating a mock resistance force which blew up passenger trains and famous monuments and killed innocents, blaming it on the true resistance – few were fooled.

The allies were also killing civilians as their planes began an intensive bombing campaign from 1942 onwards, aiming at factories, ports, ships, rail junctions etc., but often missing their target and causing incidental casualties. One daylight raid on the political police headquarters killed 100 Danes and Germans of that hated force, but also killed 114 civilians, including 87 children.

The Danes showed what they thought about such a life by constantly rioting and striking: in one riot in June 1944 the authorities shot 700 people.

On 19 September 1944 the Germans decided to disarm the police. The unit at Amalienborg Palace resisted, only giving up when shelled by a warship! For five wounded they had killed sixteen and wounded 40 Germans. The people rioted, hindering the Germans, but 12,000 police were disarmed and 1,680 were whisked away to concentration camps. Again courage had impressed the Germans: the Amalienborg guards were allowed to keep their weapons.

In early 1945 the Waffen SS conscripted the fascist militias and sent them to join the survivors of the 11th SS Division, which had evacuated Estonia by sea. It is doubtful that those who had been risking their lives since 1941 had much to talk about with those who had bullied women and children on the sidewalks of Copenhagen for the last four years.

In April both found themselves defending Hitler in Berlin surrounded by the Soviets.

On 4 May the German garrison in Denmark formally surrendered to the allies. The Resistance, wearing armbands, came out onto the streets to disarm the Germans and fascists. There were gun battles as some fascists knew they would be executed anyway and chose to go down fighting. A battalion of Danish paratroopers trained in Britain arrived to help with the pacification.

The Soviets bombed Bornholm, killing civilians, until the island's Germans agreed to surrender. This incident rankled with Danes for a generation.

Post-war Denmark was very proud of its anti-Nazi heroes: about 1,300 Resistance members killed in battle or died in custody; the armed forces members who died in 1940 and 1943; and the rioting civilians who were gunned down. Others died at the hands of the mock Resistance or in slave labour and concentration camps, having been sent there often without formal charge.

The merchant service was invaluable to the allies, but this fame cost 1,886 lives. The Faeroes had chosen to support the allies with its fishing fleet and lost 25 vessels to enemy action. The waters around Denmark remained treacherous owing to the number of sea mines, and in the first two and a half years after the war 28 Danish ships were sunk.

The Danes do not like to mention that about 4,000 civilians were killed by allied air raids, and they are not proud of their fascists: 15,500 were arrested in May 1945 and certainly some were murdered. It is believed that 11,200 Danes and 4,000 Volksdeutsch served in front-line units, with approximately a quarter of them killed.

The total death toll for the war was therefore in the region of 12,500.

See Index

EGYPT

Other names:	United Arab Republic.
Status In 1939:	independent, but under British influence.
Government in 1939:	monarchy.
Population in 1939:	19,000,000.
Make-up in 1939:	Egyptians; a few Jews; a few Arabs; small British population.
Religion:	90% Moslem, 10% Christian.
Location:	North Africa

By the time Britain declared war on Germany in September 1939 the British had been in Egypt for 60 years. The Egyptians saw them as arrogant ravishers of their produce, resources and treasures. The British saw themselves as a civilising influence, having established a civil service, medical facilities, sanitation engineering, a transport network and above all a stability. There was truth in both opinions.

The real reason the British were here was the Suez Canal. Through it sailed ships between Britain and India. Without it that voyage's length doubled, therefore so did the cost and the greater risk of shipwreck, and with German submarines on the prowl as of September 1939 no merchant seaman wanted to double his voyage time.

Also it was logical for the British to use Egypt as a half-way point staging area for troops destined for India, the Far East, the Middle East, the Near East, North Africa, East Africa and Southern Europe.

On 10 June 1940 Italy, whose colony of Libya bordered on western Egypt, declared war on Britain, and made immediate moves to seize the canal. When Italian warplanes strafed the border defences, the Egyptian troops drove off to the east, passing British troops on their way to the front. The Egyptian Army had decided to sit out this conflict. An Italian invasion in September did not change their mind, nor did raids by Italian aircraft on the ports and the Canal, though Egyptian flak gunners did help defend their cities.

The Italians were driven out by the British in December, but invaded again in April 1941: were driven out in December and re-invaded in May 1942, reaching Alamein a two-day march from the city of Alexandria. This is in fact as close as the invaders ever came to an Egyptian town. The big battles were fought in desert wasteland and only nomads were inconvenienced by the massive armies swirling about in the sand and scaring the camels.

In November 1942 the Italians were driven out again, never to return. Egypt had not declared war despite three invasions and much bombing, though Italian agents who tried to get an anti-British revolt going found no fertile soil. The Egyptians saw the Italians as just as bad as the British.

Nevertheless, when a few government ministers made what could be construed as anti-British comments, British troops surrounded the King's palace and forced him to appoint more manageable ministers.

Only when Egypt was no longer threatened from invasion did the government declare war – it was purely a gesture. Egyptian losses to air raids were light and 26 merchant ships were lost to axis action.
See Index

ESTONIA

Status in 1939:	independent.
Government in 1939:	dictatorship.
Population in 1939:	1,130,000.
Make-up in 1939:	Estonians 1,000,000;
	Russians 100,000;
	Volksdeutsch 30,000;
	Jews 4,500.
Religion:	Christian.
Location:	North-East Europe.

Estonia had a taste of freedom from Russian domination in 1917 just long enough to miss it when the Germans occupied them in March 1918, and when Germany surrendered in November, marking the end of World War I, the Estonians defended their new independence against invasion by the communist Russian Red Army. Aided by British and German forces they defeated the Red Army and sent it back to Russia.

In September 1939 Stalin, the dictator of the USSR (the Russian communist state), demanded the right to station troops in Estonia. The Estonians were in a bind: their two previous allies were now at war with each other and the Red Army had more soldiers than Estonia had people. They submitted.

Stalin had also tried to bully Finland, but that nation chose to fight and in December 1939 3,000 Estonians sailed to Finland to help her in that struggle.

The Baltic Sea was therefore a dangerous place, what with Britain at war with Germany and Finland at war with the USSR. Between September 1939 and June 1940 ten Estonian vessels were sunk by various actions.

When the Finnish War ended in March 1940 many of the Estonians remained in her Army as the Estonian Legion.

On 16 June 1940 Stalin made more demands, effectively an ultimatum to surrender. The Estonians had no choice and in a day the Red Army took over. Following behind the soldiers came the NKVD, Stalin's political police, with the mission of destroying any resistance potential the Estonians might muster. This took the form of arresting the intelligentsia – artists, writers, managers, scientists, teachers, politicians, clergy – often their entire family was sent to concentration camps or penal colonies in Siberia.

Also skilled workers were sent to factories in Russia and 20-year-old males were conscripted into the Red Army. Within a year 62,000 people had been taken away. The treatment of the intelligentsia was harsh and some were in fact executed. Moreover, the communist system often broke down. It was not unusual for a train full of prisoners to be forgotten for a week, left in a siding while its passengers starved or froze to death.

On 22 June 1941 Germany, controlled by the Nazi dictator Hitler, invaded the USSR and at once the NKVD packed their bags and fled. The Estonians saw this as their chance and broke out into open revolt: 80 German-trained Estonians parachuted into the country to help organise the resistance. However, the Red Army fled too, so quickly that many collaborators were left behind. Collaborators were a mixture of bona fide communists, ethnic Russians who saw the Red Army as a Russian liberation army, opportunists and gangsters.

The Estonians burst into the abandoned NKVD prisons to find torture chambers, fresh corpses and mass graves. Seeing this, the mobs took care of the collaborators in time honoured fashion.

The Germans announced the police could remain armed and they established a part-time militia, the Kaitseliit, while their army recruited a battalion of soldiers to hunt down Red Army stragglers and the German police recruited battalions of schumas to hunt communists. Additionally, thousands of Estonians joined the German Army, Navy, Air Force and SS as hiwis, rear-echelon volunteers.

One secretive German unit consisted of a few hundred men and women of the einsatzgruppe, whose mission was to exterminate Jews, Gypsies and communists. They too found willing volunteers from the fanatic anti-semites, criminals and morons. Once their job was done -there were few Jews and Gypsies in Estonia – the volunteers signed on as hiwis with the German concentration camp service, many becoming guards at Belzec extermination camp.

Finland had also attacked the USSR and the Estonian Legion was in the forefront of battle.

In November 1941 the Germans ordered the 9,000-strong Kaitseliit to make up a bat-talion for front line duty. Some members argued they had not joined for full-time service and not to fight, whereupon these moaners were arrested by the SS Security Police (Hitler's version of the NKVD). The battalion was formed without any further complaints.

By summer 1942 the German Air Force had created the 127th Group of Estonians to fly bombing missions against the Red Army, the German police had formed 13,000 Estonian volunteers into 25 schuma battalions to serve all over Europe, the German Army Estonian battalion had earned honours, the Kaitseliit battalion at the front was fighting bravely, and the number of hiwis was now in the tens of thousands, plus thousands of Estonians had volunteered to work in Germany. Soon, anyone without an essential job was ordered to work for the Germans, most of them shipped to Germany. They were not prisoners and their treatment was reasonably fair. However, any who failed to report for his day's work and was caught was sentenced to slave labour, tantamount to a death sentence.

In March 1943 the 969 members of the Kaitseliit battalion at the front, their casualties having been replaced by Kaitseliit 'volunteers', were honoured for their bravery by being awarded SS status, and the entire Kaitseliit was conscripted into the Waffen (combat) SS. Discounting medically unfit men this created a 6,500-man brigade. Hitherto, Estonians had been denied entrance into the SS on racial grounds, though a few Volksdeutsch had joined. In truth only the SS saw this as an honour: the German Army disliked the SS immensely.

In late 1943 the Germans bestowed another 'honour': all Estonian men born 1915-24 were conscripted into the SS brigade, and in early 1944 the age was extended to the 1904-26 birth group. Older men were called if military veterans. With this manpower the brigade became the 20th SS Division.

The division did not have far to travel to the front for the Red Army had counterattacked all the way to the Estonian border and the IIIrd SS Corps was given responsibility for defending the border at Narva. This would be truly a European battle, for in addition to the Estonian division, the corps contained two Latvian and one Danish/Norwegian divisions, a Belgian and a Dutch brigades.

The fight began in June and the SS held back the communist hordes, but on the Latvian-Russian border the Germans fell back, and on 26 July the SS were ordered to retreat. The Estonians of the 20th Division were surprised to learn that as their nation was being abandoned to the Red Army they were to sail to Germany.

In Estonia the hiwis, volunteer workers, police, schumas, anyone who had served the Germans in some capacity were fleeing along with their families and family heirlooms. Others fled too, for few were willing to trust to the goodwill of the NKVD. At the ports they found refugees packed like sardines frenetically seeking a ship while under air attack. Some chose to go into the woods to begin a guerrilla war against the Red Army.

Once they reached Germany the refugees were sorted: all males aged fifteen and a half upwards were conscripted, the fittest into the 20th SS Division, the others as hiwis to the Navy, 346, or flak batteries, 3,000, and the elderly and most of the women into factories.

The 20th SS Division received its new fellows and also the Estonian Legion, late of the Finnish Army. The division did not get much time to regroup, for on 29 August they were thrown into a major battle against partisans in Slovakia, a bitter fight which did not end until November. Thereafter, the division was put into the front line in Silesia, where the Red Army had halted for the winter.

The division came under a massive assault in March 1945 and the Estonians began a fighting withdrawal towards Prague. As Germany shrank the Estonians there tried to flee to the western front, hoping to surrender to the Americans.

On 9 May the war in Germany ended and two days later at Melnick north of Prague the 20th SS Division surrendered to the Red Army. Their fate was now in the hands of the fickle NKVD.

The British and Americans did not recognise Estonia's incorporation into the USSR and they accepted all Estonians as displaced persons awaiting a new home somewhere.

Meanwhile in Estonia the shooting had not stopped. During the German occupation anti-German guerrillas had never numbered more than about 2,000, most of them Jews, ethnic Russians and Red Army stragglers, plus some deliberately infiltrated in by the NKVD. However, once the Red Army had 'liberated' Estonia, upwards of 50,000 guerrillas harassed them, and as the Red Army passed on, leaving the rear to the NKVD, whole districts became guerrilla-controlled. Late in 1945, though, the Red Army returned with a vengeance and by 1948 the last guerrillas were captured or sailed to the west to seek sanctuary.

Total Estonian casualties 1939-48 are impossible to know, but some educated guesses can be made: a minimum of 5,000 died serving in German uniform, a few hundred in Finnish uniform and at least 6,000 died fighting as guerrillas against the Red Army; a large proportion of the 62,000 arrested in 1940-41 never survived and the NKVD arrested tens of thousands in 1944, of whom few survived; to this must be added deaths at the hands of the Germans in concentration and slave labour camps and in front of firing squads, the better part of 2,000 Jews murdered in 1941, and those who fought the Germans as members of the guerrillas and Red Army; plus there were losses to air raids and crossfires.

This comes to a round figure of about 80,000. Certainly the nation was devastated to the point that it will take well into the 21st century before it will recover.
See Index

FIJI

Status in 1939:	British colony.
Government in 1939:	British and New Zealand administration.
Population in 1939:	260,000.
Make-up in 1939:	Fijians 130,000; remainder Hindustanis and Chinese; a few British and New Zealanders.
Religion:	tribal, missionary Christian, Hindu, others.
Location:	South Pacific.

Following the declaration of war by Britain and New Zealand on Germany in 1939 ethnic Fijians were asked to volunteer for a defence force and several thousand did so. No doubt seen at first by the Fijians as a harmless game, the need for such a force was all too apparent when Japan went on the warpath across the Pacific in December 1941.

When American generals requested scouts who 'understood' the jungle sixteen Fijian commandos went to serve with them on Guadalcanal in December 1942. They remained until the Japanese evacuated eight weeks later. They impressed the Americans who asked for more 'South Sea Scouts', as they called them, and in July 1943 100 Fijian and 40 New Zealand commandos arrived on New Georgia to help capture that island. After a month's action they went to nearby Vella Lavella to hunt enemy stragglers for a month.

The Fiji 1st Infantry Battalion had been seeking Japanese on several islands to no avail, but on Bougainville there were plenty of enemy soldiers, as the Fijians found out: when they disembarked to aid the Americans they were met by enemy warplanes.

The Fijians earned a good reputation on Bougainville, so much so the Americans asked for more: a fresh commando company came and in March 1944 another infantry battalion. The Japanese showed plenty of fight on the island and as late as June the allies were forced to withdraw slightly.

In July the Fijians were relieved by Australian troops.

Fijians earned many decorations from the New Zealand and American armies, including a Victoria Cross, the British Empire's highest award.

Some Fijians served in the New Zealand armed forces on an individual basis.

See Index

FINLAND
Status in 1939: independent.
Government in 1939: democracy.
Population in 1939: 4,000,000
Make-up in 1939: Finns 3,600,000;
Swedes 400,000;
a few thousand Lapps in far north.

Religion: Christian.
Location: Northern Europe.

Finland sort of erupted on the world stage in 1917 as if from nowhere. She had always been dominated by neighbours. However, with the descent of the Russian Empire into civil war the Finns saw their chance and chose independence. Communists, including Russians, tried to spoil things and in early 1918 the Finnish Army led by General Mannerheim, a Swedish-speaking Finn late of the Russian Imperial Army, launched an offensive alongside German troops to kick the communists out as far as Karelia. Then he called a halt, for though the Karelians are Finns, orthodox Catholic rather than Lutheran, the Finnish government wanted the Russians to know that Finland had no territorial ambitions. The Karelians therefore remained under communist control – eventually known as the USSR.

The following two decades brought peace and freedom.

Stalin the USSR dictator whetted his appetite for conquest in Poland September 1939, and in November he demanded the Finns let him have air and naval bases. The Finns appraised their situation: they had fewer people than Stalin had soldiers; they had no modern equipment; their Air Force used many types of foreign planes, hence spare parts were a problem; they had no war industry of their own; the border was 900 miles long, mostly virgin forests with no roads. They told Stalin Finnish soil was not for sale.

Stalin was no doubt taken aback by this rebuff: on 30 November his Red Army invaded. The world expected Finland to collapse in days if not hours.

The Finns mobilised every man who could be spared up to the age of 60 and asked for women volunteers. This gave them a front line strength of 127,800 men, a replacement pool of 100,000 men, and a Civic Guard of 100,000 older men and 100,000 women. The Air Force had 200 planes and the Navy had 30 gunboats and five submarines.

Military theoreticians claim that putting more than 10% of a nation into uniform will destroy that nation. The Finns were desperate and put 11% into their defences.

Their main hope was in the Mannerheim Line, named after that wily old general who was still in command, but there were two flaws with this strategy: the line only consisted of 66 machine-gun nests along its 88 miles between the sea and Lake Ladoga, and north of the lake there was no line.

The dispositions of the Finns seem odd at first glance: to stop the Soviet Fourteenth Army from taking Petsamo in the frozen north was just one battalion; to hold 650 miles along the middle border against the Ninth Army was the Civic Guard; for 200 miles north of Lake Ladoga the IVth Corps' two divisions faced the Soviet Eighth Army's nine divisions and a tank brigade; and on the Karelian Isthmus the IInd and IIIrd Corps, with three divisions each, held the Mannerheim Line against the Seventh Army's thirteen divisions and five tank brigades.

The Finns did have three major advantages: the virgin terrain north of Lake Ladoga where only log cutters' tracks existed over which to carry supplies; the weather, which put deep snow in the path of the enemy and froze their vehicles, while Finnish ski troops could harass the enemy columns like ghosts appearing and disappearing at will; and the latitude, for this far north in winter there were only two hours of daylight per day, which hindered enemy movement in a strange land and restricted flying time for the dominant Red Air Force.

Foreigners heard Finland's plea for help and soon they arrived by sea – 8,000 from Sweden, 3,000 Estonians, 800 Danes, plus Norwegians, Hungarians and Americans, even anti-communist Russians.

Incredibly on 12 December General Talvela's IVth Corps counter-attacked across frozen Lake Tolva and within two days drove back the enemy 139th Division. The Soviets retreated in waist deep snow in pitch darkness through a vast forest in temperatures of -40°C. The Soviet 75th Division was sent to the rescue, but joined the retreat. About 35% of the attacking Finns were casualties, but the victory spurred on other Finns to fight harder.

On 5 January 1940 a counter attack by Civic Guard and the fresh 9th Division east of Suomosalmi destroyed the enemy 44th

and 163rd Divisions for a Finnish loss of 900 killed and 1,770 wounded.

On 6 January the IVth Corps attacked again and in a week of bitter fighting pressed the enemy 168th and 18th Divisions and a tank brigade against the north shore of Lake Ladoga and also beat off a Soviet rescue attempt by four divisions.

By 1 February the Finns in the Isthmus were in a serious hurt, six divisions trying to hold back eleven, yet by the 11th the enemy attacks had availed them nothing but casualties. Only on the 14th did the Finns begin to crack open.

The IVth Corps was going from victory to victory, taking the surrender of the Soviet 18th Division and a tank brigade, but on the Isthmus the Finns lost Viipuri on 13 March, when the Soviets outflanked them by driving across the frozen sea: it was still that cold!

When Stalin offered a deal the government felt it could live with, they surrendered. They gave up Petsamo, Viipuri and the Isthmus, a slice of the long border and a naval base at Hango. Rather than live under a communist government 450,000 people pulled up roots and walked into the country.

Tiny Finland, with a population smaller than that of Moscow, had suffered 24,923 killed and 43,557 wounded, but had defied an empire and had survived more or less in one piece. Indeed Stalin would think twice about attacking Finland again, for his victory had cost him 900 planes, 1,600 tanks, 48,000 killed and 158,000 wounded by his own admission. The Finns suspected his losses were greater, especially if one includes starvation and frostbite. Kruschev, the Soviet leader in the late 1950s, admitted Stalin lost a million men. The truth lies somewhere between.

Germany had not aided Finland, because Hitler, the German dictator, had made friends with Stalin in August 1939, but Hitler made it secretly known to Finland's President Ryti that once he had neutralised his enemies, Britain and France, he would turn on Stalin. It was 1941 before he could plan his crusade against the USSR.

The Finnish merchant service lost 32 ships to somebody's mines and torpedoes during the war with the USSR and in the following fifteen months: Germans, Soviets and British were mining the seas around Finland.

In 1940 several hundred idealistic Finns (racially Swedish) were accepted by the German SS, and the Germans provided Finland with military hardware. Hitler also offered to massacre Finland's Jews – there were about 2,000, all fully assimilated – but Ryti politely declined. His Jewish soldiers would therefore fight in Hitler's new war. To show the world this was a crusade, the Finns adopted a new insignia, the Christian symbol the hakiristi (swastika).

Hitler struck the USSR on 22 June 1941. Soviet planes hit the Finns at once, but Mannerheim withheld his offensive for a week. The recent struggle had been known as the Winter War. This new fight would be known as the Continuation War.

A division besieged Hango on the south coast, while the IVth Corps of four divisions and the IInd Corps of three divisions advanced into the Isthmus, General Talvela's VIth Corps and General Hagglund's VIIth Corps of two divisions each advanced north of Lake Ladoga, the IIIrd Corps and a German division attacked along the middle border, and a German mountain corps attacked Petsamo. German General Falkenhorst had control of his own men and IIIrd Corps and Mannerheim had direct control of the remainder.

Within days VIth and VIIth Corps were approaching the south shore of Lake Onega and north shore of Lake Ladoga respectively, hoping to trap Soviet troops against the water's edge before the lakes froze and provided an escape route. The IInd Corps aimed to do the same against Ladoga's southern shore. On 16 July VIIth Corps cut off a Soviet force at Sortavala, but the enemy evacuated across the hundred-mile-long lake in ships.

In August Viipuri was liberated: the victory was cause for celebration throughout Finland.

The Finnish advance was slow: they had only seven full-strength divisions and one tank battalion with nine different models of tank, each one inferior to the Soviet T-34. They captured Olonets in Karelia on 6 September, Lodeynoye on the 8th and Petrozavodsk on 1 October, but in the Isthmus, despite being within artillery range of

Leningrad, the Finns had called a halt. They let it be known that as in 1918 they had no territorial ambitions.

In December the Soviets in Hango evacuated by sea. The front north of Leningrad was stationary, though noisy with artillery fire. Elsewhere the Finns sent out daily patrols, but rarely encountered the enemy.

In April 1942 the VIth and VIIth Corps repelled a major Soviet assault for the loss of a thousand men. In May the IIIrd Corps repulsed an attack.

The 1,200 or so Finns who had joined the German Waffen SS, fought admirably as a battalion of the 5th SS Division, but in November 1942 they suffered badly capturing Hill 711 an insignificant dot on the map of the Caucasus. By spring 1943 they had lost 222 killed and 557 wounded, and following further losses in the Battle of Groshino they were allowed to go home for a rest. Mannerheim asked that they be transferred to the Finnish Army and Hitler agreed.

By spring 1944 it was obvious Hitler's Germany was losing the war and the Finns did not want to go down with him. They put out diplomatic feelers to learn Stalin's bottom line.

In April the IIIrd Corps beat off a Soviet attack, mowing down Soviet infantry for fifteen days, but this worried the Finns, for surely Stalin would not waste so many lives if he was willing to make peace. In May the towns of Finland came under a major enemy air offensive.

On 9 June the Finns north of Leningrad were swamped by a major Soviet offensive using over 6,000 guns and had to abandon Viipuri on the 20th. This day the Finns fell back on both sides of Lake Onega, though they did manage to destroy a Soviet division at Kuolisma.

Chief of the General Staff General Heinrichs pleaded for German help, but they sent only Foreign Minister Ribbentrop, who explained why Germany could do nothing. In fact he wanted reinforcements. The Finns let him have their Estonian volunteers.

Mannerheim, recently elected President in a free election, was already in tough negotiation with Stalin's emissaries. The result was a cease-fire on 7 September and a deal whereby the Soviets would not ask for much more than they had taken in 1940 and the Finns would expel all Germans from their soil.

If the Finns felt bad about letting down the Germans, their attitude changed when in a ridiculous move German troops invaded the island of Suursari. The Finnish garrison fought back and repelled the Germans, taking a thousand prisoners. Furthermore, as the Germans in the far north retreated across Finland towards German-occupied Norway they burned farmhouses in anger. To prevent further vandalism Mannerheim ordered army units to chase after them, to keep the pressure up so that they kept moving. The Continuation War might have ended, but Finland had a new war, the Arctic War.

On 26 September General Siilasvuo's IIIrd Corps caught up with a German column at Puolanka and the former partners fought. The Germans soon ran off, abandoning heavy equipment and supplies. On 1 October the tail of the German column reached Kemi, still 250 miles from Norway. On the 2nd they passed through Tornio leaving its houses aflame.

Not until November did the last Germans leave Finland.

The Arctic War cost the Finns about 2,000 casualties. The Continuation War had cost 55,000 killed and 3,000 civilian dead. All told, between 1939 and 1944 Finland lost 84,000 of her sons and daughters, an unbelievably high percentage of her population: e.g. two-and-a-half times that of Britain's war losses.

Defeated twice, Finland nonetheless emerged as the only fully combative axis nation to survive the war with her government and armed forces intact.
See Index

FORMOSA

Other names:	Taiwan
Status in 1931:	Japanese possession.
Government in 1931:	Japanese administration.
Population in 1931:	7,600,000.
Make-up in 1931:	Mandarin Chinese 7,400,000; aboriginal Taiwanese 160,000; Japanese colonists.
Religion:	various
Location:	off the China coast.

Conquered from China by Japan in 1894, the Formosans were subjected to a racist Japanese government in imitation of the European colonial powers. By 1931 the Formosans were also bombarded by fascist-style government and army propaganda, as were the Japanese people, but with the proviso that Formosans as second class citizens were not allowed to share in the glory of the Japanese Empire, only to work for it. Therefore, Formosan conscripts in the Army served strictly in a rear-echelon capacity. Discipline was harsh: a Japanese officer was within his rights to execute a Formosan soldier for the most rudimentary of offences if he wanted to make a point.

With the beginning of war in China Formosans served in all branches of the armed forces and the merchant navy. In 1941 Formosa became host to an army jungle warfare school. The island's ports were also used to launch invasions of French possessions in 1940 and British, Dutch and American colonies in December 1941.

As rear-echelon soldiers Formosans were not supposed to be in the firing line, but in China they had to fight off guerrillas on occasion, as they did on those islands of the Pacific where guerrillas were active, e.g. Timor and the Philippines. Moreover, the allies began a counter-offensive by invading islands without warning, so Formosan soldiers were subjected to air raids, naval bombardments and amphibious assaults. Though not armed to fight, they were expected to die rather than surrender, and in many a fight Japanese soldiers murdered the Formosans before committing suicide. Some were able to surrender, but allied troops were not always in the mood for taking prisoners.

Serious air raids began on Formosa in November 1943. The Americans did not just want to neutralise the ports and airfields, but planned to invade the island, until the plan was dropped at the end of 1944. In one raid in 1943 43 Japanese planes were destroyed. The raids stepped up and over a three-day period in October 1944 500 planes were destroyed and 40 ships sunk. Formosa provided airfields for raids against the Americans from June 1944 onwards.

In 1945 the Japanese relented and allowed Formosans to volunteer for combat units. As can be imagined few stepped forward, but some who had succumbed to Japanese propaganda did so. A handful even joined the suicide units such as the Navy's human torpedoes, the air units' kamikaze pilots and the Army's human explosives.

Formosa's airfields sent off air raids right up to the end of the war in August 1945.

See Index

FRANCE

Status in 1939:	independent.
Government in 1939:	democracy.
Population in 1939:	40,800,000.
Make-up in 1939:	French 33,300,000;
	Occitans 4,000,000;
	Germans 1,500,000;
	Bretons 800,000;
	Corsicans 200,000;
	Catalans 200,000;
	Flemish 200,000;
	Assimilated Jews 200,000;
	Basques 40,000;
	Italians 10,000;
	also large immigrant
	population including:
	100,000 Jews;
	100,000 Russians;
	several thousand North
	Africans.
Religion:	Christian.
Location:	Western Europe.

In the 1920s little boys in France thought it normal that many papas were dead and that grown-up men should be one-armed or one-legged, such was the impact of World War I on French manhood. That such a horror could be repeated was unthinkable.

Therefore, as Hitler expanded his German nation, repudiating the Versailles Treaty restrictions on his armed forces in 1935, militarising the Rhineland in 1936, waging war in Spain 1936-39, invading Austria and annexing the Sudetenland in 1938 and invading Czecho-Slovakia and annexing Memelland in 1939 the French politicians

did nothing but wring their hands in despair. This policy was called appeasement.

On 1 September 1939 Germany invaded Poland. This was too much. France had long had a respect for the Poles and had sent advisers to Poland to help her in her war against the USSR in 1920. One of them was Charles de Gaulle. On the 3rd the British government declared war on Germany: the French Chamber of Deputies forced Prime Minister Daladier to follow suit.

Mobilisation orders put 4,320,000 Frenchmen into uniform: they included those who had been little boys in the 1920s, those who had watched their older brothers march off to war in 1914 and even some who had fought in that great 'war to end all wars'.

However, Daladier did not want to fight and neither did Hitler. Hitler forbade his planes from bombing France and his ships from firing on French warships. Daladier did not bomb Germany and refused permission for British planes to use his airfields. His army advanced into Germany, true, but only for a mile to satisfy honour. There was no shooting and local farmers continued their work between the armies! The press had several names for this, such as 'Sitzkrieg' and 'Phoney War'. British troops arrived at the front and one of them was killed in December – one, after four months of world war!

The British Royal Navy did fight at sea and German submarines and mines claimed 22 French merchant ships. Daladier had planned to help Finland against the USSR, was too late and the forces were diverted to Norway when Germany invaded that nation in April 1940. His lack of commitment forced his own people to oust him and he was replaced by Paul Reynaud.

On 10 May 1940 the Germans invaded Luxemburg, Netherlands and Belgium and bombed France. Immediately the French generals went into action, sending, as part of a pre-arranged plan, the Seventh Army through Belgium to the Netherlands and the First and Ninth Armies into Belgium and the Second Army to the French-Belgian border to link the above with the main French defences along the impregnable Maginot Line, through which no German army could move.

Reynaud felt confident, as did Churchill, appointed British Prime Minister this very day, for there were 102 French, 22 Belgian, ten Dutch and ten British divisions armed with 3,100 tanks facing 133 German divisions and 2,400 tanks, moreover French tanks were bigger than German. French and German divisions contained about 17,500 men each. The others were smaller. Only in aircraft was there a shortfall: the Germans had twice as many.

Three days later there was a lack of optimism at General Gamelin's headquarters: the Seventh Army had been stopped by German paratroopers, the key to the Belgian frontier Fort Eben-Emael had fallen, the Dutch had already abandoned three-quarters of their nation and that night the German 5th Panzer Division crossed the Meuse River at Houx into France outflanking the Maginot Line.

On the 14th the Dutch surrendered, the Seventh Army retreated, elements of the Second Army were overrun west of the Meuse at Sedan, and the British and the other French armies were not yet fully into position. Heavy enemy air attacks hindered all movement. Gamelin knew he had to plug the Sedan-Houx gap or else the Germans could swing south and threaten the Maginot Line from the rear, shoot straight westward to the sea and cut off from France all the defenders in Belgium, or drive south west and seize Paris.

He ordered his armoured reserve to counter-attack at once, but there were problems: the armoured divisions had only been formed recently and were slow to respond, and almost all orders were issued via motor cycle courier not radio or telephone. As a result the counter-offensive never took place.

The Ninth Army was ordered to echelon southwards, while the British took up their vacated positions and the First Army counter-attacked southwards to slice off the German penetration, but the flaws with this plan were the Second Army was already falling back, enabling the German penetration to grow stronger, and the British had started to retreat and refused to take up the slack. By the 17th the British were planning a sea evacuation to abandon the continent of Europe.

Meanwhile German tanks were pushing westwards towards the sea, bypassing pockets of the Second Army, and reached the coast in the Abbeville-Noyelles area on the 20th. The new 4th Armoured Division commanded by General de Gaulle counter-attacked them from the south, but the Germans beat him off so easily they did not think it worth reporting.

The new plan of General Weygand, who replaced Gamelin on the 19th, was for the British to counter-attack southwards with two divisions and the First Army with eight divisions on the 21st, but instead of these 90 infantry battalions, only five made the attack, some of them a day late, and of course the move failed. On the 25th the British began evacuating from the port of Dunkirk and three days later the Belgians surrendered.

By 4 June when the Germans reached Dunkirk the ships had taken off 224,000 British and 140,000 French troops – French ships had been responsible for 30,000 of the passengers.

Weygand took stock of the situation: France had 44 divisions manning a hastily dug line running 127 miles from Abbeville to the Luxemburg border, with a British division, some Polish and Czech troops, the Maginot Line defences and a million French troops in a replacement pool. There should have been no cause for despair, but there was a paralysis, a panic, from top down so that all problems were a day late in reaching Weygand's staff, a day late in being solved, and the solution a day late in reaching the units on the ground, by which time they had a whole new set of problems.

The defenders just east of Abbeville were assaulted on 5 June and fought fiercely for days, and only on the 10th did a small German force break through, but on the 9th the defences just west of Luxemburg had been attacked and they too allowed a handful of Germans through. Once behind French lines the Germans expanded and drove for road intersections and bridges. The entire French Army now retreated.

Rather than see Paris destroyed in battle the French abandoned her on the 14th and on the 17th a new Prime Minister Marshal Pétain told his armies to cease-fire as he asked the Germans for terms. Britons, Poles, Czechs and a few French ran for the ports to escape to Britain. On the 22nd Pétain surrendered.

The image of the French fighting man of 1940 that has come down to us is of an overweight family man in his thirties, but appearing older, wearing a shabby brown uniform, carrying too much equipment, including a rifle too big for him, hoarding a piece of cheese, his only food for days, hurrying along a country lane as fast as his short legs would carry him, jumping into a ditch at every distant sound of an aeroplane, eventually throwing up his hands at the rumbling of an approaching German tank, only to suffer the humiliation of seeing the vehicle drive right past him, young blonde German infantry perched on it grinning at him and then ignoring him.

This image is not fanciful: this must have happened countless times. Over 1,800,000 Frenchmen were taken prisoner before Pétain's surrender.

But the coin had another side to it. The French suffered 92,000 killed and 250,000 wounded. Within days the British were saying they had evacuated because the French and Belgians would not fight, yet Belgian casualties were comparable to French as a percentage, while British losses were trifling. The Germans reported losses per division from French and Belgian gunfire to be far higher than from British.

Considering the magnitude of the defeat, France got off lightly. Hitler demanded reparations for having started the war, reduced the French Army in France to 100,000 and 250,000 in the colonies, disbanded the Air Force in France only, did not seize the Navy, annexed only the German-speaking part of France (Alsace-Lorraine) and none of the colonies, and put an army of occupation only in the north and on the west coast. The French breathed a sigh of relief.

In fact greater humiliation came from the surrender to Italy and the Italian occupation of a few square miles along the border.

Roosevelt, the American President, called Italy's 20 June attack on France a stab in the back, but far worse was to come as three nations chose to kick the Frenchman while he was down. The first was Britain. Anglo-French relations were already at a low ebb when a British fleet arrived off the port of Mers-el-Kebir in French Algeria and demanded the French warships there surrender, join them, scuttle or sail to a neutral port to be interned. While the French were radioing for instructions the British opened fire, destroying three battleships and a destroyer and killing 1,297. Two British airmen were wounded. Throughout the world British sailors seized French warships and merchant ships. In retaliation French air units in Morocco bombed British Gibraltar. After eight days of peace France was at war again.

On 22 September Japan invaded French Indo-China. The French resisted sternly, but the Japanese asked their pal Hitler to intervene and he asked Pétain to give in, whereupon Pétain told his troops to allow the Japanese in as 'guests'.

In November Thailand invaded French Indo-China and after three months the French were forced by the same diplomatic route to hand over some Cambodian provinces.

The French people were most concerned about the war with Britain, because British planes were soon bombing France regularly, and though they never targeted civilians their aim was terrible. In September a British fleet tried to invade Dakar in French West Africa and was repulsed: for the loss of a submarine and some shore damage the French damaged a battleship, a cruiser, two destroyers and a sloop.

Actually the sloop was French too, for de Gaulle had escaped to Britain and pleaded with his countrymen to join him in continuing the war against the Germans. He gained enough supporters to man a few warships, fly a few planes and establish an army brigade, perhaps 10,000 men and women.

Pétain took de Gaulle's effrontery personally – he had been de Gaulle's mentor – and sentenced him to death in absentia.

In October 1940 de Gaullists conquered the African colony of Gabon from its French garrison: this was true civil war.

In June 1941 the French garrison in Syria under General Dentz was bombed by British planes and on the 10th invaded from Palestine by a British, an Australian and a de

Gaullist division, while the British Royal Navy destroyed his naval flotilla. Dentz defended the large expanse with 27 battalions of colonial natives and a few whites and Foreign Legion. In the streets of Damascus légionnaire fought légionnaire. On 10 July after two Indian divisions invaded from Iraq Dentz surrendered with good terms. His men were given a choice of going to a Pétainist colony or remaining under de Gaulle: 85% chose Pétain. The battle had cost Dentz 6,000 killed and wounded.

Pétain ruled France and the empire from the resort town of Vichy. It was a nightmare job. Apart from British bombing he had 7,000,000 refugees to worry about, who would not go back to their homes in German-occupied territory. He asked Hitler for his prisoners of war: as yet only those from Alsace-Lorraine were being released as Hitler considered them to be German citizens, though 100,000 of these inhabitants refused German citizenship: of these Hitler sent the German-speakers to concentration camps and expelled the French-speakers to France adding to Pétain's refugee problem. Hitler did not accept those residents who were Jewish and expelled them and 7,500 of his own Jews to France, adding to Pétain's refugee and Jewish problems. Pétain accepted the gentile refugees, but not the Jews, his police putting them in concentration camps as 'illegal' immigrants. Most French did not know there was a Jewish problem.

In order to please Hitler Pétain dismissed his Jewish employees; 49 prefects, 58 deputy prefects and 2,282 civil servants, and urged all employers to 'purify their workforce'.

On 14 May 1941 the Paris police arrested 3,600 foreign-born Jews and put them in the newly-built Beaune la Rolande concentration camp. The facts that most had been in France since early life, had contributed to French society and some had fought for France were irrelevant. However, the law was based on race not religion and some were Catholics: the Catholic Church, normally supportive of Pétain, complained on behalf of the Catholic Jews.

On 16 July the Paris police arrested 7,000 foreign-born Jews and incarcerated them in a sports stadium without food or extra sanitation. This was too much for the elderly: some died and others committed suicide. A week later, joined by 5,800 more they were taken to Beaune la Rolande and Pithviers concentration camps. All foreign-born Jews still at large knew they were living on borrowed time, bar certain categories: essential personnel, serving soldiers and their wives, Jews with non-Jewish spouses, and of course friends of the regime, such as informers. Of the thousands of police involved one resigned in protest.

At Cabinet level there was constant intrigue: Pétain dismissed Laval, his deputy, and replaced him with Flandin; then replaced him with Darlan; then brought Laval back, all within seventeen months. Other senior positions changed hands as frequently.

Pétain quickly turned the nation into a police state: any who complained would be sent to Gurs or Rivesaltes concentration camps.

In addition to living under the heavy hand of the police, the population under German-occupation were under the scrutiny of the Abwehr, German counter-intelligence, and German SS Security Police, both of which recruited plenty of French men and women. In the first six months of occupation the French employees of Abwehr arrested 600 people in Paris alone.

There was another danger too, retaliation: in two days 150 political prisoners guarded by French police were shot by Germans in retaliation for the assassination of two Germans.

On 22 June 1941 Germany invaded the USSR. French communists had so far lost all right to call themselves patriots because neither had they taken Pétain's side nor had they resisted him, taking orders from Moscow to lie low. Now, however, Moscow ordered them to wage war against the Germans and Pétainists. There were already several resistance organisations and the communists set about trying to take control of them.

Most French were not communist but serious Catholics and, now that Germany was locked in a life or death struggle with the arch-atheist USSR, many in all conscience could not hinder the Germans.

The far right of the political spectrum saw things differently too, rallying around Pétain who promised a cleaning of the nation of the Resistance, who according to the old marshal consisted of communists, gangsters, foreigners and Jews. As for the Germans, they would leave once the British came to their senses and gave up. De Gaulle was only a British puppet and his troops were all Jews and Negroes, so no one in their right mind would support him and his British masters, who had murdered Frenchmen at Mers-el-Kebir, at Dakar, in Gabon and Syria and on the high seas plus bombed civilians nightly. In one British raid on Paris 623 people were killed and 1,500 wounded. Meantime true Frenchmen should aid the Germans in their struggle. Pétain made everything so much clearer, did he not?

On 8 July 1941 a committee raised a French Legion to fight alongside the Germans in the USSR: within a month they had 3,000 men, but their doctors had been overzealous and had rejected 6,000.

Many thought Pétain behaved as he did because Hitler was holding the French prisoners of war hostage. Pétain was concerned about them. He agreed to a German suggestion: for every three Frenchmen volunteering to work in Germany a prisoner would be released. The Germans kept their word, but in months only 240,000 volunteered, thus releasing only 80,000 soldiers. Laval had an idea: all the twenty-year-olds doing labour service would be sent to Germany under the same 'relief' system.

One problem was that the Germans had begun to force French people to work for them and they were not part of the relief system. Eventually all men aged 18-19 and 51-66 plus all unmarried women 20-35 had to report for work in France and all men 20-50 had to report in France or possibly Germany. Those in essential employment already were exempt. A total of 850,000 French workers were ordered to Germany. Treated well, their biggest worry was British air raids and police informers.

By 1942 the Resistance had become a problem and Pétain recruited the Groupes Mobiles des Réserves – fifty-seven 200-man companies of anti-terrorist police – and at the end of the year he formed the Milice, a 29,000 strong anti-terrorist army.

In the USSR the French Legion was performing well and 2,000 Frenchmen had joined the NSKK, a German paramilitary corps of drivers and mechanics. Other French citizens worked for the German armed forces and a few hundred actually joined as hiwis, rear-echelon volunteers.

Until late 1942 de Gaulle was the only focal point for anti-Pétainist French in the colonies, though he was obviously dependent on the British. When the British conquered French Madagascar from May to November 1942 they dropped all pretence at doing it for de Gaulle and used only their own soldiers.

De Gaulle called his forces Free France or Fighting France: by now 42 warships; a merchant fleet of 5,000 men and 67 ships; an air force that had put two squadrons in the Gabon campaign, one on Malta, two in Ethiopia, three in Egypt and one in Britain flying over France; a brigade in Libya and a division that had fought in Gabon, Eritrea and Syria.

But de Gaulle was not America's man. The Americans had their own saviour of France, General Giraud, who had escaped from a German prison. They had decided they needed such a man when Churchill talked Roosevelt into invading French North Africa. Conquest of this region would put an allied army in the rear of Rommel's Italian-German Army in Libya, would give allied ships a safe coast to hug in the Mediterranean and would be a springboard for further operations. De Gaulle loved the idea because it would give him access to more recruits.

On the night of 7 November 1942 the anti-Pétainist Resistance in North Africa went into action. Many were Jews who had a score to settle. General Bethouart's men arrested the German armistice commission in Casablanca, and the men of Generals Juin and Mast arrested Admiral Darlan, Pétain's Commander in Chief who was visiting a sick son in Algiers, but by dawn Bethouart and Mast were under arrest and Darlan freed. This comedy was mimicked elsewhere.

At dawn French shore guns opened fire on allied fleets off Algiers, Oran, Casablanca,

Safi, Mehdia and Fedala, but they could not prevent the Anglo-Americans from coming ashore. On the 10th Darlan surrendered North Africa: indeed he joined the allies. The little misunderstanding cost the French four destroyers and eight submarines sunk, a battleship and a destroyer damaged, 490 killed and 969 wounded. The allies lost 2,300 killed and wounded.

By chance Laval was in Germany in conference with Hitler and Mussolini, the Italian dictator, when the embarrassing news arrived. Hitler went into a tirade and ordered his army to invade unoccupied France. The only opposition they encountered was a verbal one from Pétain. The Italians took a slice of the Riviera and the island of Corsica.

Hitler demobilised the French Army, but for a ceremonial unit, then waited until the 27th to demand the fleet: in response some captains scuttled their ships, others fled to neutral ports, and some were sunk by the Germans in their attempt to escape. A few reached allied ports.

In Tunisia the French fleet surrendered to the Germans, but the army did not and joined the allies who were advancing from Algeria. German and Italian troops rushed to Tunisia to hold it.

For most French people Hitler's invasion had negated all previous treaties. They now considered themselves at war again and those who had sided with Pétain were forever damned.

Of course in North Africa the allies now had three saviours of France on their hands – de Gaulle, Giraud and Darlan, and each had their own followers. The problem was solved when a fanatic shot Darlan dead on Christmas Day. The two rivals argued, but the allies came up with a solution. De Gaulle got the jackpot, command of all Free French, while Giraud got the consolation prize, command in North Africa.

In Tunisia the French used a corps of four divisions of Tunisians, Algerians, Moroccans and a few French alongside the British First and Eighth Armies, which also had a French brigade, and US IInd Corps, but this weighty combined force took five months to cover the twelve miles between their December position and the city of Tunis. The French earned La Gloire, but it was a cack-handed campaign. The French were most impressed by the amount of allied equipment and begged for some of it, but they were not impressed by the calibre of allied generals.

When the campaign ended in May 1943, with the total surrender of the last axis troops in Africa, the French counted their losses: 2,156 killed and 10,276 wounded, a quarter of total Anglo-American-French losses. All had lost some men captured as well.

The next place on Churchill's map to Berlin was Sicily. British Eighth and US Seventh Armies landed there on 10 July 1943. The Americans soon asked for Moroccan mountain troops: de Gaulle complied. They fought admirably until the enemy evacuated 16 August.

On 8 September 1943 Italy split into civil war and though the allies had been the immediate cause of this they took no sensible action, all that is but de Gaulle. When the Corsican resistance informed him the anti-fascist Italians were fighting the fascists and Germans he immediately sent in a battle group to the island covered by a flotilla of four cruisers, four destroyers and three submarines protected by an impressive aerial umbrella. By 4 October a joint effort had forced out the fascists and Germans. The first integral department of France was free.

On mainland Italy a poor response by the allies condemned them to a slow slogging bout inching their way up the boot of Italy. They were soon asking for French help.

De Gaulle's armed forces now consisted of: a fleet of almost 50 warships; the merchant fleet; air force with 24 squadrons in the Mediterranean, seven in Britain and three in the USSR; and an army of 175,000 white troops, many of them colonial born and bred, and 275,000 natives.

In December 1943 General Juin took a corps into action in Southern Italy of the 2nd Moroccan and 3rd Algerian-Tunisian Divisions. Under US Fifth Army they made a name for themselves in the tough wintry conditions around Cassino, which was a stationary battle with even less movement than in Tunisia.

The corps, reinforced by the 4th Moroccan Division and six battalions of Moroccan Goumier mountain troops plus the Free French 1st Division, was at last given permission to advance in May 1944, but Juin was given no roads to speak of, those in the valleys being reserved for allied tank units. He told his men to keep up as best as they could, leaping from one precipitous ridge to another, a German behind every ridge. There were some rough moments: one company was trapped awhile, but the corps actually moved faster than the allies in the valleys!

In Italy all roads may lead to Rome, but Juin had no roads and his men therefore outflanked Rome while the Americans took it. The three-week advance cost the corps 10,000 casualties.

The corps continued to advance, liberating Siena on 3 July. A battlegroup invaded and liberated the island of Elba and at the end of July the entire corps was withdrawn for a new mission.

Within France the civil war had worsened as the Resistance formed actual guerrilla bands called Maquis, which faced in open combat the Milice and Groupes Mobiles. In the towns Resistance operatives dodged the police, Abwehr and SS Security Police, the latter using 32,000 French employees. In the countryside the police and gendarmerie turned a blind eye to the Resistance whenever possible and the Harvest Guards only became involved if Maquis interfered with harvest shipments. The Resistance/Maquis were outnumbered by the Pétainists two to one and this did not count the German Army which was busy watching the coast for signs of invasion.

The allies were planning an invasion and as part of the plan they stepped up their air raids to a ferocious level. Civilian casualties were extremely high and it is understandable that the Pétainists had no problem recruiting a corps of flak gunners.

In the first nine months of 1943 174 civil servants and politicians and 281 Germans were assassinated. In gunfights the security forces lost 29 killed and 69 wounded. Yet, in one three-month period 20,000 people were arrested and sent to concentration camps. Few were members of the Resistance and many were completely innocent of law breaking. In the last three months of the year 530 members of the security forces were killed in gunfights or assassinated.

On the USSR front the French Legion had exhibited outstanding courage and had to be withdrawn as early as March 1942 after suffering 50% casualties, and was assigned to anti-guerrilla operations in Poland.

In 1944 the Maquis became more active, gunning down 600 Germans in one ten-week period. Sabotage was widespread and no German truck convoy moved without a formidable escort. If the Maquis could not ambush it they informed the allied air forces by radio. Air raids were devastating especially in North-West France as every industrial plant, railyard, airfield, canal lock and bridge was bombed. In daylight near the coast every bus, train, truck and car risked being strafed by allied fighters.

The west coast was defended by a physical structure, the Atlantic Wall, built by German Organisation Todt using 15,000 German workers and 132,000 French volunteers, 94,000 foreign volunteers and thousands of forced labour and slave (i.e. prisoner) labour. The Germans manned the defences with 48 divisions, a third in the Fifteenth Army in the Pas de Calais, a third in the Seventh Army in Normandy and the remainder in Nineteenth Army covering the Biscay coast and south coast. The German Army employed 190,000 French civilians.

On 6 June 1944 the allies landed in Normandy. French aircraft and ships supported the invasion, but of the 150,000 ground troops only 300 were French. The Anglo-Americans wanted to rub it in that the French owed their liberation to them.

The Maquis rose in rebellion as per instructions from de Gaulle and took on recruits, whom they had been unable to use until now. Allied aircraft parachuted weapons and supplies to them. Unfortunately, the allies could do little else and many a Maquis band was wiped out, though in Brittany allied paratroopers dropped to aid them: two British and two French battalions and a Belgian company. All Maquis took a new name Forces Française de l'Intérieur (FFI).

As the German 2nd SS Division drove north towards Normandy it was ambushed by FFI losing fourteen killed and 21 wounded in two days. A veteran unit, it had recently taken in conscripts, 8,000 of whom were seventeen- and eighteen-year-olds from Alsace-Lorraine. Terrified, the youngsters shot in all directions, executed suspected FFI members and burned every building that housed a sniper. On their route lay Tulle, where FFI had attacked the town's garrison: the Pétainists had fled abandoning 300 Germans, who suffered 99 killed, 40 wounded and 40 missing before the division rescued them in a fight costing three killed and nine wounded. At dawn they found the missing 40 Germans, who appeared to have been tortured to death. In an act of vengeance the SS troops rounded up 400 local men. A German factory owner, horrified, managed to save 27 of them – essential workers he said – but of the rest 99 were hanged from lampposts and the others sent to concentration camps.

The division drove on against FFI ambushes and air strikes. On the 10th a Pétainist informed them a local communist village, Oradour sur Glane, had bragged they were going to execute an SS prisoner. A company was diverted to the village, found nothing, but its commander ordered all the men shot and the women and children put into a church which was then burned down. It was apt that the burning steeple fell on an officer and killed him. The village lost 190 men, 254 women and 207 children. A few survived when warned by ordinary SS soldiers.

The Waffen SS decided this was not how their troops should behave and ordered the commander to be court-martialled, but an artillery shell saved them the trouble.

It was 27 July before the Americans broke out of Normandy. At last they allowed a French unit to fight. General LeClerc's 2nd Armoured Division, a mixture of de Gaullists, Darlanists and other -ists, had been fully equipped by the Americans and they began their first action on 3 August. The German Seventh Army was on the run and the French loved this reversed blitzkrieg. By the 10th they were east of

Fougères when ordered to block the escape of the Germans. They did so and LeClerc was proud to see his men beat veteran German panzer commanders. On the 14th they held another blocking force for a week.

Meanwhile the Americans were forging ahead liberating Orléans and Chartres on the 14th, Dreux on the 15th.

Two important struggles began on the 15th. On the south coast US Seventh Army landed in the Pampelonne-St Raphael area. French ships and planes supported the invasion, but again only a few French commandos were allowed the honour of combat on the first day. Only when the Americans had conquered the defences did they allow General de Lattre de Tassigny's corps to land. His 1st Free French, 1st Armoured, 3rd Algerian-Tunisian, 4th Moroccan and 9th Colonial Divisions immediately drove for Toulon and Marseilles.

The second struggle to erupt this day was the revolt of Paris. The Police revolted, followed by civilians, and reluctantly by the Resistance. Casualties were high among this poorly armed mob as they besieged Germans and Pétainists in their barracks and offices. The FFI sent messengers looking for the Americans. De Gaulle told LeClerc to prepare to move on Paris while he asked the Americans for permission to liberate his capital. The Americans did not want to become bogged down in a city battle or to have to feed Paris, but when they realised LeClerc was going anyway, they gave him their blessing and sent a division with him. If they could not deny de Gaulle the glory of liberating Paris they would at least force him to share it.

LeClerc's men drove non-stop through 100 miles of enemy-occupied terrain, cursing every German who held them up, and on the night of the 24th reached a Paris suburb. Wisely they waited until dawn before attacking. Some telephoned loved ones in the city.

Someone must have telephoned the garrison too, for Germans and Pétainists began a mass exodus from the city. Next morning LeClerc and the Americans attacked: tank/infantry battles shared time and space with thousands of cheering, singing civilians. Many jumped onto vehicles to guide them. One German tank was destroyed directly under the Arc de Triomphe. During the day General von Choltitz surrendered, refusing his last order from Hitler to destroy the architectural treasures of the city.

The liberation of Paris cost LeClerc 628 killed and wounded and the Americans about the same. There were 600 police and civilian killed and 2,000 wounded. The FFI claimed 1,750 killed and wounded. Enemy deaths were about 2,800 and 14,800 were captured. Next day de Gaulle led a parade during which he had to avoid Pétainist snipers. In the cathedral of Notre Dame while he heard mass a Quasimodo-like Pétainist sniper interrupted the service.

On the south coast the 3rd and 4th Divisions and 3,000 FFI took Toulon on the 27th, killing 2,000 and capturing 17,000 Germans and Pétainists. Next day the 1st Free French and elements of the 3rd Divisions and 2,000 FFI took Marseilles, killed 3,000 defenders and captured 37,000.

The FFI was also liberating some towns on their own, such as Grenoble and Lyon. The German Nineteenth Army was on the run.

LeClerc had wanted to advance eastwards from Paris as soon as it had been liberated, but de Gaulle kept his division in the city to regulate the FFI, which was not de Gaullist and contained many communists. Only on 10 September did de Gaulle feel safe enough to release LeClerc, whose division now charged south-east towards Lorraine.

From the south de Tassigny's forces, now christened First Army, were also heading towards Alsace-Lorraine. It was therefore one major coincidence and with sweet justice that when the invasion forces from Normandy and the Riviera met the two linking divisions were LeClerc's and the 1st Division, both of which contained many Free French veterans.

Since landing in France de Tassigny's men had suffered 1,144 killed and 4,346 wounded, but had inflicted on the enemy about 6,000 killed and had captured 58,000. The FFI had taken 20,000 prisoners.

By mid-September the allies had run out of supplies, especially fuel and had called a halt. Eastern Alsace-Lorraine had yet to be liberated and some German port garrisons were still holding out. De Gaulle restruc-

tured his army, regularising the 250,000 FFI, the vast majority of whom had enlisted since 6 June. From them he created the 10th Division to garrison Paris, the 27th Division to man the Franco-Italian alpine border, the 19th Division to watch German-held ports and the 1st, 14th, 23rd and 25th Divisions which watched German-held ports in the south-west: plus 40,000 were taken into the air force and 100,000 assigned rear-echelon duties. Only in German-occupied Alsace-Lorraine were the FFI still operating as guerrillas. He also introduced conscription for all twenty-year-old men and recalled all reservists.

Though the allies had ceased advancing with armour, their infantry was still in action: a Czech brigade was besieging German-held Dunkirk; Canadian First Army was attacking the Breskens Pocket in south-west Netherlands; British Second Army was holding south central Netherlands; US Ninth and First Armies were attacking into the Ardennes and Rhineland; US Third and Seventh Armies were creeping into Lorraine; French First Army was in the Vosges mountains of western Alsace; on the Franco-Italian border was French Alpine Command of the 27th Division, two regiments and two US regiments; and on the west coast were five ex-FFI divisions and two US divisions of French Atlantic Command besieging enemy-held ports. The French thus had more troops facing the enemy in Western Europe than did the British. In France the allies had taken 635,000 prisoners.

At sea French warships were hunting enemy submarines, protecting convoys, attacking coastal shipping and bombarding enemy shore positions. In the air French planes were flying over the Mediterranean, Italy, Western Europe and with the Russians on the eastern front.

The Pétainists had three choices when allied troops approached them: surrender and hope for the best, fight to the death, or retreat to Germany or a German-held port. Most gave up quite peacefully, unless approached by FFI. The FFI hunted down known Pétainists and Germanophiles and imprisoned, tortured, beat and disfigured thousands. About 10,000 were executed after swift trials. Women who had dated Germans had their heads shaved.

Pétain and his government were in exile now at Sigmaringen, Germany. Pétain was still of use to the Germans. The French Legion had spent a winter on the Russian front and two years fighting partisans, and in June 1944 had gone back to the front in a pitiful attempt to hold back the Russian hordes.

In 1943 the SS had recruited a French regiment, 2,480 strong, but in its first fifteen days on the Russian front had been devastated, the 1st Battalion suffering 860 casualties. In 1944 the regiment took in more recruits, reached a strength of 1,688 and saw action again in July, losing 137 killed and 669 wounded in a month.

The 2,000 NSKK were given rifles and told to hunt partisans in Italy.

As the Pétainists fled into Germany the SS took control of this sudden influx of manhood. Darnand was told to divide his 5,000 surviving Milice into three: a third to guard Pétain, a third to enter armaments factories, and a third to join the SS regiment. Actually, 2,500 asked to join the SS and were accepted.

The 1,200 survivors of the French Legion were ordered into the SS, and 70 refused to take the oath – they were instantly arrested.

The Algemeine SS had recruited French workers in Germany for membership as reservists and now they were called to full-time duty and also assigned to the SS regiment. The NSKK were also conscripted by the SS as were Organisation Todt guards, ex-concentration camp guards, Groupes Mobiles, the 800 hiwis of the German Navy, indeed any Frenchman they could lay their hands on.

This raised the unit's strength to 7,340. It was then sent to Wildflecken for training as the 33rd Charlemagne SS Division.

On 3 November French Alpine Command liberated the village of Sospel. This month there was a major offensive in Alsace-Lorraine: the US Third Army attacked on the 8th, the US Seventh Army on the 11th and the French First Army three days later. On the 19th the French 1st Armoured Division reached the Rhine opposite Basel. Belfort was taken in a two-day fight and within days

the German Nineteenth Army was trapped in a pocket around Colmar. Deep snow in the Vosges, fog and a shortage of supplies called a halt to the offensive. However, LeClerc's division, part of Seventh Army, drove into the streets of Strasbourg on the 24th, to find German officers strolling with their girlfriends. In a two-day fight they and the FFI captured the city.

France was essential for the continuation of the allied offensive in the west that would defeat Germany, in particular her roads, bridges, rail lines, canals and ports, but the damage was unbelievable from allied air raids, FFI sabotage, German and Pétainist sabotage and overuse. As best as possible the French people maintained this network, though facing another winter of extortionate black market prices for food and heating fuel and worry about loved ones in uniform or in a camp somewhere. Prostitution and crime were rife. However, the Americans interfered so much that strikes and disobedience were constant. Not least of the problems was that the allied liberators were not as polite as the German conquerors. The Germans had paid when billeting soldiers. The allies simply commandeered and the American and British attitudes to French people were arrogant to say the least. It was a far cry from the camaraderie of World War I. Every theft of an American truck, every rape by an American or Briton made things worse.

Hitler planned a little surprise for Alsace-Lorraine. On 1 January 1945 he struck the US Seventh Army. The Americans including the French 3rd Algerian-Tunisian Division fought well, but elements retreated about twenty miles. On the 6th a German offensive came out of the Colmar Pocket. The 1st Free French and 4th Moroccan Divisions held it.

On the 20th de Tassigny launched his own surprise, attacking the pocket from the south with the 1st Armoured, 2nd Moroccan, 4th Moroccan and 9th Colonial Divisions and from the north with the 5th Armoured, 1st Free French, and US 3rd Divisions. The 10th Division held the western flank. The combat in the deep snow was so terrible that many wanted to call off the offensive, but gaining a reinforcement of three US divisions and LeClerc's division, de Tassigny continued the attack.

On 2 February the Germans collapsed and on the 9th the 1st Armoured Division reached the last enemy bridge over the upper Rhine at Chalampe just in time to see it blow up, hundreds of retreating Germans still on it.

The offensive had been a success, but had cost 6,440 US and 14,000 French casualties.

The Charlemagne Division went into action on 16 February 1945 attacking the Soviets in East Prussia. The affair was completely futile, the French were repelled easily and counter-attacked on the 22nd. On the 24th, with 10% casualties in two days the division began falling back as did flanking German units. The division made an attempt to rally at Koeslin, but was chopped up by tank/infantry assaults. One element regrouped at Kolberg and held out in that doomed city until 17 March, another element sailed to Denmark and a third reached temporary safety west of the Oder River. Roll call listed 1,100 survivors.

In March the French 5th Armoured and 3rd Algerian-Tunisian Divisions helped the Americans clear the German Rhineland, while the allies launched invasions over the Rhine: US Third Army on the 22nd, Canadian First, British Second and US Ninth Armies on the 23rd, US First Army on the 28th and US Seventh Army on the 26th at Mannheim. The allies had made no plans for the French.

On the night of the 30th the French launched their invasion of central Germany with ten men! Next day there were other similarly small crossings, but later in the day the US Seventh Army allowed the 5th Armoured Division use of a bridge and on 1 April they linked up with those already across. The French invasion could now begin for real. On the 3rd the Algerians and the 9th Colonial Division captured Karlsruhe. Then the 1st (ex-FFI) Division fanned out towards Baden Baden, the Algerians towards Pforzheim, and at Strasbourg the 1st Armoured, 4th Moroccan, 10th and 19th Divisions crossed and began climbing into the Black Forest.

On the 22nd the 2nd and 3rd Divisions with Americans took Stuttgart, encountering resistance from old men and boys. The French swept down towards the Swiss border.

De Gaulle decided it was time for the ports on the west coast to be cleared and launched an offensive in the Gironde on 15 April. While French and US bombers hit the hold-outs with bombs and napalm, a French fleet of a battleship, cruiser and fifteen smaller warships and six allied vessels bombarded them. Then the 23rd Division and LeClerc's 2nd Armoured Division attacked along with marines and naval artillery. On the 17th the Royan garrison surrendered.

In Germany French troops took Sigmaringen on the 22nd and arrested Pétain and his government. Eight days later the French cleared Lake Constance and the 1st Armoured, 5th Armoured, 2nd Moroccan and 4th Moroccan Divisions reached Austria. The invasion of central Germany was no pushover and cost the French 5,000 casualties.

Alpine Command attacked into Italy on 30 March with the 1st Free French and 27th Divisions and two regiments. On the 27th they began rolling up the towns of the Italian Riviera.

On the west coast the 23rd Division attacked La Rochelle and took Ile d'Oberon.

In April the Charlemagne was reduced to brigade status and 800 volunteers among its survivors went to Berlin to protect Hitler. One of the last soldiers decorated by Hitler, hours before he committed suicide on the 30th, was a Frenchman. On 2 May Berlin surrendered. The 120 surviving Charlemagne troops gave up too. A few miles to the west 300 Charlemagne members surrendered to the Americans.

On 8 May Germany surrendered.

In Indo-China the Japanese had dastardly attacked the French in March 1945 and a guerrilla war began against the Japanese. Already the French Navy had provided a battleship and a destroyer to help the allied navies against the Japanese.

Japan surrendered in August 1945.

De Gaulle and the French people believed they had earned the right to sit at the allied conference table. The Soviets refused to accept this, but Churchill fought for their rights. He won and France received an occupational zone in Germany and a neighbourhood of Berlin.

French losses in the conflict 1939-45 are difficult to assess, certainly when the French insist on counting colonial losses as French, but do not like considering SS and Pétainist losses as theirs. A sensible breakdown of military losses is as follows:

Battle of France 92,000 killed, 250,000 wounded;
de Gaullists 1940-42 2,000 killed;
Tunisia 2,156 killed, 10,276 wounded;
Sicily-Corsica-Italy 6,000 killed, 16,000 wounded;
France-Germany 15,281 killed 45,966 wounded.
in German prisoner of war camps 60,000 dead;
Resistance killed or executed 30,000;
Resistance died in camps 77,000;
Pétainists versus Japanese 1940 800 killed, 2,000 wounded;
Pétainists versus Japanese 1945 4,200 killed;
Pétainists 1940-43 versus allies 4,000 killed;
Pétainists in France 3,000 killed
Pétainists executed by FFI 10,000 killed;
Pétainists/SS on Eastern Front 2,500 killed, 7,000 wounded; plus civilian dead:
murdered by Pétainists/Germans in retaliation 26,000;
French-born Jews murdered by Pétainists/Nazis 26,000;
Foreign-born Jews murdered by Pétainists/Nazis 51,000;
Gypsies murdered by Pétainists/Nazis 18,000;
killed in invasion 1940 cross-fire/air raids 13,000;
killed by allied air raids 1940-45 60,000;
killed in invasion 1944 cross-fire 4,000;

Taking into consideration other military losses at sea, in the air, against the Thais, in Norway etc., plus those unfortunates from Alsace-Lorraine conscripted into German uniform who died on all fronts, plus those killed in air raids while working in Germany, we come to a figure of about 520,000 dead among French residents of 1939.
See Index

FRENCH EQUATORIAL AFRICA AND WEST AFRICA

Other names:	includes: French Cameroons; French Congo; French Guinea; French Sudan (Mali); French Togoland; Chad; Dahomey (Benin); Gabon; Ivory Coast; Mauritania; Niger; Senegal; Ubangi Chari (Central African Rep.); Upper Volta (Burkina Faso).
Status in 1939:	French colonies.
Government in 1939:	French administration.
Population in 1939:	17,600,000.
Make-up in 1939:	well over 100 ethnic groups.
Religion:	Various.
Location:	North West and West Africa.

When France declared war on Germany in 1939 all male French citizens aged 18-40 were eligible for military service. Subjects of the empire were encouraged to volunteer to fight for La Gloire de la France. Many of the volunteers from Equatorial and West Africa were placed in labour companies, but the more warlike tribes were put into infantry battalions. Their officers were French colonists. Some reached France just in time to be captured by advancing Germans in the fiasco 1940 Battle of France.

Though the government of Marshal Pétain surrendered to Germany and Italy in June 1940, General de Gaulle escaped to Britain and established a government in exile which would continue the war. He urged colonial governors to join him, thereby giving him his own soil instead of a rented office in London. The dastardly British attack on the French fleet at Mers-el-Kebir hindered de Gaulle's cause immensely.

For two months not one governor declared for de Gaulle. Then on 27 August in French Cameroons de Gaullists led by a Major LeClerc launched a coup d'état and the black and white residents of the towns cheered in jubilation. Then Governor Eboue of Chad, the first black French governor in history, declared for de Gaulle. There too the Pétainists were subdued by the size of the cheering crowds. De Gaullists also seized power in French Congo.

The borders of these colonies that faced Pétainist colonies became de facto front lines, though there was no fighting.

De Gaulle decided a show of force was needed and on 24 September a British fleet, including three de Gaullist warships and transports carrying de Gaullist troops approached the port of Dakar on the West African coast. They encountered opposition from shore guns and warships manned by Pétainist French and Senegalese. After two days the fleet retired with a battleship, cruiser, two destroyers and a de Gaullist sloop damaged. Several Pétainist ships were damaged and a submarine sunk.

This was the second major affair in the Anglo-French War and the first in the French Civil War. Pétainist governors were morally strengthened by the victory.

De Gaulle urged another strike immediately and chose a land invasion of Gabon. On 12 October 1940 from the north Colonel LeClerc led a force of Congo, Chad and Cameroons troops, while Major Koenig led a force of Congo and Senegal troops from the south. The three de Gaullist warships blockaded the port of Libreville. Gabon rearguards put up a show of resistance, but two squadrons of de Gaullist planes convinced them to retreat continually. Distance and jungle terrain were responsible for the slow advance.

Meeting on 7 November the two columns attacked Libreville. The Pétainists told their troops de Gaulle was a lackey of the British. The de Gaullists told their troops Pétain was a lackey of the Germans. No doubt most of the African soldiers simply obeyed orders. In the harbour two French sloops blasted away at each other. After four days of battle Governor Masson hanged himself and his deputy surrendered.

In early 1941 LeClerc led an invasion from Chad into Italian-occupied Libya. Ahead of the column, of a hundred Frenchmen and 300 Chad and Senegal troops riding in commandeered cars and trucks, was a scouting force of a British patrol and camel troops of the Groupe Nomade de Tibesti. Overhead flew two de Gaullist squadrons.

It took eleven days of desert driving to reach the first sign of habitation, Kufra Oasis. The column surrounded the Italian defenders and sniped at them and bombed them. On 1 March the defenders – 64 Italians and 352 Libyans – surrendered. Kufra became an important base for allied long range desert patrols.

Meanwhile a brigade of de Gaullists had been in reserve in Egypt and in February 1941 was transferred to Eritrea. Consisting of one Chad and four Senegal battalions, the 13th Demi-Brigade of the Foreign Legion (including many Germans and Italians) and some companies of African-born Frenchmen, the brigade quickly captured an Italian outpost and on 8 April captured two forts at Massawa.

Aiding the British in their war against Italy was one thing, but convincing Pétainist governors to switch sides was quite another. Fortunately, General Dentz governor of Syria-Lebanon played into de Gaulle's hands by allowing German and Italian planes to use his airfields in May 1941. The British replied with air raids, which forced him to order his guests to leave, which they did in early June. Not able to trust him, the British organised an invasion force in Palestine.

On 10 June the invaders crossed into Syria-Lebanon: an Australian and a British Division, an Indian brigade and the de Gaullist 1st Free French Division. Containing the veterans of Eritrea, minus the Chad battalion, plus a battalion of marines, three companies of Syrians and some French rear-echelon personnel, the unit was light for a division, but they intended to make up in courage what they lacked in firepower.

Dentz had 33 battalions of infantry, of which five were Senegal and three were from Equatorial and West Africa, and he had plenty of cavalry, tanks and planes.

On day two the de Gaullists took Quneitra from a rearguard, but were forced to halt that night at Kissoué. The next morning they mowed down a Pétainist cavalry charge and took the town. However, now they had to wait for supplies.

On the 21st the de Gaullists attacked Damascus and for 24 hours the Foreign Legion fought its own civil war. The Pétainist légionnaires lost.

On 10 July Dentz surrendered. His men were asked to join de Gaulle and about 15% did so.

In 1942 the British waged a ponderous campaign in Madagascar against Pétainists, most of them Senegal and local troops. Though lasting six months, total casualties were only in the hundreds and the colony surrendered in November. No de Gaullist units were involved.

The 1st Free French Division put together a large brigade under General Koenig and placed it at the disposal of the British Eighth Army in Libya. By spring 1942 it was occupying a flat desert encampment with one water well known as Bir Hakeim. Koenig had 3,600 men divided into a battalion of Pacific Islanders, a mixed company of white and native North Africans, a battalion of African-born Frenchmen, a battalion of Ubanghis, the 13th Demi-Brigade of the Foreign Legion, some French anti-tank gunners, a French artillery battalion, some French marine flak gunners and some British flak gunners. It was a ramshackle unit, to say the least.

On 26 May 1942 the enemy, General Rommel's Italian-German Army, launched an offensive and broke through at once, defeating three allied divisions and four brigades in a matter of hours. The French brigade was isolated. Under air attack at once, next day the brigade defeated an attack by Italian tanks. From now on the French created a legend as they fought off one attack after another. By 8 June Rommel, angered at the impudence of the brigade, was himself leading three divisions against the brigade – a company of Ubanghis fought to the last – and only on the 10th did Koenig even ask permission to retreat. It was granted and his brigade charged out that night. About 1,100 men were killed or captured.

Bir Hakeim was de Gaulle's greatest triumph to date and his African soldiers were as much responsible as anyone.

Bir Hakeim notwithstanding, Rommel's army continued to advance and was only stopped at Alamein, Egypt in July. Repelling an attack in September, the Eighth Army prepared a major counter-offensive for 23 October. By this date the southern flank of the army was protected by the Free French Brigade. It says a good deal about allied trust in the de Gaullists by this time, that they were given such an important position.

On the night of the 23rd the entire Eighth Army attacked, the French going up against the Italian Pavia Division. After two days the French were told to hold what they had. On the 26th the attack was renewed, but the French were brought to ground. Further along the line action continued and Rommel called it quits on 4 November.

With the Anglo-American invasion of Morocco and Algeria, and the ceasefire three days later that brought those two colonies into the de Gaullist sphere, de Gaulle no longer had to rely on negro Africans and colonial French. He now gained the excellent Moroccan and Algerian forces.

On 16 August 1944 the 9th Division, made up of six battalions of Equatorial and West Africans, three of African-born Frenchmen and French and African support troops unloaded its men and vehicles on the beaches of the French Riviera, cleared the day before by American units. At once the men began to follow the retreating Germans, liberating villagers who did not seem to mind that many of the faces in the division were black. It was not all cheese and wine, though, for there were some feisty German rearguards.

In September the division stopped in Alsace to bring up supplies. Six black African battalions were also put on the Franco-Italian border to make patrols, but when winter snow arrived were withdrawn to rest on the Riviera.

The 9th Division was not withdrawn and spent a rough freezing winter, fighting several battles including the elimination of the Colmar Pocket from 20 January to 10 February 1945.

On 1 April the 9th Division invaded central Germany by crossing the Rhine and had a serious fight for Karlsruhe which was ringed by gigantic concrete bunkers: many required aerial bombing to take them out. Following this, they advanced into the Black

Forest, a mountainous area where every bend in the road was guarded by fanatic rearguards, often manned by boys. Still, by the end of April the division was choked by thousands of prisoners as the German armies collapsed.

The six African battalions returned to the Franco-Italian border and attacked on 30 March. Within days they were advancing into Italy.

On 8 May Germany surrendered.

Native Africans had performed excellent service on behalf of their French masters and were an essential part of the de Gaullist forces in the early days and without de Gaulle the French would not have emerged as internationally respected as they did.

As Africans had helped liberate France they now expected France to liberate them. The French did not see it that way and it would be another generation before their expectations could be filled.

See Index

FRENCH POLYNESIA

Other Names:	French Oceania; includes: Futuaa; Gambiers; Marquesas; New Caledonia; Tahiti & Societies; Tubais; Tuamotus; Wallis.
Status in 1939:	French colonies.
Government in 1939:	French administration.
Population in 1939:	100,000.
Make-up in 1939:	diverse island tribes, Chinese and French colonists.
Religion:	Tribal, missionary Christians.
Location:	South Pacific.

When France declared war on Germany in 1939 nothing changed in these island paradises. A few colonists and some islanders reported for military duty for a war that frankly could not affect their placid way of life.

When France surrendered in June 1940 still nothing changed in the islands. However, a French general by the name of de Gaulle had reached Britain and was continuing the war in defiance of the French government of Marshal Pétain. By radio many islanders learned of de Gaulle's ideas, but the governors, civil servants and police took orders from Pétain. As the weeks went by de Gaullist sentiment spread until the governor of Tahiti agreed to a plebiscite: 5,564 islanders and colonists voted for de Gaulle, only 18 for Pétain. The governor proclaimed his allegiance to de Gaulle and volunteers began asking for military duty.

On New Caledonia the presence of a Pétainist warship in Noumea harbour within gun range of the government buildings was a deterrent against plebiscites until September 1940 when the Australian cruiser *Adelaide* arrived. Rather than fight a more powerful enemy the French sloop weighed anchor and sailed off. The island government was quickly convinced to opt for de Gaulle. They too put together military volunteers.

The islanders and colonists of all the French Pacific possessions created the Bataillon Pacifique, which sailed to Africa to join de Gaulle's army.

In December 1941 the Japanese began a war of conquest across the Pacific. French Polynesia seemed within their grasp and the island defence forces steeled themselves for invasion. Some islanders wanted the Bataillon Pacifique to return, but wiser heads knew they needed divisions not a battalion. The allies could not possibly provide the islands with defences: they had little enough for themselves; but New Caledonia was on the Hawaii-Australia sea/air route and as the Americans needed to defend this route they brought troops, ships and planes to New Caledonia in summer 1942. The American units were formed into a provisional division and in honour of their warm welcome took the name Americal Division. In the autumn the division went to fight the Japanese on Guadalcanal and with the American victory there in February 1943 the French islands were no longer in danger.

For men who are used to being surrounded by water the Libyan desert was a new experience for the Bataillon Pacifique. Assigned to a Free French Brigade they were positioned in a flat encampment around a well known as Bir Hakeim. The brigade consisted of 3,600 men divided into the Pacific islanders, a mixed company of white and native North Africans, a battalion of African-born Frenchmen, a battalion of Ubanghis, the 13th Demi-Brigade of the Foreign Legion, some French anti-tank gunners, a French artillery battalion, some French marine flak gunners and some British flak gunners. It was pure hodge podge.

On 26 May 1942 the enemy, General Rommel's Italian-German Army, launched an offensive against the British Eighth Army and defeated three allied divisions and four brigades in a matter of hours. The French brigade was now isolated. Under air attack at once the brigade was attacked on the 27th by an element of the Italian Ariete Division. A company of légionnaires was overrun, but the Italians were repelled twice with the loss of 32 tanks. That night the defenders drove off Italian infantry.

Over the next few days the brigade traded shells with the enemy and everyone was bombed and strafed. Several of the islanders were hit. On day four 600 Indians, captured by the enemy and then let go walked into the camp. The French sent them to the rear that night in trucks. This incident told the defenders that if they surrendered they would be treated humanely, but they fought on.

On day six they heard that a British brigade further north was overrun in 24 hours.

On day seven the Bataillon Pacifique jumped into trucks and went looking for the enemy! The following day they ran into Italian tanks, knocked one out and shot down four planes, but suffered badly and that night were ordered to return to the camp which had just refused a call to surrender.

On day nine the shelling was intense, the brigade only being able to fire 2,500 shells in return.

On day eleven after refusing a third call to surrender, the brigade was attacked by the German 90th Light Division. The defenders repulsed the Germans.

On day twelve the brigade repelled two attacks by the 90th Light and elements of the 15th Panzer Divisions, though the islanders fared badly.

On day thirteen the north perimeter fell back under German pressure.

On day fourteen the camp was attacked on all sides by the 90th Light, 15th Panzer and Italian Trieste Divisions. A company of Ubanghis was destroyed, but the others held their holes in the sand. Following this they were subjected to a raid by 60 planes. That afternoon the islanders were almost overrun by a vicious attack, but were rescued in the nick of time by a counter-attack of légionnaires. The islanders counted 250 enemy corpses in front of their holes. The enemy retaliated with another heavy air raid and one bomb landed directly on the islanders' headquarters, killing their commander and causing fearful destruction.

On day sixteen the camp fought off three divisions personally led by Rommel. Not only did they hold, but even counter-attacked. Rommel then sent 110 planes against them.

This night General Koenig asked for permission to withdraw his brigade and it was instantly given. The men climbed into trucks in the dark and drove towards the allied line, shooting up enemy tents as they came across them.

The brigade registered 1,100 killed and missing, and about 877 of the survivors were wounded.

The brigade had created a legend. Bir Hakeim was de Gaulle's greatest triumph to date and the most heroic brigade action of the three year North African campaign. The Bataillon Pacifique earned as much right to claim part of the allied victory in the war as anyone. Islanders saw further action in the war as part of the 1st Free French Division in Italy, France and Germany.
See Index

FRENCH SOMALILAND

Other names:	Djibouti.
Status in 1939:	French colony.
Government in 1939:	French administration.
Population in 1939:	45,000.
Make-up in 1939:	Danakils;
	Issas;
	Yemenis.
Religion:	Moslem.
Location:	East Africa.

When France declared war on Germany in 1939 a local defence force was created, which became necessary on 10 June 1940 when Italy declared war on France, as Italian territory bordered on the west.

On 18 June the colony was attacked by the Italians. For six days infantry, artillery and air units saw action. On the 24th France surrendered to Italy.

The Italians did not occupy the colony and things returned to normal. Over the next two years allied agents attempted to lever the colony away from loyalty to the Pétain government in France towards de Gaulle's pro-allied government in Britain. It was only in January 1943, when all other French African colonies had long since declared for de Gaulle, that the colony's government followed suit.
See Index

FRENCH WEST INDIES

Other names:	includes French Guiana; Guadeloupe; Martinique.
Status in 1939:	French Colonies.
Government in 1939:	French administration.
Population in 1939:	500,000.
Make-up in 1939:	Mostly negroes, also Chinese, white colonists, a few aboriginals.
Religion:	Christian.
Location:	Caribbean and coast of South America.

When France declared war on Germany in 1939 colonial subjects in the West Indies were encouraged to volunteer for military service. Few reached France before the collapse in June 1940. Thereafter the administrators maintained loyalty to the French government of Marshal Pétain.

There was no action here, despite Britain, an enemy of Pétain from July 1940 onwards, having forces on the border of Guiana and on many Caribbean islands. The British preferred to use diplomacy to convince the administrators to join de Gaulle as a counterfoil to Pétain.

However, it was not until July 1943 that they accepted rule by de Gaulle. The colonies' defence forces put together an infantry battalion, which went to the USA to train. Individual men also served in the French Navy and merchant fleet.
See Index

GEORGIA

Other names:	Gruziya.
Status in 1939:	member state of the USSR.
Government in 1939:	communist under Stalin dictatorship.
Population in 1939:	2,100,000.
Make-up in 1939:	almost all Georgians.
Religion:	Christian.
Location:	extreme Eastern Europe/ Central Asia.

Georgia, an ancient land whose golden age was in the 12th century, was submerged in the Russian Empire in the 19th century, re-emerged for a taste of freedom in 1917 only to be submerged in a Russian communist empire in 1921 after a shore battle.

The Russian communists suppressed all Georgian cultural, political and religious activity using the hated NKVD political police, despite the fact that the dictator of the USSR, Stalin, was a Georgian – real name Josef Djugashvili – and one of the most feared leaders of the NKVD was another Georgian, Lavrenti Beria.

No one knew the true number of innocent people arrested by the NKVD and sent to concentration camps and penal colonies in Siberia.

In June 1941 the USSR was invaded by Germany and all young Georgian men were conscripted to serve in the Red Army to defend Stalin's empire. Thrown into the great battles along the western border, whole divisions and corps were ordered to surrender by incompetent generals hindered by Stalin's megalomania. Within weeks thousands of Georgians were in German prisoner of war camps: simply open fields without shelter and only thin soup to keep them alive. With winter approaching they knew this was a death sentence.

Then out of the blue hope arrived in the form of German recruiters offering similar treatment to German soldiers, complete religious and cultural freedom and a chance to fight communists. Understandably many signed up.

There were two options for Georgians: hiwis, i.e. rear-echelon volunteers; and Osttruppen, i.e. all-Georgian battalions which hunted communist partisans, consisting of Red Army stragglers, local communists and NKVD-trained guerrillas inserted behind German lines. Georgian anti-partisan Osttruppen were not noted for taking prisoners.

In summer 1942 Hitler recognised his Georgians as worthy of their own political representation, which was especially gratifying because the German advance had almost reached Georgia by September. On the Terek River, the Germans were close enough that some people were breaking out from Georgia to come into German lines – the front was loosely patrolled here.

However, a major Soviet offensive threatened to cut off the Caucasus and in January 1943 the Germans began a full-scale retreat from the Terek River. For the 19,000 Georgian Osttruppen plus hiwis this was heartbreaking news.

This year the Georgians were sent all over German-occupied Europe, the Osttruppen ostensibly to fight local communist partisans, the hiwis simply following their German parent unit. Georgians were sent to France and given defensive duty in case of an allied sea invasion: a battalion each to Albi, Castre, Périgueux and St Nazaire, two to Normandy, one to Guernsey and one to Texel in the Netherlands.

On 6 June 1944 the allies did invade, in Normandy, and the fate of the Georgians in France was now tied to the fortunes of the German Army. In Normandy until late July they battled hard against the Americans: at St Nazaire they were besieged until the end of the war, when those on Guernsey also surrendered.

On Texel in April 1945 1,200 Georgians rebelled against the Germans and took the island for themselves. It was a week after the war was over, mid-May, before allied troops arrived. The Georgians claimed to be allies. The Canadians did not believe them and took them prisoner. British-Canadian policy was to hand over all Georgians to the NKVD. Only those who fell into American hands, or disguised their nationality, stood a chance of escaping the NKVD.

See Index

GERMANY

Other Names:	Dritte Reich (i.e. Third Commonwealth).
Status in 1933:	Independent.
Government in 1933:	Dictatorship of Adolf Hitler.
Population in 1933:	66,000,000.
Make-up in 1933:	Germans 64,175,000; Poles 1,000,000; Jews 522,000; Danes 30,000; Gypsies 28,000; Wends 20,000; Frisians 15,000; Lithuanians 10,000; Also 200,000 Russian immigrants.
Religion:	Christian
Location:	Central Europe

In January 1933 Adolf Hitler was appointed Chancellor (i.e. head of government) of Germany by President (i.e. head of state) von Hindenburg, despite the fact that the Hitler's National Socialist German Workers Party (NSDAP or Nazis) was small and he had just lost an election for President. Hindenburg, an ageing – some say senile – general put Hitler in power along with members of other parties hoping that together they could unite the Germans against the communist menace, which as the communists took orders from Stalin, the USSR dictator, was seen as a foreign attempt to usurp power in Germany. The non-Nazis in the government actually believed they could control Hitler.

Their delusion lasted barely a month. When a fanatic burned down the Reichstag parliament building Hitler declared a state of emergency and gave auxiliary police status to his party militia, the brownshirted stormtroopers of the SA. At once they began to arrest outspoken anti-Nazis and house them in makeshift concentration camps.

Within eighteen months Hindenburg was dying and Hitler had unbridled power. However, he had come to like the 'respectable' life of a Chancellor and his stormtroopers were now an embarrassment. So in July 1934 he made a deal with the Army; they provided his personal bodyguard, the SS, with weapons, whereupon in one night, 'the Night of the Long Knives', the SS arrested thousands of SA officers and butchered 2,000 of them. Because the Army had been limited to a strength of 100,000 by the Versailles Treaty imposed on the Germans at the end of World War I by the British and French, the Army had been afraid of the three million-strong SA, though the SA only had enough weapons to guard concentration camps. With the emasculation of the SA, the Army was eternally grateful to Hitler.

Yet Heinrich Himmler, the SS chief was in fact far more dangerous than the SA generals. Ostensibly a racist organisation, the SS only took in recruits of the purest German blood (i.e. they accepted Nordics and Germanics, but not Alpine Celtics), but the organisation was built on a lie from start to finish, e.g. both Hitler and Himmler were Alpine Celtics. In fact Hitler wasn't even German, but an Austrian immigrant.

Himmler used his power as Hitler's bodyguard chief to gain control of every single police department in Germany 1933–36, more often than not by blackmail and threats, so that by 1936 he was chief of the ordinary police, chief of the concentration camp service, chief of the SS, chief of SS counter-intelligence, chief of the criminal investigation police and chief of the Gestapo political police. The last three bodies were eventually merged into the SS Security Police.

Himmler never gained control of the courts and for years they plagued him, but by threats he usually got his way in the end. He had also created his own army, and in 1938 the generals and admirals were forced by Hitler to accept the SS Army (called Waffen SS) as a bona fide branch of the armed forces, though they refused to allow him access to their conscripts. This put him in the awkward position of having to declare his SS personnel as having essential civilian occupations, and if he could not prove it the SS member in question could be conscripted into the Army, Navy or Air Force.

Hitler liked the idea of his generals, admirals and SS officers at loggerheads with each other – the age old policy of divide and rule. In 1935 he repudiated the Versailles Treaty and gave his armed forces free rein to grow and he established an air force (Luftwaffe). The generals and admirals were even further in his debt. In 1936 he sent troops into the Rhineland, prohibited at Versailles. The British and French complained, but did nothing else. That year he also sent air and ground units to aid the Francoists in the Spanish Civil War. Again the French and British complained, but nought else.

In March 1938 Hitler took his greatest step. Bullying the Austrian government, he forced them into total surrender. His armies marched in to be greeted with flowers. In days Austria formally became a province of Germany. There is no doubt that the Austrians and Germans were both ecstatic – unity of these nations had been a centuries old dream.

Unfortunately, Hitler claimed that as he had inherited Austria he inherited her demands, and one of these was the return of the Sudetenland stolen by the Czechs in 1919 with Anglo-French blessing. This alarmed the British and French, not to say the Czechs. The latter mobilised their armed forces as did Hitler, and the world stared in awe. Could this mean war?

In September 1938 Chamberlain and Daladier, the British and French Prime Ministers sold out the Czechs, who were not invited to the conference. Shocked by this betrayal the Czechs withdrew their army from Sudetenland and the Germans marched in. Again they were met with flowers.

Yet Hitler had wanted war, and angry it did not come he took out his frustrations on 'the enemy in our midst' – the Jews. He unleashed his SA, much chastened since 'the Night of the Long Knives', and they smashed shop windows owned by Jews, burned synagogues and beat Jews in the street. Those who resisted were taken to concentration camps. The brutality was such that over the next year 346,000 Jews emigrated. According to Hitler's thinking a Jew was anyone who had more than two Jewish grandparents, thus 44,000 Christians including clergy were reclassified as Jews.

In March 1939 Hitler broke his agreement with Chamberlain and Daladier and invaded the Czech lands. His troops were not met with flowers, but there was no resistance. Days later he sent troops into Lithuania to take Memelland, stolen in 1919 with Anglo-French blessing.

Chamberlain and Daladier were shocked. Not only had they been made fools of, but for the first time non-German speakers, i.e. the Czechs, had been conquered by Hitler. Chamberlain's knee-jerk reaction was to tell Hitler to keep his hands off Poland, which had stolen 800,000 Germans in 1919-23 with Anglo-French blessing.

To many Germans the Czech invasion was wrong, but the liberation of German-speakers who had been 'stolen' was morally righteous – those inside the borders of Poland, Latvia, Italy, France, Belgium and Denmark had yet to be liberated. There was also the idea of revenge. In the 1920s France and Belgium had invaded Germany: being a peace-loving people the Germans had not resisted. Workers had been forced at gunpoint to send goods to the invaders' homes. Workers who protested were shot down. There was much to be set right.

Hitler proved his genius as a statesman in August 1939 by signing a non-aggression pact with the devil himself, i.e. with Stalin. Communists and Nazis alike felt betrayed. Yet this made Poland's position untenable and, Hitler believed, gave Chamberlain and Daladier a way out.

On 1 September 1939 Hitler sent his armies into Poland. The Poles resisted and there was heavy combat at once. Newsreels of the time show German troops marching to the front watched by crowds with sad faces. The German people were no longer cheering.

On 3 September Britain and France declared war on Germany. Hitler went white with shock: his brinkmanship had failed. His generals and admirals had pleaded with him not to attack and he had ignored their fears. He had only 140,000 troops on the French border, a handful of warships and seven submarines at sea and his Luftwaffe planes did not have the range to hit Britain, but four million French reservists were reporting for duty, the mighty British Royal Navy was at sea and British planes had the range to strike Germany at will – they bombed that very night.

This same evening a German submarine sighted a large vessel running without lights as a warship does and sailing in a standard British Royal Navy zig zag pattern. The submarine fired torpedoes and sank her. She turned out to be a passenger liner, the *Athenia*, with British and American civilians aboard. Such an act was perfect for Anglo-American propaganda. Hitler was truly worried – it had all gone terribly wrong.

On the 17th Stalin kept his side of the bargain and invaded Poland. The Poles were done for. But Hitler and the German people could not enjoy their victories for fear of a French invasion. Himmler told the security authorities to be specially vigilant lest the German people revolt. There were constant attempts on the lives of senior Nazis including Hitler.

In order to keep France at arm's length Hitler ordered his soldiers not to fire on French patrols, his warships not to attack French warships and the Luftwaffe not to bomb France.

By October, the reason for Chamberlain's and Daladier's rash act, the protection of Poland, no longer had substance for Poland had surrendered and neither France nor Britain had declared war on the USSR for doing the same thing Germany had done, so Hitler was sure he could negotiate peace. Certainly if France had not invaded in September she would not do so until next spring, therefore, the German people were given a breather, bar a handful of British air raids.

German losses in Poland were 16,000 killed and 32,000 wounded.

For months the German generals urged Hitler to strike France before spring. The people had not wanted war, but now that they had it they wanted to win it. With every day they imagined the French Army getting stronger. Hitler postponed the attack many times. He had been twice wounded in the trenches in France in World War I and had no wish to repeat that affair.

When the British Navy ignored Norwegian neutrality to rescue some naval prisoners, Hitler realised his iron ore route was in danger. Swedish iron ore was his biggest import and much came through Norwegian waters. If the British cut that route Germany would be in trouble. Furthermore, he learned that Britain might invade Norway. (The British were indeed planning such).

Hitler ordered an invasion of Norway in April – and of Denmark too. They had risked this since they stole German land in 1919, he said.

On 9 April the German armed forces pulled off a major victory: with one hand they engulfed Denmark so rapidly they had a signed surrender before breakfast; with the other they put troops into Norway at Oslo, Stavanger, Bergen, Trondheim, Kristiansand and Narvik. Within 24 hours they had destroyed the Norwegian Air Force, scared away their Navy and outnumbered their 90,000-man Army.

There were setbacks: the cruiser *Blücher* was sunk; and the nest day the British Royal Navy engaged (the British had been illegally mining Norwegian waters) and within two days the German Navy was short of three warships and seventeen transports; plus at Narvik the British Royal Navy sank all ten German destroyers, cutting off General Dietl's invasion force.

However, this was all the British could really do. They put a few troops ashore, who took one look and then evacuated, and a French, Polish and British force landed at Narvik, but then just sat there. Within a month most of the Norwegians had surrendered and the last enemy was cleared out on 10 June. The conquest of Norway cost Germany's land forces 1,317 killed and 1,900 wounded.

Of course, the French Army still stood on the German border like a dagger pointed at Germany's throat. Then General von Manstein, who despite his Polish origins was a friend of Hitler's, came up with a war-winning plan: basically a southern force would make a lot of noise on the Franco-German border, defended by France's famous impregnable Maginot Line, a northern force would invade the Netherlands and Belgium, which hopefully would draw many French troops to their rescue, then a third force in the centre would sneak through the Ardennes Forest, cross the Meuse River into France and charge for the sea, cutting off the main French armies from their home.

On 10 May 1940 the German armies launched the von Manstein plan. In Poland most German troops had walked and the armoured formations (panzer) had had to learn on the job how to implement the new blitzkrieg (lightning war) technique, but they had learned from their errors and now had it down pat. Ironically, blitzkrieg had been invented by two British officers, Liddell-Hart and Fuller, but the British had ignored the former and imprisoned the latter.

In its simplest form blitzkrieg meant advancing until resistance was met, then pulling back to let artillery and air power, all connected by radio, pummel the defenders, then advancing again, and if resistance was met a second time, masking it with infantry who would 'besiege' the enemy, while the panzers (tanks, self-propelled guns and truck-borne infantry) drove past the little battlefield seeking the path of least resistance. When the panzers encountered opposition the manoeuvre was repeated. Obviously the infantry were soon busy besieging scores of enemy pockets, but as the panzers advanced into the enemy rear they caused tremendous panic and disruption, and the further they advanced the greater the dislocation.

Therefore, while the key weapons for the enemy were the rifle, the machine gun and the artillery gun, the key weapons for the Germans were the radio and the internal combustion engine.

Army Group B (Sixth and Eighteenth Armies) invaded neutral Netherlands and Belgium, while paratroopers dropped on strategic sites such as bridges. The Belgians had a fort at Eben-Emael that was impregnable from all four sides: but not the topside, so German glider-borne troops landed on top, blew up the air vents and captured 700 gunners. Within minutes the panzers were driving past unscathed.

The Twelfth and Sixteenth Armies wormed their way through the thick Ardennes Forest, painstaking work using log cutters' tracks, narrow bridges over ravines and winding lanes under harassment from Belgian snipers, but after three days they reached the Meuse River. On the fourth day they fought their way across against French defences at Dinant, Houx and Sedan. On 15 May they were through and nothing stood between them and the sea but terrified French villagers.

That day the Netherlands surrendered and the British Army, which had only just arrived in Belgium turned around and retreated towards the sea at Dunkirk. Five days later the 1st and 2nd Panzer Divisions reached the sea at Noyelles, thereby cutting off from France the Belgians, the British and four French armies. French attempts to break out or reach the trapped men were feeble. The Sixteenth Army was given plenty of time to man a line north of the Aisne River between Luxemburg and the sea.

Yet on the 24th Hitler panicked. The plan had worked too well: in fact the victory was greater than any in German history. He was most afraid that his tanks would become bogged down in the mud of Flanders, i.e. a hundred mile arc around Dunkirk. When Goering his Luftwaffe chief claimed his planes could destroy Dunkirk and the allied navies so that the trapped men could not evacuate from that port, Hitler gave him the go-ahead and told his panzers not to advance towards Dunkirk.

The panzer generals were flabbergasted. There was no mud. They could reach Dunkirk in two days. They were closer to it than the British were. Their pleas were ignored. The generals blamed Hitler: he later blamed them; and everyone blamed Goering.

In northern Belgium the Sixth and Eighteenth Armies broke through the Belgian defences: the allies were on the run. Finally on the 27th Hitler rescinded his order to the panzers, but by now the French had placed a blocking force to the south of Dunkirk and the panzers ran into it. The surrender of Belgium on the 28th did little to affect the Dunkirk operation. By 4 June, when the panzers broke through, the allies had evacuated 366,000 men from the area.

Meantime, the bulk of the German armies had settled in on the Aisne line and on the 5th launched an offensive southwards into central France. On the 9th General Guderian put a panzer corps across the Somme river near the coast and other units poured through behind him. The Germans reached Châlons sur Marne on the 12th, Paris on the 14th after its garrison had withdrawn, Verdun on the 15th and Dijon on the 16th. On the 17th the new French leader Marshal Pétain asked for surrender terms.

On the 22nd the French signed the document in the same rail carriage in which the German generals had surrendered in 1918. Versailles was avenged.

In six weeks the Germans had defeated four nations (five including defenceless Luxemburg) and inflicted 3,149,000 permanent casualties at a cost of 27,000 killed and 110,000 wounded.

Hitler was not as tough on France as many wanted him to be, certainly not as tough as France had been at Versailles. He demanded heavy reparations in goods and money for having declared war on Germany, annexed Alsace-Lorraine (taken from Germany in 1919), declared his armies would occupy northern France and the west coast for a while, reduced the French Army to 350,000 men (100,000 in France), left them their Navy and all their colonies.

In the latter half of 1940 there was little moral argument among the German people and what there was went like this. Anti-Nazis claimed Germany was no longer a democracy: true, came the reply, but Germany had only had a democracy for fourteen out of the last 2,000 years, 1919-33, and what had it produced, but the loss of much territory and millions of people, starvation imposed by the British Navy blockade with its fatal effects on the elderly and infants, civil war 1919-1921, the most crippling inflation in world history, invasions by the Poles, French and Belgians 1919-23 and the Great Depression 1929-33, so who needed democracy?

Anti-Nazis claimed that Hitler had invaded neutral nations: true, came the reply, but how had Britain and France gained the two largest empires the world had ever seen, except by invading neutral nations, and had the British and French people complained? Besides Poland, Czechia, France, Denmark and Belgium could hardly be described as neutral, for they had all kicked the German and Austrian people when they were down. Hitler had ordered the invasion of Norway to keep the British out, had he not? Yes, Netherlands and Luxemburg were innocent, though according to Herr Goebbels, the minister of propaganda, the Dutch had been in league with the allies. Besides the war was over. All soldiers aged 45 were coming home, and many younger ones. All would come home once the British ceased their warmongering. Hitler had promised.

Anti-Nazis claimed that Britain and France had the moral support of the world: if so, came the reply, how come the Finns, Romanians, Hungarians, Bulgarians, Italians, Japanese, Slovakians, Swedes, Spaniards, Portuguese and Soviets were all morally supporting Germany?

Anti-Nazis claimed that official treatment of Jews was morally indefensible: true, came the reply, but whose record was cleaner? The Americans? In that nation's northern restaurants and clubs one might see the sign 'Restricted' i.e. no Negroes or Jews Allowed, and in the southern states a Negro could be lynched for just looking at a white girl. In Britain there was considerable anti-Jewish feeling, but not much colour prejudice. However, once outside his own country he was not so blameless.

No matter what the complaint, the Nazis had an answer. The anti-Nazi resistance movement had been ready to seize power once the armies became bogged down in trench warfare on the Western front, but that had not happened. They had not expected victory and they were at a loss as to what to do. They also lived in fear of the SS Security Police. Already one adult male in every hundred had been arrested, and in some famously anti-Nazi towns like Berlin, the rate was as high as one in twenty. Men and women were punished by beatings in their home and in police cells, loss of privileges and civil rights, dismissal from jobs, and some were sent to concentration camps. The mere visit by the Gestapo to one's home was enough to put fear into the household for weeks, even if the fellow had only been selling raffle tickets.

Moreover, this was the first time in German history that women had been listened to. Hitler had far more support among women than among men and he knew this when he had made such outlandish election promises in 1932, e.g. he would guarantee every woman a husband if elected president. Once he achieved power he gave medals to every mother who bore five children, made cosmetics and fashion essential war industries and rather than put women into the factories to release men for the Army he induced foreign workers to come to Germany by offering good treatment and top pay. Hundreds of thousands took up his offer. He wanted the lives of women to be as work-free as possible and loved household labour-saving devices. He launched a programme to bring in a foreign maid for every German woman member of the Nazi party paid for by the party. He listened to women's problems and that made him popular. The fact that he was considered handsome and was single (he was only 43 when he achieved power) did not hurt his image.

Britain refused to make peace. The Luftwaffe had bombed some British docks and ships off the coast using Belgian and French airfields in June and July 1940, but Hitler had refrained from damaging her cities.

Goering demanded a chance to bring the Royal Air Force to its knees so that an invasion could take place. Though German forces were now within artillery range of Britain and did shell that island on occasion, Hitler had no intention of invading Britain – the British Royal Navy would chew up any attempt, he knew – but Hitler, the great aficionado of brinkmanship decided to try to bluff the British into making peace. He told Goering to do his worst and ordered barges to assemble on the Channel coast as if for an invasion.

On 13 August 1940 the Luftwaffe launched major raids on British airfields, munitions plants and ports. It was the beginning of the Battle of Britain. London because of its high population was strictly off limits. Hitler did not want to make the British angry enough to keep fighting.

By the end of the first week the Luftwaffe was shocked into sobriety. More and more night raids were made simply to avoid British day fighters. British night fighters were not much of a threat, but this removed all pretence at accurate bombing as all British towns were blacked out.

On the night of 24 August a bomber accidentally hit London. Churchill, the new British prime minister, assumed this was deliberate, or at least said so, and ordered a retaliation against Berlin, as yet unblooded in the war. The bomb blasts shook Goering and Hitler, so Hitler delivered a speech to a vast crowd saying 'two can play at that game.' The Battle of the Capitals had begun.

Tactically this was a great mistake, for the British could place their flak guns and fighter squadrons on a direct line between the German airfields and London. Day and night the bombers flew to London, each flight advancing straight into an ambush.

At the end of October the bombers reduced their sorties and flew only at night. The invasion barges were assigned other duties. Hitler called off his bluff.

He decided to starve the British into making peace and ordered his submarine commander, Admiral Doenitz, to do everything in his power to sink every vessel going in and out of Britain – as if Doenitz wasn't doing his utmost already.

Meanwhile Hitler concentrated on his new scheme. He wanted to destroy the USSR.

In March there were two diversions that Germany did not need. Hitler had sent a party of generals to judge the political loyalty of the Italians who faced the British in North Africa, but they came back with a military report instead, which was not good, citing poor equipment, bad officers, inefficient structure. 'They could do with a couple of panzer divisions', they said. Hitler offered them, but Mussolini, the Italian dictator, refused – out of pride.

Then in December 1940 the British launched a major offensive which by February had destroyed the Italian Tenth Army and conquered half of Libya. Mussolini swallowed his pride and asked for help. In March Hitler sent two divisions under one of his favourites, General Rommel.

The second diversion came about on 27 March when the Serbian people of Yugoslavia overthrew their government, because it had signed a treaty with Germany. Hitler went berserk. He took this as a personal affront. He hadn't forgotten that the Serbians had started World War I. It was high time someone punished them, he thought. He ordered his generals to invade in one week's time.

No doubt the generals were shocked as much by the timetable as by the target, but incredibly in one of the greatest feat of logistics ever accomplished they put the Second Army in Austria and Hungary and the Twelfth Army in Romania and Bulgaria. Besides these countries, Hitler invited Italy to the party. Mussolini accepted on condition the Germans made a slight detour and invaded Greece too, where an Italian army had been bogged down in winter combat since October 1940.

On 6 April 1941 the Luftwaffe began the show with a devastating raid on Belgrade's residential section, possibly killing as many as 17,000. That day the two German armies invaded. Resistance was scattered. On the 12th they entered Belgrade, still smouldering, and on the 15th reached Sarajevo. On the 17th the Yugoslavs surrendered.

In Greece German troops chased the Greek Army and a British force of three divisions southwards, until the 21st when the British began another Dunkirk-style evacuation. By the 30th the Greeks were in the bag and the British, minus 12,820 killed and captured, had gone.

The victory was even more incredible than the previous year's conquest of West Europe. In three weeks the Germans had defeated three armies, overrun two nations and inflicted 750,000 casualties for less than 3,000 Germans killed.

To add to the good news Rommel had attacked, defeated a British armoured division, driven the British 400 miles to Egypt and trapped 30,000 men in Tobruk harbour. The German people were ecstatic. Surely the British would now see sense and make peace.

Goering had a plan. The British had retreated from Greece to the island of Crete. He wanted to take Crete from the air: bomb it, land paratroopers and glider troops, capture the airfields, then bring in troops by transport plane. German airborne troops had performed astonishingly well in Norway and the Netherlands. The concept that the sky was a direction from which the enemy might attack was not new: Napoleon had toyed with the idea of invading Britain by balloon in the 18th century, however no one had faced such as attack until the Norwegians in 1940 and they had been paralysed by it. There were two reasons Goering loved this plan: all the planes belonged to his Luftwaffe and all airborne troops also belonged to his Luftwaffe. Hitler agreed, but ordered an amphibious invasion too.

By 19 May 1941 the Luftwaffe had scared away the British Air Force from Crete and next day the paratroopers and glider troops dropped right on top of the defenders. The naval-minded British were still peering out to sea. In fact they defeated the amphibious invasion at sea, but it made no difference, for on day two the Germans began flying in troops to a captured airfield. A week later the British chose another Dunkirk-style operation and by the 30th had gone. The Germans had used two divisions to defeat four and a third divisions, had sunk three cruisers and six destroyers and damaged a carrier, two battleships and twelve other warships with air attacks and had inflicted over 25,000 permanent casualties. It was another great victory for the German press to report. However, Hitler wanted no more such victories, for the battle had cost him 3,928 killed.

The whole Yugoslav-Greece diversion had cost Germany far more than was realised at the time, except by a few army logisticians. The German mechanised forces had to drive all the way back to Poland and eastern Germany and spend weeks repairing their vehicles and as a result the invasion of the USSR was delayed until 22 June. Thus Hitler's anger and greed had inflicted damage on his panzers far beyond that which any of his present enemies could do.

He also damaged them by restructuring. The army currently had twelve panzer divisions each with a tank strength of 252: 176 light (Marks I and II) and 76 medium (35t, 38t, Marks III and IV). He altered them to 118 tanks each (30 light and 88 medium). The increase in medium tanks was appreciated, but the loss of 146 light tanks, which were ideal for encouraging infantry to surrender, was a serious blow. With other minor modifications he turned five infantry divisions into panzer and created three new panzer divisions from scratch. he also increased the Army from three mountain divisions to six, from five motorised to eleven, from 96

infantry to 132, and established several security divisions to protect lines of supply.

The additional manpower came from recalling all reservists up to age 45, taking in this year's crop of 19-year-olds, and allowing the security divisions to use infantry up to age 45. In other formations the oldest infantry were 35, except for officers and senior sergeants.

He also had Himmler's private army, the Waffen SS, which now consisted of six divisions and two brigades. The 1st, 2nd and 6th consisted of original SS members who joined in 1936 with the permission of the armed forces. The 3rd Division and the two brigades were SS reservists, whom Himmler insisted were concentration camp guards and therefore essential personnel. The 4th Division were policemen whom Himmler, wearing his hat as chief of police, had ordered to volunteer, and as policemen were essential personnel, and the 5th Division was made up of foreign volunteers, men not eligible for conscription into the German armed forces. In such a manner was Himmler able to fool the generals and admirals. The SA had not done so and most of their members had been conscripted.

On 22 June Hitler unleashed his armies on the Soviet frontier. Preceded by shelling from 7,500 guns and attacks by 2,770 planes, three million men charged forward, the Sixteenth and Eighteenth Armies and 4th Panzer Group crossing into Lithuania, conquered by the Soviets a year earlier, the Fourth and Ninth Armies and 2nd and 3rd Panzer groups crossing into eastern Poland, conquered by the Soviets two years earlier, and the Sixth, Eleventh and Seventeenth Armies and 1st Panzer Group crossing into Galicia, conquered by the Soviets two years earlier.

The Soviet defences were swamped: on day one three divisions were overrun. (Soviet divisions were half the size of German divisions). Lithuania was liberated in four days. In another nine days the Germans had Lwow, Tarnopool and Bobruisk, all of Latvia, most of Byelorussia and by 14 July all of Estonia.

Hitler had invited Finland, Romania, Bulgaria, Italy, Hungary, Croatia and Slovakia to join him in this Christian crusade against atheist communism. All these nations, Germany included, used Christian crosses on their vehicles and planes. All, but Bulgaria, accepted. The Danes, Norwegians, Dutch, Belgians, French and Spaniards sent units as well.

There was, however, one major problem, distance coupled with poor physical communications. The USSR had almost no hardtop roads and rail lines were few and far between with sidings only every 100 miles or so. Rivers were wide and subject to flooding. Only 32 German divisions were mobile (panzer or motorised), the others relying primarily on horse-drawn wagons for transportation. The mobile units might be able to drive on for days, but ultimately they had to stop and wait for the infantry and their 60,000 horses, who advanced at walking speed. The German Army of 1941 advanced no quicker than the armies of Napoleon or Caesar. They were happy if they made fifteen miles a day, but the USSR was 8,000 miles long. It would take them a year and a half just to walk across it, and that assumed they would never have to grade a road, repair a bridge, would never encounter mud or snow, and no one would ever shoot at them. Under the circumstances Hitler's promise that it would all be over by Christmas was optimistic, to say the least.

Yet at first everything went so well. Whole divisions, corps and armies were surrendering and the local peasants, Russians included, cheered on the Germans as they passed through. There was some partisan activity, mostly Soviet stragglers, and as early as July a panzer formation had to be pulled out of the advance to clear up a partisan pocket, but the security divisions did well and the advance maintained its momentum. Indeed the Germans soon recruited locals to help them fight the partisans: at first it was no effort to guard every truck, every bridge; there was plenty of manpower.

For all his faults Hitler was a political genius, but he was no military genius, and some of his actions astonished his generals. He renamed the panzer groups as panzer armies, but gave them no extra tanks.

He was correct in one thing: the target was the enemy army not cities like Moscow or Leningrad. Once Leningrad was surrounded by Germans on the south and Finns on the north he ordered it besieged not assaulted. As for Moscow he turned his back on 'the great prize' when he saw the Soviets clinging to Kiev like grim death despite being almost cut off. Against the advice of his generals he decided a sudden swing southwards by the armies in front of Moscow would trap the biggest pocket in military history. He hoped such a loss would be irreparable to the Soviets. German infantry had already identified more enemy divisions than military intelligence had said existed.

On 24 August General Guderian's panzers, 200 miles west of Moscow, swerved to the right and advanced southwards. At the same time 350 miles to the south von Kleist's panzers swerved north towards Kremenchug. On 10 September Kremenchug was cleared and Guderian was at Konotop, having made eight miles a day. On the 15th von Kleist and Guderian met at Lokhvitsa 175 miles east of Kiev, trapping 600,000 Soviet troops – only 15,000 fought their way out.

On 30 September Hitler authorised the Moscow offensive to recommence with the Second Panzer, Fourth Panzer, Second (ex-Fourth), Third and Ninth Armies. Within a week two more pockets had been trapped at Vyazma and Bryansk. However, October brought the rasputitsa, the autumn rains that turned every Russian road into a stream of mud. Vehicles sank without trace. Artillery couldn't be dragged, but had to be hand carried! Even so, in various pockets 675,000 Soviet prisoners were taken. Surely, the Germans thought, Stalin had run out of manpower by now.

In mid-November the winter freeze set in and, though the terrible spectre of frostbite raised its head, at least the roads were hard enough to be driven on and the panzers attacked. At Tula the Second Panzer Army was defeated. Had the Soviets been granted time to regroup? The answer lay in the fact that the Germans had run out of steam. They had stretched themselves to the limit and had snapped. Their trucks and tanks had been driven hard over Russian roads in the summer so dusty they clogged radiators and burned out engines, then through thick glutinous mud that ripped out transmissions and burned clutches, then over icy ruts in temperatures that cracked engine blocks. Many tanks had been knocked out by the excellent Soviet T-34 tank, which despite having no intercom and often no radio, was formidable indeed.

The soldiers were worn out too. They had been walking and fighting for 160 days and could see no end to it. Shoot one Soviet and two took his place. Capture a thousand and two thousand charged you. Day by day the casualties were not too bad, but over the months they accumulated until by early December 770,000 Germans and 230,000 others had been killed, wounded, captured or hospitalised though illness, accident or frostbite – over a quarter or the men who had crossed the border in June.

Of immediate concern was the lack of winter clothing: the men still had their summer shirts and tunics. They wrapped their feet in rags and wore shawls like elderly women. Rarely did they have the opportunity to make a fire, and this in temperatures of -36°C.

On 29 November on the south coast the Germans were forced to abandon Rostov in the face of a Soviet onslaught. Hitler was angry. On the 30th the Germans near Leningrad had to withdraw a few miles. Hitler was livid. By 5 December German patrols could see the factory chimneys of Moscow, but the next day the Soviets struck back: Third Panzer and Fourth Panzer Armies were hit north of Moscow by seventeen Soviet armies, many of them using troops who were used to Siberian winters. Waist-deep snow hindered the German foot-soldiers and trucks, but tracked vehicles were able to retreat. At Klin and Ruza German infantry clung to their foxholes like frozen statues, which they resembled. Yelets, 250 miles south of Moscow was lost on the ninth to a Soviet counter-attack and Second Panzer Army had to retreat or else. On the 15th Klin and Ruza were overrun

Hitler went into one of his customary rages, demanding no more retreats: everyone should fight where he stood. In truth this was the right idea, for if the entire front fell back in such weather they would have been lost. As it was they fell back 75 miles

from Klin and 150 miles from Yelets and lost 55,000 casualties before the Soviets halted.

The German people were worried about their sons. brothers, fathers on the Russian front. Goebbels' propaganda could not disguise the retreat from Moscow. In North Africa Rommel's troops, now three German divisions, had also retreated. Of greater concern was that Hitler had declared war on the USA, following Japan's strike against the Americans. Yet the Japanese had not attacked the USSR. That would have been worth celebrating. To be sure the Germans and Americans had been fighting at sea, but to make it formal seemed to be tempting fate. Many a German remembered the difference a million fresh American faces had made on the Western Front in 1918. This was definitely not going to be a joyful Christmas.

Conquering such a large expanse of Europe was one thing: ruling it was something else. There was no logic in how the Germans did it, almost as if they had never expected to actually conquer anyone. Denmark was turned into an axis partner. Croatia, sliced off from Yugoslavia, was given independence and also became an axis partner. The Germans had done the same to Slovakia, sliced off from Czecho-Slovakia. Though the Germans occupied over half of France, Pétain's government there was left alone and Pétain was not just an axis partner but was in full-scale war with Britain. The Norwegians, Czechs and Serbs were allowed their own governments as long as they toed the Nazi line. The Belgians and Luxemburgers were under military governors, though the latter was annexed by Germany in August 1942. Austria, Sudetenland, Memelland, eastern Silesia, Alsace-Lorraine, eastern Belgium, Western Prussia, Danzig, much of Slovenia and Banat were annexed, yet the German-speakers of Süd-Tyrol were left under Italian-occupation. In Greece there was but a token German presence. Central Poland, known as the General Government, was under Nazi party rule.

The Germans also used various methods to keep the peace. The English Channel Islands had been occupied and the 'English' people were so pleasant that the islands were used as a holiday destination for German troops. The Norwegians and Dutch were also peaceful fellows. On the opposite side of the coin, the Serbs, Poles and Soviets had vicious partisan bands that loved the idea of slitting the throat of a German sentry. In every district the Germans allocated German police advisers to oversee the local police, and generally speaking this worked well, even when it came to rounding up terrorists, communists and Jews. The German police had also created the schumas from police reservists in Germany up to age 56 and from Poles and Soviet citizens, whose duty ranged from sentry to partisan hunting. The SS Security Police poked their noses in everywhere and they too recruited foreigners: a most successful policy in France. They had nothing to do with the Abwehr, German military intelligence, who hunted saboteurs and spies. Local part-time militias were recruited everywhere. In many locales these foreign troops far outnumbered Germans. Many a German front line unit took on local rear-echelon helpers, known as hiwis.

Once convicted of a political offence, a man or woman was relegated to one of three types of punishment: local attention, incarceration or execution. Local attention would mean a beating, reduction of rights and possible local temporary imprisonment. Incarceration meant a slave labour or concentration camp. In the former prisoners were worked to death to get a job done. In the latter a job was done in order to work prisoners to death. Execution might take place locally (often in public if outside Germany) or at a concentration camp by shooting or hanging. Some Germans were beheaded on Hitler's orders.

The SS Economics Branch, which ran the slave labour camps for profit, and the SS Concentration Camp Service consisted mostly of SS reservists called up in 1939, who knew that failure to do duty could result in being sent to an SS prison, transfer to a Waffen SS unit on the Russian front, incarceration in a concentration camp or execution. This did not excuse the fact many camp bosses and guards were lunatics, sociopaths, psychotics or just downright evil. There was

a high proportion of foreigners among the guards. Very few of these men and women were Nazis.

Heavy casualties on the Russian front made recruitment of foreigners ever more necessary. In January and February 1942, though no large areas traded hands, German casualties were 175,000. Unofficially, rear-echelon men over 35 were now put into the infantry, their places being taken by hiwis. Hitler's answer was not to take on foreign helpers, indeed he did not learn of the practice for months, but to restructure the units again. On the northern and central regions of the Russian front 69 divisions were reduced from nine to seven infantry battalions, and some of these divisions reduced infantry companies from 180 to 80 men, a divisional reduction of 4,860 riflemen to 1,680.

Hitler also reduced the conscription age from 19 to 18, and the volunteer age to 17. Many 17-year-olds joined the Waffen SS, buying Himmler's propaganda that it was an elite force. Hitler demanded industry release more essential workers: 370,000 were released to be replaced by foreign workers, volunteers and forced.

The Waffen SS had been recruiting plenty of foreigners, giving him enough for replacements and two more divisions and the 17-year-old German recruits filled three more divisions. But the German Army crimped Himmler's style by conscripting all Volksdeutsch (i.e. German-speakers) in German-occupied territory. Often these fellows had simply claimed to be Volksdeutsch to get better rations for their families: a knowledge of the German language was not necessary. Thus Poles and Czechs were now forced to don German uniform.

Fear of the SS Security Police in Germany was now matched by fear of British air raids. By the end of 1940 less than a hundred German civilians had been killed by them, but in 1941 the raids stepped up, some towns being hit several nights in a row. Berlin was under constant air raid alarm. There was no logic to the raids: bombs might fall on a school, hospital, shop, house or open field. At least the raids came at night and many of these buildings were unoccupied. Cellars and air raid shelters protected most of the people, though the emergency services and flak gunners were at risk, of course.

In 1942 the size of the raids became fearful: Cologne, 13 March, 62 dead; Lübeck, 28 March, 320 dead; Cologne again, 5 April, 23 dead; Rostock, 23 April and two following nights, 204 dead; and suddenly a thousand plane raid on Cologne on 30 May, which killed 411 civilians and 58 flak gunners, wounded over 5,000 and made 45,000 homeless.

The people blamed Goering. His Luftwaffe flew the night fighters and manned all the searchlights, radar stations and flak guns. (Hitler did not trust the German Army with flak guns in case he had to bomb them now and then.) In January 1943 US heavy bombers began striking Germany in daylight. From then on the German towns were under attack day and night.

Still the summer of 1942 gave all the indication of victory for Germany. Rommel, now with four and a third German divisions and an Italian army, had chased the British all the way to Alamein, four days drive from the vital Suez canal; the Japanese had conquered British and American colonies and threatened Australia; a British division had raided the coast of France and had lost 4,500 men for its impudence; and on the Russian front the Eleventh Army and Romanians had conquered the Crimea and Hitler launched a major sweep into the Caucasus past Rostov, aiming for Stalin's oilfields. Moreover a Soviet pre-emptive strike at Kharkov had failed miserably: the First Panzer, Sixth and Seventeenth Armies had surrounded and captured 250,000, which laid open a path along the Don Valley all the way to the city of Stalingrad on the Volga River.

But in Russia all was not rosy. The new recruits were only enough to keep up adequate strengths, yet rather than fill out veteran units and use their experience to good effect, Hitler wanted to create new formations. German officers were constantly combing rear-echelon units for cannon fodder.

By August 1942 about one tenth of German troops on the Russian front were in fact hiwis, and most anti-partisan troops were also Soviet citizens. As if this wasn't enough

of a concern, the Sixth Army, which began a hellatious fight for Stalingrad on 23 August, had on its left flank, echeloning back several hundred miles, the Romanian Third, Italian Eighth and Hungarian Second Armies and on its right, also echeloning back westwards, the Romanian Fourth and German Fourth Panzer Armies. Thus they were relying heavily on axis partners – good enough soldiers in themselves, but hopelessly outclassed in terms of equipment and generalship. The final touch was the right flank of the Fourth Panzer Army, which only consisted of one motorised division and some local Kalmyk horse cavalry to patrol a front of 200 miles!

The Sixth Army was a long way from its supply base – if 400 miles of partisan-infested, dirt roads can be considered a long way – and the Luftwaffe had to fly in supplies to Stalingrad. In early November Sixth Army registered its first death from starvation.

Inside Stalingrad the Germans hunted Soviet infantry from one house to the next, one section of a factory to the next, including through the rat-populated sewers. For all concerned this was truly the devil's playground. By Hitler's law captured communist party members were to be shot at once. This was rarely done, though, for the German infantryman was in fact reticent to shoot unarmed prisoners. That duty was reserved for military police or SS execution squads. A strange camaraderie was established as the Germans called out to 'Ivan' for truces to take care of wounded. As most Germans knew some of their hiwis by name, they did not look upon the Russians as inhuman, no matter what Goebbels said. Not that anyone wanted to surrender. The Soviets had their own version of the SS, the NKVD.

At the front of this was a war to save lives. Only in the rear areas was it a war to take lives.

On the freezing morning of 19 November the Romanian Third Army was attacked by elements of four Soviet armies: next day the Romanian Fourth Army was struck by three armies. By the 21st the Soviet pincers had broken through and met, trapping Sixth Army in Stalingrad.

Not only had Hitler stuck Sixth Army out on a precarious limb, but he had no reserves.

Germans and Romanians tried their best to create ad hoc defences to stem the Soviet tide in the midst of snow blizzards. Fourth Panzer Army could not help as it too now came under attack.

On 7 December a small force, including a division of Luftwaffe personnel, repelled a Soviet assault at the Don-Chir confluence, while Fourth Panzer Army finally made a rescue attempt, though with only 35 tanks in its two lead panzer diversions, it was a miracle that on the 19th it came within 35 miles of Stalingrad. General von Paulus begged for permission to break out from Stalingrad over this short distance. After having 12,000 killed and evacuating 30,000 wounded and sick by plane, von Paulus reported he had nineteen German divisions, Luftwaffe flak gunners and ground crew, two Romanian divisions and a Croat regiment, amounting to a few hundred Dutchmen, 2,000 Croats, 13,000 Romanians, 19,300 hiwis and 253,600 Germans. Seven-eights of his trenches were manned by rear-echelon personnel. His men were dying of hypothermia and were reduced to hunting rats for food. Hitler refused permission to break out.

The next day the would-be rescuers had to fall back. Further west the Italian Eighth Army, Romanian Third Army and German formations were hit by three Soviet armies and began to retreat.

On 12 January, as if to rub it in, the Soviets swamped the Hungarian Second Army 250 miles west of Stalingrad. Five days later the last German plane left Stalingrad – the Luftwaffe had flown out 42,000 men, but 18,000 wounded still lay on the runway

On 2nd February the defenders of the Stalingrad pocket surrendered. In addition to these 42,000 wounded/sick and 288,000 killed/missing, since 19 November the Germans had lost 95,000 casualties, the Croatians 5,000, the Romanians 173,000, the Hungarians 146,000 and the Italians 105,000. This does not count sick or frostbite. Moreover, the axis forces had retreated hundreds of miles and had abandoned the Caucasus. Hitler's gamble had failed – he was totally responsible for the loss of the territory and 900,000 men, a third of his Russian front strength.

In North Africa in November 1942 Rommel had been defeated and was in full retreat across Libya, and the Anglo-Americans had invaded French-held Algeria and Morocco, won them over to their side after a three-day battle, and were entering Tunisia from the west. Goering offered to fly in German troops at the rate of a thousand a day: his planes did so, and together with Italian troops they stopped the allies cold in northern Tunisia by mid-December. North Africa had been Italy's main front for three years, but for Germany it was a side show – total German deaths there in 22 months were only 5,200. On the Russian front the Germans were losing that many per week.

But still Africa was important to Hitler in that Italy was his most important partner, plus while the British were bogged down in Africa they would not contemplate an invasion of France, a sort of Dunkirk in reverse.

In February, Rommel took advantage of the fact that the British army chasing him was a tortoise commanded by a snail, to race ahead to Tunisia and inflict a nasty little defeat on the Americans who were commanded by a timid mole.

The British coming from Libya did not attack until 20 March, but thereafter it was only a matter of time before the 300,000 Germans and Italians penned inside northern Tunisia would surrender or evacuate. Truthfully, evacuation was really out of the question as the British and American navies commanded the Mediterranean by now, but in any case Hitler and Mussolini both refused permission for a withdrawal. By 12 May it was all over. The axis troops surrendered.

It was time for Hitler, the great magician, to do some sleight of hand with his manpower. He ordered more forced workers to be brought to Germany to relieve his essential workers for military duty. Soon a fifth of his agrarian labourers and a quarter of his industrial workers would be foreigners. That summer he reduced the conscription age to 17, though these teenagers had to fulfil their six-month government labour service first. By this method Hitler could expand his Army by four panzer, one motorised, one mountain and 56 infantry divisions. After asigning self-propelled guns to his motorised formations he renamed them panzergrenadiers.

Already Goering had been allowed to create his own Luftwaffe Army. He had always had an airborne division, but in late 1942 began to form another airborne, two panzer and seventeen infantry divisions.

Hitler also allowed Himmler access to conscripts for the first time, provided that the conscript was in agreement. To Himmler's chagrin most were not. The conscription laws for foreign Volksdeutsch were also widened, and Himmler confiscated several foreign military units. His 5th SS Division had troops of 30 different nationalities.

Himmler expanded his SS with all pretence at racial discrimination tossed aside, taking in Slavs, Latins, Mongols, Arabs and Asian Indians. The SS reached a strength of 1,420,000 men and women, of which 25,000 were concentration camp guards, 24,000 slave labour camp guards, 64,000 SS Security Police, 200,000 Allgemeine full- and part-time, who helped keep the German people in line, 1,050,000 Waffen SS, i.e. the SS Army, and fully 50,000 at Himmler's headquarters doing everything from training recruits and handing out socks to studying ancient legends and managing archaeological excavations.

Within Germany fifteen-year-old boys were turned into postmen, to release adults for military duty and in a perverse method, which shows how the Nazis thought, fifteen-year-old boys who had signed up to study aviation with the Hitler Youth were conscripted as flak gunners. Parents who objected were visited by the police.

Hitler was even forced to let women take part in the war. He had already allowed them to enlist in the armed forces and SS, and now he asked them to work in industry and on farms. Eighteen-year-old girls were accepted as flak gunners.

Allied air attacks were causing serious havoc and took up a significant portion of Germany's manpower and resources. By 1943 a quarter of all German fighter pilots, 850, were engaged in defending German towns as were 33,000 guns. Entire factories were turned over to make flak guns rather than anti-tank weapons. The use of man-

power can be gauged by looking at the Leune oil refinery, which at one time was defended by the following: 3,000 TeNo emergency repair technicians, hundreds of civil defence workers, hundreds of air raid wardens to warn workers and escort them to shelters, scores of aircraft observers, a few hundred NSKK drivers and mechanics to move mobile flak guns and searchlights, 18,000 RAD government labour service 17-year-old youths to clear damage and make repairs, and 28,000 Luftwaffe flak gun, radar and searchlight troops, plus 3,900 foreign flak troops, 6,000 15-year-old boy flak troops and 3,050 female flak troops.

Several raids on Hamburg had killed 688 civilians by early 1943, but on the night of 24 July 791 British bombers killed 1,500 people. Over the next two days the Americans struck the terrified inhabitants with 320 and 150 bombers. On the night of the 27th 787 British bombers blasted them, creating a fire storm which did not so much burn people as melt them, over 40,000 of them. A million fled the city in terror. The city was hit again on the 29th and four nights later. Yet the city's great docks and industrial estates were largely untouched.

Hitler had come up with another war-winning plan. This is what he told his generals about Operation Citadelle, but he had little faith in it and secretly negotiated with the Soviets to acquire a compromise peace. Sensing weakness, Stalin called off the talks. Citadelle planned for four panzer armies and nine infantry armies to hold the Russian front, two armies of which would assault the enemy around Kursk, using a million men, 6,000 guns, 1,850 tanks and 530 self-propelled guns. The panzer divisions had been restructured yet again and now contained 132 medium tanks and a few heavies (Mark V and VI), which was excellent news, but they had few light tanks for reconnaissance. The generals calculated they would be attacking the Kursk salient with odds of 7:1 in their favour.

On 5 July the Ninth Army attacked the northern flank of the salient and the Fourth Panzer Army and Detachment Kempf attacked the southern. The Ninth advanced nine miles in three days and was brought to a halt. The Germans soon learned the problem – here Stalin had created a front line 120 miles thick! On the 12th the southern advance with 600 tanks met 900 Soviet tanks at Prokhorovka. The Germans lost 300 and the Soviets 500. The Soviets withdrew.

The Ninth Army was allowed to withdraw and on the 19th Hitler accepted that the Soviets had discovered an antidote to blitzkrieg and called off the offensive. Already the Second Panzer Army (without tanks). First Panzer Army and brand new Sixth Army were under serious pressure. Hitler diverted reinforcements to them, but they began to fall back. Effectively, from now on the Germans would never cease retreating. Kursk was the turning point of the war.

On 10 July the Anglo-Americans landed in Sicily defended by only four Italian infantry divisions and two German panzer divisions. For a month the axis troops gave the allies a run for their money and then evacuated safely to mainland Italy.

The greatest shock for Hitler took place in Rome on 26 July. Mussolini was arrested on orders of the King, who replaced him with Marshal Badoglio. Hitler was almost struck dumb: if this could happen to Mussolini, it could happen to him. He ordered Mussolini's rescue at once.

Hitler also ordered several divisions into Italy, ostensibly to help repel the allied invasion, which must surely come, but the German soldiers noted they were ordered to move south slowly, very slowly. In fact Hitler had decided to take over Italy. He was sure the King would be negotiating a surrender (he was) and he was determined to disarm or at least cripple the Italian armed forces before they turned against Germany. He issued instructions to every unit commander: upon receipt of the word 'axis' he was to disarm the nearest Italian unit.

On 3 September allied troops made a peaceful landing in the toe of Italy: the defenders had pulled back. On the 8th General Eisenhower, commander of the allies in the Mediterranean, broadcast that Italy had surrendered. The announcement took everyone – allies, Germans and Italians – totally by surprise. Only the Germans reacted with speed: Hitler issued the code word 'axis' and within an hour of the broadcast, which most Italians had not heard, Germans were calmly walking up to Italian sentries as if to ask directions, getting the drop on them, gaining the weapons racks, then arresting unarmed Italian soldiers. By nightfall tens of thousands had been taken.

The following morning an allied fleet landed troops in Italy at Salerno, but miraculously the German 16th Panzer Division had just captured the Italian defences there, whose guns pointed the wrong way, i.e. out to sea, and were able to engage the incoming allies at once. Soon six German divisions were keeping five allied divisions penned inside the tiny beachhead.

German radio broadcast on the 9th that the Italians had been peacefully disarmed. It says a lot for allied anti-Italian prejudice and stupidity that they had been disbelieving German propaganda for years, but took this announcement at face value.

It was of course a complete fabrication. The Italians were resisting fiercely. In Rome the 3rd Panzergrendier and 2nd Parachute Divisions fought two Italian divisions and civilians and only after a paratrooper jump onto Italian headquarters, the threat to bomb Rome to ruins and the guarantee that one division could remain armed were the Italians induced to surrender on the 10th. On Sardinia the 90th Panzergrenadier Division evacuated rather than test the Italian defences. German infantry spent weeks securing some Italian towns.

In Yugoslavia, Greece and Albania the Germans had tough fights overcoming Italian garrisons at such places as Corfu, Kephalonia, Zara, Rabek, Cattaro, Dubrovnik and Split. Thousands of Italian troops joined the partisans in these nations, and in Italy the Italians set up their own partisan army. On Corsica the Germans fought two Italian divisions and a French battlegroup, come to help the Italians, until the Germans evacuated in early October.

On 12 September SS commandos rescued Mussolini, who at once broadcast an appeal for his people to join the Germans and resist the allies. Italian fascists had already joined the Germans and worked avidly to help overcome Italian defences, usually by treachery. One general handed an entire corps to the Germans.

In early October the Germans abandoned Naples to partisans and pulled back to hold the Volturno River against an allied advance. It had been one hell of a month for the Germans. Hitler authorised a withdrawal to a line just south of Bologna, but no further for he needed Italy's northern industrial and food growing areas. However, Luftwaffe Field Marshal Kesselring claimed he could hold the allies south of Bologna for a year if given the opportunity. Thinking he had nothing to lose, Hitler gave his responsibility for Italy. Kesselring placed the Tenth and Fourteenth Armies along the Garigliano–Cassion–Rapido–Sangro line and ordered them to hold at all costs.

If the Germans were doing well in the Mediterranean, they were falling back constantly in Russia. This was a fearful time for their soldiers, for up until now the Germans had been calling the shots. They fought until they wanted to quit (or Hitler would allow them to), but from now on they fought until the Soviets wanted them to quit, which was never. Every day for the rest of the war the Soviets would be on the offensive somewhere on the Eastern front.

There is no doubt that at this time the average German soldier still had faith in Hitler, quite logical, for all government propaganda was geared to that end. There is also no doubt that apart from a handful of generals like von Manstein, Rommel and Guderian, no one else had the respect of the German soldier; not Goebbels 'the Poisoned Dwarf', not Goering 'Fat Hermann' and certainly not Himmler. Yet none of this mattered, for, apart from communists, even the most virulent anti-Nazis did not want to see Europe overrun by the Soviets.

New recruits were filled with the desire to protect the Fatherland, not expand it, to defend their mothers, sisters and wives, not conquer someone else's. The veterans knew that no Soviet would look upon the concentration camp service or the Einsatzgruppe execution squads as an aberration, a temporary hiccup in the history of German culture and humanity that had been a guiding light to the world for centuries. They would simply want vengeance and would take it out on anything or anyone German. The Soviet NKVD treated their own people like insects. How much more cruel would they be towards Germans?

Nor was there hope in surrender to the Anglo-Americans. In early 1943 the Anglo-Americans had announced new policies such as 'unconditional surrender' and the 'Morgenthau Plan'. These stated that they would make no deals, offer no terms, sign no truces: they would enslave all German men in labour camps outside Germany, demolish all German industry and reduce the nation to a pastoral society, where German women would become serfs at the mercy of allied soldiers and German children would be raised to hate all things German including their parents. This was no fantasy of Goebbels. This was real. Just in case any German still refused to believe the allies could be so cruel, all he had to do was tour the bombed out homes of Berlin, Hamburg, Cologne etc. There was the true face of so-called freedom loving democracy. Is it any wonder, therefore, that the Germans fought so hard?

In November fifteen German divisions fell back to Kiev, but this paper strength of 270,000 was reduced to 45,000 men. In one day of battle elements let the Soviets in and fortunately Hitler allowed them to pull out before being encircled. The excellent performance of Kesselring in Italy enabled Hitler to transfer units from Italy to Russia. However, a quarter of a million Germans and Romanians were trapped in the Crimea and Hitler refused permission for them to evacuate. Their sudden appearance on the main front would have done wonders. Instead they sat idly by. Hitler wanted them to remain ready for his spring offensive. Any corporal could have told him there would be no spring offensive.

In January 1944 the Germans besieging Leningrad were hit by a two-pronged offensive, one from inside the city, the other from the east. By 1 February they had been forced to pull back to the Estonian border. Everywhere the Germans were retreating from ethnic Russia. In the centre they were at Lutsk in Poland. In Ukrainia six divisions held onto the Korsun salient on Hitler's express order. Von Manstein urged their withdrawal before it was too late. Instead, he was ordered to rescue them. Disregarding orders 35,000 men broke out before the remaining 18,000 surrendered on 17 February.

In March the Germans in Ukrainia were assaulted along a 600-mile front! Almost at once the Fourth Panzer Army's nineteen divisions were in danger at Kamenets Podolsk. Von Manstein asked for permission to withdraw them. Further south von Kleist asked permission to withdraw to the Dniestr, considering the fact that Soviet armour was already 50 miles past it. On 31 March Hitler replied by replacing von Manstein and von Kleist by Field Marshals Model and Schoerner, two well-known Nazis.

Model was also a good general, and taking one look at the situation he too demanded a withdrawal from Kamenets Podolsk. Hitler conceded. In days the Germans fell back to Romania. The Crimea was assaulted and the Germans and Romanians fought a retreat to the port of Sevastopol, where an angry Hitler finally agreed to a Dunkirk-style evacuation. By 12 May 87,000 Germans, 40,000 Romanians and 28,000 hiwis made it out, leaving 70,000 killed and missing.

In June Kesselring lost Rome. His nineteen divisions had held back twenty-eight allied divisions including an amphibious invasion at Anzio and had inflicted 125,000 casualties. Though in retreat he was not worried. The German submarine service had been unable to blockade Britain. Not only did the British send out finished products such as tanks, planes and guns, but brought in raw materials, fuel and two million Americans with their planes, guns and vehicles. Everyone knew the Anglo-Americans were planning an invasion of France in 1944, though exactly where and when were secrets. Hitler suspected Normandy: his generals suspected Pas de Calais. Both expected May or June. The Fifteenth Army protected the Pas de Calais, the Seventh Army Normandy and the Nineteenth Army the remainder of the French west and south coasts. Constant argument altered Hitler's opinion: he accepted Pas de Calais.

Hitler had created two new panzer and 46 new infantry divisions, but most of the latter had seven rather than nine infantry battalions, about 12,500 men. The Luftwaffe had created six new airborne divisions and five new infantry divisions. To defend Western Europe Hitler assembled six panzer, 42 infantry, five airborne, three Luftwaffe, five SS panzer divisions and one SS panzer-grenadier division, plus countless independent battalions and battle groups.

On 6 June the allies invaded, in Normandy, with three divisions from the air and six divisions and eight brigades over the beaches. By noon the defenders of Normandy were outnumbered! Moreover, the Luftwaffe had replied with only 319 sorties to the allies' 10,585. Initially the allies had little artillery, but their warships could shell fifteen miles inland. By dusk the British had a thousand tanks ashore, but the nearest German panzer division, the 21st, had only 127 tanks.

The Normandy campaign was a race for reinforcements and the Germans lost it. They had to travel hundreds of miles under air attack in day and partisan attack at night. They were often short of fuel and many rail lines and bridges had been destroyed. The allies only had to sail sixty miles across a sea effectively free from German interference. It was sheer guts and determination that held back the allies.

By 1 July the 21st Panzer Division was down to 40 tanks, 12th SS Panzer from 177 to 51 tanks, next day 1st SS Panzer reported 80 tanks, by the 7th Panzer Lehr Division had lost 152 of its 182 tanks, yet by the 17th only seventeen replacement tanks had been sent to Normandy. In all the Germans had 1,347 tanks in Normandy, but the British brought in 4,157 and the Americans 2,506. By the 27th over 120,000 Germans were casualties, but only 20,000 replacements had arrived, half of them Luftwaffe ground crew. It was this day the Americans broke out of Normandy to the south.

Hitler came up with a good plan: Seventh Army were to advance due west to the sea at Avranches and cut off the advancing Americans from the British still stuck along the coast. This would have been a good idea if he had had some full-strength panzer divisions, but Hitler had retreated into a fantasy world. His divisions in France were down to 5,000 men each and his panzer divisions averaged 38 tanks apiece. American infantry divisions had twice that.

The attack failed in one day and this placed Seventh Army's 120,000 men in a bind, with Americans on their left and in front and British on their right. The British charged down from the north to cut them off and did so by 20 August: only 60,000 Germans escaped the trap. On the 15th a French and an American army landed on the coast of Southern France. The Nineteenth Army received permission to withdraw at once. France and Belgium were abandoned.

In August the entire picture on the eastern front changed swiftly: Finland surrendered and ordered German troops to march north-west hundreds of miles to Norway. The Romanian defences collapsed and the King made peace with the USSR, ordering German guest troops to leave. Hitler responded with an air attack on Bucharest, but his armies responded by fleeing west to Yugoslavia.

In September Bulgaria declared war on Germany and sent troops against the Yugoslavia garrison. In the Netherlands the allies gained bridgeheads over the Maas and the Waal by an airborne drop. The capture of a British airborne force at Arnhem could not take away the realisation that the British were just yards away from the Rhine, Germany's great natural barrier in the west. To add to the terrible news Aachen became the first German city to fall – to the Americans – and in the east German troops were defending home soil against a Soviet onslaught.

Lithuania, Estonia and Latvia were lost by October, though Hitler insisted on keeping Field Marshal Schoerner's Army Group North, almost 200,000 men, inactive on the Latvian coast.

However, there was also good news: east, west and in Italy the allies slowed to a crawl, the weather and their lengthening supply lines being responsible. In the Netherlands bad allied generalship allowed 90,000 men of Fifteenth Army to escape a certain trap and on the Franco-Italian border the allies stopped, leaving Kesselring free to concentrate on the allies south of Bologna. he had kept his promise to Hitler.

Therefore, despite losing 615,000 men, including 44 divisions, in the west since 6 June the Germans were in a secure position: holding the Netherlands against Canadians and British was Army Group H under General Student; defending the west German border down to the Ardennes against the British and Americans was Army Group B under field Marshal Model; protecting Lorraine from Americans was Army Group G under General Balck; covering Alsace against the French was Army Group Oberrhein, in theory commanded by Himmler; Kesselring held the allies in Italy; Army Group E under Luftwaffe General Loehr was holding Greece, Albania and southern Yugoslavia, though in the process of evacuating Greece; keeping back the Bulgarians, Romanians, Yugoslav partisans and Soviets in northern Yugoslavia and southern Hungary was Army Group F of General von Weichs, plus the Hungarian Army; in northern Hungary and Slovakia battling the Soviets and a Slovakian uprising was Army Group South Ukraine of General Friessner; and hanging on to the Vistula River in Poland, containing an uprising in Warsaw and fighting for German villages in East Prussia was General Harpe's Army Group A.

Hitler restructured his Army yet again: in August he expanded the conscription age from 17-45 to 16-60, the extra classes being known as Volksturm 1st Levy. The 2nd Levy was all 16-60 year old men who had essential jobs, who were expected to fight for their homes as and when attacked. In keeping with his custom of creating new units rather than rebuilding veteran ones he established 55 new divisions under the label Volksgrenadier, each one fielding only four infantry battalions, and using 10,000 men. Most of the personnel for them came from the 1st Levy. In October all boys who would turn sixteen by year's end were called up, but in reality in the German towns under attack the Nazis were arming boys as young as twelve with rifles and sending girls as young as fifteen to man flak guns, which became anti-tank guns when the time was right.

Hitler came up with another plan. He had hoarded guns, tanks, planes and his boys and old men and chose to break through the Ardennes as in 1940, this time to swerve north across the Meuse to reach Antwerp, thereby to deny the allies this much needed port and cut off the British from the Americans. His generals thought it fantasy and a hell of a waste of troops, who would be better used to slow down the allies rather than challenge superior allied firepower, but they said nothing. Too many generals were prematurely retired, in prison or worse, for the survivors to know they could get away with talking back to Hitler.

On 16 December the offensive was launched: 250,000 men and 2,567 tanks and SPGs, in nine panzer, one volksgrenadier, two airborne and eight panzer-grenadier divisions of the Fifth Panzer, Sixth SS Panzer and Seventh Armies. They did take the Americans by surprise, mashing four divisions into the snow on an eighty-mile front, taking over 9,000 prisoners and forcing a retreat, but within two weeks the courage of small American teams kept the advance to a crawl and in January the weather cleared and thereafter the allied air forces slaughtered the Germans. Two smaller offensives in Lorraine and Alsace lasted only days.

The result of the three offensives was that the Germans were short 120,000 men for the defence of their homeland and, as Hitler had allocated fully 44% of his tanks and SPGs to them, he had denuded the eastern front of replacement tanks, thereby enabling a Soviet offensive on 12 January to bore its way into Pomerania and Silesia. Here the Germans were outnumbered in infantry 9:1, in artillery 10:1, and tanks 40:1. On the 31st Soviet tanks reached Kuestrin just fifty miles from Berlin!

In the Baltic Sea millions of Germans were desperately trying to find a ship that would take them away from the insanity. Some ships were packed to the masts with civilians when they were sunk by Soviet air and naval attack. On land the people ran from Soviet soldiers who had gone crazy with bloodlust.

Hitler's reinforcements to the eastern front were now symptomatic of the state of his nation: twenty battalions of sailors with rifles; the Schwedt Division consisting of men from all branches of the armed forces, local 2nd Levy Volksturm and troops of ten nationalities, a corps of Western Europeans; and a bona fide Russian Army, belatedly recognised by Hitler.

On 24 February Third Panzer Army was attacked and within a month its 200,000 men were reduced to 40,000. At Breslau 40,000 were trapped: Hitler refused permission for them to break out. In the last week of March the allies crossed the Rhine and began slicing deep into Central Germany. The allies had only captured one bridge intact. The German officer responsible for blowing it up had failed, as he was given incorrect explosives. That was no excuse and Hitler had him executed: one of 15,000 German soldiers executed for failing to carry out orders.

On 7 April Vienna was assaulted by an overwhelming force. The garrison of old men, boys and multi-wounded veterans took ten days to die.

On the 17th Field Marshal Model committed suicide in the Ruhr Valley as his 325,000 men surrendered to the Americans. The day before the Soviets had at last launched their assault on Berlin. To defend his capital and himself Hitler had assembled a million men, 10,400 guns and 1,500 tanks, but they were attacked by 2½ million men, 45,000 guns and 6,250 tanks. By the 22nd 180,000 Germans were surrounded outside the city and on the 25th the city itself was totally encircled. Hitler waited until the 30th, when Soviet troops were a hundred yards from his bunker, to commit suicide, but not before marrying Eva Braun and executing her brother-in-law.

Hitler knowingly left the nation in the hands of Admiral Doenitz, not one of the Nazi bosses. Hitler had decided the Nazis, indeed all Germans, were not worthy of him. Doenitz negotiated a surrender to the Western Allies on 8 May and next day to all others.

Hitler's goal of achieving for Germany a justified place in the sun backfired and achieved for generations of Germans an unjustified place in hell, by labelling them with the guilt of inhumanity, something that no other nation, no matter how barbaric, has had to endure.

Just over eighteen million men and women wore German uniform from 1939-45, of which 13½ million were pre-1938 German citizens. The total loss of German-speakers (Germans, Austrians, Sudetenlanders, Volksdeutsch etc) was 2,068,000 killed and 4,760,000 wounded. Of the 3,155,000 taken prisoner by the Soviets 1,185,000 died. Of those captured by the Western Allies, the luckiest were in British hands, for the French did not treat prisoners well and allowed disease to kill several thousand, and the Americans who had the bulk of them, were caught without adequate planning: as a result at least 100,000 died of neglect by 1946. Of this total of 3,350,000 military dead, about 2,820,000 were pre-1938 German citizens.

Anglo-American air raids killed 593,000 civilians in Germany, of which 56,000 were foreign workers and 40,000 were Austrians. About 10,000 civilians died in cross-fire as the Western Allies overran the country. In the east air raids, cross-fire, ship sinkings and revenge atrocities by Soviets, Poles, Czechs and others killed 2,140,000 German-speakers by 1946 of which 619,000 were pre-1938 German citizens.

The Nazis were also responsible for the murder of Germans: 12,000 because they were of Gypsy race; 134,500 because they were of Jewish race; 50,000 because they were medically diagnosed as mentally incurable; and over a quarter of a million because they refused to accept the madness of Nazism.

Total deaths among pre-1938 German citizens was therefore in the area of 4,400,000.
See Index

GIBRALTAR

Status in 1939:	British possession.
Government in 1939:	British military administration.
Population in 1939:	22,000 civilians.
Make-up in 1939:	75% Spaniards;
	25% British and others.
Religion:	Christian.
Location:	Western end of Mediterranean.

The importance of the Straits of Gibraltar to the allied cause in World War II cannot be stressed enough. If the axis had gained control of this western approach to the Mediterranean, the final allied victory, if not in doubt, would certainly have been less definitive.

To protect the straits the British had conquered Gibraltar from the Spaniards in the 18th century and in 1940, when Italy declared war on Britain, the British Royal Navy would have sooner given up London than 'the Rock'.

Throughout the next three years the British expected an invasion of Gibraltar by Germany, Italy or possibly by Spain, which had never given up her claim, so the British evacuated non-essential civilians and the local defence force was beefed up by a large garrison. The first assault came from an unexpected quarter, France. After the British attacked the French in July 1940, the French replied with an air raid on Gibraltar. This was followed by sporadic German and Italian air raids until 1944.

Continually German and Italian submarines hovered just outside the harbour and Italian underwater swimmers, based on Spanish soil a few thousand yards away, plagued the harbour until summer 1943. British swimmers fought them in this the most silent battle.
See Index

GILBERT ISLANDS

Other names:	Kiribati
Status in 1939:	British colony.
Government in 1939:	British administration.
Population in 1939:	40,000 (1,824 Makin, 3,500 Tarawa)
Make-up in 1939:	Kiribatis.
Religion:	local, plus mission Christians.
Location:	South Pacific.

Two days after the 7 December 1941 Japanese attack on British and American possessions in Asia and the Pacific Japanese naval infantry landed on the undefended atolls (i.e. island groups) of Makin and Tarawa. Over the previous two years the islanders had known King George was at war with Germany, but it had seemed a very remote war, for nothing ever happened to disturb the placid life of the islands, bar an occasional storm.

This was different. This was invasion, and though British whites had come to the islands years earlier bringing their bible it had not been by military invasion. Individually the Japanese behaved correctly and were friendly. Official policy, however, was that the natives were to be looked upon only as workers for the Japanese Empire. Refusal to obey could result in execution.

In the forthcoming struggle between the USA and Japan, every square yard of earth in the vast Pacific was potentially a naval or air base and as the Gilberts were situated halfway between Hawaii and Australia, Japanese seaplanes based here could patrol that vital allied air-sea route.

On 17 August 1942 two companies of the US 2nd Marine Raider Battalion landed on Makin from a submarine and seized the Japanese radio station. Two days later they were gone with the loss of 21 killed: the Japanese caught nine Americans and beheaded them. Combat such as this was unparalleled in the history of Makin and the islanders were terrified. Civilised man had brought hell to paradise. The Japanese were no longer friendly, believing the islanders had aided the Americans.

The raid was a mistake, for it only alerted the Japanese, who now strengthened their garrisons to 800 men on Makin (most on Butaritari Island) and 5,000 on Tarawa (most on Betio Island) of the 6th and 7th Special Naval Landing Forces. Obviously the arrival of so many caused severe dislocation to the islanders: Butaritari was only three square miles and Betio one-and-a-quarter square miles. Betio became one vast airfield.

In November 1943 US planes began heavy air raids on the two atolls. On the morning of the 20th Betio, Butaritari and smaller Apemama each about a hundred miles apart were shelled by US warships and landing craft began coming ashore. The six tiny islets of Apemama were invaded for just four marine casualties: the marines identified a Japanese platoon and pulled back to let air power and naval guns destroy it. After five days the local islanders went to visit the Americans and told them the Japanese were all dead.

Makin was different, for the garrison of 300 Japanese and 500 Korean labour troops put up a fearsome defence against the US 27th New York Division, though outnumbered 30:1. It took three days and 66 killed and 152 wounded for the New York State troops to kill all the enemy, bar a handful of Koreans. Following this the scared islanders climbed out of their jungle hide-outs to 'surrender' to the Americans by bringing them coconuts.

Offshore a Japanese submarine torpedoed a US carrier killing 644 and an accidental explosion on a battleship killed 43.

Tarawa was even more costly. The landing craft of the US 2nd Marine Division, reinforced by five battalions, became stuck on the reef and thousands had to get out and walk across the neck-deep lagoon towards Betio for hundreds of yards in full view of the enemy. By the end of the day they had reached the island and cut it in two, but only on the fifth day did they secure the island, killing 5,000 enemy and taking 146 prisoners at a cost of 1,069 killed, 2,391 wounded and hundreds sick with heat exhaustion and jungle fevers.

Meanwhile a marine battalion had contacted Tarawa's islanders and together they searched the other islands for the enemy: they found a company on Buariki, twenty miles from Betio, and killed them all for US losses of 32 killed and 59 wounded.

The cost to the Americans to take a few dots on the map was thus 4,500 casualties and was followed by a public outcry. The name 'Tarawa' would be forever enshrined in US history.

As for the islanders, they now had to get used to occupation US-style for the next two years.

Once the war was over the islanders tried to resume their normal lives, but rusting tanks and landing craft littered their home and the social impact was irreversible. *See Index*

GREECE

Other names:	Hellas (does not include Dodecanese)
Status in 1939:	independent.
Government in 1939:	dictatorship.
Population in 1939:	7,460,000.

Make-up in 1939:	Greeks 6,900,000;
	Turks 190,000
	Vlachs 150,000;
	Macedonians 81,000
	Jews 78,000;
	Chams 30,000;
	Bulgars 30,000.
Religion:	Christian.
Location:	South-East Europe.

Having learned to expect hostility from Bulgars and Turks it came somewhat as a surprise to the Greeks when Mussolini, the Italian dictator, began anti-Greek propaganda in 1940. However, the Greek leader, General Metaxas, was a cool customer, determined not to be pushed into overreaction. Already since September 1939 eighteen Greek merchant ships had been sunk by German action, several damaged and six captured. Naturally Metaxas had protested. Once Italy declared war on Britain in June 1940 Greek merchant vessels became prey to Italian planes and warships, which claimed to have mistaken them for British. In June fifteen were sunk and five confiscated, in July seven and three, August six and two, September five sunk, in October seven sunk and two captured. Even the torpedoing of the Greek cruiser *Helle* while openly carrying a religious icon did not push Metaxas into declaring war.

Thus it was as an innocent victim that Greece was invaded by Italy across the Albanian border on 28 October 1940.

At once the Greek Air Force of 38 fighters and 85 bombers went into action and all army reservists were mobilised. Fortunately, Mussolini had chosen the worst possible time, the beginning of a cold snowy winter in the mountains.

As early as 1 November the Greek 9th Division counter-attacked in the Macedonian Mountains, spearheaded by elite Evzones and horse cavalry. On the coast on the 4th the 8th Division counter-attacked and in the Pindus Mountains the Greeks managed to cut off an Italian column by charging down from the mountain tops into the enemy rear. The Italians fought their way out, but General Papagos and his staff had learned something of value.

On the 14th after allowing several Italian divisions to advance, Papagos gave the order to charge down east of the Pindus Mountains to attack the Italian supply lines as well as their spearhead. The plan worked and the invaders were thrown into turmoil. Then Papagos ordered a complete counter-offensive with seven divisions. By the 18th the Italians were in retreat and on the 21st the Greeks chased them fifteen miles into Albania.

The war now settled down to patrols, small-scale attacks, artillery barrages and air raids. There was a Greek coastal advance in December and a Christmas battle in the mountains.

Metaxas had refused British aid, except for some air squadrons, because the Greeks had an unpleasant memory of being pushed around by the British, but in January 1941 Metaxas died of natural causes. His successor Alexander Koryzis allowed a British army (primarily a New Zealand and an Australian divisions) to enter Greece to man the Bulgarian border, thereby relieving Greek troops for the Albanian front. In January and February thirteen Greek divisions repulsed Italian offensives.

On 6 April German troops in Bulgaria invaded southern Yugoslavia, then swerved southwards into Greece – the Greek-Yugoslavia border had not been manned by the Greeks. On the 8th the Germans reached the port of Salonika, cutting off three divisions in north-east Greece, while the Greek Second Army's three divisions and the British retreated to a previously prepared position, the Aliakmon River Line.

On the 12th, the Greek Epirus and West Macedonian Armies' fourteen divisions of General Zolakoglou were attacked by the Italian Ninth and Eleventh Armies. By the 14th the British and Greek Second Army had retreated as far south as Mount Olympus, uncovering Zolakoglou's right flank, and by the 16th they had retreated 160 miles behind him. On the 18th Zolakoglou asked for terms and Koryzis shot himself. The British decided to evacuate and began to do so on the 21st. King Giorgos, who had never had real power, flew to Crete and later to Egypt. The remaining Greek authorities surrendered on the 23rd.

The Greeks had put up a resistance, the likes of which creates legends. Their Spartan ancestors would have been proud. But the British saw the Greeks only in the retreat stage and had come to Greece with a xenophobic attitude. Of 67,000 British-controlled troops 3,700 were killed, a high proportion by air raids, and 11,500 were captured. About 2,700 Greeks were killed fighting the Germans. German losses were 2,232 killed and 3,000 wounded. Greek and British sailors suffered sorely in the evacuation – two British, three Dutch and eighty-five Greek ships were sunk.

Against the Italians the Greeks had suffered 13,000 killed, 50,000 wounded and thousands maimed by frostbite. They had inflicted slightly higher casualties on the Italians.

The Greek armed forces were now in captivity in their entirety, but for a home defence division on Crete, some troops who had evacuated there with the British and a few planes, warships and merchant ships. Crete was under air attack even as the allies reached that island and they immediately set about arranging defences. The British had about 30,000 men on the island and the Greeks had about 10,000 divided into six regiments.

On 20 May the Germans came, falling from the sky by parachute and glider. On the second day they came by transport plane: the British had not bothered to defend the airfields. The British and Greeks, including civilians, fought tenaciously, but their leadership was outclassed and with the British Royal Navy offshore it was too easy to just call it quits and evacuate, which the British did after ten days. The British rescue fleet suffered terrible losses: two cruisers and fur destroyers sunk plus fifteen warships damaged, and British ground forces suffered 1,742 killed and 11,800 captured. Many of the Greek soldiers simply hid among the population. However, they had killed almost 4,000 Germans and this bothered Hitler. He wanted no more airborne battles!

In Egypt there were enough Greeks to man an infantry brigade, two air squadrons and a cruiser, six destroyers, six submarines and two torpedo boats, plus a couple of warships donated by the British.

Meanwhile in Greece the Bulgarians annexed part of Thrace and the Italians annexed the homes of the Chams and gave autonomy to the Vlachs, but the remainder of the country was allowed its own government headed by none other than General Zolakoglou. Italian troops occupied the nation and there were German troops in a few districts.

Greek soldiers and civilians had fled to the mountains to begin a partisan war against the occupiers, but for the next year they spent their time searching for food and shelter. The occupiers ignored them.

In Egypt it was not until October 1942 that the Greek brigade was given a combat mission: assigned to the British Eighth Army for an offensive at Alamein, a line in the desert. On the night of the 23rd the battle began, the Greeks going up against German paratroopers. Only after twelve days of major fighting did the Germans and Italians retreat. This was the greatest allied victory to date.

The brigade was then placed in reserve and was not called upon again until March 20 1943 at Mareth in Tunisia. As the Eighth Army attacked frontally a makeshift corps of a New Zealand Division, a French brigade and the Greek brigade was ordered to outflank the enemy. For nine days the corps fought its way through desert mountains until the enemy retired. After this the Greeks were put into reserve again.

On 10 July the allies invaded Sicily. Greek warships joined this campaign to protect transports from air and submarine attack and on occasion to bombard enemy shore installations. The campaign ended on 16 August. The Greek warships repeated these duties off the Italian shore beginning on 9 September.

In Greece the partisans had come under the spell of city intellectuals: the largest group was the National Liberation Front, which loosely controlled all left-wing political parties, calling its guerrillas National Popular Liberation Army (ELAS). They were strong in Macedonia, Roumelia and the Peloponnisos. In the Epirus Mountains Napoleon Zervas organised the National Democratic Greek League (EDES), which was liberal enough to accept all, but communists and fascists. There were many smaller groups: EEE, EKKA, EASAD and the ethnic Macedonian YVE and Kaltchev. As early as the spring of 1942 these bands began to fight, but against each other not against the invaders!

The Kaltchev made a truce with the Bulgarians in order to concentrate on battling the ELAS. It was not until June that the invaders suffered a blow: EDES ambushed a truck convoy between Arta and Yannitsa and killed sixty Italians. The YVE began raids against the Bulgarians and Italians, but left the Germans alone.

Real partisan cooperation was rare. In May 1943 British advisers convinced EDES and ELAS to get together to ambush an Italian column at Domenico, which killed eighty Italians including a general, and in June this combined force moved into Albania to surprise a German reinforcement unit, the 1st Mountain Division, but the Germans were veterans and turned the tables on the ambushers. EDES and ELAS blamed each other for the defeat.

In Athens a new leader had replaced Zolakoglou, Joannes Rallis, who recruited a battalion of a thousand anti-terrorist police and set up village militias to fight off partisan food raids. With Rallis' permission, but not Italian, the Germans entered the Peloponnisos and swept it for partisans. Rallis' battalion accompanied them and impressed the Germans so much they asked him to recruit another 14,000 such men.

In a three-day battle in Roumelia ELAS inflicted 500 casualties on the Italian Pinerolo Division. In retaliation for such activity the Italians, Germans and Bulgarians arrested people at random and sometimes executed them: e.g. in one instance at Larissa the Italians executed 118. ELAS replied by stating they would no longer take Italian prisoners. At Rovilista an EDES/ELAS ambush inflicted 120 casualties on the Italians. At Almyros the Italians repelled a partisan raid, then murdered 38 of the local villagers.

On 8 September 1943 the allies announced that Italy had surrendered. This announcement took everyone, partisans, Germans and Italians by surprise. At once the better organised Germans began arresting Italians wherever they found them. Italian fascists joined them, but anti-fascists resisted. Thousands of Italians defected to the partisans, especially to EDES. The staff

of the Pinerolo Division and Aosta Cavalry Regiment made a deal with ELAS.

However, by now ELAS was totally dominated by communists, and they weeded their new Italian allies – accepting the communists, but arresting the others by treachery. There were a few joint ELAS-Italian raids, but when they went wrong the ELAS blamed the Italians and disarmed them. By October, thousands of Italians had become slaves of ELAS, who even took the clothes off their back. Naked and friendless and facing winter the Italians began to die like flies. British advisers to ELAS were horrified and rescued the Pinerolo commander.

The other partisans accepted the Italians. If possible the partisan war against Germans, Bulgarians, Italian fascists, and Greek anti-terrorist police became even more bloody.

The British had actually returned to Greece. In late September 1943, belatedly realising that anti-fascist Italians were resisting the Germans, the British Prime Minister Churchill made a token gesture, putting 5,000 men including 350 Greeks on the Italian-occupied islands of Leros, Samos, Stampalia, Patnos, Lipsos, Nicario, Cos and Simi. The islands were under German air raids and warships could not survive in daylight – the Greek destroyer *Vasilissa Olga* found that out.

Beginning in October the Germans and fascist Italians launched amphibious invasions to take the islands one by one – Cos, Simi and Stampalia in October, Leros, Patnos, Lipsos and Nicario in November. The British and Greeks evacuated Samos, deserting the Italians. The Greek islanders who had assisted the British and Italians were also abandoned. Churchill had played at war and the result was death and destruction.

Inter-partisan fighting also went on. On occasion Britons advised both ELAS and EDES when they fought each other! In November the YVE joined the Germans and several Rallis battalions to drive ELAS out of the Macedonian Mountains, while elsewhere partisans came under assault by entire German divisions. Atrocities by the invaders and the Rallis battalions were commonplace. ELAS were also noted for atrocities. Most of the EKKA was destroyed by ELAS. In one fight Kaltchev lost fifty men to ELAS. By spring 1944 the Rallis battalions were allowed to hunt partisans on their own without German chaperons.

The Greek Civil War, for that is what it had become, stretched all the way across the sea: in April 1944 in the barracks in Egypt and among the warships political arguments ended in gunplay with a hundred killed and wounded on both sides.

Despite their political problems the Greek soldiers in Egypt insisted they were ready for combat and in September the British Eighth Army called them to Italy. The brigade was given the mission of crossing the Marano River and capturing Rimini from the Germans. The battle was tough. An advance of a hundred yards a day was considered good going. On the 17th after two weeks the Greeks reached an airfield and then took four days to cross it. Having lost 314 casualties at the airfield alone, the Greeks then crept into Rimini. It must have seemed ironic to the Greeks when Italian civilians greeted them as liberators.

In September the Soviet armies broke into Bulgaria, which declared war on Germany and withdrew its troops from Greece. The Germans in Greece were in sudden danger of being cut off and they began to pick up and pull out. On the 24th the British landed on the Peloponnisos with orders to follow, but not engage, the Germans. In one incident 1,600 members of the Rallis battalions surrendered to a handful of British, rather than be captured by partisans.

On 11 October the Germans abandoned Athens and on the 18th the Greek brigade and British troops arrived.

On several of the islands including Crete the Germans and fascist Italians were trapped, having no transport to the mainland. Greek troops made commando raids against these hold-outs over the next eight months.

ELAS made deals with German units, allowing them unhindered retreat if they paid their way in weapons and ammunition.

They needed these because the civil war was not over. In October and November as many as 5,000 people were murdered by ELAS assassination squads. EDES murdered known ELAS supporters.

On 3 December ELAS attacked Athens: the garrison resisted – police, four Greek Army battalions, including the victors of Rimini, a recently recruited National Guard, British troops, including rear-echelon personnel and air force ground crew, and EDES supporters. This was a serious affair and only a full-scale British amphibious invasion in January 1945 rescued the trapped units. ELAS claimed 4,000 casualties. The British lost 1,500 casualties and the anti-ELAS Greeks about 2,000. ELAS kidnapped 20,000 hostages when they retreated into the snowy mountains.

For Greece World War II ended on a very sour note. The major partisan factions claimed 16,000 of their members were killed fighting the invaders and 34,000 were executed or died in custody through maltreatment. In truth this figure probably includes those killed fighting each other. The smaller bands may have had a total of about 5,000 dead.

Eventually 50,000 Greeks served in Rallis battalions or village militia, of which about a thousand were killed fighting partisans. Others were murdered by partisans after the Germans left.

The regular Greek armed forces lost several hundred dead after April 1941 at sea, in the air and in Egypt, Tunisia and Italy, to add to their 15,700 killed defending Greece 1940-41 and 500 killed defending Athens 1944-45 and a few killed raiding the islands 1944-45.

The merchant service lost 2,000 dead and 283 ships sunk, about 120 after April 1941.

Civilian losses were exceedingly high: several thousand dead in cross-fire and air raids; a thousand murdered by the Rallis forces, 9,000 murdered by Italians, 21,000 by Germans, 40,000 by Bulgarians, 30,000 by ELAS, about 2,000 by others. Additionally 67,000 were murdered by the Germans because of their Jewish race.

The combination of air raids, sabotage and ambushes, which destroyed food warehouses and damaged the food transportation network and deliberate confiscation of food by whoever had a gun brought about a famine, plus the Germans stole much livestock when they retreated. This resulted in an estimated 260,000 deaths from malnutrition and related illnesses.

Total Greek war deaths 1939-45 were therefore about 515,000.

See Index

GREENLAND

Status in 1939:	Danish colony.
Government in 1939:	Danish administration.
Population in 1939:	22,000.
Make-up in 1939:	20,500 of Danish stock and many Danish-Eskimo; 500 Danes; 1,000 Eskimos.
Religion:	Christian
Location:	North Atlantic

An immense land mass, Greenland has only a few miles of coastal plain where human habitation is desirable. This territory that no one wanted suddenly became very wanted in 1939 when war broke out between Germany and the allies, for both needed weather stations and the allies needed air bases from which they could patrol for German submarines. The nation's mineral resources were equally essential to the war effort. However, Denmark remained neutral in this war.

In April 1940 Denmark was invaded by Germany, and the administration in Greenland was forced to choose between a king who was a prisoner of the Germans, neutrality or belligerency on the side of the allies. They chose the latter, but the next question was which ally? The Americans did not like the idea of the British moving into Greenland and were more likely to accept a Canadian occupation. The Greenlanders solved the dilemma by inviting the Americans in.

The Greenlanders had already created a sledge patrol to inspect the coast for signs of German incursions, but the nation was so large that one sweep would last years.

Incredibly the sledge patrol encountered a German weather station and in a skirmish a Greenlander was killed. Next day the Germans evacuated, abandoning one man who was imprisoned by the Greenlanders in a hotel.

At sea a Greenland ship was torpedoed and sunk by a German submarine.

See Index

GUAM

Status in 1939:	US possession.
Government in 1939:	US administration.
Population in 1939:	22,290.
Make-up in 1939:	Chamorros; circa 1,000 Filipinos, Japanese and Americans.
Religion:	local and Christian.
Location:	Central Pacific

Throughout 1941 the US government had been getting indications that the Japanese were planning a war. In response they reinforced their Pacific garrisons and built airstrips. These garrisons linked Hawaii with the Philippines – the island of Midway 1,250 miles west of Hawaii, Wake about the same distance again, Guam another 1,500 miles west, with the Philippines 1,200 miles further on. Such vast distances of water made even small islands of strategic importance.

Thirty-mile-long Guam was a problem, for it was only just over a hundred miles from Japanese-occupied Tinian.

On 7 December 1941 a Japanese carrier fleet sent aircraft to bomb the headquarters of the US Pacific Fleet in Hawaii. Alerted by radio the Guam garrison rushed to their defences: 153 US marines, 271 US sailors, 246 Naval Militia and 80 Insular Guards. The latter two units were manned by native islanders. For two days the island was bombed by Japanese planes and on the third day the shore was shelled by enemy warships while 5,400 troops stormed ashore from barges. The garrison commander chose to surrender. The garrison had lost nineteen killed and 39 wounded. The Japanese claimed only one of their own killed.

The entire garrison and all white civilians were taken prisoner. Their treatment was horrific, for the Japanese believed by surrendering they had lost all dignity.

The Americans had attempted to defend Guam with 753 men. The Japanese brought in 3,000 naval and air personnel, the 6th Naval Expeditionary Force and the Army's 29th Division, well over 20,000 men. Where plausible native labour was used. Anyone who refused would be answered with the bayonet.

Daily the islanders prayed for deliverance, yet knowing that when it came it would result in a ferocious battle.

In spring 1944 American carrier planes began raiding Guam and in July the raids were very heavy. Many civilians hid in caves and thick jungle to avoid being hit. A naval bombardment began on the 19th and on the 21st the Americans began coming ashore in landing craft at the towns of Agat and Asan.

Neither the islanders nor Japanese high command could have predicted the sheer size of the invasion and the firepower it brought to bear. Landing this day were the US 3rd Marine Division and 1st Marine Brigade and the Army's 77th Division, no less than 47 battalions of artillery, armoured vehicles, combat engineers and infantry. The Japanese fought for every hut in the two towns and the first day cost the Americans 1,187 casualties, but they were here to stay. As soon as pockets of islanders were liberated they began aiding the Americans as guides and porters.

By the 25th the Americans had snaked about five miles into the mountains to Fonte Ridge, where a Japanese counter-attack broke through all the way to the US headquarters before they were shot down. Fierce hand-to-hand fighting lasted three days, but after this Agano City was liberated and the Americans and local guides pushed the Japanese into the mountains of the north end of the island. On 10 August they reached the sea and the generals reported Guam secure.

The three-week affair cost the Americans 2,124 killed and 10,000 wounded and 11,000 Japanese dead were buried. However, almost at once Japanese snipers became a nuisance and at least one US battalion with local helpers remained in action. In October an entire US division swept the mountains

again. Following this American troops and local guides continued hunting the holdouts. As late as January 1945 there was a small Japanese attack.

When the war ended with Japan's total surrender in August 1945 parties went into the mountains with interpreters and loudspeakers and rounded up 1,250 Japanese prisoners. Therefore, about 8,500 Japanese had died since the American generals told the Chamorros their island was secure, their deaths being attributable to US action, disease, starvation and suicide.

The islanders had become used to a military force outnumbering them, and had to adapt to it permanently for the Americans would never again allow the island's defences to shrink below a strength of many thousand.

For years afterwards there were rumours that Japs remained in the mountains: one surrendered in 1960!
See Index

HONG KONG

Status in 1939:	British colony leased from China.
Government in 1939:	British administration.
Population in 1939:	1,200,000.
Make-up in 1939:	Chinese, including many thousands of Refugees; 6,000 British.
Religion:	various.
Location:	China coast.

Hong Kong Island had been leased in 1841 and the mainland opposite a half century later, hence its name the New Territories. The British ran the entire colony as a commercial enterprise, thus its culture remained overwhelmingly Chinese, but its laws were British. A great harbour, the colony naturally had a cosmopolitan atmosphere along the waterfront.

The Japanese invasion of China in 1931 had affected the colony little, but as the Japanese approached the border of the New Territories in 1937 many thousands of refugees fled to the protection of the tiny British garrison.

In 1937 the Japanese dared not cross that border as they would have felt the full wrath of the British Empire, but by late 1941 the British Empire was fully committed to war with Germany, Italy and France. With a naivety that can only come from a belief of racial superiority the British reinforced their garrison in November 1941 to send the Japanese a message, but did so only with 2,000 troops. Logic should have told them that if the Japanese were not afraid of millions of Chinese soldiers they would not be frightened out of their wits by 2,000 British. Then again, perhaps the British did know this, for they encouraged all white civilians to leave the colony and the troops they sent were not British at all, but Canadians, loaned by a gullible government.

Total Anglo-American defences in China consisted of a few hundred British at Tientsin and Shanghai, an American battalion at Shanghai, a gun boat each and the British Hong Kong garrison. On the morning of 8 December 1941 the Japanese attacked without warning, overrunning Tientsin and Shanghai in hours and bombing Hong Kong, where the entire British air force was destroyed at Kai Tak airfield.

On the border of the New territories one British and two Indian battalions watched Japanese soldiers walk up to them as if on parade. When the defenders opened fire the Japanese died with a surprised look on their faces. The Japanese came on again, in one place with Chinese civilians in front of them as a shield. The defenders opened fire anyway, the civilians ran, and the Japanese realised they were going to have to fight for Hong Kong. The defenders were now fired upon by artillery and they replied with their own, provided by the Hong Kong and Singapore Artillery Regiment, which despite its name was manned by Indians. Also firing on the Japanese was the gunboat HMS *Cicala*, with a crew of 40 British and eighteen Hong Kong Chinese (HKC).

On day two some British troops at the border ran and others were overrun at the Shing Mun Redoubt, forcing the outflanked Indians to withdraw. A British officer shot himself in shame. On day four it was decided by high command to retreat to Hong Kong island while the Indians held a rearguard.

Once the inhabitants of the New Territories learned they were to be abandoned they fled by the hundred thousand to the water's edge at the port of Kowloon, climbing into junks, houseboats, rowing boats, anything that could take them to the island or Macao, a nearby neutral Portuguese colony. White civilians were evacuated courtesy of the British forces.

When the Indian rearguard left the shore the Japanese infantry were close enough to try to leap into the boats and had to be fought off with rifle butts. Thousands of civilians witnessing the departure screamed and begged for rescue.

That night the troops on the island could hear a bloodcurdling screech coming from Kowloon just a mile across the water. Only after several minutes did they understand what they were listening to: the screams of thousands of HKC women being raped by Japanese soldiers.

On the island the defenders had two infantry battalions, a coast artillery regiment, a marine defence force and lots of rear-echelon personnel including air force ground crew and sailors, all British; two infantry battalions, four artillery batteries and two flak batteries, all Indian; two infantry battalions of Canadians; and a machine gun battalion, engineers and rear-echelon troops, all HKC. There was also the Hong Kong Volunteer Defence Corps, consisting of locally recruited British, HKC, Eurasians (i.e. mixed white and Chinese), and a few Portuguese – the latter could have claimed neutrality. The unit was poorly trained and seemed to have no age limit.

The island was bombed and shelled for several days and on the 18th the Japanese began to cross in barges and boats, easily gaining a beachhead all along the north coast between the towns of Victoria and Shau Kei Wan. By day two the defenders were being divided into the east, west and south of the island and some survivors were reaching their pals with stories of Japanese bayoneting wounded allied soldiers. This was not wanton, but was done at the order of several Japanese officers.

On day three the allies replied with bayonet charges, a stupid mistake for it gained nothing and wasted lives. Rear-echelon troops were sent into such charges, too, though they had no infantry training, but then again only the Indians had received serious infantry training. The British, HKC and Canadians had treated their military service so far as a big game. Many of the Canadians had never fired a rifle before, but they knew where all the night-clubs were.

When overrun even medical tents were not immune to Japanese bayonets. In one hospital patients were bayoneted in their beds and the female nurses raped. By day seven the defenders had lost all unit integrity: Canadian infantry fought shoulder to shoulder alongside British airmen and sailors, HKC engineers and Indian gunners. On day eight – it was Christmas – the British garrison commander surrendered.

Since the 8th the defenders had suffered about 3,000 killed and 9,000 defenders and 3,000 white civilians taken prisoner. The Japanese claimed 2,750 casualties.

The prisoners were now subjected to an absolute horror, because the Japanese considered anyone who surrendered beneath contempt. Treatment ranged from neglect to cruelty to murder. HKC prisoners seemed specially chosen for ill-treatment. On one occasion a Japanese officer was beheaded in front of the prisoners for having failed in his duty. Within months the soldiers were reduced to walking skeletons living mostly on unhusked rice, with if lucky a fish head once a week. The prisoners saw few of the medical supplies provided by the Japanese government and others, as often they were sold on the black market by the Japanese officers.

The Japanese used most of the prisoners to build a large airport (still in use), but embarked 1,816 onto a tramp steamer for Japan. The ship was torpedoed by a US submarine – the Japanese refused to mark prison ships with, for example, a red cross – and 840 prisoners drowned, some being deliberately pushed off life-boats by Japanese sailors.

Even without this terrible incident, by the time the prisoners were liberated in August 1945 one in five had died (four times the death rate of British prisoners in nazi hands).

Thousands of HKC merchant and navy seamen had been away from home when the colony was overrun and continued to serve

valiantly throughout the war. A company of HKC infantry fought in Burma as Chindits.

The HKC people had thought they had been oppressed by the British, but when the Japanese arrived the HKC realised they hadn't known what real oppression was. Thousands of women were conscripted by the Japanese as prostitutes and men as slaves. Any who refused was bayoneted, but in any case slaves of the Japanese did not live long. The death toll was certainly in the thousands.

When the war ended, following Japan's total surrender, British warships entered Hong Kong to be met on the wharf by smiling, bowing Japanese officers.

See Index

HUNGARY

Status in 1937:	independent.
Government in 1937:	democratic monarchy.
Population in 1937:	8,000,000.
Make-up in 1937:	Magyars 6,800,000; Volksdeutsch 560,000; Szeklers 400,000; Jews 400,000; Slovaks 160,000; very small groups of: Romanians; Ukrainians; Croats; Serbs; Gypsies.
Religion:	Christian.
Location:	Eastern Europe.

With the destruction of the Austro-Hungarian Empire in 1918 Hungary emerged independent, but with borders that did not stretch far enough to satisfy all Magyars as it left many of them out in the cold, and yet included ethnic groups. When everyone had been a citizen of the empire it did not matter, but now there was constant rabble rousing about ethnic rights. Immediately this resulted in a communist dictatorship, but Bela Kun was quickly deposed after a fiasco invasion of Czecho-Slovakia. The Hungarian people did not forget the few months of communist rule, nor did they forget that Kun was an assimilated Jew.

Assimilated Jews spoke either Magyar or German, but unassimilated Jews, about a quarter of the nation's total, spoke Yiddish (a dialect of German). Therefore, the Magyars looked upon Jews as either foreigners

(Yiddish or German) or as wolves in clothing sheep's pretending to be Magyars. Descriptions of Jews as 'Godless', 'outsiders', 'secretive' etc. were commonplace.

Such anti-semitism and a desire to liberate foreign-occupied Magyars made democratic Hungary susceptible to the ravings of Germany's nazi dictator Adolf Hitler as early as 1938.

In October of that year the timidity of Britain, France and Czecho-Slovakia allowed Hitler to send his armies into the Sudetenland province of Czecho-Slovakia. Immediately the Hungarians saw their chance and invaded too, liberating 500,000 Magyars, but also occupying the homes of 272,000 Slovakians, 67,000 Jews and 38,000 Ukrainians. There was no serious resistance.

In March 1939 Germany annexed the Czech homeland and gave Slovakia and Ruthenia independence, and a day later Hungarian troops invaded Ruthenia, liberating 175,000 Magyars and conquering 75,000 Jews and 250,000 Ukrainians. A few Ukrainians resisted, but were stifled in days.

The grateful Hungarian people re-elected the government, giving it 180 parliament seats.

In 1940 Germany restrained Romania while Hungarian troops marched into Transylvania to liberate 1,400,000 Magyars (and conquer half a million Jews, Volksdeutsch and Romanians).

In gratitude to Germany Hungary signed an alliance with that nation in November 1940. However, Hitler wanted more than just a document. He demanded the right to station troops in Hungary, ostensibly to protect the oilfields. Prime Minister Teleki, who until now had led the conquests, was alarmed, but had no support from his colleagues. He protested the only way he knew how: by committing suicide. His death was ignored and the Hungarians waved as the Germans marched in.

In April 1941 the Germans used Hungarian bases to invade Yugoslavia, which retaliated with air raids. Using this as an excuse, the Hungarian government sent in its soldiers behind the Germans to occupy areas of Magyar habitation, liberating 365,000 Magyars and occupying a few thousand Serbs and Jews.

So far, Hungarian troops had been polite in their conquests, though they had thrown non-Magyars out of jobs to give them to Magyars, but by 1941 some of the soldiers were members of the Arrow Cross fascist party, which had its own militia, and these fellows wanted to go beyond mere transference of non-Magyars from top dog to under dog. In Yugoslavia they went on the rampage, aided by local Magyars, and attacked and beat Serb and Jewish shop owners, landlords, factory owners, teachers and civil servants. In Subotica 250 were murdered: double that in Novi Sad.

The government took legal proceedings against the murderers, but Admiral Horthy the head of state stepped in and halted them. This admiral without a navy ruled as a regent without a king and increasingly his hand would be seen interfering as Hungary drifted into dictatorship.

Hitler asked a favour: he wanted Hungary to join him in a Christian crusade against the USSR. Horthy agreed. He had not minded when a few hundred of his citizens had volunteered for the Finnish Army to fight the USSR in December 1939, and he assigned a horse cavalry and two mechanised brigades to Hitler's invasion.

Currently all ethnic groups were eligible for military conscription, though the Army maintained separate ethnic units for language reasons and Jews were placed in unarmed non-fighting units.

Germany invaded the USSR on 22 June 1941 and on the 27th the Hungarian brigades advanced under General Ferenc Szombathelyi, who reported to German Seventeenth Army. By 3 August the Hungarians had overcome several rearguards at a cost of 977 casualties. The USSR was bigger than had been thought and the brigades were joined by three divisions and an armoured brigade, which soon encountered tough opposition.

By the first freeze, Horthy decided that the war was going to last through the winter and he was not going to let his soldiers die of hypothermia: he politely, but firmly, informed Hitler he was withdrawing his men out of the line until spring, though he would allow four brigades and a battalion of bicycle troops to guard German lines of supply. Horthy felt his men had done enough. In five months of action they had suffered 26,000 casualties.

In Hungarian-occupied Yugoslavia partisans had begun a low key guerrilla war and by January 1942 had killed seventeen Hungarian soldiers. In retaliation General Ferenc Feketehalmi-Czeydner unleashed his troops and Arrow Cross militia on the people of Ujvidek, forcing 550 Jews and 292 Serbs onto a frozen river until their weight broke the ice, whereupon they fell in and drowned. By other methods 2,467 Serbs, Jews and outspoken anti-fascist Magyars were butchered over a six-day period.

The Hungarian Army court-martialled the general. Horthy quashed the charges.

In summer 1942 Hitler promised a war-winning offensive against the USSR, but he was desperately short of manpower. Horthy agreed to send him a much larger force this time, the Second Army of General Jany. However, these eleven divisions contained only six infantry battalions each, whereas a German division had nine, and many of the troops were raw conscripts, not as well equipped as the Germans.

The advance began in June along the Don Valley and in September the Hungarians had to fight hard for Voronezh, but after this they took up a quiet stretch of the line north of Novaya Kalitva. Their losses in the USSR since the beginning of the war were 16,500 killed and 35,000 wounded.

In November the Soviets counter-attacked and destroyed most of two Romanian armies and trapped a German army, and in December they defeated another German army and destroyed the Italian Eighth Army on the Hungarian right flank. The Hungarians were sure their turn would come and thus they were given two months to worry about it. Their reinforcement by a Hungarian armoured division and the loan of thirty German tanks did little to increase morale.

On the freezing, snow-bound morning of 12 January 1943 the 7th Division was assaulted by waves of Soviet infantry and within 24 hours it had collapsed, its men fleeing in thigh-deep snow. Next day the 12th Division was attacked with equal force and it too folded up in hours. On the 15th the entire Second Army was attacked. The 19th and 23rd Divisions on the right flank retreated, taking neighbouring Italian troops with them. Jany had no recourse but to order a complete withdrawal: heavy equipment, frozen vehicles and guns were abandoned, the troops struggling in snow, their feet wrapped in rags. The armoured division did well in rearguard actions.

At the end of the month the Hungarians outran the chasing enemy and took roll-call: 35,000 men were known dead, 26,000 were missing and of the survivors 35,000 were wounded. Thousands were hospitalised with frostbite and respiratory illnesses. Additionally, 50,000 Jewish labour troops had been abandoned to the snow or the Soviets, neither of which showed any mercy.

Horthy told Hitler that in future Hungarian units would only be used to guard lines of supply and he ordered all but two divisions home.

In the spring seven fresh divisions went to the USSR, but Horthy had not changed his mind: they were given lines of supply duty. As a sop to Hitler he allowed him to recruit from Hungary's Volksdeutsch population. By December 1943 29,191 had entered the SS and 12,025 other organisations. The SS promised to keep the recruits together in companies of the 11th, 16th, 17th or 18th Divisions and offered better conditions, hence their monopoly on recruitment.

Also to please Hitler Hungarian generals began to solve the Jewish problem in the occupied lands by arresting them and handing them to the SS Security Police. The generals were quite aware that at best these Jewish men, women and children would be worked to death and at worst murdered outright. Ironically, complaints came from German Army generals. Thereupon, the Hungarians set up their own concentration camps. By these methods about 32,000 Jews were killed.

Horthy turned a blind eye to this, but at the same time he was secretly negotiating with the allies for a way out of the war.

Hitler learned of Horthy's treachery and poured more troops into Hungary on 17 March 1944. Horthy was ordered to put a pro-German government together; the SS Security Police arrived to arrest anti-Nazis without asking permission from the Hungarian police; and all Volksdeutsch were made eligible for German conscription.

Just two weeks later the Soviets reached Ruthenia and the Hungarian First Army was assembled to defend that province with twelve infantry and an armoured divisions and two mountain brigades. Each division now had nine infantry battalions and the armoured battalions were armed with the new Turan tank. On 17 April the Hungarians counter-attacked the Soviet 4th Ukrainian Front at Stanislav and a mighty struggle unfolded over a period of thirty-three days, at the end of which the Soviets were stopped. It was a victory, but it cost the Hungarians 12,135 killed, 25,000 wounded and 3,441 missing.

Heartbreakingly, the First Army was soon forced to fall back when flanking German units did so. In July a further withdrawal brought them to the Dniestr River.

By this time the SS aided by Hungarian police and Arrow Cross militia had arrested 400,000 Hungarian Jews. Under German law anyone with two or more Jewish grandparents was a Jew, thus 100,000 Christian Jews were among the deportees. Suddenly Horthy ordered a halt to the arrests. For the moment the SS obeyed, more or less. The Magyars were more concerned about air raids, which were getting bad, loved ones at the front and the impending Soviet invasion, to be concerned about Jews – such is human nature.

Along the front the Hungarians positioned fourteen infantry, two armoured and seven Scythian divisions: the latter being ad hoc units of rear-echelon troops and new recruits; and in September the Second Army attacked in Transylvania with two infantry, five Scythian and an armoured divisions and two mountain brigades, plus some Szekler militia. Nine days of ferocious assaults bought them nothing and the army fell back.

The eastern border was now defended by two German armies and the Hungarian First, Second and Third Armies, using one cavalry, two armoured, ten Scythian and twenty-one infantry divisions plus brigades and militia. On 6 October they were assaulted by the Soviet Sixth Guards Tank, Fifty-third and Forty-sixth and Romanian Fourth

Armies. Within days the line began to crack and the troops fell back into Hungary.

On 15 October 9,500 members of the 22nd SS Division (a third Germans, two thirds Hungarian Volksdeutsch) and SS commandos arrested Horthy's son and stormed his royal residence. Horthy broadcast to the people that he was seeking peace, but was arrested, and Hitler installed a new leader in Hungary, Count Ferenc Szalassi. Some Hungarian soldiers at the front, including three generals, accepted Horthy's declaration and defected to the Soviets, but most held their ground.

The 22nd SS Division then went on to Debrecen, but failed to hold that city against the Soviets on the 20th. By month's end the front was only seventy miles east of Budapest.

In that city the nightmare began as the SS set up two ghettos for Jews, one of them full of neutral citizens protected by Swedish diplomats. Inside the other ghetto every Jew was fair game for Arrow Cross hit squads of men and women who grabbed people at random and murdered or tortured them. Other Arrow Cross began marching Jews into the cold, wet mountains. Passing German troops registered complaints about the atrocity. By late November Soviet artillery was pounding the city, including the ghettos. Subjected to shellfire, air raids, kidnapping by Arrow Cross and an order to get to the front and dig trenches in full view of the enemy, the Hungarian Jews did not stand a chance. Other citizens had to supply men for the front line and women and children to dig anti-tank ditches in the frozen earth, line up for poor rations, dodge shells and smile every time an Arrow Cross militiaman insulted them. The enemy was within as well as without.

Nineteen Hungarian divisions were in retreat past Budapest, joined by the Germans, including the 25th and 26th SS Divisions made up of Hungarian Volksdeutsch and some Magyars. The city barricades were defended by militia and the 1st Armoured, 10th Infantry and 12th Scythian Divisions: 37,000 Hungarians; plus the German 22nd SS Division and two all-German divisions, a total of 33,000 'Germans'. In December they fought Soviet tanks in the suburb of Pest.

By 18 January almost all of Pest had fallen to the Soviets and their Hungarian communist collaborators, and now it was Buda's turn to be fought over, house by house. Hitler was afraid the ghettos would be liberated so he ordered the SS to kill the Jews. However, the SS generals here were Waffen SS, i.e. soldiers, and it took only a mild intervention by the Swedish diplomats to convince them to disobey Hitler, though it could mean their neck.

On 8 February Hitler gave the garrison permission to withdraw. Only 700 Hungarian and German soldiers made it before the city fell!

In March Hitler ordered Budapest recaptured: three Hungarian and seven German divisions made the attempt, but extraordinarily high losses only gained them twenty miles. Following this the Hungarian Army just simply began to disappear. The new German 33rd SS Division of Hungarian Volksdeutsch and Magyars received its flags, heard a few speeches and then marched to the front, never to be seen again. The Hungarian Third Army, or what was left of it, fought for Bratislava for a few days, then retreated into Austria.

In May when 8,000 Hungarians were met by advancing Americans in southern Germany the Americans treated them like allies. Once corrected the Americans took their surrender: they included six divisions! The British also ran into retreating Hungarians and treated them as allies.

For a nation that had gone along with Hitler like a novitiate in a criminal gang, Hungary eventually paid the price for her nationalist greed. After a nation has gone through a mincing machine, such as Hungary did, where gangs of starving orphans hid in forests, it is impossible to give an accurate casualty count.

About 800,000 non-Jewish pre-1938 citizens put on Hungarian uniform of which 147,000 were killed in action, several thousand died of other causes such as accident, freezing and disease, and 50,000 died in Soviet prison camps. About 65,000 Jewish labour troops also died. Perhaps half the 70,000 who donned German uniform died.

Of the 400,000 Jews and 100,000 Christian Jews in pre-1938 Hungary 203,000 civilians died from all causes, mostly murder by Hungarians or Germans. (Two-thirds of the Jews conquered by Hungary also died). The Arrow Cross and SS murdered 28,000 Hungarian Gypsies. About 40,000 other civilians died by cross fires, air raids, starvation and murder at the hands of the authorities for speaking out against the insanity.

The Soviets were brutal as they passed through and tens of thousands of women were raped and any men who defended their womenfolk were gunned down. Moreover the Soviet political police NKVD arrested an estimated 600,000 citizens and sentenced them to various lengths of imprisonment in slave labour camps. At least 10% must have died: the camps were not known for comfort.

Totalled, this gives pre-1938 Hungarian citizens a death toll of 650,000. So much for Hitler's promise of cheap victories.
See Index

ICELAND

Status in 1939:	Danish possession.
Government in 1939:	democratic monarchy.
Population in 1939:	140,000.
Make-up in 1939:	Icelandics.
Religion:	Christian.
Location:	North Atlantic

When Denmark was invaded by Germany in April 1940, the Icelandics had to chose whether to concede indirect German control or take a stand against aggression. They chose to make a stand by allowing British forces to set up air and sea bases in order to fight the German submarine fleet, which was as much a menace to Icelandic ships as it was to the British.

In July 1941 the United States took over formal protection of the nation.

The nation's location, covering the northern flank of the normal sea route between the USA and Britain was ideal for anti-submarine patrols and as a halfway stop over for convoys of allied merchant ships.

A few Icelandics joined the British armed forces and thousands of Icelandic seamen served in merchant and fishing vessels to support the allied cause. Nineteen Icelandic vessels were sunk by enemy action.
See Index

INDIA

Other names:	Indian sub-continent (subsequently Bangla Desh, India and Pakistan) excludes small French and Portuguese enclaves.
Status in 1939:	British dominion known as the Indian Empire.
Government in 1939:	part under direct British administration, remainder divided among hundreds of 'princes'.
Population in 1939:	384,000,000
Make-up in 1939:	about 65 major ethnic groups, the largest being: Baluchis; Bengalis; Gujeratis; Hindustanis; Marathas; Oriya; Pushtu; Punjabis; Tamils; Telegus; Urdus; plus several hundred thousand British colonists.
Religion:	many, but the army dominated by Moslem and Hindu.
Location:	South Asia.

India was the Jewel in the Crown, that is the most precious of the British possessions, more precious than the white-populated dominions, and as such British wartime strategy hovered around three points on the globe – Britain, India and the sea route between.

The British ruled much of India directly through a viceroy i.e. deputy to the Emperor of India, who was the King of England. Two armed forces protected the jewel, the British and the Indian. Many Indian princes also had their own troops, known for convenience sake as Indian States Forces (ISF).

Within the Indian armed forces all officers were white British, many born in India, but in the Indian Army there were three pseudo officer ranks specially reserved for native Indians. All non-officers were native Indians. After Britain declared war on Germany in September 1939 a few Indians were allowed to become actual officers.

Despite this structure, the Indian Army was seen by the native Indians as an honourable force and each regiment sternly guarded its ethnic make-up. Many of the regiments were raised in the north-west (subsequently known as Pakistan) among the more warlike ethnic groups. Yet the pride of the regiments, as far as some British were concerned, were the Gurkhas, and these fellows did not even come from India, but from Nepal. They were mercenaries, but served for honour not money.

Of course, within the ISF each prince could organise his own army as he saw fit.

As the war began slowly it was in fact the Indian seamen in the merchant service who were first in the front line as their ships had to dodge German mines, submarines, planes and warships.

The first test of the Indian Army came in British Somaliland, a large desert colony in east Africa, which was invaded by Italian troops in August 1940. Two Indian battalions, the local defence force and an East African battalion were ordered to delay the enemy at Tug Argan Pass and they did so. Unfortunately British Army officers decided the natives needed corseting by a British battalion, an ugly term meaning sending a brave unit to stiffen the backs of green or timid troops. If the Indians felt insulted, they made no fuss over it, but possibly smirked with slight satisfaction when the British battalion ran in their first encounter with the enemy. After a few days the mixed allied defenders were evacuated by ship. The Indians had passed their first test.

In Sudan, east Africa, an Indian reconnaissance unit harassed Italian soldiers along the Eritrean border for several months and in December two Indian battalions were ordered to assault Gallabat-Metemma, a town divided by the border. At the last minute Brigadier Slim was informed that a British battalion would corset his 10th Brigade Indians. As an Indian Army officer he was angered. His troops did very well, but the British ran – indeed some jumped into trucks and almost ran over Slim as he forlornly tried to stop them.

Like the Tug Argan Pass affair, this incident did nothing to alter the blinkered British Army opinion of the Indians.

The Indian 4th Division assembled in Egypt, its form being the basis for all other Indian divisions: 13,863 personnel divided into three infantry brigades, each of three infantry battalions (the British called them regiments), but the third battalion in each brigade was British Army (to corset the Indians), the artillery was usually British Army and most of the rear-echelon support was British, thus the divisions really were sort of half British half Indian. More often than not at least one of the Indian battalions was in fact Gurkha. Usually the divisional staff were Indian Army officers.

In December the division rode trucks into the cold windy desert and on the morning of the 9th began walking cautiously towards an Italian camp. Just as they started to take fire British tanks charged into the enemy rear. The fight lasted two hours and was indeed tough, and then suddenly the enemy, their leader killed, surrendered. Later in the day the division repeated the affair at another camp. Again the tanks of the British 7th Armoured Division did the trick.

The following day the two divisions assaulted the perimeter of the town of Sidi Barrani. After a 24-hour battle the enemy surrendered. This sortie into the desert was a great victory and it gave the Indians the morale booster they needed. At last they were doing something positive: winning. Unfortunately, the newspapers said it had all been a pushover, because the Italians wouldn't fight. The Indian division had suffered 200 killed and wounded, some of them in hand-to-hand combat.

In the Sudan the British planned an invasion of Eritrea and assembled the Indian 4th and 5th Divisions, the latter including Slim's brigade. The advance began on 19 January over terrain not much healthier looking than the Egyptian desert, thought the veterans of the 4th Division. Accompanying the two divisions were 3,200 Indian pioneers, unarmed labour troops to manhandle supplies. (Pioneers in the British Army were armed.)

The 5th Division overcame a paltry rearguard at Keru Gorge, taking a small brigade captive, and on the 27th the 4th Division reached Agordat to begin a battle. The affair lasted three days and the Indians were surprised by this. Still, the enemy then retreated abandoning more than a thousand sick and wounded. The 5th Division was stopped at Barentu, but when Agordat fell the Italians pulled out of Barentu as well.

On 4 February the 4th Division reached the rocky massif at the entrance to Keren Pass. Their assault was repelled. They were definitely up against a different breed of Italian, they decided. The 5th Division was brought up and together they tried and failed to break through. More British artillery arrived, Palestinian commandos and an artillery battery of the Jammu Kashmir ISF. To add to the misery of this static warfare it began to rain ceaselessly. Two Indians were awarded the Victoria Cross, the British Empire's highest award for courage.

It was only when British tanks arrived and British and Indian engineers and pioneers had cleared a road for them through the pass that the two divisions could advance on 27 March. Marching swiftly, the Indians took the city of Asmara easily on 1 April and attacked the port of Massawa on the 6th. Two days later the Italians surrendered. Eritrea was now British.

At once the 5th Division was ordered to make its way in trucks into Ethiopia, where an Italian force was holding out at Amba Alagi. On 4 May the divisions's 29th Brigade captured three mountain peaks in the rain and a few days later the 9th Brigade took Gumsa village, but was then forced back a hundred yards by a fierce Italian bayonet charge. On the 19th the trapped Italians surrendered.

Two battalions and the pioneers of the Indian Army remained in Ethiopia to besiege Italian diehards, while the 4th and 5th Divisions received orders for Egypt.

Eritrea/Ethiopia cost the Indian Army 740 killed and 4,045 wounded. Almost half the infantrymen had been hit.

The situation in Egypt had changed. The British had continued their advance into Libya and had destroyed the Italian Tenth Army, but two German divisions arrived under General Rommel, an expert on infantry tactics. He had launched an unauthorised offensive in April, defeated a British armoured division and by Easter had trapped an allied force, including an Indian armoured car unit and some pioneers, in Tobruk and had reached the Egyptian border. The Germans had discovered the Indian

3rd Brigade stuck out in the desert on their own and had crushed it in 24 hours.

The Indian 4th Division was told to dig in at Halfaya Pass alongside a British brigade, but the enemy chose not to advance further.

On 15 June the division's 11th Brigade launched an attack with the famed British 7th Armoured Division on their flank. The British had loaned the Indians nineteen tanks, but such were the German defences that sixteen were knocked out within two hours. After another two days of combat the generals called off the offensive. Total allied losses were less than a thousand, but the Indians could not afford any losses as they had received few replacements for their previous casualties.

In May 1941 other Indians had been introduced to war and for them it was more like an exercise – indeed training inflicted higher losses. The 21st Brigade of the 10th Division sailed to Basra, Iraq, to invade that country, but they came like tourists and were only held up by street peddlers and a few demonstrators. The British had not corseted this brigade, so all three battalions were Indian Army. Indian sappers and miners (engineers) flew north to work alongside a British land invasion from Trans-Jordan, building a bridge. Then reinforced by a Gurkha battalion this column attacked and captured the capital Baghdad against uncoordinated resistance. Total allied casualties in the campaign were less than 60.

The Indian 5th Brigade, temporarily separated from its parent 4th Division, was in Palestine taking in replacements when it was earmarked for the invasion of Pétainist-French Syria, together with a British cavalry and an allied-French and an Australian infantry divisions.

The invasion began on 8 June 1941 and at once the Pétainist French showed they would resist. The Indians, supported by an artillery battery from Jammu-Kashmir ISF did well reaching Kissoué on the 12th to aid French fighting French. Charged by Syrian horse cavalry the Indians rallied and easily beat off the courageous horsemen.

Next day they were through Mezze, but on the 19th the Indians were suddenly sur-rounded by an enemy equipped with tanks and artillery. The brigade and the Jammu-Kashmiris fought bravely, while the commander radioed for urgent reinforcements, and was told it would be the following day before anyone could reach him in this vast semi-arid desert. On the next afternoon, ammunition low and no sign of help, the commander chose to surrender: thinking his men would be liberated soon anyway. The Indians did not like the idea of surrender, but they prided themselves on obeying orders, even distasteful ones.

They were treated well by the French, but within days were put aboard ship for German and Italian prisoner of war camps. This they had not bargained for.

Meanwhile, that month the Indian 8th and 10th Divisions drove through roadside peddlers in northern Iraq to advance over the Syrian border. On 3 July the 21st Brigade (Slim's new command) attacked Deir ez Zor, took it in hours and drove on up the valley of the Euphrates heading for Raqqa and Jer-ablus. Near the Turkish border the 17th Brigade of the 8th Division conquered several forts.

On 10 July the Pétainist French in Syria surrendered. Part of the terms were that they should request all prisoners to be returned. The Germans and Italians honoured the agreement and returned the men of the Indian 5th Brigade.

Days later the Indian 8th and 10th Divisions were given a new mission: conquer Iran.

On 25 August the 8th Division sailed to the port of Bandur Shapur, climbed into small boats and moved to the shore amidst a naval battle. In hours they eliminated all resistance and headed inland. On the 27th they found a rearguard at Paytak Pass and overcame it in an hour.

The 10th Division invaded Iran from Iraq, taking Kermanshah by the 28th, the day the Iranian government capitulated.

Total allied casualties in Iran were less than 50.

In Egypt all allied forces were reconstituted as the British Eighth Army with the mission of rescuing the Tobruk garrison, whose composition had changed – the allies could still reach it by sea.

A preliminary move was a ride into the great desert for the 29th Brigade of the 5th Division to capture an Italian fort at Jalo. The Indians proved to be excess baggage, as the tiny garrison surrendered.

On the quiet front the 4th Division had still not received full replacements and was still short of the 5th Brigade. This was obviously a bad allocation of manpower.

The rescue was launched on 17 November by the Indian 4th, South African 1st, New Zealand 2nd and British 7th Armoured Divisions. Indian armoured cars spearheaded the advance into the desert, while the 4th Division attacked the bypassed Italian Savona Division around Sidi Barrani, which these men had conquered once already eleven months earlier. The Italians resisted stoutly, much differently than in the first battle here and, in early December the 4th Division, after repelling an attack by the German 21st Panzer Division, was ordered to follow the main advance into the desert in trucks. The 11th Brigade ran into stiff Italian opposition at Bir el Gubi on the 4th and the next day was attacked in flank by German tanks. Whole companies were overrun and the survivors jumped into trucks and fled to the east.

Notwithstanding this, the Germans and Italians were in full retreat by this stage until they reached the Gazala line. On the 13th the Eighth Army attacked the new enemy position: the 4th Division, seriously depleted by now, charging against the guns of the Italian Trieste Division. They gained only a few hundred yards, but on the 15th the enemy retreated again.

Indian armoured cars chased the enemy and nipped at their heels over the next two weeks reaching Benghazi on Christmas day. During this time the Indian 4th Division tried to regroup. During the month-long affair they had inflicted a thousand casualties on the enemy, captured 6,000, destroyed 51 tanks and shot down 27 planes, but the infantry companies were sadly shrunk by now, the whole division fielding only about 2,000 riflemen.

During 1941 the British had been concerned about Japan joining Germany, but when the Japanese invaded British Malaya on 8 December without warning it still came as a shock. The key to the British presence in Malaya was Singapore, home of the Far East Fleet, for the British believed the jungle mountains in Malaya itself would hinder any invader too much for that route to be taken seriously. Thus when the Japanese landed in northern Malaya, at first the British felt extremely confident.

In Malaya the ground forces were strong: in the north Indian Army IIIrd Corps made up of the 9th and 11th Divisions and 12th and 28th Brigades; in the south the Australian 8th and Malayan 1st Divisions. However, this was a real motley crew. The two Indian divisions only had two infantry brigades each (the third battalion in each was made up of British corseting troops, of course), and the IIIrd Corps also controlled a good deal of locally recruited militia. The Indian Army had to loan two battalions to the Malayan Division. The chief artillery component of the defences was the Hong Kong and Singapore Regiment of six field gun, seven flak and one coastal gun batteries. Though a British Army regiment, its personnel were recruited in India. The colony also had a police force heavily recruited in India.

The 9th Division counter-attacked the invaders on the 8th, but they could not prevent the enemy build up. Two days later they heard that the two capital ships of the fleet had been sunk by Japanese planes. This was a tremendous psychological blow to the generals, even if the ordinary infantry did not understand the significance.

On the 12th Indian IIIrd Corps was ordered to retreat, and within hours the men were trudging along muddy jungle trails in the monsoon rain, half-drowning in rushing streams and turning their gaze away from the despondent villagers. On the 16th they abandoned Penang. At the end of the month the Indians rested near Kuantan, disheartened, sick and exhausted after a 200-mile retreat.

Reinforcements arrived: the Indian 17th Division (with only two brigades) and elements of the 19th Division. At this time the men heard that Hong Kong had fallen. That garrison had included two Indian battalions and Indian-manned artillery of the Hong

Kong and Singapore Artillery Regiment plus British and Canadians. It was not known at the time that of the Indians most, 1,826, had fought to the death.

The retreat resumed almost at once and every day some unfortunate unit was ordered to hold a rearguard, virtually a suicide mission. In one such incident a battalion commander won the Victoria Cross.

The Indians tried to hold the Perak River, but were outflanked by Japanese in the mountains. Falling back to near the Slim River the 11th Division tried to grab some sleep, but the enemy broke past them and seized a bridge: 4,000 men of the division were cut off and abandoned.

Further Japanese amphibious invasions on the coasts outflanked any chance of making a stand and on 31 January 1942 the Indians walked over the causeway to Singapore. This 20-by-12-mile island was their last hope for survival.

On paper the defences looked strong. The north coast was swamp and not ideal for an invasion. To defend this coast General Percival put in the fresh Malayan and British 18th and battle-weary Australian 8th and Indian 11th Divisions. In reserve were the Indian 9th and 17th Divisions and 12th and 28th Brigades, Malayan and Singapore militia and a battalion each from the Indian 'princely states' of Bhawmagar, Hyderabad, Jhind, Kapurthala and Mysore. In terms of infantry battalions there were twenty Indian, fifteen British, seven Australian and five local.

On the night of 8 February three Japanese divisions (equivalent to six allied) landed on the north coast. Their losses at the hands of rifles, machine guns, mortars and artillery were devastating, but they kept coming and by dawn the allies were falling back. In truth there was no leadership, as the British high command had seemingly been paralysed since the loss of the two warships. Few orders made sense, and with every step back the defenders knew they were signing their own death warrant, for the island just wasn't that big. On the 15th General Percival surrendered.

To the people of India, the report of the fall of Hong Kong was bad enough, but the loss of Singapore was devastating news. It would have been even more demoralising had the British released the casualty statistics: 67,450 Indians were dead or missing. Certainly the British emissaries were embarrassed when they had to visit the Indian 'princes' to inform them that their armies had been 'misplaced'.

To add to the depression was fear, for the Japanese had also invaded Burma. The first real encounter took place in January. Hitherto only the Burma police (mostly manned by Indians) had sighted the invader along the thick jungle border. This month the Indian 16th Brigade fought a brief encounter and then fell back under orders.

On 9 February the Indian 46th Brigade was attacked on the Salween River and according to plan withdrew at once towards the Bilin River. The commander requested permission to withdraw further, to avoid being outflanked in this large territory, but was told to hold on. He disobeyed orders and retreated and then blew up the bridge, but this left 4,000 men stranded on the eastern bank! They swam across, but of course lost all their equipment.

On 7 March the British decided on a full-scale retreat from Burma towards India. As the artillery, engineers and rear-echelon forces withdrew the infantry – eleven Indian, eleven British and four Burmese battalions – alternated rearguards. The Indians were overtaken near Shwedaung and lost 300 men, but fought their way out courtesy of British tanks.

In mid-May the emaciated survivors reached India and slept as the monsoon rains began. The Japanese did not follow. The Indian troops still had their pride, but faith in their white masters was ebbing. They had just participated in the longest retreat in British military history, a thousand miles. It had cost 10,000 casualties and every survivor was crippled with exhaustion, jungle sores and disease.

In Libya the Indian 4th Division was not given much of a rest, for the enemy counterattacked on 25 January 1942. Ordered to retreat to Barce, some members of the division were caught by a German tank column. Elsewhere the 7th Brigade only escaped by sacrificing a rearguard. By February the division had withdrawn all the way back to Gazala, where they found that a thousand men were missing.

The 4th Division was given three months of rest after this, and the only Indians now at the 'front' was a new 3rd Brigade. They were stuck out in a camp on their own in exactly the same way as their previous namesake.

On 26 May the Germans and Italians launched a new offensive and within two days had defeated the 7th Armoured Division. If this could happen to such a powerful unit, then the members of the 3rd Brigade must have wondered what chance they might have. They should have received orders to retreat or join the main defenders on the Gazala Line, but the army's leadership was paralysed. On the 28th the Indians were attacked by the Italian Ariete Armoured Division and overrun in hours. However, the Italians decided they did not have sufficient food for all their prisoners, so they let 600 go!

Eighth Army ordered the Indian 5th Division to man the next defensive position and on 5 June the Indians, rather than wait for the enemy, advanced themselves with the 9th Brigade against Aslagh Ridge, taking it from the Ariete's infantry. Instantly German and Italian tanks counter-attacked them: two British tank brigades were brought up, but the end result was defeat for the allies. The following day the 10th Brigade stood its ground while the remainder of the 5th Division retreated. The brigade was overwhelmed by enemy tanks.

The 5th Division had suffered 4,000 killed or missing in two days! Nearby 400 unarmed Indian pioneers were scooped up by the enemy. On the 15th the 5th Division left a battalion rearguard: a move which simply put another 800 Indians into prisoner of war cages. Next day the division's 29th Brigade was caught by the German 90th Division, but managed to escape come nightfall, but elsewhere this day another Indian battalion rearguard was overrun by the German 21st Panzer division.

On the 17th the fresh Indian 20th Brigade of the 10th Division was assaulted by the 15th and 21st Panzer divisions: few escaped.

The 4th Division's 11th Brigade took refuge in Tobruk, feeling secure because the previous year the port had held out for eight months. On the 20th the perimeter came under German and Italian attack and the Indians bore the brunt of the assault by the 15th and 21st Panzer, 90th and Ariete Armoured Divisions. Miraculously they held until nightfall. Next morning some tanks broke through and late in the morning the garrison was informed the commander had surrendered. The Indians could not believe it. In fact a few Gurkhas refused to give up and fought to the death.

The whole enemy offensive had been a fiasco for the allies. The commander of the Eighth Army was relieved and General Auchinleck, Middle East commander, took personal charge, drawing a line in the sand at Alamein and implying 'no further'. Retreating past Mersa Matruh still 120 miles west of Alamein were the Indian 10th Division and the 5th Brigade. Scattered remnants of the Indian 29th Brigade, a pitiful shadow of its former self, were overrun in the desert like they didn't exist.

On the 30th the allies finally reached the Alamein Line, held by the Indian 8th Division.

The line was a series of flat camps and in one of these was the 8th Division's 18th Brigade. On 1 July the 15th and 21st Panzer Divisions slaughtered the brigade, but the battle did delay the Germans, who themselves were exhausted, and bought time for the British to bring up tanks. Thus the sacrifice of the brigade was not in vain, although the 8th Division suffered more losses this day than in its invasions of Iraq, Syria and Iran put together!

Next day the 5th Brigade was attacked, but with British aid they survived and beat off the Germans on the 4th. The enemy came on again on the 9th, but the allies held them at bay.

On the 14th the 5th Brigade and 2nd New Zealand Division were ordered to attack the Italian Brescia Division that night, when they would be reinforced by the British 1st Armoured Division. After a two-mile walk in the dark towards Ruweisat Ridge they broke into the enemy camp and fought until dawn, but there was no sign of British tanks. By that afternoon they had captured 700 prisoners, but lost 400 of their own captured, such was the confusion of the battle which they fought on their bellies in flat sand. When German tanks approached the allied troops ran for it.

Auchinleck ordered another try, this time by different New Zealanders and the Indian 161st Brigade. In the dark they walked straight into an enemy attack. One battalion of the 161st was severely mauled. At the end of July the fightng ceased.

All the Indian units requested replacements from India and Britain as their losses had been catastrophic.

A new commander arrived for the Eighth Army, General B. L. Montgomery (Monty), who at once restored the spirit of the troops with his memos, orders, and personal visits. This soon showed when the enemy came on again after a month. The Indian 5th Division, most of its ranks filled with newcomers, was attacked by the Italian Bologna Division, but the attacking nfantry did not press the attack, preferring to rely on outflanking tank forces, but the enemy tanks were defeated and by 7 September the firing died down. There was no doubt that the next battle would begin with an allied offensive.

The Eighth Army put ten rested divisions and two brigades into the line, including the Indian 4th Division, with three British armoured divisions in immediate reserve. Among the rear-echelon troops were 15,000 Indian pioneers.

The Eighth Army advanced after a twenty-minute artillery barrage on the night of 23 October. By dawn the Indian 4th Division was between Ruweisat Ridge and Miteiriya Ridge battling the Bologna Division and German paratroopers. On the 25th the Indians were told to go over to nuisance attacks only. Monty was not a broad front man and liked little set piece battles. The combination of this tactic, good military intelligence, superior air power and heavy firepower on the ground forced the enemy to began a full-scale retreat on 4 November. This third battle on the Alamein Line was the turning point in the war for Africa.

Unfortunately Monty was as methodical in movement as he was on the battlefield and this enabled the Germans and Italians to escape all the way to Tunisia, which was attacked from the west by an Anglo-American-French army in early December.

Monty did not have anyone present in Tunisia until 16 February 1943, and it was 20 March before he was able to attack. The Indian 4th Division was here and sort of went along for the ride when a makeshift corps attempted an outflanking manoeuvre. The advance was slow, but an advance it was.

The enemy fell back to a four-mile-wide coastal plain at Wadi Akarit. This is where Monty could use his talents. In the early hours of 5 April he sent the 4th Division into the mountains to outflank the enemy. In pitch blackness two Indian, a Gurkha and two British battalions crept into the Italian lines on cliff edges and overcame them, usually with the blade. It was so dark they had to feel for the headgear of a potential victim to identify him. One Gurkha earned the Victoria Cross with his kukri knife. Come dawn the outflanked enemy withdrew northwards.

Monty was now impatient and on the 29th ordered the Indian 4th and 2nd New Zealand Divisions to assault the new enemy position, the Enfidaville Line. The commanders did not want to, believing the enemy was still too strong for a frontal assault. Monty overruled them, the attack went in and gained only casualties.

Asked to provide his two best divisions to help the British First Army in west Tunisia he sent the 7th Armoured and the Indian 4th. On 5 May they attacked from Medjez el Bab towards Tunis and Cape Bon Peninsula. Entering Tunis on the 7th and the peninsula on the 8th the Indians took the surrender of General von Arnim, commander of all enemy forces in Africa, on the 12th.

It was justice that the two allied divisions that began the North African (Egypt-Libya-Tunisia) campaign were the two that finished it. This campaign had cost the Indian brigades and divisions 22,000 killed, wounded and captured, of which about 15,000 were members of the Indian Army.

This victory was important for the British in that it reaffirmed the belief that they just might win this war after all. They needed to impress this upon the people of India, for the defeats and abandonment of 80,000 of India's sons to enemy prison camps had cut to the very bone of 'white supremacy'. Most of these men had been ordered to surrender by white officers who had no other ideas. It also seemed to them the British were using Indians as cannon fodder.

German and Japanese propaganda fed on these opinions and fuelled anti-British feeling, while their secret emissaries met with Indian nationalists. One of the militant nationalists Chandra Bose came to the conclusion that whatever the Germans and Japanese wanted, it wasn't India. Only the Indians and British wanted that sub-continent. Therefore, anyone who fought alongside the Germans and Japanese was not helping them but helping India. He and his agent visited axis prisoner of war camps and gained 2,000 volunteers from men captured in North Africa to create the German-uniformed Indian Legion. The force never saw serious combat and was used for propaganda purposes until the end of the war.

From fellows in Japanese prison camps he gained over 20,000 volunteers for the Indian National Liberation Army. It must be remembered that conditions in Japanese camps were inhumane in the extreme.

Within India there was considerable unrest manifesting itself by riots, demonstrations and strikes. At one time the British and Indian Armies had 57 infantry battalions employed on internal security. To add to the fears of the people, the Japanese began air raids on Calcutta, Chittagong and other east coast towns.

Not least of the problems was famine. The vast population of India always lived on a knife-edge between plenty and starvation, and the loss of Burma, the world's greatest rice-exporting nation, cut off many Indians from their source of staple diet. There is no question that the British worked wonders, assisted by Americans, to feed the most threatened people in the north-east, at the same time as building barracks there, erecting camps, filling supply dumps, creating roads, constructing 220 airfields, laying rail track and feeding three quarters of a million soldiers and hundreds of thousands of Indi-

an workers. Yet, an estimated 1,500,000 people died of famine-related illnesses.

On the India-Burma border the Indian IVth Corps was stationed in Manipur State and the XVth Corps in the Arakan on the coast. At the end of 1942 the British launched what they called an offensive, but it was really a probe into the Arakan by four British and two Indian infantry battalions of the Indian 14th Division with a host of Indian and Burmese porters. Only after three months did the Japanese do something about it – they surrounded them. The Indian 26th Division marched up to provide an assembly point for those who broke out of the trap. At the end of April 1943 the 'offensive' was called off: losses had been 221 Indian and 171 British killed and slightly less for the Japanese, high for those engaged, but hardly likely to shake the foundations of the Japanese Empire.

The Indian 17th and 20th Divisions provided security for workers and army pioneers and engineers, who built two roads into west central Burma. Only the odd Japanese patrol interfered. A Gurkha Victoria Cross was earned in one such encounter.

On 3 September 1943 the British Eighth Army invaded the toe of Italy. The few Italians in the neighbourhood actually aided the invaders. Six days later US Fifth Army invaded at Salerno. They were met by German troops who fought back with a vengeance. Among the troops on the beach was a battalion of Jodhpur Sardar ISF.

The Eighth Army crept northwards – 'crept' is a good word here – and did not encounter a real battle until reaching the Trigno River in October. The Indian 8th Division attacked on the 22nd. After Alamein the division had not rebuilt its 18th Brigade, but had acquired a new brigade instead, corseted of course, but the division had few British as most of the division's non-infantry personnel were Indians. After two weeks of combat the Germans leisurely withdrew 25 miles to the Sangro River.

On 28 November the army launched an attack over the Sangro. The 8th Division fought its way across and in eight days pushed the enemy back about ten miles.

From then on the going got even tougher: e.g. the Indians took three days to clear the village of Villagrande. Only on 28 December did the Germans withdraw, and then only ten miles to the Riccio River.

The Indian 4th Division arrived to join the mud crawl up the Italian boot and on 11 February 1944 slipped into the foxholes of the worn out US 36th Division at Cassino, where the US Fifth Army had been stopped for two months. As the 7th Brigade was relieving the Americans the enemy attacked. It was a rough couple of hours until the Germans retired. The terrain was so rugged the entire 11th Brigade was used for porters.

The Indians attacked on the 14th and instantly they realised why the Americans had taken so many losses. The Indians were grateful to be able to scramble back to their foxholes. Three battalions suffered 441 casualties. Now came the hardest part, waiting to attack again. Each quiet day at Cassino the division lost sixty men!

The next attempt came on 15 March. For eight days they fought to their limits, one force stuck out so far in front they had to be supplied by parachute. When the generals called off the failed offensive the division counted casualties of 132 killed, 792 wounded and 155 missing.

By the end of April the area just west of Cassino was given to the 8th Division, which was comparatively fresh having only fought four one-day battles since December.

At the end of 1943 the Indian Army had grown considerably. The India-Burma border was now manned by the British Fourteenth Army commanded by none other than General Slim. Up front he had the Indian IVth Corps in the centre, with the 17th, 20th and 23rd Divisions, and the Indian XVth Corps in the Arakan, with the 5th and 7th Divisions and British 81st West African Division. In reserve were the Indian 26th Division and 254th Tank Brigade. In theory he had control of the Chinese forces in northern Burma, but they did what they liked.

In November 1943 another Arakan offensive began, not much larger than the previous one and it only encountered opposition after a week from Japanese and Indian National Liberation Army. By January 1944 the XVth Corps had suffered about 300 losses when the Japanese repeated their manoeuvre of the year before, surrounding the Indian 5th and 7th Divisions in pockets. However, this time the men were told to stand firm and they would be supplied by parachute. The bold plan worked and it was the Japanese who were forced to retreat after three weeks. The Indians counted 4,600 enemy corpses in front of their lines. The 5th Division lost 1,610 casualties and the 7th had 647. This was the first British victory over the Japanese and its effect on allied morale was out of all proportion to its effect on the Japanese.

In central Burma allied Chindit brigades moved behind Japanese lines by glider and began to raise hell through sabotage and truck convoy ambushes. Indian engineers and three Gurkha battalions were among the Chindits.

On 11 May 1944 another Cassino offensive was launched and this one succeeded. The Indian 8th Division crossed the Garigliano River under fire, succeeding because of heroism – one Indian received the Victoria Cross – and on the night of the 16th some of the men had to climb a cliff face to capture a village perched on a mountain top. Village after village, ridge after ridge, they advanced.

The rear-echelon troops had it rough too: 10,000 of them were Indian pioneers, several of whom won medals for heroism and three companies were mentioned in despatches for their bravery. In fact the main highway was officially rechristened Pioneer Way. Indians also brought supplies up to the front by mule – suffering casualties of 150 men and 500 mules killed in action.

By late June the 8th Division was on the shore of Lake Trasimene earning another Victoria Cross. On 10 July the division was diverted to take Arezzo, a tough nut to crack. Only on the 16th did the Germans pull out. It seemed to the Indians there was always one more hill, one more river, another village identical to the previous one.

The 4th Division did not go back into action until August just south of Bagnio, while the 10th Division entered the line high in the Apennines on the right flank of the 8th Division. The Indian Army 43rd Brigade was in reserve, thus three of the seventeen allied divisions in Italy were Indian.

In one instance, an enemy ambush, the 4th Division lost 70 casualties and blamed it on an allied reconnaissance unit of Italian soldiers. In truth it was simply hard for these veterans of Africa to come to terms with Italians as allies, especially as villagers often treated them like lepers – superstitious Italian women were afraid of Moslems or anyone who looked like a Moslem.

On 30 August the 4th Division pierced the Gothic Line, which, though the Germans had been building it for a year, was not as formidable as expected, but it did provide the Germans with a rallying point. One Gurkha company lost 75% casualties piercing it – they did not think it was poorly defended. In late September the 4th Division left Italy and liberated the nation of San Marino: one Gurkha earned the Victoria Cross; few of the troops realised this was a separate nation.

On 3 October while the 8th Division was fighting hard for Cavallara and the 10th Division was approaching the Fiumicino River, the 4th Division was pulled out for a rest. In its seven weeks of advancing a mile a day it had suffered 1,892 casualties: many companies were at half strength. With the 10th Division were an ISF battalion each from Nabha Akal and Jaipur.

In October the allies called a halt, but this did not stop small actions and daily barrages. The 8th Division fought on Monte San Bartolo for a week earning another Victoria Cross.

It was late November before the allies were ready again, but both 8th and 10th Divisions only made slow progress and in mid-December everyone was ordered to shut down for winter. A feeble enemy counter-attack at Christmas called the 4th Division to the line for a few days. Then the enemy too recognised the value of a quiet winter.

Slim had probed the western Burmese jungle with his IVth Corps and found no opposition until 9 March 1944 when an enemy column was sighted. Over the next few days others were seen and then it suddenly became clear

to his intelligence officers: three divisions (equivalent to six allied) had crossed the mighty Chindwin and had infiltrated into the rear of IVth Corps. Moreover, they had a two-week head start on the march to India.

Slim ordered the 5th and 7th Divisions to drop everything in the Arakan and fly up to the central Burma-India border. They were relieved by the 25th and 26th and British 36th Divisions. IVth Corps was ordered to retreat into India at once to Imphal.

On the 19th the border town of Ukruhl was attacked by a Japanese column. The garrison – an Indian infantry battalion and a parachute battalion, a Gurkha parachute battalion, some Indian and British artillery and police and rear-echelon personnel – frantically put up a makeshift defence for three days inflicting 400 casualties on the invaders, before retreating to Sanshak. Repelling assaults for another four days they then obeyed orders, destroyed their guns and, carrying their wounded in stretchers, followed local Naga tribesmen guides to retreat into the forest. They had suffered 808 casualties.

Imphal was reinforced with a third of the 5th, the 17th and 20th and elements of the 23rd Divisions, plus a battalion of Patiala ISF and the survivors from Ukruhl. In early April they were assaulted by the Japanese.

Kohima was also attacked. Here lay a brand new battalion of Assamese, the first infantry raised in that Indian province, who had yet to be trained. Together with their instructors and the local police they were astonished to see the Japanese walk in on 4 April. Reinforced in the nick of time by a British battalion they held off the enemy until nightfall. Two miles away at Jatsoma two Indian battalions of the 161st Brigade were surrounded and assaulted. The combat lasted two weeks and only on the 17th could the men at Jatsoma link up with Kohima. The defence of Kohima was heroic to say the least, for 2,000 troops, half of them raw, had fought off 10,000 Japanese for a loss of 400 casualties. The 161st Brigade suffered 300 casualties.

The British 2nd Division finally rescued the small force and counter-attacked. It took the British six weeks, 2,779 casualties and a reinforcement of two battalions of the Indian 7th Division, and their 623 casualties, to get the Japanese to move.

Therefore, by May a Japanese division had been stopped at Kohima-Jatsoma and the two others had been stopped at Imphal, where four Victoria Crosses were earned. However, it was only on 8 July that the Japanese called it quits and retreated from India. The Indian 5th, British 2nd and East African 11th Divisions followed them.

At Imphal the Indian 17th Division had suffered 4,134 casualties; the 20th Division 2,887; the 23rd Division 2,494; the 5th Division 1,603; and corps headquarters 677.

In addition to killed and wounded, all units suffered a high rate of sick, so that in the last stages of the battle companies were at platoon strength. The allies inflicted 66,000 killed on the Japanese, who retreated in such a state that many rearguards were taken alive: an unheard of thing.

In December the 5th Division was finally told to stop chasing the Japanese and rest. This year many of its companies had had a complete turnover in personnel. It was relieved by the 20th Division.

Slim's strategy now was for the 20th Division to make for Shwebo and the 19th Division for Pinlebu, under Indian XXXIIIrd Corps command. Slim hoped he could encircle the enemy on the Shwebo Plain and finish him off with tanks – he had always wanted to fight a tank battle. Pinlebu was taken on 19 December and the Irrawaddy reached by New Year. In 30 days the corps had advanced 270 miles, the swiftest movement in Burma to date. However, the Japanese fell back, denying him his tank battle. The 19th Division failed in its first attempt to cross the Irrawaddy: was successful in its second.

By 12 January the allies were now advancing southwards through Burma: Indian XVth Corps of 82nd West African and Indian 25th Divisions, Indian 50th Tank Brigade and British commando brigade along the coast: a hundred miles to their east Indian IVth Corps of British 2nd and Indian 7th and 17th Divisions, and 28th East African, Indian 268th, Burmese Lushai and Indian 255th Tank Brigades; 75 miles to their east Indian XXXIIIrd Corps of the Indian 19th and 20th and British 36th Divisions; 75 miles to

their east Chinese First Army of five divisions and an American divisional-sized unit; and 40 miles east of them Chinese Y Force.

Obviously if the Japanese could have concentrated on one of these invasions they could have defeated the entire offensive, but continuous pressure by the spearhead battalions, allied air power, including Indian squadrons, and Burmese guerrillas made sure the Japanese could not reassemble. Additionally, the allies had an ace up their sleeve: a fleet. At last the British had brought sufficient vessels including 26 Indian Navy warships to the Bay of Bengal and were readying an amphibious invasion of Burma at Rangoon. In January the 25th Division used the fleet to land on the coast at Akyab and Myebon. Informed that the Rangoon landing would take place in May just before the monsoon, which would slow Slim's advance to a crawl, Slim urged his men on. He wanted the Fourteenth Army to gain the laurels of conquering Burma. Thus the race to Rangoon was born.

By February the 25th Division had cleared the islands as far as Cheduba, the 82nd Division had taken Buthidaung and Kangaw, the 268th Brigade cleared Sabaing and the 255th Tank Brigade captured Mahlaing. But Rangoon was still 300 miles away.

On 9 March the 19th Division captured the great Burmese city of Mandalay, though a fort held out until the 20th and IVth Corps had to call up the 5th Division to fight off a Japanese surprise counter-attack. It took a month of terrible combat to defeat the Japanese here, while the 20th Division bypassed a Japanese force that had held them up several days.

Following this attempt to turn the tide the Japanese gave up and ran for it in April. IVth Corps, now with 5th, 17th and 19th Divisions and 255th Tank Brigade charged ahead, as did XXXIIIrd Corps with 7th and 20th Divisions and 254th Tank Brigade. By the 22nd 17th Division was at Toungoo, 150 miles from Rangoon.

The invasion fleet sailed on the 27th. On May Day, as the 17th Division cleared Pegu 45 miles from Rangoon, the Indian 50th Parachute Brigade jumped onto Elephant Point to secure it without resistance so that the fleet could enter Rangoon harbour.

The following day the monsoon arrived and the rains slowed down Slim's advance. Next day the fleet sailed into Rangoon, soldiers of the 26th Division jumping onto the docks to find grateful civilians. The Japanese had fled. The land advance, spearheaded by the 255th Tank Brigade was twenty miles north of the city.

In Italy the allies had planned a spring 1945 offensive that hopefully would liberate Italy from the Germans and fascists. Among the twenty-one Allied divisions were the Indian 8th and 10th.

The offensive began on 9 April, with the 8th Division aiming straight for Bologna. Resistance was heavy for a day: then the enemy fell back relying on rearguards; two Victoria Crosses were earned. On the 12th the 10th Division joined the advance on Bologna. They eventually reached the city, but at the same time as half a dozen other divisions, each one claiming to have liberated the great city. After this it was simply a matter of running to catch up with the Germans. On 2 May the enemy surrendered all forces in Italy.

The Italian campaign had cost the Indian Army 4,255 killed and 22,745 wounded: about 80% casualties among the assault troops.

The liberation of Rangoon was not the end of the Burma campaign, for thousands of Japanese were trapped west of the easternmost allied formation. Running for the Salween and Sittang Rivers, they hoped to reach Thailand and safety, where they could regroup into a formidable army again. Obviously the allies could not allow this to happen. Fortunately intelligence learned where a major portion of the enemy was going to try to cross the Sittang: a point 25 miles north east of Pegu. The 17th Division was ordered to lie in wait while others closed in and air power savaged the mass of enemy soldiers.

On 3 July the 17th Division was attacked by the retreating Japanese. The slaughter was horrific and after six days the 48th Brigade was surrounded and had to be supplied by parachute. Only on the 27th did the enemy cease attacking. The Indians counted 16,919 enemy dead and took 1,401 alive. Allied losses were 97 killed and 322 wounded.

Nineteen days later Japan surrendered and the war was over.

In Burma and India 1941-1945 the Indian armed forces suffered 8,000 killed. Other allied forces including British units in Indian formations lost 6,500 killed. Quite obviously without the Indian Army there would have been no Burma campaign.

Total war losses for the Indian armed forces were 36,092 killed, of which 10,000 were Gurkhas and 700 white officers, and 63,000 wounded. Indian civilians lost in air raids, cross-fire and the famine over 1,500,000 dead.

The 2,000 Indians who had joined the Germans survived and were peacefully captured. The Japanese-controlled Indian National Liberation Army lost 400 battle deaths, 1,500 non-battle deaths (starvation and disease), 2,000 wounded, 800 captured and 715 missing.

The British planned to execute these fellows as traitors, but there was a general outcry in India. Gandhi, the great pacifist nationalist, claimed these men had fought for India. The British backed down. Indeed the new Labour Party government in Britain began a process of granting independence to the Indian sub-continent.
See Index

INDO-CHINA

Other names:	includes Cambodia, Laos and Vietnam.
Status in 1939:	French colony.
Government in 1939:	French administration.
Population in 1939:	27,000,000
Make-up in 1939:	Vietnamese 17,500,000; Cambodians 6,000,000; Laotians 600,000; French colonists 80,000; Chinese in cities; scores of smaller ethnic groups.
Religion:	Mostly Buddhist and Christian.
Location:	South-East Asia.

When France declared war on Germany in 1939 Indo-Chinese natives were encouraged to volunteer for the French forces, to be assigned jobs according to merit not race, though the officers were all French. A few reached France in time to be handed to the Germans by the government's surrender in June 1940.

The surrender must have had an air of fantasy about it in Indo-China, for nothing changed here. Nothing, that is, until 22 September 1940, when Vietnam was suddenly attacked without warning by Japanese aircraft and a coastal invasion. The French had 50,000 troops, 12,000 of them white, and most were stationed in northern Vietnam so they sprung to their defences at once. The fighting was quite severe.

During the battle the Japanese Army put pressure on their government, which requested their friend Hitler to intervene, who asked Pétain the French head of state to do something, who ordered his forces in Indo-China to accept 40,000 Japanese as guests! The Japanese took over the bases they needed and both armies settled down to a truce. The 48-hour war cost the defenders 800 killed and 2,000 wounded. Now the people of Indo-China learned the shame of defeat.

In November 1940 Thailand thought it could mimic the Japanese and invaded Cambodia. There were few defenders here, but they easily repelled the Thais. Over the next two months Thai planes bombed several Cambodian towns and the small French air force retaliated. In January a French naval flotilla sailed to Koh Chang Island and sank five Thai warships.

Following this the Japanese stepped in, not wishing to see a yellow-skinned nation defeated by a white-skinned nation. By the same diplomatic route as before Pétain was induced to tell his troops to pull back and let the Thais have five Cambodian and Laotian provinces. French casualties were less than 200 killed and wounded in the war.

On 24 July 1941 using the same diplomatic route the Japanese forced the French into letting them have control over major elements of the colony's life: such as the transportation network. The people were quite aware that the Japanese were stealing their natural resources, such as rice and rubber, and this meant they intended to expand their empire.

In response, Britain, the USA and the Netherlands East Indies cut off all oil exports to Japan and closed the Panama Canal to Japanese ships.

The locals were correct in their assumptions. In December 1941 Japanese troop transports sailed from Vietnamese ports to launch an invasion of Thailand and British Malaya. Japan also attacked the USA.

In October 1943 American planes bombed Japanese targets at Haiphong and Hanoi. From now on air raids continued and spread. French warships, technically neutral, were hit: fortunately, naval casualties were insignificant. Moreover. the combination of Japanese theft of food, Japanese orders to plant crops they needed rather than food for the locals, and the disruption of the transportation network by bombing, condemned many regions to malnutrition.

Furthermore, the Japanese conscripted villagers: women and men to work as absolute slaves on bridge building, rail track laying and other labour-intensive projects. To refuse meant instant death. To accept meant slow death. Women were also kidnapped for prostitution.

Guerrilla bands appeared, soon coordinated by an ex-London waiter by the name of Ho Chi Minh. In early 1945 his guerrillas received help from American agents.

Despite mass starvation in the countryside, the French in the cities ate well, and on 9 March 1945 several officers were invited to dinner by their Japanese counterparts. Not much past the first course the officers were arrested and taken outside to be shot and beheaded. Simultaneously, French barracks were attacked. A hundred légionnaires at Lang Son were massacred. Others were murdered at Ha Giang and Hanoi. The Dong Nang barracks resisted for three days. The 2,000 troops of General Alessandri at Tony chose to march to allied China – it was only 500 miles of enemy-occupied jungle – but he told his native troops to doff their uniforms and melt into the population. The remainder began the march, picked up others along the way at Dien Bien Phu and fought their way to China at Tsao-Pao by 16 June.

This despicable act of Japanese treachery killed 4,200 French-uniformed servicemen and imprisoned thousands.

On 15 August Japan surrendered to the allies. Immediately, Chinese troops invaded from the north to commandeer Japanese weapons, while Ho Chi Minh seized political control. Southern Vietnam was invaded by British Empire forces who imprisoned the Japanese and released the French. However, native nationalists demonstrated that the French troops should not be re-armed and that Vietnam should become independent. The British responded by clamping down on the demonstrators, re-arming the French and even re-arming the Japanese to aid them!

On 25 October French forces arrived from France to begin taking over the colony. The Japanese were then repatriated to Japan.

In terms of human suffering two points are worthy of note: the indigenous people lost an excessively high number of lives as a result of the Japanese invasion to cross-fire, Japanese air raids, allied air raids, Japanese brutality and the combined effects on the food chain, maybe totalling as high as a million; the second point is that for this region World War II proved to be a launching pad for a half century of massacre and conflict (still extant at the time of writing).
See Index

IRAN

Other names:	Persia
Status in 1940:	independent.
Government in 1940:	dictatorship by self-styled Caesar.
Population in 1940:	16,500,000.
Make-up in 1940:	Persians 10,000,000; plus several major groups such as: Arabs; Assyrians; Azerbaijainis; Baluchis; Kurds; Turkmen.
Religion:	Moslem.
Location:	Middle East.

In 1941 there was a movement in Iran to nationalise the nation's oil resources, in belated response to the exploitation of them by Britain. Even the remote chance that this could happen scared the hell out of Churchill, the Prime Minister of a Britain cur-

rently locked in a life or death struggle with nazi Germany. Therefore, he negotiated with Stalin, the dictator of the USSR, to seize Iran. Stalin did not need asking twice: conquering innocent nations had become his favourite pastime.

On 25 August 1941 the USSR's Red Army invaded the north-west of the nation at Maku and Ardebil and the north-east at Banda Shah, while the British invaded from Iraq aiming towards Kermanshah and Ahwaz and by sea at Bandur Shapur. British planes preceded their troops dropping leaflets to inform the Iranians this was not an invasion at all, but a sort of social visit. British paratroopers dropped near the housing estates of foreign oilfield workers.

Offshore six Iranian warships challenged the might of the British Royal Navy: two were blown out of the water and four crippled and captured. Ashore Iranian naval personnel resisted – an admiral died fighting.

The British planes ceased their reliance on leaflets, when Iranian flak guns opened fire and six fighters rose to challenge them. The six were shot down and the British began dropping bombs.

In the south the Iranian Army withdrew to Paytak Pass, where they were bombed for a day and then assaulted on the 27th. They collapsed at once. The defenders of Kermanshah surrendered on the 28th and this day the Shah (Caesar) of Iran surrendered to the invaders.

Iranian forces had suffered a few hundred killed and wounded in the short war.

The USSR took over northern Iran, the British central and southern Iran, and in 1942 American troops came in to help run the oilfields. Many Iranians had refused to work for the invaders and allied troops had to do the job. This was an inglorious way to spend the war, so the British used colonial troops including thousands of Indians, and the Americans brought in negro units.

The allies continued to put pressure on Iran – the Shah was forced to abdicate – a general was kidnapped by British agents – the Soviets set up independent Azerbaijan and Kurd states.

Allied troops in Iran were plagued by bandits and black marketeers, because this became the main route by which the Anglo-Americans supplied the Soviets.

Following the invasion, the Germans recruited about 200 Iranians, mostly students, to fight against the allies.

In 1945 when the war ended, the Anglo-Americans pulled out, but it was 1946 before the Soviets did so, under Anglo-American diplomatic pressure. Thereupon, the Iranian Army invaded the Kurd and Azerbaijani lands and destroyed their Soviet-trained forces.

Churchill's rash act created a serious anti-western feeling in Iran for the remainder of the century.

See Index

IRAQ

Other names:	Mesopotamia
Status in 1940:	independent.
Government in 1940:	monarchy.
Population in 1940:	4,500,000.
Make-up in 1940:	Arabs 3,500,000;
	Kurds 700,000;
	also: Assyrians; Azerbaijanis;
	Persians.
Religion:	Moslem.
Location:	Middle East.

Iraq gained full independence from Britain in 1932, but the British retained the right to exploit the nation's oil wealth unmercifully, to keep a small garrison and to cross the nation with troops at any time.

Freed from British restrictions the Iraqi Arabs celebrated by turning on the Assyrian minority and massacring thousands, and when the King died, leaving a four-year-old heir, the perpetrators of the massacre gained control of the government.

The British dealt with such butchers as long as they got their oil, but in April 1941 a coup put the Golden Square, four pro-German politicians, in power. The British replied at once by reinforcing their garrison at Basra and alerting their air base at Habbaniyah, protected by Kurd and Assyrian troops. The Golden Square responded angrily, calling upon the Iraqi Army of 368,000, saying that the reinforcement was a violation of the treaty, which it was, but the British continued to come in.

On 2 May Iraqi soldiers watched British planes take off from Habbiniyah, circle, then drop bombs on them. The British had started a war.

By day's end Iraqi flak and fighters had shot down seven British planes, but the 100-plane Iraqi air force was destroyed. On the 5th the two Iraqi brigades at Habbaniyah were attacked by the British garrison. Next day the British troops in Basra began an upriver advance. On the 10th a British column invaded from Trans-Jordan to link up with the Habbaniyah garrison and on the 18th the Iraqis could not prevent the reinforced Habbaniyah garrison from crossing the Euphrates and capturing Fallujah. An Iraqi counter-attack on the 22nd failed.

Falling back on their capital, Baghdad, the Iraqis set up trenches, barbed wire, artillery emplacements and received the allied attack on the 28th. German and Italian planes gave assistance to the Iraqis. However, on the night of the 30th the Golden Square fled the country and the new government surrendered.

Iraqi casualties in the 29-day war were about 100 killed and 500 wounded. Allied losses were fewer than sixty.

About a hundred Iraqis fled to Syria, where they joined the German Arab Legion.

Iraq gave no further trouble to the British, but the British knee-jerk reaction had made no friends in the Arab world.

IRELAND, SOUTHERN

Other names:	Irish Free State, Eire
Status in 1939:	dominion of the British
	Commonwealth
Government in 1939:	democratic monarchy.
Population in 1939:	2,900,000.
Make-up in 1939:	Celtic;
	a few descendants of Norse,
	Normans and English.
Religion:	Christian.
Location:	edge of Western Europe.

In 1921 following 700 years of English domination, Ireland, or at least three quarters of it, was granted autonomy likened to that of Canada, and it took a two-year guerrilla war to get that much. In 1922 a civil war was fought between those who accepted the treaty and those who wanted greater independence as a republic without a king. The pro-treaty faction won and the Irish Free State settled down to a peaceful life.

Ironically, when Canada gained de facto independence a decade later, therefore so did the Free State, thus in 1939 when the British declared war on Germany, for the first time in centuries the people of southern Ireland had a choice whether or not to fight in Britain's wars.

By chance in 1939 the Free State Prime Minister was Eamon de Valera, who had barely escaped an British firing squad in 1916, had been hunted by the British during the guerrilla war, and had been hunted by the Free Staters during the civil war as one of the leaders of the anti-treaty faction. Therefore, it came as no surprise when his government voted not to join Britain in the war for the following reasons: the British had refused to allow the Free State control over Northern Ireland, on the grounds that most of its people were descended from Scots and English; Churchill, a hated man in Ireland, was a member of the current British government (he would soon become Prime Minister); de Valera saw this as Britain's war not Ireland's; and the most important of all, as an ally Britain would demand the right to put troops into the Free State, and they had only just left a year earlier.

Living in an integral part of the United Kingdom of Great Britain and Northern Ireland, the Northern Irish had no such choice: they were at war, however the British government was wise enough not to introduce conscription there for fear the Celtic minority would riot against the idea.

A small group of Irish believed themselves to be still at war with Britain: the Irish Republican Army (IRA - taking the name of the original rebels in 1921). Consisting of about 2,000 men and women, mostly Celts from Northern Ireland, they waged a comedy-of-errors terrorist campaign against the British, though it was no laughing matter when they blew up English housewives in a shopping centre in Coventry in August 1939.

The IRA saw Britain's discomfort with Germany as their advantage and they sent workers to Germany and IRA agents to broadcast, write and teach German spies how to pass as Irish or British. They also offered safe houses in the Free State for German spies.

De Valera was adamant that Free State soil was off limits to Germans, so his police hunted down the spies and their IRA friends. However, he wanted the British to know that his soil was off limits to them too, so he put his army along the northern border. There were no incidents, which is interesting as the Free State uniforms were very similar to German.

If de Valera's government was neutral, his people were not. Even after 1921 enlistment in the British Army was popular as a method of relieving poverty and unemployment, though it was officially proscribed. The tiny Free State Army never had room for recruits. When Britain and Germany went to war fully 60,000 Free Staters enlisted in the British armed forces, others joined the merchant fleet and thousands went to Britain to work. Enlistments among Northern Irish, with half the population, were 30,000.

If this mass movement was based on personal gain, it was nonetheless welcome, and as the war progressed the Free State people became decidedly anti-German. This was caused by the sinking of Free State ships by German submarines - sixteen during the war - and the German bombing of the Free State: in August 1940 killing three, twice in January 1941 killing three and once on Dublin in May killing 34. German excuses that their planes were lost were not believed. Therefore, some of the enlistments in the British forces could well have been from a moral stance.

There has never been any indication that Free Staters in the British forces did not pull their weight. Plenty were decorated for bravery, including eight with the Victoria Cross, the empire's highest award. German officers and their IRA friends toured the prison camps looking for Free Staters among British prisoners, offering free booze and prostitutes to any who joined the anti-British legion - powerful inducements to an Irishman - but not enough volunteered to fill a truck, so the idea was dropped.

Throughout the war, wherever there was a British ship, platoon or air squadron, there was a Free Stater.

Despite provocation by the Germans, de Valera steered a true course of neutrality. He even refused an offer from Churchill of Northern Ireland in return for British bases in the Free State: it had taken the southern Irish 700 years to get rid of British troops and de Valera was not going to be known as the man who invited them to return.

Allied airmen and sailors and their German counterparts who reached Free State soil after surviving a wreck were interned, but this imprisonment was not all that unpleasant: one American courted and married a local girl while imprisoned.

The Free State press had to obey de Valera's rules, so whenever a Free Stater in British uniform was killed in action it was reported that he/she had died while working in Britain.

ITALIAN EAST AFRICA

Other names:	includes Eritrea, Ethiopia and Somaliland.
Status in 1939:	Italian colony.
Government in 1939:	Italian administration.
Population in 1939:	16,000,000.
Make-up IN 1939:	Somalis 3,500,000; Tigreans 1,500,000; a hundred other groups; 300,000 Italian colonists.
Religion:	Christian, some Moslems, tribal
Location:	Horn of Africa

Eritrea had become an Italian colony in the nineteenth century and Somaliland in the early twentieth century. Ethiopia had only been conquered in the period 1935-36 in a war of massed charges by Ethiopians, some armed with spears and swords, against Italian machine-guns. Eritrean soldiers in the Italian Army had gained laurels in that conflict.

Though Ethiopia was far from pacified - there were still guerrillas in the mountains - Mussolini the Italian dictator convinced thousands of Italian to colonise the area, in the same manner as previous generations of Italians had colonised Somaliland and Eritrea. Part of the civilising process, as far as Mussolini was concerned was to establish

the largest army in Africa. By 1939 he had 92,000 Italians and 250,000 natives in uniform in East Africa under the command of the Duke d'Aosta, a playboy nobleman known in international society.

Natives served either as ascaris: clones of Italian soldiers, distinguishable at a distance only by their hats, and were formed into battalions, brigades etc; or as bande: men who were equipped by the Italians, but who obeyed their tribal leaders more than their Italian officers, wore traditional garb and fought in their traditional style, i.e. anarchic. When the mood took them they would go home for a few days.

Italians served as officers for the native units, in Italian Army rear-echelon units and the Savoia Division, in the Air Force, the Navy and the Blackshirts, the latter being the fascist party militia. Many were colonists who were in the reserves and were only called up in emergency.

Mussolini provided the emergency when he declared war on Britain and France on 19 June 1940. The Duke, who loved the British, was angered by this move, not least because East Africa was surrounded by British and French territory and had no hope of being relieved by an Italian fleet or land advance. He was on his own.

He reacted by sending his planes against the enemy colonies and launching pre-emptive strikes, sending Ethiopian ascaris against French Somaliland, Eritrean and Ethiopian ascaris against the British in Sudan and Ethiopian ascaris and bande against the British in Kenya. Because of what was happening in Europe France surrendered on 24 June, but this still left Britain, which for the Duke was the more threatening of the two.

For a few hundred killed and wounded his strikes did the trick, throwing the British into a panic, and in August he sent a mixed force into British Somaliland, which overran the colony in two weeks. However, before the British evacuated by sea under Italian air attack they had given one of his columns a bloody nose at Tug Argan Pass. His Ethiopian ascaris had not done well and he had to thrown in Colonel Lorenzini's 2nd Colonial Brigade of Eritreans. Tug Argan cost 2,000 killed and wounded.

Of great portent for the future was the knowledge that some generals had refused to aid the Tug Argan column, owing to petty jealousies and political differences. The Duke was forbidden by Mussolini to take disciplinary action.

Over the next five months his forces did exceptionally well in border skirmishes. The bande excelled in this type of warfare, for it differed hardly at all from their traditional tribal warfare.

However, the Duke knew it was only a matter of time. On 16 January the British invaded Eritrea from Sudan. General Frusci ordered his forces there to fall back at once. A rearguard of an Ethiopian brigade at Keru Gorge performed poorly and its commander surrendered, but nearby 500 Ethiopian horse cavalry under Italian officers charged British and Indian infantry: their misplaced bravery cost them 478 casualties.

Frusci brought Lorenzini's brigade to this front, gave him another Eritrean brigade, three Italian battalions, some artillery and engineers and christened the whole the 4th Division with orders to fall back through Agordat to Keren Pass. Further south General Bergonzi's 2nd Division of Eritreans and Ethiopians was to fall back to Keren through Barentu.

On January 28 both Lorenzini and Bergonzi stood and fought for three days each against an Indian Army division, then Lorenzini pulled out of Agordat, abandoning 1,000 sick and wounded. Bergonzi, outflanked by this, had to retreat from Barentu, abandoning his sick and wounded.

They both reached Keren, where Lorenzini was given overall command. His men felt confident, for this position was a natural barrier of sheer mountains, precipitous peaks, knife-like ridges and few tracks and the seasonal rains had just begun. The defenders were quickly attacked at the beginning of February by the two divisions, reinforced, and brought under constant artillery and air bombardment. Attacks and counter-attacks gained and lost the same ground over and over again. World War I veterans on both sides compared it to the trench warfare of that conflict.

The second allied invasion came from Kenya in early February: two British divisions of black Africans and a division of the white South African Army. At Beles Gugnani oasis Somali bande fled when attacked by three battalions. This was not a skirmish and the bande had no stomach for a full-scale battle. When fifteen allied planes bombed Afmadu the garrison of ascari and bande both panicked and ran. On the 13th a bande at Bulo Erillo fought three battalions for a few hours and then ran: 130 gave up. However, Jelib on the Jaba River was defended by a battalion of the 102nd (Yemeni and Somali) Division and they repelled an attack by three battalions.

General de Simone panicked worse than his bande and ordered Kismayu abandoned. Thus the allies found an intact port, 330,000 gallons of fuel, full warehouses and 25 ships. The Somali and Italian residents both cheered the British!

At Gobwen Somali ascaris repelled an attack by white South Africans and then counter-attacked for two days. Only the arrival of South African armoured cars forced them to retreat.

By now de Simone ordered Brava and Mogadishu, both under allied air and naval bombardment, to be abandoned. The allies found an even greater treasure here. De Simone ordered the 101st and 102nd Divisions and bande to abandon their homeland and retreat north towards Ethiopia. Needless to say, many deserted.

Over the next weeks De Simone led them 800 miles, the 101st to Neghelli and the 102nd to the Bisidimo River, where they held an attack for two days then fell back, abandoning the city of Harar. In late March de Simone reported to the Duke that out of his army of 15,000 Italians and 43,000 ascaris and bande, he had left 4,000 Italians and 1,000 natives. The allies registered 10,350 Italian and 11,732 native prisoners, many caught because they were too sick to run. Thus 30,000 native troops had deserted. The Duke would have been thoroughly disheartened had he known that de Simone had only inflicted 445 killed and wounded on the allies.

A third invasion came from Sudan into Ethiopia in February, a small British force named Gideon Force accompanied by two British-trained battalions of Ethiopians.

Their first attack, on the 27th at Burie was a failure, and the Italians of Colonel Natale almost caught the allied commander Major Wingate. Wingate rethought his tactics and called in an air-strike on Burie. Though only a few planes showed up they panicked 1,500 bande into declaring neutrality. Disgusted, Natale felt he had no choice but to retreat. On 4 March he hit the road with 500 Italians, 3,500 Eritrean and Ethiopian ascaris and 4,000 bande, plus several hundred Italian and native civilians. Each night some bande deserted and an attack by Ethiopian guerrillas killed 250 men. When the column reached Debra Markos they found 75% of the bande had left.

The Duke believed Natale could have done better and he dismissed him, telling Colonel Maraventano to add the column to his garrison at Debra Markos and to counter-attack. This gave Maraventano 1,200 Italians, 2,500 Eritrean ascaris, 7,500 Ethiopian ascaris, 3,000 Ethiopian bande. He also had 2,000 Italian and native civilians to look after.

He counter-attacked on the 25th, hoping to push Gideon Force, the Ethiopian battalions and the guerrillas into the arms of the Bahrdar garrison of five Ethiopian battalions and 1,000 bande, but after five days of battle the plan failed. It cost Maraventano 3,000 bande and 3,000 ascaris killed or deserted. On 3 April Maraventano decided to join the Duke.

The Duke knew his time was up. De Simone had abandoned Somaliland and eastern Ethiopia. The police chief of Diredawa radioed the British asking them to come to protect the local Italian women and children from Ethiopian guerrillas. At Jijiga an entire Ethiopian brigade deserted. Relief sentries were finding the previous sentries disappeared - gone to join the guerrillas. He was worried about the 18,000 Italian civilians in Addis Ababa, so he made the bold decision to declare the city 'open' and to hit the road himself with the garrison, heading north to link up with Frusci, who was still holding at Keren.

At Keren eight Ethiopian, eight Eritrean and six Italian battalions were holding back nineteen British and Indian battalions. Both sides had artillery and engineers and the British had air power. But 40 % of the Ethiopians had deserted by 15 March and this day Lorenzini was killed while leading an attack. By the 27th when the British broke through with tanks most defending battalions were at less than quarter strength. Frusci approved a withdrawal. He abandoned Asmara and ordered his men to head for Massawa or join him to try to reach the Duke.

On 6 April survivors from Keren together with local troops, sailors and police fought for Massawa against two divisions, commandos and French Foreign Legion. On the 8th the garrison commander surrendered.

Frusci had lost 5,500 ascari and bande and 7,500 Italians killed and wounded trying to hold Eritrea. He reached the Duke at Amba Alagi, a mountainous position where they decided to make their last stand. Between them they had three Italian and four Ethiopian battalions and a mob of men from a score of units including airmen, police and sailors. They were all diseased and exhausted. At nearby Dessie no less than 8,000 bedridden sick and wounded were abandoned. The Duke and Frusci repelled their first attack on 27 April. Soon they were fighting off an Indian/British brigade and a South African division and from 11 May assaults by thousands of Ethiopian guerrillas led by Lord Seyoum of Tigre. On 19 May the Duke finally surrendered: he had 412 natives and 4,677 Italians still standing. The allies gave them full honours and played music at their disarming in respect for their courage.

The wily Duke had refused to surrender others who were still holding out - and there were plenty: garrisons at Debra Tabor, Wolchefit Pass, Gondar (which included the Bahrdar garrison which had broken out and reached this town), Chilga, Kulkaber, Addis Dera, Wadera, Jimmu and Soddu. All were besieged by guerrillas and the latter four by British forces too.

Maraventano's column had reached Addis Dera, but could move no further. On 23 May he contacted Wingate, agreeing to surrender if Wingate protected his troops and civilians from the bloodthirsty guerrillas. It was agreed.

The garrison of Debra Tabor surrendered to the allies on the same terms.

At Soddu two divisions surrendered to British forces when they ran out of food. Other garrisons also did the same. General Gazzera abandoned Jimmu and 15,000 sick, starving and wounded and with his fittest tried to outrun two chasing British brigades. He gave then a drubbing at Demli and Gimbi, but finding a Belgian force trapping him in front he surrendered his 6,500 men on 6 July.

After repulsing several attacks by a British brigade the garrison at Wolchefit Pass surrendered on 27 September, but only because they had run out of food.

The allies now concentrated their attacks on General Nasi's diehards at Kulkaber, Chilga and Gondar. In October the garrisons came under attack by three brigades, artillery, armoured cars, aircraft and thousands of guerrillas. Kulkaber bore the brunt of the assaults in November and finally gave up on the 19th: 775 Ethiopian ascaris and 1,648 Italians put up their hands.

On the 27th Nasi surrendered all remaining defenders in East Africa.

The defence of Mussolini's east African empire cost 5,000 Italian and 15,000 ascari and bande lives, and a total of about 60,000 wounded. Allied casualties were about a thousand killed and 5,000 wounded, but guerrilla casualties must have been in the region of 100,000. About 100,000 Ethiopians had been killed and wounded in the defence of their homeland during the Italian invasion 1935-36 and about 50,000 fighting against the Italians between June 1936 and June 1940, plus several thousand civilians had been deliberately murdered. It had cost Mussolini 10,600 killed and wounded, about a third of them Eritrean, to conquer Ethiopia and 8,600 casualties, most of them Ethiopian, Somali and Eritrean to hold on to it from June 1935 to June 1940.

The Duke had been cut off from all hope of rescue or supply since day one, but his men had held for a year and a half. This is all the more unbelievable when the desertion problem is brought into light, and absolutely incredible when it is realised that the British codebreakers had been reading all the Duke's commands to his men! It is indeed sad to report that the Duke, still in his thirties, died in a British prison.

A courage and stamina existed here among the Italians and their native soldiers (once the faint hearts had run off) that is hard to match elsewhere. Allied soldiers who went on to fight both Germans and Japanese claimed Keren was their toughest battle.

Of course one should not ask why did some native soldiers ran away, but rather why did any of them fight for a regime that had oppressed them? Not only was the regime a racist one, as all white regimes in Africa were, but it was fascist. The answer probably lies in the belief among some that loyalty is more respectable than politics. *See Index*

ITALY

Other names:	
Status in 1939:	independent .
Government in 1939:	dictatorship of Benito Mussolini.
Population:	40,000,000;
Make-up in 1939:	Italians 37,600,000;
	Friulis 1,000,000
	Sardinians 1,000,000
	Volksdeutsch 200,000
	French 50,000
	Slovenians 60,000
	Croats 60,000
	Catalans 15,000
	Greeks 15,000
	Albanians 15,000
Religion:	Christian
Location:	Central Mediterranean.

By August 1939 when Hitler was planning the invasion of Poland he believed he had Mussolini's Italy firmly in hand as a partner. He was, therefore, shocked when Mussolini's foreign minister and son-in-law Galeazo Ciano visited him with an urgent statement: if Hitler expected Italy to keep Britain and France off his back while he dealt with Poland, he would have to ship to Italy immediately sufficient equipment to do the job. A list was supplied. A long list, so long in fact that it would have been impossible for Hitler to fill it.

How could this be, Hitler asked? The answer was that while Hitler's only war to date had been sending about 2,000 personnel to help Franco in the Spanish Civil War, Mussolini had been fully engaged militarily. Mussolini had achieved power in 1922 and had inherited a war in Libya that took until 1932 to win. Then Mussolini had invaded Ethiopia in 1935, which had soaked up fifteen Italian and three colonial divisions and cost him 10,600 casualties by May 1936, and a guerrilla war since then had kept two Italian divisions and a quarter of a million colonial troops busy and had cost another 8,000 casualties.

In June 1936 Mussolini had become much more involved in Spain than Hitler, sending five divisions and elements of three others, plus air force and navy. Victory there in March 1939 had cost Italy 14,400 casualties. In April 1939 Mussolini had sent four divisions to invade Albania: the fighting only lasted a weekend, but the troops had to remain to protect the cities from guerrillas. In Spain 270 Italian planes had been shot down or ruined and hundreds of tanks destroyed, and Mussolini had given to Franco 763 planes, 1,930 artillery pieces and 10,000 machine guns. As a result of all this the Italian Army would not be fully equipped again for at least another year.

Thus while those young men of Germany who dreamed of glory in battle, a group which all nations possess, were straining at the leash, that faction in Italy had long since been sated in Libya, Ethiopia, Spain or Albania. Thus at the moment when Hitler expected Mussolini to risk war with the two largest empires in the world Mussolini had few glory hunters, but millions of ordinary men who wished for a quiet life to raise their families.

Hitler made a deal with the USSR instead, invaded Poland and ignored the French and British declarations of war against him. His gamble paid off, for Poland was destroyed without Anglo-French interference.

Mussolini was hailed as a saviour by the Italians for keeping them out of the war, but on 10 June 1940 he betrayed them all. Seeing the French reeling in the face of a German invasion and the British all but kicked off the mainland, he declared war on France and Britain. It was a despicable act which most Italians abhorred: it was sort of like kicking a man when he was down.

Still the armed forces obeyed orders and reacted accordingly. In East Africa the Duke d'Aosta mobilised his 340,000 Italian and native troops, small air force and naval flotilla. This colony was totally surrounded by British territory and cut off from all succour by Italy. In one fell swoop Mussolini had denied his empire (technically speaking King Vittorio Emmanuele's empire) a large colony and access to the 92,000 Italian servicemen there.

In Libya Marshal Italo Balbo mobilised one army on the western border facing French Tunisia and another on the eastern border facing British Egypt.

On the Franco-Italian border the Prince of Piedmont formed the First and Fourth Armies of 25 divisions with orders to invade France.

At sea the Navy got ready to fight the French Navy with its ports in Southern France, Tunisia, Morocco, Corsica and Algeria and the British Royal Navy, the biggest navy in the world, with its ports in Gibraltar, Malta, Cyprus and Egypt. The Air Force began raids on Malta at once.

All in all Italy faced a daunting challenge. On 20 June the Assietta, Cosseria, Livorno and Modeno divisions crossed the Franco-Italian border. Coming up against fixed defences the Italian generals proved they had learned nothing in their wars: they shoved men through the alpine passes like meat through a grinder. The Italian soldier deserved better. On the 22nd France surrendered to Germany and on the 24th signed a surrender to Italy. The prince reported his casualties: 1,247 killed, 2,631 wounded, 3,878 captured, many after being wounded, 2,151 maimed by frostbite. They had killed 37 Frenchmen. For this terrible price Italy gained a few mountain villages and the coast as far as Monaco.

There were two types of Italian general: those in the regular Army, who invariably had to have good family, connections with the nobility and a mentor; the others were the Blackshirts, members of the fascist party militia, who when in combat took orders from the Army, to their chagrin. Blackshirts fought in their own units, their uniform consisting of black shirt covered by an army tunic with black trim. The Blackshirts were democratic, hated the class system and were loyal to the party. Thus, neither Army nor blackshirts promoted men on tactical know-how, which boded ill for the Italian fighting man.

Mussolini could not disguise the sour aftertaste left by the 'victory' over France, especially as the northern Italian cities now came under sporadic air attack by British bombers. Further bad news came from Libya where Balbo was killed when his aircraft was shot down by his own flak gunners.

At sea in the first three weeks of war the Italian Navy sank a British cruiser and four destroyers and lost a destroyer and nine submarines. Obviously there was something seriously wrong with the submarine fleet.

On 9 July the Italian battle fleet set out after a British convoy with battleships *Giulio Cesare* and *Conti di Cavour* with twelve cruisers and sixteen destroyers, and off Calabria ran into the British battle fleet with battleships *Warspite*, *Malaya* and *Royal Sovereign*, an aircraft carrier, four cruisers and seventeen destroyers, but this was 1940 not 1914 and the carrier proved the most decisive weapon, for not only could her aircraft inflict punishment, but the Italian ships had to dodge these aircraft, thereby interfering with their gunnery accuracy. When the *Giulio Cesare* was struck by a shell the Italians called it a day and the British did not follow.

It was not glory, but the Italians had met the famed Royal Navy and had survived. Also in several destroyer actions the Italians were holding their own.

In September much was made of the Italian advance into Egypt. Balbo's replacement, Marshal Graziani, one of history's great survivors, had come out of medical retirement to lead the Tenth Army to victory according to the newsreels. Actually, his men had wandered into Egypt, harassed unmercifully by British planes and armoured cars, suffering 3,500 sick, wounded, missing and dead and had halted after fifty miles. Graziani refused to go further until he had more tanks: not the L3, which was a joke, or the M11 with its gun in the hull; but the M13, which alone could stand up to a British tank. As more tanks were not forthcoming, Graziani stayed where he was.

Unable to prevent Britain's Royal Air Force from bombing his cities or Royal Navy from sinking his submarines, and unable to get to grips with their army in Egypt, Mussolini showed how his mind worked by invading a nation he thought he could defeat: Greece.

He had been antagonising the Greeks since spring by sinking their ships, but it was not until October that he decided to invade, ordering his generals to put eight divisions into Albania and be ready to invade in eight days. His generals pleaded it could not be done, but in fact they did it, showing that when they needed to the Italians could execute seemingly impossible logistical tasks in swift order.

On the 28th without warning the Italians crossed the border and 463 planes challenged the Greeks' 123 aircraft. Of course this was the wrong time, heading into a freezing winter, the wrong place, high mountains, and the wrong method, sticking to the narrow valleys and not clearing the peaks.

11 November 1940 began as a day of celebration, for it was the 22nd anniversary of the victory over Germany in World War I, but this day would henceforth be remembered with sorrow. Over Britain thirteen Italian planes were shot down in minutes, the highest loss to date. Off Albania four merchant ships were sunk in minutes by British warships. Southern Italy was bombed for the first time. And worst of all just after dusk the naval base at Taranto was attacked by a handful of flimsy biplanes from a British carrier. Two were shot down, but they left a destroyer and a cruiser damaged, the battleships *Conti di Cavour* and *Littorio* sinking and the *Caio Duilio* crippled. It was the first time in history that a battle fleet had been knocked out by planes and it shocked the world.

Three days later, the Greeks charged down the mountainsides into the rear of the Italian columns. The Italians had to fight their way out in a total fiasco devoid of emergency procedures and support, though they did exhibit uncommon bravery in quarters. By the time the fighting died down the

Italians had been forced back fifteen miles inside Albania. Casualties were high: 20% killed and wounded and 20% missing in some units.

The entire world laughed at Italy. French kids in Italian-occupied France wrote on walls 'Greeks! Stop here!'

The Italian Navy had to regain their pride immediately and they sortied out after a British convoy on 20 November with the large battleship *Vittorio Veneto* and smaller *Giulio Cesare*, six cruisers and fourteen destroyers. On the 27th off Cape Spartivento they engaged a flotilla of British cruisers, then came under attack by carrier planes and eventually fought with the battleships *Renown* and *Ramillies*. Running low on fuel both sides withdrew. An Italian destroyer and a British cruiser had been damaged.

An even greater humiliation than the Greek fiasco lay waiting in Egypt. Graziani had put his men into flat desert camps, a standard practice in the desert for all belligerents, with the idea that each camp should help defend its neighbour. Therefore, communication and mobility were of paramount importance, neither of which were Italian strengths. On the morning of 9 December 1940 General Malletti in command of Nibeiwa camp was awakened by British artillery shells blasting his camp. As his men ran for their tanks they were cut down by shrapnel, and as most of the vehicles had two-man crews, a tank could not operate one man short. Eventually the two Italian and one Libyan tank battalions managed to get a few tanks out of the camp to advance towards British infantry seen in the distance. In the camp the gunners opened fire on the British while the infantry waited. After two hours of shelling the camp was suddenly assaulted by British tanks from the rear. Soon Libyan infantry were battling tanks with rifles and Italian gunners were fighting infantry with crowbars and ramrods. By 11.00am, with Malletti and scores of others dead, the camp surrendered to elements of an infantry and an armoured division.

This was repeated at the Tummar West camp, where 2,000 Libyan troops were attacked by 2,000 British and 40 tanks. The camp surrendered by mid-afternoon.

That afternoon the remainder of the 2nd Libyan Division was attacked at Tummar East by three Indian and British battalions and tanks. By dusk the Libyans were giving up, but some of the one hundred Italian cadre chose to run for it across the cold windy desert.

At Sidi Barrani the 4th Blackshirt Division prepared to receive an assault, and sure enough next morning the garrison was hit by air attack, a bombardment by British warships and artillery and an assault by an infantry brigade and an armoured brigade. That night some Italians chose to run for it across the desert. Come morning after a 24-hour battle the commander capitulated: 500 defenders had been killed and wounded, and 15,000 Italians and Libyans were ordered to surrender.

Throughout the 10th, 11th and 12th the 1st Libyan Division in the open desert was bombed, strafed and shelled by artillery and warships. To stop the murder its commander surrendered his panicky 5,000 Libyans and 150 Italians.

At Azzaziya an armoured brigade was slaughtered by a British armoured brigade: the British actually felt sorry for the Italians in their little tin-pot tanks.

At Buq Buq a blackshirt formation was attacked by an armoured brigade. For 52 killed and 200 wounded the blackshirts managed to knock out 13 tanks, but at this rate they would run out of flesh before the enemy ran out of tanks. With no help in sight the 4,000 fascists surrendered.

When General Berti, commander of the Tenth Army, returned from leave to his headquarters in Tobruk he was informed by his embarrassed staff that in four days 30,000 men were missing. Stunned, he regained his composure and told everyone to concentrate on holding Bardia, which had an Italian population. The 1st Blackshirt Division was told to put a rearguard at Sidi Omar: the 900 blackshirts were steamrollered by a British armoured brigade.

In Bardia General Bergonzolli, a hero from previous wars respected by his men, had the Cirene and Marmarica Divisions of Italian colonists, the 1st and 2nd Blackshirt Divisions, part of the Catanzaro Division of conscripts, a brigade of useless tanks and the survivors from the foot race with British tanks. The city was under air and naval bombardment and there was panic in the air.

Following two days of serious bombardment the perimeter was attacked in 3 January 1941 by British 7th Armoured and Australian 6th Divisions, the depleted 1st Blackshirt Division bearing the brunt of the assault. Within hours the defenders were chopped up into pockets. Fighting was severe: a counter-attack by Marmarica drove back the Australians for awhile. The following evening Bergonzolli organised a break out and they ran across the desert. Next day after a sixty-hour battle the garrison gave up: a thousand killed and wounded and 35,949 soldiers, blackshirts, airmen, sailors and police taken prisoner.

Bergonzolli, no spring chicken, ran with his diehards for 75 miles to reach Tobruk. Without resting he inspected the only defences: the Sirte colonists' Division, a brigade of useless tanks and a badly bombed cruiser in the harbour. Berti and his Tenth Army staff had already fled. For the next two weeks the defenders bluffed the enemy by aggressive patrolling while under bombardment.

On the 21st the weak defences were attacked by the victors of Bardia, yet by late afternoon a counter-attack had regained some ground. Come dusk Bergonzolli decided it was time for another marathon across the desert. His diehards joined him. Next morning the garrison capitulated: several hundred had been killed and wounded and 25,000 soldiers, blackshirts, airmen, police and sailors surrendered.

Derna, held by elements of the Sabratha and Catanzaro Divisions, repelled a probe by British armour on the 22nd and continued to do so day after day. The remainder of the Sabratha defended Mechili on the 24th and on the 25th General Babini's tanks actually defeated a British tank force. Next day the Mechili garrison withdrew. On the 29th after repelling all probes, the Derna garrison evacuated.

Every Italian in eastern Libya was now on the run, but unknown to them British tanks had bypassed them, intent on heading them off, thus on 5 February the Tenth Army, now under General Tellera as Berti had been dismissed, found the British blocking them at Beda Fomm. He ordered an assault at once. His men obeyed for three days; casualties were high, Tellera was killed and Babini lost almost all of his 110 tanks. Finally the 25,000 Italians, Bergonzolli among them, threw up their hands.

Mussolini tried to hide the truth from his people. He blamed Graziani and accepted his resignation. He fired others. His Tenth Army was gone: 90,000 Italians and 30,000 Libyans were prisoners, 20,000 were dead and only 7,000 had reached safety. Total allied casualties were 1,900.

On 28 March 1941 the Italian battle fleet was at sea with *Vittorio Veneto*, eight cruisers and eleven destroyers hoping the British would accept the challenge. They did. Meeting British cruisers the Italian cruisers retreated, standard Italian practice – to sucker the enemy in. The British fell into the trap and in a few hours the *Vittorio Veneto* opened fire at the incredible range of 26 miles. However, the British had their usual ace up their sleeve: carrier planes. Italian shore-based bombers arrived, as did British bombers, as did German bombers. It was a total mêlée. Most of the Italian ships were bombed and the *Vittorio Veneto* was badly damaged. Admiral Iachino ordered the fleet to retire at nightfall, abandoning the cruiser *Pola*, which was dead in the water.

However, Admiral Cattaneo disobeyed orders and took two cruisers and five destroyers back to rescue the *Pola*, but he was caught in a radar/searchlight ambush by battleships *Barham*, *Warspite* and *Valiant*. The three cruisers and two destroyers were sunk. About 1,200 survivors were picked up and the *Pola*'s crew were captured, meaning Cattaneo and 2,400 men had gone down.

The outcome of the Battle of Cape Matapan, not realised at first, was that the Italian battle fleet could not sail in daylight for fear of allied aircraft and could not sail at night for fear of allied radar.

What the Italians did not know was British code-breakers could read most Italian naval signals. They knew who was sailing when and where to. Much of Italian army radio traffic was also being read, as were almost every one of Hitler's orders to his armed forces. To confuse the Italians the British let a few Italian ships go by unmolested and usually approached their victims first with a reconnaissance plane, making it appear that it really was luck that enabled them to intercept Italian submarines, ships and aircraft: while the British explained their land victories to the people of the world by claiming all Italian soldiers were cowards and would not fight. The highly prejudiced and gullible people of the 1940s did not ask if Italian sailors were heroic, how come their soldiers were not?

In March Mussolini had swallowed his pride and allowed a German armoured division to help him in Libya. Led by Rommel, the Germans were told to defend the 'line', but Rommel was not a defensive general. He attacked at once and within days defeated a British armoured division. Then, with the British running away from him and the Italians running after him, he assaulted Tobruk, failed and besieged it. The Italian Ariete Armoured Division now arrived and though Rommel told them Tobruk was too strong, they attacked anyway. They failed and lost a thousand men. It was a matter of honour, they explained. They too settled down to a siege.

The Italian soldiers were not angry that Germans had succeeded where they had failed, for it vindicated them. Using the same tactics as the British had used, the Germans defeated a brand new armoured division and an infantry brigade and had taken thousands of prisoners. So many British tanks had been abandoned that whole Italian tank companies could be equipped with them.

In March the Yugoslavian people revolted against a pro-German government and Hitler went into a rage. He demanded his Army crush them and invited Mussolini to help. The Italian was flattered and soon talked Hitler into diverting some troops to Greece as well.

On 6 April 1941 the Germans invaded Yugoslavia from Austria, Hungary, Romania and Bulgaria. The latter column then swerved south into Greece and forced the Greeks into retreat to the right rear of the army which was fighting the Italians in Albania.

The Italian Second Army of eight divisions invaded northern Yugoslavia from Italy and the Ninth Army with four divisions invaded southern Yugoslavia from Albania. A Yugoslav riposte into Albania was easily held. Italian marines invaded the coast and the Zara Division attacked out of the Italian enclave of that name.

On the 12th sixteen divisions of the Italian Ninth and Eleventh Armies attacked the Greeks. They broke through in a few days. The Yugoslavs surrendered on the 17th and the Greeks on the 21st.

In Yugoslavia the Italians had done well, taking 30,000 prisoners for a few hundred casualties. In Greece they took stock of their enterprise. It had cost them 13,755 killed, 12,368 maimed by frostbite, 20,000 captured (and sent to Egypt, therefore not returned) and over 50,000 wounded. The Greek campaign proved four truths: the incompetence of most of Mussolini's generals, many of whom concentrated on writing music, seeking favours and dallying with their mistresses; the arrogance of Mussolini; the shoddiness of Italian equipment, which either did not work, wore out quickly or was no comparison to enemy equipment when it did work; and the courage and stamina of the ordinary Italian who had to risk his life in the face of the above three adversities.

Still, for the Italians April was a great month: victory in Libya, Yugoslavia and Greece, and May was excellent news too for a German airborne invasion kicked a British Army out of Crete and the British Royal Navy suffered excessive losses: to Italian mines a submarine and a destroyer, to Italian destroyers a submarine, and to Italian and German air raids five torpedo boats, two motor launches, four submarines, seven destroyers and four cruisers sunk and nine destroyers, a carrier, five cruisers and battleships *Barham*, *Warspite* and *Valiant* damaged. It really did look like the Mediterranean was going to become what Mussolini claimed it was: Mare Nostrum (Our Sea).

Though Hitler was the more prominent dictator in the mind of the world, he had in fact modelled himself on Mussolini. The German Nazi party, with its extreme right nationalist philosophy based on past glories (the ancient Germanic tribes) and emphasis on will, physical strength, athletics and the virtues of a pastoral upbringing mirrored the Italian fascist party, though the fascists naturally harked back to the days of the Roman Empire, hence the fasces symbol and use of Roman ranks and unit designations among the Blackshirts. Hitler's version of the Blackshirts were the SA brownshirt stormtroopers. Indeed the only key difference between the two philosophies was racism. The Nazis believed Germans were superior, the fascists did not feel the same way about Italians. Hence some of Italy's fully assimilated Jews were fascists and blackshirts, generals and admirals. It was with a sad farewell that Mussolini dismissed them (and his Jewish mistress) simply to please Hitler.

Both dictators had also risen to power by battling the communists in the streets. Thus, when Hitler invited Mussolini to join with him and invade the USSR, the den of the communist wolf, he could hardly refuse. Besides, it fell into place nicely. Mussolini had been trying to convince his people that the Germans had not pulled his chestnuts out of the fire in Libya or Greece, it was coincidence that Germans were present on loan when the victories were won, and now he could claim that Italian soldiers were going to be loaned to the Germans in return – no one would ever seriously suggest the Italians were being sent to save the Germans!

German armies invaded the USSR on 22 June 1941. Mussolini at once sent his contingent: a flotilla of MAS torpedo boats and six midget submarines, three squadrons of planes, and 55,000 troops divided into the Pasubio and Torino Infantry and the Amedeo di Aosta Mobile Divisions and some blackshirt battalions.

In two months the Italians advanced five hundred miles, overcoming sporadic resistance, and by late August were the spearhead of an entire group of German armies. It was elixir of glory to the Italian people that their troops had beaten the famed Red Army. Unfortunately, this elixir did not spread far enough to the soldiers them- selves, for by the autumn rains it was getting cold in Russia and no one had any winter clothing. Mussolini had not provided any.

There was another group of Italian soldiers who were fed up. The Ninth Army of eight divisions was stationed in that part of Yugoslavia that Mussolini had confiscated: Montenegro, Kosovo and much of the coast. The Second Army of eight divisions was in Slovenia. In July, just three months after the Yugoslav Army had been destroyed, the Montenegrans rose in revolt: not in a riot sense, but by ambushing truck convoys and attacking barracks. One Italian battalion suffered 200 casualties in an ambush. Within days Mussolini realised he had a full-scale rebellion on his hands and he ordered Ninth Army to go into the field and put it down harshly. Spearheaded by the Venezia Division the army did as ordered.

In November a major guerrilla army – partisans led by 'Tito' – was thrown out of German-occupied Serbia into Montenegro, but the Germans had not bothered to inform the Italians. Caught off guard, the Italians nonetheless recovered quickly and made it so hot for Tito he chose to re-invade Serbia and try his luck against the Germans.

At sea the Italian admirals tried their luck once more with the repaired battleships *Littorio* and *Caio Duilio*, and *Andrea Doria* and *Giulio Cesare*, and a large cruiser/destroyer escort. On 17 December 1941 they encountered ten British cruisers and six destroyers, but when one Italian destroyer was damaged both fleets broke off the action. It was a poor showing by the Italian admirals and can only be explained by the fact that they had their binoculars trained on the sky.

However, as so often happens in war, a tiny dedicated team pulled off what the admirals and their mighty forces fail to do. The Italians had developed undersea chariots, which swimmers rode. The idea was for the swimmer to place the chariot, which was nothing but a bomb, under an enemy ship and them swim like hell before the concussion of the explosion squashed his brain like a paper bag. Even if he lived, he had to throw himself on the tender mercies of the enemy. Needless to say, Italian admirals called the chariots suicide craft. The men who rode them nicknamed them pigs. But considering the fact that most who signed up were killed in the first year of operation, for the sole gain of sinking two oil tankers in Gibraltar harbour, the admirals were probably right.

On the night of 18 December six volunteers on a one-way trip aboard three chariots entered the harbour of Alexandria, Egypt and placed their bombs under three vessels. Two of them were caught – when they refused to talk they were taken to the lowest part of a battleship in case a bomb was under it – a war crime, of course – but still refused to talk, though they knew darn well the bomb was under them. An admiral ordered them brought back on deck for another interrogation, during which the bombs blew up, rupturing an oil tanker, damaging a destroyer and sinking the battleship *Queen Elizabeth.* The battleship *Valiant* was out of commission for six months. The other four swimmers were caught later.

On 17 November the British Eighth Army launched a major offensive in Libya with the mission of relieving the siege of Tobruk. Bearing the immediate attack was the Savona Division and some smaller German units around Bardia. Like most Italian divisions the Savona only had six infantry battalions. Most of the allies drove past this battlefield and headed for Tobruk. General Bastico ordered Rommel to take the Italian Ariete Armoured Division and his German Afrika Korps (DAK) of the 15th and 21st Panzer Divisions and intercept the British armour.

The interception took place at Sidi Rezegh airfield. It was the largest battle seen in the desert to date. The Ariete encountered a brand new British armoured brigade and turned and ran: the British speedily chased after them, straight into an Ariete ambush, which destroyed a quarter of the British tanks before they could back out. Obviously the eager newcomers had believed their government's propaganda about Italians being cowards.

On the Tobruk perimeter the garrison attempted to break out: the German 90th

and the Italian Brescia, Trieste, Pavia, Trento and Bologna Divisions held them in.

After a week of battle at Sidi Rezegh the axis partners had the British on the run and caught up with the famed Desert Rats 7th Armoured Division and a South African infantry brigade on a plateau. An afternoon assault by the DAK and the Ariete drove the Desert Rats into retreat and the 3,000 South Africans were taken prisoner.

Despite Italian Bersaglieri (light infantry) doing a powerful job of holding a New Zealand brigade, Rommel conferred with Bastico about withdrawing and on the 18th day of battle the orders were given.

A Pavia rearguard held off the allies, while the army retreated to the Gazala Line: a handful of slit trenches in the sand. Everyone was completely exhausted and worn out. Casualties had been heavy. Ariete's infantry were at 10% strength!

Yet in 48 hours the Brescia, Trento, Pavia, Trieste and Ariete rushed to their defences to fight off an enemy attack at odds of 9:1 against. They held for three days and then the order to retreat was given. The Germans now panicked – many stole Italian vehicles at gunpoint. The Italians had few enough vehicles as it was and almost every one of them had to walk across the desert in a cold wind, open to every allied plane in the sky.

The generals had forgotten about the Savona: they were still holding under periodic attacks and constant bombardment, even though they had to throw airmen and sailors into the front. Rommel expressed surprise they were holding so long. Only on 2 January 1942, by which time Rommel and Bastico had retreated over 400 miles, did the Savona defenders give up, one pocket holding out to the 12th and a few Germans until the 17th.

The winter campaign cost the allies 2,900 dead, 7,300 wounded and 7,500 captured. German losses were 1,100 dead, 3,400 wounded and 6,100 captured and Italian losses were 2,300 killed, 2,700 wounded and 6,000 prisoners, plus around Bardia 4,000 Germans and 13,800 Italians surrendered. The disparity in the percentage of German and Italian wounded shows that many Italian wounded were abandoned and are therefore included in the prisoner total. One must also realise that a German in a truck can retreat faster than an Italian on foot.

In March 1942 the battle fleet sortied again: *Littorio* leading three cruisers and eight destroyers, covered this time by Italian and German planes. On the 22nd off Sirte they fought a convoy of four merchant ships, four cruisers, a flak cruiser and eighteen destroyers. After damaging a cruiser and three destroyers, and suffering a cruiser and the *Littorio* damaged, the Italians withdrew, knowing a storm was brewing. Before they reached harbour two Italian destroyers were sunk in the storm with only seven men surviving.

In late spring 1942 the Second Army tired of being ambushed by partisans in Slovenia and took the field. The combat was ferocious, but few and far between as partisans were usually found only when they wanted to be. This same spring Eleventh Army on occupation duty in Greece was also attacked by partisans, thus Italian divisions were in action against partisans throughout Yugoslavia, Albania and Greece.

Rommel had led a riposte in January and had thoroughly routed a British armoured force.

In May he planned another attack and this time he would take the Italians along as he was given command of the army (Armoured Army Africa). He launched the offensive on the 26th with the German 90th Division and two divisions of the DAK plus the Italian Ariete Armoured, Trieste, Brescia, Pavia, Trento and Sabratha Divisions. The Germans, Ariete and Trieste, which were mobile, swung round the inland desert flank, while the other divisions charged the British lines frontally.

The mobile forces defeated the British armour on the first day and overran two infantry brigades by day six. The fighting was constant with no let up and day after day the Italians and Germans were victorious – only the French at Bir Hakeim camp were a fly in the ointment – and by 20 June the axis partners had crippled three British brigades and totally destroyed eight and were at the gates of Tobruk.

That very afternoon Sabratha, Trento, Pavia, Trieste, Ariete, 90th and DAK assaulted the city perimeter. The fighting lasted all night and next morning German tanks felt they could break through if engineers lifted mines in front of them under fire! Italian engineers advanced and together they and the German tanks broke through. By noon it was all over: Tobruk and its Italian/Arab population was in Italian hands for the first time in seventeen months. Naturally the Italians were deliriously happy to wipe out the stain on their honour. They also captured 5,000 tons of supplies, 1,400 tons of fuel, 400 guns, 1,000 armoured vehicles and 35,500 prisoners

Rommel, who had sent armour ahead to reach the new allied line at Alamein, was reinforced by a fresh Italian armoured division the Littorio, which joined the Ariete and Trieste and DAK to fight towards Alamein. They almost cracked the defences on 1 July: they did destroy a brigade; but in days Rommel came to realise everyone was totally clapped out. He allowed his men to rest.

In return for 8,000 permanent casualties the Italians and Germans had inflicted 58,000 permanent casualties on the allies and had advanced across eastern Libya and western Egypt and were now just sixty miles from the great naval base of Alexandria and 130 miles from the Suez Canal.

In the Mediterranean the naval war progressed. Italy's merchant vessels were constantly being intercepted, but her warships did well when given a chance, e.g. in April and May 1942 the Italians lost a cruiser and a destroyer, but they sank two submarines, one of their mines sank a destroyer and joint Italian-German air raids sank five destroyers and a submarine and damaged a cruiser and two destroyers.

Therefore, when Italian spies in Gibraltar and Alexandria informed Rome that an allied convoy was about to sail from each for Malta the Italians put their battle fleet in motion with *Vittorio Veneto* and *Littorio*, six cruisers, five destroyers and fourteen submarines. The British no longer underestimated the Italians and to escort six merchant ships from Gibraltar they had two carriers, battleship *Malaya*, three cruisers, a minelayer, six motor gun boats, two corvettes, ten minesweepers and twenty-seven destroyers, and to escort eleven vessels from Alexandria they had a phoney battleship, seven cruisers and twenty-six minesweepers, corvettes and destroyers.

The battle of the twin convoys began on 14 June with Italian and German air strikes, followed that night by German submarines and torpedo boats, and next day the Italian battle fleet encountered the Gibraltar convoy, catching it with only part of its escort. The result was the greatest axis naval victory in the Mediterranean. An Italian cruiser was sunk and the *Littorio*, two cruisers and two destroyers were damaged, but the axis forces damaged three merchantmen, three cruisers, a destroyer, three minesweepers and the phoney battleship and sank six merchantmen and five destroyers. Only two merchantmen safely reached Malta.

At Alamein the Italians could sense victory: they could almost smell the odours from the bazaar in Cairo ; metaphorically that is. They knew one more push would do it: the British Royal Navy was withdrawing its ships from Alexandria and clerks were burning secret papers.

Yet one more push just wasn't in them or the Germans. Even the fresh Littorio Division had been driving for two weeks over primitive terrain under air attack.

They tried: the German DAK, 90th Division and fresh 164th Division and the Italian Littorio, Ariete, Trieste, Sabratha, Trento, Pavia and Brescia Divisions butted their heads against six allied divisions, but after a month Rommel called off the slaughter. The Sabratha was withdrawn: a destroyed division. The Trento's engineer battalion was down to sixteen men! Alamein cost Rommel 3,000 killed and captured and about 5,000 wounded.

During August Rommel received replacements and patched-up wounded veterans and fresh units until he had 25,000 Germans and 82,000 Italians. He chose to make his second attempt to break through on 31 August. The German 164th Division and Ramcke Parachute Brigade and Italian Bologna, Brescia and Trento and elements of

the Folgore Divisions attacked frontally against four divisions, while the DAK, Ariete and Littorio swept round the supposed open flank. However, Rommel realised after three days and many casualties, including three generals, his armour was not going to get past the allied armour. He withdrew his tanks and sent the 90th and Trieste Divisions to hold back the enemy armour. By 7 September the fighting had died down. The failure cost Rommel 1,154 Italian and 1,969 German killed and wounded. The capture of an enemy brigade commander by green Folgore infantry was no compensation.

Over the next two months Rommel built up his strength to 71,000 Germans and 90,000 Italians, but he had a pretty good idea he was losing the supply race. On the night of 23rd October he learned this only too well, when he received a telephone call while on leave in Germany: the allies were launching an offensive accompanied by the heaviest artillery barrage yet seen in the desert war.

Bearing the brunt of this sudden onslaught were the Trento, 164th, Bologna, Brescia, Folgore, and Pavia Divisions and Ramcke Brigade, facing poor odds: two Bersaglieri battalions against six allied, nine German against twelve, nine Trento against fifteen, six Bologna against nine, three German lightly armed paratooper against three, six Brescia against nine, six Folgore lightly armed paratrooper against nine, and only the Pavia outnumbered its attackers.

By dawn three British armoured divisions were almost breaking through. The DAK and 90th, Ariete, Littorio, and Trieste Divisions moved up to aid the infantry. There would be no flank sweeps this time just frontal assaults. Rommel's army had 1,219 guns, 424 tanks worthy of the name and 350 planes versus allied 2,311 guns 1,100 tanks and 530 planes.

Rommel was back within hours and he masterminded the battle for the next ten days. His casualties were horrific and his officers protested that their units were disappearing before their very eyes: in the Folgore by 2 November thirteen of eighteen field grade officers had been killed or wounded; and his tank strength was down to 66 German and 196 Italian.

Knowing when he was whipped, he ordered a retreat on 3 November, telling the Bologna and Brescia to leave first as they had no vehicles. They spent a day walking to the rear under air attack, then Hitler countermanded the order and they returned, also under air attack. On the next morning Rommel countermanded Hitler's countermand and they retreated again. This time so did everyone else.

Rommel threw in the Ariete to hold off three armoured divisions while the army escaped. The Ariete did as told: the division was sacrificed.

On the retreat Rommel's staff tried to take stock of the situation: they had less than seventy German and Italian tanks. Their casualties were 1,100 Germans killed, 3,900 wounded and 7,900 missing or abandoned, and 2,000 Italians killed, 1,600 wounded and 20,000 missing or abandoned. The entire Folgore Division had been captured: actually it only had 304 men still standing when it was!

The Italian people took weeks to get used to the idea that they were in full retreat in North Africa and would not win that campaign, and while many were just entering mourning came news of another, far worse defeat.

Hitler had asked Mussolini for help in the USSR and the proud Italian eagerly sent more troops, expanding his expedition to 270,000 strong and renamed it the Eighth Army of General Gariboldi of the original Pasubio, Torino and Amedeo di Aosta, plus the Sforesca, Ravenna, Cosseria, Julia, Tridentina, Cuneense and Vicenza Divisions, plus eight blackshirt battalions.

They did very well in the 1942 summer offensive. Near Yagodny the horse cavalry of the Amedeo got into the act with a sabre charge, routing an entire regiment and killing 150 and capturing 600 for a loss of 39 killed and 74 wounded and 170 horses killed.

By September the Eighth Army was told to hold what it had, while the German Sixth Army struggled for Stalingrad. Patrols broke the monotony as in time autumn rains were traded for freezing snow.

On 19 November the Romanians were attacked, two armies being thrown into confusion and forced to retreat, thereby abandoning the Sixth Army. Some Romanian troops edged their way into the Italian positions for safety. The Italians had held off light thrusts.

On 11 December the Ravenna, a flanking German division and the blackshirts were hit by a Soviet attack. It was heart-stopping, but they held.

It had been a Soviet test. On the morning of the 16th came the real attack. It was so cold Soviet tanks drove across frozen rivers. The Italians were hit by no less than 425,000 Soviets armed with 5,000 guns and a thousand tanks. The Julia, Tridentina and Cuneense Divisions fared best, because as alpine troops they were equipped and trained to move in snow: and the Vicenza was currently in the rear; but the other divisions did not stand a chance. Everyone fought and ran, fought and ran, until hours blended into days and days into weeks.

It was almost a month before they stopped retreating and manned a line drawn in the snow: the defences built around the alpine troops, the Vicenza and a mob of survivors from the others. The Germans did not blame Gariboldi and indeed entrusted five of their divisions to him.

But on 12 January the neighbouring Hungarian Second Army began to collapse under Soviet assaults, and two days later the Germans and Italians were attacked too. A thousand Cosseria survivors were cut down by twelve battalions of sabre-wielding horse cavalry. The snowy white retreat began again. Someone, somewhere suddenly remembered that the last time Italian troops had retreated in Russia was 1812 under that other Italian megalomaniac, Napoleon.

After another two weeks, the Soviets stopped owing to stretched supply lines and timely German counter-thrusts.

Mussolini had to call his army home: 80,000 of his men were dead or missing, 30,000 were wounded and over 10,000 maimed by frostbite. Thousands of others had pneumonia. The alpine troops were the least affected: the Tridentina had only 65% casualties, the Julia 80% and the Cuneense 88%.

In November the Anglo-Americans had invaded French Algeria and convinced the French to join them and then had advanced into Tunisia. In reaction Hitler sent his armies into southern France and Mussolini ever on the lookout for new conquests occupied more of the French Riviera and Corsica. The Germans began flying troops to Tunisia at the rate of a thousand a day and Mussolini sent troops there by sea and from Libya. At the beginning of December the Germans repelled the allied advance into western Tunisia.

Meanwhile Rommel had decided to retreat across Libya into Tunisia. Mussolini's dreams of African empire would live or die in the rainy mountains of Tunisia.

By mid-December the Germans had two divisions holding the west Tunisia line twelve miles from the city of Tunis and were joined by the Italian Superga and Giovanni Fascisti Divisions and 50th Brigade. Their opponents were a US corps, a French corps and the British First Army.

The fighting was static, charge and counter-charge trading ownership of hilltops that a tourist would never look at twice.

In February Rommel reached Tunisia weeks ahead of the chasing British and launched an attack against the Americans, using the 10th and 21st Panzer and the Italian Centauro Armoured Divisions. They put the fear of god into the Americans and forced them back through Kasserine Pass almost to Algeria, but Rommel called off the attacks on the 21st when he saw he could gain no more.

He was also eager to turn back and hit the British Eighth Army with a pre-emptive strike, before that force could fully arrive from Libya. However, his weak tank forces failed in this on 6 March at Medennine and he called it off at once.

Rommel now returned to Europe to plead with Hitler and Mussolini to abandon Tunisia before it was too late. Naturally they ignored his pleas.

General Messe took over Rommel's army of 25,000 Germans and 55,000 Italians (now renamed Italian First Army), which held their lines for a week in late March under the Eighth Army's assaults, but thereafter the army began to retreat. By now the troops were fighting in battle groups, each one containing Germans and Italians from several divisions: Giovanni Fascisti, Spezia, Pistoia, 90th, Trieste, DAK, 164th, Centauro and a mere handful of survivors from divisions destroyed at Alamein.

As always the retreat was under constant air assault and by mid-April Messe's forces were fighting on the left flank of the German and Italian defenders of west Tunisia. By May they had their backs to the sea and on 9 May Fifth Panzer Army surrendered. Messe gave up three days later. The axis presence in Africa was over. A quarter of a million Italians and Germans, evenly divided, walked into captivity.

The allies had already been bombing Sicily and the island's meagre coastal defences manned by blackshirts and reservists up to age 55 were under serious pressure to desert, for their officers were of poor quality and the bombardment was killing men for no gain. It is surprising, therefore, that many fought back when the allies invaded southern Sicily on 10 July 1943 with the largest allied amphibious invasion of the war: 160,000 men. One coastal 'division' suffered 50% casualties before folding up.

General Guzzoni's Sixth Army relied for the real defence of Sicily in its manoeuvre force of the Aosta, Assietta, Napoli and Livorno Divisions aided by the German 15th Panzergrenadier and Hermann Goering Panzer Divisions: but 'aided' is not the right word. By this date the Italians and Germans were barely on speaking terms. Hitler even had the gall to send Guzzoni a German 'adviser'.

The Italians and Germans counter-attacked: neither made any dent in the allies; although one Italian force almost made it to the coast, but US naval gunfire slaughtered the infantry in heaps and blew their tiny tanks into oblivion.

In Rome on 24 July the members of the fascist grand council, including Ciano, Mussolini's son-in-law, voted no confidence in Mussolini's war leadership. That is all: just a vote that meant nothing legally; but it shook the dictator. It was his first experience of rejection in over twenty years. He went to visit the King to explain and was grabbed by a group of police on the King's orders. It was a coup: the King named Marshal Badoglio as the new Prime Minister.

In hours the Italian people were thronging the streets by the thousand, tearing down posters and statues of Mussolini and singing proscribed songs. Fascists hid indoors. Everyone was sure peace would come.

On 16 August the last defenders left Sicily. The Germans and Italians were quite successful in bringing out 42,000 Germans and 62,000 Italians – but in separate evacuations: there was almost no contact between the two 'partners'.

Sicily cost the Italians 3,000 dead and 226,000 missing, a third of the missing being Sicilians who deserted. Many had joined the allies! By this date 13,000 Italians were serving in the British armed forces!

As soon as he deposed Mussolini the King sent emissaries to the allies seeking peace. In August they came to an agreement: there would be two invasions of Italy, the first by the British Eighth Army in the south, which the Italians would not oppose, and the second made with fifteen divisions including an airborne drop near Rome. The second invasion would be preceded by certain code words broadcast on British radio. Then the Italians would exit the axis and demand the Germans leave. Hitler was pouring troops into Italy and the joint allied Italian action should trap the Germans in Italy, free Italy from fascist-nazi influence and perhaps even cause Germany to rethink her war aims and seek peace.

Inside Italy the Italians had the remnants of the four divisions from Sicily plus the Piceno, Mantova and Legnano Divisions in the south, the remnants of the Russian veterans in the north and eleven divisions in the Rome area, of which the Centauro, Ariete and Littorio were new and not fully formed. Also in the north were the Fifth and Fourth Armies and around Naples the Seventh Army, but again many of the divisions were only partly formed. The coast was defended by so-called coastal divisions, but their fixed defences all pointed out to sea, of course.

Hitler suspected the Italians were going to betray him – he had just finished trying to make peace with the USSR, which would have been a betrayal of Italy – and he ordered all commanders to arrest the nearest Italians upon the issue of one code-word 'axis'.

The invasion of the toe came on 3 September as planned. Local Italians actually helped unload supplies. On the afternoon of the 8th, without the British radio code-word warning, the allies announced to the world that the Italians had surrendered! Everyone, Germans, Italians and allied troops were taken by surprise.

Immediately Hitler issued 'axis' and in response Germans walked up to Italian sentries, as if to ask a question, and got the drop on them, then commandeered the barracks weapons and arrested the unarmed bewildered Italian soldiers and sailors. Within hours a hundred thousand or more were easily captured.

Italian officers told their men to ignore the radio broadcast as it was an allied trick. Fascist officers, who suspected it was true, deliberately connived with the Germans. General Gambara at Fiume handed an entire corps to the Germans. When General Pentimalli surrendered his corps near Naples, one of his staff officers shot himself in shame. Lowly ranking fascists and blackshirts joined the Germans. That evening Badoglio spoke on the radio: it was true. Thus, the Italian Civil War was born.

Near Rome the Sardinian Grenadiers and Piacenza Divisions were attacked by the German 2nd Parachute Division, the Ariete was attacked by the 3rd Panzergrenadier Division and the Pasubio Division was attacked by the 15th Panzer Division. The naval base at Gaeta was attacked by the Hermann Goering Panzer Division. In each case civilians joined the defenders. By midnight there was combat with Italians fighting Germans and fascists in Pisa, Bolzano, Futa Pass, Livorno, Ascoli Piceno, La Spezia, Florence, Verona, Piombino, Teramo, Orbetello, Udine, Reggio nell Emilia, Piacenza, Cremona, Mantova, Bologna, Modena, Chiusi, Orvieto, Viterbo, Tarquinia, Torino, Tortona, Cuneo, Bergamo, Savona, Genoa, Parma, Pavia, Trieste, Fiume, Naples, Averso, Treviso and Trento.

The allies had blown it. Moreover, they invaded not with fifteen divisions, but four, and not near Rome, but south of Naples at Salerno and there was no airborne drop. The 16th Panzergrenadier Division, which had just shot its way into the rear of Italian coastal defences, fought the invaders on the Salerno beaches and stopped them.

The following day the Italian Navy made its way to allied ports under German air attack. The new battleship *La Roma* was sunk with 1,365 lives lost.

On Sardinia civil war broke out inside the Nembo Division barracks. The fascists joined the Germans, who seeing the amount of opposition against them decided to evacuate the island. On Corsica the Cremona and Friuli Divisions began fighting the Germans. The local resistance movement called for French regular forces to come help drive the Germans off that island. On Crete fascists surrendered the Siena Division after a German air raid.

The Italians defending Rome surrendered on the 10th, but only after a German airborne assault, the promise that one division could remain armed and that Rome would not be occupied and the German threat that if the Italians did not give up Rome would be bombed to ruins.

By the end of the 11th on mainland Italy the only resistance to the fascists and Germans was at Piombino, Teramo, Orbetello, Udine, Reggio nell Emilia, Piacenza, Cremona, Mantova, Bologna, Modena and Naples. However, large numbers of troops and civilians had begun fleeing into the mountains determined to wage war as partisans.

In the ports 168 merchant ships scuttled rather than surrender to the Germans. If caught their captains were shot.

In Greece, Albania and Yugoslavia thousands of Italians defected to the partisans, while the fascists joined the Germans. In some places the anti-fascists could not reach the partisans so they resisted German attack: the Zara Division at Zara, the Bergamo Division at Split, the Taurinense Division at several locations, the Isonzo, Lombardia and Cacciatore Divisions in the Slovenian mountains, the Marche Division in Dubrovnik, smaller units at Rabek and

Cattaro, and countless tiny units in small, but bloody engagements. Over the next weeks these garrisons fought until they ran out of ammunition. Mussolini was rescued by Germans on the 12th and he announced a new government and that any Italian officers who ordered resistance against the Germans and fascists would be shot. The fascists put this order into practice and over the next months thousands of soldiers and officers were executed for having shown resistance.

In October the Germans began invading the Greek islands one by one. It was December before they rounded up the last Italian hold-outs.

The king's army had been put through the wringer: in September and October 522,000 were captured by the Germans by one method or another, 35,000 had been killed in action against the Germans/fascists, 60,000 had joined partisans in Greece, Albania and Yugoslavia, tens of thousands had joined the Germans, and countless numbers had either gone home to hide or had become partisans in Italy. The remainder were those who had been reached by the allies, who were now put under the command of Marshal Messe, recently released by the British.

Meanwhile the allies had to protect Sicily, Sardinia, Naples and southern Italy from air raids, amphibious commando assaults and possible invasion. By late September they had decided to let the Italians do this for them.

King Vittorio Emmanuele's navy with 75,000 sailors was now serving the allies and his 28,000-man air force was preparing to fly again under allied orders.

By October his army had the Calabria, Cremona, Friuli, Bari, and Nembo Divisions and several coastal formations in Sardinia, the Sabauda Division and coastal units in Sicily, and in southern Italy coastal units and the Piceno, Legnano and Mantova Divisions. One might suspect that these coastal formations were redundant, but the allies did not think so: they reinforced them with their own coastal troops! Many of the coastal troops operated flak guns and searchlights against German air raids. Moreover, there were 19,000 Italian flak troops doing the same and about 40,000 Carabinieri (military police) were involved in traffic control, security, and hunting black marketeers and fascist partisans and saboteurs.

Counting rear-echelon personnel, about 550,000 Italians were in the King's uniform serving the allied cause.

In addition among the Italians in allied prisoner of war camps 110,000 had volunteered to serve the King. Reclassified as 'cooperators' they were given rear-echelon or civilian duties in their land of incarceration: USA, Britain, Australia, Egypt, Libya (and some would follow the US Army into France in 1944), but almost none were allowed to join the King's forces in Italy. British civilians, many of whom knew nothing of politics, did not realise that these Italians were now allied troops allowed to spend their pay in the town: the civilians simply thought the authorities were getting soft on prisoners! Fascists refused to cooperate, of course, and remained locked up.

Aditionally, 16,000 Italians were now wearing British uniform.

The British government did not want to use Italians in the front line, though, because they were in a dilemma. They knew the myth of Italian cowardice was hokum, but they had told their people this. If they used Italian soldiers now, it would be evidence that either they had been lying or that the allied armies were so sorely tried that even Italians had to be put into the line. The British government would admit to neither. Therefore, they suggested to the Americans, their joint partners in the Italian campaign, that they accept the King's offer of troops, but use them for rear-echelon duties only.

However, the US Fifth Army was already using 4,000 Italian soldiers at the front as porters, stretcher bearers, medics, scouts etc., and they asked for a combat unit. The British relented and sent a provisional division, which had several names given to it by the British, who wanted to fool their own journalists. The unit went into action near the Cassino front in December 1943 and held its own. By April 1944 the US Fifth Army was using 17,300 Italians at the front (including the provisional division) and 23,000 in the rear, and the British were using 4,000 Italians at the front and 30,000 in the rear.

That month the provisional division received an official name, the Utili, after its commander, and was coupled with the Nembo Division to make a small corps of about 22,000 men. In May the corps shifted from US Fifth Army to British Eighth Army. Obviously the British had overcome their prejudice and their fear of British public opinion. The corps fought well alongside Poles, who praised them.

Mussolini controlled most of Italy through the use of German troops and fascists – the latter formed about 100,000 Carabinieri and police and 40,000 National Guard and there were many smaller self-proclaimed units. Mussolini also had 47,000 troops in his new army to be divided among the new Monte Rosa, Littorio, and Italia Divisions; 12,000 marines of the San Marco Division; a small air force to face the great allied air armada; and 13,000 sailors of the Condotierri Division, who began hunting partisans in the northern mountains. By December 1943 Mussolini had about 275,000 armed personnel on security duty or in training. A fascist infantry unit performed well at the siege of Anzio.

By November about 100,000 Italians had put on German uniform, many in independent platoons at the front, but most in rear-echelon or anti-partisan units in Italy, Yugoslavia and Greece.

Hitler annexed the Sud-Tirol and northeast Italy, giving all male inhabitants a choice of putting on German or fascist uniform. The partisan war was brutal. Mussolini would have no debate about how to treat them. He proved this when he executed Ciano, his son-in-law for having voted against him the previous July! If he was willing to murder the father of his grandchildren, imagine how he treated captured partisans.

By late 1944 Mussolini had the following troops hunting partisans: 68,000 National Guard, 100,000 Black Brigades, 80,000 Carabinieri and 13,000 Condotierri. He also had 20,000 flak gunners throughout northern Italy, and a marine and three army divisions manning the Franco-Italian border against French and US troops.

The German Army had recruited 100,000 Italians: and there were 10,000 in their navy, 90,000 in their air force, mostly serving as flak gunners, and 105,000 in the SS as camp guards, sentries and in two anti-partisan divisions; plus several thousand served in paramilitary organisations. Thus about 665,000 Italians were taking a direct part in the axis war effort.

The allies only pushed north of Naples to take Rome in June 1944 and by August they were creeping just south of Bologna. They were to remain there until April 1945: the Italian campaign was as frustrating for the allied front line soldier as it was for the partisans.

In December 1944 Mussolini tried his own offensive, which failed miserably: he blamed the accompanying German troops and they blamed the Italia and Monterosa Divisions; but the two divisions settled into the line and stayed there until spring.

The allies had withdrawn the Italian corps from the line – the Poles were sad to see them go, but in January 1945 the allies began to feed into the line the first of six Italian divisions. By now the US Fifth and British Eighth Armies were preparing for their April offensive with 600,000 personnel, of which fully one third were Italian! And this did not count the 500,000 Italian troops, sailors and airmen serving elsewhere. Behind the axis lines 250,000 partisans were waiting to attack. Thus, 950,000 Italians were taking a direct role in the allied war effort.

On 1 April preliminary attacks began and in days blended into the spring offensive. The allies were attacking with twelve independent brigades and twenty divisions, including the Mantova, Legnano, Folgore, Cremona and Friuli Divisions.

Generally the axis lines crumbled, though each allied soldier had his 'one rough fight' to get through before the war ended. On the 21st several divisions entered Bologna and others aimed for the mighty Po River. The Germans and fascists hoped they would be safe on the north bank, but few

made it and in any case the partisans soon controlled every town. The Italian divisions received the unheard of praise from the British that they were 'invaluable'.

At the end of April Mussolini was arrested by partisans: they held him for a day, were scared of a fascist rescue attempt and finally executed him, his mistress and most of his government ministers near Lake Como. Already the Germans were negotiating a surrender. By 2 May it was all over.

The world's image of the Italian male is that of a happy-go-lucky, artistic, opera loving gourmet much obsessed with the opposite sex. This image is so strong, and so accurate, that anything that challenges it seems unbelievable fantasy; thus in films and books Mafia gangsters are actually seen as almost harmless. The truth is Italians are human and possess all the human characteristics: humanity, cruelty, bravery, fear, greed and generosity. Sitting in an armchair a half century after World War II it is still easy to imagine some Germans behaving cruelly in that conflict, but odd to think of Italians behaving as such, yet some Italians behaved with bestiality of a despicable nature, massacring and raping foreigners and their own people with abandon.

Many Italians performed badly on the battlefield owing to inept leadership, poor equipment and a lack of serious training, and many exhibited great courage on the battlefield. The closest that allied war correspondents came to describing any Europeans as 'suicide warriors' was their description of Italian underwater chariot riders.

Anti-Italian prejudice among some so-called historians stinks to high heaven even a half century after the war, with such nonsense as describing an Italian destroyer sailing into battle 'reluctantly'. How on earth a ship can sail 'reluctantly', is beyond this author. A ship either sails forward or backward.

Other so-called combat veterans have described Italian dive-bombers as obviously less aggressive than German, though how the veteran could tell the difference between an Italian Stuka and a German Stuka is beyond this author, for who is it who sticks his head out of a foxhole during an air raid to read insignia?

German generals say the Italians let them down: German generals have yet to blame any of their defeats on themselves!

Yes, some Italians ran, and so did some Americans, Germans and Britons. In September 1943 the British Eighth Army lazily sauntered up the Italian peninsula despite facing no opposition, while just miles away Italian housewives battled German troops with their bare hands. How dare those 'saunterers' denigrate the courage of the Italians.

When British high command in Italy in 1944 suggested the US Fifth Army get rid of their Italian combat soldiers, General Clark the commander replied his army could not operate without them!

Incidentally, every twelfth American soldier was racially Italian and they were known for reckless bravery.

No one has calculated Italian war casualties fully, but the following is as thorough as can be and does not include 15,000 African soldiers of the Italian Army killed in East Africa:

200,000 who died fighting the allies (163,000 June 1940 to the morning of 8 September 1943 including those who died in prisoner of war camps from maltreatment, with an estimated 20,000 killed fighting the allies after that date, a minimum of 10,000 murdered by partisans in the last days and about 7,000 killed wearing German uniform);

130,000 who died fighting the fascists (35,000 regulars 8 September to end of 1943, 4,729 killed and wounded after that date, 20,000 partisans killed in Greece, Albania and Yugoslavia, 45,000 partisans killed in Italy, and 30,000 Italian prisoners of war, who died from German maltreatment, because they would not volunteer to serve them);

150,000 civilians dead (64,000 civilians killed in allied bombing raids 1940-45 and 80,000 from cross fire, axis air raids and murder by fascists and Germans in retaliation for partisan activity, plus 4,500 murdered because of their Jewish race):

a total of 480,000 minimum. •

See Index

JAPAN

Other names:	Nippon, Greater East Asia Co-prosperity Sphere
Status in 1931:	independent
Government in 1931:	oligarchy
Population in 1931:	73,000,000 in the home islands.
Make-up in 1931:	Japanese; a tiny number of Ainu.
Religion:	primarily Buddhist, some Christians.
Location:	islands off the edge of Eastern Asia

In the 19th century the Europeans turned their gaze towards eastern Asia, and began to gobble up these nations and milk them dry for profit, with the exception of China, which was too big. Soon China was ruled indirectly by the international community of thieves and looters, who were politely known as the colonial powers.

The Japanese knew they were next on the list: as early as the mid-19th century the British and Americans had attacked Japanese ports. The Japanese decided that the only way to survive was to take the mantle of a colonial power for themselves.

There is nothing inherently cruel or warmongering in the Japanese character. Indeed in the 17th century when they saw the calamitous casualties that firearms could inflict on the battlefield, they repudiated this invention brought to them by foreign Christians, and made it an offence punishable by death to possess a firearm. In such a way was warfare made more humane. No other nation had done this.

It is all the more sad to relate that the Japanese became the victims of the most horrific firearm known to man: the atomic weapon.

To take the disguise of colonial power the Japanese began to imitate the British: after all both were islands off the coast of a threatening land mass and needed secure sea lanes and a source of raw materials to supply their factories. In 1894 the Japanese warred with China and won the island of Taiwan and a place in the international settlements of China, so that just six years later when the Chinese revolted against the Europeans, Japanese troops were allowed to participate in the war alongside European and American troops. This sealed Japanese membership of the club.

In 1898 the Americans turned on Spain, a fellow colonial power, and stole the Philippines. The Japanese were keen learners: in 1904 they turned on Russia and stole the Kuriles and Southern Sakhalin.

In 1914 everyone turned on the Germans and stole their colonies: the Japanese gained some Pacific islands as a result.

However, in 1931 the Japanese upset the colonial game. It had been a gentleman's agreement that as China was big enough for everybody, no one colonial power should attempt to conquer that nation for themselves. The Japanese broke the rules by attacking Chinese warlords in Manchuria and occupying that province. In punishment the colonial powers threw Japan out of the League of Nations, despite the plea of the Japanese government that its generals had usurped their authority.

The government had indeed ordered the Army to cease its war in China, but the generals took no notice. In fact they became greedy and began a ponderous village by village conquest.

The Navy took sides with the government and refused to aid the Army. The politicians were embarrassed by this insolence, but terrified of civil war between the Navy and Army, for each had its own 'army' and 'air force' and 'merchant fleet', though the army possessed no warships.

The militants within the Japanese Army organised youth clubs, parades, demonstrations and other community relations programmes to propagandise the people. The most militant of the army faction was Colonel Hideki Tojo, who wielded far more power than his rank suggests. Using military police, intimidation and murder Tojo and friends gained tremendous influence.

In July 1937 the Navy reluctantly began to help the generals in their expansion of the China war by enabling fifteen divisions of the First and Second Armies to land in China to reinforce the Kwantung Army. In November they transported the Tenth Army to China. Despite this massive increase in manpower, the Japanese were still outnumbered

by the Chinese ten times, so the advance was slow.

Yet, the biggest reason why the generals made war piecemeal was because they did not want to have to conscript additional classes above the normal intake and upset the Japanese people, nor did they have the means to fully supply a larger force in China. In other words their eyes were bigger than their stomach.

The mounting casualties were a problem. Propaganda played down the number, 75,000 dead by late 1937, and made heroes of the fallen. Many a village family wore mourning clothes as a result of the generals' greed in China.

Yet the generals' arrogance grew. They began to launch 'accidental' attacks on American and British ships and installations in China and in 1938 they probed the USSR: the Soviet riposte inflicted a serious defeat on the little division-sized force. In 1939 they tried again, this time with a corps, and in August suffered 11,000 casualties when the Soviets responded. Days after this defeat, Germany, one of Japan's few friends by this date, signed a treaty with the USSR. The generals were taken by surprise and felt totally isolated and betrayed.

The immediate result was the installation of Prime Minister Abe, a vociferous, anti-Army, anti-war politician. He hoped that the loss of face suffered by the generals would cause them to listen to him and pull out of China.

It may have done so, but Hitler secretly contacted the generals and told them not to worry: the USSR treaty was just a ploy to keep the Soviets off his back while he defeated Britain and France. Relieved by this message, the generals snubbed Abe and the pacifists. There were further 'accidental' attacks on British and American personnel in China. The American reply: an embargo on war materials did not impress the generals. Abe resigned in late 1939. His successor, Prime Minister Yonai, vowed to halt all 'accidental' attacks and surprisingly the generals agreed. It had probably occurred to them that if Germany was defeated by Britain and France, the British and Americans might assault Japan's sea lanes and starve her into submission. The generals, therefore, straightened up their act.

However, in June 1940 the Germans defeated France and kicked Britain out of Europe, while the Americans sat back. Germany appeared invincible and, the Japanese generals assumed, would now turn on the USSR. This gave the Japanese generals tremendous confidence. In fact some young hot-head army officers tried to kill Yonai and were arrested for their impudence.

The generals used more subtle means, forcing Yonai to resign and replacing him with their own man, Prince Konoye. Immediately, using the Kempai Tai political police he began a serious crackdown on opposition.

The generals decided that China continued to resist primarily because she had hope in the colonial powers, not because they were suddenly amiable towards the Chinese, but because they still considered China to be communal property. Therefore, the generals studied each power in turn and formed the following opinions.

France was helpless, having been defeated by the Germans and then kicked in the teeth by the British at Mers-el-Kebir. France would be no problem.

Britain was weak in Asia, because she concentrated on her German, French and Italian enemies, even to the point of absorbing troops from her Pacific dominions of New Zealand, Canada and Australia.

The Dutch possessed a large force in Asia, but as the motherland was under German occupation they would not resist too hard, for fear of the Germans taking hostages upon Japanese request.

The Portuguese were so corrupt they would not even notice a Japanese invasion in their colonies, let alone resist it.

The USSR would soon have its hands full fending off Germany.

This left only the Americans with their powerful Pacific Fleet and a large army in the Philippines. Konoye and Tojo gave the Navy a mission: devise a plan to destroy the US Navy's Pacific Fleet, which would in turn isolate the Philippines from succour, so that this island colony could be conquered. Meanwhile the army would gain a stepping stone in French Indo-China.

On 22 September 1940 the Japanese invaded Indo-China. Immediately, they asked Hitler to intervene, who spoke with the French leader Pétain, who ordered his troops in Indo-China to cease fire and invite 40,000 Japanese troops into Indo-China as guests. It was typical of the thinking of the generals that they invaded and then negotiated, rather than the other way around, thereby suffering about 2,000 killed and wounded needlessly.

In July 1941 the generals seized administration of Indo-China. In response the Americans, British and Dutch cut off all oil exports to Japan. This reaction, though not unexpected, put a timetable on events, something that had not been done before: the reason being Japan only had enough oil reserves to last to the end of the year. Indo-Chinese oil was insufficient. In other words, Tojo told the Navy, if his diplomats could not convince the allied nations to lift their embargo by December, the Navy would have to attack the Americans.

In October Prince Konoye was forced to resign: his diplomatic efforts had failed and time was running out. He was replaced by none other than Tojo himself, who now chose to rule publicly, not from behind the scenes. Yet, even with this fanatic in charge, the government ministers did not vote on the peace or war issue until 25 November, by which time the fleet was at sea. The vote was for war.

To conquer the American, British and Dutch bases in China, Malaya, Burma, Philippines and East Indies, the Army and Navy put together a force of 240,000 troops, while the main battle fleet was on its way to strike Hawaii to cripple the US Pacific Fleet. Ever the imitators, the Japanese had studied the British carrier plane raid on the Italian fleet at Taranto the previous year and believed they could repeat the success, i.e. hurt the American fleet hard enough that their admirals would fear to sail.

The overall purpose of the war plan was to put the allies into such a no win situation early on that they agreed to terms: loss of their oil- and rubber-rich colonies to Japan and denial of aid to the Chinese. With a little bit of luck this should be achieved in six months.

The code of Bushido, expanded and warped by Tojo and pals, gave every Japanese citizen one goal, that of conquest. Victory in battle was the supreme achievement and death in battle the supreme glory. Failure was not tolerated and suicide expected of all who did fail. The ordinary soldier and sailor did not accept this creed: his religion – Buddhism or Christianity – would not allow him to, hence the brutality with which sergeants and officers ruled their men. Beatings were commonplace and execution of officers and men for dereliction of duty, usually by beheading, took place in public.

Treatment of enemy prisoners was despicable for according to this new warped philosophy, a man, woman or child who surrendered gave up their rights to be treated as humans. Likewise any Japanese who surrendered would be executed if caught.

At first glance this seems a horrific creed, but in the USA every schoolboy learned of Davy Crockett and his colleagues at the Alamo, who fought to the death rather than surrender or retreat. When fighting native American Indians, white American men would murder their women and children rather than let them fall into Indian hands. During World War II it was the done thing in the British Army for an officer's disgrace for a sex or theft reason to be answered with suicide.

The new Japanese method of waging war meant that captured enemy wounded were often bayoneted and those who were taken prisoner were worked, beaten and starved to death.

The army infantry division carried over 24,000 men on its rolls, but its combat echelon of nine infantry, three artillery, three engineer and a reconnaissance battalion was not much larger than that of an allied division half this size. There were also independent brigades of 5,600 men divided into five infantry and one artillery battalion, an engineer company and rear-echelon support. The independent regiment was a slimmed-down version of the brigade with 3,800 personnel. The Japanese omitted the normal structure 'division, corps, army, army group' and preferred 'division, army, area army'.

As befitting their Pacific Ocean aspirations the US Navy and Japanese Navy both had their own armies. Japanese naval troops were divided into Special Naval Landing Forces, each of two infantry and two artillery companies manned by 1,060 personnel.

In the early hours of 8 December 1941 General Takumi's task force landed on the north-east coast of British Malaya. There was little opposition. Less than an hour later just after sunrise on 7 December (Hawaii time) the carrier planes of Admiral Nagumo's carrier task force signalled Admiral Yamamoto, Chief of the Combined Fleet: "Tora! Tora! Tora!"; meaning the Americans below were unaware. The Japanese had taken the Americans completely by surprise. Minutes later Americans began to die as the Japanese hit without warning, a trick they had learned from the British, who had made this sort of sneak attack famous as 'Copenhagen-ing' in 1801.

Actually a pseudo-declaration of war was supposed to have been handed to the American government in the nick of time, but it was not. Later Japanese assertions that it had not been intended as a sneak attack were lies: otherwise the attack would not have been launched on a Sunday and the code signal to Yamamoto would have been unnecessary. The manner of the attack was the greatest mistake any Japanese government has ever made. Yamamoto had warned the generals of this. They refused to listen.

Within hours of the offensive the Japanese Fifteenth Army invaded Thailand overland from Indo-China and by six amphibious invasions; Japanese troops overcame British and American forces at Shanghai; and the 38th Division invaded British Hong Kong. Takumi's force in Malaya was counter-attacked, but easily repelled the British. In Hawaii the Japanese had sunk or crippled all eight American battleships and three cruisers and seven other warships, destroyed 188 planes and caused havoc with docks and barracks, for the loss of a few planes and six midget submarines.

On the third day Japanese planes caught the so-called British Far Eastern Fleet off Malaya and sank both its capital ships. The Japanese had therefore not only destroyed all enemy battleships in the Pacific and its tributary seas, but had in fact replaced all battleships of every navy, including the Japanese Navy, with the aircraft carrier as the queen of the high seas. The Japanese naval aviators understood this at once, but their admirals, raised in the tradition of battleships, did not understand. The aviators did not dare point out to these men of higher rank that the two air assaults had rendered the mighty Japanese battleships obsolete, for by definition it rendered the admirals obsolete too. The irony is that by destroying the allied battleships the Japanese made the US Pacific Fleet with its five carriers more equal to the Japanese Navy with its twelve carriers than the two fleets were prior to the attack. In fact, with hindsight the Japanese attack on Hawaii was the worst thing they could possibly have done.

By 11 December Thailand was firmly under the Japanese thumb; Japanese planes flying from Taiwan had destroyed American air power in the Philippines; and General Homma's Fourteenth Army had invaded the Philippines island of Luzon at Aparri and Vigan. On the 12th a force landed at the south end of Luzon at Legaspi.

By the 13th the 38th Division had driven the British from mainland Hong Kong and was preparing to invade Hong Kong island.

The 5th and 18th Divisions under General Yamashita's Twenty-Fifth Army crossed from Thailand into north-west Malaya, many of the troops using bicycles, and took Penang on the 16th: the British were in full retreat.

On the night of the 18th the 38th Division invaded Hong Kong island.

General Homma's landings on Luzon had been feints designed to draw enemy forces northwards and southwards. On the 22nd he landed his 48th Division at Lingayen Gulf a hundred miles south of Vigan. He also put a force ashore on Mindanao Island on the 20th. On the 24th he sent the 16th Division into Luzon at Lamon Bay seventy miles south-east of Manilla. He hoped to squeeze the American and Filipino forces at Manilla. On the 25th he landed men on Jolo Island.

On the island of Borneo a special naval landing force of the 3rd Fleet invaded Kuching on 24 December during which a Japanese destroyer was sunk by a Dutch submarine: the British garrison fled into the jungle.

On the 25th Hong Kong surrendered. For 2,750 casualties the Japanese had killed 3,000 and captured 9,000, and interned 3,000 white civilians.

The year ended with most of the enemy on Luzon fleeing westwards to the Bataan Peninsula, where Homma easily cornered them. On 2 January the 16th Division entered the streets of Manilla to find the enemy evacuated. On the night of the 10th Fourteenth Army suffered its first serious losses attacking the enemy at the neck of the Bataan Peninsula and by the 25th Homma had to order his men to hold what they had – after all the Americans and Filipinos weren't going anywhere.

As early as 16 December elements of the Southern Army had crept into Burma from Thailand, but it was January before this force and the 55th Division really invaded that oil-, rice- and rubber-rich British colony. The British defences were quickly beaten back.

In Malaya the 5th and 18th Divisions steadily advanced southwards, aided by five amphibious invasions to outflank the enemy defence lines, so that by 16 January on the west coast they were only fifty miles from the southern tip of the peninsula. Later in the month on the east coast the Takumi Force reached Endau, about eighty miles from the tip. Only two British destroyers were able to interfere with the landing and one was sunk by Japanese warships.

Further landings on Borneo by naval troops of the 3rd Fleet's Central Force took place at Labuan 1 January, undefended by the British, and Tarakan on the 11th, where a Dutch force resisted for a few days.

Also on the 11th troops of the 3rd Fleet's Eastern Force landed on Celebes at Manado and Kema. Dutch opposition was easily overcome. Further landings took place by Central Force on Borneo at Sandakan on the 19th and Balikpapan on the 24th, where the first successful allied naval counter-attack took place: US destroyers sank four Japanese destroyers. The Eastern Force landed at Kendari, Celebes on the 24th. Dutch resistance was slight.

On the 23rd naval troops from the 4th Fleet landed in the Solomons on New Britain, New Ireland and Bougainville sitting astride the route Australia-Hawaii. Rabaul on New Britain, captured from 1,400 Australians, who quickly surrendered, was immediately turned into a major base.

On the 30th naval troops of the 3rd Fleet's Eastern Force invaded Ambon and in two days overran two battalions of Australians and Dutch.

On 1 February Yamashita's Twenty-fifth Army troops scouted the southern Malaya shore, peering at Singapore Island, where the British had retreated. The Japanese were exhausted and low on supplies. The far shore, swampy and dark, looked uninviting.

On 4 February Japanese planes attacked the Dutch East Indies Fleet, which beefed up by British, Australian and American warships contained six cruisers, fifteen destroyers and some smaller vessels, a body that could seriously interfere with an amphibious landing. However, the planes damaged several ships and forced the fleet to head for port. The cruiser USS *Marblehead* had to return to the USA for repair.

On the night of 8 February the 5th, 18th and Imperial Guards Divisions crossed the narrow waterway to Singapore in barges and rafts: allied firepower was heavy, causing many casualties, but wave after wave of soldiers were sent forward until by dawn they had a foothold. Come daylight Japanese aircraft made a difference and by noon the infantry were swiftly moving inland.

Makassar, the last Dutch-held town on Celebes, was invaded on the 9th by the men who had taken Kendari and was overrun in a day.

On the 10th Banjarmasin on Borneo's south coast was invaded by the units that had overrun Balikpapan.

On the 14th 3rd Fleet's Western Force went into action for the first time landing on Banka island and making a combined paratroop and amphibious invasion of Sumatra near Palembang. The Japanese sank a Dutch destroyer off Banka.

The news of their landing was overshadowed by the news of the surrender of the British on Singapore on the 15th, just hours before Yamashita was to make up his mind

whether or not to retreat: he was outnumbered two to one and almost out of ammunition! Because of the prestige placed on Singapore the Japanese considered this to be their greatest victory to date. For 3,500 killed and 6,000 wounded in Malaya-Singapore they had inflicted 141,000 casualties on the British.

On the 19th troops of 3rd Fleet's Eastern Force left Makassar for Bali, taking that exotic island without opposition. However, the Japanese task force was counter-attacked by the Dutch Fleet at night in the Lombok Straits. The Japanese recovered swiftly and drove off the enemy, sinking a destroyer, for only minor damage to themselves. The Japanese Navy excelled at night gunnery.

Also on the 19th Admiral Nagumo's task force repeated his Hawaii success by striking Darwin, Australia, bombing the port, sinking a destroyer and eight transports and causing serious psychological damage to Australian morale. The Japanese had no intention of invading Australia, but deliberately gave the opposite impression.

On the 20th Eastern Force troops including elements of the 38th Division invaded Timor by two amphibious and one paratroop landings. The Japanese had made a deal with the Portuguese, who allowed them to enter their half of the island. The Dutch half did not resist either, its Dutch and Australian garrison choosing to go bush and wage guerrilla war.

On the 27th in the Java Sea between Java and Borneo the Japanese invasion force of the 3rd Fleet, bound for Java, ran into the Dutch Fleet: with no air support the Japanese had four cruisers and fourteen destroyers against five allied cruisers and twelve destroyers. The battle stretched into the evening and ended with several Japanese vessels damaged, but they sank two cruisers and three destroyers and crippled a cruiser.

The following day the Japanese were attacked by two cruisers and ten destroyers in Bantam Bay. Without air support the Japanese warships sank both cruisers and crippled a destroyer. Within days aircraft and warships sank another five allied destroyers.

On 1 March 3rd Fleet's Western Force and the 2nd Division invaded Java at Merak and Eretan and Central Force with the 48th Division invaded at Kragan. On the 7th the Dutch command surrendered 70,000 men.

This same day the British abandoned Rangoon to the Japanese Fifteenth Army and began retreating across Burma towards India chased by the 18th, 56th, 33rd and 55th Divisions. A Chinese force entered Burma, but soon retreated.

On 9 April the 80,000 defenders of Bataan surrendered to Homma's 30,000.

In April Admiral Nagumo's task force sailed into the Indian Ocean with five carriers, four battleships, four cruisers and eight destroyers against the remnants of the British Far Eastern Fleet. Nagumo's aircraft sank two cruisers, a destroyer and a carrier, plus several merchant ships and damaged two harbours in Ceylon.

On 6 May Homma conquered Corregidor Island off Bataan and convinced the American General Wainwright to surrender all defenders throughout the Philippines by telling him he would massacre his prisoners otherwise.

It was done. In exactly five months the Japanese had conquered the American, Dutch and British possessions between India and the Solomons. By now there was nothing to stop the Japanese from invading any island in this area. They took several without opposition.

They had inflicted 375,000 killed or captured for less than 40,000 killed and wounded: an incredibly cheap victory, the Japanese generals thought, considering they had lost 185,000 dead in China to date. The Navy was also happy for they had crippled the US Pacific Fleet and British Far Eastern Fleet and destroyed the Dutch East Indies Fleet for the total loss of five destroyers.

Yet at the height of their empire building things began to go wrong for the Japanese. Allied submarines and aircraft were sinking merchant vessels – not many at first, only twelve in December, but enough to worry the Japanese who needed them more than ever to feed the troops they had put on countless islands.

Another facet of the sea war that aggravated the situation was that the Army and Navy not only had their own merchant fleets, as did civilian organisations, but no one bothered to coordinate their efforts and the Army and Navy refused to assist each other. Thus, some ships were travelling back to port empty while others were overworked.

The most immediate danger was from the carriers of the US Pacific Fleet. In January they had sailed from Hawaii to bombard the Marshall Islands and in February struck the Marshalls, the Gilberts and Rabaul. In March they raided several island bases. But it was on 18 April that they made their most important psychological impact. Eighteen US B-25 twin engine medium bombers bombed Japan, including Tokyo! Japanese army intelligence was sure they had flown from a carrier, though the Navy said it couldn't be done – the planes were too big. Captured American fliers refused to talk. Some were executed by the Japanese after a show trial for 'crimes against humanity'.

The Japanese finally got a chance to engage the American carriers in May, when the US Pacific Fleet with the carriers *Lexington* and *Yorktown* tried to interfere with Admiral Goto's landing in southern New Guinea. Admiral Takagi's covering force also joined the four-day fight in the Coral Sea. The Japanese sank the *Lexington*, crippled the *Yorktown* and sank two destroyers, but the carrier *Shoho* was sunk and the *Shokaku* damaged, and most important of all Goto retreated.

This was the first naval engagement in history in which no warship sighted the enemy: proof that the Japanese aviators had been correct in their judgement following the Hawaii strike, that the day of the battleship was over.

Yamamoto knew he had to draw the US Pacific Fleet out again and wanted to do it while the *Yorktown* was too crippled to sail, leaving the Americans with only the carriers *Enterprise* and *Hornet*. He chose a two-pronged invasion across the Pacific with a northern prong aiming to invade the islands off Alaska, while the central prong, led by Nagumo's four carriers, two battleships and three cruisers, would occupy Midway Island, north-west of Hawaii. Not far behind Nagumo was Yamamoto himself with five battleships, four cruisers and thirty destroyers.

Yamamoto did not know that the Americans had begun to read his signals and thus knew all about the plan, but funnily enough this would have pleased the wily old admiral, for he knew he had to bring the American carriers to battle to sink them.

On 4 June Nagumo's veteran airmen flew off to bomb Midway. Midway-based planes retaliated against Nagumo, but hit nothing, his flak and defensive fighters being far too good. When Nagumo beat off American carrier planes Yamamoto knew the plan was going according to schedule: the American carriers had left Hawaii.

However, in mid-morning as Nagumo's defensive fighters were refuelling and his bombers were arming with torpedoes in order to hit the American carriers, another flight of American carrier dive bombers arrived: the carriers *Kaga*, *Akagi* and *Soryu* were devastated as the American bombs fell on torpedoes and fuel on the flight decks. The *Soryu* went down in just twenty minutes. Nagumo had to transfer from the burning *Akagi* to a cruiser.

One flight of Japanese planes from the *Hiryu* found the *Yorktown*, not as damaged as the Japanese had thought, and crippled her and sank a destroyer. But that afternoon more American carrier planes arrived to sink the *Hiryu*. The *Akagi* burned out and sank and the *Kaga* was sunk by an American submarine.

The next day an American plane crashed into the cruiser *Mikuma*, sinking her. On the 6th a Japanese submarine sank the *Yorktown*.

The immediate result of the battle was the retreat of the Midway invasion force – the Alaskan invasion went ahead – but the long term result was that the Americans were now in pole position to win the race to establish naval supremacy. It would be a long race, but Japanese warship construction, especially carrier construction, could not hope to win the race. In 1943 the Japanese would launch one carrier, three cruisers, twenty destroyers and 37 submarines, but the Americans would launch 34 carriers, two battleships, eleven cruisers, 347 destroyers

and 56 submarines. Perhaps of greater importance was the loss of the veteran Japanese air crews and aircraft maintenance crews.

On the island of New Guinea the Japanese Seventeenth Army's 20th and 51st Divisions began a land campaign, which took the form of Japanese infantry battling at distances of a few feet with Australian and American infantry in primitive, steaming jungle. It was a disgusting, inglorious campaign.

On 7 August the Americans began calling the shots as they put a reinforced marine division ashore on Guadalcanal and Tulagi. Only Japanese rear-echelon troops were here and were overrun in a week, so the Japanese Seventeenth Army decided to throw the Ichiki Regiment and the Yosuka Naval Landing Force onto Guadalcanal to retake the airfield. The regiment was totally destroyed in one attack – the commander committed suicide – and a larger ground force, the 2nd Division and the 35th Brigade, had to be sent to Guadalcanal.

This was the first evidence the allies had that the Japanese ground forces might not be as invincible as they seemed. It is this author's opinion that the Japanese ground forces were in fact not very good. Their generals were incompetent in basic tactics, though their strategy was not bad at times. Most infantry officers had neither initiative nor tactical knowledge. Their victories over the poorly armed and ill-coordinated Chinese and over poorly trained and badly led allied colonial troops had given them a cockiness that was most unwarranted. Their favourite manoeuvre was a direct frontal assault, the infantry yelling 'Banzai' at the top of their voices, but at Milne Bay, New Guinea and at Bloody Ridge, Guadalcanal, this failed disastrously as the allies stood their ground and mowed down the Japanese with machine gun and rifle fire. The Japanese supply system ranged in quality from poor to non-existent. As early as 1942 Japanese soldiers were going into battle suffering from malnutrition. Their equipment was shoddy, their rifles lacked stopping power and they were untrained for jungle warfare: without a senior sergeant they were hopelessly inadequate.

Then why, one may ask, did it take so long to defeat them? The answer lies in the morale of the average Japanese soldier. On the one hand he was afraid of his officers, on the other he was afraid of shaming his family and his unit. There is no doubt that the little fellow from Tokyo was the toughest individual any army has ever fielded. He could be starved, shot, blown up and burned and still resist.

At sea it was a different matter, especially at night. On 8 August the 8th Fleet sent a night patrol into the waters off Guadalcanal and sank four allied cruisers near Savo Island. Next day planes sank an American destroyer.

On the 24th the 8th Fleet put to sea again and tangled in daylight with an American task force in the Eastern Solomons. After losing a carrier and a destroyer the Japanese withdrew.

In mid-September a Japanese submarine claimed a US carrier.

On the night of 7 October Japanese forces bringing reinforcements to Guadalcanal met US warships. The Japanese sank a destroyer, but lost a cruiser and a destroyer.

In the next fleet engagement, off Santa Cruz 24-26 October, for two Japanese carriers damaged, they sank an American carrier and crippled another.

Beginning in November Japanese warships tried to influence the stalemate on Guadalcanal by their expert night naval gunnery and long lance torpedoes, but the Americans were gaining radar sets that somewhat offset the inequality. In the first engagement on the 12th two battleships, a cruiser and fourteen destroyers challenged five US cruisers and eight destroyers. The Japanese lost two destroyers and the battleship *Hiei* was badly damaged, but they sank four destroyers and crippled four cruisers and three destroyers. Next day the Japanese found and sank a cruiser, but had to scuttle the *Hiei*.

The next night Japanese cruisers shelled the Americans ashore, but homeward bound they were caught by US planes and a cruiser was sunk.

On the night of the 14th the Japanese tried again, this time with a battleship, four cruisers and nine destroyers. They ran into two US battleships and four destroyers, and the Japanese damaged a battleship and sank three destroyers almost at once, but the battleship *Kirishima* was reduced to a wreck and a destroyer was sunk.

That same night eleven transports tried to reinforce Guadalcanal with the 38th Division: all the transports were sunk or beached and only 20% of the troops survived to reach the shore.

After this disaster the generals began to appreciate what the admirals had been telling them: Guadalcanal was not worth it. In December Imperial Headquarters overruled Seventeenth Army's protests: the troops would be evacuated.

Between 14 January and 8 February 1943 the Navy performed wonders, bringing off over 10,000 troops from Guadalcanal without allied knowledge.

The land battle of Guadalcanal claimed 21,700 Japanese dead, for an American loss of 1,600 dead.

The Japanese naval loss was severe, but again the real importance of the losses, over 2,300 of the Navy's 4,000 flyers, was not understood!

New Guinea was not going well. The northern coastal area of the extreme east of the island was lost in January 1943 along with 3,600 Japanese lives. The arrival of part of the 41st Division was not of much real help, for it was not enough. In February the remainder of the division set out across the Bismarck Sea for New Guinea aboard eight transports escorted by eight destroyers. Between 1-4 March the convoy came under devastating US and Australian air attack: a destroyer and all the transports were sunk.

When the news of the terrible tragedy reached the generals and admirals, they went white with shock. Casualties had never meant much to Japan's leaders, but middle-ranking officers and certainly the enlisted men were staggered by the news, though propaganda tried to minimise it, of course.

On 18 April came the worst loss. Admiral Yamamoto was killed near Rabaul when his passenger plane was shot down by US fighters.

On 11 May came the next allied offensive: the 2,380 defenders of Attu, one of the Alaskan islands occupied the previous June, were attacked by a reinforced US division accompanied by a naval and air bombardment. Unlike most Pacific islands, Attu has no vegetation, not even a bush, and with only fog to hide behind this was a brutal toe-to-toe struggle. By 30 May only about 500 Japanese were still alive lying in a gully, many of them wounded. The realisation that they could be thoroughly defeated was too much for their minds to comprehend: it betrayed their government propaganda and said something about the inadequacies of their race, they thought. This warped attitude resulted in most of them committing suicide. Only 28 badly wounded were taken prisoner by the Americans.

However, the Japanese generals and admirals were learning humility and they chose to evacuate their remaining troops off Alaska. They did it so successfully that the Americans were astonished to find them gone when they invaded.

There were other incidents that called for humility. On one day in June 94 Japanese planes were lost in air battle over the Solomons, for the American loss of six planes.

The Japanese did not know where the Americans would invade next. Those on New Georgia in the Solomons were the first to find out. Seventeenth Army decided to reinforce the 229th Regiment and 7th Yokosuka and Kure Naval Landing Forces on New Georgia at once and on the night of 5 July in Kula Gulf the convoy ran into a US task force. They lost three destroyers and only managed to put 850 members of the 13th Regiment ashore on Kolombangara Island, but they sank a US cruiser. Reinforcements did get in over the next few nights and on the 12th there was another naval engagement in Kula Gulf: for a cruiser sunk the Japanese sank a destroyer and crippled three cruisers. The last reinforcement attempt was on 7 August: three Japanese destroyers were ambushed and sunk and the transports turned back.

Ashore the Japanese were pressed back to the coast of New Georgia and then fled to Arundel Island just yards away. There they were hunted down. A handful survived by fleeing to Kolombangara a mile from Arundel. These few managed to evacuate in September.

In September a major allied amphibious invasion of New Guinea bypassed the front line defences, seized Lae and Salamaua and threw the 20th Division and the Sasebo, Maizeru and 5th Yokosuka Naval Landing Forces into retreat. By November 12,000 Japanese had died on New Guinea. Over the next two months another 3,000 would die, but half of them from starvation. Some Japanese resorted to eating their fallen comrades!

The next American invasion came at Bougainville in the Solomons on 1 November, where, after the 42,000 men of the 38th Brigade and 6th Division were surprised by the landing, the 23rd Regiment settled down to a static struggle over tree-covered hill slopes to contain the beachhead. The Japanese Navy counter-attacked at once with four cruisers and four destroyers into Empress Augusta Bay, but were ambushed by a US Navy task force, losing a cruiser and a destroyer and were forced to withdraw.

Bougainville was not all that much of a surprise, but the next American attack was: the Gilbert Islands in the Central Pacific on 20 November. It only took four days for the 5,800 men of the 6th Yokosuka and 7th Sasebo Naval Landing Forces and base troops on Makin and Tarawa to be wiped out, but they inflicted 4,456 casualties on the Americans and damaged a carrier, all for fewer square miles than a Tokyo suburb. Indeed over the next few days US newspapers argued whom to blame!

On 15 December US troops invaded New Britain at Arawe, 300 miles from Rabaul at the opposite end of the island, where General Imamura's Eighth Area Army ordered air strikes at once. On the first day 400 sorties were flown against the US transports. Eleven days later US marines landed fifty miles further away from Rabaul at Cape Gloucester.

It was clear to Imamura that the Americans planned not to conquer the island, but to share it with the 90,000 Japanese of the 17th Division and 39th and 65th Brigades. American air raids on Rabaul would be used to neutralise the Japanese air units.

One thing was obvious to all. The Japanese did not respond with a naval counter-attack. Japanese warship losses and most importantly merchant ship losses (552 sunk by 31 October 1943) meant there were fewer warships to manoeuvre and less fuel and supplies to enable them to manoeuvre.

In their great offensive beginning in 1941 the Japanese had leapfrogged islands, thus throwing the allies off balance, and bypassed large pockets of troops, the biggest pocket being on New Guinea. Now the Americans were doing the same – and were claiming to have invented the technique, e.g. they bypassed 11,000 Japanese on New Ireland.

In keeping with this strategy, the Americans bypassed the Japanese front line on New Guinea by landing at Saidor, 120 miles further up the coast.

The next American offensive was in the Central Pacific. Beginning on 30 January 1944 they invaded several of the Marshall Islands. In February they also landed in the Admiralties. In terms of manpower these garrisons were not large, a total of about 20,000 Japanese, so they could be written off without too much of a dent in the Japanese generals' consciences. They fought to the death, the last succumbing in April. The generals were not always heartless: they had evacuated their men from Guadalcanal, New Georgia, Kolombangara, Vella Lavella and several smaller islands, but the Marshalls and Admiralties were just too isolated.

The Burma Area Army had had a peaceful time since May 1942, bar a few air raids and some guerrilla activity, but they knew that 1944 would bring three major allied invasions, two across the Burma-India border, one on the coast and one in the centre, and one from China. The defensive strategy they came up with was quite good: counter-attack the coastal invasion by a flanking move, counter-attack the central invasion by infiltration and hold back the China invasion by steady rearguard actions.

In February the coastal counter-attack went ahead with the Twenty-eighth Army's 55th Division advancing along a route twenty miles inland and parallel to the coast and then swerving seaward to assault Taung Bazaar with one force and advance to the sea with two others.

It would have worked, except for one thing: allied control of the air in western Burma. The allied troops formed boxes, stood their ground and, supplied by air, used firepower to stop all assaults. The result was 4,600 Japanese dead and a Japanese retreat.

In March General Mutaguchi's Fifteenth Army advanced against the centre invasion with the 33rd Division over the middle Chindwin towards Imphal, the 15th Division over the upper Chindwin towards Imphal and the 31st Division further up the Chindwin through Ukruhl towards Kohima.

The 18th Division made short counter-thrusts against the Chinese invasion, but eventually had to be reinforced with the 2nd, 53rd and 56th Divisions.

In China the Japanese went over to the offensive for the first time in years, their prime goal to overrun the American airfields, which would keep the Japanese home islands out of aircraft range. The offensive involved no less than the First, Eleventh, Twelfth and Twenty-third Armies. That they should launch such a major affair is evidence that the Japanese leaders were afraid that air raids on Japanese cities would lose them prestige and authority among the normally docile population.

In April and May the Americans landed at Hollandia and Aitape on New Guinea and Wakde and Biak Islands off New Guinea. By these moves 60,000 Japanese soldiers of the 35th and 36th Divisions of the Eighteenth Army on New Guinea were bypassed.

In June came the next American assault. It was no surprise they went for the Marianas. Indeed, the Japanese had prepared a welcoming committee: on Guam the Navy's 6th Expeditionary Force and the Army's 29th Division; on Saipan the Army's 43rd Division, 47th Brigade and 3rd Artillery Regiment and the Navy's 1st Special Naval Landing Unit and 55th Guard Unit; and on Tinian the Army's 50th Regiment and a battalion of the 135th regiment; a total of

60,000 troops under the Thirty-first Army; plus 600 aircraft were on the islands or in range; and lastly Admiral Ozawa had the 1st Mobile Fleet with 450 carrier planes.

The Marianas fight began when US carrier planes bombed the islands on 11 June, followed by an invasion of Saipan on the 15th. Ozawa responded with a counter-thrust on the 19th. However, he had few veteran pilots, their ranks replaced by eager, but poorly trained, youngsters. The American pilots were mostly green too, but far better trained by instructors, who had been at the sharp end of battle themselves. Moreover, in the vicinity the Americans had no less than 26 carriers.

In one day 350 of Ozawa's 450 carrier planes were shot down by enemy fighters and flak. During the day the carriers *Taihu* and *Shokaku* were sunk by submarines. That night crews on Ozawa's ships peered into the sky, assuming the 350 missing planes had landed on an island to refuel.

Next day another 65 were shot down and the carrier *Hiyo* was sunk by American planes and three other carriers damaged. Also within a few days 280 Japanese shore-based planes were shot down. American losses were trifling.

From here on it was only a matter of time before the Marianas garrison was destroyed.

The Japanese city of Yawata was bombed by American long-range bombers flying from China. The first raid on Japan since the 'experiment' in April 1942, it heralded a major bombing campaign for all Japanese cities. Soon American bombers would be arriving from island bases in the Pacific. This more than anything else told the Japanese people that their leaders had failed them. On 18 July Tojo was forced to resign by his back-stabbing pals.

By August the Fifteenth Army was in retreat in Burma, having failed to overcome fanatic resistance by the allies and losing 66,000 dead. The Burma Area Army still had over 200,000 troops in the Twenty-eighth and Thirty-third Armies, but obviously the Japanese in Burma could not afford many more defeats such as this. Their starving, ragged survivors began to fight a withdraw-al, relentlessly pursued by the enemy right through the monsoon.

The Philippines were invaded by the US Sixth Army at Leyte on 20 October 1944. The Japanese planned a strategy of three parts: a rugged defence by the 430,000 defenders of the Fourteenth Army of General Yamashita on Luzon and the Thirty-fifth Army of General Suzuki on the other Philippine islands; a naval counter-attack at night by surface warships; and the kamikaze surprise.

The counter-attack was ingenious, but the losses of veteran naval air crew now dictated tactics. Admiral Ozawa, who had obliged the Americans in June, sailed with his almost empty carriers past Leyte to the north. The Americans took the bait and sped after him with Halsey's carrier force. The real attack was by Admiral Kurita's, Admiral Nishimura's and Admiral Shima's task forces: the former north of Leyte; the others to the south. Neither had carriers and were to rely on gunfire alone.

Kurita was intercepted by American submarines, losing three cruisers and two destroyers and by Halsey's planes on the morning of the 24th losing a cruiser and the *Musashi*, at 64,000 tons the biggest battleship in the world, whereupon Kurita turned back. That night Nishimura entered Leyte Gulf with the battleship *Fuso*, two cruisers and four destroyers and was met by the US Navy's main bombardment force. In the last great surface action of the war fought without planes Nishimura died and only a cruiser and a destroyer escaped. Shima lost a destroyer and a cruiser and retreated.

However, Kurita returned at dawn and surprised the American close shore support unit, but Kurita failed to take complete advantage of the situation and with gunfire only sank two destroyers and damaged some ships, including two carriers. All his ships damaged by air attack, Kurita retreated.

This morning Halsey's planes found Ozawa's force and sank four carriers, a cruiser and three destroyers.

Among the retreating Japanese task forces a battleship, three cruisers and two destroyers later sank from battle damage.

The admirals defeated, they now put their hopes in the kamikazes. It had occurred to the logical Japanese that their pilots were effectively doomed. Losses were horrendous: 160 shot down in one day over Taiwan; 600 to American fighters and flak over the Philippines in a few days. The cost to the allies was minimal. Therefore, it was decided to ask some pilots to deliberately turn their planes into human bombs and ram the enemy. This had certain advantages. Any old plane including trainers could be used; pilots did not have to be trained too well, about two weeks should do it; and in theory with each life sacrificed an American bomber would go down or a ship would be hit. The Japanese remembered losing a cruiser to one American suicide pilot in 1942.

The kamikazes were launched against the Leyte invasion fleet and they definitely came as a surprise to the Americans. To mentally stay sane in the face of this horrific reality, the Americans came up with stories: the pilots were doped up; they were trained to take off but not land; they had insufficient fuel to return to base; their families would be killed if they refused; they were cemented into their planes. None of which was true.

The planes were shot to pieces by flak and fighters, yet they kept on coming. Not all Japanese planes were kamikaze and the allies never knew who they were up against. In the first few days the suicide pilots crippled two cruisers and three carriers and sank a carrier.

The other Japanese services got into the act: the submarine force created human-guided torpedoes, the surface forces created human-guided ramming boats full of explosives and the Army created human bombs, who would throw themselves against enemy tanks.

All in all this simply shows how desperate the Japanese had become to survive as a nation. Not even those arch fanatics Stalin and Hitler had asked their men to form suicide units.

Between 13 December 1944 and 13 January 1945 in the waters of the Philippines during the small American invasion of Mindoro and the larger invasion of Luzon by the US Sixth Army, kamikaze planes sank or crippled 79 warships including three battleships and five carriers.

In February the US Eighth Army began occupying these Philippine Islands defended by the Thirty-fifth Army.

The biggest shock to the Americans came on 19 February 1945 when they landed on Iwo Jima. Here the Japanese Imperial Headquarters had placed under its direct command the Army's 109th Division and a naval guard force, 23,000 men each one dedicated to taking as many enemy with him as possible. They cleared the tiny four-square-mile island of all vegetation and dug caves into its volcanic rock. The Americans knew it would be a tough nut and invaded the island with three marine divisions. There was barely enough room for the 80,000 combatants. It was 35 days before the Americans could stand erect without getting a bullet in the head and four months before they could truly call the island secure. It cost the American ground troops 26,000 killed and wounded. Only 1,083 Japanese were taken prisoner, most of them too badly wounded to resist.

About 200,000 Japanese troops of the Thirty-second Army were preparing to defend the Ryukyu Islands. Only 350 miles from Japan itself they were within range of Japan-based aircraft and were seen as a doorstep for the coming allied invasion of Japan. On the main island, Okinawa, there were 122,700 troops manning the 62nd and 24th Divisions, 44th Brigade and 27th Tank Regiment, of which a portion were native Okinawans (7,600 conscripted into the Army, 2,000 into the Navy, a home guard of 3,050, 1,100 naval militia and 16,600 army militia, some as young as fifteen).

Though these were not indigenous Japanese islands, the Japanese authorities chose to make an example of them, by fighting as if they were. Their only hope now of staving off an invasion of Japan proper was to make the allies think that it would be too costly for them, and the only way to do that was to fight like the devil himself.

The Americans began landing on small islands in March and on 1 April they invaded Okinawa with four divisions of the Tenth Army.

General Ushijima allowed them to come ashore with only a few snipers for company. Imperial Headquarters had decided on a strategy of letting the Americans become embroiled in a ground battle of attrition, while cutting them off from their fleet. This was to be done by conventional and kamikaze air raids and a naval counter-attack.

At first it looked as if it was going to work. Kamikazes slammed into four carriers, a battleship, a cruiser and four destroyers. On the 6th the Americans infantry reached the main defence line and the ground combat attained a ferocity as terrible as any seen in the war. The towns were not untouched and thousands of civilians fled into the mountains, many to hide without food for weeks and others retreated with the Japanese troops, some times at gunpoint. Where a last ditch stand was called for Japanese officers ordered the local civilians butchered: no one was to be allowed to surrender.

At sea the largest battleship afloat, the *Yamato*, sailed with a small escort towards Okinawa with only enough fuel to reach her target, the US transports. On the 7th she and four of her escorts were sent to the bottom by US carrier planes.

Each day air raids devastated the US fleet off Okinawa and on the island in the Shuri area Ushijima's men fought their final battle. On 21 June he committed suicide, when his command was down to a few diehards.

Of the 92,350 defenders who were actually Japanese 10,000 were taken prisoner, many of them unwounded and glad to be out of the war. Of the 30,350 Okinawan troops 8,000 surrendered. The air assaults cost the Japanese 7,800 flight crew killed, about a third of them kamikazes. Over 120,000 civilians were killed from American firepower, starvation and murder by the Japanese.

The Japanese had succeeded all too well in shocking the Americans: 763 American planes were lost, the Tenth Army lost its commander and 52,600 casualties, and the Navy and merchant fleet lost 9,731 casualties with 36 destroyers and smaller vessels

sunk and 376 vessels of all sizes damaged, many requiring lengthy repair.

The Japanese ruling clique had ordered children to be evacuated from the cities and all men and women fifteen and over to enrol in the militia. By creating this defence force of 50 million, they hoped to make the Americans think twice about invasion. A by-product was to make American air raids on Japanese cities a legitimate act of war, as they were now effectively 'military installations', though the Americans would have bombed anyway. The Americans had found that incendiary bombs burned the Japanese towns like matchwood, resulting in firestorms that actually melted people. On 9 March US bombers had set fire to Tokyo, killing and maiming 125,000 inhabitants and rendering a million homeless. In these air raids Japanese fighters and flak claimed some bombers, but not enough to make any difference.

Once Germany was defeated in May the Japanese generals assumed the USSR would attack Japan, so they restructured their forces on the Asian mainland. In Manchuria facing the Soviet border they put the Third, Fourth, Fifth, Thirtieth and Forty-fourth Armies. However, of the 25 divisions here, eight were brand new and most of the others had older troops. It was not a very effective force, really. Sakhalin and the Kuriles were defended by the Twenty-seventh Army and Korea was held by the Thirty-fourth and Fifty-ninth Armies.

In China the Japanese were in retreat, but their strength of nine armies was still formidable.

On 6 August an American bomber dropped a bomb on Hiroshima, the centre of Japanese Christianity. First reports to Tokyo were confused and alarmist. It was only on the 8th that the truth reached the Emperor, who ghost-like lived in the bomb-damaged Imperial Palace: the single bomb had destroyed the city.

Next day reports came in of a Soviet attack into Manchuria and a second single bomb raid on Nagasaki, which disappeared in a cloud of dust.

The Emperor now stepped in and over the next few days argued with the generals and admirals. He wanted to surrender.

The arguments for holding out were that the Japanese Army was still very large and the allies probably did not have too many more atomic bombs, otherwise they would not be continuing with conventional bombing – a thousand planes raided Tokyo on the 14th – plus their threat to invade Japan might be a bluff.

The arguments for a surrender were overwhelming: there were no more island outposts, therefore Japan was the next invasion target; the Navy had been destroyed and was without fuel; the air forces were all but wiped out – 3,000 planes had been lost over the Philippines and 6,900 over Okinawa; Japan's cities were dying under conventional air attack and a quarter of Japan's homes had been destroyed or damaged; the Americans may have a hundred atomic bombs; Japan could no longer feed herself or supply her factories, because of the terrible destruction of her merchant fleet by American submarines and to a lesser extent by other methods – 229 ships sunk in 1942, 434 in 1943, 969 in 1944, 744 in 1945 to date, condemning 30,000 merchant sailors to a watery grave.

The Emperor won the argument, though there was an attempted coup, and to pre-empt further coups he recorded a radio message to his people calling off the war. It was the first time they had heard him. It was not a body blow to the Japanese people, but a blow to their very soul. Effectively, it was the destruction of a religion.

The allies were informed and on 2 September in Tokyo Bay aboard the battleship USS *Missouri* the delegates signed the surrender.

For months allied teams of interpreters with loudspeakers roamed the islands of the Pacific and the jungles of Burma looking for Japanese hold-outs. In the Ryukyus 87,000 eventually gave up, 35,000 on Borneo, 70,000 on New Britain, on Bougainville 23,750, on Luzon 58,000, in the other Philippine islands 50,000, in Burma 118,000, on New Guinea 13,500, on New Ireland 11,000, in the Halmaheras 37,000 and so on.

In China since December 7 1941 203,0000 Japanese had been killed by the Chinese plus American air raids; in Burma

and Malaya 190,000 were killed by British Empire, American and Chinese forces; in the East Indies 13,000 had been killed; 80,000 were killed fighting the Soviets in the last few days of the war and 300,000 of those who surrendered to the Soviets were never returned; about 1,130,000 Japanese died serving against the American and allied forces in the Pacific island campaigns at sea, in the air and on land. The Japanese estimate that 81,000 of thee above died after the Emperor's surrender: killed by local guerrillas, killed by local villagers in revenge for massacres, and dead from malnutrition, disease and suicide.

In Japan American air raids killed 10,500 uniformed personnel and 183,000 civilians, half of them in Tokyo; plus 140,000 died from the effects of the bomb at Hiroshima and 70,000 at Nagasaki.

The lust for glory on the part of a handful of fanatic generals in 1931 had resulted in the deaths of 2,670,000 of their fellow citizens and the imposition of a foreign occupation. *See Index*

JEWS AND GYPSIES

Status in 1939:   stateless

Jews and Gypsies appear in this work as if they were a separate state, because the Nazis treated them as such. Hitler took away all citizenship rights from any German who had more than two Jewish grandparents or was of Gypsy race. In Germany this covered 566,000 Jews, of whom 44,000 were Christians including priests and nuns, and 28,000 Gypsies. Germans who had one or two Jewish grandparents lived on a knife-edge.

The Gypsy that the nazi law was aimed at was a member of the Romany ethnic group. A non-Romany who travelled the countryside living on petty theft and trading may call himself a Gypsy, rather than tramp, but he had no more right to use the term Gypsy than a Norwegian has to call himself a Zulu. Thus the law discriminated against Romanies, who might be living very productive, socially acceptable lives, but protected tramps.

As Hitler expanded his empire he extended his laws to all conquered peoples.

Anti-semitism (i.e. hatred of Jews) was nothing new to Germany, but was no stronger there when Hitler came to power in 1933 than it was in France, Britain or the USA. However, Hitler and his nazi supporters began to increasingly oppress the Jews so that by September 1939 346,000 had emigrated, most of them with only the clothes on their backs as the Nazis had confiscated their property, jewels and money. Of these, about 90,000 were 'reconquered' when Hitler's armies overran their new homes.

Within Nazi-controlled areas all Jews and Gypsies were under constant suspicion of being anti-Nazi, which of course they were, and therefore suffered a higher rate of arrest by Heinrich Himmler's SS and incarceration in concentration camps than did the gentiles (Christians), but apart from a few beatings and a handful of killings the true nazi 'war' against them did not start until the nazi invasion of Poland in September 1939.

In Eastern Europe lived a different kind of Jew, the unassimilated, i.e. those who kept their own culture, spoke Yiddish or Ladino and were considered a separate ethnic group, just as Poles were different from Greeks. Assimilated Jews in these areas, i.e. those who lived as Poles or whatever, but kept their faith were mistrusted and those who lived as Christians were usually considered wolves in sheep's clothing as they often changed their name to hide their ethnicity.

Gypsies may have been the darlings of the intellectual set in the fashionable districts of Paris or Berlin, but among the uneducated and superstitious Christian peasantry of Eastern Europe, who still kept garlic on their window sills to thwart vampires, the Gypsies were feared as evil incarnate!

In Poland in September 1939 Hitler gave the SS the mission of rounding up Jews and housing them in city ghettos, where homes built for four people were soon holding four per room. Only menial jobs were open to them under the nazi system and in any case the SS took their salaries in return for starvation rations. Jewish police ran the ghettos. The perimeters were guarded by Polish police, who had orders to shoot attempted escapees.

Some SS members went further than their brief and murdered Jews, whereupon they were arrested and court-martialled by the SS generals, who considered themselves to be in an 'army': but Himmler either quashed the proceedings or commuted the sentences. The generals soon learned that when it came to Jews and Gypsies as far as Himmler and Hitler were concerned 'anything goes'.

As Hitler's armies invaded other nations the Jews there were rounded up and sent to the Polish ghettos, making overcrowding so bad that disease ravaged the ghettos. Thousands died.

In spring 1941 as his armies prepared to invade the USSR, Hitler asked Himmler to create an extermination unit of 3,000 men, who would follow the troops into the USSR and shoot Jews, Gypsies and communists. Himmler used normal, ethical recruitment practices, but reversed, to pick 3,000 killers from his 140,000 strong SS, but to his embarrassment he could not recruit enough killers – guarding a concentration camp full of traitors, communists and gangsters was one thing, murdering children was quite another! He had to resort to recruiting from the ordinary German police and even among female SS members to make up his numbers.

On 22 June these killers, divided into four einsatzgruppe, entered the USSR and began their murders. Every nation has its psychopaths, sociopaths and morons and the USSR was no exception. Within days the einsatzgruppe began to recruit such people to help them, called hiwis. In time the hiwis began to do some shooting under light supervision.

Mathematically the campaign was successful: e.g. 20,000 Jews and Gypsies were shot in two months in the Vilnius area, 6,000 in the Kovno district, 6,000 at Borisov in one day, over 12,000 in two weeks at Kishinev. The largest 'aktion' was at Babi Yar, where 34,000 were shot in two days. By December well over 250,000 men, women and children had been executed, and this did not count the thousands of Jews and Gypsies murdered by the Romanians and Croatians who preferred to do their own killing rather than hand the intended victims to the einsatzgruppe as other nations did.

In Himmler's opinion this was not success. Potential victims were escaping: hidden by local villagers, allowed to escape by German police and soldiers or deliberately saved by German industrialists as cheap labour. Moreover, ordinary German soldiers were complaining about the massacres. The so-called secret executions were being filmed and photographed by spectators and in some areas local villagers brought picnic baskets to watch the Jews and Gypsies get what was coming to them. It was most undisciplined. In many shootings a solitary German corporal supervised a dozen or more hiwis, now fully uniformed with their own rank structure. Most importantly, the killers themselves were suffering a host of reactions: mutiny, insanity, suicide and most of them remaining permanently drunk. In letters home they described themselves as 'soldiers at the front': what an insult to the real German soldier.

Himmler turned to his T4 medical doctors for advice on an alternative. T4 was Hitler's campaign of euthanasia on any German deemed mentally or physically incurable, which had become a public scandal when the German people found out about it. Since then the T4 doctors had become ever more secretive in order to continue the programme. In late 1941 under the chairmanship of Reinhard Heydrich, Himmler's deputy, T4 doctors, scientists and members of the crematorium industry established extermination camps – corpse factories, which would be fed like some mythical beast requiring human sacrifice.

Manned by a handful of volunteers from the concentration camp service of the SS and a considerable number of hiwi volunteers, many of them ex-hiwis of the einsatzgruppe, all of the camps would be erected in the conquered territories of the east: Chelmnitz was opened in early 1942, followed by Belzec, Sobibor, Treblinka and others, and the most insatiable beast of all, Birkenau, which was part of the Auschwitz group of concentration, slave labour and prisoner of war camps.

The initial method of execution was a van, which had its exhaust piped into the rear. Victims were loaded, then the van driven around until the screaming and banging ceased. The van was then emptied of corpses and driven to pick up its next load of one-way ticket passengers. The corpses were handled by prisoners, who had been promised salvation.

The most efficient system was the gas chamber. Looking like communal showers, and labelled as such, they took in several hundred naked frightened victims, women and children in one, men in an another, who had arrived minutes earlier by train. Expecting water, the shower heads spewed forth Zyklon B crystal gas. After a few minutes the chambers were ventilated so that prisoners could drag out the corpses. They were buried at first, but later crematorium ovens were constructed. Everything of value was taken from the dead such as spectacles, jewellery, gold teeth, hair and tattoos: the camps were run on a tight budget and every saleable commodity was salvaged.

In the ghettos Jews were subjected to forced labour, which in itself was no bad thing for it got them out of the ghetto on a daily basis and gave them purpose, but in 1941 many graduated to the concentration camp or slave labour camp: the former, run by the concentration camp service of the SS, worked prisoners to death as punishment, the latter, run by the economics department of the SS, worked prisoners to death for profit. In practice there was little difference. At best camp commanders were indifferent to suffering, at worst they were absolute madmen, such as Amon Goeth the butcher of Plaszow labour camp.

The main difference between a Christian inmate of a camp and a Jew or Gypsy, was that ultimately if the camp didn't kill him/her first the Jew or Gypsy was destined for a train ride to oblivion. Some knew, some didn't, some pretended not to know in order to live a day at a time. Every few weeks local police aided the German police and SS to arrest Jews and Gypsies from the ghetto or camp and crammed them on freight trains like sardines – the beast was hungry, the beast must be fed.

Ironically, in autumn 1944 when the Soviets began to overrun the extermination camps, the SS guards suddenly needed their prisoners. They marched them in cold weather across high mountains with little food and no warm clothing, murdering those who could not keep up, their destination being concentration camps in Germany. The reason the guards did this was because they would have been drafted for the front line otherwise. This way, they could claim they had an essential occupation. Like most bullies they were cowards. These men and women were not Nazis: true Nazis were fighting and dying at the front for the cause. For these guards the only cause was self-preservation. Thus in some cases Germans, who may have fought for Germany in World War I, were herded with rifle-butt blows like cattle by Ukrainians or Russians wearing SS hiwi uniform, as a result of Hitler's insane policies.

Once arriving at the concentration camps in Germany the prisoners found such overcrowding that disease devastated them. In spring 1945 when the allies reached these camps they found more unburied corpses than live prisoners, intermingled with each other, the living too weak to crawl away from the dead.

The image that has come down to post-war generations is of Jews and Gypsies meekly led to the slaughter like lambs. This happened, but it is not the whole story. Many served in the allied forces: 10,500 American Jews including General Rose were killed in action; over 40,000 Jews served in British uniform; German Jews served in the British forces as spies, scouts, interpreters and commandos and joined the French Foreign Legion; French Jews were remarkably active in their army; 65,000 of the Polish troops and 85,000 of the Soviet troops captured by the Germans were Jews – all were executed. Throughout Eastern Europe Jews and Gypsies formed their own partisan bands. Communist partisans would accept them, but most Christian bands would not: indeed some hunted down Jews and Gypsies as avidly as they ambushed German convoys.

In 1943 in the Warsaw ghetto a few Jews armed themselves with home-made weapons and handguns bought and smuggled from the Polish resistance movement, and when the next round up squad came in to fulfil the beast's weekly quota they attacked the Germans. The Germans responded with a military style attack using a few Polish police, 375 Ukrainian factory guards, 234 German police and 800 teenage recruits to the Waffen SS (i.e. combat soldiers), who were told they were going up against communist terrorists. They attacked with grenades, machine guns, flame throwers and armoured vehicles. It took an entire month at a cost of eighteen killed and 89 wounded to kill or disarm the 'terrorists' and arrest 55,000 men, women and children to feed the beast.

The world blames the Germans for the Holocaust (i.e. the genocide of Jews and Gypsies), but everywhere Hitler's killers went, including Germany, they received local help as well as hindrance. Many a German saved lives. Many a foreigner took them. Not only did the SS use a Jewish police in the ghetto, but had Jewish Gestapo agents seeking out troublemakers.

There is no doubt that if Hitler's armies had invaded Britain and the USA his killers would have gained aid from the British Union of Fascists and the Ku Klux Klan.

The Holocaust was not a German, or even a European or even a Christian phenomenon. At the end of the twentieth century genocide is still popular in this world of ours.

Economically, morally and militarily the Holocaust was a terrible error on Hitler's part. Morally it put him outside all socially acceptable decency. Trains that should have carried medicine, ammunition and German wounded, carried prisoners destined for the camps – such cargo had priority! Germany's war effort was denied great experts in the field of science, engineering, medicine and economics, because they were racially unacceptable.

This crime against humanity must be placed in a perspective that can make it real, otherwise the number of six million Jews and 200,000 Gypsies becomes just that, a statistic.

Put it this way. If Hitler had succeeded in his plan to rid the world of such people, in the post-war years there would have been no Bob Dylan, Barbra Streisand, Neil Diamond, Jerry Lewis, Michael Douglas, Woody Allen, Yves Montand, Topol, Peter Sellers, Tony Curtis, James Caan, Paul Newman, Gene Wilder, Michael Caine, Paul Simon, Art Garfunkel, Dustin Hoffman, Oscar Hammerstein, Lerner & Loewe, Neil Simon, Joan Collins, Lawrence Harvey, Sid James, Steven Spielberg, or Mel Brooks.

One wonders how many of those who died would have given the world as much pleasure as the above if given a chance at life.

See Index

KAZAKHSTAN

Status in 1939:	member state of the USSR
Government in 1939:	communist under Stalin dictatorship.
Population in 1939:	5,000,000
Make-up in 1939:	mostly Kazakhs; a few smaller ethnic groups; a few Russian colonists.
Religion:	Moslem
Location:	Central Asia.

Kazakhstan is a massive area, roughly the size of the USA east of the Mississippi. When the Russians conquered the region in the 19th century they did not suppress the proud ancient traditions of the Kazakhs, but under Stalin's communist Russian government in the 1920s the Kazakhs were oppressed, their religion and culture becoming officially proscribed.

When the communist oppression resulted in mass starvation the Kazakhs rebelled in 1931, but were bloodily defeated by Stalin's Soviet Red Army and Red Air force.

Therefore, when thousands of young Kazakhs were conscripted by the Red Army in 1941 to fight the Germans they understandably were reluctant to risk their lives for Stalin.

However, not much risk was called for as Soviet generals surrendered entire divisions to the Germans. Once inside fenced fields under German guard with no shelter or medicines the Kazakhs saw there was no risk –

death was certain, for the German treatment was negligent to say the least.

Just before winter hope arrived in the form of German recruiters, who offered to volunteers treatment comparable to that of German soldiers, complete religious and cultural freedom and a chance to fight communists. Needless to say, many signed up.

Kazakhs could serve as hiwis, i.e. rear-echelon troops in German units, or as Osttruppen, i.e. combat soldiers in their own units. Both had their own rank and medal structure.

Hiwis followed their parent German unit throughout Europe, but the osttruppen were divided into battalions to serve in the German-occupied USSR against communist partisans (guerrilla bands).

In autumn 1943 some Kazakh osttruppen were sent to Albania and Yugoslavia to fight communist partisans. In May 1945 when Germany surrendered, Kazakhs tried not to fall into Soviet hands, knowing they would be executed or sent to concentration camps. Those who fell into American or French hands usually survived, but those who were captured by the British were handed to the Soviets.

About 30,000 Kazakhs served in German uniform. Kazakhstan remained firmly under Soviet control and the majority of Kazakh men served in the Red Army throughout the war.

See Index

KOREA

Other names:	Chosen.
Status in 1931:	Japanese colony.
Government in 1931:	Japanese administration.
Population in 1931:	25,000,000
Make-up in 1931:	Koreans; some Japanese colonists.
Religion:	Buddhist
Location:	Eastern Asia

Conquered by the Japanese at the turn of the century, the Korean people were supposed to be happy about this according to Japanese propaganda with its emphasis on Asian brotherhood, but in practice the Japanese were racist and the Japanese Army gained prominence in Korea over the years to rule with an iron hand.

When Japan became embroiled in war in China Koreans were conscripted to do their military duty, but, denied the rights of Japanese conscripts, they were placed in manual labour units, something which was judged to be beneath the Japanese 'warrior'. Most of the officers of these units were Japanese, who saw their assignment as some sort of punishment, almost a disgrace, and accordingly they took out their anger on their Korean troops. Beatings were commonplace and executions were not infrequent.

When prisoners of war began coming in, Koreans were assigned to guard them and they in turn took out their frustrations on the helpless prisoners, e.g. Americans in their care suffered a fatality rate of 8% per annum, whereas in nazi hands it was 1.2%.

There was little danger for Korean troops until early 1942 when allied aircraft began to raid the rear areas. Starting with the allied invasion of the Pacific islands in August 1942 Korean troops were suddenly thrust into the firing line. This manifested itself as bombing and shelling, but the Japanese consistently refused to form Korean fighting units. However, when the Japanese realised they had lost a battle and were in danger of capture they butchered their Koreans if possible before committing suicide.

Naturally Koreans did not want to fight for Japan and they often hid until the fighting was over. Of the 41,500 Japanese who surrendered prior to the end of the war, 75% were in fact Koreans.

Just before the war ended the desperate Japanese formed Korean combat units and some brain-washed Korean youngsters even volunteered for suicide units.

In August 1945 ten Japanese divisions were in Korea preparing to fight to the death against the invading Soviet Army, but on the 15th the Japanese Emperor called it quits. Soviet forces entered northern Korea and American forces entered the south. There was little opposition from the Japanese.

Probably about 70,000 Koreans died as a result of the war in air raids and as members of the Japanese armed forces and merchant fleet.

After shaking hands once, the Americans and Soviets began to argue and each created a Korea in their own image. In less than five years the two Koreas were at war with each other.

See Index

KYRGYZSTAN

Status in 1939:	member state of the USSR.
Government in 1939:	communist under Stalin dictatorship.
Population in 1939:	1,500,000.
Make-up in 1939:	mostly Kyrgyz; substantial minorities of Kazakhs; Tajikhs; Uzbekhs; and Russian colonists
Religion:	Moslem.
Location:	Central Asia.

This ancient land fell to the Russian empire in the 19th century and to the communist Russian state of Stalin at the end of World War I. A devoutly religious people, they had no time for the atheist communists and in 1931 this animosity caused bloody war between poorly armed villagers and the Red Army and Red Air Force. The rebels were crushed.

Therefore, in 1941 when the young men were conscripted into the Red Army to fight the Germans their heart was not in it. Once at the front whole divisions were surrendered by incompetent Russian generals and thousands of Kyrgyzstan natives found themselves in fenced fields under German guard with no shelter or medicines and facing certain death come winter.

Then hope arrived in the form of German recruiters offering volunteers treatment similar to that of German soldiers, complete religious and cultural freedom and a chance to fight communists. Naturally many signed up.

They could serve as hiwis, i.e. rear-echelon troops in German units, or as osttruppen, i.e. combat soldiers in their own battalions trained to fight communist partisans (guerrilla bands) in the German-occupied USSR.

Hiwis followed their parent German unit throughout Europe and in 1943 osttruppen were sent to Yugoslavia and Greece to fight communist partisans.

In May 1945 when Germany surrendered, Kyrgyz in German uniform tried to stay out of the way of the Red Army, knowing they would be executed or sent to concentration camps if caught. Once in American or French hands they were usually safe, but if caught by the British they were handed to the Red Army.

Firmly under Soviet control most Kyrgyz men served in the Red Army throughout the war.

See Index

LATVIA

Other names:	Kurland and Livonia.
Status in 1939:	independent.
Government in 1939:	dictatorship.
Population in 1939:	2,000,000
Make-up in 1939:	1,800,000 Latvians;
	100,000 Jews;
	a few thousand Russians;
	a few thousand Volksdeutsch.
Religion:	Christian
Location:	North-East Europe

The latter part of World War I was complete turmoil for Latvia. In November 1917 the Russian empire divided into civil war between communists and anti-communists. Latvians chose independence, were occupied by Germany in March 1918, achieved independence again eight months later and then fought alongside German and British troops to repel an invasion by the Soviet communist Red Army. After this there was peace for twenty years.

In October 1939, flushed with his victory over the Poles, Stalin the Soviet dictator demanded Latvia allow him military bases. Prime Minister Karlis Ulmannis felt he had no choice but to allow this, for Latvia's previous allies Germany and Britain were now at war with each other.

On 16 June 1940 Soviet troops attacked a border post and in response to this 'incident' Stalin demanded Latvia surrender. Ulmannis agreed and the Red Army invaded.

At once Stalin's NKVD political police began arresting all potential resistance organisers: teachers, doctors, scientists, engineers, lawyers, politicians, managers, artists, writers etc.; also young men were conscripted into the Red Army – to refuse meant arrest for one's whole family; and skilled workers were ordered to Russia. Freight trains took them on weeks-long journeys across Russia in winter. Often entire trains of wretches froze to death. A conservative guess is that 60,000 people were taken from their homes.

As part of a deal between Stalin and Hitler all Volksdeutsch were expelled to Germany, where they had to live in camps run by the SS until homes could be found for them.

On 22 June 1941 the German Army invaded the USSR and within four days reached Latvia. The NKVD shot their prisoners and ran away, quickly followed by the Red Army. Latvians harassed them as they fled. Other Latvians, often relatives of the 'disappeared ones', ransacked the prisons looking for bodies – they found plenty – and then hunted down known collaborators. As many of the communists were Jews this soon degenerated into an anti-Jewish riot, in which victims were publicly beaten to death to the cheers of crowds and the astonishment of arriving German soldiers.

Actually, one German unit, the Einsatzgruppe, had the mission of murdering all Jews, and seeing the rioters they instantly recruited some of them to serve as hiwis (helpers). Other German formations took on hiwis to do rear-echelon duty.

The German authorities retained the armed Latvian police and the German police recruited battalions of schumas to fight communist partisan guerrillas. A part-time militia, the Aiszargi, was also set up to protect villages from partisan raids and the German Army recruited a Sicherungsabteilung (anti-partisan battalion). Latvians were also asked to volunteer for work in Germany and thousands did so.

The Volksdeutsch were allowed to return to their homes and jobs, though many men had volunteered for the German forces. Eventually they were subjected to conscription.

As winter approached the 94,000 strong Aiszargi was asked to put a battalion into the front line. Its leaders refused, saying their members had only volunteered to serve part-time in their own towns, whereupon they were arrested and sent to concentration camps. The Aiszargi learned that a German request was as good as an order. The battalion was hastily formed as the Latvian Legion and sent to fight near Lake Ilmen.

In January 1942 the legion fought bravely to rescue a German unit in deep snow in temperatures of -68˚C. Combat under such conditions is mindless and the force was quickly whittled down. The Germans were so impressed they gave them specially struck medals.

By 1942 forty battalions of Latvian schumas, about 20,000 men, had been recruited and were assigned to duty all over eastern Europe. One battalion was ordered to Warsaw, where among other jobs it had to round up Jews and put them on freight trains destined for extermination camps. Feelings were mixed about such a horrific order, but most obeyed, knowing the consequences of disobeying, and some extreme anti-semites actually enjoyed it, shooting down runaways.

In the winter 1942-43 several thousand Latvian schumas swept the forests of Latvia searching for partisans: about 4,000 were operating here, almost all of them Jews and Russians.

The Latvian Legion was rebuilt using Aiszargi 'volunteers', but in February 1943 was trapped for six days and suffered 75% casualties before fighting its way out.

Heinrich Himmler the SS chief had always fancied himself a general and had created his own army, the Waffen SS. Ever on the look-out for recruits he noticed the bravery of the Latvian Legion and confiscated the entire unit in March 1943. Adding to it more 'volunteers' from the Aiszargi and four Latvian schuma battalions he began to build a 15,000 man division, the 15th SS. One consolation for the Latvians was that they received better pay and conditions. Volksdeutsch who had been serving in the SS were transferred to the unit.

Impressed with his 15th SS Division, Himmler created a second Latvian division, the 19th SS, by taking advantage of the new conscription law, which called up all Latvian men 19-28, who were not employed on essential jobs. In early 1944 the age was expanded to 18-40. Rudolf Bangerskis a Latvian hero was made Inspector General of Latvian SS. The new division was given to SS General Bruno Streckenbach, a man known to brook no complaints: his last job had been to murder Polish dissidents.

There were enough conscripts left over to be put into the German Air Force, most of them as flak gunners and 628 into an air legion of three bomber squadrons. Others went to the German Army as hiwis or to the Aiszargi.

In spring 1944 the IIIrd SS Corps of the 11th Danish-Norwegian, 15th Latvian, 19th Latvian and 20th Estonian Divisions and a Dutch and a Belgian brigade was ordered to defend the Estonian-Russian border against an expected Red Army assault. The Latvian border was to be held by the German Sixteenth and Eighteenth Armies.

The offensive came on 25 June and for weeks the SS troops stood like a rock, but the German armies fell back uncovering the right flank of the SS, who had to withdraw in late July. Thousands of Latvian civilians fled the advancing Red Army: anyone who had aided the Germans, or had relatives who had, was terrified of the NKVD. With household goods on carts and in baby carriages they hit the road, periodically strafed by Soviet planes.

By the end of October only a sliver of Kurland was still held by the Latvian and German defenders, including the 19th SS Division. The 15th SS Division had been evacuated to Germany.

Thousands of Latvian civilians and Aiszargi had managed to reach Germany by ship, dodging Soviet planes and submarines. Some were welcomed by Latvian relatives working in Germany, but others had to be aided by German welfare organisations. All men aged fifteen and older were conscripted into uniform or industry: 3,614 going to the Air Force to join the 6,400 Latvians already serving as flak gunners. Women were given factory jobs and teenage girls were encouraged to volunteer for the flak guns. Some men were drafted into the SS as guards or to replace casualties in the two divisions.

As eastern Germany was invaded by the Red Army the Latvian refugees fled again. The 15th SS Division was put into the line to help stop the enemy and was soon joined in early 1945 by members of the 19th SS Division, which had been disbanded following a mutiny. Hitler had allowed these SS and 64,000 German wounded to be evacuated from Kurland, but replaced them with 28,000 fresh troops. Even the Latvian Aiszargi, hiwis and police still holding out there alongside the Germans knew it was a waste of manpower to fight such a dead-end campaign.

In February 1945 the Soviets attacked the Latvian SS and severely hurt them. Constant retreat was the order of the day and by April the Latvians had withdrawn to Frankfurt an der Oder and on the 16th were attacked by the greatest small area offensive in history. Within hours they were falling back towards Berlin's Tempelhof airport. There they regrouped and fought for five days and on the 28th retreated to Anhalter Rail Station a thousand yards from Hitler's bunker. By now the thousands of Latvian SS had been slimmed down to a few hundred.

On 2 May with Hitler dead the Berlin garrison surrendered. The few Latvian survivors became prisoners of the NKVD. Days later the war in Germany was over.

Though the Kurland Pocket defenders, 183,000 Germans and 14,000 Latvians, surrendered on 16 May, there were about 60,000 Latvians hiding in the Latvian woods, determined to fight on as guerrillas. Those who were caught were sent to NKVD camps in Siberia, but there some of the Latvians led revolts.

Latvians captured by the Western Allies were treated as displaced persons and not handed to the NKVD. Thus began a diaspora to Germany, Britain and North America.

It was 1948 before the last Latvian guerrillas were killed or captured by the NKVD.

It is impossible to know Latvia's wartime losses. About 125,000 Latvians wore German uniform and how many lived to talk about it is unknown. Counting air raids, massacres by German and Soviet forces, it is fair to assume that between 1940 and 1948 Latvia lost about 200,000 dead.
See Index

LIBYA

Other names:	includes Cyrenaica, Fezzan, Sirte and Tripolitania.
Status in 1939:	Italian colony.
Government in 1939:	Italian administration.
Population in 1939:	800,000.
Make-up in 1939:	Arabs 630,000 Italians 100,000; Jews 40,000; a few Berbers.
Religion:	Moslem
Location:	North Africa

The coastal towns of Libya have accommodated many invaders. As early as 1804 American marines were earning a name for themselves here. The Italians had first come 2,000 years before that. They came again in 1911, seizing the towns from the Turks. However, inland Libya is rocky desert and no one had conquered this area in over a millennium. The Italians were convinced they could do it, by taking the oases and holding them against the nomadic desert tribesmen until they submitted, and they did in fact manage it, and it only took them twenty-one years of warfare. In 1932 tanks and planes killed off the last Libyan resisters.

The nomads had suffered a terrible defeat bordering on genocide, so by June 1940, when Italy declared war on Britain, not many Libyans were all that enthused about fighting for the Italians.

The first they really knew about this new war was when the towns were raided by British aircraft. They caused little damage. For three months the Italians skirmished with British armour on the Libya-Egyptian border, but the troops, most of them Libyans, were ill-equipped to fight armour and suffered accordingly, e.g. Fort Capuzzo's 200 Libyans and 26 Italians surrendered after a few shots. The Libyans had no respect for their Italian officers. One Italian general was captured while drivng with his mistress. The incident in which the Italians accidentally shot down their commander's plane and killed him summed up the campaign nicely.

The Italian Tenth Army invaded Egypt in September, occupied 50 miles of worthless scrub and settled down to pat each other on the back. The army had inflicted 160 casualties on the British, but had suffered 3,500 losses to battle, illness, injury and missing.

General Graziani, the new commander, knew the desert well: it was he who had defeated the nomads; and he demanded good tanks from Italy. Mussolini, the Italian dictator, refused and told him to win with what he had.

At 5.40am 9 December 1940 at Nibeiwa camp a few miles inside Egypt General Malletti was still in his tent when artillery shells began falling. His men, of two Italian and one Libyan tank battalions, ran to their tanks, some being cut down before reaching them. The L3s, 3-ton vehicles with machine guns, and the M11s, with a 37mm gun in the hull, were hopelessly inadequate to fight British tanks, but there were a few M13s which were adequate as they carried a 47mm gun.

For an hour the men took the punishment and then sighted advancing British troops and the tanks took after them, while the artillerymen began firing. Minutes later the camp was assaulted from the rear by a tank battalion and three infantry battalions. For four and a half hours the artillerymen fought with bare hands against British infantry while the Italian tanks rushed back to fight the better British vehicles. Malletti died fighting. At 11.30 the 2000 Libyans and Italians began giving up.

Meanwhile at Tumar West camp about four miles away General Pescatori and 2,000 men of the 2nd Libyan Division were attacked at 11.25am by an equal infantry force and a battalion of tanks. The Italian officers cursed and cajoled their Libyans to resist and they did so, but a tank charge can make a hell of a dent in a thin line of infantry in a flat desert and within a couple of hours the Libyans began throwing up their hands.

The remainder of the division was at Tumar East four miles away and was attacked in the afternoon. Come dark about a hundred Italians and a few Libyans ran for it across the desert. The others gave up.

Graziani had lost 8,000 men for a British cost of 125 casualties.

The next day at Sidi Barrani an Italian division and Libyan rear-echelon soldiers,

15,000 men all told, were attacked. They fought for 24 hours and then surrendered.

The 1st Libyan Division of 150 Italians and 5,000 Libyans retreated after sitting under a British air, artillery and naval barrage for a day. In panic some men ran into the open desert to die of thirst. Surprisingly they formed a rearguard on the 11th which held off a British attack. The following day they were shelled by three British destroyers, so the Italian commander surrendered.

At Azzaziyah three battalions of L3s and M11s were wiped out by British tanks and at Buq Buq an Italian division was crushed by tanks suffering 56 killed and 4,000 prisoners.

The next defensive position was Bardia, which was not just a Libyan city, but had an Italian quarter. Its main defenders were the Cirene and Marmarica Divisions of Italian colonists and a host of Libyan and Italian rear-echelon personnel including airmen and sailors. Subjected to air raids and naval bombardment the city was finally attacked on 3 January 1941. At one point the Marmarica counter-attacked and actually drove back the British Empire forces. On the night of the 4th a large party of diehards ran out into the open desert to escape and the next morning the garrison surrendered 35,949 personnel. Upwards of a thousand had been killed and they had inflicted 456 casualties.

The Libyan inhabitants were ecstatic at being liberated by the British.

The diehards had run to Tobruk defended by the Sirte Division of colonists. After resisting a few days the city surrendered on the 22nd: 25,000 prisoners; they had inflicted 355 casualties.

Derna's and Mechili's garrisons fought off the British and then retreated. Benghazi was abandoned without a fight and the Libyan inhabitants turned on the Italian colonists. The police did what they could to suppress the riot and when British troops entered they joined the police to fight the rioters.

In February the Tenth Army fought a last stand at Beda Fomm and then surrendered 25,000 men.

The Libyans were astonished how quickly Cyrenaica province was overrun. The defenders had lost 20,000 killed (a few hundred of them Libyans) and 120,000 captured a quarter of them Libyans). Allied losses were only 1,900.

Many Libyans had joined the British, but few were accepted. Those that were received labour unit jobs and there was an infantry force, but the British used them as sentries only.

On 31 March a single German armoured division trounced the British and drove them all the way back to Egypt within days. The Libyan people were astounded to see Italian soldiers returning so quickly. The Italians colonists were now cockier than ever.

The inhabitants of Tobruk were terrified as German and Italian planes raided the port and the perimeter was attacked by Germans and Italians in mid-April. The city settled down to a siege defended by a British garrison. The Libyan labour troops of the British began to desert and hide in the town. On 20 July the British evacuated these units lest they lose them all.

By now the Italians too had put almost all their Libyan troops into rear duties. The only action they saw now was from air attack and commando raids.

Two British attempts to re-enter Libya in May and June were defeated, but the third attempt finally broke through to Tobruk in December. The Italians and Germans retreated.

Now it was the turn of the Libyans to ransack the Italian quarters of their cities again.

On 21 January 1942 the Italians and Germans counter-attacked and within days recaptured Benghazi, Derna and smaller communities. It was the turn of the Italian colonists to be cocky again.

In May the Italians and Germans attacked again and drove the British out of Libya completely. Tobruk fell in a day.

In late November the Italians and Germans came through Libya again, this time heading in the opposite direction. Tobruk was freed from Italian rule for the second time and Bardia and Benghazi for the third time. However, Mersa Bregha was abandoned on 11 December, Beurat on 14 January 1943 and Tripoli on the 19th. Within days the Italians abandoned Libya for good.

The belligerents had traversed Cyrenaica province like a floormat: it must have been confusing for the Libyan people as to who was winning on any given day.

Generally the Libyans had performed poorly as soldiers for British and Italians alike, but then again why should they have risked their lives for either colonial power? Much of Libya's post-war attitude to foreigners stems from her treatment at their hands. *See Index*

LITHUANIA

Status in 1938:	independent.
Government in 1938:	dictatorship.
Population in 1938:	2,500,000.
Make-up in 1938:	Lithuanians 1,800,000;
	Volksdeutsch 500,000;
	Jews 168,000;
	some Russian colonists.
Religion:	Christian.
Location:	North-East Europe.

A part of the Russian empire, Lithuania was occupied in March 1918 by Germany, declared its independence in November that year and managed to fight off both Poles and Russian communists (Soviets) to maintain that independence. By 1923 the Lithuanian government also controlled a segment of Germany, the Memelland, but had lost its main city, Vilnius, to the Poles.

Peace existed after this and by 1938 Lithuania was a stable and relatively happy nation.

In March 1939 Hitler's German forces liberated the Memelland: the Lithuanian Army did not resist. Soon Memelland's Volksdeutsch inhabitants were wondering if oppression under the Lithuanians had not been preferable to freedom under the Nazis.

In September the Soviet Red Army invaded eastern Poland, including Vilnius, and in October demanded the right to put bases in Lithuania. Jona Cernius, Lithuania's leader, felt he had no choice but to agree, especially as Stalin, the Soviet dictator, dangled Vilnius as a carrot. The deal was made. Lithuanian troops entered Vilnius to the cheers of the 200,000 inhabitants, while 50,000 Red Army troops entered Lithuania to silence.

In June 1940 came the demand many had been apprehensive about: Stalin wanted complete Lithuanian surrender. The government caved in, and at once more Red Army troops marched in. A new government of communists, most of them brought in by the Red Army, signed the surrender.

Behind the Red Army followed the NKVD, Stalin's political police, with the mission of nipping in the bud any potential resistance: their method being to arrest anyone who had shown the ability to think – doctors, scientists, engineers, teachers, artists, writers, politicians, managers, and so on – and send them to concentration camps and penal colonies in Siberia. Skilled workers were sent to Russian factories. A combination of neglect and downright murder killed most of the estimated 60,000 deportees. 19- and 20-year-old men were conscripted into the Red Army.

On 22 June 1941 the German Army invaded the USSR, charging across Lithuania in hours. The people cheered as NKVD and Red Army fled in commandeered vehicles. At once Lithuanians, many of whom had lost loved ones, opened the prisons finding fresh corpses, victims of the communists. In a rage they sought out known collaborators. As many of the collaborators and NKVD were Jews the affair soon turned into an anti-Jewish riot. It took German troops a day or two to restore discipline.

Lithuanians volunteered to aid the Germans and many were taken on by the army as hiwis, rear-echelon soldiers. The Germans retained the Lithuanian police and recruited several battalions of schumas, anti-guerrilla police, who initially searched for Red Army stragglers hiding in the forests. To defend every town and village against guerrilla raids the Germans created a part-time militia, the Siauliai, and a full-time anti-guerrilla (i.e. anti-partisan) force to go into Russia behind the German Army. The Germans also asked for volunteers to go to Germany to work – thousands signed up.

Like the Memellanders, the Volksdeutsch of Lithuania proper were subject to conscription just as any German.

One of the invading German units was the Einsatzgruppe, whose mission was to murder all Jews, Gypsies and communists, regardless of sex and age. A law unto themselves, no better than the NKVD, they nonetheless attracted some Lithuanian followers from among the sociopaths, psychopaths and morons, who were soon doing much of the killing. By late August the Einsatzgruppe had shot about 20,000 innocents.

The Jews were placed in ghettos in the towns, from which the Einsatzgruppe would periodically extract a few for extermination. Any who tried to escape the ghetto were shot down by the Lithuanian police or schumas. In September 13,000 were taken from Vilnius and shot and 15,000 from Kaunas.

In November the Einsatzgruppe moved on, leaving the remaining Jews safe, if living in hovels with little food could be considered safe. On one occasion there was an embarrassing mass escape of Jews from Vilnius.

In early 1942 the 23 schuma battalions (12,000 men) received orders to go to various towns in Europe. One battalion was sent to Warsaw, where one of its jobs was periodically to arrest Jews from the city's ghetto to be executed. Most of these schumas went through the motions like zombies, but there were some who enjoyed the work, even shooting at ghetto residents for fun.

The Germans demanded the 32,000 strong Siauliai put together a full-time force. Some fellows refused and were promptly arrested. After this there was no further argument. The unit, known as the Legion, was given anti-partisan duty. By now there were about 2,000 partisans in Lithuania, almost all Jews and Russians. Later the Legion went to Russian to hunt partisans.

In 1943 the Legion recruited 3,000 construction engineers.

However, in spring 1944 the Red Army was knocking on Lithuania's eastern border and the nation mobilised its defences. On the border itself were German troops, many with Lithuanian hiwis. Internally, ready to fight a partisan uprising were the police schumas, Siauliai, the Legion, and a Lithuanian section of the NSKK, a corps of military drivers and mechanics.

The awaited offensive came on 23 June and in a hellatious three-week battle the Third Panzer Army was shattered. Vilnius was abandoned as the Germans and Lithuanians retreated. Any Lithuanian who had the remotest connections with the Germans fled, for fear of the NKVD, who had never been too fussy about catching the right person, just as long as someone was caught. About 120,000 Lithuanians were cut off and fled into the forests to wage guerrilla war. Kaunas fell on 1 August.

The refugees fled into Germany. Some gained help from Lithuanians working in Germany, both volunteer and forced labour, and others relied on German welfare organisations. All males aged fifteen and older were conscripted into factories or uniform: most as flak gunners and hiwis. The 27,000 members of the Legion and the Siauliai who reached Germany were also turned into hiwis. Women were placed in factories and teenage girls encouraged to volunteer to serve flak guns.

As the Red Army invaded eastern Germany the Lithuanians had to flee again. Many did so by sea, from East Prussia, but the Red Air Force and Navy were waiting. One ship, the *Wilhelm Gustloff*, went down with 7,700 Germans, Lithuanians and others.

In May 1945 Germany surrendered. Lithuanians caught by the Red Army were turned over to the mercy of the NKVD. Those who managed to reach the American or British armies were safe. Some Lithuanians became hiwis of the US Army.

With Germany defeated the Red Army could return to Lithuania to hunt down the guerrillas. They set up a 7,000 man unit of People's Defenders, recruited from Lithuanian-born Russians, and the Armed Party Activists, recruited from the few hundred Lithuanian communists. Most of the hunting was done by the NKVD and Red Army.

Not until 1953 were the last hold-outs run to ground.

It is believed that 68,000 ethnic Lithuanians wore some sort of German uniform and about 50,000 Volksdeutsch did so. A rough estimate of a quarter of them being killed in the war would not be too far out.

Civilian losses were terrible: c 60,000 at the hands of the NKVD in 1940-41 and more in 1944; 143,000 Jews and Gypsies massacred by the Nazis; and thousands killed in cross-fire, air raids and dislocation in 1944-45. According to Soviet sources they suffered 20,000 killed at the hands of Lithuanian guerrillas 1944-53 and killed 50,000 guerrillas.

This comes to a minimum of 300,000 dead among pre-1939 Lithuanian citizens. *See Index*

LUXEMBURG

Status in 1939:	independent.
Government in 1939:	democratic monarchy.
Population in 1939:	290,000.
Make-up in 1939:	the national language is Letzeburgesch; significant minorities French- and German-speaking; 2,000 assimilated Jews.
Religion:	Christian.
Location:	Western Europe.

On the morning of 10 May 1940 German troops crossed the border without warning. Government and royal persons had minutes to decide whether to remain or flee. The 82-man ceremonial Army could offer no real resistance: seven were wounded.

Following the German Army was the SS Security Police looking for German anti-Nazi refugees, of which there were about 2,000 in the country, and also arresting outspoken Luxemburgers.

The Waffen SS, the combat branch of the SS, came looking for recruits among the German- and Letzeburgesch-speaking population. They found a few. German labour recruiters convinced many Luxemburgers to take jobs in Germany. The NSKK, a corps of military drivers and mechanics, took on volunteers. Organisation Todt recruited construction workers. Even the SS Security Police soon found willing helpers and informers.

On 5 September all Jewish property was confiscated and the Jews denied human rights. In 1941 the police and SS Security Police arrested them and put them on trains for destinations unknown.

When Germany invaded the USSR in 1941, thereby becoming the Christian crusaders against the atheist communists, many devout Christian Luxemburgers saw their way clear to aid the Germans. By late 1941 about 2,000 Luxemburgers were wearing some sort of German uniform.

However, in August 1942 Hitler announced that Luxemburg was annexed, that all were now German citizens and the use of any other language than German was illegal. The nation responded with a general strike and demonstrations, yelling "Mir woelle bleiwe wat mir sin" (we want to remain what we are); a courageous move in the face of German guns. However, when the police and SS Security Police began to arrest the strike leaders and send them to concentration camps, the strike collapsed.

As 'Germans' the young men were eligible for conscription into the German Army and 13,000 were inducted by year's end. In 1943 the conscription age was expanded to 17-45 and thousands more were called up. Such oppression created a small resistance movement, which coordinated its activities with the Belgian anti-Nazi resistance.

When the allies invaded German-occupied France in June 1944 a score or so of their troops were Luxemburg commandos. Recruited from escapees and men who had been abroad in May 1940, they were happy at last to be on the road back to Luxemburg.

The fighting was rough and not until September 1944 did the American armies reach Luxemburg. The Luxemburg resistance rose in open revolt to harass the retreating Germans. Within days the nation was free.

A military force was raised to guard American headquarters in Luxemburg city.

However, a chord of terror struck the hearts of the Luxemburgers on 16 December, when the Germans counter-attacked. Over the next three days the entire northern third of the country was re-occupied. The civilians fled, suspecting the SS Security Police and their informers would return, wanting to know who had been friendly with the Americans. It took six weeks of bitter fighting in the snow before the Americans aided by Luxemburg

resistance kicked the Germans out. The villages were devastated.

Luxemburg's war losses were not great in numbers. Of the 20,000 or so who wore German uniform, some 4,000 were killed. About 4,000 died in SS custody, having been arrested for resistance activity or for simply standing up for human decency. Half the nation's Jews were murdered. In addition there were deaths from air raids including workers in Germany and battlefield crossfire. This is a total of about 10,000 dead.
See Index

MADAGASCAR

Other names:	Malagassy.
Status in 1939:	French colony.
Government in 1939:	French administration.
Population in 1939:	4,000,000
Make-up in 1939:	Malgache;
	60,000 French colonists;
	a few negro tribes.
Religion:	various including Christianity.
Location:	Indian Ocean.

As part of the French Empire the Malgache were thrust into war in 1939, but apart from the danger to Malgache sailors the war seemed remote. Few Malgache soldiers of the French Army saw action.   When France surrendered in June 1940, the people considered the war over.

They were wrong. On 5 May 1942 British planes struck the port of Diego Suarez, sinking a sloop, three submarines and a merchant cruiser. This was followed by a British landing. The garrison of sailors, one Senegalese and three Malgache battalions and French-manned artillery fought them for two days, suffering 200 killed and 500 wounded, before withdrawing inland. The British, who had lost 109 killed and 284 wounded, did not pursue.

The island garrison of 20,000 troops was mobilised, but on an island as big as Britain they knew they were insufficient for the task. Fortunately the British left them alone.

In September the British changed their minds and launched an offensive from Diego Suarez and by several amphibious invasions. The French command ordered a steady withdrawal along the primitive dirt roads, with rearguards to slow down the invaders. Usually the rearguards gave up after a few shots in their direction. At one place 200 defenders surrendered.

After two months of exhausting retreat the French commander surrendered on 5 November.

All told the defenders had suffered about 1,200 killed and wounded, of which about 600 were Malgache. A vote was held and the majority of troops chose to join de Gaulle, a British-sponsored French general. The island administration was turned over to de Gaulle's French followers.

Everything was soon back to normal.
See Index

MALAYSIA AND SINGAPORE

Other names:	see below
Status in 1939:	British colonies.
Government in 1939:	British administrations.
Population in 1939:	6,063,000.
Make-up in 1939:	Brunei: various tribes 40,000;
	Malaya: Malays 2,250,000, Chinese 1,700,000, Tamils 500,000;
	North Borneo (Sabah): various tribes 331,000;
	Sarawak: Chinese 130,000, various tribes 416,000;
	Singapore: Chinese 580,000, Malays 48,000, Tamils, 48,000;
	All – British colonists about 20,000.
Religion:	Moslem plus many others
Location:	Malaya-Singapore in South-East Asia; others on the Pacific island of Borneo.

In 1939 when Britain went to war against Germany colonial subjects of the above were asked to volunteer for their home defence units and for the merchant fleet. The war did not touch the colonies otherwise.

The fact that the Japanese invaded Indo-China in 1940 did not create a sense of urgency within the colonies, though in late 1941, just to be safe, some reinforcements were brought to Singapore Island. It did not seem sensible for British colonists to sail home risking German submarines on the way to get to Britain and risk German air raids, because of the slight risk that the Japanese might attack.

Besides, they said, the British Far Eastern Fleet could stop any amphibious landing, the air force could shoot down any raiders, the 7000 foot jungle-clad mountains of Malaya would stop any invader and the massive army could repel any assault on Singapore, and no attack could take place in winter, because of the monsoon. They were also fortunate that the current commander, General Percival, had helped design the defences and knew them intimately.

With hindsight the naivety of the British, who were convinced they had thought of everything, is only overshadowed by the child-like trust the indigenous natives had in their British masters.

In northern Malaya was the newly assembled Indian IIIrd Corps of the 9th and 11th Divisions and 12th and 28th Brigades. In central Malaya was the Australian 8th Division. At Singapore was the Malay Division.

The Malay Division was a real hodge-podge: three infantry brigades – one of a Malay, an Indian and a British battalion; one of an Indian and two British battalions; and one of a British and two Indian battalions; plus two autonomous Indian states' battalions, three battalions of the Singapore Straits Settlement Volunteers SSSVF, British artillery, two Indian-manned artillery batteries of the Hong Kong & Singapore Artillery HK&SA; Singapore engineers and signallers; and British rear-echelon troops.

In addition to the above formations there was a considerable number of indigenous troops: the Federated Malay States Volunteers of four infantry battalions and an artillery battery, all recently called to full-time duty; and some militia units – the Kelantan Volunteer Force, Perak River Platoon, Sultan Idris Company and Johore forces of infantry, artillery and engineers. Other Malay troops were in six labour battalions, rear-echelon companies, medical units, two infantry companies attached to the 11th division and one to the 9th division, and there was one battalion of the SSSVF at Penang. Almost all the indigenous units were recruited from Malays, though the SSSVF had British colonists and Chinese. There was also a Chinese transport company.

Much of the artillery was provided by the Indian-manned HK&SA: one shore gun, seven flak and six field gun batteries. The military police in Malaya was mostly Indian-manned.

The total number of ground troops was 37,000 Indians, 19,000 British and colonists, 16,800 indigenous and 15,000 Australians.

Malaya's air defences consisted of 150 planes: three Australian squadrons, Malay Volunteer Air Force and Singapore Straits Settlement Volunteer Air Force.

The Far Eastern Fleet was built around the *Prince of Wales* and the *Repulse*, just arriving in early December.

On paper this was a formidable force, but in truth with only two capital ships the fleet was inadequate, the planes were obsolete and their crews poorly trained, and the army was an administrative shambles responsible to too many governments and pseudo-governments and had not had a chance to train as a force.

At 45 minutes past midnight on 8 December 1941 Japanese troopships landed men at Kota Bharu in north east Malaya. By dawn the 9th Division and aircraft were counter-attacking the invaders, but they failed to hold the port and airfield. This first day several towns were raided by Japanese planes. In Singapore's first attack 61 civilians were killed.

Hours later the Air Force withdrew their planes from the north to cover the navy's counter-assault. However, Admiral Phillips had no air cover on the 10th when 85 enemy aircraft began to bomb his ships: 140 minutes later both capital ships were on the bottom along with Phillips and 839 of his men. Three planes had been shot down.

With the destruction of this so-called fleet, North Borneo was defenceless, so the British there destroyed the oilfields. At Sarawak the indigenous Rangers and Volunteer Force, reinforced by an Indian battalion, peered out to sea awaiting invasion. On 18 December the Japanese came, and the defenders retreated into the jungle almost at once to march south towards Dutch territory, hoping for safety in numbers. On the march the British officers told their indigenous troops to go home. The jungle was just too vast to defend. The British and Indians fought as guerrillas for a few days, then surrendered.

Within days all of Brunei, North Borneo and Sarawak were overrun.

On 11 December about 50,000 Japanese troops invaded north-west Malaya from Thailand and all the defenders were ordered to fall back. The allied soldiers of different skin complexions stumbled together along primitive tracks under a heavy rain, turning their faces away from the villagers they were abandoning. No one likes to retreat. Here and there men were ordered to man rear-guards, effectively a suicide mission. The Japanese were moving fast, rebuilding bridges and grading roads in record time. Some advanced on bicycles!

Air reinforcements from Britain and New Zealand made no difference. Ground reinforcements came too, but the three Indian brigades were put into reserve in the south.

After three weeks of war the IIIrd Corps had retreated 200 miles and unfortunately as often happens in retreat the skins of different hue began to blame each other: Britons complaining the Malays deserted and Indians ran away: Indians saying the British wouldn't fight. All blamed the lack of leadership. When the enemy outflanked the Perak River line, the troops retreated again, their generals abandoning 4,000 men on the north bank.

As soon as a form of defence line was built, the troops heard Japanese forces had landed on the coast behind them and the retreat began again.

On 31 January 1942 the last troops crossed the causeway from the mainland to Singapore Island. The loss of Malaya was a tremendous blow: half the world's tin; a third of the world's rubber; but more importantly it was the loss of prestige for the British that hurt the most. The Indian and indigenous troops could not understand what had gone wrong: how a white-led army could have been so decisively defeated by a yellow-skinned army.

The defenders had inflicted about 4,600 killed and wounded on the Japanese, but suffered 6,000 killed, 11,000 wounded and 8,000 missing. Some of the missing were indigenous troops who had gone home to wage guerrilla war.

The 20-by-12-mile island of Singapore was overcrowded with about 400,000 civilian refugees and ships were leaving crammed to the funnels with civilians. Meanwhile Percival tried to put his units into some sort of order: Australian 8th, Indian 11th, British 18th and Malay Divisions. Counting units crippled in the mainland fighting he had an infantry strength of twenty Indian, fifteen British, seven Australian and five indigenous battalions.

On the night of 8 February 21 Japanese battalions crossed the straits in barges and rafts to land on the swampy north coast. Allied firepower slaughtered them, but they kept coming and by dawn had a foothold. The Australians began a fighting withdrawal. The next day the causeway was lost and the enemy now began pouring across it. There was no longer any allied air strength to hinder them. Allied counter-attacks were quickly repulsed.

Percival ordered everyone to fall back to Singapore City, where incredibly some troops were still awaiting orders. A Malay unit refused to retreat at first. All ships were ordered to leave. In the streets, half-blinded by smoke from air raids and shellfire, the people were panicky. Soldiers tried to move, but were hindered by the mass of people and the total confusion. On the 13th a Malay battalion was all but wiped out by a ferocious assault.

Percival had abandoned his source of fresh water and decided that the Japanese might turn off the taps. On the 15th he surrendered.

General Yamashita of the Twenty-fifth Army was taken by surprise. Outnumbered by Percival 2:1 and having run out of ammunition he was contemplating retreat!

Apart from Dunkirk, this was the greatest defeat in British history. It had the effect of proving to everyone in Asia that a yellow-skinned people could defeat the most powerful empire in the history of the world. Never again would the white man be able to convince Asians that he was superior.

Depending on how the computation is made the number of casualties vary. Probably, counting police and air, sea and ground personnel of all descriptions (i.e. 67,450 Indians, 38,450 Britons and colonists, 18,350 Australians and 16,800 indigenous) 6,000 were killed in Malaya and 2,700 on Singapore, over a thousand escaped to Sumatra and some of the indigenous troops hid in the crowds, 8,000 were captured or missing in Malaya and 122,350 surrendered on Singapore. Japanese losses in the two months were 3,500 killed and 6,000 wounded.

All white civilians, about 15,000, were arrested as were several thousand Chinese businessmen and community leaders.

The end of the campaign did not mean an end to the killing. The very next day, 16 February, the Japanese murdered 64 Australian soldiers – all female. Within two weeks 5,000 prominent Chinese had been murdered, many by ritual decapitation. Random killings continued.

The conditions in which the military and civilian prisoners were kept ranged from disgusting to fatal. The death rate was exceedingly high.

The Japanese recruited tens of thousands of workers by various methods for great building projects and then proceeded to work them to death without a spark of humanity. The racial Chinese suffered most. Most likely, 100,000 people found death in this manner. Thousands of women were conscripted as prostitutes for the Japanese soldiers.

Natives in Borneo were also drafted to work for the conqueror. To refuse meant instant execution by a bayonet or sword.

To be sure the Japanese found collaborators, but none of them were ever trusted enough to soldier for the empire, bar some Indians who had come to the conclusion that the British were finished as an empire.

Another way in which the killing went on was guerrilla war. No Japanese went on sentry duty without fear of having his throat slit.

Under British authority natives of the above colonies serving at sea continued to fight, plus some Malays and Chinese from these colonies served as army scouts and commandos. Most of them finished up serving in China as part of a British military mission.

On 6 June 1945 Australian troops landed in Brunei. They were resisted for two weeks and then the surviving Japanese fled into the jungle. Unfortunately, the coastal towns were severely damaged.

In mid-August the war ended with Japan's surrender. On Borneo Australians accepted the surrender of thousands of Japanese, but learning of the unspeakable horrors they had inflicted on the locals and allied prisoners, the Australian guards had a tendency to turn a blind eye to local villagers who wanted revenge. How many Japanese prisoners were killed is unknown – hundreds, thousands?

See Index

MALTA

Status in 1939:	British possession.
Government in 1939:	British administration.
Population in 1939:	278,000.
Make-up in 1939:	Maltese;
	a few Italians.
Religion:	Christian.
Location:	Central Mediterranean.

The Malta islands have been militarily strategic for millennia, because of their location, and conqueror after conqueror has left his mark, to make the Maltese people a unique blend of races. In 1939 the British were here because they wanted a naval base to link Gibraltar with the Suez Canal. Of all conquerors they were the most benevolent to date.

When Britain declared war on Germany in 1939 Maltese entered the British Royal Air Force, merchant fleet, Royal Navy and Army, most of the latter in the Malta Artillery and the King's Own Malta Regiments. Many of the artillery gunners went to protect the Suez Canal.

On 10 June 1940 Italy declared war on Britain and the very next day the sky over Malta was full of Italian planes, their airfields just twenty minutes away. The flak gunners manned their weapons and the three biplane fighters took off to give battle. Day after day the Italians returned. The main target seemed to be Grand Harbour in Valetta.

On 31 July twelve British fighters flew to Malta from a carrier, but one was shot down by an Italian fighter as it arrived. The pilots found thousands of Maltese civilians moving into caves in the hills to escape the bombs but that they aided the defenders in every way possible. Maltese troops were manning flak guns and others worked ceaselessly at the bases, despite the constant raids. Army conscription was introduced, but most Maltese soldiers were volunteers. Eventually 15,000 served. There were also 5,000 special constables doing duty as sentries, aircraft observers and air raid wardens.

It was November before the first merchant ship reached Malta with supplies. She was welcomed as if she had brought treasure: indeed she had – the everyday items without which man cannot survive.

In 1941 German flyers joined the Italians and quickly learned why the Italians preferred any target to Malta: the concentration of flak was awesome.

On 20 April 1942 Malta received a major air reinforcement as 47 carrier fighters flew in, but by the end of the day 37 had been bombed to bits.

On 9 May another 62 fighters flew in. British, Australian, New Zealand, South African, Canadian, French and American pilots learned to love the Maltese people. There certainly was no shortage of excitement: one Yank shot down twelve planes during a tour at Malta.

In May 1942 the islands were struck by no less than 5,715 sorties. Maltese and British flak gunners were knocking down a hundred planes a week.

On 15 August 1942 an American oil tanker reached Malta, an absolute godsend. The Americans were fêted, especially as they had run such a gauntlet of fire that their ship had to be scrapped. By now Grand Harbour was littered with half-sunken vessels.

On 13 September came the ultimate accolade. George VI, the British King, awarded the entire Malta nation the George Cross, the highest medal for civilian bravery.

It was with a profound sense of justice that Malta became a staging area for the allied invasion of Italy in July 1943. By mid-

July the airfields that had sent planes to Malta daily were in allied hands. The siege of Malta was over.

The air raids were responsible for the deaths of 1,493 Maltese and the wounding of 3,764 – as a percentage of population four times the British blitz casualties. The enemy had dropped 10lb of explosives for every piece of ground twelve yards by twelve.
See Index

MARIANAS ISLANDS

Other names:	includes Saipan and Tinian.
Status in 1939:	Japanese colony.
Government in 1939:	Japanese administration.
Population in 1939:	23,000 on Saipan and Tinian.
Make-up in 1939:	the indigenous Chamorros were outnumbered by Japanese colonists.
Religion:	Buddhists, tribal and Christians
Location:	Central Pacific.

Colonisation by the Japanese a generation earlier was really no worse than by Europeans, except for the numbers, but in December 1941 when the Japanese used these islands as bases to seize US-occupied Guam, the Chamorros (who had race brothers on Guam) knew things would change quickly.

Their fears were real enough. If they had thought the islands crowded before, they were now practically pushed off by incoming Japanese troops. By early 1944 Tinian twelve by four miles was garrisoned by 9,000 men of the 50th and 135th Regiments. Slightly larger Saipan, three miles away, was held by 31,500 Japanese troops of the 43rd Division, 47th Brigade, 3rd Artillery regiment, 1st Special Naval Landing Force and 55th Naval Guard Unit. In fact the Tinian Chamorros were shoved off and sent to other islands.

There was no doubt in anyone's mind the Americans were coming. In an American air raid on 22 February 1944 much damage was done to the airfields and 168 Japanese aircraft were destroyed.

On 11 June American planes began daily attacks and on the 13th warships shelled the Saipan beaches. The civilians fled inland to the mountains. Japanese colonists and Chamorros alike prayed to their god for the horror to stop. It had only just begun.

On the 15th the Americans reached the beach in landing craft; the 2nd and 4th Marine Divisions reinforced by seven battalions supported by the largest fleet ever seen in the Pacific.

Ashore the Japanese fought as if it was their last act on earth, which of course it was. Despite ferocious American firepower the Japanese had been relatively unharmed and they massacred the incoming Americans, inflicting 30% losses on their assault troops by midnight.

The next day the dazed Americans could not advance. On the 17th they charged again, reinforced by the army 27th Division and three extra battalions. By day's end the Japanese had inflicted 2,200 casualties so far on the 4th Division alone, but had lost over 3,000 dead.

On day four the Americans began to advance and soon liberated the southern half of the island and Charan Kanoa town. By the 22nd the Americans had lost 6,000 killed and wounded and the Japanese 7,000 killed. Here and there a few Chamorros began cautiously to approach the Americans. They found friendly faces and offers of medical aid. In return they helped guide the Americans into the mountains.

But the Japanese were still full of fight and one of their counter-attacks on the 26th broke through the infantry line and reached the artillery, before it was wiped out. This second week the Americans lost 3,200 casualties, but over 8,000 Japanese were killed.

On 7 July another counter-attack broke through the American infantry, reaching their rear, but 4,300 Japanese were shot down doing this.

As the Americans approached the last square mile held by the defenders at the northern end of the island the Japanese colonists were in turmoil. Their menfolk were in uniform here or elsewhere, so they consisted mostly of the elderly, women and children. Terrified of what would happen to them in American hands, for Japanese propaganda had scared them to death with wild stories, they reached the cliffs overlooking the sea. With American infantry in sight they asked Japanese soldiers for grenades. Whole families blew themselves up. Others joined hands and leapt into the sea hundreds of feet below. The Americans from private to general shook their heads in disbelief.

Not all Japanese civilians chose death. Some surrendered alongside Chamorros. They were 'tortured' by the Americans with coffee, food and chocolate.

On Saipan 14,735 Chamorros and Japanese civilians surrendered. The battle cost the Americans 16,500 killed and wounded and the Japanese defenders 29,000 dead.

On 24 July the two American marine divisions invaded Tinian. It took nine days of battle to secure the island. Over 8,400 Japanese defenders were killed for 1,867 American casualties.

On Tinian some Japanese colonists committed suicide, but 4,000 surrendered. They and the civilians on Saipan were held in guarded camps, because Japanese soldiers hiding in the hills periodically came down looking for food and trying to contact them.

Skirmishes continued even while the Americans brought in air force and navy rear-echelon personnel. In November American marines swept the mountains of Saipan and suffered 49 casualties in skirmishes. On Tinian between 2 August, when the Americans first thought they had killed all the defenders, and 31 December 163 Americans were killed and wounded and they killed 500 Japanese.

On 9 March 1945 American B-29 bombers began flying from Tinian to bomb Japan. On 6 August one of the B-29s, the *Enola Gay*, left Tinian with an atomic bomb bound for Hiroshima. A week later the war was over.

Japanese colonists now helped the Americans search the mountains for hold-outs. They talked fifty into surrendering on Tinian and 1,800 on Saipan. Small garrisons on the other Marianas islands now gave up.
See Index

MARSHALL ISLANDS

Status in 1939:	Japanese mandate.
Government in 1939:	Japanese administration.
Population in 1939:	10,000.
Make-up in 1939:	Indigenous islanders; a few Japanese colonists.
Religion:	tribal and mission Christians.
Location:	Central Pacific.

Japanese intrusion into these islands, which are strung out for hundreds of miles across the Pacific, a generation earlier had made little impact on the islanders, but this changed in December 1941 when Japan began a war against the USA. At once they began to garrison the Marshalls: after all nothing stood between them and Hawaii, but water.

In February 1942 American carrier planes raided the atolls (island groups) of Kwajaelin, Maloelap and Wotje. The islanders were frightened out of their wits. The raid only confirmed Japanese fears of an American invasion and they increased their Marshalls garrison to over 20,000 troops, basing them primarily on Roi-Namur, Kwajalein, Eniwetok, Wotje, Maloelap, Jaluit, Majuro and Mili. In December 1943 the American planes returned, striking Kwajalein and Wotje, and on 19 January 1944 most of the islands were hit, especially those with small airstrips. The raids continued daily. It was obvious the Americans were coming.

On 30 January the islanders of Majuro watched the Americans land. They walked up to the invaders on the beach and told them that all the Japanese but four men had left. At once scores of ships began anchoring in the lagoon. The islanders had not known there were so many ships in the world.

On the 31st the islands of Mallu, Ennuebing, Ennubin, Ennumenet and Ennugarett were invaded by companies of the US 4th Marine Division. The total of 135 Japanese on these islands fought to the death, inflicting 64 casualties on the Americans, while the natives, perhaps 100 per island, hid in clumps of trees.

This day the US Army 7th Division put troops onto Gehh, Nina, Gea, Ennubuj and Ennylabegan. The 200 or so Japanese fought to the death inflicting a few score casualties. Here too natives hid in sheer terror.

On 1 February three-mile-long Kwajalein Island was invaded by three of the 7th Division's battalions. This was a different ball game, for the garrison numbered 7,850. The combat was bloody and fought at ranges of a few feet. The 300 or so natives hid under palm leaves and in gullies terrified at the noise and horror of it all. They did not like the foreigner's way of waging war.

At the same time the 4th Marine Division invaded Roi-Namur, two very small islands joined by a causeway. The 3,840 Japanese fought like wildcats. Yet within 36 hours the marines had killed the last of the defenders, except for 91 taken prisoner. About a hundred natives surrendered. It had cost the Americans 737 casualties.

On Kwajalein the Americans had to bring in two more battalions on the 2nd and another on the 3rd. After five days of battle the Americans killed the last defender. They took prisoner 130 defenders, mostly Koreans, and a few natives. It cost the Americans 940 casualties.

The 7th Division now cleared several smaller islands and killed 700 Japanese for a hundred casualties and the 4th Division cleared some islands for a similar casualty rate. On each island natives eagerly gave the Americans information, often pointing out Japanese snipers and machine gun nests.

On the 17th a mixed American army and marine force invaded Eniwetok. Here too a hellatious battle was fought and it was six days before the Americans killed the last of the defenders at a cost of 600 casualties.

The US 22nd Marine Regiment invaded Engebi and fought a major struggle for five days killing 1,250 Japanese for 303 casualties. Some natives cautiously went up to the Americans with food as a peace offering. They were relieved to find the Americans were friendly.

The 22nd Marines took Parry in two days at a cost of 334 casualties. On Eniwetok, Engebi and Parry the Americans counted 2,600 dead Japanese and took 64 prisoners.

Over the next three months the 22nd Marines invaded twenty-nine lesser islands. On each one natives pointed out the enemy – a dozen or so riflemen and a machine gun. Some natives accompanied the Americans in landing craft to other islands as guides. Less than 50 American casualties were incurred.

The natives and Japanese on Wotje, Maloelap, Jaluit and Mili tensely awaited their turn, but it never came. The Americans allowed them to wither on the vine until the end of the war, when they surrendered.

After the war the foreigners moved on, leaving the islands littered with rusting burned-out vehicles, crashed planes and crippled landing craft. The island paradise had been turned into a scrap yard and as for the natives, it was impossible to readjust. They would never be the same gain.
See Index

MAURITIUS, RODRIGUEZ AND SEYCHELLES

Status in 1939:	British possessions.
Government in 1939:	British administrations.
Population in 1939:	Mauritius 385,000;
	Rodriguez 11,000;
	Seychelles 34,000.
Make-up in 1939:	one third Europeans with a
	French Creole culture;
	remainder a mixture of
	Chinese, Hindus, Bhojpuris
	Urdus and others.
Religion:	various.
Location:	Indian Ocean

Upon declaring war on Germany in 1939 Britain asked her subjects in the above colonies to volunteer for military service. Some entered the merchant fleet, Royal Navy and Royal Air Force on an individual basis. Those who joined the British Army were placed in the Pioneer Corps, with the duty of stringing barbed-wire, filling sand bags, digging trenches, repairing roads, unloading trucks, indeed anything soldiers hate to do.

Mauritius raised 4,000 pioneers and Rodriguez and Seychelles 400 each to serve in Egypt. On 10 April 1941 800 Mauritians embarked aboard ship and set sail from Egypt. Next day, as their ship entered Tobruk harbour, they could see smoke drifting from air raid damage. Suddenly geysers of water shot upwards: they were being bombed. Minutes later bombs slammed into the vessel, killing 26 Mauritians and wounding 48. Once berthed the Mauritians were informed that as rear-echelon troops they should not have come. They turned around and went back to Egypt.

In early 1942 the pioneers followed the British Eighth Army into Libya, only to be told to retreat within days. In May they received retreat orders again and did so by truck under air attack. On 20 June 400 Mauritians were in Tobruk when they learned the town was surrounded. They worked in the harbour that day and the next under air raids. Others were at the perimeter preparing defences. Just before noon they were informed the garrison commander had surrendered: they were prisoners of war!

The Pioneer Corps earned respect from the Eighth Army soldiers, more so than any other rear-echelon troops. They stayed with the Eighth throughout the Alamein battles, the advance across Libya and the Tunisian campaign.

On 3 September when the Eighth Army invaded Italy 800 Mauritians hit the beaches alongside the infantry. There was no opposition, but for air raids.

Six days later the US Fifth Army invaded Italy at Salerno, where the Germans put up fierce resistance. 400 Mauritius and 400 Seychelles pioneers hit the beaches right behind the infantry. They spent the next three weeks unloading landing ships under shellfire.

The Rodriguez pioneers and another 400 Mauritians arrived in Italy in the autumn. The Mauritians were mentioned in despatches for their bravery under fire especially in the Cassino battles in 1944.

The pioneers spent the remainder of the war to May 1945 supporting the allied forces in Italy.
See Index

MEXICO

Status in 1941:	independent.
Government in 1941:	dictatorship.
Population in 1941:	19,600,000.
Make-up in 1941:	Mestizos (European-Indian mix) 10,500,000;
	Indians 5,500,000;
	Creoles (Basques, Catalans, Spanish) 3,000,000.
Religion:	Christian.
Location:	North America

For the allies the prime benefit of Mexico's declaration of war on the axis powers in 1942 was the denial of her ports and goods to the axis.

At sea six Mexican merchant ships were sunk by German submarines.

By 1944 the Mexican government felt that to cement their relationship with the USA, which had never been good, they should do something positive in the war effort. They chose to send a squadron of fighters to join the allied air forces.

The fighters reached the Philippines in summer 1945 and saw action attacking Japanese ground forces on Luzon.
See Index

MICRONESIA

Other names:	600 islands in the Carolines and the Palaus.
Status in 1939:	Japanese mandates.
Government in 1939:	Japanese administration.
Population in 1939:	50,000.
Make-up in 1939:	tribal islanders; a small number of Japanese colonists.
Religion:	tribal and mission Christians.
Location:	West Central Pacific.

The relationship between the islanders and the Japanese, who had arrived a generation earlier, seemed to be placid and did not alter the islanders' way of life, but in December 1941 when the Japanese made war on the USA, they began to put troops onto select islands. They knew the islands could be used as stepping stones for an American invasion across the Pacific between Hawaii and the Philippines. Truk in the Carolines was the finest natural harbour in the world and naturally the Americans would want that.

Centred on Truk the Japanese fleet could pivot to repel offensives against the Marshalls, Gilberts, Admiralties or the Marianas. Therefore, as long as the fleet was in being the actual ground forces in these islands were irrelevant. The fleet assembled at Truk in April 1942.

American long-range bombers harassed Truk, but they were notoriously inaccurate. Natives watched the bombs fall with curiosity. Not only was Truk heavily defended with flak guns and fighter airfields, but the fleet's own flak guns were formidable.

In 1943 the Americans decided on the neutralisation of Truk rather than its occupation, which would be costly in terms of lives. As part of this strategy their submarines began to sink everything going in and out.

On 17 February 1944 American carrier planes struck Truk: it proved to be one of the greatest allied air victories of the war, as they sank thirty merchant vessels and fifteen warships, shot down 45 Japanese fighters and destroyed 220 planes on their runways, plus blew up facilities, fuel dumps, warehouses, docks, for the loss of twenty-five American planes.

The natives could not believe what they saw. The Japanese fleet abandoned Truk, the linchpin of their Pacific war strategy.

American long-range bombers began striking Ponape in the Palaus. On 30 March American carrier planes attacked the Palaus and two days later hit Woleai. Scores of merchant ships were sunk.

In September the carrier planes returned to the Palaus, for the Americans had decided that to assist their invasion of the Philippines they needed a harbour: possible sites were Peleliu, Anguar, Yap and Ulithi.

On 15 September the US 1st Marine Division invaded four-square-mile Peleliu. Despite a massive air and naval bombardment General Nakagawa's 14th Division was waiting on the beach to mow down the Americans as they leapt from landing craft. Only after two days of slaughter could the Americans begin cautiously moving inland. The invaders had lost 2,000 killed and wounded, but it looked like the Japanese were whipped.

On the 17th two-square-mile Anguar, six miles from Peleliu, was invaded by the US Army 81st Division. They came ashore fairly easily, the 1,600 defenders of the 59th Division having chosen to hold a hilly position, the Bowl, in the north west of the island. After six days of battle the Americans could reduce their assault frontage from six battalions to one, and they began mopping up the last resisters, which took a month. The island cost the Americans 1,600 casualties.

However, on Peleliu the defenders had withdrawn to a mountainous position called the Umurbrogol Ridge. The first assault on the ridge cost the Americans 2,000 men. The 81st Division was asked to send reinforcements.

Not until 26 November could the Americans consider Peleliu secure, for a total cost of 7,550 killed and wounded and 15,000 sick. They killed 13,600 Japanese.

The US Navy now decided they didn't need Anguar or Peleliu: Ulithi would be the best base – 400 natives met the Americans on the beach with coconuts. There were no Japanese.

On Anguar and Peleliu a tiny number of Japanese hold-outs hid and periodically crept into an American camp looking for food. A few Japanese from another island raided Peleliu in early 1945.

The remainder of the natives and Japanese on the other islands sat out the war without interference.
See Index

MONACO

Status in 1939:	independent.
Government in 1939:	monarchy.
Population in 1939:	19,000.
Make-up in 1939:	Monagasque 2,000; French and other immigrants 17,000.
Religion:	Christian.
Location:	0.75 square mile on the French Riviera

Smaller than some city parks, with its people and language completely engulfed by immigrants and tourists, the nation was a sort of reminder of what an ancient city-state used to look like. As its revenue came from gambling, it really did have the appearance of a theme park.

However, the Monagasque take themselves seriously and, when France declared war on Germany in 1939, they notified the world they wanted no part of it. Their business was bringing pleasure not death.

In June 1940 Mussolini's fascist Italian Army ignored this and invaded the nation. There was no resistance: the police were left alone.

Over the next three years refugees escaping the German Nazis entered Monaco under Italian protection. The locals made them welcome, though it put a strain on the economy.

In September 1943 the Italians collapsed into civil war and German troops arrived. At once their SS Security Police began screening the refugees. Arrests were made and the locals now realised how isolated they had been from the realities of nazi-occupied Europe.

In August 1944 the Americans invaded the French Riviera and shelled warships in Monaco harbour and a German barracks, in hopes of levering the Germans out without a ground battle that would have destroyed the picturesque nation. The tactic worked, and Monaco was in fact liberated by two scruffy American GIs, who wandered into the country by mistake!

The monarch Prince Rainier now declared war on Germany and authorised his citizens to enlist in the French Army. He served as a captain and won medals for bravery.

See Index

MONGOLIA

Other Names:	includes, inner and outer Buryat.
Status in 1931:	see text.
Government in 1931:	see text.
Population in 1931:	Buryat 1,000,000; Inner 2,000,000; Outer 1,000,000.
Make-up in 1931:	Mongolian tribes; some Kazakhs in the West; some Chinese in Inner.
Religion:	Lamaists and Buddhists.
Location:	Eastern Asia

The rise and fall of military empires can be nowhere more evident than Mongolia. In the late medieval period the Mongols under Genghis Khan and successors conquered much of China, Eastern Europe, the Holy Land and Persia. Everyone fell to their swift horsemen.

Yet by 1919 the Soviet Red Army (Russian communist) could scatter the Mongolian horsemen. Occupying Buryat and Outer Mongolia they found only a few tribal goatherds living in huts made from goatskins. Their capital Ulan Bator was nothing more than a market place.

The Soviets annexed Buryat, but left Outer Mongolia under the puppet government of Bogd, a lamaist leader. This state gave the Soviets a diplomatic window through which they could talk to the western world.

Inner Mongolia remained under Mongolian and Chinese warlords, where there was constant fighting.

In 1928 the Buryat Mongols revolted against the atheist communists: the Soviet Red Army massacred 35,000 rebels.

In 1931 a Japanese army destroyed the Chinese warlords in Manchuria and befriended the 100,000 anti-communist Russian refugees living there. The Japanese soon set up a puppet state, Manchutukuo, ruled by Henry P'u-Yi, the last Emperor of China. They also intrigued with warlords in Charar and Suiyan in Inner Mongolia. The Mongol princes had the following choices: allow warlords to continue to ravage their lands; ask Chiang-Kai-Shek the most powerful Chinese warlord for protection; sell out to the Chinese communists of Mao-Zhe-Dung; invite the Soviets in; or negotiate with the Japanese. The latter seemed the lesser of many evils.

By 1935 the Japanese were in effect the protectors of Charar. In July 1937 the Japanese invaded Chiang-Kai-Shek's China, Charar and Suiyan. The warlords fled and the princes ordered their people not to resist. It was late October before the Japanese entered all the provinces of Inner Mongolia, simply because of its size. Some horse cavalry columns had covered 500 miles of desert and steppe.

The Japanese established the Mongolian Federated Autonomous Government at Kuesui in Suiyan to rule all of Inner Mongolia.

In July 1938 the Japanese sent a division-sized force, including an anti-communist Russian brigade, into the USSR from Korea. They clashed with the Red Army at Changkufeng and were thoroughly defeated.

In May 1939 the Japanese sent a corps, their Russians and a unit of the Inner Mongolian Army across the unguarded border to Nomonhan in Outer Mongolia. It took two months for the Soviets to respond, as it was 400 miles from the railhead, but in August the Outer Mongolian Army and the Red Army counter-attacked. In a ten-day battle the Japanese-controlled forces were decisively beaten, losing upwards of 15,000 casualties. The situation remained tense along the border, but there were no further battles.

In June 1941 Germany invaded the USSR, drawing off Soviet forces westwards. The Red Army conscripted Buryat Mongols to fight the Germans. Outer Mongolia remained neutral, but many a Red Army recruiter crossed the border to grab young men.

The big battles against the Germans went badly at first and whole units were ordered to surrender. Many a Mongol found himself starving to death in a German prison camp. However, German recruiters now came along, promising him treatment comparable to that of German soldiers, and cultural and religious freedom, if he volunteered to fight the communists. Naturally many signed up. They were formed into anti-guerrilla battalions and sent all over Europe.

Buryat Mongols in the Red Army fought in the victorious battle in front of Moscow in December 1941.

In June 1944 when the allies invaded France they found several Mongol battalions. The Germans preferred to use Mongols for their original purpose, fighting guerrillas, and encouraged them to be as ferocious as possible. On occasion Mongols raped and massacred innocents: they knew they could expect no quarter if caught by the French Resistance, and in any case this was how they had waged war for centuries.

Yet the word soon got out that the Americans would treat them well, so whenever possible they surrendered to them: some Americans actually thought they were Japanese!

Most Buryat Mongols served valiantly in the Red Army. Their primitive behaviour was laughable. When they invaded Germany they stole light bulbs, not realising they required electricity. They stole watches and threw them away when they ceased to tick, not knowing they had to be wound. They raped unmercifully and savagely. Their Russian officers treated them like cattle.

In summer 1945 the Red Army assembled to take care of unfinished business: the destruction of the Japanese. They put the 1st Far Eastern Front with four armies in the Vladivostok area, the 2nd Far Eastern Front of two armies north of Manchutukuo and the Trans-Baikal Front with six armies and the few thousand strong Outer Mongolian Army on the west of Manchutukuo and north of Inner Mongolia. They had 28,000 guns, 5,550 tanks, 4,370 planes and 1,500,000 troops.

In defence were the Manchutukuo Army, the Inner Mongolian Army, the North Chinese Republican Army, the anti-communist Russians, and nine Japanese armies. In total they had 5,360 guns, 1,115 tanks, 1,800 planes and 1,000,000 troops, of which 840,000 were Japanese. However, the tanks were useless compared to Soviet T-34s and Stalins.

On 9 August the Soviets attacked. The Trans-Baikal Front advanced at the rate of fifty miles a day, brushing aside all resistance, over the 6000-foot Great Hingan mountains to Mukden. A column of tanks and horse cavalry including Mongols crossed the Gobi Desert for 200 miles into Inner Mongolia to reach Changpeh in eleven days. By this time the other Soviet armies had advanced a hundred miles into Manchutukuo.

On the 15th the Japanese Emperor had surrendered, but on the 17th had to send an emissary to personally order the Japanese generals to cease fire against the Soviets. Many Japanese soldiers fought on, but the puppet state armies collapsed. It was early September before the shooting stopped.

The Red Army and Outer Mongolia Army lost 8,219 killed and 27,000 wounded. About 80,000 Japanese and about 3,000 puppet troops were killed and 800,000 taken prisoner, of which only about 60% survived Soviet captivity.

Peace returned to Buryat and Outer Mongolia, but Inner Mongolia returned to its natural state of internecine war.
See Index

MOROCCO

Other names:	French Morocco (does not include Ceuta, Ifni or Tangiers)
Status in 1939:	French colony.
Government in 1939:	French administration.

Population in 1939:	18,000,000
Make-up in 1939:	Berbers 10,800,000;
	Arabs 6,950,000;
	Jews 200,000;
	French Colonists 50,000.
Religion:	Moslem.
Location:	North West Africa.

When France declared war on Germany in 1939 French male colonists were subject to recall as reservists or conscription, but native Moroccans had to volunteer. Many did so, serving in their own units with French officers.

When Belgium was invaded by the Germans in May 1940 Moroccan troops were part of the French forces sent north into Belgium to help repel the invader. Arriving near Cambrai they were attacked by General Rommel's 7th Panzer Division. Ordered to hold at all costs they did so. Whole companies were destroyed before they got the word to retreat. During the next two weeks they were constantly on the move, their rearguards overrun, so that by the time the French were evacuating from Dunkirk, there were few Moroccans left.

Other Moroccan troops were in central France when the Germans attacked that region on 5 June. On the 17th the French government of Marshal Pétain began surrender negotiations, but that did not stop some Moroccans from fighting to the death. On the 22nd it was all over. About 15,000 Moroccans had been killed or captured.

Under the armistice terms Morocco retained a French garrison of 50,000, air squadrons and a naval flotilla. It seemed to everyone the fighting was over, but just a week later the British attacked the French fleet. In response French planes took off from Morocco and bombed Gibraltar.

In Morocco the troops were put on alert in case of a British invasion. The invasions came, but elsewhere in the French empire, and in June 1941 it was the turn of Syria, where part of the garrison consisted of a Moroccan infantry battalion and a horse cavalry squadron. They resisted for a month until the French commander surrendered. The prisoners were given a choice of going home or joining the British and 'their'

French general, de Gaulle. Most chose home.

Morocco itself was peaceful, though the Pétainist regime was a strict police state and introduced anti-Jewish legislation.

On the night of 7 November 1942, in agreement with the British, anti-Pétainist officers arrested the German Armistice Commission in Casablanca and set up welcoming committees on the Moroccan beaches for an Anglo-American invasion the next morning. They also occupied Army Headquarters.

Just before dawn the coast at Mehdia, Safi and Fedala was invaded by the American 2nd Armoured, 9th and 3rd Divisions. But the rebels had been only partially successful. French- and Moroccan-manned shore defences opened fire on the landing craft and the navy sortied out of Casablanca to do battle.

Throughout the day there was much confusion as the defenders received conflicting orders to resist and cease resistance and this let the Americans get a good foothold. The next day resistance stiffened, but on the 10th Admiral Darlan, French Commander-in-Chief, ordered a ceasefire.

The Moroccan troops had suffered a few hundred losses, but were not disarmed. On the contrary, they were now given orders to join the Americans.

By December the Anglo-Americans were trying to take Tunisia from a German-Italian army and the French organised a corps to help them. The Moroccan Division was formed as part of this effort, plus Moroccan camel troops were sent to patrol the southern desert of Tunisia, and three battalions of Goumiers, mountain experts who fought in traditional robes, were organised to fight in the central mountainous portion of Tunisia.

The first major effort came on 8 January 1943 when Moroccan camel troops defeated the Italians at Temout Mellor and advanced all the way into Libya at Tanoui Mellek. Meanwhile in the mountains the other Moroccans settled into a static defence.

In late February in northern Tunisia a Moroccan force aided the British to repel an Italian attack at Siliano.

On 28 March Moroccans took Jebel Abiod and a few days later Goumiers captured Sejanene. Others took Cap Serrat.

On 19 April the allies launched a major offensive. The Moroccan mission was to occupy Point du Fahs, which they did after a week of combat. However, now the Anglo-Americans hogged the glory as their advance squeezed out the French corps. They were calling the shots and the French had to obey.

On 12 May the Italians and Germans gave up. Their forces included a battalion of Moroccans, who had obviously backed the wrong side.

Moroccan casualties in Tunisia were about 3,000.

It was with satisfaction that the Goumiers responded to an American call in late July. The Americans had become embroiled in a mountain campaign in Sicily and they needed mountain experts. The 6,000 Goumiers did very well: the Americans noted their special fondness for the bayonet.

The enemy evacuated Sicily on 16 August and on 3 September the allies invaded Italy. Five days later Italy broke apart in civil war and on the French island of Corsica the Italians began fighting the Germans. The Corsican resistance movement asked for French help against the Germans and on 13 September a party of Frenchmen landed to see for themselves. They recommended a landing at once and on the 15th a regiment of the 4th Moroccan Division sailed to Corsica, accompanied by French warships and aircraft.

Linking up with the anti-German forces on the 17th they took Ajaccio, repelled German counter-attacks at Serbe and Linsecca and on the 23rd began to advance across the island. By the 26th 6,600 Moroccans were ashore. On 3 October the Germans evacuated. The Moroccans had been the first allied troops to liberate a department of France.

The allies soon needed help in Italy and General Juin put together a corps, which entered the freezing cold line near Cassino in December with General Dody's 2nd Moroccan Division and six battalions of Goumiers. Despite such inclement weather and tough resistance by Austrian mountain troops, they captured three mountains in three weeks. A major offensive was launched on 14 January 1944 and in five days they crossed the Rapido river and took the strategic Monte Il Lago and repulsed all German efforts to retake it. But now the Moroccans were told to hold what they had until the allies captured Monte Cassino. It was to take four months!

In March General Sevez's 4th Moroccan Division entered the static line. The unit was powerful with 19,652 men and 3,900 mules.

When the allies gave the go-ahead for an advance in May they gave the Moroccans rough mountain ridges, while they themselves used valley roads. Using the 4th Division and the Goumiers as spearheads the French corps not only advanced, but moved quicker than the allies on the valley roads. They bypassed Rome and chased the enemy up central Italy.

Elements of the 4th Division were withdrawn and used for an amphibious invasion of Elba Island. They took it 17-19 June at a cost of 500 casualties.

In late July, Juin's corps was withdrawn from Italy and embarked aboard ship for the invasion of southern France. The 4th Division had a solid mission: to take the great port of Toulon.

After landing behind American troops on 16 August the Moroccans drove to Toulon and battled against the forts ringing the city and took the surrender of the German garrison on the 27th.

The French, now designated First Army, drove north up the Rhône-Saône Valley: the 2nd and 4th Moroccan Divisions making record time, about fifteen miles a day against opposition, through the Dijon area by 12 September into Alsace. They halted to bring up supplies, not because of resistance, and in October elements of the army advanced again to reach the Rhine River. The First Army settled down to a static cold winter.

On 6 January 1945 in deep snow the 4th Moroccan Division beat back a German attack by a division of Austrian mountain troops. On the 20th it was their turn, as the army went over to the offensive, with the

2nd Moroccan Division struggling in thigh-deep snow to take Pulversheim and the 4th Moroccan Division attacking Cernay and Rouffach in blinding snow blizzards and wind that cut like a knife. This was the Moroccans' toughest fight to date.

For seventeen days the troops fought and cursed the weather, the enemy and their officers until meeting American troops coming down from the north.

The affair cost the two Moroccan divisions 5,000 killed and wounded and thousands hospitalised with respiratory ailments and frostbite. It was fortunate that they were now given a respite from major battle for two months.

On 4 April the 4th Division crossed the Rhine at Strasbourg. They found only light opposition as they climbed into the mountains of the Black Forest, but day by day they encountered some fanatic rearguards, often defended by mere boys with no training. From the 9th to the 12th the division only covered seven miles.

Then suddenly the defences collapsed and on some days there was almost no opposition. By late April they were easily clearing the Swiss border region, though on the 28th the 4th Division had to fight off a counter-attack. On the 30th the Moroccans entered Austria. A week later the war was over.

Moroccans had fought in most of France's campaigns of the war and had proven themselves to be superb soldiers in every affair. It remained to be seen how the French would reward the Moroccan people.
See Index

NEPAL

Status in 1939:	independent
Government in 1939:	ruling clan
Population in 1939:	6,200,000.
Make-up in 1939:	Nepali tribes.
Religion:	Hindu
Location:	north of the Indian sub-continent.

Nepal is one of the few nations that successfully repelled the British, who for two centuries had an insatiable hunger to conquer far away places. Nepal is certainly far away

from Britain, and far up too, for it encompasses part of the Himalayas.

The Gurkhas, who come from a small tribal group, were so respected by the British as warriors that in the 19th century they were invited to form permanent regiments in the British-controlled Indian Army. They accepted. There is no doubt that as an ethnic group the Gurkhas provided consistently the best soldiers for the allies in World War II. Some achieved junior officer rank, but usually they fought under British officers. Technically mercenaries, as they served whether their government agreed or not, they fought for honour and tradition, rather than their pay. Over 10,000 were killed in the war fighting in Africa, Burma, Malaya, and Italy. Eleven earned the Victoria Cross, Britain's highest award for bravery: a percentage five times greater than that of British soldiers.

In spring 1942 the government of Nepal watched closely the Japanese advance across Burma, for by June only the shattered remnants of a couple of British divisions stood between Nepal and the Japanese. The Nepalese did not know that the Japanese had no intention of invading Nepal.

Therefore, the Nepalese offered their Army to the British. The offer was graciously accepted and the Nepalese received training from the Indian Army.

In spring 1944 the Nepalese units were assigned security duty just behind the front. In August they followed the British advance into Burma.

In December 1944 a battalion was assigned to the Indian Army 268th Brigade, which was given the mission of patrolling the Irrawaddy River's west bank. On several occasions the Nepalese ran into Japanese patrols and stragglers. Their training proved worthwhile in these tiny, but bloody actions.

Having proved themselves, they were ordered to attack over the river. They did so and cleared the far bank and then aided in the capture of Sabaing.

The Nepalese troops continued to perform security duty, which included hunting down Japanese snipers and stragglers, until the end of the war in August 1945.
See Index

NETHERLANDS

Other names:	Holland.
Status IN 1939:	independent
Government in 1939:	democratic monarchy.
Population in 1939:	8,900,000.
Make-up in 1939:	Dutch 8,460,000;
	Frisians 300,000;
	Jews 140,000
Religion:	Christian.
Location:	Western Europe

Having escaped participation in all European wars for over a century, the Dutch were not ready for World War II in 1939, but their military intelligence suspected they would have no choice. Hitler, the German dictator, seemed to be planning an invasion.

At sea Dutch merchant ships were in constant danger from German submarines and mines and allied mines. In the seven months preceding May 1940, 31 Dutch merchantmen were sunk and several damaged and a navy minesweeper was blown up with the loss of 30 lives.

The Netherlands defences consisted of a hundred-plane air force and an army of ten divisions, almost all the soldiers being reservists, who required a couple of days to report and receive equipment.

On the morning of 10 May 1940 without warning Dutch ports, air fields and border defences were bombed by German planes. Reports came in to the high command that German paratroopers were dropping near the Lek, Waal and Maas bridges, seventy miles from the German border. At 7.00am the Dutch government asked the British and French for assistance.

Mobilisation was ordered at once, but many men had to walk or take trains and buses to their reporting stations. There they had to await hand-outs from supply sergeants, and there was of course the required form filling. All this took time, and time was one thing the Dutch did not have.

By noon the German 9th Panzer Division was leading the Eighteenth Army across the middle Maas River.

Confusion was the word everyone would later use to describe the first day of war, and every man and woman who was prevented from doing their duty suspected Fifth Column action, i.e. traitors or Germans in disguise giving wrong instructions and directions. Traffic cops, railway officials, housewives, even nuns were arrested as suspected fifth columnists. German air strikes added to the confusion and of course created terror.

On day two, serious combat was taking place as the Dutch counter-attacked the paratroopers and tried to stop the Germans in the eastern part of the nation. One German formation covered forty miles this day. By day's end Apeldoorn had fallen.

On day three the townsfolk of Tilburg and Breda watched German trucks drive through. Some civilians had fled with a hastily packed suitcase, but the roads were unhealthy as German fighters were strafing them. This day the Dutch learned that the French relief force had been stopped by German paratroopers on the lower Maas.

On day four the Dutch troops at last began to impress the Germans with a tenacious defence. Queen Wilhelmina personally telephoned the British for air support and a rescue for herself. She got the rescue, but not the air support.

On day five Hitler, angry at the steadfast Dutch resistance, authorised a ruse. German planes were ordered to strike the defences inside Rotterdam, a highly populated city, unless the Dutch gave up. The Dutch refused, whereupon the Germans called off the air strike, except the planes did not get the message or understand the ruse. They bombed and 814 civilians died.

The Dutch government had to make a decision: the Army was fighting well, but falling back and civilian refugees were crowding into the western cities; civilian losses to future bombing and starvation could become enormous; and confusion reigned supreme. (The Germans were also confused. One of them accidentally shot their paratroop general.)

On day six the Navy and merchant fleet sailed for Britain. At 9.00pm the government announced a surrender.

Dutch losses were 2,100 killed and 2,700 wounded, and about 2,000 civilians had been killed.

Those Dutch who reached Britain vowed to fight on. Eleven merchantmen had been sunk and six captured, but the rest of the merchant fleet reached Britain, taking with them 26 captured German ships. Within days the merchant fleet made its first great contribution to the war effort, rescuing 20,000 allied soldiers at Dunkirk and taking them to Britain under air attack.

Enough flyers reached Britain to form two anti-shipping bomber squadrons.

Of the Dutch Navy a destroyer and a sloop had been sunk, but three cruisers, two destroyers, a sloop and a minelayer, some submarines and small craft placed themselves under British Royal Navy orders. There were sufficient extra sailors to man five minelayers and some submarines borrowed from the British. The navy was soon in action again: a submarine was lost in June, another in November and a minelayer in June 1941. Small craft based in Britain raided the Dutch coast at night looking for German merchant traffic.

In 1941 the destroyer *Isaac Sweers* in company with three British destroyers met two Italian cruisers and a German E-boat, and sank all three axis vessels. In November 1942 the *Isaac Sweers* took part in the invasion of French North Africa, but five days later her courageous career came to an end when she was torpedoed and sunk by a German submarine.

Several Dutch ocean liners were converted to troopships in British shipyards. The *Westerland* and *Pennland* took part in the failed invasion of Dakar in September 1940, and in April 1941 the *Pennland, Costa Rica* and *Slamat* were sunk by German planes while trying to rescue British soldiers from Greece. Few of the crew survived: they had strongly suspected it was a suicide mission.

In 1942 the *Nieuw Zeeland* was torpedoed, but survived to take her soldier passengers to their destination.

In the German-occupied Netherlands some felt they could adapt to the situation. Eighty Germans in Dutch uniform and thirty Dutch fascists had aided the Germans during the invasion, so the Fifth Column scare did have a sound foundation. However, not all Dutch fascists were pro-German. The Dutch fascist party had one major difference with the German Nazi party: they were not racist and

indeed several Jews had risen to high party rank.

In September 1940 someone murdered a member of the unarmed Dutch fascist militia. The people knew it was time to take sides. Soon 93,000 Dutch had volunteered to work in Germany and thousands of others for the Germans in the Netherlands. The German Waffen SS took on Dutch recruits to form an infantry battalion. In imitation, the Dutch created their own SS to guard government buildings. By February 1941 one adult in seven had joined a fascist or pro-German political organisation.

There were benefits to collaboration. The Germans began to release most of the 300,000 Dutch prisoners they had taken.

In response to the murder of a second fascist, the fascist militia barricaded the Jewish quarter of Amsterdam, turning it into a ghetto. Every few days the militia and German SS Security Police (including Dutch members) arrested a few Jews and sent them off to a concentration camp guarded by Dutch and German SS guards.

In June 1941 Germany invaded the USSR and many a devout Christian, who had refrained from helping the Germans, now felt it right that as long as Germany was in a life or death struggle with the atheist communists it was their Christian duty to aid the Germans.

The Waffen SS took advantage of this belief to take on more recruits to join the Dutch battalion which was already in the forefront of the invasion of the USSR. Within months the 5th SS Division had three Dutch battalions.

The NSKK, a German corps of paramilitary drivers and mechanics, took on Dutch recruits and they too went to Russia.

In response to this feeling the ex-Chief of the Army General Staff raised the Netherlands Legion to fight alongside the Germans in Russia. The 2,500 strong unit entered the line in Russia in November 1941.

After the Germans had conquered a large territory in the USSR they invited Dutch civilians to settle there. Some took up the offer, moving into homes and jobs stolen from some poor unfortunate Russian.

At the front survival not colonisation was on everyone's mind. The Legion had good need of the Netherlands Field Hospital that joined them. In the Battle of Gusi Gora in March 1942 the Legion suffered 80% casualties. The Dutch fascist party was ordered to provide 2,600 replacements at once.

In June the reconstituted Legion smashed their way through the Soviet Eleventh Army and captured its commander. In July, down to a strength of 1,755 the Legion was pulled out for a well-earned rest in the Netherlands.

In August 1942 in Russia a Dutch NSKK convoy was attacked by communist partisans. The drivers retaliated by counterattacking with their rifles and took over a thousand prisoners! The astonished Germans handed out 25 medals for bravery.

Not all Dutch NSKK were so fortunate: some were trapped with the Germans inside Stalingrad. The Dutch of the 5th SS Division were among the soldiers who tried to rescue them, but they failed and in January 1943 the entire German Sixth Army and its few hundred Dutch NSKK were lost.

The Netherlands Legion went back into the line in late 1942 and settled down for a long cold winter. Beginning Christmas Day they suffered high losses to Soviet assaults. They held their trenches and in January were rewarded with another leave in the Netherlands.

In March 1943 the survivors of the Legion were awarded SS membership – it was prudent to accept the 'honour'. Amalgamated with the Dutch members of the 5th SS Division they formed a new formation, the SS Brigade Nederland. Their first assignment was to hunt communist partisans in Yugoslavia.

In December 1943 they were sent to the Russian front.

In spring 1944 the brigade was assigned to the IIIrd SS Corps with responsibility for defending the Estonian-Russian border. They fought courageously and withstood several assaults in June and July, but German forces on the southern flank were not as fortunate and fell back. Therefore the Dutch were ordered to begin a fighting withdrawal to the Baltic coast. One third of the brigade was cut off and chopped to pieces. The Dutch fascist party was ordered to provide 'volunteers' for the brigade and by September, despite serious losses, the brigade had 9,000 men facing the Soviet hordes.

The Free Dutch Navy, as those under British orders called themselves, were also fighting a tough war, dodging planes, mines, warships and submarines. They took part in the allied invasion of Sicily in July 1943, one warship being lost, and in the invasion of Italy at Salerno. From then on the Dutch warships remained off the Italian coast for months, bombarding the enemy on request.

In March 1943 the anti-shipping bombers of the Free Dutch Air Force switched to land targets, sometimes in the Netherlands. This year three Dutch reconnaissance squadrons began operations.

The Dutch people had to live with these air raids, which were dangerous for the bombers of the 1940s were rarely accurate. It got so that even a car journey was dangerous for allied fighters roamed the skies shooting up anything that moved.

Another danger for the Dutch people was the oppression of the police state. An anti-German resistance movement had been created and in one incident they blew up a German Navy officers club. In retaliation the Dutch police arrested 300 Jews and sent them to a concentration camp.

To combat the 'terrorists' German police were brought in to aid the Dutch police, and the German police recruited Dutch members, plus the fascist militia was given arms. Moreover, all male members of the fascist party aged 18-40 were conscripted into the militia to form twelve brigades. Later the age limit was expanded to 17-50. They were to arrest anyone suspected of aiding the terrorists. In April 1943 250 of these suspects were shot in retaliation for a terrorist incident.

Forced labour was also introduced, meaning that any Dutch man or woman who did not have an essential job would be found a job, usually in Germany. Eventually 410,000 were assigned forced labour.

In 1943 the authorities ordered all ex-prisoners of war to return to their prison camps, unless they were doing something essential.

When the allies invaded Western Europe at Normandy, France in June 1944 Free Dutch aircraft and ships were there, and the Free Dutch Army's Princess Irene Brigade was alerted. Some of its members had become so tired of waiting in Britain, they had organised a commando force and begged the British for action.

Only in mid-August did the brigade get the word. Their introduction to combat was in fact anti-climactic, for they simply chased Germans along the French coast into Belgium.

The allies came up with a major plan for the liberation of the Netherlands and the invasion of northern Germany. They would do what the Germans had done in 1940, i.e. seize bridges on the Maas, Waal and Lek using paratroopers and glider-borne troops. Armoured forces would then drive along a thin narrow road linking up with all of them. This would create a salient into the Netherlands a mile wide and sixty miles long terminating at Arnhem.

On the afternoon of 17 September the US 101st Airborne Division dropped onto Eindhoven, to the north the US 82nd Airborne Division dropped onto Nijmegen and still further north the British 1st Airborne Division dropped west of Arnhem. Dutch liaison teams dropped with the divisions and they were met by the Dutch resistance.

The Germans and fascists were taken completely by surprise and were dumbstruck. They stood and stared at more planes than they thought existed. German flak gunners shot down 75 of them, but didn't make a dent in the air armada.

Yet, within a few hours they actually had the upper hand: they blew up a vital bridge at Eindhoven and trapped a solitary British battalion in Arnhem. Waffen SS General Bittrich, Paratrooper General Student, whose last visit to these bridges was in 1940 where he was shot by one of his own men, and Army Field Marshal Model coordinated their defences, having learned the allied intentions by finding the entire plan on a dead British officer. They ordered every SS man, policeman, soldier, airman and sailor to surround and attack the enemy airborne divisions. These orders included Dutchmen of the NSKK, RAD labour units and the fascist

militia, now called the Landstorm. A Landstorm battlegroup assaulted the British on the west of Arnhem.

After three days British armour had cut through to reach the Americans, and a Polish brigade parachuted south of Arnhem and engaged a second Landstorm battlegroup. On the 23rd British armour broke through to Elst, hitting the second Landstorm battlegroup in the rear. The Dutchmen had to run.

However, this was the most the British could do and they ordered the 1st Airborne Division to escape as best it could to the south of the Lek. By the 27th the Germans and Landstorm were rounding up British stragglers.

The major result of the allied failure to take Arnhem was that there would be no allied liberation of the Netherlands in 1944.

However, South Beveland and Walcheren islands were liberated in November. Dutch commandos were among the liberators.

The Dutch people proved where they stood: the rail workers went on strike and refused all threats and arrests to return to work. The Germans brought in their own rail workers to make sure they had enough rail transport for their own needs at least. As a result the nation became short of food and heating fuel. The people supported the strikers, though their stomachs got smaller and their fingers bluer as winter came on.

The front line in southern Netherlands was held in part by the Princess Irene Brigade. It was quiet.

The Russian front was not quiet: indeed it now lay across eastern Germany and one of the units ordered to help stop the Soviet steamroller was SS Brigade Nederland, pulled out of Estonia and in January 1945 renamed 23rd SS Division, but without benefit of replacements. In February the Dutch SS counter-attacked the Soviets at Koeslin and did well until 5 March, when they had to fall back or disintegrate. From here on it was a matter of a steady fighting withdrawal towards Berlin.

In late March the allies crossed the Rhine (Lek) into Germany and swung along the north bank into the eastern Netherlands.

Reaching Arnhem on 12 April the British 49th and Canadian 5th Armoured Divisions attacked the devastated town: among the defenders were the 34th SS Division (the new name of the Landstorm). After a two day battle the Dutchmen retreated westwards towards the coast.

On the 25th the Princess Irene Brigade shot their way across the Maas.

Already the German commander in the Netherlands had asked for a truce, saying he would allow allied parachute drops of food to the starving people if the allies ceased to advance. This was agreed and it came into effect on the 28th.

Hundreds of bombers flew over the Netherlands, but for the first time in five years the people did not take cover. The bombers dropped food and medicines.

A few days later Germany surrendered.

The Princess Irene Brigade had only lost 23 killed and 104 wounded. The Free Dutch Air Force had lost more men than this and the Navy had lost several hundred dead. The merchant fleet lost 1,914 lives, with 232 ships sunk in Free Dutch service.

The resistance claimed 5,500 of its members killed in action or died in fascist/German custody. A thousand civilians had been deliberately murdered by the fascists/Germans in retaliation for terrorist acts and thousands of ordinary Dutch people had been sent to concentration or slave labour camps for having spoken out against oppression. Camp inmates suffered a high fatality rate.

About 46,000 Dutch wore German uniform and several thousand aided the Germans in a uniformed capacity (e.g. fifty were chauffeurs for German officers) and the 23,000 man police force had obeyed German orders. Probably about 10,000 of the fascists and pro-Germans were killed in action. The official figures are that after the liberation the allied Free Dutch government executed 36 fascists and imprisoned 113,000 men and 37,000 women. However, how many were murdered by the resistance groups is anybody's guess.

About 10,000 civilians died in air raids and in battle cross-fire. An estimated 15,000 died of starvation and related illnesses in the winter 1944-45. Additionally many of the Dutch colonists in the conquered lands of the USSR were killed by one method or another.

Of the 140,000 Jewish Dutch, 102,000 died at the hands of the fascists/Germans.

In the war against Japan (see Netherlands East Indies) about 21,000 Dutch died, half of them civilians.

The total war dead of the Netherlands was, therefore, about 175,000.

See Index

NETHERLANDS EAST INDIES

Other names:	Indonesia
Status in 1939:	Dutch colony.
Government in 1939:	Dutch administration.
Population in 1939:	70,000,000
Make-up in 1939:	a plethora of ethnic groups, speaking over 250 languages; 80,000 Dutch colonists.
Religion:	Moslem, some Christians.
Location:	South West Pacific

The Dutch had made this region a colony in the 16th century and by 1941 had not yet explored all of it. Some areas were civilised, indeed had been long before the Dutch arrived. Other areas contained primitive cannibals. The islands included Sumatra, a 1,500 mile walk from end to end, Java, over 600 miles in length and where the greatest interests of the Dutch lay, exotic Bali, Celebes, a thousand miles from Manado town to Makassar City, and hundreds of smaller islands, plus half of Timor (the Portuguese had the other half), three-quarters of Borneo (the British had the rest) and half of New Guinea (the Australians had the remainder).

Economically it was a wonderful colony to possess: militarily it was a nightmare to defend. The Dutch had defended it in the past and always by use of their navy. Their defences of 1941 centred on a fleet of two cruisers, the *Java* and *de Ruyter*, the defence vessel *Sourabaya*, nine destroyers, two minelayers and some gunboats. Admiral Helfrich commanded the navy and Admiral Doorman led the battle fleet.

General van Oyen's air force by comparison was small and obsolete. The army of

General Ter Poorten had small forces on each major island and the bulk of them in two divisions on Java; but these divisions were not modern fighting machines; the 1st had two infantry, a mechanised, a horse cavalry and an artillery regiments. The 3rd had three infantry regiments, the Barisan corps (really a regiment), the Legion of Mankunegoro (two companies), a mechanised detachment and six artillery batteries. In total 25,000 Dutch and 40,000 native troops.

Most of the native troops were Christians and therefore not representative of the people. Moreover, there had been a mutiny a few years earlier and the repercussions were still being felt.

The threat to Dutch rule came from outside, however, from Japan. In response to the Japanese seizure of French Indo-China, the Dutch had refused to ship goods and oil to Japan. The Japanese needed that oil and would not back down. Hence the Dutch prepared for a possible invasion.

On 8 December 1941 the Japanese attacked the American and British possessions in the Pacific and Asia. It did not take a prophet to figure out they would attack the Dutch soon. The Dutch asked for foreign aid: there would be none from the motherland, which had been occupied by the Germans eighteen months earlier.

The reinforcements came: 2,200 Australian troops to Java, 800 to Ambon and a thousand to Timor; and an American artillery battalion and sixteen British tanks to Java. Some American planes arrived and the Dutch fleet received two American cruisers and seven destroyers, an Australian cruiser and a sloop and a British cruiser and four destroyers.

Dutch planes flew from Sumatra to attack Japanese forces in Malaya and on 2 January 1942 the minelayer *Prince van Oranje* ran into a Japanese fleet: she was blown to bits as were her crew of 121.

On 11 January came the first invasion: the 1,100 Dutch troops on Tarakan Island had no choice but to flee into the swamps when 5,000 Japanese arrived. This same day Japanese paratroopers dropped onto Celebes at Manada and Kema. The Dutch garrison withdrew at once.

On the 24th Balikpapan on Borneo was invaded. The infantry resisted while the engineers blew up the oilfields. This day the garrison at Kendari, Celebes was assaulted from the sea. They withdrew inland. Two days later Dutch troops in western Borneo went into the jungle to wage guerrilla war.

On the 30th Ambon was invaded. The 300 Dutch, 600 Ambonese and 800 Australians fought for four days, then totally without any chance of rescue the commander surrendered.

On Sumatra the Dutch planes were joined by the remnants of the allied air units from Malaya. They were completely outnumbered and outclassed by the Japanese.

Doorman saw a chance to sortie with his battle fleet, but on 4 February he was attacked by enemy aircraft. The USS *Houston* was hit with sixty killed and the USS *Marblehead* received such damage she had to return to the USA for repairs. The other ships were lightly damaged.

On 9 February another Japanese fleet invaded Celebes and on the 10th they landed on Borneo at Bandjarmasin. On the 13th Doorman took his fleet to sea again, but five waves of Japanese bombers drove him back to port. On the 14th the Japanese invaded Banka Island and Sumatra.

The following day the Dutch learned that the British had surrendered at Singapore. With the Americans trapped on Bataan Peninsula in the Philippines, this left only Australia as an ally for the Dutch, and the Australians were naturally enough concerned for their own land.

Further invasions and parachute drops took place on Sumatra, where only 25 aircraft of all the air forces were still in action.

A Dutch destroyer and a minelayer were sunk and on the 18th an air raid sank the defence vessel *Sourabaya*.

The following night Doorman chose to attack a Japanese fleet invading Bali. Sailing with part of his force he struck the Japanese in the Lombok Straits in darkness, while no planes could interfere. However, Japanese night gunnery was excellent and Doorman came off worst. While he damaged two destroyers and a transport, one of the Dutch destroyers was blown apart.

On the 26th Doorman was informed another enemy fleet was approaching Java and on the afternoon of the 27th in the Java Sea with five cruisers and twelve destroyers he encountered four enemy cruisers and fourteen destroyers. For an hour they shelled each other: the British cruiser *Exeter* took an 8" shell and had to retire and a Dutch destroyer was hit by a torpedo and sank.

The Australian *Perth,* USS *Houston* and Dutch *Java* followed the *Exeter,* thinking they had missed a signal. Doorman, aboard the *de Ruyter,* angrily had to follow with the rest of the fleet to set things right.

Sending a Dutch destroyer to escort the *Exeter,* he regrouped his fleet and charged the enemy again, this time in darkness. A British destroyer was hit and blew up. Then the American destroyers reported they were low on fuel and had to withdraw.

Reduced to two Dutch cruisers and the RAN *Perth* and USS *Houston* and two British destroyers, he could have turned for home with honour, but he knew this was probably the last opportunity his fleet would have to fight without enemy air interference. He ordered another charge.

The first victim was a British destroyer, which ran headlong into a mine and blew up. The other destroyer stopped to look for survivors. The cruisers were met by torpedoes. The *Java* and *de Ruyter* were hit and went down in minutes, Doorman and most of the crewmen being lost. The *Perth* and *Houston* retired.

Hours later on the 28th the *Houston,* *Perth,* the American destroyers, a Dutch and two British destroyers challenged the Japanese fleet in Bantam Bay. By the time that 359 crewmen on the *Perth* were dead or dying out of a compliment of 676 the Australians abandoned ship. Minutes later the *Houston* went down. The Dutch destroyer was crippled and forced to beach.

The same day Java was invaded at Kragen and Eretan. The 3rd Division fought back.

Over the next few days most of the remaining allied warships were sunk or crippled by enemy warships and air raids. The survivors of the allied fleet: four American and one British destroyers sailed for Australia. For a loss of twenty-five warships the fleet had sunk only four Japanese destroyers.

On the 4th elements of the 3rd Division fell back from Kragen. Next day Java was invaded at Batavia, defended by the 1st Division. On the 7th elements of the 3rd Division abandoned Sourabaya.

On the 9th General Ter Poorten agreed to surrender. A few Dutchmen scrambled for ships to escape to Australia, but the seas were crawling with enemy warships and the sky was dotted with enemy planes.

The Netherlands East Indies were no more. The few hundred Dutch who reached Australia were more of an embarrassment to the Australians than a help. About 2,500 Dutch armed forces personnel had been killed in action. The Japanese took prisoner over 60,000 soldiers and 80,000 Dutch colonists.

The Dutch flyers in Australia eventually received equipment for a bomber squadron from the allies and flew missions for the rest of the war against the occupied Indies. Dutch infantry reinforced the Dutch-Australian garrison of Timor who were fighting as guerrillas against the Japanese invaders: they were all finally evacuated in February 1943.

It was 1945 before the allies got around to liberating the Indies. Their first invasion was in May on Tarakan, and on 1 July they invaded Balikpapan. The war ended when the Japanese surrendered in mid-August.

Arriving in the Indies to take the surrender of the Japanese garrisons, the allies found evidence of the terror inflicted by the sons of Nippon. On Ambon half the allied soldiers taken prisoner had been murdered. Each island had its horror story. In fact 8,000 prisoners of war and 10,500 civilian men, women and children had died in captivity: e.g. executed for breaking a rule, worked to death, denied medical treatment for curable diseases, starved and tortured to death for sport.

Throughout the Indies the Japanese had enslaved the native people to work on various projects. Women were forced to become prostitutes for the Japanese soldiers. Refusal was met with the bayonet. Post-war

United Nations investigators decided that 300,000 natives had been murdered or worked to death.

Additionally, the Japanese had commandeered all sea traffic for themselves, and much was destroyed by the allies later in the war, so that whole communities were left without food shipments. Malnutrition claimed entire villages. Post-war investigators were satisfied that the claim of 3,700,000 dead as a result was accurate.

Naturally the natives had not taken this lying down and had formed guerrilla bands, sometimes using traditional tribal weapons and tactics. However, in 1945 Achmed Sukarno, a guerrilla leader on Java, had actually negotiated a truce with the Japanese. When British troops arrived in September 1945 to take the surrender of the 75,000 Japanese on Java, Sukarno's people came out into the open and declared independence. The British decided they had to hold the colony for the Dutch so they fought the demonstrators. When the British realised they were outnumbered they re-armed the Japanese and sent them against the people!

Sukarno's forces resumed their guerrilla activity. Before the British could be relieved by Dutch troops they suffered 2,120 killed and wounded and killed several thousand natives.

See Index

NEWFOUNDLAND

Other names:	includes a portion of Labrador.
Status in 1939:	autonomous state of the British Empire.
Government in 1939:	democracy influenced by a British Royal Commission.
Population in 1939:	314,000.
Make-up in 1939:	mostly Irish and Scottish stock; small aboriginal population.
Religion:	Christian.
Location:	North America.

Though lying on the coast of Canada and belonging to the British not the Canadians, Newfoundland was neither one nor the other: the British people had never heard of Newfoundland and the Canadians looked upon the 'Newfies' with humour and derision.

Britain's declaration of war on Germany in September 1939 spoke for the Newfoundlanders, whether they liked the idea or not. The citizens volunteered for service with the British Royal Navy, Royal Air Force and Army, but their immediate contribution was at sea as fishermen and merchant seamen. Their job was already dangerous – the North Atlantic is not an understanding sea – and now they had to face German submarines, planes, warships and mines.

Others worked as civilians at the air bases set up by the Royal Canadian Air Force. Indeed one of the greatest problems for the German submarines was the air patrol from Newfoundland. In 1940 American long-range bombers began flying from these bases. An excellent rapport grew between the natives and the foreigners.

On 11 August 1941 Churchill, the British Prime Minster, and Roosevelt, the American President, met in conference in Placentia Bay, having come here in their warships, to produce the Atlantic Charter. It was certainly the most dramatically staged of all their meetings.

Newfoundland army recruits were placed into the 59th and 166th Artillery Regiments (one battalion each). The 59th was eventually sent to south-east Britain, which was under constant shellfire from German guns in France! In early 1943 the 166th received orders for Tunisia: they entered the line in March and supplied fire missions for the British First Army until 12 May.

In autumn 1943 the 166th transferred to the British Eighth Army and went into action in Italy.

By now the British Royal Air Force had formed the all-Newfoundland 125 Squadron, which flew Mosquito night fighters over Britain. Most Newfoundlanders, however, remained in British squadrons.

In August 1944 the 59th Artillery was assigned to the Canadian First Army to help shoot that force across northern France into Belgium by September. Transferred to British Second Army they helped shoot the American 82nd Airborne Division across the Waal River at Nijmegen. Following this, they fought in the Rhineland in the autumn and returned there in February 1945. In March they shot the British across the Rhine, then followed them, finishing their war at Bremerhaven in May.

The 166th remained in action in Italy until May 1945.

Newfoundland members of the armed forces lost seventy-two killed in action. Additionally, there were merchant and fishing fleet losses.
See Index

NEW ZEALAND

Status in 1939:	Dominion of the British Commonwealth.
Government in 1939:	democratic monarchy.
Population in 1939:	1,700,000.
Make-up in 1939:	British and Irish stock; 95,000 Maori aboriginals.
Religion :	Christian.
Location:	South Pacific.

Within hours of the British declaration of war on Germany on 3 September 1939 the New Zealand government did so too. As 'Britons' they thought it their duty and immediately mobilised their armed forces, which consisted of a tiny Air Force, a reservist Army trained for home defence and the Navy (officially a division of the British Royal Navy), which was already at sea and ready for action.

It was this Navy that would gain first laurels. The cruiser *Achilles* in company with the British *Ajax* and *Exeter* encountered a German pocket battleship in the South Atlantic. They fought her until she ran for a neutral port. Later she scuttled. It was the first allied naval victory. It cost the *Achilles* a piece of her superstructure, her captain wounded and several crew killed.

Meanwhile 75 Squadron Royal New Zealand Air Force (RNZAF) went off to Britain to fly patrol missions: the first non-British squadron to arrive to help the British. Other New Zealanders served in British squadrons and indeed any Kiwi, as the New Zealanders were known, who before the war had wanted to fly full-time had joined the British Royal Air Force (RAF). The RAF's first fighter ace was a Kiwi, 'Cobber' Kain. The

New Zealanders were notching up a good number of 'firsts'.

The government placed the New Zealand 2nd Division at the disposal of the British and the formation of about 17,000 men reached Egypt under the command of General Freyberg, a Kiwi who was an officer in the British Army. Eager to get to grips with the enemy (in Egypt it was the Italians) some Kiwis joined the Long Range Desert Group, who poked their noses behind enemy lines. When the 2nd Division's truck drivers drove some Australians to a battle, many could not resist joining the fight.

The 2nd Division was surprised to be ordered to Greece in March 1941 and put into reserve. This was not to the men's liking, but just a few days after arrival on 6 April the Germans obliged them by invading Greece. Suddenly the Kiwis were shown the true face of war, for they were ordered to fall back. This they could not understand, especially when they started to lose guys to air attack. Rearguards fought for a few hours each, but the retreat continued. On the 24th they neared Athens after walking 200 miles under air raids and were told to evacuate by ship. The Kiwis cursed the British general who had thought this one up. They did not know that they were given priority in the evacuation, because of a New Zealand-British agreement.

Reaching Crete in several ships under air attack the division took a roll call: 2,000 men were dead or missing with 200 of the evacuees wounded. Yet Crete was not safe, for German planes had total air supremacy. The men were split up into battlegroups to prepare for an amphibious invasion at Maleme: the British and Australians would defend Suda Bay twelve miles east; more Australians were at Rethimnon another twenty miles east and at Iraklion another 30 miles east. Cretan troops were everywhere. No one was happy with these positions.

They proved even less impressive than the men had thought, when on 20 May the Germans invaded from the air! German paratroopers and gliders landed at several locations. The following day the Germans arrived by transport plane at an airfield that the British generals had chosen not to defend. On the 25th the word went round: there was to be another evacuation.

The survivors reached Egypt by ship and made roll call again: over a third of the men were dead or missing. It would have been more, but New Zealand's Prime Minister Fraser had pleaded with the British Royal Navy and gained an extra night of evacuation.

At sea the New Zealand cruiser *Leander* made a name for herself, driving off a flotilla of destroyers, repelling a submarine, surviving air strikes and sinking a surface raider. However, the cruiser *Auckland* was sunk by aircraft and the destroyer *Neptune* went down like a rock when she struck a mine, taking 147 New Zealanders and 32 Britons with her – only one man lived.

In Egypt the 2nd Division rested and received replacements to come back up to strength. In November 1941 the division was assigned a combat mission in the desert under British Eighth Army.

On 20 November they swamped a handful of Italians at Fort Capuzzo. This was more like it, the men thought: so far they had a poor opinion of British generals. On the 23rd, minus the 5th Brigade (i.e. a third of the division's infantry) the Kiwi division riding in trucks drove into a German camp and shot up the tents and vehicles. Upon interrogation of prisoners they were astonished to find they had captured the headquarters of General Rommel's German Afrika Korps. Here was a fight worth writing home about, even if it had been an accidental victory.

That night they attacked Sidi Rezegh ridge – Rommel was personally directing the Italian-German defence – and they were repulsed. They continued to attack in a cold wind for the next two days and got nowhere.

On the night of the 26th the 5th Brigade which was parked in the open desert in the allied rear was suddenly attacked by the 21st Panzer Division. In sheer terror the Kiwis fought back with whatever was at hand. The Germans were repelled and the Kiwis breathed a sigh of relief, but fifteen minutes later the 15th Panzer Division attacked them. By dawn the enemy had

gone, but so had 800 Kiwis including the brigade commander – captured and taken away in trucks.

Two days later at the ridge the 2nd Division knocked out a German tank attack on their rear, taking prisoner the commander of the 21st Panzer Division.

On the 30th the 6th Brigade was assaulted at the ridge by the 5th Panzer Regiment. Infantry cannot fight tanks for long and the men had to fall back, leaving 600 to be captured. Next morning part of the divisional headquarters including a field hospital was overrun by the Germans. Freyberg asked for permission to retreat: it was given.

However, the Eighth Army had in fact won the battle and chased the enemy to the Gazala line. The Kiwis were ordered to follow.

On the 13th the 2nd Division attacked the enemy line. They got nowhere, but after two days Rommel withdrew his forces anyway. The Kiwis followed them cautiously and soon stopped to resupply.

On 7 December 1941 without warning the Japanese attacked allied forces in Asia and the Pacific. Suddenly the New Zealanders felt very vulnerable as there was nothing between their shores and the Japanese fleet but water. Naturally they informed the British they needed the return of their air, sea and land forces, but the British were reluctant! The New Zealanders were astonished, even though a similar Australian request was also turned down. The New Zealand government had entered the war to aid Britain and now they too needed help. While the bickering continued the Japanese were getting closer to New Zealand by the day.

The best New Zealand could do was send some fighter planes to Malaya: they proved inadequate against the Japanese; and four air squadrons were sent to Fiji along with some cadre to defend those islands. The New Zealand Army had the home defence 1st Division and would soon expand through conscription aged 21-40 for overseas duty and 18-20 and 41-45 for home defence.

A compromise was finally reached with the British: the New Zealanders could have their Navy back, but their airmen and 2nd Division would remain under British control. In fact New Zealand was to send more airmen. Soon the RNZAF would have three fighter, two anti-shipping and two bomber squadrons flying from Britain. The British would not reinforce New Zealand with any of their own forces. This agreement was based on the British opinion that the Japanese probably didn't want to invade New Zealand anyway.

The most important result of the agreement was the New Zealanders stopped thinking of themselves as Britons, for the British had shown where their priorities lay.

The New Zealand 2nd Division took in another 2,000 replacements in early 1942 and introduced them to the fleshpots of Cairo. By now there were few original members left. In June they were alerted: Rommel had attacked and broken through.

The British generals described the situation to Freyberg as 'fluid'. On 26 June he learned what this meant: the 21st Panzer Division destroyed his transport column. Freyberg replied by counter-attacking with his artillery! Notwithstanding this unorthodox behaviour, he knew when to run, and this was one of those times. They ran right through the 104th Panzergrenadier Regiment at night. By the 29th they had reached the new defence line at Alamein.

He ordered his 6th Brigade to dig in. They were not impressed by the so-called defence line: on their right were seven miles of sand then an Indian brigade; on their left were fourteen miles of sand then another Indian brigade. They were all that stood between the enemy and Alexandria naval base, Cairo and the Suez Canal.

Incredibly on 1 July the enemy was happy just to crush one of the Indian brigades and two days later British tanks reinforced the line. From now on there was constant fighting, but the enemy could not break through, though on the 9th the 6th Brigade were forced out of their holes for a while.

On the 14th the 2nd Division, minus the 6th Brigade, attacked at night and hurt the Italian Brescia and Pavia Divisions, but without tanks they could do no more. The British tanks had become lost. The following day

after losing several hundred men, the Kiwis had no choice but to retreat when counter-attacked by tanks.

Freyberg was told he would have to do it again. This time the 6th Brigade attacked at night and ran straight into attacking enemy tanks. British tanks did come to the rescue this time, but were promptly wiped out. The Kiwis fell back.

In August both sides rested at Alamein and Rommel attacked only on the 30th. Within two days his tanks were crippled and he fell back. On 4 September the 2nd Division was ordered to counter-attack. They were held up by a fanatic defence by Germans and Italians. A Kiwi brigade commander was captured by Italians. On the 7th General Montgomery, the Eighth Army commander, called off the attack.

Montgomery was planning his own offensive and he prepared thoroughly. For almost two months the Kiwis watched replacements and equipment arrive. By 23 October there were seven allied divisions and two brigades in the line and three British armoured divisions waiting in the rear. They faced four and a third German and eight Italian divisions. That night they opened fire with the largest artillery barrage seen in the desert war.

Just twenty minutes later the infantry and combat engineers went forward in the dark: the nightmarish scene lit by lightning-like gunflashes. The noise was deafening. The first enemy the Kiwis met were Italians of the Trento Division suffering from shell-shock and easily taken prisoner, but after an hour the Kiwis encountered toughening resistance and by dawn they were pinned to the ground by machine gun fire in the middle of a minefield.

The slugging match continued until the 27th when the Kiwis were thankfully pulled out of the slaughterhouse.

Unfortunately, they were withdrawn to regroup in order to attack again. At 1.00am on 2 November they charged forward alongside British tanks. The battle was ferocious – 200 of the tanks were blown up and hundreds of men shot down, but they won the field.

On the 4th Rommel ordered a complete retreat and the Kiwis were given the honour of chasing him, but told by Montgomery to do it cautiously. They needed no reminding. On the 12th Montgomery called a halt.

In their five days of full-scale battle the division had lost 266 killed, 876 wounded and 37 missing.

In November 1942 three RNZAF bomber squadrons began flying from the island of Guadalcanal against the Japanese, their airfield five minutes flying time from the front line held by American marines. Offshore the cruiser *Achilles* and three corvettes were helping the American navy to fight for this island. Daily the ships fought off enemy planes and nightly they hunted for Japanese warships. The *Achilles* was bombed in December and in January the corvettes sank a Japanese submarine.

In 1943 after Guadalcanal was taken the American marines were given a rest in New Zealand: it was the beginning of a long friendship between the two peoples.

The New Zealand 2nd Division took in another 1,000 replacements then followed the Eighth Army for 1,500 miles across primitive rocky desert to Tunisia. On 6 March 1943 they were shelled for a few hours, and then told they had won the Battle of Medenine. It was not much of an affair, said the veterans, however the replacements were scared to death.

On the 20th Freyberg was reinforced with some British, Greek and French troops and ordered to fight his way through the mountains to outflank the enemy's Mareth Line. It took nine days to do it, most of the time spent sitting in trucks waiting.

On 29 April Freyberg was ordered to assault the enemy frontally, but he argued against the order. Montgomery was adamant. Freyberg caved in, the attack was made and failed. Days later the army was able to advance and on 12 May the last enemy soldiers in Tunisia (and in Africa) surrendered.

By April 1943 another three corvettes arrived off Guadalcanal, for the Japanese air and sea forces were still busy, even if they had lost the island. On 1 April the fleet was attacked by 117 Japanese planes. A 500lb bomb sank the New Zealand corvette *Moa*.

Two RNZAF fighter squadrons reinforced the Americans. They were heartily welcomed, especially when one squadron shot down six enemy planes on its first operation.

In July New Zealand air and sea forces took part in the American invasion of New Georgia and on the 11th just offshore the *Leander* was torpedoed and five American warships damaged in a surface engagement. They sank a Japanese cruiser. The *Leander*, fortunately with only seven dead, retired for repairs.

The Americans chose to occupy Vella Lavella, during which two New Zealand corvettes sank a submarine. Following the Japanese retreat from the beaches, the New Zealand 3rd Division, minus its 8th Brigade, was brought in to seek out Japanese stragglers.

This division had been eager to earn as much glory in the Pacific as the 2nd Division had in the desert. The Kiwis found no glory on Vella Lavella though, as they had to walk deliberately into Jap-infested jungle until the enemy showed himself. Two platoons were cut off for five days and had to be rescued by landing craft, with the vessel's machine gunner shooting at sharks while the Japanese shot at the Kiwis in the water. It seemed that even mother nature was at war with the Kiwis.

On 7 October it was over. This little exercise, which gained no newspaper headlines, cost the Kiwis 48 killed and 32 wounded.

General Barrowclough had been arguing for a real mission for his division and he finally got one: the liberation of the Treasury Islands. On 27 October the division, minus the 14th Brigade, invaded Mono, 21 square miles of thick vegetation with the Japanese under the beach – literally. Finding no opposition on the beach the infantry moved inland, whereupon the Japanese came out of bunkers underneath the beach and shot at the rear-echelon boys. It cost 91 Kiwi and 24 American killed and wounded to kill the Japanese.

It then took another 94 New Zealand and 17 American casualties to secure the island by 30 November. They had killed 200 Japanese.

The next mission for the division, minus the 14th Brigade, was the liberation of the Green Islands in February 1944 supported by five RNZAF squadrons. It cost just twenty casualties.

Barrowclough's next order was heartbreaking: the division was to be disbanded. Eventually 12,069 men were returned to civilian life to work on farms, 38 went to Britain, 1,798 transferred to a home defence unit and 3,228 were sent to the 2nd Division as replacements.

The 2nd Division needed these replacements. The division had been sent to Italy after a six-month rest and on 28 November had attacked a German river line. Freyberg had become leery of promises of British tank support, so he had talked his government into letting him create his own tank force. Nonetheless the advance was slow, 180 yards a day, as the Kiwis had to fight for every rock, bush, olive tree and village. Only in January were they told to halt, but this still subjected them to daily sniping and artillery barrages.

The problem was the enemy position at Cassino, which the Americans had failed to take. In early February Freyberg was reinforced with the Indian 4th Division and told to move to Cassino. The Kiwis would have the honour of taking it – they were getting tired of such 'honours'.

Just before the attack the US Air Force blew apart the historic monastery on Monte Cassino, just in case the Germans were using it – they weren't – having notified the monks to leave – they hadn't – so that the Germans would no longer use it – they did. It was all part of the Cassino fiasco.

The Kiwis experienced the fiasco at first hand when they attacked. They were brought to a halt in minutes. Now the Kiwis realised how the Yank battalions had been whittled down to platoon strength.

While waiting for the generals to come up with another plan the Kiwis were losing sixty casualties a day to snipers and artillery salvoes.

On 15 March the US Air Force did to Cassino what they had done to the monastery (fortunately the townsfolk had evacuated), whereupon Freyberg sent his men forward, Kiwis, Indians, Britons, with Kiwi and American tanks. After eight days of battle the allied ground forces commander in Italy, General Alexander, visited the front and agreed with Freyberg that the failed affair should be called off. Freyberg had lost 2,100 casualties: 940 of them were Kiwis.

The Kiwis were glad when they were pulled out, for the problem became someone else's headache.

In May the allies advanced at last and the Kiwis joined them. In this mobile warfare village upon village began to blur into the memory, as they all looked alike, and soon no one could remember in which village it was that private so and so was killed, or corporal so and so lost a leg, or sergeant so and so was blinded. In August they helped liberate Florence. It was nice to fight in a town someone had heard of before.

They rested a month, then attacked again, but this time they were on the Gothic Line. It was almost as bad as Cassino. They soon shut down operations for the winter.

On 9 April 1945 the 2nd Division launched its part in the great spring offensive, the one that would win the war, some officer had said. If so, then no one wanted to be hit at this stage of the proceedings, therefore they fought cautiously. However, within two days the Germans were on the run. They did not want to die either. On the 30th as they crossed the Piave River the Kiwis heard that the enemy was surrendering Italy. Entering Venice they found it in partisan hands.

On 2 May they entered Trieste, but found partisans of a different hue: Yugoslavian communists; and the German garrison wouldn't give into them. The Kiwis worked out a deal. The partisans would make one more attack, whereupon the Germans would surrender to the Kiwis. It worked, but sadly the Kiwis took casualties in this their last encounter with an armed enemy. Six days later Germany surrendered.

The last New Zealanders to see action were navy pilots flying missions to Japan right up to the Japanese surrender in August.

New Zealand's fallen were as follows: Army 6,793 dead and 15,324 wounded; Navy

3,341 dead and 274 wounded; Air Force 2,875 dead and 1,123 wounded; Merchant Fleet 72 dead. This includes a handful of Fijians and 606 Maori soldiers, but does not include New Zealanders who served in British uniform.

Taken at face value as a percentage of population these 13,081 dead represent a 20% greater loss than that suffered by the British armed forces and double that of the American armed forces. The 2nd Division suffered over 200% casualties, more than any other division of the Western Allies. *See Index*

NORWAY,

Status in 1939:	independent.
Government in 1939:	democratic monarchy.
Population in 1939:	3,100,000.
Make-up in 1939:	Norwegians;
	a tiny number of Lapps in far north;
	1,700 Jews.
Religion:	Christian
Location:	Northern Europe.

Despite being descended from Vikings, the Norwegians of 1939 were a placid isolated people who practised a policy of peaceful coexistence with everyone. They had not joined the European scramble for colonies, though they had claimed a few far north islands, and had separated from Denmark on amicable terms at the beginning of the century and had stayed out of World War I.

The idea they would be dragged into World War II when it began in September 1939 was preposterous, they thought. Yet within days Norwegian seamen were at risk from German submarines, planes and mines and allied mines. Over the next seven months 51 ships were sunk and many damaged.

On 30 November the USSR invaded Finland, a serious blow at Norway's attempt at peaceful coexistence, because if Finland fell Soviet atheist communist troops would be on the Norwegian border with no guarantee they would stop there. Several hundred Norwegians went to Finland to serve in her army, thereby indirectly defending Norway and Christianity.

In March 1940 the Finns surrendered and Soviet troops did indeed reach the border, but stopped there.

There was another threat: in February 1940 a British warship had put sailors on board a German ship hiding in Norwegian waters. This incident may have pleased the British as being straight out of 'Boy's Own' magazine, but it was a violation of Norwegian neutrality by both belligerents. For the first time Norwegians realised they might be forced into war, but on who's side?

Unknown to them the British were planning an invasion. Currently Swedish iron ore crossed Norway by rail in winter and then sailed down the Norwegian coast to Germany. The British planned to cross Norway and destroy the Swedish iron mines.

In March, though the British decided to simply mine Norwegian waters: obviously this would sink Norwegian ships.

The mining flotilla left Britain in early April at the same time as a German invasion fleet. In the early hours of 9 April British forces sank two of the German ships and before dawn Norwegian patrol boats signalled the German fleet asking its intention. The Germans answered with point-blank gunfire. The gunners of the Oscarborg gun battery in Oslofjord ran to their battle stations, still disbelieving they were going to defend their homeland, the first to do so in more than a century. Their gunfire was accurate and astonishingly they sank the German cruiser and flagship *Blücher*.

Already German paratroopers were dropping on Fornebu Airport near Oslo and Sola Airport near Stavanger, followed by transport planes. The Norwegians were subjected to the first airborne invasion in history and naturally were taken completely off guard. In any case the Army, which consisted mostly of reservists was only just now reporting for duty. The Germans marched into Oslo at the head of a brass band!

This morning King Haakon learned that his brother had surrendered his kingdom of Denmark. Haakon chose to resist and fled north from Oslo. By the end of the day he would have 90,000 troops in six divisions.

Germans were coming ashore at Bergen, Trondheim, Kristiansand and Narvik. At the latter town in the far north two defence ships were sunk by the invaders and the garrison commander then surrendered. At Bergen, shore batteries damaged two German vessels before they were overrun.

The British reacted with great speed: as has been seen their flotilla was already in the area; within a couple of days they sank two German warships at sea, a cruiser at Bergen, ten destroyers at Narvik and seventeen transports at various places for just two British destroyers lost. However, 249 German ships made a successful trip and 108,000 troops were put ashore.

On the ground the Norwegian 1st Division began resisting a German advance out of Oslo, one element protecting the road to Trondheim and the other the road to Bergen, while the 4th Division was trying to keep the Germans inside Bergen. In cold snowy conditions the fighting consisted of light Norwegian rearguards firing on the Germans, whereupon the Germans replied with artillery and dive-bombers and then attacked again. The Norwegians were falling back at the rate of six miles a day. This in itself was not a bad thing, for the Norwegians had a lot more space than they did manpower.

At Dombaas thirty miles south of Andalsnes German paratroopers dropped on the 14th, but in a six-day fight the local Norwegians forced them to surrender.

British troops had landed with Norwegian permission at Namsos on the 14th and Andalsnes on the 18th, but were easily repelled by Germans on the 20th.

By the 21st the 1st Division had retreated as far north as Lillehammer. On the 30th the British began to evacuate by sea.

This day the Norwegian 5th Division, falling back from Trondheim and the 1st Division falling back from Oslo stepped aside and let the two German columns meet at Berkaak. Next day the Norwegian Southern Command surrendered at Lomen. On the 5th most of the remaining Norwegian Army surrendered at Hegra.

At Narvik the Germans had been cut off since the destruction of their invasion fleet by the British and on 13 May an allied force of a French division and a brigade and a British and a Polish brigades attacked them. The fighting was low intensity and on 8 June the allies evacuated. Two days later the last Norwegian troops gave up.

In the campaign the British Royal Navy had lost a carrier, two cruisers, eight destroyers, five submarines, 110 aircraft and 2,500 killed at sea and 1,869 casualties on land. The French lost a destroyer and about 500 casualties on sea and land and the Poles lost a destroyer and a submarine and about 400 casualties. Total Norwegian casualties were 1,335 killed and wounded, and about 400 civilians had been killed in cross-fire and air raids. The conquest of Norway cost the Germans three cruisers, ten destroyers, six submarines, thirty transports, 200 aircraft, 2,375 killed at sea and 1,317 on land with 1,900 wounded.

Once in control the Germans did not behave all that badly: they released most of the surrendered Norwegians to civilian life. A group of prominent citizens including church leaders publicly preached cooperation with the Germans, though Vidkun Quisling an internationally respected politician and humanitarian who broadcast on national radio that he was setting up a pro-German government was not only ignored by the Norwegian people but also by the Germans.

King Haakon had fled to Britain and vowed to fight on with his Free Norwegians as they called themselves. Enough airmen joined him to form two fighter and a patrol squadrons, and 58 warships arrived in Britain to create the Free Norwegian Navy, which began to patrol Britain's coast, protect Atlantic convoys, hunt for German submarines and warships and raid the Norwegian coast looking for German vessels.

Despite the merchant fleet losing 31 ships sunk and 29 captured during the invasion of Norway, no less than 1,876 vessels reached allied ports!

Quisling lobbied in Berlin and eventually won recognition in September 1940, his National Unity Party taking control of an autonomous Norway. The Germans in Norway concentrated on setting up large air and sea bases, while the Norwegian police kept order.

German recruiters also arrived, accepting 100,000 Norwegians who volunteered to work in Germany. The NSKK, a corps of paramilitary drivers and mechanics, accepted several hundred Norwegian volunteers and the Waffen SS recruited two infantry battalions.

The first glimpse of an anti-Quisling resistance movement appeared. Not only had Norway been unable to avoid war, but she now settled into civil war.

In June 1941 Germany invaded the USSR, immediately forcing the Soviets back from the Norwegian border. Many a devout Christian Norwegian, who had harboured no thoughts of aiding the Germans or Quisling now decided that as Germany had chosen the path of anti-atheism, he/she had to help the Germans. It was their Christian duty. Some clergymen preached as much.

Already the two Norwegian SS battalions were in the thick of the fighting as part of the 5th SS Division.

Quisling recruited a legion to fight in the USSR, consisting of 1,200 volunteers, many of them policemen. They were trained by the Germans and entered the front line near Leningrad in February 1942. The unit did well, though a few complainers were sent home by the Germans – i.e. complainers about nazi methods in Russia.

In August 1942 a new Norwegian SS battalion went into action as ski troops in northern Russia, serving under German General Dietl, the hero of Narvik.

By early 1943 the legion had suffered 158 killed and several hundred wounded. So far there had always been enough volunteers to make good the casualties.

However, in March 1943 the legion was confiscated by the SS and renamed the 1st Battalion SS Regiment Norge. The regiment's other two battalions were the Norwegian SS from the 5th SS Division. Together with a Danish SS Regiment the Norwegians were placed into the new 11th SS Division Nordland. Germans and Hungarian Volksdeutsch made up the other components. The division was sent to the front in southern Russia.

In spring 1944 the division was sent to defend the Estonian-Russian border from a coming Soviet offensive. They battled throughout July and held their ground, but Germans on their southern flank collapsed

and they were eventually ordered to fall back to Kurland on the coast. Trapped there by August they were put on short rations as they dug in, their backs to the sea under air and artillery barrages. The fact that their German commander Fritz Knochlein was a sadist made things even tougher.

Life in Norway had also been getting tough. Quisling had 100,000 members in his party and he placed half of them in a uniformed unarmed militia, the Hird. Acting as auxiliaries to the police they enforced his increasingly draconian laws. In retaliation for the killing of two Germans by the resistance at Televaag, the entire village was burned to the ground and all menfolk sent to a German concentration camp.

When the schoolteachers refused to teach his propaganda, the police arrested a thousand of them and put them in a slave labour camp in the frozen north.

Though the islands of Jan Mayen and Spitsbergen were occupied for a time by Free Norwegian troops, most of the northern islands had a small German garrison. In March 1941 the Lofoten Islands were raided by British and Free Norwegian commandos. The islanders cheered when 215 Germans surrendered and were marched to the ships, and cheered even louder when 60 Quislings they had pointed out were also arrested. The commandos took with them 315 recruits.

Free Norwegian commando raids continued and they usually took away with them local volunteers. However, they were incensed when John Nygaardsvold, King Haakon's Prime Minister, complained about the raids, saying it would only cause the Germans to reinforce Norway, which would make it more difficult to liberate.

The Germans did indeed reinforce Norway to protect their air and sea bases, but that is exactly what the allies wanted, for they had no intention of liberating Norway!

Quisling created his own SS in imitation of the Germans. Their first duty was to confiscate all homes and property owned by Jews. Norwegian Jews lived as Norwegians, indeed were Norwegians. Only their choice of faith distinguished them. Most people were outraged.

On the coast the German Organisation Todt began constructing defensive bunkers and took on thousands of Norwegian workers. Some were made armed guards to protect sites from sabotage. The authorities ordered all Norwegians not employed in essential industries to report for forced labour. Many worked on the bunkers, but others were sent to Germany. Any who refused were arrested and dispatched to slave labour: a far different matter.

In September 1942 the police, Hird and Norwegian SS arrested the nation's Jews. Actually they only caught half: the resistance spirited the other half across the mountains to neutral Sweden.

The Hird were constantly complaining that the police were not doing their job, e.g. allowing some people to evade forced labour. Quisling finally acted: the Hird and his SS, both now armed, arrested 470 policemen and sent them off to German concentration camps.

By the end of 1944 Soviet forces were once again on the Norwegian border, but following a diplomatic agreement they allowed a Free Norwegian brigade to take over the advance, which consisted of a few patrols into the vast Arctic expanse.

In response the Germans ordered all civilians to evacuate the northern region and their homes were burned down to deny shelter to the liberators. Many civilians fled into the forests.

It was January 1945 before the Free Norwegians fought their first skirmish here. Ironically, the soldiers they met were Norwegian volunteers serving the Germans.

This was the only campaign the Free Norwegian Army was to fight, though their commandos continued raids. Norwegian commandos also fought on Walcheren in the Netherlands. The Americans had raised a battalion of Norwegians from immigrants and used it to good effect in Central France, Rhineland, Ardennes and Germany.

In March 1945 the Norwegian Resistance welcomed British and Free Norwegian paratroopers and commandos at several locations and began major sabotage raids, culminating in the destruction of the rail lines to Stavanger, Bergen and Kristiansand, forcing the Germans to use ships for resupply, and of course the allied navies were waiting.

Other Norwegians were defending Germany by early 1945, the SS ski battalion in the west, the 11th SS Division in the east. By April the division was reduced to a few hundred survivors and was battling in Berlin to protect Hitler himself.

On 4 May, with Hitler dead, the new German government surrendered their forces in Norway, but such was the confusion that the Germans in Norway were not sure what to do. The Resistance came out into the open and were joined by 10,000 Norwegians, who had escaped to Sweden and had been armed and trained by the Swedes for just such an eventuality. Together they demanded the Germans disarm. It took four days of arguing before the Germans agreed. Quisling's forces disarmed too, though a few hid.

The Norwegians are not a boastful people and as a result the world quickly forgot that this peace-loving nation had ever been inconvenienced by the war. About 25,000 Norwegians served in the Free Norwegian armed forces, of which 1,150 were killed: four warships were lost in the Battle of the Atlantic and one was sunk in the Normandy invasion. The Free Merchant Fleet lost 367 ships sunk after the German invasion and 3,640 sailors died between September 1939 and May 1945.

The 40,000 resistance members suffered 162 killed on operations and 1,226 who died in custody, plus 93 died trying to escape across the sea.

Over a thousand civilians died in Quisling/German concentration and slave labour camps or were executed; others died in air raids and some died as a result of the dislocation in the north; and 762 were murdered because they were Jewish.

About 3,000 Norwegians were killed in action in Quisling or German uniform. After the German surrender King Haakon's government returned and executed Quisling and 24 others and imprisoned 46,000 of his supporters.

Total deaths in the six years were therefore about 12,000.

In the post-war years the anti-German resistance movement was berated for not having done more, but exactly what they could have accomplished other than destruction of property and retaliation on the people is never explained by their detractors. It is noticeable that their detractors never had to live in fear of the midnight knock, for they were either safe in another land or they did not take up the gauntlet themselves. Certainly the allies had no complaints, for the Resistance always did what was required of them. Their most important contribution to the war effort was helping to destroy Hitler's nuclear weapons programme!

See Index

PALESTINE

Other names:	Israel
Status in 1939:	British mandate.
Government in 1939:	British administration.
Population in 1939:	1,600,000.
Make-up in 1939:	Arabs; Jewish population growing rapidly by immigration.
Religion:	Moslem; large Christian minority; growing Jewish population.
Location:	Near East

Palestine's problem was that it had been promised by the British to both Arabs (i.e. Moslem and Christian Semites) and to the Jews (i.e. Jewish Semites). A three year Arab revolt against British rule ended in 1939 with the British promise to curtail Jewish immigration. The Arabs did not just see Jews as different in terms of religion, but as European invaders, no different than any other European colonial power.

However, once this latest British promise had been made the Jews revolted, demanding the right to bring in as many of their religious brothers and sisters as they saw fit, with the avowed purpose of creating Israel, an independent nation run by Jews, with selective rights for Christians and Moslems. In 1939 11,000 Jews were allowed in by the British, but an estimated 17,000 came in illegally assisted by the Jewish rebels. Needless to say, Arab families who had farmed the land for a thousand years could not understand a German's or a Russian's claim that this was his land, promised to him by God.

Palestine was not so much the promised land as a land of promises.

However, another problem arose in September 1939, when Britain declared war on Germany, a state run by Hitler who was dedicated to enslaving all Jews. The more moderate Jewish rebels, the Palmach of the Hagenau, realised that as bad as the British were, they were saints compared to Hitler's Nazis. Therefore, they agreed to a truce.

Two fanatic rebel groups led by Josef Stern and Menachem Begin refused to cease-fire against the British. Therefore, when Jews such as Moshe Dayan enlisted into the British armed forces to fight the Nazis, they were de facto at war with the Jewish fanatics.

Palestinian volunteers were accepted by the British Royal Air Force and Royal Navy. The Army took them into all-Palestinian pioneer companies, which were to be used for manual labour only. Two thirds of the volunteers were Jews, the remaining third were Arabs: the British did not separate them!

A Palestinian pioneer company was sent to France in time to be told to run for it and had to fight off advancing Germans.

In July 1940 Haifa in Palestine was bombed by Italian planes. Tel Aviv suffered an air raid in September. Palestinian pioneers were sent to Egypt to support the British forces facing the Italian enemy.

The Palestinians had demanded a combat role, and probably taking into consideration the fact that some of the Palestinian volunteers had recently been shooting at British troops as Arab rebels or Jewish rebels, the British created a Palestinian commando force. They saw action in Eritrea against the Italians in March/April 1941.

Meanwhile a Palestinian pioneer unit was sent to work in Greece at the port of Salonika. Despairing that the war would pass them by, they got all the action they wanted when German forces broke through the front line and entered the city on 8 April. Unarmed or poorly armed and not trained to fight, the pioneers had to run or give up. They began the long retreat, walking along dusty roads under air attack for eighteen days, only to be told the army would be evacuating by ship.

Reaching safety in Egypt and Crete they took roll call: of the 2,170 Palestinians who had gone to Greece only 400 were left! Those who had reached Crete were not really safe, and on 20 May the Germans invaded the island by parachute and glider. Another sea evacuation was called for. Few made it to Egypt.

The Germans treated their Palestinian Jewish prisoners badly, but did not kill them.

On 10 June 1941 the British used Palestine as the springboard for their invasion of French Syria. French planes retaliated at once and bombed the ports. In Syria the first serious opposition was encountered by Australian troops at the Litani River. This was overcome when Palestinian commandos invaded the coast on the far side of the river, outflanking the defences and winning the battle. Here Moshe Dayan, one of the commando officers, lost an eye.

The British had exiled Fawzi al Kawukji for his activity in the Arab revolt and he had gathered together a guerrilla band in Syria. During the British conquest of this nation, complete by 10 July, the British fought with Kawukji's men, some of whom escaped to German territory and were accepted as the nucleus of an Arab Legion. Another exile from British 'justice' was Hajj Amin al Hussein, the Grand Mufti (religious judge) of Jerusalem, who had gone to seek solace in Germany, where Hitler honoured him with SS rank. He became the spiritual leader of the Arab Legion.

By 1942 4,500 Palestinian pioneers were serving in Egypt, with Jews and Arabs separated into their own companies. Other Palestinian pioneers served in Palestine, where Begin's Irgun Zwei Leume had at last called a truce. As sentries, pioneers, flak gunners, airmen, sailors, artillerymen and commandos 30,000 Palestinians were now in British uniform.

One of the commando organisations was the Special Interrogation Group, who used their knowledge of the German language (many were German Jews who had emigrated to Palestine) not just to interrogate prisoners, but to fight behind the lines in German uniform. On one occasion a raiding party stopped off at a German air force mess to get something to eat!

The German Arab Legion under various names served in Russia, Sicily and Tunisia, where it gathered strength. By 1944, it was reduced to about a thousand men and sent on anti-guerrilla operations in Greece. During the German retreat the unit disappeared.

Despite having airmen, sailors and soldiers in combat the Jewish organisations in Palestine and Britain knew that it would all be forgotten unless they created a major unit with obvious Jewish connections. They immediately ran into anti-semitic elements in Britain, in government and the Army. Only in October 1944 with Churchill's help did they get the go-ahead.

Cadred by British officers the Jewish Brigade was to recruit Palestinian and European Jews who were already serving. Some of the German and Austrian Jews had enlisted into the British Army straight from British internment camps: Hitler may have denied German citizenship to them, but the British civil servants of the immigration department had not and had imprisoned these refugees as enemy aliens! It took months of arguing to be accepted.

Eventually, the brigade consisted of three infantry battalions of the Palestine Regiment, a Palestinian flak battery retrained as field artillery, Palestinian engineers and rear-echelon personnel and 216 members of a Palestinian coastal artillery regiment. The Hebrew language was used as a lingua-franca. Yet not enough Jews had volunteered: the brigade was still short a thousand men; so some British Christians voluntarily transferred to the brigade, though one group refused to wear the brigade shoulder patch – the Star of David. High Command got over this hurdle by attaching these men rather than assigning them.

The Jewish Brigade entered the line in Italy in March 1945. After three weeks they took part in the great spring offensive. They fought for five days without a hitch and then were placed in reserve.

Casualties were seven Jews killed and 130 wounded with 31 Christians wounded. The British deliberately kept the brigade in Italy when the rest of the army entered Austria, for fear the Jews would retaliate against the Austrian people.

227

At the surrender of Germany on 8 May 1945 there was still only one Palestine and two distinct claims as to who should control it. The problem had simply been put on ice for awhile, though already Begin's mob were on the warpath. At the time of writing (1995) this problem has yet to be solved.
See Index

PANAMA

Status in 1939:	Independent.
Government in 1939:	dictatorship supported by USA.
Population in 1939:	650,000.
Make-up in 1939:	Mestizos 455,000; Indians 60,000; Negroes 95,000; Europeans 39,000; a few US citizens in the US-leased territory.
Religion:	Christian
Location:	Junction of North and South America.

The USA dug a canal across the Isthmus of Panama at the turn of the century, overcoming financial problems, jungle terrain, yellow fever and the Venezuelan government. By connecting the Pacific and Atlantic this enabled merchant traffic to sail from the eastern seaboard of the USA to the western without making the long treacherous Cape Horn passage, and it effectively enabled the USA to use one fleet to suffice for either coast's defence. Naturally the canal had to be protected and the USA leased land on both banks and established military bases, turning it into a miniature USA.

Throughout World War II a considerable US military presence had to remain here.

Panama's economy was tied to the canal, hence to the USA, and she possessed a considerable merchant fleet of her own, though truthfully it was often used as a flag of convenience by US companies. The crews were Panamanian and US, but included others too, like most merchant fleets.

When German submarines went on the prowl in 1939 Panamanian ships, though neutral, were at their mercy. By November 1941 24 ships had been sunk, several damaged and three captured with 60 seamen killed. When Panama declared war against Japan, following the Japanese attack on the USA on 7 December 1941, this effectively put Panama on the anti-German side, which obviously she was already.

Panama's war effort was valuable in that her merchant marine supplied all the allied belligerents including making the dangerous Atlantic convoy run to Britain and the exceedingly dangerous Arctic Ocean run to Russia. By the end of the war in August 1945 the Panamanian merchant marine had lost 88 ships sunk and 21 captured. Her losses were double that of all other Spanish-speaking American nations combined.
See Index

PAPUA-NEW GUINEA

Other names:	includes Admiralties and Biak. (For Bougainville and New Britain see Solomon Islands chapter.
Status in 1939:	Australian colonies (Biak was a Dutch colony).
Government in 1939:	Australian administration (Biak was Dutch).
Population in 1939:	Admiralties 12,400; Biak 21,000; Papua-New Guinea 1,250,000.
Make-up in 1939:	hundreds of tribal languages spoken; small Australian population mostly at Port Moresby.
Religion:	tribal, some mission Christians.
Location:	South West Pacific.

British and Australian colonists and missionaries had laid a thin veneer of civilisation over this territory by 1939, but many areas were unexplored and some tribes were still practising cannibalism.

In 1941 the Australians shuddered to think that the island of New Guinea could become a modern war zone, but if Japan did attack as seemed likely, this land would become Australia's first line of defence.

In December 1941 the Japanese attacked the Americans and British without warning. At once the Australians rushed troops to defend Malaya and the East Indies, knowing that if these regions fell, the Australian Army would have to fall back to Australia. New Guinea was just far too primitive a land in which to wage a successful defence.

The natives wondered what all the fuss was about: they had spears, they would frighten away 'Japan Man'.

On 3 February Port Moresby, the only real town on New Guinea, was raided by Japanese planes. The natives panicked and ran into the jungle. In time they drifted back, and were soon treating the air raids as just a nuisance. Most of the white colonist women and children were evacuated to Australia, their menfolk becoming Australian soldiers.

The Japanese approached New Guinea cautiously, leap-frogging along the north coast from the west to as far east as Buna. The Australians offered no resistance.

However, in March after the fall of Malaya and the East Indies the Australians swallowed their pride and placed themselves under American command. General MacArthur immediately said there would be no further talk of withdrawing to Australia: they would stop the Japanese in New Guinea, no matter how primitive it was.

On 23 May 1942 a company of Australian commandos flew to Wau airstrip and were soon joined by 250 members of the New Guinea Volunteer Force, fuzzy-haired natives from central New Guinea, who had volunteered to fight for 'the king'. Their combat equipment consisted of rifle, ammo, and knife. Pants were optional. Their mission was to scout the enemy rear, not fight. They performed excellent reconnaissance, keeping MacArthur informed of exactly what the advancing Japanese were doing. On 28 June, though, they couldn't resist attacking the 'town' of Salamaua, destroying supplies and a bridge and inflicting a hundred casualties. Indeed, despite their brief, by August they had killed or wounded 500 enemy for the loss of twelve men.

By now the natives of New Guinea had learned that 'Japan Man' was a brute, forcing them to work for him and killing those who refused or tried to run away. The villagers were only too happy to tell the commandos and NGVF all they knew of Japanese strengths and dispositions.

The allies had chosen to fight their way from Port Moresby to the north coast over the Owen Stanley mountains and they hired native porters by the thousand. Many an Australian and American soldier cursed the 'fuzzy-wuzzies', when he found evidence of pilfering, but it is also true to say that without the native porters the allies could not have maintained their effort. Over the next three years thousands of allied soldiers would owe their lives to native stretcher bearers, who sometimes carried a wounded or sick soldier for days on end over terrain that would defeat the hardiest explorer.

The first units the allies put across the Stanleys were the 39th Militia Battalion, made of white colonists, and the Papuan Light Infantry, recruited from the natives of eastern New Guinea. They retreated in the face of the Japanese advance, but maintained contact for a month, during which they inflicted about 2,000 casualties. The Australians who relieved them also had to fall back.

There were some racist comments about the Papuans' value in combat, but to be fair in October the Australian command decided to give them another chance. They were asked to root out a small Japanese force that had become trapped south of the Kumasi River. Over a week the Papuans killed 200 enemy for small loss to themselves.

In December and January a counter-offensive by Australian and American troops liberated the north coast, including Buna, Gona and Sanananda.

In October the commandos and NGVF at Wau had been reinforced as Australian infantry, engineers, rear-echelon troops etc. flew in. The big war had caught up with them. All this activity just a few miles from the enemy could hardly go unnoticed and the airstrip was assaulted. Local natives alerted the garrison and the whole, NGVF included, fought a full-scale battle with artillery and air strikes used on both sides. Only on 30 January 1943 did the Japanese withdraw. The NGVF followed them, picking off lone stragglers.

In June 1943 an American amphibious force landed at Nassau Bay on New Guinea's north coast behind the retreating Japanese. The allies were so cocky by now they began to build airstrips in the enemy rear! These strips were guarded by the 39th Militia Battalion and the Papuan Light Infantry. No matter where the allies went, there were always plenty of willing natives to do manual labour.

In September 1943 an Australian amphibious invasion near Lae outflanked the enemy base at Salamaua and within days the Japanese had to retreat westwards. The Papuan Light Infantry followed them, hunting for stragglers and overcoming rearguards. In mid-October the Papuans ran into a major defensive position at Shaggy Ridge. Australians came up and tried to outflank it for a month.

An American amphibious invasion in the enemy rear was intended to outflank Shaggy Ridge. It did and the enemy withdrew. Again the Papuans were told to maintain contact. In one incident three Papuans stumbled into the Japanese and killed 43 of them. In another incident Papuans and colonists killed 99 Japanese. In neither incident were any allied personnel wounded. Searching the ruined camps the Papuans found evidence of cannibalism. The Japanese were starving and were killing and eating natives and in some cases eating their own fallen comrades. The Papuans looked around them. They could identify food in the jungle, but the office clerk from Osaka or the plumber from Tokyo was lost here.

In 29 February 1944 the Americans landed on Los Negros in the Admiralty Islands, having been led to believe there would be almost no opposition. The 1st Cavalry Division (dismounted) reported only five casualties on landing. MacArthur's intelligence chief was well pleased. On 2 March, the Japanese showed themselves. Counter-attacking, they began a tough fight: rear-echelon troops and navy 'Seabees' had to be thrown in. In 36 hours the Americans had 258 casualties.

Still the Americans advanced and entered plantations where the local natives gave them plenty of information and provided guides. After a week and 550 casualties the Americans could honestly inform the natives they were here to stay. On the 11th they landed on nearby Manus, clearing it in two weeks for 164 casualties. Landing on nearby Rambutyo, they met natives who asked for weapons. They were given them and the natives took care of the Japanese garrison that had been oppressing them for two years. In June the last serious opposition was overcome in the Admiralties.

Following his success in the Admiralties MacArthur ordered American landings on New Guinea at Hollandia and Aitape in April, so far behind Japanese lines that only a few rear-echelon troops were found. In May they landed at Toem and Wakde Island opposite. There was an enemy garrison here, but it was overcome in a week. Then the Americans advanced westwards towards Sarmi.

On 27 May the US 41st Division invaded Biak Island. This 120-mile long tangled jungle of caves and ridges was a nightmare and reinforcements had to be rushed in. Impatient as ever, MacArthur sent a force to hit New Guinea at Cape Sansapor 800 miles west of Hollandia. There was no opposition. Biak took three months to secure and cost the Americans 2,025 killed and wounded and 4,000 hospitalised with sickness. They felled 6,200 Japanese and captured 765, most of them Koreans.

These invasions not only bypassed thousands of Japanese, but also the Australians who were still fighting them. It was frustrating for the Australians to risk their lives in an affair of which the newspapers back home said little or nothing, but the Papuan Light Infantry, New Guinea Volunteer Force, colonists, and native civilians felt differently, for this was their home.

The Japanese in New Guinea were only brought to heel by the surrender of Japan herself in August 1945. Tribal headhunters, who had been selling Japanese heads to the Australians, did not at first understand that they were supposed to take the enemy prisoner now.

The liberation of the island of New Guinea cost the allies about 7,500 lives. About 40,000 Japanese died. The native people suffered greatly. Their dislocation, enslavement, air raids, battlefield cross-fire, and the attraction of work for the allies was just as unsettling as it was for any of the victims of the war in Europe. To the Western World a tribal native who only possesses a hut and a few beads cannot be as dislocated in time of war as a civilised person, but this is false. After all, home is home. Certainly the Australian soldiers were disgusted when they found natives tied to trees, having been tortured and murdered by the Japanese. No matter how uncivilised, a life is a life.

The impact of the war on the native population is most starkly exemplified by the birth of the cargo cult. Primitive natives watched as white men climbed into giant birds to be wafted away to paradise. With a certain cunning, they made replicas of the birds out of stones, hoping to attract one of them, so that they could pounce on it and go straight to heaven. A whole new religion was created by the Douglas C-47 transport aircraft.

See Index

PHILIPPINES

Status in 1939:	on the road to independence from the USA.
Government in 1939:	democracy
Population in 1939:	19,200,000.
Make-up in 1939:	113 languages spoken, the most prevalent being Tagalog, Visayan and Llokane; small American and Spanish populations.
Religion:	Christian, but Moslems dominate in southern islands.
Location:	Western Pacific.

When the Americans invaded the Philippines in 1898 and defeated the Spanish, the Filipino people said 'thank you and goodbye', but to their alarm the Americans had come as conquerors not liberators. The result was intermittent warfare between the Filipinos and the Americans until 1913. At times American soldiers behaved abominably.

There were Americans who genuinely loved the country and its people, and coupled with the fact that despotism has never sat well on a United States government, these two factors created a climate by the 1930s in which the Americans agreed to let the Filipinos have full independence come 1946. Thus in 1941 the Republic of the Philippines had its own government and armed forces, but was still a US colony.

The Filipinos had hired retired US General Douglas MacArthur to be their first field marshal and his training programme was only partially under way when in 1941 he was recalled to duty in the US Army and given command of all US and Filipino forces in the Philippines. This stemmed directly from the sabre-rattling in Tokyo. American civilians were encouraged to go home. After all, Luzon Island was within range of Japanese airfields.

On 8 December 1941 MacArthur and President Quezon in Manilla City, Luzon were informed that the US Pacific Fleet at Pearl Harbor was under Japanese air attack (7 December Pearl Harbor time). Just hours later Clark Field and Nichols Field on Luzon were attacked by Japanese planes. Over half the Filipino and US air strength in the Philippines was destroyed at one fell swoop.

MacArthur urged that the islands of Luzon and Mindanao should be defended and the Filipinos deferred to his experience, though many wondered if 650-mile-long Luzon wasn't too big to defend. On the 10th the extreme north of Luzon was invaded and two days later Legaspi in the extreme south was invaded. Only American and Filipino light formations were able to scout the enemy.

On the 20th an enemy force landed at Davao City on Mindanao.

On the 22nd the Japanese showed some strategic thinking by invading Luzon at Lingayen a hundred miles north of Manilla and two days later at Lamon Bay 60 miles southeast of the city. With the bulk of their Fourteenth Army ashore, the Japanese now converged on Manilla.

MacArthur ordered his forces to retreat at once: from the north the US Army's 26th Cavalry Regiment (horsed), consisting of Americans and Filipinos, and an all-American tank group, and the Philippines Army 11th, 21st, 31st, 71st and 91st Divisions; from the south the US Army's Philippines Division, consisting of Americans and Filipinos, and the Philippines Army 1st, 41st and 51st Divisions. None of the Filipino divisions were fully formed. All units were plagued by air raids.

MacArthur finally realised he could not fight a two-front campaign, so he chose to evacuate to Bataan Peninsula west of Manilla, though no supplies had been stockpiled there and it was known to be a disease-ridden area. He told his superiors in Washington he would hold out until the rescue expedition arrived.

By early January the troops began filing into the peninsula, and on the 9th they turned to repel Japanese attempts to break through. They then steadily fell back under pressure, inflicting serious losses on the Japanese until the 26th. Thereafter the Japanese ceased attacking. The three US formations and the Filipino 1st, 2nd, 11th, 21st, 31st, 41st, 51st, 71st and 91st Divisions settled down to a siege.

MacArthur made his headquarters in a big cave on Corregidor Island protected by the US 4th Marine Regiment. MacArthur began to get the blame for everything. He invited it, as he never left his cave to see his troops. He was soon known as 'Dug-out Doug' and his soldiers created a little rhyme calling themselves 'the Battered Bastards of Bataan, no Papa, no Mama, no Uncle Sam'!

And battered they were: jungle sores, dysentery, tropical diseases, starvation rations, artillery salvoes, sniping, air raids and nightly infiltration by silent assassins.

When MacArthur was ordered to leave the Philippines he at first refused, but convinced by his staff that he was to go to Australia to command the rescue expedition he agreed. President Quezon had already left in a submarine. As a direct snub to the US Navy, who said it was too dangerous to supply Bataan except by submarine, MacArthur chose to leave by surface vessel on 11 March.

When he arrived in Australia he found two surprises: one, President Roosevelt awarded him the Medal of Honour; and two, there was no rescue expedition.

When Dug-out Doug skeedaddled the morale of the men he left behind was at an all-time low.

On Corregidor, General Wainwright held a commanders meeting – most of the Filipino units had American commanders on loan – and the decision reached was for a do-or-die counter-attack on Bataan. It was launched on 4 April. Not everyone could attack, for many were too weak to stand let alone fight. Those who did attack suffered a loss of one in five to shot and shell. Within 24 hours the Japanese had pushed them back and broken through. The cavalrymen fought as infantry, having long since eaten their horses.

On the 9th the commanders on Bataan surrendered.

Since the first day of war the allies had suffered on Luzon 17% killed and missing, including desertions by Filipinos, and about the same percentage wounded. Of the 63,000 Filipinos (of both the US and Philippines Armies) and 12,000 Americans taken prisoner that day, 24,000 were bedridden.

The reason the American generals surrendered was to save lives and they expected their surrendered men to be rested, fed and medically treated. Instead, they were ordered to walk out of the peninsula. Any who could not walk would have to be carried by the others, though few were strong enough to do this. Their complaints ignored, the march began: men who fell out and couldn't be revived were bayoneted. Some Filipinos were bayoneted for the fun of it. The Bataan Death March lasted seven days. Only then were the prisoners allowed to build their own prison. Probably one American in twenty died on the march. One Filipino in twelve died.

In April the Japanese began invasions of the other Philippines Islands, defended by elements of the Filipino 61st, 81st and 101st Divisions.

Corregidor Island and its 13,000 man and woman garrison still held out under artillery and air barrages. Just over three miles in length and a few yards wide there was nowhere to hide but inside the big cave, Doug's dug-out.

Just after midnight on 6 May the island was invaded. Marines, soldiers and sailors battled for eleven hours, some companies losing 30% casualties. At noon General Wainwright surrendered. The island garrison had suffered 800 dead in the barrages and the invasion. Convinced that the Japanese would kill all their prisoners unless his surrender spoke for the remainder of the Philippines too, Wainwright broadcast his surrender order to all. Another few hundred Americans and 35,000 Filipinos laid down their arms. A total of 7,000 American civilians were also imprisoned.

Wainwright would spend the next three years in captivity convinced that if liberated he would be court-martialled for cowardice.

The prisoners received treatment that can only be described as horrific. Of those who survived to reach a prison camp one American in eleven died in the first six months. The Filipino death rate was one in three!

The Japanese set up a puppet government, claiming to have liberated the Filipinos, ignoring the fact that the Filipinos were only four years off independence. Their disgusting treatment of Filipino prisoners of war, their execution of Filipino men who refused to work for them, their brutal treatment of those who did work, their enslavement of thousands of Filipino women as prostitutes for over 400,000 Japanese soldiers, said more than any speeches about Asian brotherhood. The Filipinos knew they were in a life or death struggle with the Japanese.

Actually not all Filipino troops had surrendered. Some were waging guerrilla war and those who had earlier deserted now joined them. A few American servicemen and civilians fought with them. One American civilian engineer created a veritable private army.

At first it was sentry stabbing and mild sabotage. The guerrillas had not the means to do ought else. MacArthur in his radio contact with them discouraged even this much, claiming the activity would bring down Japanese wrath on the people. This is exactly what happened. The Japanese massacred villages in response to guerrilla activity. But what MacArthur did not realise was the Japanese were already massacring the Filipinos anyway.

MacArthur was in fact bringing a rescue expedition to the Philippines, though no one knew it, not even the US government. He had said on the radio to the Filipinos 'I shall return' and he was a man of his word. One of his units was the US Army's 1st Filipino Regiment recruited from Filipinos living in the USA.

By autumn of 1944 the guerrillas, whom the Americans insisted on referring to as 'scouts', had begun to receive air-dropped and submarine-carried supplies and had become a bona fide army, their size and scope having become quite alarming to the Japanese. However, the Japanese were too busy watching for the American liberation, which they knew was coming. They were sure the US invasions of Morotai and the Palaus in mid-September were preliminary moves.

They were, but it had taken MacArthur some powerful lobbying to get the American government to agree to a Philippines invasion. As it was, they only approved an operation on the island of Leyte.

On Leyte the Japanese had their 16th Division and a brigade; on Mindanao two divisions and a brigade; on Luzon eight divisions and a brigade; and on other islands three divisions. Including the army air force, navy and navy air force the Japanese Philippines garrison stood at 430,000.

To liberate the nation from these fourteen divisions and three brigades MacArthur had fifteen divisions and some smaller units, but at about 15,000 men a US division was smaller than a 24,000 man Japanese division. Moreover, MacArthur knew he might be called upon to use his troops for other things besides his personal expedition to the Philippines. Military theory calls for an attacker to have twice if not thrice the defender's strength. Obviously the Americans would need all the help the Filipino guerrillas could give them.

The liberation got off to a good start. In September US Navy carrier planes knocked out 478 Japanese planes over the Philippines.

The guerrillas on Leyte were informed their 120-by-20-miles island was to be the first to be liberated: the invasion would begin on 20 October and they were to alert civilians in the fighting zone. The US fleet was too big to surprise the Japanese, so secrecy did not matter.

The Americans came ashore with the Sixth Army's 1st Cavalry (dismounted) and 7th, 24th and 96th Divisions. The Japanese chose to await them further inland. MacArthur waded ashore for the newsreel cameras (several times until his public relations people were satisfied with the shots)

233

and then broadcast on the radio to the Filipino people that he had returned, failing to mention he had not done it alone, and then ordered the guerrillas to "strike, strike, strike!" They needed no urging. The Filipino government-in-exile also returned with much less fanfare.

On Leyte guerrillas provided the Americans with invaluable guides and reconnaissance patrols.

The Japanese reinforced Leyte with their 1st and 26th Divisions. The Americans countered by reinforcing with their 11th Airborne, 32nd and 38th Divisions. In December the Americans made a full-scale invasion of the opposite side of the island with the 7th and 77th Divisions, liberating Ormoc City on the 10th. The Japanese replied by bringing in elements of their 8th Division.

Upwards of 200,000 Americans had fought on Leyte by year's end, but the Americans were now able to reduce their Leyte front to the Americal, 77th and 96th Divisions and put 55,000 rear-echelon personnel onto the island to turn it into a major air and naval base.

In spring 1945 the Americans on Leyte turned over most of the front to the guerrillas. There was fierce action as late as May. The liberation of Leyte cost several hundred Filipino and 11,000 American casualties. Japanese losses were 60,000 killed.

On 24 December 1944 the US 24th Division invaded Mindoro Island, where aided by guerrillas they neutralised the thousand or so Japanese garrison.

This was a stepping stone to Luzon, for MacArthur had finally convinced his government to let him take that island. However, he was to let the Japanese on the other Philippine islands wither on the vine.

The US Sixth Army invaded Luzon on 9 January 1945 at Lingayen Gulf, meeting little opposition. Filipino guerrillas told them the strength and locations of the Japanese: the 2nd Armoured, 8th, 10th, 19th, 23rd, 39th, 103rd, and 105th Divisions, a brigade and depot troops to make 200,000 Japanese defenders.

The Filipino guerrilla Tarlac Regiment had liberated Tarlac town already and informed the US 37th and 40th Divisions that 30,000 Japanese were waiting at Clark Field. On the 24th the Americans and the guerrillas attacked.

On the 28th the US 6th, 25th and 43rd Divisions and the Filipino guerrilla Yay Regiment were counter-attacked at San Manuel, but swiftly saw off the Japanese.

By 1 February Clark Field had been taken with its garrison pushed into the western mountains. Over the next two months Filipino guerrillas and one at a time the US 38th, then 40th then 43rd Divisions would battle these hold-outs.

The Yay Regiment and US 6th, 25th and 32nd Divisions were counter-attacked by the Japanese 2nd Armoured Division: anti-tank guns, aircraft and hand-held bazookas destroyed the tiny Japanese tanks. The three US divisions then chased the retreating Japanese into the eastern mountains. With them went the Filipino guerrilla Buena Vista Regiment, serving as a fourth infantry regiment for the 32nd Division.

MacArthur was impatient. He wanted Manilla. He ordered the US 1st Cavalry and 37th Divisions to ignore enemy rearguards and drive south into the city. The US 11th Airborne Division landed on the coast below Manilla and was ordered to push north to the city.

On 4 February the Americans and Filipino guerrillas joyfully reached the city and liberated 3,500 American civilian prisoners. The city inhabitants were ecstatic. The Japanese Army had evacuated the city, but the Navy's 17,000 sailors had not and their admiral was determined to take the city to hell with him.

The fighting stretched into the next day and the next. Artillery was needed to blast the die-hard sailors out of their buildings. Many Japanese took civilian hostages and then butchered them when they saw the Americans would attack anyway. Sheer terror reigned for two weeks. By the 17th the last hold-outs were inside the Intramuros fort. A twinge of conscience made them release 3,000 civilian hostages, after which they fought to the death.

The liberation of MacArthur's favourite city cost him a thousand guerrilla and 6,500 American casualties, but the real losers were the inhabitants, over 100,000 died in the madness.

Other units were getting on with the war. The US 503rd Parachute Regiment jumped on top of Corregidor and a battalion of the US 24th Division invaded. It took over two weeks, the addition of the US 151st Regiment and 1,200 American casualties to destroy the garrison and wipe the shame of Corregidor from American and Filipino history. Tiny Caballo Island took eighteen days of death to overcome.

The US 38th Division cleared Bataan, wiping out the stain but not the memory of the Bataan Death March.

On 6 March the US 1st Cavalry and 6th Divisions advanced into the Sierra Madre mountains in northern Luzon, where after a week of bloody losses, including a divisional commander, they had to be relieved by the US 43rd Division and Filipino Yay Regiment.

Part of the US 40th Division invaded Luzon at Legaspi to find the guerrillas had been in fierce combat for a week.

In the Baguio-Bambang area the Filipino Tarlac and Buena Vista Regiments and US 25th, 32nd and 33rd Divisions fought a tough campaign and had to be joined by the US 37th Division in mid-April. Baguio town was finally liberated on the 26th. They then concentrated on Bambang.

In early May the Filipino Yay Regiment and US 43rd Division waited for three days while aircraft dropped napalm on their target and then they attacked for twelve days straight to capture Ipo Dam. Meanwhile the Filipino 2nd Regiment and the US 38th Division assaulted Wawa Dam. The action was so rough that tanks and flamethrowers had to be used on individual Japanese, but on 28 May they took the dam.

American intelligence now decided there were only 15,000 Japanese left near the dams – only 15,000! Therefore, they pulled out and left them to the Yay and 2nd Regiments, which continued to attack for the next three months using infantry, artillery, engineers and horse cavalry.

Bambang was liberated at last on 10 June and its defenders ran northwards chased by the US 6th, 32nd, 33rd and 37th Divisions and the Filipino Tarlac and Buena Vista Regiments. In nine days the allies advanced a

hundred miles. On the 23rd the US 11th Airborne Division dropped on the north coast ahead of the retreating Japanese and advanced towards the 37th Division, meeting them on the 26th. This trapped 50,000 Japanese in a 6,000-square-mile pocket.

By 1 February 1945 the US government were happy they were well on their way to capturing the Luzon airfields, which is all they wanted. MacArthur asked permission to fulfil the Philippine government's request to liberate the remainder of their nation. His superiors did not refuse him, but they did begin to take units away from him and told him that in any future operations he was to use Filipino troops not Americans.

MacArthur proceeded to ignore Washington and assigned the entire US Eighth Army to the liberation of the other Philippine islands!

On 80 by 30 miles Samar Island on 14 February the locals were surprised to find their liberators were the US Army's 1st Filipino Regiment as well as elements of the 41st Division. They quickly captured Allen town and then chased the enemy into the interior.

On 250-by-30-mile Palawan the Filipino guerrillas of the 105th Division had been fighting for months against 2,700 Japanese and had captured an airstrip and a base, into which they had been receiving American airlifts. On 28 February an element of the US 41st Division landed and together they captured Puerto Princessa town, finding the bodies of 79 murdered American prisoners. After another five days only a hundred Japanese were still alive.

By February guerrillas had gained control of Buria, Siniara and Romblon. American reinforcements who arrived in March were hardly necessary.

On 3 March the Americal Division invaded 50 by 10 miles Masbate Island and together with the local guerrillas hounded the Japanese for weeks, until the Americans were sure the Filipinos could handle the remainder.

On 18 March the US 40th Division invaded 60 by 30 miles Panay to be welcomed by a parade formation of Filipino troops on the beach! The Filipinos told the newcomers there were 2,800 Japanese on the island, but that they could take care of them.

On 80-by-30-mile Negros the Filipinos had surrounded eight air strips defended in total by the 14,500 strong Japanese 102nd Division. On 29 March the US 40th Division and 503rd Parachute Regiment joined them and together launched an offensive. Over a two-month period the Americans and Filipinos killed 7,000 Japanese. In June the 40th Division withdrew and the others continued attacking.

On 26 March the Americal Division invaded 80 by 10 miles Cebu, where 13,000 Japanese were waiting for them on the beach; of the first wave's fifteen landing craft ten were destroyed, but the Americans persevered and within a day liberated Cebu City. With guerrilla aid and American engineers fighting as infantry they pressed forward, until in late April the Americans were happy to leave the enemy to the Filipinos.

On 2 April part of the US 41st Division invaded Tawi Tawi and within two days decided the locals could handle the enemy garrison.

On 11 April troops of the Americal Division invaded 30 by 30 miles Bohol and found the Filipinos had the enemy penned in. They assisted them for two weeks and then returned to their parent division on Cebu.

On 20 by 5 miles Jolo the guerrillas had been battling 4,000 Japanese for years and by April had liberated their capital city, the airfield and most of the countryside. After a regiment of the US 41st Division joined them on 9 April they launched an offensive which in three weeks eliminated the Japanese as a viable force.

On Mindanao (200 by 100 miles excluding the Zamboanga Peninsula) in October 1944 open warfare had broken out between 40,000 Filipinos of the 106th, 107th, 108th (Moslem) 109th and 110th Divisions and the Japanese 30th and 100th Divisions, a brigade and depot troops, about 80,000 men. On 10 March 1945 the 108th Division in the peninsula killed 250 Japanese for a loss of seventeen killed and 21 wounded in order to facilitate the landing of the US 41st Division. Then together the two divisions assaulted Zamboanga City.

In April the Japanese commander of Mindanao, General Morozumi withdrew his forces into three pockets at Davao City, the Zamboanga Peninsula and along the Sayre Highway, which dissected the island. On 17 April the US 24th and 31st Divisions landed in safety and liberated Kabaken on the 23rd separating Davao from the highway. Then the US 24th and Filipino 107th Divisions besieged the city, while the US 41st and Filipino 106th, 109th and 110th Divisions advanced northwards along the highway.

On 10 May the 40th Division landed where the highway meets the north coast and began advancing along it southwards. On the 23rd the two advancing columns met at Impalatao town.

On 24 May the US 41st Division relieved the Filipino 107th Division, so that the Filipinos could root out small bypassed enemy pockets.

In late May the Filipino 106th, 109th and 110th and US 31st, 24th and 41st Divisions turned off the highway to chase the enemy into the jungle. After a month of heavy combat, the Americans retired to let the Filipinos carry on alone. Between 1 July and 16 August the Filipino 109th and 110th Divisions killed 2,325 Japanese.

The last major amphibious landing in the Philippines was on 12 July in Sarangani Bay, Mindanao where a battalion of the US 24th Division linked up with local guerrillas to crush 2,000 Japanese over a period of two weeks.

On 15 August the Japanese Emperor surrendered. Now a psychological campaign began as Filipinos and Japanese prisoners roamed the jungle with loudspeakers trying to convince the hold-outs the war was over. This went on for months and not all Japanese surrendered peacefully.

In defence of the Philippines 1941-42 the Philippines armed forces lost about 7,000 killed and the US armed forces 3,000, of which some were Filipinos. Probably a thousand civilians died in air raids and cross-fire. Of the 8,580 Filipinos in US uniform taken prisoner 4,500 died in confinement. Of the 17,000 actual American servicemen taken prisoner 6,000 died in confinement. Of the American civilians interned about one in eight died. Of the 98,000 Filipino troops captured 42,000 died in Japanese custody.

During the occupation about 5,000 Filipino guerrillas were killed in action. Thousands of Filipinos were arrested for suspected guerrilla connections and murdered or worked to death. Innocents were killed in reprisals or worked to death on building projects. A figure of 80,000 civilian deaths at the hands of the Japanese is probably too low.

During the liberation about 1,000 guerrillas were killed in action operating on their own and 1,670 were killed and 5,000 wounded operating under US orders. US ground forces casualties, including those of their 1st Filipino Regiment, were 10,330 killed and 37,500 wounded.

Besides the 100,000 civilian deaths in Manilla another 20,000 or so civilians throughout the islands were killed in crossfire, air raids and murdered by the Japanese. Manilla was the second most damaged allied city in World War II.

It cost the Japanese about 10,000 killed conquering the Philippines and 330,000 dead trying to hold on to it. After the war 97,500 Japanese surrendered.

Total Filipino war dead was thus about 200,000 civilians and 62,500 in uniform.

Historians continue to argue whether the liberation of the Philippines was worth the time, effort and lives and if it had any bearing on the defeat of Japan. Some argue that the neutralisation of the airfields on Luzon was necessary and possibly the capture of a few ports, too, but that is all. To be sure MacArthur went out on a limb waging his own private war. President Roosevelt was a very ill man in February-March 1945 (he died in April) and no one else was strong enough to stand up to MacArthur. With hindsight one might assume the allies would have won the war on the same date had they not invaded the Philippines, but wars are not fought with hindsight. MacArthur was driven by personal ambition, we know, wanting to appear as a saint to the Filipinos, but despite this the ordinary Filipino families were grateful for the liberation for they are the ones who had to endure a terrifying occupation by the Japanese and they could not care less why MacArthur returned, just as long as he did.

See Index

POLAND

Status in 1938:	independent.
Government in 1938:	dictatorship.
Population in 1938:	34,325,000.
Make-up in 1938:	Poles 24,358,000;
	Ukrainians 4,857,000;
	Jews 2,880,000;
	Byelorussians 1,100,000;
	Volksdeutsch 794,000;
	Lithuanians 200,000;
	Kashubians 100,000;
	Gypsies 36,000.
Religion:	Christian.
Location:	Eastern Europe.

Long oppressed by Germany, Russia and Austria until 1918, the Poles then turned the tables and by force of arms conquered tracts of land where other ethnic groups were living. A Soviet invasion added to these troubles and it was not until 1923 that there was peace. A mini-civil war notwithstanding, the Poles more or less settled down to a fairly mild oppression of their ethnic minorities.

However, Polish ultra-nationalism was never far below the surface and in 1938 they took advantage of Czecho-Slovakia's difficulties with Germany to take Teschen an area of 75,000 Poles, 20,000 Volksdeutsch and 133,000 Czechs.

During summer 1939 the Poles realised that Hitler, Germany's dictatorial leader, wanted to free the Volksdeutsch. France and Britain guaranteed Poland's borders, but frankly only one nation could help Poland against Germany and that was Stalin's Soviet empire. Yet, with Stalin as an ally, who needs an enemy, the Poles thought. Therefore, they chose to go it alone, believing their 40 divisions and sixteen brigades, 475 tanks and 315 planes should quickly put a damper on Hitler's ambitions.

On 1 September without warning the Germans invaded. General Smigly-Ridz had placed his Polish forces in a ring around the western borders to defend every acre of Polish soil, including the Volksdeutsch areas, and this was his first mistake, for any break through by the Germans put them inside the Polish circle.

In the north along the border with East Prussia (a German province) Army Modlin's two infantry divisions and two cavalry

237

brigades were attacked by German Third Army's one panzer and seven infantry divisions; west of East Prussia Army Pomorze's five infantry divisions and a cavalry brigade were attacked by Fourth Army's one panzer and seven infantry divisions; in the west Army Poznan's four infantry divisions and two cavalry brigades were not attacked; in the south west Armies Lodz's and Prosy's one mountain and fourteen infantry divisions with a cavalry and three mountain brigades were attacked by the Eighth and Tenth Armies's two panzer and fifteen infantry divisions; in the south Armies Krakow's and Karpathy's one mountain and eight infantry divisions and one cavalry, two mechanised and three mountain brigades were attacked by the Fourteenth Army's two panzer, two mountain and seven infantry divisions.

On paper this did not look good for the Poles: on the ground it looked even worse. Though each Polish division was the same size as a German division, the Germans outnumbered the Poles in tanks 6:1, in field guns 3:1 and planes 4:1. Polish cavalry with their massed horsemen were trained to fight a kind of war that the Germans did not offer.

The Poles fought well, but they were barely mobile. The Germans were not as mobile as their propaganda proclaimed: each infantry division relied on horse-drawn wagons, but German officers had been trained to use initiative; Polish officers had not .

The Poles prayed for rain: it would aid their horses and turn their dirt roads into mud and stop the enemy tanks. It did not rain.

By 5 September Army Pomorze was cut off, Armies Lodz and Prosy had retreated 75 miles, part of Army Krakow was besieged in Krakow City and Army Poznan still not engaged was retreating.

By the 8th Army Karpathy (now called Malopolska) was retreating towards Lwow, Army Prosy was falling back towards Deblin on the Vistula south of Warsaw, Army Lodz was withdrawing to the Vistula north of Warsaw, and Army Modlin was on the move to Warsaw.

The Warsaw garrison repelled an impudent German thrust and on the 9th Army Poznan ran into the rear of the German Eighth Army, defeating two divisions. However, the Germans responded far quicker than the Poles to this turn of events and in two days surrounded Armies Poznan, Modlin, Lodz and Prosy in one massive pocket centred on the Bzura River. Armies Krakow and Malopolska were also surrounded.

On the 17th the 200,000 or so Polish troops on the Soviet border were swamped by a Soviet offensive of 34 divisions. The Polish High Command was so shocked by this stab in the back some officers committed suicide.

On the 20th Armies Malopolska and Krakow and the Bzura pocket all collapsed. Hundreds of thousands of Poles walked into captivity. Next day the Soviets shook hands with the Germans at Brest Litovsk.

On the 23rd Warsaw was assaulted, its garrison reinforced by elements of Armies Modlin and Lodz to a strength of 150,000 men. On the 27th after a ferocious battle the commander surrendered.

In the south 80,000 Polish troops fled across the border into neutral Romania. Elsewhere diehards fought on for a week, but it was all over.

The destruction of Poland cost the Soviets 2,600 killed and wounded, with 5,000 Poles killed fighting them and 180,000 taken prisoner; and the Germans 16,000 killed and 32,000 wounded, with 66,300 Poles killed fighting them and 600,000 taken prisoner. Some Polish villages had been overrun before their menfolk could be mobilised; some Volksdeutsch had defected to the Germans at once; some Poles hid rather than surrender.

Civilian casualties were high as German planes had strafed refugees on the roads and many towns had become a battleground. Some towns were visited by German fanatics who murdered Poles and Jews. In places Poles had murdered Volksdeutsch. About 25,000 civilians died in the campaign.

In the Soviet-occupied zone lived 4,500,000 Ukrainians, 5,300,000 Poles, 134,000 Volksdeutsch, 200,000 Lithuanians, 1,100,000 Byelorussians and 1,100,000 Jews. Behind the Soviet Red Army had come Stalin's NKVD political police with the mission of destroying any potential anti-communist resistance: their method was to arrest doctors, lawyers, architects, bankers, artists, writers, teachers, managers etc. and haul them off to concentration camps. Skilled workers were ordered to work in Russia and 19-20-year-old youths were conscripted into the Red Army. By June 1941 1,060,000 people had been forcibly removed from their homes.

Stalin wanted the captured Polish officers removed, for after all most were reservists and in civilian life were artists, engineers, lawyers etc. The NKVD shot 15,000, before someone decided it was not a good idea.

Thousands of people fled the Germans and entered the Soviet zone. Stalin ordered them all arrested in case one was a German spy.

The 134,000 Volksdeutsch were the luckiest. By agreement they were expelled to the German zone.

If life was terrifying in the Soviet zone, it was equally so in the German zone, which was now divided into the 'Volksdeutsch' region annexed by Germany, containing 133,000 Czechs, 100,000 Kashubians, 580,000 Jews, 620,000 Volksdeutsch and 9,200,000 Poles, and the 'Polish' region called the General Government, where lived 9,800,000 Poles, 357,000 Ukrainians, 1,200,000 Jews and 60,000 Volksdeutsch.

The German version of the NKVD, the SS Security Police, kept a lookout for anti-German activity. They too had their concentration camps and firing squads, and they arrested 50,000 members of the professional classes. The SS had the added role of racial selection: Volksdeutsch were given rations of German standard, Jews received a pittance, others something in between. Volksdeutsch were also given good jobs and homes at the expense of others.

The General Government retained the Polish police who aided the SS to round up all Jews and place them in town ghettos. Jews were expelled from the annexed region and forced to crowd into the General Government's ghettos.

This was idiocy. During the invasion some of the German soldiers were Polish-speakers and some of the Polish soldiers were German-speakers, i.e. Volksdeutsch.

Soon the Poles were allowed to register as Volksdeutsch (as if they had just remembered they were Germans!) Knowledge of the German language was not necessary! The advantages were that a husband sitting in a German prisoner of war camp would be released, a better job would be offered, a better home perhaps, certainly better food rations. Hungry kids can temper one's national pride. Czechs nick-named these men and women 'Margarine Germans' i.e. they did it for food. Jews and Gypsies were not eligible to sign up as Volksdeutsch.

Warsaw became quite crowded as Jews and Poles arrived from the annexed region looking for shelter and others came to exploit. In June 1940 its civilian population, broken down into ethnicity, was 895,000 Poles, 393,500 Jews (in the ghetto) 5,000 Ukrainians, 2,500 Germans, 5,000 foreigners and 5,500 Volksdeutsch and Margarine Germans.

Naturally, resistance movements sprang up to fight Germans and Soviets, and to combat them the NKVD recruited informers and agents, many of them Jews. The Germans brought in 36 battalions of police and took on Volksdeutsch recruits. By summer 1940 they had also recruited 33 Ukrainian and three Polish battalions of anti-terrorist police.

The Germans made sure everyone had a job (Jews were not paid for their labour) and by summer 1940 had sent 1,000,000 Poles to work in German factories, of which 200,000 had volunteered. Volksdeutsch were exempt from forced labour, but they had a different problem: soon all their men aged 19-45 were conscripted into the German armed forces. This law included the Margarine Germans.

In the German annexed region 850,000 Poles had become Margarine Germans and 1,200,000 Poles had been expelled to the General Government because they had not been born in the region. In 1942 all Poles who had lived under German rule prior to 1918 and their children were declared to be Volksdeutsch citizens. The law did not apply to Jews, Gypsies, Czechs and Kashubians. This law gave them much better treatment and indeed saved lives, but it also made their menfolk 19-45 eligible for military conscription. About 200,000 Poles refused to be labelled 'Germans' and moved to the General Government.

The Poles who had escaped to Romania eventually made their way to France and reformed as soldiers, sailors and airmen. A brigade and the navy fought in Norway in April-June 1940, and when Germany invaded France Polish flyers went into action, shooting down 55 planes. In June Polish troops fought the advancing Germans and when the French surrendered they tried to make it to the ports to escape to Britain: 24,000 did so. Of the rest 6,000 were killed and wounded and 60,000 captured.

Among those who reached Britain were 147 fighter pilots, soon proving their worth in the Battle of Britain. In one 30-day period a Polish squadron was the highest scoring allied squadron. The 147 suffered 30 killed, but shot down 220 planes.

The Polish Air Force in Britain expanded to two ground attack, two bomber and nine fighter squadrons.

The Polish Army in Britain lobbied constantly to be sent into action and in August 1941 the British finally relented, sending a brigade to reinforce the besieged garrison of Tobruk in North Africa. One of its battalions was made up entirely of officers, who willingly served as privates to get to grips with the Germans: actually most of their time at Tobruk they were up against Italians. Tobruk was relieved in December and the Poles helped chase the enemy to the Gazala Line. The allies attacked the line on the 14th and 15th and the Poles were the only unit to break through, but without support they had to fall back under German counter-attack. Having lost 585 casualties in Africa the brigade was withdrawn.

The Polish Navy and merchant fleet performed wonders. One destroyer was among the ships that sank the *Bismarck*, Germany's prized battleship. Polish vessels protected convoys, hunted enemy vessels and raided the European coast.

On 22 June 1941 Germany invaded the USSR. Polish conscripts in the Red Army fought the Germans, but within days the Red Army was denied further conscription of Poles as the Polish areas were overrun. Whole Soviet divisions were captured in the Soviet zone of Poland, which now became the new German zone.

However, Stalin did have thousands of Poles in his prisoner of war camps. He sent delegates to them asking for a new Polish Army to be created. They volunteered at once in order to get out of the disgusting camps and to fight Germans, but soon two factions emerged: General Anders' faction who would only fight alongside the British and General Berling's group who agreed to fight alongside the Red Army. Stalin allowed Anders men to make their own way to British Iran, but gave them little assistance. Some men, already starved and still on half rations crossed 5,000 miles to reach Iran. Anders assembled 77,500 men, 500 female soldiers and 35,000 civilians. Most of the Jews in the army had joined Anders' faction and he did have a few Ukrainians and Byelorussians from eastern Poland.

Berling's group passed inspection in 1943 and in May his 1st Kosciusko Division put its 15,400 men and 600 women into line in the Vyazma Salient. A sprinkling of his men had seen action already as Red Army soldiers, but most had only seen action very briefly in 1939 against the Red Army.

In July the Poles were informed that their senior political leader in Britain, General Sikorski, had been killed in a plane crash. As he had many enemies, Germans, Soviets and Poles, sabotage was rumoured.

At the end of August the 1st Division attacked: above them flew Polish air squadrons. The fighting was frantic and seemingly went on forever, literally driving some men insane. Only on 25 September did the Germans retreat. The Poles eagerly followed them for every step put them closer to home.

In November, during a halt caused by the autumn rains, Berling formed the Ist Corps of the 1st and the 2nd Dombrowski Divisions. Under Red Army orders they held a stable front during the winter.

In March 1944 the corps received the 3rd Romauld Traugut Division.

Polish commandos fought in the invasion of Italy at Salerno in September 1943, helping the allies gain a solid foothold. One of the German formations holding them back in Italy was the 65th Division, consisting mostly of Polish Volksdeutsch and Margarine Germans.

Anders men reached the Italian front on 20 February 1944, the 3rd Karpathy Division slipping into foxholes near San Angelo, soon joined by the 5th Kresowa Division and 2nd Armoured Brigade to make up the IInd Corps.

In April he was informed he was to assault Monte Cassino. He wondered if this honour came from allied desperation. In five months the Cassino position had repelled Americans, British, Indians and New Zealanders.

The Poles attacked on the night of 11 May, unfortunately running into two German regiments instead of one, and within hours Anders took the courageous step of cancelling the attack. He knew the world's eyes were on his Poles and he did not want to fail. On the 16th he attacked again. The combat was extremely desperate: at one point some Poles ran out of ammunition and threw rocks at the Germans; in another area tanks advanced into a minefield under fire with engineers crawling underneath with bayonets prodding for mines, risking being shot, blown up or run over. The courage of the Poles not only captured Monte Cassino, but created a legend.

After this the allies advanced, the Poles with them. Each village blurred in the memory as they all looked alike. Throughout the summer they advanced, each bend in the road possibly containing a rearguard, each tree a sniper, each ridge an artillery battery.

Polish warships continued to make a name for themselves. They bombarded the enemy during the invasions of Sicily, Salerno and Normandy. Three destroyers were sunk, but by January 1944 the Poles had sunk a cruiser, two destroyers and four minesweepers. Polish submarines were also praised. In the last quarter of 1943 the submarine *Sokol* sank 13 ships. By January 1944 the submarine *Dzik* had sunk 21 ships.

By this date the Polish Air Force reborn in Britain had reached a strength of 12,000 men and women, had flown 703 bombing missions and had shot down 610 planes.

In spring 1944 the Red Army began its second invasion of Poland in five years. By now about 250,000 resistance members had acknowledged rule by the government in Britain, calling themselves the Home Army. Aditionally were the communists who owed allegiance to Stalin and the NSZ and WIN, who had waged war against the Red Army as well as the Germans and who also fought Polish communists. Normally, Lithuanians, Byelorussians and Ukrainians, though Polish citizens pre-1939, did not join Polish resistance movements, but had their own.

In April the Polish anti-German resistance movement in Volhynia declared itself to be the 27th Division of the Home Army and made open war against the Germans. After three weeks they broke clear of a German encirclement attempt and reached the Red Army. They were met by friendly faces, but given a choice of joining Berling's men or demobilisation.

On 6 July the Home Army in Vilno revolted, but a Red Army unit was only a day away and the two allied units soon linked up. In a six-day fight they pushed the Germans out.

On 23 July the Lwow Home Army revolted and defeated the Germans before the Red Army arrived. On 24 July the Home Army captured Lublin.

Berling's men were aimed straight at Warsaw and by 31 July were crossing the Vistula at Pulawy. However, they met determined opposition and had to withdraw on 4 August after losing a thousand casualties. Their goal had been to outflank Warsaw and lever the garrison out. No one wanted to see Warsaw destroyed in a battle.

Yet for some in Warsaw the waiting was unbearable. Each day some poor fellow was arrested and the arrogance of the Germans had not diminished with their defeats on the Russian front. By now the population had altered: a net increase of 26,000 Poles having come to the city after being displaced by Volksdeutsch in the countryside, a net increase of 13,500 Germans who came to steal good jobs and a net increase of 11,182 Volksdeutsch (most probably Poles who had become Margarine Germans). There were no

Jews: all had been deported to extermination camps.

On 31 July General Bor, the Warsaw Home Army commander, gave in to the hotheads: as the Red Army was only 20 miles away he agreed to a revolt. Next day the Home Army swelled by members from the countryside to 40,000 men and 4,000 women openly revolted against the Germans in Warsaw.

The German garrison consisted of the police: (2,080 Polish and Volksdeutsch ordinary police, 280 Ukrainian ordinary police, 1,170 Volksdeutsch and Polish, 2,400 German and 800 Ukrainian anti-terrorist police, 310 German rural police and 150 German and Volksdeutsch SS Security Police); the paramilitaries (30 German SS officials and 600 Volksdeutsch stormtroopers); and the armed forces (500 Waffen SS German and Volksdeutsch combat soldiers, 1,300 German airmen and flak gunners, a thousand German Army rear-echelon troops and eight infantry battalions, two Turkestani and one Azerbaijani battalions and a Russian company).

The first incidents went well: Poles shot up trucks, gunned down patrols, shot unarmed rear-echelon soldiers and machine-gunned female secretaries at their typewriters; but in a couple of hours they began to assault defended buildings and suffer accordingly. In the first 24 hours 500 of the garrison were shot or stabbed to death, but 2,000 Home Army members were casualties. The civilians were caught in the middle.

Three German battalions entered the city as reinforcements, but Bor got reinforcements too when the 2,000 strong communist resistance joined him.

On 4 August the Germans were reinforced by Kaminski's Russian SS RONA Brigade and 2,695 German police. German planes were now bombing suspected Home Army positions. Next day Dirlewanger's SS brigade arrived, all of them criminals recruited in prison, 40% of them Russians and Ukrainians. Dirlewanger's and Kaminski's men were responsible for sickening atrocities: e.g. raping and murdering female patients of a cancer hospital.

Over the next week more reinforcements arrived for the garrison: police (a Cossack regiment and three German battalions) and army (two Azerbaijani Regiments, nine Cossack and two Caucasian battalions).

By now the garrison was using artillery to flatten whole blocks. Civilian losses were terrible and they soon ran out of food. The German garrison commanders, who were Air Force and Army not SS or police decidedly straightened up their act: they organised food shipments, evacuated civilians where possible, took Home Army prisoners alive and shot SS General Kaminski.

On 7 September in the middle of the battle the German 19th Panzer Division retreated across the Vistula to the city, the Red Army right behind them. So far Stalin had not aided the Home Army: no air supply drops, no air support, no artillery support. Allied and Polish Air Force planes had been flying aid to the Home Army, and when they were shot down Stalin complained that the wreckage fell on 'his' soil!

However, on 12 September just as the 25th Panzer Division retreated to Warsaw, Stalin was forced by Anglo-American pressure to help the Home Army. He authorised Berling to make a liberation attempt.

On the night of the 16th Berling's 3rd Division crossed the river in boats with fire support from the 1st Division. The assault troops were wiped out. Next night they tried again and this time gained a toe-hold and by the 19th were 400 yards from the Home Army. Yet for four days it proved impossible to cross that 400 yards and on the 22nd Berling recalled his gallant men.

On the morning of 4 October the Home Army surrendered: 9,000 dirty, thin, sick men and women. The Germans kept their word and treated them as bona fide prisoners of war. Indeed in parts of the city Home Army prisoners were saluted by the Germans. 6,000 Home Army fighters had already been captured and 16,000 killed. The others had escaped. The garrison lost 2,000 killed and 9,000 wounded.

Warsaw's civilians suffered most. About 200,000 died from cross-fire, starvation, murder and disease. On Hitler's orders the entire city was evacuated and blown up by engineers.

In Britain the Polish 1st Armoured Division was given the word in August 1944 to join the battle in France. Their first mission was to help shut the Falaise-Argentan gap. This they did in four days, trapping thousands of Germans. Then they advanced into Belgium, where they had to fight for every river and canal. Along with everyone else they came to a halt at the Netherlands border on 10 September.

The allies chose to break into the Netherlands using airborne troops on the 17th. The most forward unit, the British 1st Airborne Division, was dropped on the north side of the Rhine near Arnhem bridge, as everyone said 'a bridge too far'. Counter-attacked by heavy enemy forces they were soon in trouble.

In Britain General Sosabowski had followed the Arnhem situation with keen interest and on the 20th he discussed a rescue attempt with his British superiors, who asked him to drop his brigade of paratroopers on the south side of the Rhine near the British and thus link them with advancing British armour. His problems were, he could not take his whole brigade at once, fog might trap his first echelon without air supply, the British armour might never reach him and in any case every German in the area including flak gunners would be waiting for him. He agreed to go at once.

That afternoon he and his first echelon parachuted and fought their way into a tiny pocket. The second echelon jumped the next day, but thereafter bad weather grounded the third echelon. Fortunately this day the advancing British reached the Poles. Some Poles had swum the river and contacted the British paratroopers. On the night of the 25th the British paratroopers withdrew, partly covered by the Poles. Then Sosabowski's men were withdrawn, having lost 220 killed or missing and 158 wounded.

Anders had lost many men and of course he had no reserve manpower, but then he found out that among the German prisoners taken in France were some Poles. He asked them to volunteer; 30,000 did so.

In Poland Berling had been dismissed by Stalin for his too zealous attempt to reach the Home Army, though legally Stalin had no right to do this. Using Berling's men and ex-Home Army soldiers Stalin created two Polish armies, the First and Second. In January 1945 the Soviets and Poles launched a major offensive, liberating the rubble that was Warsaw, Kielce on the 15th, Radom on the 16th, Krakow on the 19th and reaching the Oder River in Germany on the 22nd. By now the German conscription age was 16-60 and this included all Poles who had German/Volksdeutsch citizenship. Naturally many deserted.

In February the Polish Second Army captured Poznan and the First Army battled for Danzig, finally taking the city on 30 March. Polish planes flew ground support in these battles.

In April came great offensives in Netherlands, Italy and eastern Germany. The Polish 1st Armoured Division swept through eastern Netherlands, liberating Hengelo and Westerbork and running into fanatic opposition at Delfzijl. Leaving a force to besiege this town, the division swerved east and invaded northern Germany, taking the defences of Aschendorf and Pappenburg. They were surprised to liberate a prison camp of 1,700 Home Army soldiers, all women. On the 24th they entered Leer. The name means empty, but it wasn't: they found fanaticism at its worst and had to call for Canadian reinforcements.

In Italy the allies attacked on the 9th, Anders' corps making good progress until the 14th when they ran into German teenaged paratroopers at Imola. Using a plethora of firepower the Poles aided by others captured the town in a day. They then charged ahead for Bologna, liberating rebellious Italian partisans there on the 20th. After this they chased the running Germans north towards Austria.

In eastern Germany the great offensive began on the 16th. Polish planes aided Soviet troops to break into Berlin. The Polish First Army assaulted Stettin, while the Second Army conquered the Dresden region then turned south towards Prague.

Anders' war ended when the Germans surrendered in Italy 2 May. The 1st Armoured Division ceased fire when the northern Germany defences surrendered on 4 May. The First Army took the German surrender on the 9th and the Second Army fought its last diehards on the 11th near Prague.

But the dying did not stop. The Soviets reclaimed the land they had conquered in 1939 and the NKVD went to work again. The NSZ and WIN fought them. The remainder of Poland, nominally independent under Stalin-sponsored President Bierut, reclaimed all soil taken by the Germans and annexed a large part of Germany. The Poles decided to kick out all Volksdeutsch from old Poland and the native Germans from the newly conquered lands, except for select cases. Towns like Danzig (renamed Gdansk) became ghost towns. Germans who refused to go were beaten, imprisoned or murdered. As usual in such ethnic cleansing the innocents suffered most.

The Poles overseas in Anders and other armies were allowed to return, but 150,000 chose not to do so. Those who did were closely watched by the NKVD and their new Polish offspring. Some Jews had survived, but they were not welcomed back. Many were murdered by neighbours. The fact that many communists and NKVD were Jews had something to do with this. Each town's communist party headquarters was jokingly referred to as the Jewish ghetto.

In November 1945 Polish troops surrounded a large pocket of NSZ and WIN and massacred them. The Polish Army now concentrated on destroying ethnic Ukrainian guerrillas. In this combat General Swieczewski was killed in an ambush on 23 March 1947. The government's immediate reaction was an offensive by three Polish divisions and some NKVD in the Peremyshl area. They destroyed one Ukrainian unit. However, by the end of 1948 almost all the guerrillas had fled to Slovakia. At last Poland achieved a peace of sorts.

For armed forces that according to Hitler did not exist, the Poles notched up some pretty fair battle honours: Norway, France 1940, Battle of Britain, the Atlantic, Tobruk, Air Offensive Europe, Arctic Convoys, Tunisia, Sicily, Salerno, Cassino, Normandy, Vyazma, Vistula River, Falaise-Argentan, Italy's Gothic Line, Arnhem, Danzig, Bologna, Delfzijl and Berlin.

The 1st Armoured Division had suffered 1000 killed and 3,870 wounded. Anders corps lost 2,900 killed, 7,675 wounded and 4,300 captured. The Polish Air Force reborn in Britain lost 2,000 killed. Altogether at sea, in the air, in France 1940 and other combat zones the British-supported Polish forces lost 8,300 dead.

Soviet-sponsored Polish forces lost 13,000 killed and 26,000 wounded.

The Polish security forces admitted to 32,400 killed fighting guerrillas 1945-48. The true figure may have been higher.

Together with losses in 1939 this makes uniformed Polish losses 125,000 killed. Plus the Soviets murdered 30,000 of their prisoners and the Germans 200,000 of theirs.

Resistance losses can only be approximated. The Home Army claim 80,000 dead and wounded, probably in equal numbers. At least 2,000 other guerrillas must have died by late 1944 and guerrilla casualties 1945-48 must have equalled the security forces: hence another 30,000 dead, though it must be noted most were ethnic Ukrainians. One suspects another 10,000 would have died in custody.

This would give a total of 82,000 dead guerrillas.

Some historians estimate that 200,000 Polish-speakers served in German uniform. This author suspects it was far higher. About 80,000 Volksdeutsch wore German uniform and tens of thousands of ethnic Ukrainians did so. Deaths among these 350,000 or so pre-1939 Polish citizens must surely have been a tenth.

Together with Poles killed while wearing Red Army uniform, this brings total military deaths to approximately 480,000.

Civilian losses dwarf this figure. In late 1945 380,000 Jews were accounted for. The other 2,500,000 had disappeared. Certainly about 90,000 died in Polish or Red Army uniform, but civilian Jews died from air raids, cross-fire, NKVD execution and maltreatment, and German-caused starvation, disease and execution.

Another 2,900,000 non-Jewish civilians died: 200,000 in the insanity of the Warsaw uprising, 250,000 at the hands of the communists in 1939-41 and another 50,000 minimum 1944-48; many starved in the communist created famine of 1945-46; the others died at the hands of the Germans by one method or another e.g. two-thirds of all Gypsies were deliberately murdered. Tens of thousands of Volksdeutsch and Margarine Germans were murdered by Poles 1944-46.

The civilian death toll 1939-48 stands at 5,300,000 at least. With military deaths this makes Poland's loss 5,780,000 – one person in six.

See Index

ROMANIA AND MOLDOVA

Other names:	Greater Romania.
Status in 1938:	independent.
Government in 1938:	fragile democracy.
Population in 1938:	17,400,000.
Make-up in 1938:	Romanians 12,840,000;
	Hungarians 1,400,000;
	Volksdeutsch 750,000;
	Ukrainians 780,000;
	Jews 728,000;
	Bulgars 366,000;
	Gypsies 260,000;
	Turks 177,000;
	Gagaus 100,000.
Religion:	Christian.
Location:	Eastern Europe.

Having been on the winning side in World War I Romania emerged with considerable territory and a host of ethnic minorities who lived in the conquered areas, making a Greater Romania. Among all these peoples were significant minorities of Gypsies and Jews. There were two types of Jew, those who had assimilated into Romanian or other cultures and dominated business and the law, and the unassimilated who spoke Yiddish or Ladino and kept to themselves. Some towns had large neighbourhoods of unassimilated Jews, e.g. half of the city of Jassy. Not surprisingly in the 1937 election the racist ethnic Romanian fascists took 29% of the vote. King Carol was alarmed at the growth of fascism and in 1938 he dismissed the government to rule directly and cracked down on the fascists.

In 1940 with Romania's traditional friends, Britain and France, completely whipped by the Germans, Carol had nowhere to turn for support except to Germany. However, Hitler, that nation's dictator, forced Carol to pay a high price for this friendship: he was forced to dismantle Greater Romania; i.e. cede Dobrudja to Bulgaria, Transylvania to Hungary and North Bukovina and Bessarabia (Moldova) to the USSR.

After such a shameful surrender, not even the Royal Guards were willing to protect their King. General Ion Antonescu seized power and cornered Carol into abdicating in favour of his son.

Antonescu was not about to be dictated to by the fascists, though, and in winter 1940/1 he put them in their place after short but bloody street battles.

In spring 1941 Hitler invited Antonescu to a crusade against the USSR. The Romanian dictator accepted, but only to regain North Bukovina and Bessarabia. He knew the people would support him, for the Soviet NKVD political police had behaved despicably in their annexed regions, arresting any resident who could think for himself. As many as 100,000 had been sent to Soviet concentration camps. Refugees related unbelievable horror stories.

As part of the new friendship with Germany Antonescu turned a blind eye when 1,600 of his Volksdeutsch citizens joined the German SS, e.g. General Phleps became an SS colonel.

On 22 June 1941 the Germans launched their massive offensive against Germany. The Romanian Third Army drove into North Bukovina with two divisions and three mountain and three horse cavalry brigades. The Fourth Army with one guards and four infantry divisions, an armoured brigade and a cavalry brigade marched into Bessarabia. A Romanian brigade at 8,000 men was almost as large as a Soviet division. A Romanian division had 17,500 troops. In the air the Romanians were outnumbered and their fleet was tiny.

It looked like Antonescu hoped the Germans would win the war for him, especially when Antonescu agreed to subordinate himself to Field Marshal von Runstedt's German Army Group. The Romanian armies contained several ethnic minorities, but no Jews or Gypsies.

The Soviets ran or collapsed in panic. The first victories were easy, too easy, and Antonescu became greedy. He reinforced Fourth Army and ordered them to continue.

Following the combat troops Romanian rear-echelon forces and fascist militia began to celebrate in the liberated lands by the age-old method of massacring Jews. The fact that many of the NKVD and local communist informers were Jews added fuel to long-standing racial hatreds. In one incident 8,000 Jews were placed aboard a freight train and driven for days until they starved to death! Others were hanged. Some Jewish corpses were exhibited in butcher shop windows as a joke. After the initial surge of violence subsided the police arrested all the Jews and imprisoned them in barbaric conditions.

Soon all Jews in Romania were arrested.

By August the Romanian troops had crossed the Dniestr River into Ukrainia and were calling this region their new province of Transniestra, but to maintain their hold they had to have the port of Odessa, which the Soviet garrison denied them. The Fourth Army was brought up to assault the city with six divisions.

The Odessa battle was a horrid, bloody affair in which the Romanians with their Latin blood and culture drew upon emotions rather than logic and threw themselves into the guns time and again, their generals bankrupt of all strategic ideas.

When nothing was gained by the slaughter Antonescu sent reinforcements. By October sixteen divisions were bashing their heads against the walls of Odessa. At last on the 16th the Soviets evacuated by sea.

The generals congratulated themselves on their victory: it had cost them 98,000 casualties!

Meanwhile the Third Army was still advancing, though they lost a mountain brigade to a Soviet riposte on 26 September at the entrance to the Crimea Peninsula. Together with the German Eleventh Army the Third Army, now with four divisions and six brigades, attacked against the Ukrainian coast, trapped an enemy army and took 107,000 prisoners.

In December the Third Army took up positions on the Crimea and Ukrainian coasts and drove back a Soviet counter-attack in an eighteen day battle. In February they repelled another counter-attack.

In 1942 Hitler planned an ambitious offensive to enter the Caucasus and also reach Stalingrad on the Volga River. Indeed it was so ambitious that he did not have the manpower to accomplish it. He invited his partners to aid him.

Despite the Odessa fiasco, Antonescu fully supported Hitler in his venture, giving him the Third and Fourth Armies to protect the flanks of the German Sixth Army which was to capture Stalingrad. Additional Romanian units would aid the German Eleventh Army to clear the Crimea.

In May the Crimea fight began with two Romanian divisions and a brigade and six German divisions crushing the Soviets in the Kerch area, taking 170,000 prisoners. Simultaneously other Germans and three Romanian divisions attacked the port of Sevastopol. It was 4 July before the last Soviets gave up. Romanian losses were 8,454.

The fight for Stalingrad began in August, though for the Romanian armies things were usually quiet. By autumn it was cold and icy, but nothing else had changed. The Germans were still fighting inside Stalingrad and were running out of food.

On 19 November as some Third Army men were preparing breakfast they were suddenly attacked in the darkness by the greatest Soviet counter-offensive to date.

The 1st Cavalry Division was hit by an entire Soviet army; and five other divisions were struck by two armies. The new Romanian 1st Armoured Division rushed up their tanks immediately, only to be crushed by bigger and better Soviet tanks. By day's end every Romanian was either surrounded, running or dead. Only the IInd Corps, as yet untouched, was able to withdraw in good order.

Running is not the right word, though, for in snow the fellows stumbled and struggled, not sure which direction they were headed: it was enough effort to put one foot in front of the other without worrying about navigation.

On the 20th, 50 miles south the Romanian Fourth Army was attacked by three Soviet armies. The VIth Corps bore the brunt and simply ceased to exist. The 1st Cavalry and 20th Divisions sought refuge inside Stalingrad.

In Third Army, Ist Corps side-slipped into the lines of the Italian Eighth Army for safety, while the other units decided to try to reach the Chir River 70 miles in the rear. By the 22nd Stalingrad was surrounded.

General von Paulus in Stalingrad ordered his 300,000 Germans to conserve all food. He did not blame the Romanians – he was no racist, he had a Romanian wife. He blamed Hitler for having eyes bigger than his stomach.

The Third Army reached the Chir and began to build a line: they were missing 40,000 men, 30,000 horses and the equipment of five divisions.

In days the Romanians were under assault by 22 Soviet divisions and fifteen brigades. On the 25th the 6th Romanian Division, surrounded for a week, capitulated.

On 18 December the neighbouring Italians were struck by a massive offensive, which also hit the Romanian Ist Corps. The whole line began to fall back in thigh deep snow.

Yet there was a Stalingrad rescue attempt by German Fourth Panzer Army and Romanian VIth and VIIth Corps. By the 19th they were within 30 miles of Stalingrad, but down to 35 tanks and the line behind them retreating, they could do no more, especially as Hitler ordered von Paulus not to break out towards them. On the 27th the would-be rescuers retreated.

The axis partners tried to anchor on the Hungarian Second Army in mid-January, but the Hungarians were themselves hit by a heavy offensive and fell back. Everyone had to retreat again.

It was February before the line finally stabilised, by which time Stalingrad had fallen.

The Romanian share of the winter débâcle was 120,000 casualties.

Antonescu continually gave in to Hitler's demands and suggestions, e.g. in April 1943 he allowed the SS to take female Volksdeutsch volunteers and actually conscript teenage boys (older Volksdeutsch men were already holding essential jobs or wore Romanian uniform). In this way another 44,000 entered SS ranks in 1943 and by August 1944 14,000 more had entered and 15,000 had entered other German organisations.

This relationship was highlighted in August 1943, when hundreds of American bombers raided the Ploesti oil refineries in daylight: 43 bombers were shot down and 66 badly damaged by Romanian flak gunners and Romanian, Bulgarian and German fighter pilots. Hitler knew that without Romanian oil he was done for: Antonescu knew that without the German armed forces he was done for. He recalled his fighters from the Russian front to defend the refineries. Allied air raids continued, but on a lesser scale.

By early 1944 the Romanian Army was guarding the Ukrainian and Crimean coasts with nine divisions, but the Germans had suffered further serious defeats and were falling back. It was heartbreaking when the Romanians were told to march west into the Crimea or past Odessa to Bessarabia.

Inside the Crimea five German and seven Romanian divisions plus airmen and sailors awaited orders. They were no good to anyone there. On 7 April the Romanian 10th Division was hurt in a Soviet invasion of the peninsula and Hitler now agreed the Crimea should be evacuated. Five Romanian divisions were told to fight a withdrawal action, while the others made their way quickly to Sevastopol. In one week 17,652 Romanians were lost. In late April the Germans held Sevastopol, while the Romanians evacuated by ship in swift but disciplined order. On 13 May the port was abandoned.

This was a noteworthy achievement: in the face of enemy assaults by land, air and sea 87,000 Germans, 40,000 Romanians, 28,000 hiwis (anti-communist soldiers recruited in the USSR), 72,000 horses and 21,000 vehicles safely evacuated by ship to Romania. Unfortunately, casualties were high: 6,300 Romanians killed and wounded and 25,000 missing; 31,700 Germans and hiwis wounded and 22,500 killed or missing.

Even as Romanians were sailing home to safety the Romanian Army was rushing to defend the border: the Third Army of five divisions anchored on the coast with the new German Sixth Army to its north, both under Romanian General Dumitrescu. To their north were the German Eighth and Romanian Fourth Armies, the latter containing eleven divisions. In reserve Antonescu had five divisions and the Crimea survivors.

Inside Romania were hundreds of thousands of refugees from Ukrainia, Transniestra and Bessarabia, but they had sought shelter under a cracking dam.

Secretly Antonescu was talking to the allies to seek a way out of this mess.

On 20 August the Third Army along the Dniestr River was assaulted by three Soviet armies and a corps. The German Sixth and Romanian Fourth Armies were also attacked by heavy forces. Miraculously the defenders stood for two days before the dam broke. Two days later the Sixth Army was surrounded.

King Mihail, who had taken a back seat since Antonescu deposed his father, announced on the radio he was going to ask the Soviets for peace terms and he asked all Germans based in or retreating through his nation to leave at once. Everywhere Romanians turned on the fascists. Antonescu was arrested as were some German generals.

Hitler responded with a rage at his staff officers and ordered Bucharest to be bombed and attacked at once. On the morning of the 24th German planes struck the city as Germans, Volksdeutsch and fascists battled against the Romanian army and police. Mihail declared war on Germany.

On the 26th the Soviets reached the lower Danube; and Focsani next day. Everywhere the Romanian forces were surrendering to, indeed welcoming, the Soviets. On the 28th the Soviets entered Transylvania from the north and landed on the coast at Constanta. Ploesti fell on the 30th; and on the 31st the Soviets, including a Romanian communist division, entered Bucharest.

In these few days 130,000 Romanians were taken prisoner by the Soviets. Now, however, Stalin issued instructions that the Romanians were to be treated as allies! Instantly Soviet troops joined the Romanians who were battling the retreating Germans.

Over the next few days the Soviets assigned political watchdogs to all Romanian forces and restructured them to fit the Soviet style of administration, e.g. divisions were shrunk to about 9,000 men. This was a remarkable achievement in the midst of a battle as Romanians and Soviets fought side by side against a German-Hungarian counter-attack from the Romanian-Hungarian border.

The Germans combed the Volksdeutsch villages for able-bodied men who were conscripted into the SS. The Romanian fascists were also given SS status as the 1st and 2nd Romanian Regiments.

On 9 October the Soviets launched a fresh offensive with three armies aiming towards Hungary. On their northern flank the Romanian Fourth and First Armies attacked the Hungarian First and Second Armies. The fighting was very bitter: Romanian-Hungarian animosity was far older than the current conflict. Ethnic Romanians serving in the Hungarian Army defected to the Romanians. In just six days the Romanians and Soviets overran eastern Hungary, but the front soon shut down as the Soviets had to wait until they could bring up more supplies.

The next offensive did not come until 1 November in freezing wintry conditions. The Romanian Fourth Army attacked the Hungarian Second Army again pushing towards Budapest from the north east and by 13th December were only six miles from the city; but two weeks later they were still at the same spot: Hungarian resistance was fanatical.

At year's end the Fourth Army had to face west as German counter-attacks tried to smash them. Despite high losses they remained in their holes in the snow.

Budapest did not fall until 13 February 1945.

In March the First and Fourth Armies advanced up the Danube against a mix of Germans, Hungarians and Slovakians, capturing Prievidza, Banovce, Svatoy Martin and Vrutky by 11 April and Zilina on the 13th. They then moved steadily forward against tough opposition into the Moravska-Ostrava industrial basin.

By early May the Romanians had cleared the industrial basin and were attacking towards Prague, the last capital city in enemy hands. On 9 May the Germans surrendered. It was over.

For emerging on the winning side Romania gained international recognition of her right to Transylvania and Dobrudja, but Northern Bukovina and Bessarabia were ceded to the USSR. In those two provinces the NKVD had returned to finish their murderous terror begun in 1940. They also had full sway throughout Romania, because the new Romanian government was a Soviet puppet. In order to find enough communists to make up this government the Soviets had to resort to Romanians born outside Romania proper and to Jews, Bulgarians and Hungarians born inside Romania.

The Volksdeutsch people were hounded mercilessly, in spite of the fact the bulk of them had remained loyal citizens. Their support during the war against Germany was not taken into consideration. As many as a million Volksdeutsch and other Romanian citizens were arrested or punished in some way by the NKVD.

Romanian military losses versus the Soviets and allies were 300,000 dead and 250,000 wounded. This includes those who died in Soviet captivity, e.g. of those captured 1942-43 only a tiny number survived to be released. Of the 130,000 captured in August 1944, 95,000 lived to be released.

Fighting alongside the Soviets August 1944 onwards the Romanians lost 60,000 killed and 90,000 wounded.

An estimated base figure of 10,000 dead among those pre-1940 Romanian citizens who served in the uniform of another nation (Hungarian, German, Soviet, Bulgarian) is as good as any.

Tens of thousands of citizens were killed in air raids, cross-fire and through war's dislocation. An absolute minimum of 75,000 died in NKVD custody. In addition to those who died at the hands of Antonescu's police for treason against him, 420,000 Jews and perhaps as many as 36,000 Gypsies were murdered by Romanians, Hungarians and Germans simply because of their race.

This comes to a total of just under 900,000 dead for the pre-1940 citizenship. In truth it must have been greater. Coupled with Romanian losses in World War I, these casualties devastated the nation's intellectual future to the point that even by the late 20th century Romania is a primitive land struggling to achieve basic human freedoms and social programmes that other Europeans take for granted.

See Index

RUSSIA

Status in 1938:	the cornerstone ethnicity of the USSR.
Government in 1938:	communist under Stalin dictatorship.
Population in 1938:	100,000,000
Religion:	Christian
Location:	Extreme Eastern Europe into Western Asia.

At first it may seem odd to look at Russians as a separate nation, when there is a chapter on the USSR below, but preceding and following the USSR the Russian state was a powerful entity. Moreover, Russians achieved a limited international recognition as an independent nation during World War II.

When the Russian communists attacked other nations to establish their empire, the USSR, they took their Russian ethnicity with them. Often the communist bosses in the newly conquered states were Russians either brought in for the purpose or recruited from the small group of Russian colonists already living there.

The fact that Stalin the Soviet dictator was not a Russian but a Georgian was irrelevant: after all Hitler wasn't a German, Napoleon wasn't a Frenchman and Catherine the Great wasn't a Russian. There was no doubt in anyone's mind that the expansion of the Soviet state was the expansion of a Russian empire under a new name.

And yet Russian nationalism was stifled by Stalin. Expressions of Russian culture were strictly monitored by the NKVD, Stalin's political police. The Orthodox religion was also monitored for in Russia it is as tied to Russian culture as Anglicanism is to English culture in England.

Hundreds of thousands of anti-communist Russians had fled the USSR following their military defeat in 1921, and as emigrés they lived all over the world. Tens of thousands lived peacefully in Germany. Indeed Hitler, the German dictator as of 1933, used them: they were allowed to join his stormtroopers, though their shirts were white not brown.

Without doubt the claims of the German woman Anna Anderson to be none other than Princess Anastasia Romanov and to have survived a communist murder squad would have been seriously investigated by Hitler's Gestapo. They must have concluded her claims to be false; otherwise Hitler would have used her for propaganda as he used other Russian aristocrats and military heroes. Some of the Russians were sent to the USSR as spies: known as V-men.

This policy seemed to fall flat on its face in August 1939 when Hitler made a treaty with Stalin, but in truth Hitler simply needed his rear covered while he dealt with France and Britain, which he did by June 1940. Thereafter he planned to turn on the USSR.

The Japanese had also found Russian emigrés useful and when they inherited 100,000 of them by conquering Manchuria in 1931 they established a brigade of Russian soldiers, which they used to test the Soviet border on occasion, most notably in 1938 and 1939.

When Germany invaded the USSR in June 1941 the V-men worked overtime. As German troops entered the USSR they found the villagers to be friendly. The Russians saw the Germans riding in vehicles bearing a Christian cross, bringing their own clergy, opening churches, holding mass and shooting at communists. What else were they to think, but that they were being liberated? At once they asked to help the Germans. Many units took on helpers, known as hiwis, i.e. rear-echelon soldiers, at first wearing armbands and paid out of unit funds.

The Germans also retained the ordinary Russian police and quickly formed a part-time village militia, known in north Russia as the Indigenous Fighting Bands and in southern Russia as the Order Service, whose job was to repel raids by communist partisans who had been sent behind German lines by the NKVD. Soon in north Russia the Germans created full-time anti-partisan units known as Security Detachments.

On 22 August at Mogilev an entire Soviet Cossack infantry regiment defected to the Germans asking to be allowed to fight the communists. Cossacks were Russians who lived in a semi-nomadic horse culture, sort of like Russia's version of wild west cowboys. Tested by the Germans, they proved loyal, were renamed the 102nd Regiment and sent to the front.

In November the Germans convinced Russian Colonel Sakharov to recruit a unit from among his fellow prisoners of war: he got 350 men at once. The Germans nicknamed the unit the Grey Head Battalion after its middle-aged commander.

By now the word Osttruppen (eastern troops) was being used to describe German-sponsored units consisting entirely of Soviet citizens. Colonel von Pannwitz, a Polish Volksdeutsch in the German Army, wanted to recruit Cossacks, who had been captured while serving in the Soviet army. Touring the prison camps he recruited several sotni, i.e. 100-man companies. Equipped by the Germans they patrolled the rear on horseback.

German Second Panzer Army went one step further, establishing an autonomous Russian state, Lokot, in the Orel-Kursk-Bryansk region. With a population of 1,700,000 the state was governed by Russians and had its own defensive militia. They introduced freedoms that under Stalin one could not even dream about.

By spring 1942 the German army, SS, air force and navy were using 100,000 hiwis, about half of them ethnic Russians. In April Hitler formally acknowledged the recruitment of hiwis, recognising a fait accompli. From now on they were fully uniformed and equipped with their own rank and medal structure. Where necessary they were armed.

The Osttruppen were also issued with German uniforms and treated more or less as 'Germans'. Soon hiwis and Osttruppen were distinguishable from Germans only by national shoulder patches, e.g. Russia, Ukrainia, Azerbaijan. Unlike Osttruppen hiwis were not authorised to wear the armed forces eagle patch.

With such support from Hitler himself many units expanded their use of Soviet citizens. Von Pannwitz restructured his Cossacks into two regiments and toured the Don, Kuban and Terek regions recruiting more Cossacks.

When the ruler of Lokot was assassinated by partisans, Bronislaw Kaminsky took over: half Russian, quarter Pole, quarter Jew and completely insane. He set up a full-time military unit with the rather presumptuous title of Russian National Liberation Army RONA to hunt down the partisans.

The Grey Head Battalion proved itself in action against partisans and was renamed the Reconnaissance Brigade, but called itself the Russian National People's Army RNNA.

In June the Druzhina entered the front line, a force of Russian commandos raised by the SS.

In the upper Don Valley Sergei Pavlov formed a Cossack unit under German police authority and by August they were patrolling the valley. This month Hitler formally recognised the Osttruppen, again simply acknowledging what his officers had already done.

German generals were becoming bolder in their friendliness with the Russians. General Wagner established an autonomous state in the Kuban ruled by Cossack leader Timophey Domanov with his own militia.

When the German Sixth Army was surrounded in Stalingrad it reported its ration strength at one stage as 253,600 Germans and 19,300 hiwis. There is no reason to assume the Sixth Army took on a higher percentage of hiwis than any other German formation. Thus it looks like about 7% of the fighting strength of the Germans in Russia in November 1942 were hiwis. This did not count hiwis serving at Army group level or in the rear. The 134th Division once reported that half its men were hiwis!

When the Soviet forces began to advance in November 1942 every man Jack was put into the line to stop them. This included a Russian horse cavalry unit, which fought Soviet horse cavalry at Kotelnikovo.

On the political front Russian politicians were constantly lobbying Hitler for recognition. He recognised a Cossack National Council to look after Cossack welfare. It was a first step. As a result von Pannwitz felt justified in expanding his two regiments into a division.

On 15 December 1942 Hitler appointed General Hellmich to be the first Inspector General of Osttruppen (not hiwis). His first job was to count them: the RNNA now had 10,000 Russians including artillery; von Pannwitz had 15,000 Cossacks (a few were Ukrainians); the RONA had 20,000 Russians; the Kuban Cossack Militia was a few thousand strong; and the Russian Order Service was quite large. Army Group North had got rid of its Indigenous Fighting Bands, but had expanded its Russian Security Detachments to several thousand men. Together with smaller units this made up about 55,000 Russian Osttruppen serving the German Army. Non-Russian citizens of the USSR made up another 495,000 Osttruppen serving the German Army.

The German police had 5,000 Russian hiwas (sentries) and Pavlov's Russian regiment which was currently guarding the headquarters of Field Marshal von Manstein. The SS had the 2,000 strong Russian Druzhina. Thus the SS and police had about 10,000 Russians. Non-Russian citizens of the USSR provided another 140,000 men for the SS and police.

It was impossible to accurately count the hiwis as they served on an individual basis. When Hitler pressed him for a number, Hellmich estimated 310,000. However, the Army Chief of Staff General Zeitzler, who wanted to play down the reliance on non-Germans, said there were no more than 220,000 hiwis. A compromise figure of 250,000, not counting the 20,000 or so lost at Stalingrad, is probably accurate. About a third of the hiwis were Russian.

Counting 40,000 Volksdeutsch citizens of the USSR, considered to be German soldiers (though they hadn't been to Germany for 200 years), all the hiwis and all the Osttruppen, a million Soviet citizens were serving in German uniform by early 1943, of which about 150,000 were Russians.

In February 1943 Hitler recognised the Russian Liberation Army ROA, led by General Vlasov who had been captured by Dutch troops the previous summer. Most of the Russian troops joined the ROA, which was more like a trade union than an army, for it could not give orders.

Jealous of the German Army's control of the ROA, Himmler had his SS execute 28 Russian officers for 'treason'. Such was life in Hitler's empire.

Von Pannwitz continued to recruit Cossacks and gained the entire 102nd Regiment.

As the Germans lost territory to the Soviet advance they actually gained more local recruits. Many Russians did not want to trust to the goodwill of the NKVD, who would soon know from their spies who had aided the Germans. Giving a German soldier a drink of water could be considered treason. Once on the road it was better for the refugees to put on German uniform. This gave them training, weapons, safety in numbers, money and secure accommodation for their families who travelled with them, e.g. practically the entire population of Lokot was on the move.

In June 1943 Hitler in one of his moods ordered no more recruitment of Soviet citizens. He was one of the first to disobey his own order. When Himmler suggested the Osttruppen be disbanded, the German generals hurriedly replied that currently of 253,000 men on anti-partisan sweeps only 15,000 were Germans. On another occasion in one of his rages Hitler ordered all Soviet citizens dismissed. His shocked generals stood up to him, saying that if that happened they might lose the war!

At the end of 1943 General Koestring succeeded Hellmich. The job was an eye-opener for the general: he learned that of 600,000 anti-partisan troops in the east 480,000 were Osttruppen. Additionally, tens of thousands of Osttruppen were fighting partisans in Yugoslavia, Albania, Greece, Italy and France. There were also Osttruppen at the front in the east and in Italy, and there were 350,000 hiwis. The Air Force even had Russian air units. The total was about 1,150,000 Soviet citizens in German uniform.

When the Germans evacuated the Crimea in May 1944 they lost 57,000 men, but 115,000 escaped, of which 28,000 were hiwis: more evidence of the extreme reliance of the Germans on Soviet citizens.

When the allies invaded France in June 1944 they not only had to fight Germans but Osttruppen: 123,000 of them, and that did not count hiwis who had accompanied their German parent unit from Russia to France. Cossacks held up the Americans on Omaha Beach.

On 1 August 1944 the 20,000-man German garrison of Warsaw, of which 3,400 were Osttruppen, was suddenly attacked by rebellious Poles. The garrison was reinforced by a regiment and six battalions of Germans and the Dirlewanger SS Brigade, of which 40% were Osttruppen, and by a brigade, three regiments and eleven battalions of Osttruppen. Clearly there was a major reliance on Soviet citizens.

On 28 January 1945, by which time not a square yard of Russian soil remained under his control, Hitler recognised Vlasov's ROA as a sovereign state. Vlasov at once called upon his ROA members to assemble into a real Russian Army. Many a German officer tried to hold onto his Russians, as sometimes he had little else. Still the 13,000 Russians of the 600th Panzergrenadier Division in Germany joined en masse and became the ROA 1st Division. The Russian 650th Panzergrenadier Division in Norway joined en masse and became the 2nd Division. The 599th Brigade of 13,000 Russians stationed in Denmark joined as the 3rd Division. The 4,000 Russian Osttruppen in the German Air Force became the nucleus of Vlasov's air force. Within days Vlasov had 54,000 troops.

The Cossack National Council now joined Vlasov and offered their 82,000 troops, though von Pannwitz's Cossacks (now a corps of two divisions currently fighting at the front in Yugoslavia) joined the SS instead.

By February there were 650,000 Osttruppen (counting Vlasov's men). As for hiwis, the German Navy reported they had 15,000, the Air Force 50,000, the Army and SS had 600,000: and this after 240,734 hiwi and Osttruppen casualties to date (not counting police casualties).

In March in Slovakia the Germans ordered the ROA 1st Division to attack. General Buniachenko, its commander, caused considerable consternation when he refused, saying he took orders from his own government. Vlasov stepped in and asked him to attack. This was done.

On 5 May Vlasov was frantic with worry. His ROA had assembled near Prague, where a million Germans were still fighting on, though almost all of Germany had been overrun by the enemy. In Prague the people had revolted. As a last chance to save his men, he accepted an offer from the Czech resistance to enter Prague and attack the Germans! His 1st Division quickly captured the airport and radio station. However, they then joined the Germans after a deal was made by which they could leave unhindered by the rebels to make their way to the west and surrender to the Americans.

It almost worked, but within days the Soviets, advancing from the north, had cut off the Russians. Vlasov and the others surrendered, hoping beyond hope for clemency from the NKVD.

On 19 May von Pannwitz managed to surrender his 39,000 Cossack soldiers and 12,000 civilian dependants to the British. Within days the British handed all of them, von Pannwitz included, to the NKVD.

In all 1,800,000 Soviet citizens had put on German uniform to fight communism. Actual Russians probably numbered about 200,000. A high number were caught by the Soviets or handed to the NKVD by the British. A smaller number were given to the NKVD by the Americans and French.
See Index

SAN MARINO

Status in 1944:	independent.
Government in 1944:	democracy.
Population in 1944:	14,000.
Make-up in 1944:	Italians; considerable number of refugees.
Religion:	Christian.
Location:	Italian Peninsula.

San Marino was a left-over from the days when the Italian peninsula consisted of nothing but city states. In the 1860s San Marino had honoured Abraham Lincoln

with citizenship – he graciously accepted.

By the 1920s the nation had been absorbed into Mussolini's fascist Italian dictatorship and its young men were forced to serve in the Italian Army.

When Mussolini was deposed in July 1943 the nation reaffirmed its independence and the Germans acknowledged this.

However, as the Germans steadily retreated north up the peninsula they reached the border in September 1944 and requested permission to place artillery observers in the country. The San Marinese refused, whereupon the Germans invaded. The 300-man San Marinese Army was defeated by the 993rd Panzergrenadier Regiment and the nation was occupied.

Just days later on the 18th the Indian 4th Division crossed the border at the Marano River and in two days kicked out the Germans. This was the most brief of Hitler's occupations.

On the 23rd San Marino formally declared war on Germany.
See Index

SOLOMON ISLANDS

Other names:	includes Bougainville, New Britain and New Ireland.
Status in 1939:	British colonies
Government in 1939:	British administration.
Population in 1939:	New Britain 80,000; Bougainville 40,000; New Ireland 19,000; remainder of islands 150,000.
Make-up in 1939:	a hundred languages spoken.
Religion:	tribal, mission Christians.
Location:	South West Pacific.

When Britain went to war against Germany in 1939 some natives entered the Solomon Islands Defence Force SIDF, but certainly many saw this as unnecessary. The few white settlers were quite convinced no German would come to the Solomons. They referred to the force as the Gilbert and Sullivan Defence Force (a play on the words Gilbert Islands and Solomon Islands).

In December 1941, when the Japanese suddenly began invading allied possessions in the Pacific, all laughter about island defence ceased.

On 23 January 1942 Japanese troops waded ashore on New Ireland, New Britain and Bougainville. Each island's defence unit went bush, i.e. headed into the mountains to begin a guerrilla war. Their most valuable contribution to the war effort, they were told, would be to keep radio contact with the allies and report what they saw.

From 300-mile long New Britain and slightly smaller New Ireland the Solomons stretched south east. First encountered was Bougainville 120 miles from New Ireland with the tiny Green Islands between. Further south-east just 80 miles was the New Georgia group, with the tiny Treasury Islands between and hefty Choiseul and Santa Isabel off to the north. Still further south east was the Guadalcanal group, Malaita, San Christobal and Rennell.

By 3 May the Japanese had reached as far as the Guadalcanal group, where they began to install a seaplane base on tiny Tulagi Island and an airfield on Guadalcanal itself. The Tulagi unit of the SIDF had only just been evacuated in time – five Chinese, fifteen Britons and Australians and 150 natives. On 80- by 40-mile Guadalcanal Island the local SIDF covertly watched the Japanese building the airfield.

The liberation of the Solomons began on 7 August 1942. This area of the world, beautiful at first sight is in fact hot, humid, malarial and insect ridden, where the grass was so sharp it could slice the skin. The 14,000 natives on Guadalcanal had so far kept their distance from the Japanese. This Godforsaken island was about to become one of the world's greatest battlefields.

On the 7th the US 1st Marine Division (reinforced) landed five battalions on Guadalcanal, one on Tulagi, one on Florida and three on tiny Gavutu-Tanambogo. The airfield was captured for a half dozen casualties and Florida offered no opposition, but the others had garrisons of Japanese who were prepared to fight to the death, and did. It took a week and 200 US casualties to destroy them.

The Japanese replied with air strikes and naval activity. The sea battles of Guadalcanal were to be as bloody as the land battles.

The Japanese rushed the Ichiki Regiment and the Yosuka Naval Landing Force to Guadalcanal to reconquer the airfield, which the Americans called Henderson Field. The American marines wiped them out, so the Japanese sent the 35th Brigade. By September the Americans had the 1st and 2nd Marine Divisions and the Japanese had reinforced with the 2nd and 38th Divisions. By November the Americans had brought in the 25th and Americal Divisions.

The SIDF reached the American lines and provided them with guides for reconnaissance patrols and local native civilians provided labour. The Americans were extremely grateful for the aid and they praised the native troops, which they called South Sea Scouts.

The Guadalcanal campaign ended in February 1943 when the Japanese evacuated. The entire affair had been fought along a 30-mile strip of the coast for the sake of that one airfield. It cost the Americans 1,600 killed and the Japanese 21,700 dead.

The Americans were consistently aided by the coast watchers, who had been purposely inserted or left behind on the enemy-occupied islands. Consisting usually of a lone Australian or Briton aided by local natives, they would radio to the allies every sighting of a ship or plane, its type and course. Whites and natives both knew that if caught they would be executed. Some were.

The Australians had also set up Z Force, made up of 1,500 whites and 6,000 natives who knew these islands (including New Guinea). Their mission was to make reconnaissance and sabotage raids.

The natives on these islands had grown to hate the Japanese. When possible they hid from the invader, for the Japanese often entered villages demanding labourers and any who refused would be bayoneted on the spot. Wherever Z Force raided they always found willing help from the local natives.

The next allied target for liberation was the New Georgia group, population 7,000. The SIDF unit here had waged guerrilla war against the Japanese for over a year, killing 54 by June 1943.

The Americans invaded New Georgia Island on 21 June 1943 at Segi town. Natives confirmed that the main enemy posts were the Kure Naval Landing Force and 229th Regiment at Munda, a 90-mile walk from Segi, and the 13th Regiment and Yokosuka Naval Landing Force at Vila town on Kolombangara Island. Within days the Americans had the 25th, 37th and 43rd Divisions ashore plus smaller units, all subjected to air raids.

It was July before the ground fighting began when US forces skipped along the coast to Munda. Quickly the Americans asked for South Sea Scouts and received a 200-man detachment of the SIDF drawn from New Georgia, Guadalcanal and other islands.

On 15 August the Americans put a regiment on Vella Lavella Island 50 miles northwest of New Georgia. The 400 Japanese on the island retreated and the Americans brought in New Zealand troops to follow and kill them.

By late August the Japanese survivors on New Georgia retreated to Arundel Island, just a few yards across the water. On the 27th the US forces followed them.

By 21 September Arundel was cleared. This left Kolombangara, but on the 29th the enemy garrison evacuated.

In the New Georgia group the SIDF had lost eleven killed and twenty wounded helping the Americans with their reconnaissance patrols. The allies suffered about 5,000 casualties.

A SIDF raiding party to the Treasury Islands brought back six natives to help allied planners and then they returned to organise a guerrilla force to fight the 250 Japanese. On 27 October the Treasuries were invaded by New Zealand troops and liberated for 226 casualties.

The next target was Bougainville, invaded by the US 3rd Marine Division at Cape Torokina on 1 November. The bulk of the 50,000 Japanese on the island, the 6th Division, 38th Brigade and the survivors from New Georgia and Guadalcanal, who outnumbered the 40,000 natives, were stationed on the opposite side of the 120- by 60-mile island. The local SIDF operated as guerrillas in the Jaba River area, so were not on hand to welcome the Americans. The welcome was provided by the Japanese 23rd Regiment. They kept the Americans in a beachhead of 7000 by 5000 yards, but this still gave the Americans two airfields.

In December the Americans invaded New Britain, taking the Japanese by surprise, who thought the Americans would clear Bougainville first. The US 112th Cavalry Regiment landed at Arawe on the 15th and the US 1st Marine Division at Cape Gloucester on the 26th. Opposition was light, for the bulk of the 90,000 personnel of the 17th Division, 39th and 65th Brigades and base units were at Rabaul at the opposite end of the 300-mile long island. After three weeks and a thousand casualties the Americans were happy with what they had and soon handed the beachhead to their 40th Division.

On New Britain Z Force, the SIDF guerrillas and the native population of 80,000 continued on as normal.

On both New Britain and Bougainville the Americans moved units through, a few at a time, almost using these front lines as a school. By late summer 1944 both were the preserve of Australian forces, which advanced and occupied large tracts of land. The Japanese suffered terribly, for they were cut off from supplies, began to starve and suffer from a myriad of diseases and were harassed by air raids and the guerrillas.

When Japan surrendered in August 1945 the true picture of Japanese conditions was revealed. Bougainville cost 2,850 American and 2,100 Australian casualties and the Japanese 20,000 dead. At war's end 23,750 gave up. New Britain cost the Americans 2,000 and the Australians 200 casualties and the Japanese 20,000 dead. At war's end 70,000 gave up. About 12,000 Japanese surrendered on the other islands that had not been invaded.

The allies could have liberated these islands without local help, but it would have been a far longer and bloodier affair. Native guides, soldiers, raiders, saboteurs, spies and coast watchers were priceless. Many an allied victory at sea, in the air and on land was a direct result of native intelligence reports.

See Index

SOUTH AFRICA

Other names:	includes Namibia.
Status in 1939:	dominion of the British Commonwealth.
Government in 1939:	democratic monarchy (whites only).
Population in 1939:	11,400,000.
Make-up in 1939:	9,000,000 in tribes, scores of languages;
	1,200,000 Afrikaners (i.e. Dutch and French stock)
	1,000,000 British stock;
	several thousand Indians and Chinese;
	a few thousand Germans.
Religion:	tribal and Christian.
Location:	Southern Africa.

When Britain declared war on Germany on 3 September 1939 there was an emergency debate in the South African parliament. Most whites were pro-British, but within the Afrikaner community there was an extreme right faction led by Balthazar Vorster and Hendrik Verwoerd, heavily supported by the Dutch Reformed Church, that had actually sent young men to Germany to be trained by Hitler's stormtroopers. Naturally they voted against war.

On the 6th General Jan Christian Smuts became Prime Minister, a man with great credibility in the British and Afrikaner communities: he had fought aganst the British 37 years earlier and for them 21 years earlier. He led parliament to declare war on Germany. Vorster and Verwoerd were arrested.

Now came the question: who would fight? The British armed forces already had a sprinkling of white South Africans, who had wanted to serve in a full-time service, e.g. as pilots. South Africa's own Air Force and Navy were tiny and the Army was just a reserve force. Moreover, the nation had little manpower to draw on because of the racist rule that kept blacks from handling weapons. To make things even more difficult the Dutch Reformed Church threatened to excommunicate anyone who fought the Nazi Germans. As a result, volunteers were accepted for service in Africa only, which in September 1939 was a pretty safe bet as there were no German forces in Africa. A

unit of police was accepted by the Army to make up the numbers.

On 10 June 1940 Italy declared war on Britain. Now there was real chance of South Africans getting into the war, for Italy had the African colonies of Ethiopia, Eritrea, Somaliland and Libya.

Within weeks South African planes were on their way to defend Egypt from an Italian invasion.

Late in the year the South African 1st Division arrived in Kenya to form a British expedition against the Italians. About 15% of the division's troops were black, all of them serving in a rear-echelon capacity. The division's 1st Brigade was loaned to the British 12th (black African) Division. The British Army had no qualms about putting blacks from their East and West Africa colonies into combat units.

Along Kenya's north border the South Africans skirmished with Italian native troops and it came to the attention of the British area commanders that the South Africans were woefully inadequate. On one occasion some South Africans retreated when a mob of natives walked past. At El Waq they and British Army black African soldiers defeated the enemy, but their performance was still poor. It seemed that the South African government, believing its men would never actually fight anyone, had discarded all thoughts of training them.

In February 1941 the British attacked out of Kenya into Somaliland. At Mega the 1st Division defeated enemy native soldiers.

At Gobaen on the Jaba River in Somaliland the South Africans met their first serious opposition as they tried for five days to cross the river in the face of resistance by Italian Somali troops. One element finally managed it and beat off counter-attacks for 24 hours. South African planes and armoured cars were of paramount importance here. When the enemy withdrew, the South Africans jumped into trucks and chased them.

The British expedition conquered Somaliland by use of the truck, and in March everyone prepared to invade Ethiopia. The 1st Brigade was now attached to the British 11th (black African) Division.

On 18 April the 1st Brigade was surprised by an Italian counter-attack at Kombolchia and lost nine killed and 30 wounded, their worst casualties to date. However, joined by thousands of Ethiopian guerrillas they attacked on the 26th and rounded up 8,000 prisoners, many of them bedridden with wounds and sickness.

After a month and several hundred miles of driving, the South Africans were sick to death of staring at the Ethiopian countryside, a primitive trackless wasteland that seemed to go on forever.

On 13 May the 1st Brigade entered an actual front line for the first time, at Amba Alagi, where a few thousand Italians and natives were holed up. In a disciplined attack the South Africans captured a major feature, the Triangle, and on the 19th the enemy surrendered.

All South Africans were now ordered to Egypt, where the enemy was knocking on the border door. One South African fighter squadron had done well over Egypt, strafing enemy columns for nine months and shooting down fifty planes. By late 1941 there were six South African squadrons in Egypt.

The 1st Division (with its 1st Brigade returned) was ordered to take part in Operation Crusader, a British attempt to relieve Tobruk in Libya, surrounded on land by an Italian-German Army since April.

On 17 November the offensive began with South African armoured cars leading the British 7th Armoured Division. Within a day they had broken through and were shooting up aircraft at Sidi Rezegh airfield.

On the 22nd the divisions's 5th Brigade captured a plateau from a German force and then camped. Next day the lone South African brigade felt much better when the 7th Armoured Division joined them, especially as that same afternoon the plateau was attacked by the 15th and 21st Panzer and Ariete Armoured Divisions. However, before dusk the British division drove off, abandoning the South Africans. Disgusted, almost 3,000 men put up their hands in surrender.

On the 24th the 1st Brigade at Taieb el Esem was attacked by the Ariete, but here British tanks stayed with them and they won the day.

In December the fresh South African 2nd Division entered the trenches facing the Italian Savona Division and a German battle-group at Bardia-Lower Sollum-Halfaya Pass. They patrolled nightly and made a few light attacks. Artillery salvoes were constant.

On 2 January Bardia surrendered, Lower Sollum on the 11th and Halfaya on the 17th: a total of 13,800 Italians and 4,000 Germans were taken prisoner.

In the air during the winter the three South African fighter and three bomber squadrons had been extremely busy. They lost 65 planes shot down.

In May 1942 the Italians-Germans launched a major offensive in Libya. The nine South African squadrons in the area went into action at once. The 1st Division, holding a forward line, was attacked by the Trento and Sabratha Divisions.

After three weeks of battle the division was given permission to withdraw. They had courageously held their own, despite German armour having defeated other allied units in their rear, and it was evident they were a far different unit than that which first fought in Kenya.

As the German armour continued to advance, General Klopper was told to take his South African 2nd Division and hold Tobruk. The previous year this port city had withstood a siege in Italian hands for sixteen days and another in allied hands for 240 days. Therefore, the South Africans were not worried, especially as they were reinforced by a British tank brigade and an Indian infantry brigade, plus the garrison already had rear-echelon troops.

On the 20th the defenders watched the enemy arrive, and that very afternoon they were attacked by five Italian and three German divisions, albeit worn-down divisions.

Next morning Italian engineers cleared a path for German tanks, which broke through. Before noon Klopper surrendered!

At first no one believed the order. Some refused to obey and fought a few hours more. By afternoon the guns were silent. The prisoners totalled 200 Czechs, 2,500 Indians, 10,720 South Africans (of which 1,760 were black) and 21,600 British: a total of 35,000 men, over a hundred tanks, scores of guns, 2,000 vehicles, warehouses full of supplies and an intact port.

South Africa's military reputation, such as it was, also went into the bag. The shortcomings of South African troops in eastern Africa had been glossed over and hidden from the public. The surrender of the 5th Brigade during Crusader had been blamed on the British who abandoned them. The capture of the Italians and Germans at Bardia et al by the 2nd Division was hailed as a great victory, but they had in fact surrendered only because they had been surrounded for two months and were out of food and ammunition. The South African surrender of Tobruk could not be kept from the public. The surrender of a division with everything going for it after just seventeen hours of battle suggested serious weaknesses in South Africa's military structure.

The 1st Division was still fighting for its life, having dug in at a line drawn in the sand at Alamein. On their right was the sea, on their left five miles of desert to the next unit. It was not much of a defensive position. Fortunately, when the enemy approached on 1 July artillery managed to keep him at bay.

Over the next few weeks the enemy tried to break through the line by choosing one unit to concentrate against on any given day, and on the 13th it was the turn of the South Africans. They repelled the attack. Later the South Africans were moved into the desert.

In the air during the May-July battles the South African Air Force in Egypt lost 90 aircraft, over 60%.

South African planes were also in action against the French on Madagascar, where a British force had invaded in May 1942. This gigantic island was seen as a possible link between the Germans-Italians and the Japanese. A Japanese submarine did raid British ships in one of the island's harbours and a Japanese plane flew over Durban, South Africa on a reconnaissance.

In September the British decided they had to have all of Madagascar, and if the French resisted, so be it. The 7th Brigade and an armoured car unit both of the South African Army were brought to the island and they proceeded to advance from Diego Suarez down extremely long jungle roads overcoming half-hearted rearguards. Another South African armoured car unit aided British black African troops to advance from Majunga inland and on the 29th a battalion of the 7th Brigade landed at Tulear and began advancing inland.

In November the French gave up. South African losses were a few score killed and wounded.

The men of the South African 1st Division, who had had a quiet August at Alamein, were rudely awakened from their daydreams by an artillery barrage on the 31st. An hour later they were attacked by the Trento Division and German Ramcke Parachute Brigade. Yet they held their positions. After a couple of days the shooting faded to a desultory skirmish and on 7 September it was quiet again.

In the air the action had been quite ferocious: the South Africans lost 39 planes. By now of the 96 allied squadrons in Egypt, eleven were South African.

On the evening of 23 October it was the turn of the allies to go over to the offensive at Alamein. A tremendous artillery barrage shattered the night's serenity and just twenty minutes later the infantry and combat engineers of seven divisions and two brigades began walking forward: the South Africans went into action against their old antagonists the Trento Division. By dawn they were pinned down by murderous fire.

The following afternoon South African armoured cars scouted for the British 1st Armoured Division which was hoping to break through. Enemy resistance continued to be very effective.

It was only on 4 November that the enemy called it quits and began to retreat.

The twelve-day affair cost the 1st Division just under a thousand casualties. Fifty South African planes were shot down.

South African flyers had proven themselves time and again, and at last on the Alamein line South African troops had done the same. On-the-job training had honed them into a lean fighting formation.

South African armoured cars chased the enemy out of Egypt and right across Libya. Beginning in March they scouted for British armour in the Tunisian campaign.

The South African government had been forced into a total rethink about the state of their Army. They decided to put their best eggs in one basket: the 6th Armoured Division, made up of volunteers to fight in Europe. Combat veterans were brought into the unit and they were made responsible for training the new guys. The unit would have much more punch than a British armoured division: a strength of 20,500, of which 3,000 were blacks. In addition 1,500 white Rhodesians were attached.

The division, which took the nickname Springboks (a name for all white South Africans), went into action in Sicily in August 1943. The enemy was already on the run and evacuated on the 16th. The Springboks did not get a chance to show their mettle.

Indeed the next year was frustrating as the allies in Italy were stuck in the mud: Italy with its narrow, winding mountain roads was no place for an armoured division, but the British insisted on keeping the formation here without using it.

Only with the allied break out in May 1944 and the capture of Rome on 5 June, were the Springboks finally unleashed. Meeting a strong German force at Viterlo the tanks charged straight through and left it to the division's infantry. Next day the tanks trapped a German formation at Monte Fiascone and rounded them up in a day. The division fought a successful three-day encounter at Bagnioregio. By late June they were mopping up along the eastern shore of Lake Trasimene.

On 17 July the lead tanks reached the Arno River to find German engineers rigging a bridge for demolition. Shooting them, the tanks crossed. They were now further ahead than any allied unit in Italy and were ordered to wait.

On the 23rd they charged ahead again, crossed the Greve River and ran into tough resistance, so much so they had to call for reinforcements for the first time.

At San Cascaiano the division was counter-attacked by Tiger tanks – the allies had nothing to match the Tiger, so the Springboks withdrew over the river.

On the 27th they crossed the river at Mercatale, made it to Impruneta on the 28th and advanced to the Ema River by 3 August. Next day they drove into Florence. Thousands of laughing, ecstatic civilians informed the Springboks that the Germans were still in the city on the north bank of the river.

The division was now transferred from British Eighth Army to US Fifth Army and placed in reserve on the west coast.

In late September they went into action again, reaching Lagaro on 3 October. They were now advancing in pouring rain.

On the 8th they ran into the 16th SS Panzergrenadier Division at Ripoli-Monte Vigese. This was quite a battle and was followed by another equally sanguinary affair at Monte Stanco until the 13th, and then by a similar engagement at Monte Pezza until the 20th and then Monte Salvaro. The Germans were fighting every hour of the day and night for every building, every copse of trees, every farm. On the 28th Fifth Army called a halt to the slaughter.

By now the South African Air Force had eleven squadrons supporting the Eighth Army in Italy; two supporting the Fifth Army in Italy; three attacking the enemy in Greece; three attacking the enemy in the Balkan nations; two bombing Austria and Germany; and four patrolling the Mediterranean. Other squadrons were patrolling the sea from African bases searching for German submarines.

At sea a few South African vessels were escorting allied convoys.

In Italy the Springboks waited all winter for action, but did not get the go-ahead until 14 April 1945. Driving into the enemy rear: the divisional column of jeeps, trucks, bulldozers, mobile cranes, armoured cars, tanks, and self-propelled guns was thirty miles long; they entered Bologna alongside other formations on the 20th.

Having inched their way through the delirious crowds, who jumped onto the vehicles to kiss and shake hands, they reached the open countryside and charged forward again. The enemy was on the run and on 2 May surrendered.

Generally speaking, South Africa's military contribution to the war has been overlooked.

The lack of international recognition is understandable, because the South African Navy was small, the Army never had more than two divisions in action at a time, and the Air Force, though strong, was under British orders and was therefore denied publicity to the advantage of British squadrons.

The contribution was made by men with integrity, who had to put up with a hostile minority at home, a government that apparently did not take war seriously and a recruitment base of just over two million whites.

South Africa's losses were 3,863 killed and 14,363 wounded.

See Index

SPAIN

Other names:	
Status in 1940:	independent.
Government in 1940:	dictatorship of General Franco.
Population in 1940:	25,800,000.
Make-up in 1940:	Spaniards c 18,800,000; Catalans c 6,000,000; Basques c 500,000; Gallegos c 500,000.
Religion:	Christian.
Location:	South Western Europe

In one sense Spain fought World War II before it happened. The Spanish Civil War of 1936-39 has been called a dress rehearsal for World War II. On one side were General Franco's fascists, extreme nationalists, devout Christians, Mussolini's Italians and Hitler's Germans; and on the other were communists, socialists, Stalin's Soviet troops, Catalans and Basques. Britons and Americans also fought on an individual basis for Franco's side and in their own battalions for his opponents.

By March 1939 when Franco won the war the nation was in an absolute shambles with hundreds of thousands of casualties, a devastated economy and ruined cities.

Six months later Germany was at war with France and Britain and Hitler called in his marker: he had aided Franco with about 2,000 ground troops in a tank unit and with airpower, not to mention a mountain of equipment. Franco should help him now.

But Franco refused. He could hardly do differently. His nation was in no mood for another war, nor was it capable. It was bad enough that his merchant ships had to run the gauntlet of the British Royal Navy. What Spain needed now was peace.

Many of the defeated Spanish leftists had fled into France and now some of them joined the French, either the Foreign Legion as fighters or the Army as labourers. About 2,000 joined British Army labour companies.

In June 1940 France was overrun by the Germans. Those Spaniards in the French Army who were not caught, hid among the population. When the British evacuated they only took 10% of their Spaniards with them: the others were abandoned like so many used tools!

When a French anti-German clandestine resistance movement was formed some Spaniards joined it. Catalans and Basques were especially useful for they spoke the languages of both sides of the French-Spanish border and could smuggle goods into France and endangered agents and downed allied fliers into Spain.

Franco's police were always on the lookout for these agents and allied fliers: what they wanted from them was information about Spaniards serving in the French Resistance, for occasionally these Spaniards crossed into Spain to ambush and commit sabotage.

In June 1941 Germany invaded the USSR. Franco was now between a rock and a hard place. He could not afford war with Britain, though his people longed to reclaim Gibraltar conquered by the British two centuries earlier. Yet the USSR was the lair of the communist wolf, the nation that had supported the leftists in the civil war, the champion of atheism and the arch enemy of the Catholic church.

He compromised. He asked for a few volunteers to join the Germans, hoping the British would not notice them. He also agreed to let Italian underwater swimmers use his soil to raid British shipping in Gibraltar harbour.

General Munoz-Grandes found he had enough volunteers to form a division,

18,700. Uniformed by the Germans (though retaining a blue shirt) and equipped and trained by them at Grafenwoehr, the Germans called it the 250th Infantry Division. The Spaniards called it the Blue Division.

The Blue Air Legion of five fighter squadrons was formed to fly alongside the Germans.

The Spaniards got some idea of the task ahead of them when they were ordered to walk to the ever moving front: it took them two months and 600 miles to reach the sound of the guns!

In October 1941 the division was assigned a 30-mile sector from the Volkhov River to Lake Ilmen. This was awesome, for 30 miles is far too much for one division. Combat began on the 12th with a day of victory, followed by two days of advance to take Dubrovka, and then three weeks of defending it against heavy counter-attacks.

In Passad a Soviet riposte trapped men. After three days 200 wounded were brought out on snow sleds, but the others held on.

On 4 December the division was attacked by twice their number in temperatures of -40°C, but they held their ground, though by now infantry casualties were 18%. In one area they came across some of their wounded, who had been captured by the Soviets and tortured to death. It was just like old times from the civil war!

A sudden rush forward pushed a Soviet infantry battalion onto a frozen river where Spanish machine gunners gleefully mowed them down.

In January 1942, when the German 290th Division was cut off, a team was put together to break through to them: 370 Spaniards on skis and horse-drawn sleds with 70 Russian hiwis (helpers). In temperatures of -55°C they crossed frozen Lake Ilmen: in the two-day trip 102 men were maimed by frostbite. Joined by 40 Latvians the team fought a skirmish.

Casualties and the weather whittled down the team until by the 20th there were but twenty-two Spaniards still standing. Nonetheless, they joined in a Latvian attack, after which there were only fourteen still standing. Such was war on the Russian Front.

In 1942 the Germans launched a major spring offensive as the snow thawed. The Blue Division attacked east of the Keresti River. At Bolshoye Shamolshe they encountered stubborn resistance: the reconnaissance battalion had 50% casualties. Then they took Maloye Shamoshe, where for 274 casualties they killed several hundred and took 5,097 prisoners.

The Spanish government decided that a year on the Russian front was long enough and General Munoz-Grandes and his original members were brought home, so that the division now consisted of newcomers, those who had already arrived to replace casualties and a few diehards who asked for a second tour.

In August General Infantes led the division into line near Leningrad on an eighteen-mile sector. The outgoing Germans told them it was quiet here: they had only been losing twenty men a day.

On 21 January 1943 a battalion was flattened into the snow by a heavy Soviet assault. After 24 hours only 70 of the 800 men reached safety and some of them were wounded. Over the next three days 42 of those were lost!

On 10 February the Blue Division caught the brunt of a major Soviet offensive and within hours everyone from infantrymen to cooks and laundry troops were retreating in a blinding snowstorm. A German-Belgian-Latvian counter-attack saved them, but the division had to fight for another week to hold their new positions along the Ishora River. When the Soviets at last retraced their steps, the Spaniards counted 3,645 casualties. Their infantry companies were at quarter strength.

In March the division repelled an attack.

In May the division shrank its sector to just fifteen miles, thereby reducing 'normal' attrition to just twelve to fifteen men a day.

On 6 October 1943 the division was withdrawn and the men informed they were all going home. Evidently the British had finally noticed the division and had complained. Franco did not explain that the real reason was that Italy had disintegrated into civil war, the Germans were losing the war and he feared a British-American amphibious invasion.

About 30,000 men had served in the division. Its casualties were 3,934 killed, 8,466 wounded and 326 missing. The air legion had strafed many a Soviet column and had shot down 156 planes for a loss of 22 flyers.

However, Franco compromised again. A new unit, the Blue Legion of three battalions, was formed for anti-partisan duty behind German lines. Some of its members were veterans of the Blue Division. The legion was sent to the Estonian-Russian border.

In December 1943 the legion was rushed to the front by the Germans, in violation of its contract, and ordered to hold six and half miles of front at Kostovo. With just one rifleman for every fifteen feet of snow the legion could not hope to repel a major attack, yet that is exactly what happened on 25 December, and they held their holes in the snow, shooting Soviet infantry as fast as they could reload. Over the days and then weeks the killing became mechanical as they lay there freezing, dreaming of the Costa del Sol.

Then they were ordered to retreat: the worst kind of retreat, in a blizzard. They stumbled one step at a time for thirteen days. Reaching safety they were reassigned to watch the Estonian coast.

On 21 March under British diplomatic pressure Franco recalled the legion. Spain would no longer participate in the war.

However, individual Spaniards continued to work for the Germans. Thousands were employed in German-occupied France. Many laboured at the submarine pens at La Pallice and Bordeaux. The Germans commented on their efficiency and bravery during air raids.

Almost a thousand Spaniards joined the Waffen SS. Formed into a battalion they were assigned to a division of devoutly catholic Belgians (a good move).

In February 1945 the Spanish SS fought a major struggle against Soviet hordes at Stargard in eastern Germany. Forced to retreat, they suffered badly at Lindenburg holding a rearguard for the Belgians.

By April the surviving 200 Spanish SS were trapped in Berlin. Almost all died there.

In April 1954 the last of 248 Spanish prisoners of the Soviets were released, 22 of them SS.

They came home to a different world. By this date the British were partners with a German Army in an anti-Soviet alliance, their citizens beginning to visit Spain for its beaches. No one seemed to mind that Franco was still in charge, the only fascist dictator who made war on the allies and lived to tell the tale.

See Index

SUDAN

Other names:	Anglo-Egyptian Sudan
Status in 1939:	British colony.
Government in 1939:	British administration.
Population in 1939:	8,000,000.
Make-up in 1939:	Arabs in the north; many tribes in the south.
Religion:	Moslem in the north; Christian and tribal in the south.
Location:	North East Africa.

Two things made Sudan's worthless desert valuable to the British once war broke out with Germany in 1939 and Italy joined Germany in June 1940: through it flowed the Nile, the life-giver of Egypt, and whoever controlled the flow controlled Egypt; secondly it separated the two Italian colonies of East Africa and Libya.

There was another reason, less obvious but influential: Britain had fought long and hard to conquer the Sudan in the previous century and it was a matter of honour to keep it: indeed personal honour, for Churchill, the British Prime Minister, had fought in that conflict.

Sudanese joined the British Army either as labourers in pioneer companies or as fighting men in the Sudan Defence Force (SDF). Their officers were British.

At Metemma-Gallabat on the eastern Sudanese border there was shooting on 14 June between the SDF and Italians: the war for Africa had begun.

On the 28th 30 SDF troops and some Ethiopian guerrillas entered Ethiopia and ambushed an Italian column, but the affair backfired and the SDF had to run for it. An inauspicious beginning to say the least.

Within days SDF troops captured an Italian outpost on the Gilo River, but others lost Gallabat; camel-mounted SDF troops sniped at the Italians; at Kassala SDF and British inflicted 157 casualties on the Italians; at Karora and Kurmuk Sudanese police were overrun by the enemy.

Though these incidents were hardly world shattering, Churchill ordered Khartoum, Sudan's capital, strenuously guarded and sent reinforcements to Sudan.

In January 1941 the British invaded Italian East Africa from Sudan. SDF troops scouted for the columns. Additionally, a British officer, Major Wingate, had formed a few hundred SDF and a thousand or so Ethiopians into Gideon Force, which invaded Ethiopia in February. Within days, however, the Ethiopians ignored Wingate's discipline and joined the guerrillas and on the 27th he was almost caught when an attack on Burie went wrong. He and the SDF fell back.

Fortunately, the Italians retreated in the face of guerrilla pressure. The SDF followed and overcame several rearguards.

From 24 to 28 March near Debra Markos the SDF and the guerrillas were involved in a major battle as ten Italian battalions counter-attacked. Even with a mob of guerrillas on hand the SDF were hard put to retain their mountain positions. The Italians withdrew.

At Addis Dera Wingate negotiated with an Italian column. If they surrendered to his SDF he would guarantee their safety from the guerrillas. This was agreed and 1,100 Italian and 7,000 native soldiers gave up.

By October the SDF was still acting as scouts for the British in Ethiopia, and Sudanese pioneers were breaking their backs hauling supplies, grading roads, repairing captured encampments etc. A few Italian outposts were still holding out and the British had insufficient manpower to overcome them, bar the mass of guerrillas. The SDF was put into major attacks at Gondar, Kulkaber and Chilga, suffering badly on 11 November at the latter.

The British decided to concentrate on Kulkaber and ordered Sudanese pioneers to drop their shovels, pick up their rifles and attack as a feint. The trick worked, the

enemy reserves went to meet them, and the SDF and two British Army black African brigades attacked elsewhere. The position was taken: 1,648 Italian and 775 native troops surrendered. Days later the last Italians in East Africa capitulated.

SDF patrols had been penetrating southern Libya since 1940 and in November 1941 an SDF column captured Jalo oasis. SDF were used to garrison several captured oases.

In spring 1942 they had to abandon Jalo in the face of an Italian advance, but they returned to it in September. Unfortunately, these Italians were not as obliging and after a five day fight the SDF retired.

About 10,000 Sudanese served in the British Army during the war and performed exceedingly well under British officers.
See Index

SWAZILAND

Status in 1939:	British possession.
Government in 1939:	British administration.
Population in 1939:	186,000.
Make-up in 1939:	Siswati.
Religion:	tribal, mission Christians.
Location:	Southern Africa.

In 1939 when Britain declared war on Germany she asked her colonial subjects to volunteer for military service. About 3,600 Swazis joined the Army and were placed in nine pioneer companies under white officers, whose job was manual labour such as road grading, trench digging, truck unloading.

They served in the rear areas, their only action an occasional air raid.

This changed when the allies returned to mainland Europe in September 1943. Landing at Salerno with US Fifth Army in the teeth of heavy German fire were thirteen pioneer companies, one of them of Swazis. Obviously the Swazi's dedication to duty must have impressed someone for them to be entrusted to such a crucial battle to work on the beach under fire.

On day three of the battle German tanks reached the beach and the allied pioneers had to fight them, 139 being killed before other units restored the situation. The Swazis remained under fire for three weeks.

As the infantry moved inland the Swazi company followed them to work closely behind the front.

In January 1944 the Swazi company was chosen for another amphibious invasion, Anzio, and was the only non-British pioneer company on the beach. They worked under shellfire for four months. The Swazis and four British companies at Anzio suffered 128 casualties and received a unit citation for bravery from President Roosevelt.

The Swazis certainly proved themselves. They served in the breakout to Rome, the advance up Italy and the struggle for the Gothic Line. In late 1944 eight more companies of Swazis arrived in Italy. They spent the winter preparing the allies for the spring offensive.

The Swazi people could be justly proud of their men's contribution towards the destruction of fascism.

See Index

SWEDEN

Status in 1939:	independent.
Government in 1939:	democratic monarchy.
Population in 1939:	6,500,000.
Make-up in 1939:	Swedes; a few thousand Lapps in the north.
Religion:	Christian.
Location:	Northern Europe

Almost all books about World War II do not even mention Sweden and those that do, do not discuss the pros and cons of her involvement, and that is exactly how the Swedes like it.

Yet in 1939 things did not look so trivial when war broke out between Britain and Germany. Sweden supplied iron ore to Germany. Indeed this was Germany's number one import and without it the factories of Essen, Wuppertal, Solingen etc. could never have produced the tanks, guns and planes that made Hitler's fighting machine.

Half the ore was carried in Swedish ships. In the depths of winter when many of the ports were iced-up the iron ore was transported by rail across Norway to Narvik and thence along the Norwegian coast to Germany in German ships. Swedish vessels also delivered timber to Germany.

Having made the conscious decision to supply Hitler with such a crucial element of his war-making capacity the Swedes could hardly shut off the tap when Germany was involved in war with Britain and France, without incurring Hitler's wrath, which no Swede wanted to do, despite the fact that Swedish ships were thus made a target for British mines, submarines and aircraft. After all, when trading in British waters the ships were subjected to harassment by German forces. In the first ninety days of the war nine vessels were lost.

Now came another spice to the recipe: the USSR invaded Finland. Friendly relations existed between Sweden and Finland, because they were neighbours and because a tenth of Finland's population were racial Swedes. Sweden was not strong enough to challenge the USSR, but couldn't stand by and watch Finland fight the bully alone. A compromise was reached when Sweden allowed 8,000 of her men to volunteer for the Finnish armed forces.

It was March 1940 before they were trained and could see action, by which time Finland was surrendering. Most of the volunteers came home, but a thousand or so remained in Finnish uniform as they did not trust the Soviets to honour the peace terms.

Meanwhile the British had been worrying themselves silly over the iron ore, at one time contemplating an invasion of Sweden through Narvik to destroy the mines, under the guise of aiding Finland.

Hitler knew they were up to something and ordered an invasion of Norway in April 1940 in part to secure his winter iron ore route. The presence of German forces in Norway would also put pressure on Sweden.

Sweden was well and truly hemmed in. On the one hand, after April, German troops were on her western border and on the other hand a beaten Finnish Army was all that stood between her and the USSR.

During the Norwegian campaign German troops were cut off at Narvik. The Swedes gained a diplomatic favour from Germany by sending supplies to the trapped Germans: they were only 30 miles from the Swedish border.

At the same time Swedish border guards did not turn away obvious refugees from Hitler's police state. This laxity did not apply to uniformed personnel, though. Allied airmen and sailors who accidentally reached Swedish soil were interned, pleasantly but securely. Swedish fighter planes and flak guns were always on the lookout for allied aircraft lost or crippled and looking for a flat place to land.

In June 1940 Hitler conquered the iron ore mines of France, meaning he should have been less dependent on Sweden, but in truth his greed made him as dependent as ever.

He informed the Swedes why he needed the extra iron ore when he invited them to join him in a crusade against the USSR. The Swedes politely declined to overtly make war, but they were willing to help in many other ways: iron ore would still be available; the Swedish merchant fleet, despite suffering mounting losses, would still be available; the Swedes would not complain if the Swedish battalion of the Finnish Army attacked the USSR; the Swedes would allow supplies bound for German forces in northern Russia to cross Swedish territory by rail; they would also allow the soldiers themselves to cross Sweden by rail; Swedish warships would escort their troop transports from Germany to Sweden; and lastly Sweden would not object to Swedish volunteers joining the German forces.

Several hundred Swedish volunteers joined the Germania Regiment of the 5th SS Division.

On 22 June 1941 the Germans invaded the USSR. Their 163rd Division crossed to Sweden escorted by Swedish warships and thence went by rail to northern Finland to join the Finns who were also invading the USSR. The Swedish battalion of the Finnish Army besieged the Soviet base at Hango.

The axis forces were successful and in September the Finns called a halt. They had reached the suburbs of Leningrad and that's as far as they wanted to go. In December the Soviets evacuated Hango. The Swedes now asked for the release of the Swedish battalion, as its mission had been accomplished, and the Finns complied.

However, by the summer of 1943 it was obvious that Germany was not going to win the war against Britain or the USSR. The Swedes wondered how to gain allied acceptance without incurring Hitler's anger too strongly. In July they made their first move: they denied the German Army in north Russia access to the Swedish rail network for resupply.

They also decided not to allow any more Swedes to join the German forces. The Swedish SS had been transferred to the 11th SS Division and as their casualties were no longer being replaced their numbers shrank.

Another move the Swedes made was to recruit several thousand Danish and Norwegian refugees in their country into 'police' units and train and equip them for the day when those two countries would be free of German occupation. This seemingly pro-allied move, was false for the personnel would not be allowed to actually fight Germans.

In early 1944 the Swedes became bolder, telling Hitler that he could still have his iron ore and timber, but Swedish ships would no longer transport them to Germany. So far their 'neutral' merchant fleet had lost 172 ships sunk and 26 captured. Also a Swedish Navy patrol boat and a submarine had been blown up by mines.

This was a serious blow to the Germans, for their merchant fleet had also been devastated. It became still more aggravating when the Germans lost the French iron ore mines in the autumn.

In Budapest when that city was besieged by Soviet forces in winter 1944-45 the Swedish embassy staff with the approval of the Swedish government issued phoney passports to as many Jews as possible, who were in dire danger of being executed by Hungarian and German Nazis. No less than 35,000 were saved. Thankfully, the Swede Raoul Wallenberg was able to convince the local SS to disobey Hitler's order to kill all Jews.

When the Soviets captured the city they released the Jews, but arrested and murdered Wallenberg on the grounds that if he would do that for refugees from nazism, maybe he would also do it for refugees from communism?

In March 1945 the Swedish government turned a blind eye when Norwegian commandos used Swedish soil to raid German installations in Norway.

After Germany surrendered in May 1945 the Swedes let their Danish and Norwegian 'police' into those nations to round up capitulating Germans.

During the war 202 Swedish merchant vessels were sunk and scores damaged. So many mines had been laid about her coast that over the next two years seven more ships were sunk by them.

See Index

SWITZERLAND

Other names:	Helvetia.
Status in 1939:	independent.
Government in 1939:	democracy.
Population in 1939:	4,700,000.
Make-up in 1939:	German-speakers 3,470,000; French-speakers 940,000; Italian-speakers 190,000; Romansch-speakers 100,000.
Religion:	Christian.
Location: central	Europe.

The reasons why one would expect Switzerland to have become involved in World War II were that she sat in the middle of the belligerents and had a linguistic affinity with three of them. But the Swiss are Swiss, not French or Germans or Italians. The numbers of Swiss who volunteered for the belligerent armies was small, a few hundred, most of them into the German forces as they had been swayed by German and Swiss fascist propaganda.

However, the Swiss did put on uniform, when war broke out in 1939, their own, as mass mobilisation was ordered. Their mission was to patrol the borders and skies and keep the nation out of the fighting.

Occasionally German planes overflew Swiss airspace. However, it was British and American aircraft that caused the most problems by flying over Switzerland, sometimes quite deliberately to shorten a route and thus save fuel. As a result the Swiss government introduced the blackout in November 1940.

Swiss flak gunners and fighter pilots always opened fire. In one incident an American fighter squadron bounced a Swiss squadron – understandable as the Swiss were flying German-built Messerschmidt Bf 109s.

During the war three Swiss planes were shot down by German fighters. Swiss fighters shot down seven German aircraft. Swiss fighters also shot down eight allied planes, and flak gunners shot down nine.

The Swiss had to fight to protect their neutrality, because allied planes often bombed Swiss territory by mistake, the most serious incidents being British raids on Basel and Zurich in December 1940, and again in May 1943, and American raids on Schaffhausen in January 1944 and on Rafz and Stein in February.

One of the many problems was caused by allied bombers, crippled by German action, wandering over Switzerland looking for a place to land. No less than 250 crashed or force-landed in Switzerland. One of them crashed into the house of Max Huber, the President of the International Red Cross. Fortunately he was not home. Foreign airmen were medically treated and interned.

In October 1944 the ground war came near as American and French troops chased Germans past the Swiss border. Swiss troops dodged artillery shells to mark out the border.

In April 1945 Germans, retreating in Italy, reached the Swiss border, hoping to hide in the Alps to avoid the allies. Swiss troops refused to allow any Germans or fascists into Switzerland, even unarmed refugees. Their diligence assisted the allies.

Of great importance was the activity of the International Red Cross based in Switzerland. Swiss members worked tirelessly to aid prisoners of war and civilian refugees. Though their inspections of camps were often controlled by the camp authorities, without them the conditions of the prisoners would have been even more intolerable than they were.

The Swiss people hosted upwards of 400,000 refugees, a tremendous number for such a small nation. The German government constantly tried to bring Switzerland into the war as a partner, therefore Swiss counter-intelligence was always on the lookout for trouble. The authorities executed fifteen Swiss, a Frenchman and a Lichtensteiner for spying.

See Index

SYRIA AND LEBANON

Status in 1939:	French mandate.
Government in 1939:	French administration.
Population in 1939:	4,100,000.
Make-up in 1939:	Mostly Arabs:
	a few Circassians;
	Assyrians; Turks;
	Druze; Jews.
Religion:	c80% Moslem, 20%
	Christian,
Location:	Near East.

From 1920 to 1939 French rule in Syria was dogged by revolts and disturbances, for no one had asked the French to conquer them. Lebanon was far more peaceful and had achieved autonomy governed by a council of Maronite Christian Arabs. Its capital, Beirut, was known as the Paris of the Near East.

When France declared war on Germany in 1939 Syrians and Lebanese volunteered for the French forces, but few saw action.

In June 1940 when the French government of Marshal Pétain surrendered, French General de Gaulle made it to Britain and proclaimed a government in exile that would carry on the fight. Polish soldiers training in Syria moved into British-controlled Palestine and a few Syrians and French went with them.

Days later the British attacked the French fleet and the two allies were suddenly in de facto war with each other. Syrian troops loyal to Pétain manned the Palestine border, expecting invasion.

German intelligence agents arrived in Syria with the blessing of Pétain, bent on fermenting an Arab war against the British. A group of Arabs led by Fawzi al Kawukji, who had fought the British just a year earlier were licking their wounds in Syria. The Germans negotiated with Fawzi.

An indirect result of this work was a coup in Iraq, which placed a pro-German regime in power. The British reacted in May 1941 by invading that nation. Pétain ordered the French commander in Syria, General Dentz, to allow German and Italian planes to use his airfields to bomb the British. Dentz complied, but ordered his troops to be alert, believing this would invite a British invasion.

The British did indeed complain through diplomatic channels and then bombed the Syrian airfields. Naturally, Dentz's fighter planes and flak gunners defended Syrian airspace.

Dentz backed down and ordered the Italians and Germans to leave, which they did on 6 June 1941. Next day the skies were clear and the Syrians thanked God.

But on the 8th the British invaded with three divisions and a brigade and their planes attacked everywhere. One of the invading divisions consisted of de Gaullist troops, some of them Syrians.

To defend Syria Dentz had eight Syrian, three Lebanese, five Senegalese, six Algerian, three Tunisian, four foreign legion, one Moroccan, and three black African battalions of infantry, a Tunisian, a Moroccan, an Algerian and twelve Circassian squadrons of horse cavalry, 6,700 French artillerymen, ninety tanks, some armoured cars, and an air force of twenty-one squadrons: with rear-echelon personnel a total of 38,000 men.

In Lebanon the defenders tried to hold the Australian 7th Division at the Litani River, but failed when Palestinian commandos invaded the coast behind them. They did halt some of the Australians further inland and even drove them back.

In Syria, Quneitra was lost to the de Gaullists, but at Kissoué they were stopped on the 11th. On the 12th horse cavalry charged the de Gaullists and an Indian brigade, but were scythed down by machine gun fire.

In Lebanon Sidon was lost when British warships aided the Australians, but inland the Australians were held at Merjuym and the Indians were surrounded on the 19th. Next day they surrendered.

This seemed like a victory, but in concentrating on the Indians Dentz had left open the road to Damascus, his capital, and on the 21st de Gaullists and Australians reached the city: foreign legion fought foreign legion. Next day Dentz ordered a retreat.

British forces now invaded from Trans-Jordan and two companies of foreign legion were ordered to stop them at Palmyra: they did for nine days.

In early July British forces invaded from Iraq capturing Deir ez Zor on the 3rd, Al Qamishiye on the 7th and El Haseke on the

8th. The British at Palmyra advanced westwards to take Homs on the 9th.

Dentz studied the situation. He was cut off from France by the British Royal Navy, he had lost Lebanon, the British were advancing up the Euphrates and along the Syrian-Turkish border.

He asked for terms. They were generous. In return for surrender, his men could opt to be sent to other French colonies or join de Gaulle.

Dentz surrendered on the 10th. He had lost 6,000 killed and wounded. De Gaulle recruited 5,668 of his men. Most of the Syrians and Lebanese refused to join de Gaulle.

Allied casualties were 4,500. The colony was turned over to the de Gaullists.

Fawzi's men had been thoroughly defeated by the British at Raqqa on 9 July, but a few of his men, some Syrians and German agents fled through Turkey to German territory to form the 300-man German Army Arab Legion.

The de Gaullists rewarded Lebanon with independence in February 1945, which only highlighted the French domination of the Syrians. Understandably the Syrians demonstrated against French rule and some took to guerrilla war. De Gaullist French proved just as callous as the Pétainist French in this affair, but Syria did emerge an independent state.

See Index

TAJIKISTAN

Status in 1939:	member state of the USSR.
Government in 1939:	communist under Stalin dictatorship.
Population in 1939:	2,500,000.
Make-up in 1939:	Tajiks; a few smaller groups.
Religion:	Moslem
Location:	Central Asia

Tajikistan, a celebrated nation for centuries, part of the great Khanate of Kiva in the Middle Ages, had obviously known better days when they were conquered by the Russians in the 19th century.

The fall of the Russian empire in 1917 gave them a brief glimpse of freedom, but in a couple of years the Russians were back:

this time with a communist philosophy as the USSR.

Soviet rule was terrible, atheistic, brutal. Periodically Tajiks rebelled.

In 1941 when Germany invaded the USSR thousands of Tajik men were conscripted into the Soviet Army, but alongside millions of others they were abandoned to the advancing Germans by an incompetent military system. After brief but bloody battles many a Tajik found himself in a German prison camp: an open field with no shelter or medical provisions to help him survive the coming Russian winter. It seemed like a death sentence.

Then hope arrived in the form of German recruiters, who offered treatment comparable to German soldiers, complete religious and cultural freedom and a chance to kill communists. Understandably many volunteered.

Tajiks were formed into their own units to hunt communist partisans behind German lines.

In 1943 Tajik companies were sent all over German-occupied Europe: e.g. a half-Tajik, half-Kazakh battalion fought well in Albania against communists. However, when they were sent against Moslem Albanians a hundred Tajiks defected.

At the end of the war few Tajiks in German uniform survived, for they were either caught by the advancing Soviets or by British troops, who handed them to the Soviets. Only those who surrendered to Americans or French had a chance of survival.

See Index

THAILAND

Other names:	Siam.
Status in 1939:	independent.
Government in 1939:	dictatorship, ostensibly a monarchy.
Population in 1939:	17,000,000.
Make-up in 1939:	Thais 15,300,000; Tachew Chinese 1,000,000; Malay 500,000; small tribal groups.
Religion:	Buddhist.
Location:	South East Asia

By a combination of diplomacy and luck Thailand had managed to remain free of

European colonial domination, although at times the French had dictated policy and had forced the Thais to cede certain non-Thai provinces to French Indo-China and British Malaya.

Thailand aped modern society, even sending an air unit to help France in World War I.

On 12 June 1940 the dictator Field Marshal Songram signed a non-aggression pact with Britain and France. Ten days later France capitulated to Germany. In September the Japanese bullied their way into French Indo-China. Songram decided that the French had lost all pretence at greatness and despite his non-aggression treaty he came to the conclusion he could regain Thailand's lost provinces.

On 20 October he mobilised 50,000 troops. He had 290 planes, but they were obsolete, therefore he dealt with the Japanese for 93 modern aircraft. His Navy consisted of ten destroyers, two gunboats, two minesweepers, nine minelayers, two defence ships and four submarines. The Navy controlled two battalions of marines and coastal guns.

In Indo-China the French had 38,000 locally raised troops, 7,000 French and 5,000 Foreign Legion. They had about a hundred aircraft and their navy was smaller than the Thai. Currently, the French had their hands full, staring down the Japanese 'guests', putting down a revolt in the Mekong Delta and maintaining security elsewhere, therefore only fourteen battalions could be spared to defend Battambang, which is where the Thais placed their Army.

In November 1940 the Thais sent patrols across the Mekong into Cambodia and skirmished with the French. By day Thai planes bombed the towns of Cambodia and Laos. By night the French bombed the towns of Thailand.

On 16 January 1941 the Thais advanced and at Yang Dam Koum ran into a major French force. Thai tanks hurt the French, but both sides withdrew at the end of the day.

The following day off Koh-Chang Island a French plane bombed the Thai navy, alerting them to the presence of a French flotilla of a cruiser, two sloops and two gunboats. At 6.15am the opposing fleets opened fire.

Within thirty minutes three Thai destroyers and two defence ships were burning and sinking. The French retired without damage.

The Japanese did not want to see a yellow-skinned people bested by a white-skinned people, so they stepped in and through diplomatic channels arranged for the French surrender of three Cambodian and two Laotian provinces.

Thailand was thus indebted to Japan. On 8 December 1941 the Japanese asked for this debt to be paid, demanding a formal alliance against Britain. To enforce the agreement, the Japanese invaded Thailand. Some Thais resisted, but next day in Bangkok the treaty was signed.

Over the next few months Thai aircraft flew against the British in Malaya and Burma.

In spring 1942 three Thai divisions invaded Burma's Shan province. No British were there, but Chinese troops had come down to aid the British and the Thais ran into them. Rather than open a whole new war against China, the Thais talked and they and the Chinese soon came to an arrangement. Together with the local Shans they created a Golden Triangle, where trade took place in any and everything with no questions asked.

Meanwhile the Japanese had decided they needed a rail line across Thailand and to build it they commandeered their prisoners of war and enslaved thousands of Malays and Burmese. Thai men and women were induced to volunteer to work on the line, but their treatment was brutal. Thais, who refused to work under such conditions, were imprisoned or murdered. Ally or no, the Japanese wanted the line built and did not care whose life it cost. About 66,000 people died building the line.

In 1943 the Japanese kept the Thai government happy by allowing them to regain the Malayan provinces, but at grassroots level the Japanese were seen as invaders. Some villagers began a low-key guerrilla war.

Bangkok and the new rail line were targets for allied bombers. Thai flak gunners and fighter pilots defended their airspace. In June 1945 the rail line was cut when bombers destroyed the bridge over the River Kwai.

On 15 August 1945 the Japanese Emperor surrendered. The Thais now negotiated a peace with the allies, the last axis government to do so. They had secretly sent information to the allies and now expected to be allowed to keep their French and British provinces as a reward. They were quickly brought out of their fantasy world by allied threats.

British troops entered Thailand, but only as a formality. The Thai soldiers were not disarmed and they were used to guard disarmed Japanese.

See Index

TONGA

Other names:	The Friendly Islands
Status in 1939:	British protected state.
Government in 1939:	monarchy.
Population in 1939:	45,000.
Make-up in 1939:	Tongans.
Religion:	Indigenous.
Location:	South Pacific

When the British had first arrived bringing their new god and their sense of civilisation, the islanders must have been amused and overawed at the same time. When the British said they would protect them, they must have thought to themselves, from what? Hurricanes?

In December 1941 when the Japanese suddenly began conquering Pacific islands the idea of protection became real enough. Tonga lay on the direct route between New Zealand and Hawaii, a route that Americans and New Zealanders both needed.

In gratitude for New Zealand protection (the Tongans looked upon the New Zealanders as 'British'), the Tongans raised an army to fight 'Japan Man' – twenty-eight warriors should do the trick, they decided.

Neither New Zealanders nor Americans treated this offer with disdain and accepted the 'Army of Tonga' with good grace. In 1943 the Army was taken to an American training camp on Guadalcanal. No doubt the sight of so many armed men astonished the Tongans.

In July they were taken to New Georgia Island, where Japanese were currently resisting the Americans at Munda town, while others had been bypassed and the Tongans were ordered to find them in the tall grass and jungle-clad hillsides.

The Tongans found the Japanese on their first patrol, by walking into an ambush. The Tongan leader was killed, but his men charged the enemy and drove them off. So this was war, they said to each other?

The Tongans continued to send out patrols and each day gained experience. After a month they were pulled out for a rest.

The Americans then asked the Tongans to go to Vella Lavella Island, where an American invasion had forced a few hundred Japanese inland. On 31 August the Tongans began searching the steep cliffs and caves of the island. Those who remained in camp were subjected to nightly air raids. For twenty-six days the Tongans challenged the Japanese to ambushes and sniping.

Following this operation the Tongans were released to go home: they hoped they had been of service. They had. They were mentioned in American dispatches several times for their excellence: one fellow was decorated for bravery by the New Zealanders and one by the Americans. Considering its size it was the most decorated 'army' in World War II.

See Index

TRANS-JORDAN

Other names:	Jordan
Status in 1939:	British mandate.
Government in 1939:	British administration.
Population in 1939:	450,000.
Make-up in 1939:	Arabs.
Religion:	Moslem.
Location:	Near East

The British mandate was super-imposed over Emir Abdullah's government, hence the nation had its own Army, the Arab Legion led by a British adventurer John Glubb. The locally raised British Army unit was called the Trans-Jordan Frontier Force TJFF, aptly named for its prime mission was to prevent border smuggling.

In May 1941 the British put together a column, Habforce, to invade Iraq. It was to consist of a brigade of the British 1st Cavalry Division, some infantry and three squadrons (i.e. companies) of the TJFF and an element of the Arab Legion, loaned to the British by the Emir. However, when the TJFF members learned they were to go up against fellow Arabs, they mutinied. This caused great embarrassment to the British officers, especially as the Arab Legion, known by British soldiers as Glubb's Girls, because of their headdress, did not mutiny.

Led by the jeep-mounted Arab Legion, the column drove into Rutba on 10 May and spent two days collecting supplies especially water. Their destination was the British base at Habbaniyah, currently besieged by Iraqis, which lay at the end of a five-day drive across inhospitable desert in 120˚F.

Almost as soon as the vehicles moved out they were strafed by German planes. The constant watch for aircraft, the ever-present sickening heat, the monotony of the landscape and the uncomfortable ride frayed everyone's nerves. They reached a canal and had to wait for Indian engineers to fly in to build a bridge. Aircraft easily landed in the flat terrain. On the 18th they reached Habbaniyah.

On the 19th the column joined with the garrison of British, Kurd and Assyrian troops to fight their way across the Euphrates River by bridge and boat. After four days of fighting the enemy was in retreat.

On the morning of the 28th the allies approached the city of Baghdad, where the Arab Legion wiped out several outposts. Iraqi artillery forced the prudent Arab Legion to fall back, but on the 30th the entire force, including the Arab Legion, launched a full-scale attack. They went up against trenches, barbed wire, machine guns, artillery and aerial strafing. The next day the Iraqis surrendered.

German and Italian air raids continued for a few more days as the troops spread out to occupy the country. A few of the Arab Legion had been wounded.

Habforce was reprovisioned in June for another campaign: the British invaded French Syria on the 8th.

The TJFF had overcome their mutiny and wisely the British chose to more or less forget it. TJFF vehicle-mounted and horsed troops entered the vast desert of Syria to locate the enemy. At Ezraa they ran into French armoured vehicles. Obviously they had to withdraw at once, and did so while two anti-tank rifle teams held off the French long enough. Their mission was to reconnoitre not fight.

Habforce invaded Syria on the 21st, the long thin vehicle column repeating its desert drive of the previous month. French planes strafed them and a few burned-out vehicles had to be left behind to mar the clean scenery. For one British brigadier the heat, flies, monotony and terror of the air raids was just too much and he had to be relieved.

Habforce reached Palmyra on the 25th and attacked the city at once. The Arab Legion was told to scout the area to prevent any surprises.

On 1 July the Arab Legion ran into a French vehicle column and drove back and forth in their jeeps machine gunning the trucks. For one killed and one wounded they took seventy prisoners.

On 3 July Habforce took Palmyra, finding they had only been up against two companies of foreign legion.

Habforce drove on to take Homs and on the 10th the French surrendered.

Glubb's Girls had proved invaluable in two campaigns and the Trans-Jordan Frontier Force had regained their honour.
See Index

TUNISIA

Status in 1939:	French colony.
Government in 1939:	French administration.
Population in 1939:	3,200,000.
Make-up in 1939:	Arabs; 2,840,000
	French 155,000;
	Italians 85,000;
	Jews 85,000;
	Berbers 30,000;
	Maltese 6,500.
Religion:	Moslem.
Location:	North Africa.

Really in 1939 there were three Tunisias: the coastal plain with the cities of Bizerte and Tunis, more European with Arab quarters than vice versa; the Arab towns inland which held a densely packed population that was far more educated and aware than the Europeans gave them credit for; and the double-spined north-south mountains, known as the western and eastern dorsals, with an open desert in the south of the country – the land of the nomad.

The Nomads took no notice of the French, as they had taken no notice of the Turks, the Romans, the Carthaginians before them.

War against Germany in 1939 put French citizens into uniform and native Tunisians volunteered for the Tunisia Division, to serve under French officers. They got little chance to show their prowess in France before the government of Marshal Pétain surrendered in June 1940. Ostensibly life would return to normal.

However, there was a new enemy, Britain, following a dastardly British attack on the French fleet, and in June 1941 Tunisian soldiers (three infantry battalions and a cavalry squadron) fought the British in Syria.

On 9 November 1942 British and American forces (i.e. the allies) invaded Algeria and Morocco. In Tunisia the soldiers looked to their French officers, but they seemed confused: who was fighting whom? In violation of the peace terms of 1940, German and Italian soldiers began arriving in Tunisia at the rate of a thousand a day. The Tunisians watched them warily.

On the 18th an outpost of the Tunisia Division at Medjez el Bab, forty miles west of Tunis, was approached by an advanced party of the allies. They shook hands.

Next day the Germans demanded Admiral Darien and General Barre surrender their forces: Darien agreed. Barre did not. When German paratroopers walked towards the Tunisian soldiers, the Tunisians opened fire. Within hours there were skirmishes all over northern Tunisia.

For three days the fighting was undisciplined, but 7,000 Tunisian troops managed to reach the allies at Medjez el Bab.

Sbeitla was lost to the Germans, who gave it to the Italians, who lost it to the Americans: the townsfolk had been occupied by soldiers of four nations in 24 hours.

The allies began to sort out the mess, eventually creating the following: two British corps in the north under their First Army of General Anderson, with the Tunisia Division attached; in the southern desert the US IInd Corps of General Fredendall; and linking them along the western dorsal General Koeltz's French XIXth Corps of the Moroccan, the Algiers and Constantine Divisions.

The British and Tunisians attacked in late November and by the 29th were just twelve miles from Tunis. Then a small German force counter-attacked on 1 December and pushed back the British. Within days the Tunisia Division was back at Medjez el Bab and only their artillery prevented the British from being routed.

The seasonal rains arrived, too early for the allies' liking, and brought the armies to a halt as the dirt roads became mud traps. From now on no one was going anywhere.

Within the German-occupied sector all Jews were arrested and their menfolk placed in labour gangs. Draconian policies were introduced and the people were for once united – in anger against the invaders.

Nonetheless, a few were convinced to see things Hitler's way: 274 French and 132 Tunisians enlisted into the Phalange Africain and 1,200 Tunisians joined the German Arab Legion.

On 17 January 1943 the British and Tunisians were attacked by Germans at Bou Arada Valley and the XIXth Corps was struck at Robaa and Ouseltia. By the 20th the 10th Panzer Division had defeated the Constantine Division and repelled the US 1st Armoured Division.

On 31 January the XIXth Corps was hit at Faid Pass by the 21st Panzer Division and had to withdraw.

On 14 February the Americans were attacked by the 10th, 15th and 21st Panzer and Centauro Armoured divisions. The Americans collapsed and Koeltz had to pull back his right flank and rush reinforcements to Kasserine Pass. Gafsa and Sbeitla were abandoned along with many supplies. Things looked so bleak Koeltz sent the Constantine Division to hold Tebessa in Algeria, but the British 6th Armoured Division, Koeltz's troops and an ad hoc force of Americans finally stopped the enemy on the 22nd at Sbiba-Thala-Kasserine.

The Germans next tried an attack against British Eighth Army entering Tunisia from

Libya. It failed and on 20 March the Eighth Army attacked at Mareth and began to inch their way north. By the 27th the Germans were retreating through Gabes.

On 11 April British Eighth Army at last linked with the other allies, thus pinning the Germans and Italians in a pocket from Medjez el Bab to Enfidaville. On the 19th the Eighth Army attacked, followed a day later by the XIXth Corps, then First Army.

On 7 May after some serious combat the Americans, now on the north coast, reached Bizerte. The population went wild mobbing the Americans with kisses. British troops found a similar welcome in Tunis. Almost all of the German Arab Legion and Phalange Africain deserted.

On the 9th Fifth Panzer Army surrendered. Three days later Italian First Army surrendered. There were no more armed axis troops in Africa.

The Tunisian troops remembered when they and the allies had been just twelve miles west of Tunis. It had taken the allies six months to cover that twelve miles. It had also cost the allies 83,000 casualties, of which the French Army share was 2,156 killed, 10,276 wounded and about 10,000 captured, most of the latter in the early days.

The ports had been damaged by allied air raids, but fortunately much of the fighting had taken place away from populated areas.

Over the next months a 3,500 strong Tunisian regiment was organised to carry on the war. Assigned to the 3rd North African Division of Algerians they saw fierce action in 1944 in Italy near Cassino, the break out in May, the advance up Italy June-July, the capture of Toulon, France, the advance up the Rhône-Saône Valley, the winter line in Alsace, the Colmar Pocket in January-February 1945, the clearing of the Rhineland in March and the invasion of central Germany in April, finishing up on the Austrian border.

Just about everywhere the French were fighting, there were Tunisians. Mutual respect developed between them and the French soldiers, and though there were some post-war troubles, generally speaking French-Tunisian relations remained good for the remainder of the century.
See Index

TURKMENISTAN

Status in 1939:	member state of the USSR.
Government in 1939:	communist under Stalin dictatorship.
Population in 1939:	2,000,000.
Make-up in 1939:	Turkmen.
Religion:	Moslem.
Location:	Central Asia

When the Turks advanced out of central Asia to settle Asia Minor (Turkey) they left a few relatives behind, and a thousand years later these Turkics (speaking languages akin to Turkish) were part of the Russian Empire.

The collapse of the Russian empire in 1917 gave the Turkmen of Turkmenistan, one of the Turkic-speaking group, a chance to savour freedom, but in 1920 the Russians returned, this time as communists calling their empire the USSR and introducing an austerity not known in the worst days of the previous empire, with atheist policies aimed at destroying the Turkmen's culture and religion.

In June 1941 when Germany invaded the USSR, the communists conscripted thousands of Turkmen into their Red Army, but an inadequate military system abandoned many to the advancing Germans. By autumn Turkmen were in German camps, little more than fenced fields open to the elements with poor food and no medicine. No one was looking forward to a Russian winter in such conditions.

Hitler, the German dictator, wanted Turkey as an ally and was bending over backwards to please that country. When someone mentioned that Turkic-speaking troops of the Red Army had been captured, he hit upon the idea of recruiting them into a Turkestani Legion to please the Turkish government. Truthfully, this was like recruiting Saxon German troops to please the English (Anglo-Saxons), but Hitler never dealt in truths.

His recruiters established the legion by offering the prisoners treatment comparable to Germans, complete religious and cultural freedom and a chance to kill communists. The alternative was to rot in the death camps.

There was one flaw: how could a German tell a Turkic-speaker from the mass of humanity huddled together in the open fields. The result was the recruitment of Altays, Azerbaijanis, Balkars, Dolganys, Karachais, Karagas, Karakalpaks, Kazakhs, Khakass, Khyrgyz, Kumyks, Nogays, Tofalarys, Tuvunians, Uzbeks, Yakuts as well as Turkmen: about 20,500 men all told. Language diversity was solved by putting all of one language in their own battalions. These battalions were then scattered all over German-occupied USSR and put on anti-partisan operations.

In 1942 Hitler went further to please Turkey by allowing the legion a political representation: the Turkestani Liberation Movement led by Veli Gajun Chan. Under very trying circumstances, Chan worked wonders. One of his problems was that SS murder squads had killed Turkic-speaking people, mistaking them for Jews. His complaints fell on deaf ears, for officially the murder squads did not exist.

One victory of the movement was to establish a full division, the 162nd: specifically six battalions of infantry, each of 950 Turkic-speakers and 27 Germans. The remainder of the division was a mixture of such people. This was a victory, because a division would receive far more publicity than a single battalion.

Himmler, head of the SS, had always fancied himself a general and had created his own army, the Waffen SS, not to be confused with his murder squads. The German Army restricted his recruitment, so he was ever on the lookout for new blood. When he learned that Hitler was trying to please Turkey and the German Army had created an entire division of Turkic-speakers, Himmler went one better creating a new East Turkic Legion recruited from Soviet soldiers recently captured.

In 1943 the German Army's Turkestani Legion sent battalions all over Europe. Some ended up fighting the Anglo-American invaders in France. The 162nd Division was sent to Italy and put into the front line: e.g. on 19 September 1944 the Germans were holding San Fortunato Ridge with eight battalions: two of army infantry, two of army panzer-grenadiers, one of air force paratroopers, one of air force infantry and two of Turkic-speakers; when they were assaulted by the Canadian 1st Division. Within twenty-four hours the

Turkic-speakers were falling back. As a result the ridge defenders had to fall back, then so had the corps, thus so had the Tenth Army, thus so had all the axis forces in Italy.

The 162nd Division was ordered to man a rearguard. They did not do well, but the Germans at last turned and stopped the allies.

The Germans complained bitterly of the division, but it must be remembered how they were recruited and that they had been trained for partisan hunting, not front line battle, and had been promised combat against communists, not allied troops.

In early 1945 Himmler assembled his East Turkic Legion and a Tatar brigade into a division-sized force and placed them into the front line in eastern Germany to stop the Red Army.

The 162nd Division was given some training and put back into the line in Italy to hold the east coast and the Commachio Lagoon. On 1 April 1945 British commandos and Italian partisans began sailing in small boats into the lagoon, which had scores of tiny islets, on each of which were Turkic soldiers. For a week this most unusual battle raged. Generally each islet's defenders gave up after being attacked. The division was destroyed.

By the time of the German surrender in May 1945 about 110,000 men had served in the Turkestani Legion or the East Turkic Legion. A large number were caught by the Red Army and punished by execution or a long sentence in a concentration camp. Those who were caught by the British were handed to the Red Army. When these fellows were identified Stalin's political police, the NKVD, arrested their relatives back home and sent them to concentration camps. In this manner tens of thousands of innocents were done to death.

A few who gave up to Americans and French survived.

See Index

UKRAINE

Other names:	Little Russia, includes Crimea.
Status in 1939:	member state of the USSR.
Government in 1939:	communist under Stalin dictatorship.
Population in 1939:	18,000,000.

Make-up in 1939:   Ukrainians 15,400,000;
Jews 1,500,000;
Volksdeutsch 340,000;
Tatars 300,000;
Bulgars 200,000;
Greeks 125,000;
Gagaus 100,000;
thousands of Russian
colonists.
Religion: Christian.
Location: eastern Europe

The twentieth century has been a century of genocide. Armenians, Jews, Gypsies, Timorese, Rwandans and others have suffered nation murder. Yet the genocide of the Ukrainians is rarely mentioned.

The Ukrainians had achieved their independence at the fall of the Russian empire in 1917 and had fought all and sundry to keep it, but soon lost: Ruthenia to Czecho-Slovakia, Bessarabia and Bukovina to Romania and Galicia to Poland. The remainder, including the Crimea, was lost in 1921 to the new breed of Russian, the Soviet communists of the USSR.

After the communist Red Army defeated the Ukrainians, their political police (later called NKVD) came to arrest anyone who had the intellectual power to resist communism: musicians, artists, writers, businessmen, managers, lawyers etc. For official matters the Russian language replaced the Ukrainian. The atheist state replaced Christianity: 20,000 priests were taken away to NKVD concentration camps.

In the late 1920s Stalin, the USSR dictator, ordered all small farmers kicked off their land so that it could be collectivised, i.e. turned into state run operations. If lucky the farmers were employed to work their own land, if not they wandered the countryside with their families, homeless and starving. Any poor wretch who tried to steal food from a barn was shot down by NKVD guards. The food was destined for employees of farms, factories and mines, and for communists of course, the remaining portion going to feed the Russians, and the surplus to the western world to trade for tractors, machinery, expertise etc.

The starving Ukrainians made a nuisance of themselves: they attacked the guards, they stole rifles and revolted. By 1933 650,000 of them had been sent to concentration camps. By this date, though, the Russian people were learning the truth of the genocide, for that is exactly what it was. NKVD tried to prevent Russians from sending food to Ukraine.

Stalin knew he could not keep the lid on this any more, so he publicly admitted it but blamed the Ukrainian communists: his NKVD arrested 27,000 of them!

A conservative estimate is that 3,000,000 Ukrainians died of starvation and related illnesses, but it could have been as high as 8,000,000.

In September 1939 the Red Army invaded Poland and together with the Germans carved up that nation. Part of the Soviet share was Eastern Galicia and at once the NKVD began to arrest the local Ukrainian intelligentsia.

In 1940 the Red Army invaded Romania to take over Northern Bukovina and Bessarabia. There too, the NKVD indulged themselves with the local Ukrainian intelligentsia.

As a result by 22 June 1941, the day Hitler, the German dictator, ordered the invasion of the USSR, the Ukrainians hated the communists. Many also hated Jews: a high proportion of the communists were Jews; Christian-Jewish relations had never been good in this part of the world and by now they were positively vindictive.

The Soviet defences were hopelessly inadequate as Germans, Romanians and Hungarians poured across the border.

In March 1939 Ruthenia had been allowed exactly twenty-four hours of independence, whereupon Hungarian troops put an end to it. The Sich, Ruthenia's 'army' of a few hundred, fled to German territory and were welcomed. Re-equipped by the Germans, they fought alongside them in Poland in September 1939. After this they became sentries for the Germans in Western Galicia, where the Germans also raised thirty-three battalions of auxiliary police (schumas) from the ethnic Ukrainians.

Thus there was a precedent for the Germans to use Ukrainians and in June 1941 when they invaded Soviet-controlled Eastern

Galicia and then Ukraine it seemed natural they should do so with Ukrainian support. This included two infantry battalions, Roland, which helped capture Kishinev, and Nachtigall, which fought for Vynnitsa.

In Lwow the NKVD fled at the approach of the Germans, following which the Ukrainian inhabitants broke into the prisons: they found 3,500 corpses; victims of communist inhumanity! Understandably, their relatives went berserk, hunting down known collaborators and communists and beating them to death or hanging them from lampposts. Some were Jews. Within hours this mob rule turned into a Jew hunt. Hundreds of Jewish men, most innocent of communist activity, were murdered.

In every town and village the Germans were met by grateful Ukrainians. The Germans recruited many as hiwis, i.e. rear-echelon soldiers at first distinguishable only by an armband. (Months later they received uniforms and their own rank system)

One of the German rear-echelon units was the Einsatzgruppe, whose express purpose was to murder all Jews, Gypsies and communists: men, women and children. While most city Ukrainians thought this to be abhorrent, some did not, and in the small villages, where superstition and illiteracy were commonplace, many loved the concept. The German einsatzgruppe killers were a combination of machine-like asocials, psychopaths and moronic bullies, who did not actually hate Jews: they would have murdered red-headed people had that been the order; and as such they were astonished at the hatred of Jews in some villages. Not only did some villagers drag their Jewish neighbours, men, women and children, to the death sites, but brought their own children to watch the shooting with picnic baskets! Many a Ukrainian signed on as an einsatzgruppe hiwi.

In 1942 when the Jew killing switched from mobile firing squads to permanent extermination camps, the Ukrainian hiwis of the einsatzgruppe became camp guards, e.g. at Sobibor and Treblinka camps 90% of the staff were Ukrainians.

To occupy the vast Ukraine the Germans needed help. The German police brought with them some of their Galician Ukrainian schuma battalions, retained the Ukrainian ordinary police, recruited 10,000 Ukrainians as sentries, known as hiwas, and thousands of others into the schumas. The Roland and Nachtigall battalions were transferred from the German Army to the police as schuma battalions. Eventually fifty-two schuma battalions were raised among the Ukrainians of Eastern Galicia and Ukraine to add to the thirty-three raised in Western Galicia.

The German Army recruited a part-time militia in each town to fight off raids by communist partisans who had been deliberately inserted behind German lines by the NKVD. The German Army also recruited entire battalions of Ukrainian labour troops.

In the Crimea, which the Germans reached in October, they found the Tatars. These people had revolted against the communists in 1931 and had suffered the arrest of 40,000 as a result. They despised communists and when the Germans arrived they were welcomed as liberators: about 500 Tatars joined the einsatzgruppe as hiwis; thousands more joined the ordinary German army as hiwis; six battalions of Tatar antipartisan troops were formed; a village militia was created with a strength of 10,000; and 3,000 Tatars were recruited into the police schumas.

By late 1941 Soviet citizens serving in their own German-sponsored units were known collectively as Osttruppen, to distinguish them from the hiwis who served on an individual basis: e.g. a German engineer platoon might have one hiwi as a cook and one as an interpreter.

By late 1941 the Ukrainian National Revolutionary Army, which despite its name was a mere militia force in Olevskie, had become disillusioned with German rule. They found the antics of the einsatzgruppe and SS Security Police (the German NKVD) to be little different than that of the communists. They revolted and became partisans.

By this date all the various militias were unified into the Ukrainian Popular Self-Defence Corps UNS with 180,000 members.

The Germans ordered all Ukrainian men and women into essential work. Any who could not find such jobs themselves were given jobs, often in Germany. One plan was for a half million Ukrainian women to go to Germany as maids for nazi party members. By late 1942 3,000,000 Ukrainians were forcibly working away from home. Any who refused to go were arrested and sentenced to slave labour, a totally different matter. Few survived as long as a year in a slave labour camp.

The Germans found willing recruits among the Volksdeutsch minority. Stalin caused this: his NKVD were arresting all Volksdeutsh regardless of loyalty. Purely for survival Volksdeutsch men entered the German forces as 'German' citizens, though they had not 'seen' Germany for two hundred years.

In July 1943 the Germans suffered a terrible defeat at Kursk. Everyone now knew that the Germans would never vanquish the USSR. The Red Army and NKVD would return. Recruitment for the anti-communist units actually increased, for many Ukrainians, though innocent of pro-German behaviour, were terrified they would suffer nonetheless, and many a family would rather have a few armed men to call upon than trust to the goodwill of the NKVD.

The German SS had waived its racial restrictions on recruitment and in 1943 Ukrainians were allowed to join (as different from being hiwis attached to the SS). The 14th SS Division was established ostensibly to recruit from Galicia only, but any Ukrainian was welcome.

As the Red Army advanced, the UNS militia, now 380,000 strong, retreated with their families. The men were organised into full-time regiments.

The schumas were sent all over Europe to hunt partisans or man coastal defences. The Tatar anti-partisan troops entered the Savage Division in Italy to fight partisans.

Ukrainians, who had become disillusioned with the Germans, had created partisan bands to fight them, but these were not friendly with Soviet partisans. Indeed when the Red Army began advancing across Ukraine, the Ukrainian nationalist partisans fought them. By 1944 these partisans had coalesced into one organisation, the Ukrainian Partisan Army UPA. By April 1944 the UPA was also rebelling against Romanian rule in Bukovina and Bessarabia, Hungarian rule in Ruthenia and against the Germans in Galicia.

On 28 June 1944 following a Soviet breakthrough the 14th SS Division was taken off anti-partisan operations, reinforced with fifteen battalions of Ukrainian schumas and sent against the Red Army at Brody. For two weeks they repulsed cavalry assaults, but then were attacked by tanks: the men were ordered to withdraw. On 22 July they rested and took count; they were missing 7,000 men.

During this summer Galicia, Bukovina and Bessarabia were lost to the Red Army, therefore the UPA began fighting the new Soviet occupiers.

In October the SS took in 5,953 Ukrainians from other organisations to make up losses in the 14th SS Division. The SS also set up the 1st SS Mountain Brigade from Tatar volunteers. There were now about 39,000 Tatars in German uniform.

In January 1945 General Pavlo Shandruk was lobbying Berlin harder than ever to seek sovereignty for Ukraine: Russian anti-communists had just achieved it for their government.

In March the 14th SS Division, in battle against Titoist partisans in Yugoslavia, was suddenly ordered to Austria: at last Hitler had recognised Ukraine as a sovereign state and a Ukrainian Army UVV was to be formed. President Livytsky's chief aim was to liberate some part of ethnic Ukraine from which to operate. The recently lost Ruthenia was probably the best bet. The 14th SS Division changed its name to the 1st Division UVV and asked for orders. A formation of Ukrainians planning to defend Berlin was renamed the 2nd Division. Other formations of Ukrainians pledged their allegiance: a brigade in Denmark, two regiments in the Netherlands and smaller units that gave Livytsky and Shandruk about 50,000 men overnight. German interference still dogged events. The German Air Force asked for weapons for 2,500 of their men at the expense of arming Ukrainians. Naturally, Livytsky refused.

In mid-April the 1st Division UVV went into action in Austria, while the 2nd Division fought in Czechia against the Polish Second Army and suffered 50% casualties.

On 6 May the Germans in Austria surrendered to the British and the 1st Division UVV contacted the British. A surrender was agreed: as the Ukrainians entered British encampments they did so under Soviet artillery fire and air strikes.

Throughout Central Europe Ukrainians who fell into Red Army hands were sent to the NKVD for execution or a sentence to a concentration camp. Those who reached the allies stood a chance of survival, though the British handed some to the NKVD. The British planned to hand the 1st Division UVV to them en masse, but the prisoners learned of this and barricaded themselves in their huts. Negotiations provided a solution. As the SS had called the division 'Galizien', referring to West Galicia, which had been part of pre-1939 Poland, the division claimed its members were Polish citizens. The Polish Army in Italy, currently at loggerheads with the Soviet-sponsored Poles in Poland, needed all the support they could get so they accepted the divisions. The division was released as an 'allied' force and eventually the men were allowed to settle in Britain.

During the war about 780,000 Ukrainians (including minorities, such as Volksdeutsch and 50,000 Tatars) wore German uniform. Others wore Hungarian or Romanian uniform. Of these about half died prior to the German surrender or fell into NKVD hands in May-June 1945. Of the remaining 400,000 or so, about 200,000 managed to survive by one method or another, and 200,000 ethnic Ukrainians had joined the UPA as partisans in areas occupied by Soviet or Soviet-sponsored forces.

The UPA partisans (many were women) had no choice but to fight on. The NKVD would butcher them if they surrendered. Already in the Crimea the NKVD had deported 200,000 Tatar civilians to penal colonies, because their relatives had aided the Germans.

In West Galicia ethnic Poles, now under a communist government, began to kick 200,000 Ukrainian civilians out of their homes and farms. With no place to seek refuge some joined the UPA partisans.

Thus by late summer 1945 the UPA was in combat against the Poles and NKVD in Western Galicia, the NKVD and Red Army in Eastern Galicia, Ruthenia, Bessarabia, Bukovina and Ukraine. In Slovakia there were periodic UPA ambushes of Red Army convoys and Czecho-Slovakian patrols.

The combat was ferocious. By 1948 about 30,000 Poles and NKVD had been killed in Western Galicia by UPA, with a comparable loss to the UPA.

In early 1949 the UPA command realised they were not going to win and ordered their members to fight their way through Czecho-Slovakia to Western Germany, currently under US occupation. Thousands made it, some joining the US Army as hiwis.

Not all could safely move or wanted to. Diehards continued to ambush military convoys especially in the mountains of Ruthenia, Galicia and Slovakia.

In 1957 the last fanatics made their way to western Germany.

See Index

UNION OF SOVIET SOCIALIST REPUBLICS (USSR)

Other names:	often referred to as 'Russia'.
Status in 1939:	independent.
Government in 1939:	communist under Stalin dictatorship.
Population in 1939:	190,000,000.
Make-up in 1939:	100,000,000 Russians; remainder divided into a hundred ethnic groups.
Religion:	officially none.
Location:	Eastern Europe, Central and Northern Asia.

When Lenin established his own Bolshevik (communist) government and army (Red Army) in 1917 to gain control of all Russia he had in mind to recreate the Russian Empire: he called it a prison of nations. He accomplished this with great bloodshed and his successor, Stalin, put the finishing touches to the new empire. No matter that Stalin was a Georgian, not a Russian, he ruled the Russian empire under the title Union of Soviet Socialist Republics.

Union suggests voluntary membership: there was none. Soviet means council or congress: in truth Stalin ruled like an emperor. Socialist means keeping the welfare of the people in prime position: in truth the people were murdered, imprisoned, starved and turned into a zombie-like workforce, while communist party members lived high off the hog. Republic suggests autonomy. In truth there was none.

Therefore, the very name of the country was a lie: as was everything else. This two-faced society insisted on portraying the beautiful face to foreigners and through the mass media to its own people: a face of education, jobs and homes for all, peace, a land of plenty, security from the cradle to the grave. Every citizen knew that the other face, the ugly one, was the reality: the world of the NKVD, Stalin's political police, with their concentration camps, informers, midnight arrests and big brother surveillance, resulting in a nation-wide epidemic of fear, alcoholism and despair.

According to Stalin the people's greatest enemy was fascism, especially the variety led by Hitler in Germany and Mussolini in Italy. However, anyone who complained was labelled fascist by Stalin and imprisoned. Stalin's own family was not immune to his paranoia. One of his problems was that communism, even if correctly applied, which it never was, does not work. However, he could hardly admit he had chosen the wrong system, for that would remove the credibility that he enjoyed among a few devoted followers. If the nation was built on a lie then either the lie must go or the nation. Stalin demanded that the lie, which he named 'truth', must survive, even at the expense of the nation: e.g. if commandeering the farms in Ukraine to create state-owned cooperatives meant throwing millions of people out of their homes to starve or freeze to death, then so be it: who cares if millions die, as long as the lie is allowed to survive?

Religion was officially illegal. Any Moslem imam, Christian priest or other religion's clergy who tried to perform rites was arrested.

The NKVD ruled the state on Stalin's behalf like medieval robber barons. Of course the people revolted now and then

and the NKVD had to bring in the Red Army, for like most bullies the NKVD had no stomach for a fight. The Red Army put down rebellions in Yakut 1928, Ukraine 1928-33, Buryat 1929, Kazakh 1931, Crimea 1929-33, and Chechen, Ossetia, Kabardin, Avar, Dargin, Lak and Lezghin in 1935. In all, several hundred thousand were killed in fights ranging from ambushes to full-scale battles with artillery and air strikes. The world knew nothing of this and chose to know even less.

In 1937 the NKVD turned on the Red Army, arresting three-quarters of the Supreme Military Soviet, thirteen of nineteen army commanders and 110 of 135 divisional commanders. Most were executed.

Then they turned on the civil service with equally bloody results; then on industry, murdering and imprisoning those bosses whose workforce had not produced their quota, refusing to take into consideration such things as obsolete machinery, shortages of raw materials and the poor transportation network.

Then the NKVD turned on the communists: arresting 98 of 179 members of the Central Committee and 1,108 of 1,966 delegates to the 17th Party Congress. The NKVD also sent agents abroad to assassinate foreign communists.

By 1939 Stalin had murdered directly or indirectly 20,000,000 people and had imprisoned 8,000,000. When the NKVD loyally reported to Stalin that they had taken care of his enemies, he ordered them to murder their commander, which they dutifully did. Not since the days of Tsar Ivan the Terrible had the Russian Empire seen such insanity.

Stalin had played at war abroad. When Spain erupted in civil war in 1936, he had sent 2,000 advisers, some planes and tanks. However, it was not until August 1939, when the Red Army defeated a Japanese encroachment for a few thousand casualties and he had made a deal with Hitler that same month, that he really felt ready to unleash the dogs of war.

On 17 September, while the Poles were desperately fighting a German invasion, Stalin ordered the Red Army to attack the Polish rear. The Red Army was divided into 'fronts' or 'districts' each of which contained 'armies', each of which in turn contained 'corps' or 'divisions'. A division consisted of about 9,000 troops. A corps had about the same, divided into four brigades. In this supposedly classless army officers had no insignia, unit pride was discouraged, campaign decorations and medals were non-existent.

On the 17th the Red Army drove for Vilnius, Bialystok, Sokol and the upper Dniestr River with fifteen infantry and nineteen cavalry divisions and ten armoured brigades. The Red Army was proud of its horse cavalry and refused to see them as obsolete.

Within two weeks all serious resistance had been crushed and 12,300,000 people were introduced to life Stalin-style. The invasion cost the Red Army about 2,600 killed and wounded.

His victories over the Japanese and the Poles convinced Stalin that his 1937 massacre of the generals had been a good idea. Armed with this cockiness he bullied Lithuania, Latvia, Estonia and Finland demanding military bases. Only Finland chose to fight.

On 30 November 1939 the Red Air Force began bombing Finland and the Red Army invaded with twenty-three divisions and six armoured brigades.

The attack took place in the dead of winter, in frozen forests, with waist deep snow, incredibly low temperatures and only three hours of daylight per day. Stalin must have believed that like Moses before him he could command the elements.

Within days the Soviets were stopped by determined resistance. The war proved a terrible burden on the Red Army and in March 1940 Stalin settled for a consolation prize: a few slices of land along the border.

His generals were shocked. Tiny Finland, its population smaller than the Red Army, had stood up to Stalin. True, the Red Army had killed almost 25,000 Finns, but Stalin had had to replace General Meretskov with Marshall Timoshenko and reinforce him with another twenty divisions. Stalin admitted to losses of 48,000 killed and 158,000 wounded. Kruschev, a later Soviet leader, admitted to a million losses including frostbite and sickness. Most likely the Red Army suffered about 200,000 killed and 400,000 maimed by wounds and frostbite. All Red Army prisoners were released by the Finns, whereupon the NKVD arrested them for having surrendered.

Yet Stalin bounced back. In summer 1940 he conquered Lithuania, Estonia and Latvia and took over North Bukovina and Bessarabia without firing a shot – except for NKVD firing squads which were soon busy in the newly conquered territories.

Stalin now played for time. He knew his next confrontation would be against Hitler's Germany. As part of the game he traded with Germany, his oil going into Hitler's tanks. He also ordered his border troops not to make overt moves.

Meanwhile, Stalin personally worked with Timoshenko to restore the Red Army and some excellent equipment was issued including the T-34 tank. Stalin soon had 4,500,000 soldiers, 21,000 tanks, and 14,500 aircraft. The bulk of his Army was 18-22 year old conscripts, though he did call up some as old as 36.

In spring 1941 Stalin's spies and British intelligence told Stalin Hitler was about ready to attack. Some of his spies were highly placed in British intelligence, so he knew the British were not lying to him. Yet he did nothing. His inactivity at this time has been blamed on many things, but it does seem that he well and truly did not know what to do. When all is said and done, Stalin was a survivor, but he was not an intelligent man.

On 22 June the invasion began. The Odessa Special Military District in Bessarabia and North Bukovina was attacked by two Romanian armies. The Kiev Special Military District in west Ukraine was attacked by four German armies. North of the Pripet Marsh the Western Special Military District was assaulted by four German armies. In Lithuania the Baltic Special Military District was hit by three German armies. These districts commanded a total of eleven armies and sixteen corps.

On the 22nd as much as three-quarters of the Soviet armour was undergoing repair and a high percentage of the Air Force was undergoing maintenance or awaiting spare parts.

This first day the Germans advanced sixty miles in places. Entire divisions were overrun. Vilnius was lost on the third day. For the first eleven days Stalin did nothing: paralysed with indecision and panic.

By the 30th all of Lithuania and half of Latvia had been lost and Minsk the capital of Byelorussia and Tarnopol in Ukraine were besieged. Red Army headquarters (Stavka) had lost contact with twenty-one divisions. Over 2,000 planes were lost, many of them bombed on the ground.

On 1 July Leningrad Special Military District with three armies was attacked by the Finnish Army all along the border and by German troops in the Arctic north.

By 9 July Latvia and Estonia had been overrun, three divisions were trapped in Pinsk, the Germans had registered their 287,704th Red Army prisoner and had knocked out their 2,585th tank.

At last Stalin emerged from his trance and worked with Stavka to gather reinforcements.

In Ukraine the Soviet Fifth and Sixth Armies counter-attacked. By the 14th the Baltic Special Military District, renamed North West Front under Marshal Voroshilov, had withdrawn to the Luga River. The Western Special Military District, renamed Western Front under Marshal Timoshenko, was trying to hold Polotsk, Vitebsk and the upper Dniepr. South of the Pripet Marsh Marshal Budenny's Odessa Special Military District, renamed South West Front, was pulling out of Bessarabia.

By the end of July over a million Soviet troops were missing or dead.

However, by early August it did appear the German steamroller was running out of steam. The Soviet counter-attack in Ukraine had worried the Germans and the Odessa garrison was shooting down countless waves of Romanians.

Then 100,000 men on the upper Dniepr surrendered on the 5th! On the 10th 103,000 surrendered at Uman.

Kiev was outflanked north and south, but as the capital of Ukraine Stalin insisted it be held. By mid-August Timoshenko had fallen back to the Desna River and Voroshilov slowed the German advance in his sector to just 130 miles for the month.

In Leningrad the generals wanted to withdraw: the Finns blocked them on the north and the Germans on the south were just 20 miles away. The city was under air and artillery bombardment and winter was approaching. Stalin replied that he could no more surrender a city named after Lenin than Stalingrad, named after himself. Thus for purely prestige reasons Kiev and Leningrad were to be held at all costs.

On 8 September Leningrad was surrounded, but for Lake Ladoga. Inside were three million civilians and thirty divisions. A week later five of the North West front's divisions surrendered.

Timoshenko was not worried, for, though he sat just 180 miles west of Moscow, no German assaults came his way in September. The main German effort was now in Ukraine. There Budenny could not prevent the enemy from cutting off the Crimea, because he was too busy holding onto Kiev. General Yeremenko's new Bryansk Front protected Kiev on the north, but his position was precarious. The Twenty-first Army counter-attacked at Gomel and failed. South of Kiev Kremenchug was besieged.

Budenny pleaded with Stalin: he had to pull out now or else the greatest debacle to befall a Russian army would occur. His political commissar (watchdog), General Kruschev, agreed with him (a rarity, for all commissars were Stalin sycophants). Stalin replied by firing Budenny and told Timoshenko to sort out the mess.

On 15 September at Lohvitsa the German pincers met behind Kiev, trapping five Soviet armies in a pocket of 22,000 square miles. Four days later Stalin decided it might be a good idea to abandon Kiev after all. For some this would mean walking 150 miles under air attack before they could engage the enemy!

At the end of September the Kiev pocket simply collapsed: 600,000 men walked into German prison camps!

Stalin authorised the defenders of Odessa to sail away: 120,000 made it by 16 October.

During October the Crimea was lost, but for Kerch and Sevastopol. On the 6th Yeremenko's Bryansk Front lost Bryansk and on the 9th his Third and Thirteenth Armies were cut off.

On the 7th six armies were trapped at Vyazma. On the 13th they surrendered 675,000 men.

West Front, down to 90,000 men under General Koniev, defended the approaches to Moscow as the Germans resumed their advance on the capital of the USSR. On 10 October General Zhukov was given command of West Front. Kaluga was lost on the 12th, but now heavy seasonal rains aided the Soviets when they turned Russia's dirt roads into rivers of mud slimy enough to swallow a truck whole. The Germans were astonished, never having experienced the Russian rasputitsa.

Along the north shore of the Sea of Azov three Soviet armies were trapped on the 20th when the Germans reached the Mius River.

On the 24th Timoshenko, now leading South West Front, abandoned Kharkov.

By the 28th West Front was just forty miles from Moscow. Stalin remained in the city and this encouraged the inhabitants to stay and fight too: that and the fact that the NKVD arrested anyone who tried to leave. Men and women marched out to the suburbs to dig anti-tank ditches. Under air raids since June, the Muscovites were not fighting for Stalin or communism, but for Mother Russia.

In November the rains ceased and the mud ruts froze, enabling German vehicles to move again. On the 9th North West Front now under General Kurochkin lost Tikhvin east of Lake Ladoga. Timoshenko's South West Front lost Kursk, Yets and Stalinogorsk, but the Fiftieth Army held Tula and simply refused to budge. The IInd Cavalry Corps actually regained some ground.

North of Moscow General Koniev's new Kalinin Front lost Kalinin and was pressed back just fifteen miles from Moscow in temperatures of 30°C.

On the north shore of the Sea of Azov three armies counter-attacked the First Panzer Army, forcing it back 30 miles to the Mius. Though hardly showing on the map of the USSR, this seemed like a great victory to the hard-pushed Soviets.

Stalin was planning something much more impressive. Learning from a spy that the Japanese were preparing to attack the Anglo-Americans in the Pacific, he emptied his eastern border defences of troops and brought them to Moscow.

On 6 December these troops were ready and Stalin gave the order. The Kalinin and West Fronts attacked from the Volga River north of Moscow towards the south-west. Next day Timoshenko's South West Front launched a major offensive from Yelets and Tula between 120 and 250 miles south of Moscow. Attacking in heavy snow, the troops from the east, equipped and trained to handle Siberian winters, overran German troops who were still clad in summer uniforms. The Red Army inflicted 55,000 casualties on the Germans, advanced up to 200 miles and put an end to all thoughts of the Germans taking Moscow.

It was a good end to a bad year. The Soviets had lost 7,000 aircraft, twenty-seven corps and scores of divisions: a total of 2,700,000 dead, 3,800,000 captured and 2,000,000 wounded.

A major Soviet programme of saving everything of value was underway. The authorities dismantled and transported 1,360 factories from out of the path of the Germans – machinery, workers, tools – and in newly built premises began turning out essential goods before the roof was complete. The entire economy was geared to war production. Women entered factories and mines.

The military conscription age was now 17-50 for men and childless females. Only a deformity or essential job kept one out of uniform. At one time half the entire population was under enemy occupation, but these were eligible for conscription too and were grabbed when partisans raided their homes. Partisan conscripts went into their first action without weapons! Only after proving themselves were they armed.

Women in the armed forces usually served in all-female units; gunners, infantry, engineers, cavalry, tankers, flyers: there were some very good women fighter pilots. There were some mixed units. A tank might have a crew of three men and a woman. In mixed units no provision was made for female hygiene requirements. In the Red Army life was primitive, to say the least.

Women soldiers were told that if they became pregnant they would be treated by the NKVD as malingerers. Partisans simply shot any member who became pregnant.

Stalin's victory in December only made him lose reason again. He ordered a complete offensive by everyone along the 1,700 mile front from the Crimea to the Arctic. Zhukov's West Front gained Kirov, but even with parachute assaults could do little else. Timoshenko's South West Front gained 50 miles. Stalin had yet to learn that shoving the enemy back a few miles was not nearly as effective as levering him out of each town one a time.

In the Crimea the Caucasus Front was holding Kerch and Sevastopol, aided greatly by the Black Sea Fleet, though in January alone this cost 6,700 killed and 10,000 missing. Rather than use recruits to replace casualties the Red Army preferred to create new units, sometimes with the numbers of lost formations, so by February they had twenty-one divisions in the Crimea.

A so-called spring offensive in the Arctic in April, in the middle of a snowstorm, cost the Karelian Front 30,000 in dead alone and gained nothing and inflicted only 5,700 dead on the Germans and Finns.

Stalin urged a spring offensive everywhere, but his generals convinced him he should attack only in the Belgorod-Lozovaya region. Even this operation would have a frontage of 150 miles.

The affair began on 12 May as Timoshenko launched his Sixth and Twenty-eighth Armies to trap the German Sixth Army and by the 17th his Sixth Army had advanced 20 miles towards Kharkov: then suddenly the German Sixth and two other armies retaliated and within a week not only had the Sixth Army fallen back to its jump-off position but 70 miles past it. The spring offensive was a total fiasco costing the Red Army tens of thousands killed and 241,000 captured.

A German-Romanian offensive in the Crimea could not be stopped and on 3 July

the last Soviets got out of Sevastopol by ship: trying to hold the peninsula cost the Red Army 286,000 killed and missing.

On 7 July as Voronezh was lost to a major enemy offensive, General Vatutin was given command of Voronezh Front with the mission of retaking the city.

Stavka soon recognised that the Germans were trying to pry open the 250-mile wide gate to the Caucasus. The southern gatepost was Rostov: the northern was Stalingrad. The Voronezh Front offered stubborn resistance and not until the 23rd did its two armies fall back.

By the end of July the First and Seventh Armies were defending the approaches to Stalingrad and the Sixty-second and Sixty-fourth armies were trying to keep the gate shut. However, south of these armies the German First Panzer Army reached Rostov and cut off three armies and totally destroyed four others. When the German Fourth Panzer and Sixth Armies destroyed the Soviet Twenty-first Army, this left only the Fifth and Sixth Armies and Fourth Tank Armies to restore the situation, and they were mere shadows of armies. The gate was wide open.

Stalin effectively recognised this defeat when he created the Trans-Caucasus Front under General Tyulenev with the obvious inference that the Germans would soon own the Caucasus.

Throughout August the Sixty-second and Sixty-fourth Armies fought the German Sixth Army in Stalingrad, while Budenny's Caucasus Front's four armies fell back south of Rostov into the Kuban and the Trans-Caucasus Front of four armies fell back into the Caucasus.

In September General Meretskov's Volkhov Front tried to rescue General Govorov's forces inside Leningrad. The attack was a failure and cost 60,000 Soviet lives.

Though he failed in the north, Stalin was determined he would not fail at Stalingrad. Inside the ruined city the Soviet Sixty-second and Sixty-fourth Armies fought the German Sixth Army for every building like it was a castle. Stalin had placed Zhukov in control of the Stalingrad operation, who chose to supply the city's defenders with the bare minimum of replacements, in order to husband his resources for a pincer counter-offensive. He placed Yeremenko in charge of the new Stalingrad Front to fight for the city and an 80-mile stretch of the Volga south of the city. The German Sixth Army with no available reserves now whistled to Zhukov's tune.

On 19 November the South West Front of General Vatutin and the Don Front of General Rokossovsky (totalling five armies and five corps) opened fire with 3,500 guns and slammed into the Romanian Third Army north west of Stalingrad. Next day Stalingrad Front with three armies struck the Romanian Fourth Army south of Stalingrad. Despite bitterly cold, snowy weather the Soviets broke through and on the 22nd their pincers met. A million Soviet troops had surrounded a third of a million Germans in Stalingrad.

After much bickering at Stavka the Second Guards Army was sent to hold the immediate rear of the German Sixth Army to prevent a German relief force reaching the city, while the two fronts continued their attack south west towards Rostov. They hoped to close the gate behind the Germans in the Caucasus. The term 'Guards' was an honour: evidence that the so-called classless society was melting in favour of overt elitism.

In mid-December just as the Romanians were able to stop retreating and anchor on the Italian Eighth Army in the Don Valley, the First and Third Guards Armies struck the Italians, shifting them out of their snowy trenches as quickly as the Romanians had been dislodged. By year's end the Soviets were at the Donets 100 miles from Rostov, though it had cost 90% of their attacking tanks.

However, the Germans had been forced to abandon the Caucasus and were preparing to defend the Kuban. One more Soviet sword-like thrust towards Rostov should do it, but now Stalin demanded a shove rather than a stab: the Bryansk Front under General Reiter would aim for Voronezh, the Voronezh Front under General Golikov would attack towards Kharkov, Rokossovsky's Don Front would aim for Rostov from the north, Vatutin's South West Front would aim for Rostov from the north-east and Yeremenko's Stalingrad Front (renamed South Front) would attack Rostov from the east.

The great offensive was launched in January 1943 with the Bryansk and Voronezh Fronts severely mauling the German Second and Hungarian Second Armies and taking Voronezh on the 25th. However, Rostov was only taken on 14 February. Moreover, the Voronezh and South West Fronts were hurt in savage German counter-attacks. Still, by March the Red Army held the Donets River and a salient at Kursk.

The winter campaign was undoubtedly one of the greatest victories in Russian history, with a net advance of 435 miles along a 750-mile front, which inflicted 825,000 casualties on the invaders. The Italians and Hungarians were hurt so badly they withdrew from the Russian front. The Red Army had about 750,000 casualties.

Only when the Soviet soldiers began to liberate their homes did they discover the true horror of fascist occupation. Oddly enough, it was actually worse than Soviet propaganda had described it. They found entire villages erased, their inhabitants disappeared. They found mass graves. The Jews and Gypsies had been annihilated, though Soviet propaganda denied Jews were singled out for worse treatment than other Soviet citizens. Many towns were devoid of all but children and the elderly: the Germans had forced millions to go to Germany to work for them. Soviet soldiers already knew that some of their citizens had joined the Germans, but officially this was denied. Many a soldier arrived home to find his/her family dead of starvation or war-related disease.

A new spirit arose in early 1943: a spirit spread wide by the affirmation that the Red Army was fighting for Mother Russia. Everyone still hated the NKVD, but if they could not kill them and get away with it they could at least kill the invaders, who were just as bad. Stalin contributed to the mood by releasing his tyrannical grip: he introduced officer's rank insignia in the armed forces; unit pride was encouraged; medals and campaign decorations were handed out.

Stalin's spies informed him that Hitler was planning a spring offensive against the Kursk salient. Kursk was not a logical choice, for it led nowhere, not to Moscow, Rostov or Leningrad. It was simply Hitler's way of throwing down the gauntlet and challenging Stalin to a fight to the death.

This time Stalin listened to his generals. They decided there would be no pre-emptive offensive, giving German machine gunners a target of waves of Soviet infantry. This time the Soviets would wait patiently, their defences consisting of line upon line stretching back towards the rear. Normally a defence front is a half mile thick at most and often much less. At Kursk it was 120 miles thick!

This would be one hell of a surprise for a German tank crew. The Soviets had another surprise too, 2,000 aircraft, including a newly-designed tank hunter.

On the ground awaiting the enemy were Rokossovsky's Central (ex-Don) Front, Vatutin's Voronezh Front and Koniev's Steppe Front: 5,000 tanks and 28,000 guns. The Soviets outnumbered the attackers 2:1 in planes, 2.8:1 in guns and 2:1 in tanks.

Stalin felt very confident for another reason too: Hitler had asked for peace talks. After a few meetings, Stalin sensed victory and told his emissaries to break off.

The Germans attacked on 5 July. The Central Front held the German Ninth Army in the north to an advance of just three miles a day. The Voronezh Front allowed the Fourth Panzer Army and Detachment Kempf to cover 30 miles in a few days, but in an area of rolling steppe and few trees the fighting was bloody in the hot summer sun. On the 12th at Prokhorovka the Soviets lost 500 tanks, but knocked out 300 German. This day General Popov's Bryansk Front and General Sokolovsky's West Front attacked towards Orel in the rear of German Ninth Army. On the 17th the Voronezh and Steppe Fronts counter-attacked. Two days later the Germans admitted defeat and began to fall back.

Kursk was the most important battle fought by Germany in World War II, because after its outcome was known every German, even the most rabid Nazi, knew that total victory was out of the question. The Soviets had found an antidote to the blitzkrieg (lightning war) of the German panzers: defence in depth was the answer.

Stalin was not about to let the Germans off the hook: Bryansk Front attacked to seize Orel; Central Front aimed for Sevsk; Voronezh Front aimed to cut off Kharkov; Steppe and South West Fronts attacked Kharkov. This was not blitzkrieg in reverse: the Germans were usually able to retreat in good order. The offensive was not a series of thrusts, but was more like a ham slicer, shaving off a piece of German-occupied territory every day.

By the end of September the Soviets had reached the Dniepr, but one law Stalin had to obey was the supply rule: the further the Red Army advanced, the fewer supplies it had, the more men had to be assigned to guard those long supply lines, the less were available to continue the advance.

One notable achievement was the levering of the Germans out of the Kuban. This released the troops of Petrov's Caucasus Front for action on the main front.

In late October the 150,000 troops of General Tolbukhin's 4th Ukrainian (ex-South) Front attacked between the Crimea and Zaporozhye, cutting off almost 300,000 enemy in the Crimea by 1 November.

Two weeks later and 300 miles north the 400,000 soldiers of the 1st (ex-Voronezh) Ukrainian and 2nd (ex-Steppe) Ukrainian Fronts launched a major offensive to reach Poland – they had to be satisfied with Kiev.

Elsewhere smaller offensives continued. Every day the Red Army was attacking somewhere.

In January 1944 the Volkhov Front attacked with 290,000 troops, 1,200 tanks against 50,000 Germans and 200 tanks and broke through to the defenders of Leningrad on the 27th. It had taken 880 days to cover the 30 miles between them. Though hundreds of thousands of the population of Leningrad had been evacuated by air and over the lake, the city had lost a million lives.

With the Leningrad Front released for mobile operations it joined the Volkhov Front in advancing westwards towards Estonia. To their south the 2nd Baltic Front of

General Popov helped them capture Luga on 13 February and by March they surrounded the Germans in Pskov and reached Lake Peipus. This 80-mile water barrier gave the Soviets the opportunity to disband the Volkhov Front, its troops to be sent to reimburse other fronts. Thus ended the Leningrad offensive.

The Western Ukraine offensive in January resulted in the 1st Ukrainian Front taking Lutsk and Rovno in Poland by 2 February. The 2nd Ukrainian Front took Korsun, capturing 18,200 Germans and killing or wounding 55,000 at a cost of 70,000 killed and wounded. The 3rd and 4th Ukrainian Fronts attacked with 257,000 troops and 1,400 tanks to capture Krivoi Rog with a pincer movement.

Stavka could sense a sweeping victory in the Ukraine, and they ordered attacks while the Germans were still off balance and the spring thaw had yet to arrive. In the Ukraine the Red Army had increased to 25 armies with 890,000 soldiers and 6,400 tanks to attack the enemy's 107,000 men and 1,300 tanks.

While the 2nd Byelorussian Front of General Kurochkin made a strong feint towards Brest Litovsk, the 1st Ukrainian Front (personally led by Zhukov since Vatutin had been killed by anti-communist partisans) attacked towards Tarnopol, Marshal Koniev's 2nd Ukrainian Front aimed for the upper Dniestr, the 3rd Ukrainian Front of Marshal Malinovsky attempted to seize the lower Dniestr and General Tolbukhin's 4th Ukrainian Front rolled up the Black Sea coast while masking the Crimea.

The offensive gained ground on 6 March and by the 12th Soviet troops were crossing the Yuzhni Bug River. Zhukov trapped a German force near Tarnopol, Koniev's troops crossed the Dniestr, and between them Koniev and Zhukov trapped a German element at Kamenets-Podolsky east of the Dniestr by the 27th. Stalin urged his generals towards the Prut River, before the supply officers yelled 'not one step further'.

Koniev's fellows made a supreme effort and crossed the Prut in the face of strong Romanian resistance on 10 April.

On the coast Tolbukhin's divisions launched two offensives in the fine spring weather: one towards Odessa and the other into the Crimea. On the 10th Malinovsky's forces charged down from the north to take Odessa, thereupon Tolbukhin concentrated on the Crimea.

The Western Ukraine offensive had wiped out eighteen enemy divisions and inflicted 50% or more casualties on sixty-eight.

Tolbukhin threw all of his thirty divisions, 475,000 troops, 6,000 guns, 500 tanks and 1,250 planes into the Crimea on 8 April. He steadily squeezed the Romanians and Germans back to Sevastopol, which they evacuated by 12 May. The Red Army inflicted 108,000 casualties on the enemy.

The Red Army of 1944 was a far different animal than that of 1941. The Soviets were winning not just because they had more manpower and equipment: they had had that in 1941; but because they were applying this overwhelming force where it would do the most good.

Nonetheless the discrepancy between the Soviets and Germans is noteworthy. Both Germany and the USSR had few long range bombers, preferring to use their air force as an extension of their army. As a result Soviet factories were practically immune from aerial damage. As long as the Soviets could transplant a factory out of the way of enemy ground forces they could produce a mountain of equipment for their war machine. However, German factories were under devastating Anglo-American air attack.

During 1941-45 the USSR out-produced Germany in tanks 95,000 to 54,000, guns 188,000 to 102,000, mortars 348,000 to 68,000 and planes 108,000 to 79,000. More to the point, the Germans had to fight nuisance campaigns in Africa and Italy, and a serious campaign in the west as of June 1944.

The Germans' raw materials came from their own soil, their friends and neighbours and from soil they conquered. The USSR via the Arctic Ocean and Iran had access to the entire world's raw materials, courtesy of the USA and Britain. Indeed the Soviets only had to place the order and the allies would ensure they got it. The USSR also had access to Anglo-American industry. The American truck proved to be the most important item shipped to the USSR.

Once the steel was in Stalin's hands he and his generals had the option of turning it into a sword or a hammer. In early 1944 Stalin had at last begun to listen regularly to his generals, especially Zhukov, who urged him to forge a sword. The result was instead of the broad push and shove offensive of 1943, 1944 saw rapier-like thrusts, which sliced off whole regiments, divisions, corps and armies.

Of course distance still had to be overcome and each day the Soviet advance stretched the supply system like an elastic band. If stretched far enough it would snap. In the Ukraine the Soviets stretched their supply line 400 miles and in late April had to shut down or else. The enemy was, however, falling back on his supplies.

Now Stavka released the armies in the centre, who had been raring to go for weeks. For this Byelorussia offensive Stavka assembled the 1st Baltic Front of General Bagramyan which would aim for Usachi from the north to cut off Vitebsk, the 3rd Byelorussian Front under General Chernyakovsky which would attack south of Vitebsk, the 2nd Byelorussian Front of General Zakharov which had Mogilev and the Berezina River as its targets, and the 1st Byelorussian Front of Marshal Rokossovsky which planned to take Slutsk. Together these four generals controlled 1,245,000 troops, 2,715 tanks, 23,355 guns and 5,327 aircraft.

The offensive began on 22 June and caught the Germans by surprise. In five days Vitebsk and forty-six enemy divisions were encircled. In another two days Chernyakovsky had troops across the Berezina and had surrounded two corps at Mogilev, and Rokossovsky's divisions were battling for Slutsk 100 miles from his start line.

By 6 July the 1st Byelorussian Front was in Kovel, Poland, and between them Zakharov and Chernyakovsky had surrounded 105,000 enemy in Minsk. Bagramyan had a pocket trapped at Polotsk. Like dam water

pouring through cracks, the Soviets advanced.

On the 13th Koniev's 1st Ukrainian Front joined the battle with eighty divisions, 1,200,000 soldiers, 2,050 tanks, 20,000 guns and 3,250 planes, and pushed into Przemysl on the 23rd, the day that Rokossovsky's divisions entered Lublin. Four days later Bagramyan took Dvinsk in Lithuania and Chernyakovsky surrounded Vilnius.

By now Yeremenko's 2nd Baltic Front had attacked south of Lake Peipus into Latvia. By the end of July Rokossovsky had a Polish corps across the Vistula and other troops in Praga opposite Warsaw. Most pleasing of all Chernyakovsky had tanks 50 miles from Hitler's headquarters in Rastenburg, Germany!

As noted above it was now the habit of the Soviets to bypass German held cities and let the garrison starve or surrender. The anti-German resistance in Warsaw did not know this and openly rebelled on 1 August. By this date the supply line was stretched again and the Poles were being forced back to the east bank of the Vistula.

Thus ended the Byelorussian offensive, which destroyed seventeen enemy divisions and halved another fifty, (a total of 825,000 enemy casualties) at a cost to the Red Army of 600,000 casualties.

The advance could continue, but only in the Baltic states where distances were shorter: there the enemy was pushed into the coastal area of Latvia.

The 1st Baltic Front entered Germany and now began to exact a terrible revenge on the largely innocent inhabitants.

The Romanians were talking peace when the 2nd and 3rd Ukrainian Fronts decided to settle the issue by invading Romania on 19 August with 900,000 troops, 1,850 tanks, 19,000 guns and 3,200 planes. The defences collapsed in two days: the Germans running and the Romanians surrendering. In two weeks most of Romania was overrun and the Red Army invaded Bulgaria meeting no resistance and approached the eastern borders of Yugoslavia and Hungary.

This month the Finns called it quits. This freed forty-one Soviet divisions for operations elsewhere, minus the Fourteenth Army, which attacked Kirkenes in German-occupied Norway and for 15,000 casualties gained a permanent foothold.

Not only had Bulgaria and Romania surrendered but had joined the Soviets, placing their armies under Soviet orders. This forced the Germans to evacuate Greece and Albania.

Only on 19 October were the 3rd Ukrainian Front and Bulgarians and communist partisans of Yugoslavia (Titoists) able to conquer southern Yugoslavia and Belgrade. The effort spent was so costly that the 175 miles between Belgrade and the sea would remain in German hands for another six months.

For political reasons Stalin wanted Budapest, the Hungarian capital, and was prepared to pay almost any price to get it. 2nd Ukrainian Front and the Romanians battled Germans and Hungarians while the armoured formations of both sides danced in waltz-like manoeuvres. The result was a noisy, bloody stalemate with three Soviet corps trapped at Nyiregyhaza on 24 October.

On the 31st the Red Army finally broke through the Hungarian defences and on 5 November began shelling Budapest. Malinovsky was content for his men to make lunges in the area, slowly but certainly encircling the city.

By year's end the encirclement was complete, trapping 70,000 defenders.

On 14 September the Red Army tried to free Latvia of axis forces by attacking with the 1st, 2nd and 3rd Baltic Fronts: one hundred and twenty-five Soviet divisions and 3,000 tanks, but they failed as a good-sized German force held on like grim death. A second attempt launched on 2 October captured Riga by the 15th, but the Germans still held the coast.

The Anglo-Americans waged war one offensive at a time with breaks in between. Stavka hit upon the strategy of always having one pot on the boil. A look at the dates of the 1944 offensives explains this approach: Western Ukraine January to 17 April, Crimea 8 April to 12 May; Byelorussia 22 June to 29 August; Lwow 13 July to 29 August; Romania 19 August to 14 October; Latvia 14 Sep-

tember to 20 November; Budapest 20 October into 1945. The Germans never knew where the next offensive was coming and often their reserves only reached a threatened area simply to find they were needed more urgently elsewhere.

The front line south of Latvia was only 930 miles long now. Here were 3,900,000 Soviet soldiers divided into five fronts, containing 68 armies, 9,760 tanks and 74,000 guns. They also had allies now: a Czech corps, a Bulgarian army, two Polish and two Romanian armies.

On 12 January the Red Army launched a new offensive into western Poland. From south to north the 1st Ukrainian Front of General Koniev was aiming for Cracow, the 1st Byelorussian Front of Marshal Zhukov was to bypass Warsaw, Rokossovsky's 2nd Byelorussian Front targeted Danzig, Chernyakovsky's 3rd Byelorussian Front was swinging north towards Koenigsburg and Bagramyan's 1st Baltic Front was sweeping along the Baltic coast.

Chernyakovsky's forces managed only three miles a day over frozen ground in the face of fierce resistance by German boys as young as twelve defending their villages. Rokossovsky's divisions cut behind them and reached the sea on the 28th.

Zhukov put the Polish First Army into Warsaw on the first day of the offensive, passed Lodz, encircled Poznan and, by the time supply restrictions halted him on the 31st, had tanks on the Oder fifty miles from Berlin! Berliners could hear the battle.

Koniev's troops swept into Cracow on the 19th then began a siege of Breslau on the 24th.

The Poland offensive has been called the peak of Soviet military achievement, not least because the commanders from front down to division were allowed to show initiative. They also showed flair and on occasion bare-faced cheek. So far it had cost them 150,000 casualties.

Furthermore when the supply officers said an assault over the Oder was out of the question, especially as there was an unusually early thaw, the generals turned to major mopping up operations, with the 1st and 2nd Byelorussian Fronts swerving hard right and marching to the sea.

There is the firm possibility that the generals preferred to see their men in action than become bored and frustrated with inaction. Alcoholism and poor discipline were constant problems. The generals did not mind if their soldiers looted, raped and murdered: the locals were after all Germans; but only as long as the soldiers did it under orders. They had come too far to see their armies disintegrate into mobs of drunken thieves.

By 5 March Zhukov's warriors had taken Stargard and on the 18th they stormed the fortress city of Kolberg. Danzig was claimed by Rokossovsky's divisions on the 30th.

Though Budapest was occupied on 18 February, its garrison being totally destroyed, the Germans tried to recapture that prestigious city on 6 March. For a week the 2nd and 3rd Ukrainian Fronts slaughtered the Germans: then it was all over.

The 2nd Ukrainian Front now began inching their way up the Danube on which lay two capital cities, Bratislava and Vienna. On their northern flank Yeremenko's 4th Ukrainian Front aimed for Zilina, Moravska Ostrava, Brno and Prague.

It was only in April that the Titoists, Bulgarians and 3rd Ukrainian Front were able to push the enemy out of north east Yugoslavia, so that they were in Austria by the middle of the month, by which time the 2nd Ukrainian Front had captured Vienna.

Meanwhile along the Oder the Red Army had been stockpiling supplies for their Berlin operation. The generals were becoming anxious: by 11 April the Americans were only 75 miles west of Berlin. On the 16th the Soviets opened fire with 45,000 guns: the night becoming day, with gunners suffering such concussion they bled from the ears. Then 6,250 tanks and 2,500,000 troops of Zhukov's 1st Byelorussians and Koniev's 1st Ukrainians charged over the top into the mouths of 10,400 guns, 950 tanks and a million men. Koniev was under orders to pass Berlin, but he wanted that city for his own men and women: thinking they deserved such a prize.

Yet as early as the 21st Zhukov had troops in the suburbs. So Koniev reluctantly ordered a resumption of his original orders.

On the 25th his Fifth Guards Army met US First Army: the Americans and Soviets danced with each other.

The streets of Berlin were an absolute nightmare for everyone. Some Germans surrendered eagerly, only to be fired upon by boys filled with nazi propaganda, the bullets killing Germans and Soviets alike. Smoke seemed to hide so much of the combat. It was a big city, but for the infantry it was a tiny, lonely battle. Only on 2 May with Hitler dead did the garrison commander surrender.

Berlin cost Koniev and Zhukov 100,000 killed and 200,000 wounded. (For comparison, these were higher losses than that of US ground forces against Japan in the entire war).

On 2 May Rokossovsky's divisions met the British at Wismar. On the 7th the Germans surrendered to the western allies and formally to the Soviets on the 8th. It was in fact the 11th before all major fighting around Prague ceased. Not counting Berlin, the last twenty-six days cost the Red Army a quarter of a million casualties.

Stalin announced the Great Patriotic War was at an end, but this did not mean the fighting was over. Red Army and NKVD were in action against anti-communist partisans and bypassed axis soldiers in Latvia, Estonia, Lithuania, Poland, Ukrainia, Ruthenia, Bukovina and Bessarabia. Many units freed from the war against Germany's regular forces now retraced their steps to fight the partisans. It was heartbreaking to see someone, who had survived battle after battle since 1941, succumb to a sniper's bullet. The fighting was bitter with no quarter expected on either side.

The Karelian Front, which had fought Finns and Germans was transferred to Siberia and renamed 1st Far Eastern Front. Stalin had promised the allies he would attack Japan three months after Germany surrendered. He was a man of his word when it came to invading someone. The 1st Far Eastern Front put four armies north of Vladivostok; the 2nd Far Eastern front had three armies and a corps to the north of Manchuria; and the Trans-Baikal Front had five armies and a corps on the west side. In total 1,500,000 troops, 28,000 guns, 5,550 tanks and 4,370 planes were facing a million Japanese, 5,360 guns, 1,115 tanks and 1,800 planes.

More important than numbers was quality: the Soviets had excellent tanks and aircraft and a well-honed fighting force of proven leaders and combat veterans. The Japanese had inferior quality equipment, poor leaders and few veterans. Frankly the Japanese did not stand a cat's chance in hell.

On 9 August the Soviets invaded. Within six days the Trans-Baikal Front was 150 miles inside China and 100 miles inside Manchuria. The 1st Far Eastern Front was 50 miles inside Manchuria and entering Korea.

On the 15th Japan surrendered to the allies, but many an individual Japanese fought on, not relishing the thought of life in a Soviet prison camp. By the 19th the Trans-Baikal Front was 560 miles inside China having crossed the Gobi desert. Other Soviet troops invaded Sakhalin Island, learning at first hand the type of Pacific island warfare the Americans had been fighting.

The fighting ended in early September. Soviet losses were 8,000 killed and 27,000 wounded.

The war against the partisans continued until 1948, with some Lithuanian partisans not giving up until 1953 and a few diehard Ukrainians in the Carpathian Mountains fighting until 1957. At least 40,000 Soviet troops were killed in anti-partisan combat after May 1945.

Soviet casualties for the war years will never be known with even a modicum of accuracy. Poor record keeping coupled with deliberate falsification for propaganda reasons has seen to this.

From 1939 to 1949 Soviet uniformed and partisan personnel suffered roughly 10,000,000 deaths from battle, accident (e.g. plane crashes), disease and starvation. Red Army soldiers often went into battle hungry.

Additionally, of the 5,700,000 soldiers taken prisoner, about 500,000 subsequently escaped and at least 1,000,000 joined the Germans, but 3,300,000 died in enemy custody. The death rate among those who did not join the Germans was about 70%. (For comparison Russian prisoners in German hands in World War I suffered 5.4% deaths)

The invaders killed about 1,500,000 pre-1939 Soviet civilians, plus at least 5,000,000 died from starvation, freezing, war-related illnesses, cross-fires and air raids.

In 1939-1949 circa 9,000,000 pre-1939 Soviet citizens died in NKVD hands (i.e. this does not count the hundreds of thousands of victims who came from the lands conquered from September 1939 on).

Thus Stalin's wars in this ten year period claimed at least 29 million lives among his pre-1939 citizens.

Stalin's popularity increased because of the victory, the communist party enrolling record numbers: giving it almost 3% of the population!

Statistically the Soviets fought the bulk of Hitler's war machine and suffered accordingly: in December 1941 they were fighting 75% of Hitler's divisions; in December 1943 67% and in March 1945 64%. They were also fighting Germany's partners.

However, things must be seen in perspective. During the twenty-one months following Germany's invasion of Poland, the Soviets actually aided Germany. Finland and Romania would never have become axis belligerents if it was not for Stalin. The Soviets did not tangle with Germany's navy : the western allies did that; and as has been seen the Anglo-American air offensive had significant influence on Hitler's ability to fight Stalin, not least of which keeping 100,000 flak guns busy. When the allied war against Japan and Italy is taken into consideration the perspective changes again. Claims that Japan was no threat to the USSR are nonsense, the Japanese invasions of the USSR in 1938 and 1939 proved that. When Stalin made war on Japan in August 1945 he did it for himself, not as a favour to the allies.

Still, the sheer scale of the horror suffered by the Soviet people is indefinable, too big to be truly understood. As Napoleon said: "One death is a tragedy: a million are statistics."

See Index

UNITED KINGDOM OF GREAT BRITAIN
AND NORTHERN IRELAND (UK)

Other names:	often referred to as Britain or England.(author includes Isle of Man and Channel Islands)
Status in 1939:	independent.
Population in 1939:	46,000,000.
Make-up in 1939:	Northern Ireland = Scottish and Anglo-Saxon stock, c 1,000,000; Irish-Celtic stock c 500,000; Great Britain = Scotland basically Celtic stock, c 4,000,000; Wales basically Celtic stock, c 2,500,000; England basically Anglo-Saxons c 38,000,000.
Languages:	2% of Scots Gaelic-speaking; 30% of Welsh Welsh-speaking; all others use English with dialect variations.
Religion:	Christian.
Location:	off west coast of Europe

By the 1930s the British (culturally and politically dominated by the English) had achieved the largest empire the world has ever seen. This had been gained by possessing the world's finest navy, a magnificent merchant fleet, a keen sense of opportunism, a flair for trade and the willingness to challenge anyone who got in the way.

The British honestly believed they were bringing to the conquered a British sense of fair play and justice; and armed with such a belief the average Briton viewed colonial wars, an average of one a year for over 100 years, as a regrettable side effect of their mission to civilise the world.

This attitude thrived as long as the wars did not infringe upon the lifestyle of the average Briton. The only ones who fought on land or sea were volunteers: officers, recruited from a poorly educated aristocracy/landed gentry; and other ranks recruited from the uneducated underclass. While the people always cheered the Army and stood in awe of officers, they despised common soldiers.

Even when fighting Europeans the British had been extremely loath to commit large armies. At Waterloo, the greatest British victory of the 19th century, only a quarter of the winning troops were in fact British.

British historians played down the other fellows, disgracefully.

When Britain declared war on Russia in 1854 she initially mobilised an army of only 25,000.

This all changed in 1914. With a naivety that with hindsight is astonishing the British generals marched into the Great War (World War I) to maintain the balance of power by imitating the Europeans, who raised their armies by conscription and thought in terms of millions not a few thousand. Every recruiters' trick was used to gain volunteers. Women were encouraged to spurn advances from any man not in uniform, but by 1916 the government had to resort to conscription.

The Western Front of Belgium and France slaughtered British manhood. To this day British village war memorials are stark reminders of the tragedy: their list of names seemingly far too long for the size of the community.

Thus it is understandable that less than twenty years later, when Hitler rearmed Germany and annexed Austria, the British politicians did little but wring their hands and hope for the best. No elected official dared suggest that British manhood repeat 'the Great War'.

In 1938 British Prime Minister Chamberlain met Hitler, begging him, almost on bended knee, not to start a war with Czecho-Slovakia, and when Hitler agreed to take just a slice of Czecho-Slovakia, the British and French governments eagerly handed it to him. The British public cheered Chamberlain when he returned.

In March 1939 Hitler took over the rest of Czecho-Slovakia, and this angered the British parliament so much, knowing their Prime Minister had been made to look like a fool, they responded with a knee-jerk reaction: they guaranteed the Polish border. As usual their prime purpose was to maintain the balance of power in Europe: i.e. the British were terrified of Europe becoming united under one dictator. As far as the British were concerned Hitler was the reincarnation of the Kaiser, Napoleon, Louis XIV and William the Conqueror.

When Hitler ignored the British guarantee and invaded Poland on 1 September

1939, parliament urged Chamberlain to declare war: Hitler had called their bluff and it was a matter of honour that they meet their obligations. After two days of argument a despondent Chamberlain agreed and informed his empire they were now at war.

Once done, the British politicians wondered what had happened. Almost without thinking they had plunged into another war: in effect a repeat of the Great War. City folk evacuated their children to the countryside, as everyone expected German air raids. An air raid false alarm on the 3rd panicked Londoners. Wiser heads knew that no German plane had the range to bomb Britain!

The government was not about to make the same mistakes as in 1914. The regular Army was small and spread all over the empire and there were a few divisions of reservists, who were called to full-time duty. Traditionally, the people were never asked for their opinion by a government consisting of men from the upper classes, therefore Britons had developed a habit of voting with their feet. The government suspected that if allowed to remain out of uniform the vast majority of British males would do so. Perhaps they were no longer as gullible as they had been in 1914. Therefore, conscription into the reserves was introduced in July and in September all men from nineteen into their forties were informed they would be called to full-time service eventually, the youngest first. Unlike 1914 the armed forces need not rely on recruiters' tricks.

Moreover, everyone was ordered into essential jobs, women included: cosmetics assistants found themselves making shells; traditional male jobs fell to women; 200,000 men were conscripted into coal mines. The government issued severe rationing for almost all items and issued every citizen with a gas mask in case the Germans dropped gas bombs.

The generals were willing to fight the Great War again, but only if a significantly smaller Army was used, with the obvious intention of keeping casualties low. Only ten divisions, at 13,863 men each, were at first sent to France to aid France's hundred divisions. Neither nation was eager to begin hostilities and after declaring war on Germany

the British and French armies spent the next eight months staring at the German border. Only after a hundred days of what the British press called 'world war' was a British soldier killed. The disgusted press soon renamed it the 'Phoney War'.

Not that Britons weren't fighting. The Royal Air Force, whose planes had greater range than German ones, began bombing the Germans on the first night of the war. At sea British merchant and naval vessels alike were in danger from German submarines, surface warships, mines and aircraft, but apart from a surprise submarine raid on the British naval base at Scapa Flow, which sank a battleship, the sea war was one area which caused the British no worries – as yet.

In February 1940 the war at sea took a new turn when Churchill, the political boss of the Royal Navy, announced that all British merchant ships would be armed. He had lost 170 merchant ships in five months and did not want to lose more. However, this removed any moral qualms from the Germans about sinking merchant vessels. Hitherto, they had at least allowed the crews to evacuate before doing so. Now they could not afford to order a merchant ship to stop, for fear it would open fire. From now on they would shoot first and ask questions never.

Churchill was constantly coming up with controversial stratagems. One was to invade neutral Norway and Sweden to destroy Sweden's iron ore mines. Chamberlain modified it to simply mining Norwegian waters. Even this would be an act of war on a friendly state.

Chamberlain had actually toyed with sending an expedition to fight the USSR in Finland. Fortunately, the Finns surrendered before this disastrous move was made.

On 9 April as the Royal Navy began to secretly mine Norwegian waters, the Germans invaded Norway. This was an unbelievable coincidence. The Royal Navy had sailed as an enemy of Norway and arrived as a rescuer.

As the Finland expedition troops were no longer needed, Chamberlain despatched them to Norway at once, but this was another knee-jerk reaction with no planning. Colonels and majors had to improvise on the spot. The result was a complete shambles. Within weeks the British were rapidly coming home. British losses on land were 1,869 killed, wounded and missing, and at sea a carrier, two cruisers, eight destroyers and five submarines and 2,500 lives.

On 10 May 1940 Churchill eased into the driving seat. Parliament was angry at Chamberlain, for he had failed to keep the peace and then had failed to wage war. Still as despondent as he had been in September, he stepped down. Churchill ostensibly set up an all-party government, but in truth as prime minister put his personal stamp on everything.

By coincidence this same morning the Germans invaded Belgium. Following a contingency plan the British Expeditionary Force (BEF) in France of the 1st, 2nd, 3rd, 4th, 5th, 12th, 23rd, 42nd, 44th, 46th, 48th, 50th and 51st Divisions began driving into Belgium.

The worst nightmare of the British, a return to the battlefields of the Great War, had become reality. The generals were panicky. Their government was brand new. The troops were apprehensive. Their equipment was poor. There was a shortage of junior officers: aristocrats these days were choosing the RAF. The sergeants were Great War veterans and did not look forward to combat. A few younger regulars had seen colonial wars, but most had spent their time in bazaars and night clubs. The reservists had been given no serious training.

A look at the fate of one British infantry battalion, chosen at random, gives a good account of how the British Army met its obligation. The German attack was four days old before the 1st Battalion South Lancashires (4th Division) boarded trucks for Belgium. They arrived at Veldkant on the night of the 14th under air attack and entered the line at 10.30 next morning anchoring the entire BEF to the Belgian Army. Thirty-one hours later without having seen a German, they were ordered to retreat. Seemingly the British generals were not going to fight here after all!

That night this battalion fought its first skirmish - with the Belgians - losing one killed and two wounded! A clear case of inexperience.

On the 20th still in retreat the battalion was shelled and suffered four wounded. On the 22nd they finally set up a defensive position at Okkerwijk. They spent the day under light shellfire and air raids, losing two killed, but that night were ordered to retreat again.

On the 23rd they set up defences at Triez-Cailloux and were lightly shelled for four days. Already the entire BEF was evacuating from Dunkirk to Britain.

Ordered to retreat on the 27th the battalion left a rearguard at Ploegstreet which at 4.00pm on the 28th fired a shot at advancing Germans: the first of the battalion to do so! That night two companies got lost.

On the 29th the battalion reassembled at Nieuport and was shelled for three days, suffering eight casualties. On the 30th they shot two enemy scouts.

On the 31st they fought off their first enemy attack at a cost of fourteen casualties.

Next day they retreated to the beach near Dunkirk and embarked aboard ship under air attack. They were in England by 5.30pm.

The above is representative of the fate of most of the British battalions. They spent their time running: under orders to be sure; but running nonetheless. Their generals had lost all aggressive spirit. The troops deserved better.

When this battalion reached England their brigade commander told them 'You fought like Tigers', an obvious morale-boosting overstatement if there ever was one. In three weeks of combat the battalion lost 40 killed and wounded: 4½%.

When British soldiers returned from Dunkirk they expected their people to abuse them as cowards: they were astonished to be cheered as heroes. The government was telling the people that the British lads had shown courage, but that the Belgians and French wouldn't fight. The former was true and the latter was not, but Churchill couldn't very well admit his generals had no stomach for a fight. Lord Gort, the commander of the BEF, was given a desk job. Churchill refused to authorise a combat decoration for the affair.

The campaign had been the most shameful in British history. The BEF had suffered about 5,000 killed and wounded in ground fighting, inflicting negligible casualties on the Germans. However, 2,000 troops had died in the short sea crossing when German planes bombed their ships. The Dunkirk Spirit was born in the waters off Dunkirk, as vessels of all sizes made their way there to rescue the lads. Even private yachts and motor boats were commandeered, many of their owners going with them, to carry troops between the beaches and the larger ships. German shellfire and bombing was constant: 250 vessels were sunk, but 224,000 British and 142,000 French soldiers were rescued by 4 June.

The battle now switched to France where elements of the BEF were being reinforced. However, few Britons encountered the enemy. The 51st Division was forced to surrender. On 17 June, when French Prime Minister Pétain announced he was seeking terms, the British made for the ports: 144,000 Britons were evacuated, but 6,000 died when their ships were bombed.

In May and June the BEF lost 11,000 killed and 100 tanks, 2,500 guns, 64,000 vehicles and 41,340 men abandoned.

Churchill had begun a propaganda campaign against the French to hide his generals' shortcomings and on 3 July he turned this into all-out war, when a British fleet opened fire without warning on a French fleet at Mers-el-Kebir, while French ships in British ports were boarded. It was a cack-handed way of trying to woo the French Navy. From this day onward Britain was at war with the France of Pétain.

Churchill knew from his excellent intelligence network of radio eavesdroppers and codebreakers that Hitler had no intention of invading. However, Churchill knew Hitler was an opportunist par excellence who would invade if he got the opportunity. Churchill intended to deny him that opportunity. He had refused to send his new Spitfire planes to France and now he protected the Hurricanes and Spitfires of Fighter Command like a mother hen, for he knew the Germans would have to gain control of the air before invading.

During July British fighters protected convoys sailing the Channel under the very noses of the Germans, who standing on the French coast could quite literally see England and the water between. German artillery began to shell England!

The public braced themselves for invasion: everyone expected Herr Hitler to come calling. As yet most men had not been called to duty. Films of football games of the time show thousands of young men in civilian clothes, almost none in uniform. This was because the armed forces did not have any equipment for them. The BEF had come back with rifles at most: having abandoned everything else.

As part of the invasion plans a Home Guard was formed, which contained volunteers between sixteen and whatever. Serving a few hours a week, these fellows were initially ill-equipped but made up for this with enthusiasm and courage.

Success was now foreseen in the air and it was to the fighter pilot whom everyone looked for salvation.

German planes now had the range to hit Britain for they were flying from Belgium and Norway, and in July they struck ports in Wales and south-east England. However, it was 12 August when the Germans came for real, wave after wave of bombers and fighters: they had 3,000. Fighter Command had just over 600 pilots to meet them. The day's tally was 22 British to 31 German planes shot down. Airfields in south-east England were bombed.

Next day airfields all over England were struck, but the score in the air was thirteen British to 45 German. Only seven of the British pilots were killed and this proved to be the most important point from now on. Half or more of the British pilots survived being shot down and parachuted onto friendly soil. Some were in action again within hours. However, every one of the flyers in a shot down German plane was lost, whether he died or parachuted onto English soil.

British towns were bombed day and night: Belfast in Northern Ireland, Glasgow in Scotland, the Welsh cities and all English towns of industrial importance.

Surprisingly Hitler had placed London off limits, for fear the bombers would cause massive civilian casualties, but on the night of the 24th a German bomber accidentally dropped its load on London. In retaliation the RAF bombed Berlin.

Hitler accepted the challenge and on 7 September he ordered raids on London. From now on London was very much a target.

At the end of October the Germans admitted defeat. Fighter Command and flak gunners had shot down or irreparably damaged 1,530 planes. Fighter Command had lost 787 planes, but thanks to recruitment and use of allies now had more pilots than ever and fighter production was keeping pace. Hitler ordered night bombing to continue. The few British night fighters were no threat.

Thus the Battle of Britain (daylight aerial dogfights) was over. The Blitz (the bombing of cities) continued.

Fending off a German 'invasion' of Britain was one thing, waging war was something else. Britain now had three enemies: Germany and France, both of whom Britain had chosen to fight, and Italy, which had declared war on Britain on 10 June 1940. Churchill and his military leaders divided their efforts into four parts: the Battle of the Atlantic; the German War; the French War; and the Italian War.

The Atlantic Battle would continue to be fought with the Royal Navy protecting merchant convoys, while seeking out enemy forces before they could do damage. Throughout the war the British merchant fleet would lose an average of ten ships a week.

The Germans were too smart to risk their fleet in one go, such as at Jutland in 1916, preferring to send out a couple of warships at a time and rely primarily on submarines and mines.

The British would fight the German War by the age-old method she had used against other European powers, such as Spain, namely pin-prick jabs against enemy-held territory: in this war by the use of commando raids and air attacks. Churchill was so confident in his commandos he gave them half Britain's Thompson sub-machine guns: 25!

The RAF bombers, which had lately spent most of their time dropping propaganda leaflets, were now ordered to take the war to down-town Germany. The bombers flew without fighter escort at night. Like the Germans over Britain, they had found daylight bombing to be too risky.

The British would wage the war against France by using General de Gaulle, who had fled France to Britain to carry on the struggle.

With him on their side they preached a sort of crusade to the French colonies and with a little military help here and there they knocked down French colonies like dominoes.

This left the Italian War. It would be fought in two theatres: at sea the Royal Navy would enter the Mediterranean and fight a do-or-die campaign against the powerful Italian Navy; on land the British would have to use as many non-British troops as possible to occupy Italian East Africa and Italian Libya.

By the end of 1940 they had two divisions of Indians, two of black Africans, one of white South Africans and several African brigades ready to invade East Africa. No British infantry formations larger than a battalion were present.

To fight in Libya the British gathered the 7th Armoured Division, a brigade, and the Indian 4th Division. A third of the infantry in an Indian division was British. Soon the Indians were replaced by an Australian division. Thus even in Libya few of the combat soldiers were British.

In other words Britain's new policy was to keep their Army small until there was sufficient equipment to conscript more men and to keep most of the Army out of combat until all the conscripts were trained.

In Egypt General Wavell, theatre commander, allowed General O'Connor to raid the Italians along the Libyan border in December 1940. O'Connor tried to imitate the German blitzkrieg (lightning war) tactics that had been so successful in Poland and France. He defeated the enemy so easily, he was astonished. Wavell now approved a full-scale offensive.

A combination of these tactics, the initial Italian use of poor quality Libyan troops and the fact that the British could read many of the enemy's messages gave the British one of the greatest victories in history by February 1941. Actual British casualties were but a few score.

In East Africa the British relied almost exclusively on non-British troops, but kept a firm rein on all units through British officers. General Cunningham won a startling victory over the Italians, though here it took longer. Not until November 1941 did the last Italians give up.

Italy's dictator, Mussolini, not satisfied with challenging the British Empire, had invaded Greece in October 1940. Churchill offered troops to the Greeks, seeing a way of sneaking into Europe via the back door as it were, but the Greeks only allowed British planes to aid them.

However, in March 1941 the Greeks gave in to Churchill: but where was Churchill to get this new expedition from? He could not use many British troops without undermining his policy of keeping the army secure. He ordered Wavell to send a New Zealand and an Australian divisions and a British armoured brigade. Wavell complained: this left him with only two British armoured and two Australian divisions in Libya. Churchill overruled him, gambling that the Italians would make no trouble for Wavell.

Churchill lost: just days after the troops left for Greece General Rommel arrived in Libya with a German division, took one look at the brand new British 2nd Armoured Division in front of him, attacked and completely destroyed it. This time O'Connor was on the receiving end of blitzkrieg tactics, and like the Italian generals he had scooped up, he too was meekly captured.

Churchill demanded the Libyan port of Tobruk be held, even if the country had to be abandoned. Wavell rushed the Australians to the port and they settled into a siege, supplied by the Royal Navy.

The Germans also intervened in Greece on 6 April 1941. The British generals there ordered an immediate retreat and within two weeks a naval evacuation. This seemed like a repeat of the BEF fiasco, but it wasn't. The British commanders were justified in their decisions. Nonetheless 11,500 men were abandoned, about 5,000 of them British, and the Royal Navy was angered at losing warships in yet another 'army mishmash'.

The Royal Navy had a base on Crete Island and took the evacuees there. The survivors, together with a Greek division and a British marine division, peered out to sea, awaiting the Germans. They need not have bothered: the Germans came by parachute and within a week the British generals were ordering another sea evacuation. The Royal Navy was extremely angry by now. Their losses in bringing out 29,000 troops were three cruisers and

six destroyers sunk and many warships damaged: most of the Greeks and 13,500 allied troops were killed or abandoned.

Churchill continued his policy of looking for soft targets. He sent expeditions of mostly non-British forces to conquer Iraq and French Syria in spring 1941, which gave Britain control of oilfields and considerable influence in the region. The British public did not complain that their Army was invading neutral nations. No one had ever asked them what they thought before: it never occurred to them they should be asked now.

When Hitler launched his armies against the USSR on 22 June 1941, Britain felt the benefits at once as most of the German bombers turned their backs on Britain. Without asking for anything in return, Churchill guaranteed Stalin he would supply the USSR with everything possible, even to the detriment of his own Army: and why not?

The British were already complaining that the Americans were willing to provide equipment but not willing to shed blood: yet that was their own policy with regard to colonial subjects, the dominions and now the Soviets.

It served Churchill's purpose that the Germans were now fighting the Soviets, for not only were both his ideological enemies slaughtering each other, but the Germans would suffer far more damage at the hands of the Soviets than the British could ever inflict. The disparity between war Soviet style and war British style is easy to show: in June-July 1941 the Soviets lost over 100,000 killed in action. In this same period total British ground losses at Tobruk, Libya-Egypt border, Syria, East Africa and commando raids was less than 500 killed. Put another way, the Soviets killed more Germans in a week than the British had in almost two years of war.

The Australians in Tobruk were holding on bravely and in August 1941 Churchill decided that it was time for a real British commitment to the desert war, as it was known in Libya-Egypt. Perhaps the reports of Soviet losses embarrassed him.

Wavell had become the scapegoat after Churchill's defeats in Greece and Libya and was replaced by General Auchinleck. General Cunningham, fresh from his victory in

East Africa, was brought to Egypt to command all allied combat formations under the new British Eighth Army, while in Tobruk, still accessible by sea, the Australians were slowly replaced by Czechs and Poles and the British 70th Division: the first British infantry division to see action since France!

Cunningham planned Operation Crusader to rescue Tobruk by an overland attack using the 7th Armoured Division and three brigades of Britons and the New Zealand 2nd, Indian 4th and South African 1st and 2nd Divisions. A high proportion of Cunningham's rear-echelon personnel were non-British.

Crusader began on 18 November 1941 and over the next six weeks the allied army (with troops of twelve nations it obviously should have been named allied not British) fought a tremendous campaign that ended with the Germans and Italians falling back to their kick-off line of the previous March. For 18,000 casualties the allies inflicted 33,000 casualties.

It was a great victory, that unfortunately was soured when three weeks later, on 21 January 1942, the enemy counter-attacked, severely mauled the British 1st Armoured and Indian 4th Divisions and regained 400 miles of Libya.

The naval war against Germany was largely defensive, but the British air war against Germany became offensive when the Germans withdrew from British skies to attack the USSR. The last big raids on Britain were in May 1941. About 50,000 British civilians had been killed in air raids, 80% of them Londoners.

Fighter Command now began flying over enemy-held coasts shooting up targets of opportunity in daylight, while Bomber Command concentrated on night raids on German targets all over Europe including German cities.

The idea of bombing German cities, where civilians made items of war had always been a bone of contention. One school thought it was alright to hit factories and kill workers while they were making the goods, but not alright to hit their homes and kill them while they were asleep. To some this was silly, yet it must be remembered that the children and the elderly stayed at home and were not part of the enemy's war-making effort. Moreover, a bomb that hits a house does no damage to the military-industrial complex, but a bomb that hits a factory or rail yard does.

Air Marshal Harris took over Bomber Command in February 1942 with the avowed purpose of terrorising civilians. He was not interested in killing soldiers or blowing up equipment or derailing a train. The more homes he flattened the better. This was a shocking and unsettling attitude to some.

The excuse for this strategy was that reconnaissance proved the night bombers were fortunate if they hit the right town let alone the right factory. They flew blind. Harris decided that if his men were risking their lives – he was losing 200 a month – they might as well hit something, so he created Pathfinder units that would light up the centre of a city with incendiaries. The bombers would then mass bomb the conflagration, taking out entire neighbourhoods.

The British public did not know of this policy, but no doubt they would have approved. They had dropped leaflets, until the Germans raised the stakes by bombing cities, so the British did the same. When the Germans bombed London, they bombed Berlin. Tit for tat. Now that the Germans had killed 50,000 British civilians, the British were prepared to kill 50,000 or more Germans.

The airmen did not concern themselves with the morality question. They were too concerned about surviving. When Harris calculated half his crews would be lost in fifteen missions, he gave his men a tour of thirty missions. It was low enough to give them hope: high enough to get the most use out of them before they died. The odds of them surviving a tour were 2:1 against. Certainly no one could call the German people 'defenceless'. On many raids the loss of British flight crew outnumbered the civilian loss on the ground.

Now that the Germans were locked in a life or death struggle with the Soviets, Churchill thought he could finish off Italy and France and be in a fair position to be in on the peace talks when Germany surrendered to the USSR.

There were two flies in this buttermilk: first by December the Germans were in sight of Moscow, thus there was no guarantee the

Soviets would win the war; and secondly Japan was sabre-rattling. The British reinforced their Asian garrisons in 1941: but these were British-style reinforcements, i.e. penny packets: two capital ships to scare aware the might of the Japanese Navy, two battalions of Canadians to Hong Kong to challenge the Japanese Army, and Indian recruits to hold Malaya-Singapore. Needless to say, the Japanese were not frightened.

On 7 December 1941 (8th local time) the Japanese invaded Malaya and Hong Kong without warning. Hong Kong fell on Christmas Day. In Malaya four colonial-dominion divisions fought the invaders. Then on 15 February 1942 Percival, the commander in Malaya, surrendered his entire army of 130,000 on Singapore to a Japanese force half the size.

There is no doubt that Churchill was shocked white by this. Singapore had been his baby: he had called it a fortress.

In Burma colonial forces were in full retreat. The reinforcement of a British armoured brigade made no impact.

Yet on the day Japan began her war, Churchill slept more peacefully than ever, for the Japanese had attacked the Americans as well, and this meant the Americans were now an ally of Britain. Churchill knew the Americans would fight Germany, because they were already doing so at sea. Churchill and the American President, Roosevelt, had become friends and had cemented this alliance in summer of 1941. The Japanese attack on the USA, and then a convenient declaration of war by Germany, removed all legal barriers from Roosevelt's undeclared war on Germany.

Churchill dreamed: with American soldiers and equipment and British generals he could fight the Germans on their own terms and beat them: but not in France. No, his generals would never go for that. There they had been slaughtered in 1914-18 and humiliated in 1940: they were not eager to return there.

Churchill went to Washington at once, to make sure that the American generals and admirals did not convince Roosevelt to focus solely on Japan, but assist in the defeat of Germany too.

The Eighth Army now under General Ritchie had been reinforced and stood at British 1st and 7th Armoured and 50th Divisions, South African 1st and 2nd Divisions, one de Gaullist French, two British and an Indian brigades. On 26 May 1942 General Rommel led his Italian-German army into battle against Ritchie and proved he was the strategic master by far. In a series of leap-frog moves the British were totally outgeneralled.

They brought in the Indian 5th and 10th and New Zealand 2nd Divisions to no effect. In late June General Auchinleck, the theatre commander, personally took battlefield command, but it was already too late to stop the enemy west of Alamein. By 1 July a third of the army had been lost: 35,000 at Tobruk alone.

Auchinleck drew a line in the sand at Alamein and fought the enemy to a standstill. It cost him another 13,000 casualties, but with a timely reinforcement by an Australian division he held fast.

Churchill provided the Americans with a battlefield. The Americans were adamant they wanted to liberate the French. Churchill, a brilliant orator, talked them into attacking the French! Namely, invading French Algeria and Morocco: this would wind up his war against France, put allied troops in Tunisia behind Rommel's back, protect allied shipping in the western half of the Mediterranean, and most importantly of all it would bog down the Americans in the Mediterranean, where they could help Britain defeat Italy, rather than drag Britain into a second front in France.

On 9 November 1942 six American divisions and a British brigade landed on the coast of Algeria and Morocco and in a three-day battle convinced the French to join them. British planes flew with US markings, as Churchill thought a Frenchman might surrender to Americans quicker if he thought his traditional enemy, the English, were not involved.

Churchill's plan was working. By 11 November 1942 eight UK divisions had launched attacks on Britain's enemies, but eleven American divisions had done so. British troops were involved in smaller packets, to be sure, but this was evidence that American manpower had taken over the war effort. The trick was to retain British control of that effort. With Algeria firmly in hand the allies advanced into Tunisia.

The invasion could not have been timed better, for things were looking up in Egypt. Auchinleck had been replaced by General Alexander and Ritchie was to be replaced by Gott. Unfortunately, a plane crash ended Gott's life and Eighth Army was given to Montgomery, a poor second choice. One thing Montgomery had going for him was his attitude. He could make troops do anything.

Monty, as he was affectionately known, was given the greatest desert forces seen yet: seven infantry divisions, including the British 44th, 50th, and 51st, and three British armoured divisions (1st, 7th and 10th) and two brigades. About half his rear-echelon forces were British. In total he had 220,000 men, 900 guns, 1,400 anti-tank guns and 910 tanks. He outnumbered Rommel 4:1 in tanks, 2:1 in anti-tank guns and 2:1 in manpower. It was the first large number of actual Britons to go into action in two and a half years.

In twelve days of battle at Alamein, beginning 23 October, Montgomery inflicted 36,000 casualties at a cost of 13,500 (58% of which were British).

However, if Montgomery was the king of morale-building and the master of the set piece battle, he was no huntsman. Once Rommel ordered a retreat on 4 November Montgomery was content to send a few armoured cars after him for a week or so. Rommel's army, so devastated that a puff of wind would have destroyed it, was allowed to escape.

The Tunisian campaign was plagued by many problems: the allies landed too far from Tunisia to rush the country, giving the Germans and Italians leave to enter; the rains were due to start soon and they would ruin any chance of an advance; and the allies were on a learning curve in terms of cooperation. The British had put their First Army of General Anderson into Tunisia: he had the 6th Armoured, 1st, 46th, 56th and 78th Divisions and four brigades; the first all-British army to launch an offensive in the war. They had thought Fredendall's US II Corps and the French would be placed under Anderson, but found the Americans hostile to that idea, as were the French. Each wanted to run his own show. To the British this boded ill: a sign that the Americans thought they could win where the British had failed. To make matters worse Anderson was not a likeable fellow.

All air, land and sea forces in Tunisia were under American General Eisenhower. A nice man and very diplomatic, the British saw him as a weak strategist. They insisted Alexander be given command of land forces. Eisenhower agreed, to the chagrin of the Americans, but Alexander commanded by the common British method of making suggestions rather than issuing orders. As a result the Americans ignored him, not realising when they had been ordered to do something.

Things came to a head when Rommel attacked the Americans on 14 February. Immediately, the Yanks ran and the British had to provide their 6th Armoured Division and the French some of their troops in order to stop Rommel near Kasserine Pass on the 21st.

The British were angry that the cocky American newcomers had shown no eagerness to fight. The Americans were angry because Monty was supposed to be fighting Rommel in Libya, yet here was Rommel able to attack with his desert veterans without hindrance from the snail-like Montgomery. Monty's Eighth Army of three British armoured (1st, 7th and 10th), three British infantry (4th, 50th, and 51st), a New Zealand and an Indian division and a French and a Greek brigade, was indeed following Rommel, but the overcautious Monty would not be willing to attack for another month.

However, the Americans had taken note of their poor showing and had replaced Fredendall with Patton.

Facing dogged resistance all the way, the allies finally brought about the axis surrender in Tunisia on 12 May. The campaign cost 80,000 allied casualties, of which actual British were about 6,000 killed, 20,000 wounded and 10,000 captured, and it took six months instead of six days as planned. Allied propaganda made much of the 250,000 enemy taken prisoner, but this was mainly for public consumption.

The British had ignored the Japanese since retreating into India, except for a probe by two brigades into the Arakan at a cost of 171

British dead, and a penetration behind Japanese lines by a mixed Chindit brigade. In August 1943 Admiral Mountbatten was placed in command of South-East Asia including Burma. A lesser member of the royal family, he had specialised in commando operations for the last two years. Undoubtedly, Churchill expected him to organise cheap, headline-grabbing operations, but not to risk his Army.

Mountbatten built his army to 800,000 men, a quarter of whom were British, including two all-British divisions, but he was not at liberty to use his army. Churchill and Co. had decided that Japan was not their prime concern. Mountbatten would only be allowed to probe and launch another Chindit operation until after the 1944 summer monsoon.

Churchill did send a British Far Eastern Fleet to fight the Japanese, but from September 1943 one thing he could spare was warships. In fact over twenty of the ships were not British, including six American. This was another example of Churchill using his propaganda machine to give the impression the whole operation was purely a UK affair.

After several months aiding Mountbatten, Churchill agreed the fleet should be divided in two, part to remain with Mountbatten, the remainder, under the pretentious title British Pacific Fleet, to aid the Americans, who gave this small remnant a simple task force number, 57.

While Tunisia was being conquered the Americans began talking about France again, so Churchill pointed them towards Sicily. Sicily would be a good base only if one was going to go somewhere else in the Mediterranean, which the Americans did not want to do. Churchill's friendship with Roosevelt overcame American objections.

On 10 July 1943 the allies invaded Sicily, using forces the Americans wanted to use in France; 2,500 ships carried the US Seventh and British Eighth Armies: 160,000 men, 14,000 vehicles, 600 tanks, 1,800 guns, with more to follow. Of the twelve divisions and four brigades used in the campaign, the 5th, 50th, 51st, 78th and 1st Airborne Divisions and two brigades were British.

The Eighth Army became stuck in the marshy lowlands around Catania and around the dominating Mount Etna, while the Americans, once they were inland, met mostly Italian rear-echelon troops. The British were angered that Patton, the US commander, turned the campaign into a race, and even more angered when he won it.

However, Eisenhower, the campaign commander, and Alexander, the ground commander, had both proved diplomatic and had stilled troubled waters time and again.

Sicily led to the best result Churchill could have hoped for: the surrender of Italy. Unfortunately, it was negotiated by men on both sides who were uneasy in cloak and dagger methods and handled it badly. Much of it was bluff on the British part. They promised an invasion the likes of which, especially right after Sicily, they could not hope to deliver. Eisenhower was so angry at the deception, he refused to put his signature to it: his deputy signed.

To carry out their obligations, at least to a degree, the British talked the Americans into invading Italy, even offering to provide the bulk of the troops. Montgomery's Eighth Army invaded the toe on 3 September and found no opposition. On the 9th the US Fifth Army invaded Italy at Salerno: of its five divisions the 46th and 56th were British. Against German resistance they barely held on: this was a rough battle. The American commander kept asking 'where is Monty'. The Eighth Army were advancing slower than walking speed despite no opposition, acting like tourists. Monty refused to urge his men on. Indeed he reined them in.

By 1 October the Fifth Army had broken out of the beachhead, had reached Naples, and were advancing towards Cassino, while the Eighth Army finally got into the act on the right flank.

Italy became a muddy, static, bloody campaign. The Italians may have collapsed, but the Germans were full of fight. Churchill had chosen this battlefield. It led nowhere, for even if Italy was conquered that would only put the allies in the Alps, where no one wanted to fight. However, Churchill liked the idea of a short line – Italy was only 80 miles wide in places – for that meant it would take few divisions to man it, and as the British intended to draw upon units of several nationalities so that the British did not bear too much of the burden, Italy seemed the right place to fight.

Italy was a trap from which the allies never escaped. Of the thirty-nine allied divisions that fought here only eight were British, yet it would cost the British alone 90,000 casualties.

Churchill had hoped that Italy was the only place he would have to fight in Europe, but the Americans eventually forced him to concede to an invasion of France.

One concession the British got was that the Americans had to accept Montgomery as ground commander.

On 6 June 1944, D-Day, the allies invaded the Normandy Peninsula of France with an equal number of British and American assault battalions, plus fourteen Canadian battalions.

Anglo-American cooperation was at its best now, with Eisenhower in charge and on his staff every American had a British deputy and vice versa. The 7,000 vessels and 10,000 planes that put 155,000 men ashore by nightfall were unstoppable.

Once ashore Montgomery fought his set-piece battle and he did it methodically, though his policy of drawing the enemy armour onto the British and Canadian forces while the Americans mostly fought infantry caused raised eyebrows at home. Yet with Cherbourg on the American right flank, it was essential they be free to capture that port as soon as possible, which they did on the 29th.

In any case as German reinforcements came in from the east they naturally engaged the British first. The Germans fed these units in piecemeal, yet were able to inflict Russian Front-sized losses on the allies; losses that the British couldn't afford.

The British had farmed out many men to rear-echelon forces for non-British infantry, had 200,000 men in Burma fighting off a major Japanese offensive, an army in Italy, had 170,000 in enemy prison camps, and manned the extremely large RAF and Royal Navy. The British would eventually put 8,186,000 (including 640,000 women) into uniform, but it wasn't enough to meet commitments. While the Americans were still creating divisions, the British had already disbanded eight.

Moreover, of the thirteen British divisions that fought in Normandy (6th Airborne, 7th, 11th and Guards Armoured, and 3rd, 15th, 43rd, 49th, 50th, 51st, 52nd, 53rd and 59th Infantry) only five had seen action and two of those only a few days in June 1940. The troops had sat in Britain for the last four years and there is every indication that much of that time was wasted for they certainly were not adequately trained and they suffered as a result. Normandy honed a force of confident veterans, but at a cost in blood the British could not afford.

By mid-August when the British broke out of Normandy into northern France they had lost about 12% casualties among the fighting echelon, and some battalions were grievously hurt. The 59th Division had to be disbanded just to attempt to keep the other divisions at a strength of 18,347. As it was, many infantry battalions were reduced from four rifle companies to three.

The British Second Army charged across the Great War battlefields in just two weeks, seizing Brussels and Antwerp, and trapping over 100,000 Germans to the west: but Montgomery more or less forgot about them and they escaped to fight again. By now Montgomery only controlled the British Second and Canadian First Armies. It had been previously agreed that in September the Americans would take over command of their own troops, but even before the handover date they had begun to ignore Montgomery.

In early September Monty urged a lightning-like thrust into the Netherlands using airborne troops. It was so unlike him to urge speed that he took everyone off guard. In a week the operation was prepared and launched: two US and a British airborne divisions dropped on top of the southern Netherlands bridges. However, the British 1st Airborne Division fell into a cauldron at Arnhem. As British armour rescued the American paratroopers, the operation was not a total failure, but without the Arnhem bridge it was not a success. The bridges gained by the Americans were never needed. 6,327 British paratroopers were killed or captured.

Of the 92 allied divisions and 48 brigade-sized units that fought on the Western front fourteen divisions and nine brigades were British. Even then, the British practically shut down for the autumn and winter, leaving the Canadians, French and Americans to carry on.

In December the Americans were struck by a major German counter-offensive in the Ardennes. Montgomery as senior general in the north was given command of the northern flank, but while the Americans in the south under Bradley and Patton sliced into the enemy flanks, cutting off units, Monty preferred shovelling them back into Germany. Furthermore, he was late.

To the Americans this was bad strategy typical of Montgomery. Monty made things worse when he told the press how he had saved the Americans: failing to mention the troops he used were the US Ninth Army. He claimed it was an American intelligence failure to be caught with their pants down, but did not mention he had applied for leave just before the German onslaught.

British officers cringed when they heard Monty. He was told he had gone too far this time. Eisenhower offered his resignation: 'him or me'! Churchill and Roosevelt smoothed things over and Monty made a public apology.

As Monty's 21st Army Group was sitting north of the mountains, facing the Rhine lowlands and the north German plain beyond, he suggested he be given all necessary forces to enable him to charge to Berlin, while the Americans protected his flank. Following on the press incident, this was too much. Eisenhower refused. He opted for an all-out push by everyone. The Americans thought Monty too cautious to 'charge' to Berlin.

Besides, Berlin was no longer a goal. Eisenhower had been informed by Churchill and Roosevelt that the city would be jointly ruled by the Soviets, British and Americans, no matter who took the losses to capture it. He chose to let the Soviets take the losses.

Monty planned the crossing of the Rhine like he had the Channel in the previous June. He required weeks of planning, a mountain of supplies and airborne divisions to pave his way. Patton and his US Third Army deliberately crossed the Rhine without preparation in one night, hours before Monty's big push, just to make Monty look foolish. Patton failed to mention to the press that there were few Germans in his sector.

On the 24 March 1945 Monty crossed the Rhine with British Second Army, US Ninth Army, US 17th and British 6th Airborne Divisions. Perhaps the Americans had been right about Monty's lack of speed. By 10 April the Americans were at Hanover, but the British on their immediate left flank were way behind, not coming even until a week later. By the 21st the Americans had run out of targets and were resting, but the British were still advancing ten days later.

Even now Monty asked for American aid to cross the Elbe. The US 82nd Division wondered why Monty had needed their help: they met almost no resistance and took upwards of 100,000 prisoners!

Monty did have his day, though, on 4 May when a group of German generals approached offering to surrender. He negotiated for a complete German surrender. Once the generals had agreed to talk on this matter he sent them to Eisenhower. The surrender was signed on 7 May.

The campaign from D-Day to the end cost the British 30,280 killed and 96,670 wounded. British infantry battalions averaged 63% killed and wounded.

When informed of the surrender, the British public went berserk for a day, ecstatic, euphoric. They did not think about the war against Japan. The public had already relegated that war to the same status as a minor colonial war. British servicemen in Burma had good reason to call themselves the 'Forgotten Army'.

It was said at the time that the British had never been a finer people than during the war. This is undoubtedly true. It was their peak.

United Kingdom deaths in their greatest war were 362,950: Army 146,350; Royal Air Force 72,700; Royal Navy 51,100; Merchant Service 28,800; civilians 64,000 (air raids, ship passengers, in Japanese camps).
See Index

days. The plane dropped depth charges, which only made the submarine commander angry. He fired a brace of torpedoes at the *Greer*, which missed. The *Greer* depth-charged the submarine and missed.

Next day another American merchant-man was sunk.

On 11 September Roosevelt ordered all US forces to shoot at German submarines on sight.

Four days later a US destroyer in a convoy action was torpedoed by a German submarine, suffering severe damage and eleven killed.

In October another US merchantman was sunk. On the 30th the US destroyer *Reuben James*, escorting a British convoy, was torpedoed. She went down swiftly, of her 160 crew 115 died.

On 13 November Congress authorised the arming of all US merchant ships and the removal of war zone restrictions.

In early December two US merchantmen were sunk.

In the Atlantic the US Navy was fighting and dying, but at the Pacific base of Pearl Harbor in Hawaii they were wining and dining, worried about promotion and getting a date on Saturday night.

On Saturday 6 December 1941 US code interceptors learned that the Japanese government was to send a crucial message to the embassy in Washington answering US demands. Later, the Americans were informed by their own submarines and British intelligence that a Japanese task force was on its way to Malaya or Thailand.

At 3.42am on the 7th off Hawaii, while the servicemen ashore were sleeping off their Saturday night binge, the patrol vessel *Condor* sighted a periscope in a restricted zone. At 6.30am a supply ship sighted a 'suspicious object' and fifteen minutes later the destroyer *Ward* opened fire on it, thinking it a submarine – it submerged. Five minutes later a navy plane joined the *Ward* in depth charging the area.

At 7.02am a radar operator in Hawaii on his own time reported a swarm of aircraft and was told 'Don't worry about it.'

At 7.48am Japanese planes began attacking Kanoehe Naval Air Station. Startled marines fired at them with rifles. At 7.53am planes began strafing Ewa Marine Air Station. A minute later planes bombed Ford Island Naval Air Station. Several warships at Pearl Harbor saw this and sounded the alarm.

Seconds later the harbour which contained the Pacific Fleet comprising nine battleships, nine cruisers and smaller vessels, was attacked by dive bombers and torpedo bombers.

A minute later planes struck Hickam Airfield. Sentries fired back with pistols.

Within thirteen minutes of the beginning of the strike on the harbour the Japanese pilots could see that of the nine battleships, *Utah* and *Oklahoma* were capsizing and *California*, *Arizona* and *West Virginia* were sinking.

Japanese planes were also attacking Bellows and Wheeler Airfields, Forts Weaver, Shafter, Kamehameha, de Russy and Ruger, Schofield Barracks and Camp Malakole.

The last Japanese planes left at 9.26am. The destruction was unbelievable: five battleships, three destroyers and four other ships lost; four battleships, six cruisers, three destroyers and six other ships damaged, 170 planes destroyed, 71 civilians and 2,403 service personnel killed and 1,178 hospitalised.

Japanese losses were ten midget submarines, 30 planes, 79 lives.

The impact on the American public of such an attack cannot be over emphasised. The fact that it was made by orientals rather than whites was a major underlying current in the American reaction to the dastardly attack, as Roosevelt called it. It was as if all the subconscious fears of the white population of Negro revolt and Indian scalp raids had merged into one nightmare.

Germany and Italy declared war on the Americans within two days, but no harm came to German and Italian immigrants. With a third of Americans descended from Germans and Italians, e.g. the military leaders Nimitz, Krueger, Spaatz, Wedemeyer, Eisenhower, no race hatred could emerge. However, not only were Japanese immigrants arrested, but all Americans of Japanese race, the Nisei, were also arrested and sent to specially erected camps in wilderness areas, their property confiscated. Roosevelt was no racist, but he felt he had to allow white Americans their 'revenge'.

December brought more bad news: the loss of garrisons at Shanghai, Guam and Wake and the invasion of the Philippines. The navy informed Roosevelt that with no battleships, three carriers, sixteen cruisers and 40 destroyers in the Pacific compared to the Japanese ten battleships, ten carriers, 38 cruisers and 112 destroyers, they could not rescue the Philippines: those men were doomed.

Roosevelt's first job was to create a war-winning team and then expand the armed forces rapidly. His manner of presidency was unusual. He loved using informal 'eyes and ears' people, who would report to him what was really happening. He was often at loggerheads with his senior people, but he had put them there for that purpose. He would not tolerate sycophants.

Many of his personnel decisions seemed odd. Ultimately most of them proved correct. One of the few presidents to take his title of Commander in Chief of the armed forces seriously, he set up the Joint Chiefs of Staff: General Marshall of the Army, his sidekick General Arnold of the Army Air Force, Admiral King of the Navy and his non-voting sidekick the commandant of the Marine Corps. Chairing the four was retired Admiral Leahy as Roosevelt's representative. Through Leahy the President kept tabs on the meetings and he also spoke with each member every few days. Roosevelt gave these men an order and they decided how to implement it. It had been Roosevelt's war up until now: it would remain so.

This was bad news as far as the admirals were concerned, because Churchill arrived in Washington within days and talked Roosevelt into naming Britain's enemies in Europe as America's priority enemies. Japan would have to be left to lesser forces. Of course, Roosevelt was really only continuing his already established policy of making war on Germany.

The armed forces consisted of the Army (including the Air Force), which was selectively conscripting men within the 21-31 age group, later expanded to 18-35. Volunteers

to age 45 were accepted. The Navy and Marines took only volunteers (they began conscripting in 1943). Those who wanted to join the Army, but were of conscription age were told to go home and wait, though there was no guarantee they would be called. The prime reason for this policy was that the Army did not have enough equipment as yet.

The National Guard had already been training for over a year. These state soldiers, not to be confused with US Army reservists, had originally enlisted with the agreement that they would be called to duty from their civilian jobs only for riots and to curtail looting during floods and other natural disasters and only within their state. However, the fact that they were now expected to fight alongside the US Army did not surprise them. In previous centuries in every major American war state soldiers had always born more of the action than the US Army. Even in World War I state soldiers had made up a third of the battlefront. The Hawaii National Guard had already seen action on 7 December, of course.

Roosevelt also had to mobilise industry, though not so much with rules and laws as in other nations, but with persuasion. His first requests were laughed at, being deemed unrealistic 'pie in the sky' figures. Yet over the next four years US industry would produce these figures and more, culminating in ten battleships, 137 aircraft carriers, 48 cruisers, 349 destroyers, 203 submarines, 279,512 warplanes, 2,382,311 military trucks, 257,390 artillery guns, 88,410 tanks and self-propelled guns and 43,383,000 tons of merchant shipping.

The USA outproduced all enemy nations combined. In 1941 the USA had made only 4,052 tanks and SPGs and launched only 1,972,000 tons of merchant shipping.

The nation equipped 669,000 marines including airmen, 4,183,000 navy personnel including airmen and 11,260,000 army personnel including airmen. By 1943 the Army would have more lieutenants than the pre-1939 Army had personnel!

Eventually the Americans divided the war into five zones. Admiral Nimitz commanded the Pacific Ocean area and was ordered to secure Hawaii, the US coast and Midway and use ground forces to invade the

Solomon, Gilbert, Marshall, Marianas and Ryukyu Islands, using them as stepping stones to Japan. With no battleships Nimitz was forced to rely on carriers and submarines, which he soon learned were in fact his two most valuable weapons.

Roosevelt ordered General MacArthur to leave the Philippines in March 1942 for Australia where he was given command of South West Pacific area. He was to use primarily Australian forces at first to secure Australia. MacArthur hated to leave the Philippines and Roosevelt soothed his damaged ego with the award of the Medal of Honor. MacArthur's ego was such that Roosevelt often referred to him as 'His Majesty'.

The third zone was the United Kingdom, which became a combat zone for the Americans on 7 December 1941. The British public was surprised to see Americans in uniform within hours: obviously they were already there and had been wearing civilian clothes. In this zone the Navy was ordered to aid the British in securing the sea lanes, and on 4 July 1942 US Eighth Air Force began flying bombing missions from British airfields.

The fourth zone was the Mediterranean, which in summer 1942 saw US warships arrive and American planes begin action at Alamein.

The smallest zone was the China-Burma-India theatre commanded by General Stillwell. By February 1942 US advisers and cadre were fighting alongside the Chinese army in Burma and China. General Chennault of the Flying Tigers soon formed the 14th Air Force to bomb Japanese targets in Asia. The 10th Air Force was to aid the British in India.

In June 1942 the Japanese invaded the USA, namely the Aleutian Islands off Alaska, from which the inhabitants had fortunately been evacuated. Despite this Roosevelt saw this month's victory at Midway as crucial to the Japanese war, for four Japanese carriers were destroyed. Sensing what Napoleon called the moment of balance, Roosevelt approved offensive operations in the Pacific. Nimitz was ordered to invade the Solomons, while using air and sea forces to harass the Japanese in the Aleutians.

On 7 August 1942 Admiral Ghormley put the 1st Marine Division ashore on Guadalcanal in the Solomons. Over the next six months this would become a bloody and frustrating affair.

MacArthur went over to the offensive on New Guinea in October with Australian troops. Both he and Ghormley were reinforced by units consisting mostly of National Guard state troops: the 32ndNG Division to New Guinea; the Americal NG and 25th Divisions to Guadalcanal. Divisions normally had about 14,000 men, but marine divisions were somewhat larger. The state soldiers noted with satisfaction that they had gone into offensive action before the regular US Army.

Guadalcanal sucked in the US and Japanese navies and over five months a series of naval engagements saw US and Japanese fortunes swing like a pendulum. Fortunately for the Americans Admiral Halsey took over the campaign in October. The Japanese Navy lost two battleships, a carrier and fifteen other warships to the US two carriers and twenty-one other warships. Despite this imbalance, the Japanese surrendered their capability to seriously interfere with any US naval operations in the future.

Roosevelt wanted to go onto the offensive in Europe too, but the British opposed his suggestion to liberate France. He let Churchill provide him with a battlefield: French North Africa. A good many Americans were angry that instead of concentrating on the Japanese they were making war on the French. It would not be the last time the generals cussed out Churchill and deplored his influence on Roosevelt.

The generals were also surprised by Roosevelt's choice of commander for North Africa: General Eisenhower, a junior desk officer, who had never seen action. MacArthur said of him: 'Best clerk I ever had.'

On 8 November the 1st and 2nd Armoured and 1st, 3rd, 9th and 34thNG Divisions with a British brigade invaded Morocco and Algeria. Waving gigantic flags and wearing US emblems on their uniforms the Americans wanted the French to know they weren't British. Many French eagerly joined the Americans. Most did not, until ordered to do so on the 10th. The little affair cost the Americans over 2,000 casualties.

Eisenhower's next goal was Tunisia, which he could have had for a song if he had landed close enough, but he hadn't. By the time his forces reached Tunisia the Germans and Italians were waiting for him.

Insisting at first on being his own ground commander, Eisenhower had the British First Army, a French corps and Fredendall's US IInd Corps. With the campaign soon reduced to a slugging match in heavy rain the British suggested one of their own as ground commander, a polite way of saying they knew best. The Americans were perturbed when Eisenhower agreed.

Eisenhower had 'spies' at Fredendall's headquarters, who reported that Fredendall was showing no signs of aggression and was building a personal concrete bunker to rival the pyramids. As early as 1 December the 1st Armoured Division was held up by air attacks! US 12th Air Force was obviously unable to provide air security. The troops soon settled down, but on 21 January the 1st Armoured was again repulsed by an air attack! Then the division was repelled by Italian infantry.

The next problem with the British occurred on 14 February. Rommel's army was supposedly in Libya restrained by Montgomery's British Eighth Army, yet IInd Corps was attacked by Rommel's army. Americans from battalion commander on down fought bravely, but their colonels and generals ordered a retreat. After a week a mixed bag of Americans, including cooks, clerks and engineers, together with French and British repelled Rommel's Italians and Germans at Kasserine Pass. A near disaster was barely averted.

IInd Corps had performed badly: 1st Armoured Division lost 2,800 wounded and 3,000 dead or missing; 34thNG Division had over 2,500 casualties.

Obviously Fredendall had to go. He was replaced by George S. Patton, America's leading tank expert, known for his spit and polish and professionalism. He was also a dandy, a prima donna, who wanted headlines as much as he wanted victory. He went through II Corps like 'crap through a goose'

- his words - removing the considerable deadweight that a peacetime army gathers and sending home these hangers-on by the proverbial boatload. He promoted juniors and rewarded bravery.

His kick-ass discipline transformed the corps so that by 30 March the 1st (Infantry) Division was able to defeat the 10th Panzer Division. From now on IInd Corps, soon passed to General Bradley, would bring the enemy face to face with the American tradition of Yorktown, Gettysburg, Belleau Wood. The pride lost at Kasserine Pass would be regained a hundredfold.

Tunisia was wrapped up in May. The six-month campaign cost the allies 80,000 casualties: of which 11,700 killed and wounded and 10,600 missing were American.

Already Churchill had talked Roosevelt into invading Sicily and on 10 July 1943 in the largest amphibious operation to date, US 8th Fleet and 12th Air Force put Patton's Seventh Army ashore with the 82nd Airborne, 1st, 3rd, 9th, and 45thNG Divisions. The British invaded with an equally large force.

American airmen were now taking the war to Europe: the 8th Air Force flying from Britain and the 15th Air Force from North Africa. Heavy bomber crews were given a tour of just 25 missions, which seemed too few to the recruits until they began to fly through flak and fighter defences.

By the end of 1942 the 8th Air Force had lost just 37 planes, but had not struck inside Germany yet. In January they began to do so in daylight escorted by allied fighters as far as the German border. Fighters did not have the range to go further, but the arrogant 'bomber generals' said they did not want them, adamant that an American bomber could survive anywhere in daylight. In just two months their losses doubled and during the summer of 1943 the 8th Air Force lost 366 bombers.

The 15th Air Force lost 51 bombers and 58 severely damaged in one raid over Romania!

Meanwhile Americans were liberating their soil. In Nimitz's area on 11 May 1943 Admiral Kinkaid's task force landed the 7th Division on Attu Island off Alaska, where the tundra covered, cold, foggy land offered the 2,380 Japanese nowhere to hide. However, what was supposed to be a simple matter of shooting fish in a barrel turned into a nightmare. It took four weeks and American losses of 1,697 killed and wounded and 2,100 hospitalised with frostbite and respiratory ailments to kill all defenders, but for 28 who surrendered.

Attu was Nimitz's right flank. On 21 June he also attacked on his left flank thousands of miles to the south. This was phase two of the liberation of the Solomons. Over the next nine months under the overall command of Admiral Halsey the 3rd Fleet supported by the 13th Air Force would put the 1st and 3rd Marine, Americal NG, 25th, 37thNG, 40thNG, 43rdNG and 93rd Divisions and a New Zealand division onto islands of malaria infested, steaming jungle.

While the Solomons campaign was in full sway Nimitz launched his long-awaited central offensive in November against the Gilberts with his 5th Fleet and 7th Air force. The 27th New York National Guard Division took tiny Makin Island for 218 casualties, but the 2nd Marine Division found itself in a brutal, gory contest for Tarawa. Over five days they killed 5,000 Japanese and suffered 3,551 casualties. Nimitz was brought up sharply when the newspapers demanded a scapegoat for this pyrrhic victory. Six months on Guadalcanal had cost only a thousand more casualties.

Eisenhower had also got the USA into a mess, but he tried to distance himself as much as possible from affairs he felt were out of his control. Churchill had convinced Roosevelt to invade Italy as part of a deal to negotiate an Italian secret surrender, using bluff and threats against the Italians that disgusted Eisenhower, who refused to sign the documents.

Moreover, when he learned that jurnalists knew of the terms, he chose to go public on the radio without informing the Italians! The result was a total collapse in Italy as Italians began to shoot each other. The Germans simply picked up the pieces and they also used unfair means: e.g. they threatened to bomb Rome to ruins if Italian soldiers did not surrender. The British had said exactly the same thing to the Italians two weeks earlier.

When Eisenhower made his broadcast on 8 September 1943 Montgomery already had a British army in southern Italy, so Eisenhower perhaps thought his US Fifth Army, scheduled to invade Italy at Salerno that night with the 82nd Airborne and 36thNG and 45thNG Divisions and two British divisions, would not be in too much danger. If so he was wrong. Salerno was a terrible affair and Montgomery did nothing to relieve the men on the beach.

Clark's Fifth Army broke out of Salerno after three weeks and began an advance north against stiffening German resistance.

Cassino proved to be the next stumbling block in Italy, and Americans, then French, then British, Indian and New Zealanders tried to smash their way through the position. It was May 1944 before Poles broke through.

The Americans had been suckered into Italy and could not get out. They eventually committed their 1st Armoured, 82nd Airborne, 3rd, 10th, 34thNG, 36thNG, 45thNG, 85th, 88th, 91st, and 92nd Divisions. It would cost the Americans 111,740 killed and wounded. The Texas National Guard 36th Division lost 1,700 casualties in one night!

MacArthur's South West Pacific command had been strengthened. He now had the 5th Air force, 7th Fleet and the 1st Cavalry, 6th, 24th, 31stNG, 32ndNG, 33rdNG, part 40thNG, and part 41stNG Divisions and the Australian Armed Forces, with which to continue his New Guinea campaign and take the Admiralties and Biak.

In 1944 he talked Roosevelt into allowing him to enter the Philippines with the intention of at least liberating Luzon, the main island.

Nimitz handed over the mopping up operations in the Solomons to MacArthur, who handed them to the Australians, while Nimitz concentrated on his central offensive. His 5th Fleet and 7th Air Force put the 4th Marine and 7th Divisions and smaller forces into the Marshalls in early 1944.

With several airfields in the Marshalls quickly secured, Nimitz authorised the Marianas invasion. On 15 June 1944 the 5th Fleet and 7th Air Force put ground forces onto Saipan. The Marianas soon involved the 2nd, 3rd and 4th Divisions and 1st Brigade of the Marines and the 27thNG and 77th Divisions of the Army.

American carrier pilots met their enemy counterparts in the Marianas and proceeded to devastate the Japanese carrier force. The air casualties were so one-sided, the American navy pilots called it the Marianas Turkey Shoot. However, ashore the fighting lasted for the rest of the year and cost 31,000 American casualties.

Despite the massive effort to invade the Marianas – over a thousand planes and over 2,000 vessels – the USA was also providing almost half the effort to invade France the same month: i.e. almost 3,000 vessels of the 12th Fleet and Merchant Marine and 5,000 planes of the 8th and 9th Air Forces.

On 6 June they put the 82nd and 101st Airborne and 1st, 4th and 29th Divisions ashore in Normandy. That the USA could make two such unbelievable invasions at the same time on opposite sides of the planet was astounding even to the men and women who planned them.

Familiar faces made up the Normandy team. Eisenhower in overall command, Montgomery in ground command and Bradley handling the American troops. Patton, who had been sent to the doghouse for several months for having slapped a couple of his men, was waiting secretly in the wings now for the word to bust out of the beachhead with his new Third Army. He became frustrated as day after day the allies did not seem to be going anywhere. Normandy was rough. Not until late July when the 9th Air Force and planes borrowed from the 8th blew a hole in the enemy line could Patton be unleashed.

Once turned loose by Bradley's 12th Army Group, Patton's Third Army fought one of the most lightning campaigns in history. In less than three weeks they had fanned out south 100 miles, west 150 miles and east 200 miles. Bradley gave General Hodges the First Army and they did fantas-

tically well too. In two weeks they crossed northern France and Belgium and took Aachen in Germany.

General Patch's US Seventh Army invaded Southern France on 15 August and met the Third Army in September. However, the allies were soon stuck at the German border having run out of supplies. By now Montgomery controlled British 21st Army Group with the Canadian First Army eliminating German forces along the Belgian coast and the British Second Army standing on the Belgian-Netherlands border; Bradley's US 12th Army Group had Simpson's US Ninth Army, Hodges' US First Army and Patton's US Third Army on the German border between the Netherlands and Lorraine; and General Devers' US 6th Army Group controlled Patch's US Seventh and the French First Armies in Alsace.

Patton was angry when he learned all spare fuel was to be sent to Montgomery for an airborne project 'Market Garden' in mid-September. It failed and cost the US 82nd and 101st Airborne Divisions 3,542 casualties. Moreover, Montgomery kept the two American divisions, as he said he did not have enough British troops. In the next two months they would suffer another 3,594 casualties.

Eisenhower, the boss of Devers, Bradley and Montgomery, had once again assumed the role of ground commander and truthfully he should have picked someone else, for he was better suited to diplomacy than running a battle. Aware that Roosevelt was coming up for election in November and afraid, as many generals were, that Roosevelt would lose to a compromise peace faction, he ordered his men to keep up the pressure fuel or no fuel, supplies or no supplies. This led to a bloody two-month battle of attrition between American and German infantry.

The Americans would eventually have in Western Europe three airborne, fifteen armoured and 43 infantry divisions (nine of them National Guard) and a host of smaller units.

Roosevelt won the election.

MacArthur was not stuck. Reinforced to seventeen divisions (nine of them NG), he

UNITED STATES OF AMERICA (USA)

invaded the Philippines in October 1944, first on Leyte Island, moving to Luzon in January. He then divided his ground forces into the Sixth and Eighth Armies and effectively ignored Roosevelt by going beyond his brief to only liberate Luzon to liberate all the islands.

Three big battles awaited the Americans before the inevitable end was in sight: the Ardennes, Iwo Jima and Okinawa.

On the German border the front had shut down in the snowy, freezing conditions of early December. It was soon so quiet that many generals went on leave. On the foggy morning of 16 December the Germans launched a major offensive using the best part of three armies against four of Hodges' divisions along an 80-mile stretch of the Ardennes Forest. Outnumbered 6:1 and outgunned by gigantic Tiger tanks the Americans were simply mashed into the snow if they did not run.

Within a day the Americans had fallen back to create a bulge in the line. On the 18th parts of the 101st Airborne and 9th and 10th Armoured Divisions were surrounded at Bastogne.

Montgomery was asked how soon he could take over the US Ninth Army on the northern edge of the battlefield and counterattack: he replied 'a couple of weeks'. When Patton was asked how soon his Third Army could pull out of his current battle, regroup, resupply, plan a route, drive 100 miles and counter-attack: he replied 72 hours!

Third Army relieved Bastogne on the 26th, but though the trapped men had suffered 3,000 casualties they continued to fight. It was in fact 30 January before the Americans could rest easy. The Battle of the Bulge scared the allies and cost 100,000 American casualties.

The second big battle was the occupation of an eight square mile sulphurous rock in the Pacific called Iwo Jima. On 19 February Nimitz's 5th Fleet put the 3rd, 4th and 5th Marine Divisions on the island. The marines met a terrifying ordeal: it was weeks before they could stand erect without being shot. They called the island 'secure' at the end of March, but an army regiment had to come in

and clear out snipers for another three months. It was a high cost for a sulphurous rock: 26,000 American casualties.

The third battle was fought in the next island group on Nimitz's list, the Ryukyus dominated by Okinawa. The 5th Fleet put the US Tenth Army ashore on 26 March 1945. The Marine Corps' 1st, 2nd and 6th and the Army's 7th, 27NGth and 77th Divisions waded into a blood bath that killed over 100,000 of the enemy and cost 62,000 American casualties.

Once the Americans recovered from the Bulge they and the allies advanced over the Rhine into Germany. The outcome, bar the bleeding and dying, was a foregone conclusion. By April 1945 the German Army was reduced to a shadow and individual Americans found themselves guarding thousands of prisoners!

On 7 May German emissaries signed the surrender at Eisenhower's headquarters.

The Western Europe campaign cost the Americans 523,000 casualties. The five US divisions that had kicked it off on D-Day suffered a 300% turnover in personnel.

The most grieved of America's casualties was Roosevelt. On 12 April it all became too much for him. Though of weak constitution and wheelchair-bound, he had worked miracles, but this day he slipped away. His Vice President, Harry Truman, was visibly shocked by the news of his death, for he had never expected to inherit the country let alone the greatest war in history.

Truman was fortunate that Germany was all but beaten. The Japanese were a different matter. Their merchant fleet had been devastated by American submarines and planes, and their cities were being burned out by the 10th, 11th and 20th Air Forces, but they still packed quite a punch in the form of soldiers ready to fight to the death. By summer 1945 the Americans had overcome a million Japanese troops at a cost of 9,000 aircraft shot down, hundreds of vessels sunk or crippled and 217,000 casualties. In Japan the enemy had over six million troops, who at this rate could inflict well more than a million casualties on the

Americans, and if the Japanese militia of 50 million was included then US casualties could become astronomical.

The Americans would not share out these casualties either, for the other allied nations would not or could not join them in the invasion of Japan in significant numbers.

A further problem was the shortage of American combat troops. Already, airmen had been thrown into infantry combat without retraining; the Navy was retraining sailors as infantrymen; and only two US divisions had not been crippled by combat.

The Japanese problem dogged Truman day and night. Then he was informed of a new weapon that just might solve the problem: the atomic bomb.

By August 1945 the Japanese were willing to concede to all allied terms, but they wanted to retain their Emperor. This in itself was not a hitch, but it did seem that every time peace was suggested the Japanese had one more demand. Following advice from the British government, Truman decided to use the bomb.

It was dropped on Hiroshima on the 6th. The city disappeared. Yet unbelievably, many Japanese generals did not want to surrender. Truman ordered a second bomb dropped on Nagasaki. The city disappeared. Still the Japanese bickered. Only a week later did they agree to surrender.

During the war the US armed forces were racist in the sense that promotion for members of non-acceptable ethnic groups such as Spanish-speaking Americans, Jews and native American Indians was rare, and negroes and nisei were segregated into their own units. Recruits from the northern states found all military bases to be a real culture shock. However, recruits from the southern states, where racism was encoded in law, found the military bases to be extremely liberal. As most military bases were located in the south, they were in fact oases of justice and fair play.

Nisei volunteers were placed primarily in the 442nd Regiment, 100th Battalion and 522nd Artillery Battalion, and fought courageously in Italy and France. These racial Japanese assumed that upon enlistment

their families would be released from the internment camps. In fact not until 1944 were they released, when the Supreme Court told the government it had acted illegally, by which time many a nisei had paid in blood for the right to be buried in an American grave. The 442nd was the most decorated regiment of the Army.

The negroes of the USA were a large enough body to have all of the classes that white society had, from illiterates to college professors. The majority of negroes in the Army were deliberately kept out of combat by white officers, who should have known better: negroes had fought bravely in every American war.

Of the few negro combat units that were raised, the 92nd Division and 366th Regiment did not perform well in Italy, though they did far better after they were weeded of illiterate and deficient soldiers. The 93rd Division and 24th Regiment might have done well in the Pacific if given a chance, but instead were assigned inglorious mopping up operations on bypassed islands. The 2nd Cavalry Division was actually disbanded before seeing combat, the only US division to be disbanded.

Several smaller combat units did very well: five tank, six artillery, two anti-tank and a combat engineer battalions. When Patton was asked if he wanted a new (white) tank battalion to replace one of his negro units he refused. In March 1945 negro infantry platoons were assigned to almost every regiment fighting in Germany.

In the Army Air Force integration was introduced when some negroes were made aerial gunners. Negro fighter pilots earned an enviable record in Italy.

At sea negro sailors started winning medals at Pearl Harbor and continued to do so. The Marines were the most apprehensive about using negroes in combat, but were surprised when they finally did: a negro unit earned praise on Iwo Jima.

Only one negro became a general, but many served with distinction up to the rank of colonel.

It was heartbreaking for bemedalled negro veterans to return to their southern homes and be refused service at a whites only restaurant. It was worse for the nisei, who returned to find their homes had been sold by the government to 'decent' Americans.

The United States sneaked into the war like a gate crasher, but exited with the most dramatic finale in military history. The armed forces had come a long way, from horse cavalry to atomic weapons in four years. The war cost 409,200 American lives: Army including National Guard and airmen 318,274; Marines including airmen 21,078; Navy including airmen 62,614; Coast Guard including airmen 574; Merchant Marine 5,662; civilians *c.*1,000 (air raids, ship passengers, Japanese camps)
See Index

UZBEKISTAN

Status in 1939:	member state of the USSR.
Government in 1939:	communist under Stalin dictatorship.
Population in 1939:	10,000,000
Make-up in 1939:	Uzbekis; small number of Russian colonists.
Religion:	Moslem.
Location:	Central Asia.

Part of the great Khanate of Khiva in the middle ages, the Uzbekis had fallen to the Tsarist Russians in the early 19th century, achieved independence under the Emir of Bukhara in 1917, only to fall to communist Russians in the early 1920s and be absorbed into the USSR in 1924.

The communists suppressed all public religious and cultural activity and introduced measures that terrorised the people. Understandably, when the Red Army conscripted Uzbekis to fight the Germans in 1941, they did not want to go, but to refuse could mean the arrest of one's entire family.

Yet the recruits did little fighting in the beginning as entire divisions surrendered. Thousands of dejected Uzbekis found themselves facing a bleak winter in German prison camps. They knew few would survive.

Suddenly German recruiters came through the camps, offering complete religious and cultural freedom, treatment comparable to German soldiers and the chance to kill communists. The majority of Uzbekis signed up.

They were trained in their own battalions as anti-partisan hunters and served in the German rear in the USSR. As of 1943 battalions were sent all over Europe either as anti-guerrilla units or as coastal defence.

When Germany surrendered in 1945, these men, who had done nothing but attempt to survive, serve their nation and obey God, were on the run from the Red Army. If caught not only would they be executed, but their relatives back home would be arrested. Those who survived did so by 'melting' into the vast mass of displaced persons, stateless and friendless.
See Index

YUGOSLAVIA

Other names:	includes Bosnia, Croatia, Kosovo, Macedonia, Montenegro, Serbia, Slovenia.
Status in 1939:	independent.
Government in 1939:	democratic monarchy.
Population in 1939:	16,500,000.
Make-up in 1939:	Serbs 6,600,000; Croats 4,000,000; Slovenians 1,353,000; Macedonians 924,000; Bosnian Moslems 870,000; Volksdeutsch 710,000; Albanians 700,000; Hungarians 500,000; Montenegrans 412,000 Romanians 100,000; Gypsies 100,000; Italians 100,000; Jews 78,000; Bulgarians 50,000;
Religion:	Christian, but adverse sect differences.
Location:	South Eastern Europe.

One look at the above ethnic make-up explains that there really was no such place as Yugoslavia, except in the minds of the British and French politicians in 1919, who allowed the Serbs to extend their boundaries to encompass the above people. Obviously this provoked considerable civil unrest and in 1934 a Macedonian nationalist assassinated the Serbian king.

By June 1940 the Serbs saw their traditional friends, the British and French, decisively beaten by German armies, and as a result they felt they could not stand up to Hitler, the German dictator. On 25 March 1941 the Serb leaders formally signed an alliance with Hitler.

The Serb people quite literally revolted in anger, setting up their own government and repudiating the treaty.

Hitler reacted in the same way as the Austrians had reacted in 1914, when the Serbs assassinated the Austrian heir. Hitler took this as a personal insult and his anger overcame all reason. He ordered an invasion at once.

On Palm Sunday 6 April the capital Belgrade was struck without warning by German planes, which killed an estimated 17,000 inhabitants, and the nation was invaded by German forces. The Yugoslavs mobilised their forces, calling up reservists: the Seventh Army in the north to repel the German Second Army; the Fourth Army to hold Banat, Novi Sad and Belgrade under assault by German Panzer Group Kleist; the Fifth Army in Macedonia to hold back the invading German Twelfth Army; and the Sixth and First Armies along the eastern border, as yet not under serious attack.

However, soon the coast was under attack from Italians coming out of Zara (an Italian enclave) and from the sea. The Third Army ordered a pre-emptive strike against Italian-held Albania at once.

On the 8th the Fifth Army lost Skopje and on the 10th the Seventh Army fell back from Zagreb and Ljubljana, where thousands of Croatian and Slovenian troops actually welcomed the invaders.

On the 9th the Third Army in Montenegro was attacked by the Italian Ninth Army. On the 11th the Italian Second Army invaded western Slovenia. The Bulgarians and Hungarians also invaded.

On the 12th the citizens of Belgrade, their homes still smouldering from the bombing, watched helplessly as Germans entered. The people of Sarajevo saw a similar awesome sight on the 16th.

On the 17th members of the government fled the country: the remaining ministers surrendered.

The twelve-day war cost the Italians just over a thousand casualties and the Germans 151 dead. The Yugoslav armed forces of 344,000 men were completely destroyed.

Areas of Hungarian ethnicity were occupied by Hungarian troops. The Bulgarians claimed all of Macedonia, though the Italians grabbed a few villages. The Italians also annexed all Albanian towns, Montenegro, western Slovenia and most of the coast. The Germans were not greedy: they annexed Banat, where a Volksdeutsch population lived, and eastern Slovenia; and placed Serbia under their protection. Immediately, 109,000 Volksdeutsch were recruited to work in factories in Germany.

Surprisingly, the axis powers agreed to independence for Croatia and allowed the Croats control of Bosnia.

The first to suffer under the new regimes were the Jews: the Volksdeutsch expelled them from their towns; the Serb police arrested them as troublemakers; and the Hungarians murdered several hundred as part of their liberation celebrations. However, it was in Croatia where the most horrible fate awaited them, for this new state was based on a Roman Catholic government with strong support from local bishops. Ante Pavelic, the Croat Prime Minister, created a militia called the ustaci, who on 26 June began arresting all Jews and Gypsies. At one camp at Danica 6,000 of these bewildered men, women and children were murdered.

The ustaci soon turned on their Serb neighbours: ordering all Serbs to go 'home' to Serbia or convert to Roman Catholicism. To create a sense of urgency the ustaci shot a few Serbs out of hand.

Milovan Acimovich, the Serbian Prime Minister, had only 22,600 police and frontier guards and 600 German police, 250 Volksdeutsch factory guards and some Serb and Russian immigrant factory guards with which to keep order in his new state, so he could do nothing to help his Serb brothers in Croatia and Bosnia. The Croats had their ustaci and a new army of ex-Yugoslavian army soldiers recently released by the invaders.

In Macedonia three Bulgarian divisions and a police force kept strict discipline.

In German-occupied Slovenia the Germans recruited Slovenes into a self-defence militia. By July the German army had reduced its entire presence in Yugoslavia to just four divisions of middle-aged reservists.

Things were much more peaceful in the Italian zones, though there were still sixteen Italian divisions here. They recruited the locals, whether Slovenes, Montenegrans or Albanians, into militias, and they welcomed all refugees, whether they be Serbs, Gypsies or Jews.

It is surprising, therefore, that the first revolt came in Italian-held Montenegro. On 13 July Montenegran partisans shot up an Italian truck convoy near Kolasin and besieged garrisons at Bioca and Danilovgrad. The Italian Ninth Army was ordered to put down the revolt ruthlessly. Yugoslavia had a new war.

Partisans also began actions in Serbia, and in September the Germans replaced Acimovich with General Nedic, ex-Yugoslavian Minister of War, who at once offered amnesty to the partisans. In the mountains Draza Mihailovich had formed a body of army officers into guerrillas and had then allied with Cetniks, i.e. refugee Serbs fleeing Croatia and Bosnia. Some of these Serbs accepted the amnesty and joined Nedic's police or factory guards, but several thousand remained with Mihailovich in the mountains.

There was another guerrilla leader, Josip Broz, a communist who changed his name to Tito in order to hide his communist affiliations. He told his recruits he would accept all political voices except fascists and all ethnic groups. Tito also accepted women as fighters.

No one was fooled by Tito, and in response to this communist partisan army, the Russian immigrants created a self-defence force. Moreover, the Germans brought in an infantry division and swept the mountains. After thirty Germans were killed in Kraljevo, they responded by massacring 1,700 villagers. In Kragujevac for the deaths of ten Germans, 2,300 were murdered. In Belgrade the Germans and Serb police murdered 4,750.

Mihailovich was sickened by this retaliation and he called off all attacks. Tito refused to call off attacks. On 28 October Cetniks and Titoists argued about this attitude and the debate ended in gunplay. From now on Mihailovich's Cetniks and Tito's partisans were at war.

Tito withdrew his partisans into Montenegro to link up with the partisans there and to gain a breather from German and Cetnik harassment, but they ran foul of the Italians, losing 300 killed and 600 wounded at Plevlja in early December. On the 12th Tito himself was almost caught by an Italian assault.

Faced with determined resistance, Tito chose to go back to Serbia. It was the right move: the Germans and Serbs were caught off balance and had to ask for Bulgarian aid.

By now Tito had gained influence over partisans throughout Yugoslavia. In Slovenia his people were known as reds. The German-and Italian-sponsored militias were known as whites. Non-communist partisans were called blues. This three ring circus soon turned bloody with no quarter asked or given.

In Bosnia the ustaci preferred throwing elderly Serb ladies out of their homes and butchering unarmed Jews and Gypsies, to risking their lives fighting partisans. They stayed out of the way of Titoists and Cetniks if possible. When the German army requested Jure Francetic be dismissed from the ustaci for his unbridled cruelty, Pavelic replied by promoting him, to show the Germans who was boss.

The Bosnian Moslems created their own guerrillas who defended villages and raided Serbs and Croats alike.

The axis partners launched their final offensive to destroy Tito with Nedic's new army (Serbian Volunteer Corps), Serbian police, two German divisions and the Croatian Army IIIrd Corps. From 4,900 foot Mount Zlatar to Prijepolje, west to Foca, thence north east over the Lim River to Sandzak the Titoists retreated in snow, losing hundreds to frostbite, pneumonia, German air attacks, Croatian and German artillery salvoes, sniping by Cetniks and Moslems, and near Prijepolje an Italian attack.

Suddenly the Titoists disappeared. In the month-long affair the Germans had lost only 25 killed, but 300 maimed with frostbite, such were the conditions. The Germans counted 521 dead Titoists and caught 1,331. The Serbs and Croats had a similar experience.

German aerial reconnaissance picked up Tito's main force at Valjevo only 55 miles south west of Belgrade. The axis forces now launched their final offensive to destroy Tito and for 500 German casualties they claimed to have killed 3,500 partisans, though the body count included elderly and children who had starved or died of illness. Yet, not only did Tito himself escape but he did so with enough followers that they repelled a Cetnik attack at Borac.

Throughout Yugoslavia there were partisan ambushes and sabotage raids. Between 16 February and 20 March 1942 the Germans lost 37 killed, 65 wounded and 45 missing; the Croats lost 75 killed, 305 wounded; the Serbs lost fifteen killed and thirteen wounded; the Bulgarians lost fifteen killed and thirteen wounded. The Hungarians were losing about one killed per week. Italian losses were similar.

The true measure of partisan activity is that the Italians had not reduced their garrison and the Germans and Bulgarians had increased theirs, plus the Croatian Army had been brought into play.

Come spring Tito defeated a Cetnik band at Kolasin, but on 16 April the axis partners launched their final all-out attack to destroy Tito with a German division, ten Croat army and ustaci battalions and three Italian divisions. Tito's main force fell back southwards, his columns strafed by German and Italian planes and straddled by artillery salvoes.

Unbelievably, a month later Tito was able to counter-attack two Italian divisions near Kolasin, though he failed and lost many partisans.

In June Tito broke out of the encirclement by invading Croat-held Bosnia. His intention was not just to escape, but to rescue a Titoist band that had been assaulted by a German and a Croat division. In this Bosnia fighting the Croats suffered 200 killed, 250 wounded and 169 missing and the Germans lost nineteen killed, 31 wounded and six missing, but they killed 1,748 partisans and captured 713 of which 275 were executed. Probably the executed were real partisans and the others were elderly and children. It was obvious that Tito's people with their hand-held weapons could not match artillery and planes.

As Tito's main force entered Bosnia his initial opposition came from Croat police and ustaci. Some villages like Kalinovich were so well defended they could not be captured. In early July as the main force moved west of Sarajevo, the Croat IIIrd Corps and ustaci battalions sortied out of that city to do battle. They surrounded Tito's main force in the Bugojno Valley, where local Croat farmers joined the fight with shotguns. Soon Cetniks arrived and attacked in waves of infantry and horse cavalry, waving gigantic flags so that axis aircraft would recognise them as anti-Tito forces. The Cetniks had sworn not to cut their hair until they were free, so their appearance was that of barbarian cavalry of a millennium earlier. The Titoists were disgusted by the sight of this unholy alliance of Croats and Cetniks, hitherto sworn enemies. Tito fell back over the Vrbas River.

An ustaci battalion, following Tito, massacred the village of Hurije for having fed the Titoists as they passed through. The Croat 1st Mountain Division was severely hurt by a Titoist riposte in the Kozara Mountains losing 235 killed, 182 wounded and 521 missing. Two Croat mountain brigades had to be brought up.

In August aerial reconnaissance discovered Tito's main force near Mount Malovan. They had retreated eighty miles over trackless mountains. At Livno Tito took 700 ustaci reservists prisoner, hoping to trade them, but at Kupres he was repelled by ustaci losing 250 casualties.

Tito's invasion of Bosnia had been a bloody affair: Croats losing 552 killed, 835 wounded, 1,572 missing; Germans 73 killed, 188 wounded and eight missing. Cetnik losses are unknown. Together they killed 10,729 partisans and captured 21,362 of which 558 were executed. Again a high proportion of the captured were elderly and children who had not been able to keep up the mountainous trek. Many of those executed were wounded who were 'finished off'. The ustaci were known for this.

By autumn the axis forces were powerful. To add to the German army garrison of four divisions the German SS had raised the Prinz Eugen Division from Yugoslavian Volksdeutsch, the German police had recruited thirty battalions of Croats, and the German Army established the 369th Devil's Division of Croat volunteers.

In Slovenia the Italians had been forced to sweep the mountains with three divisions and their whites looking for reds. The blues sat this one out.

The Croat army created a field force of four brigades and a regiment, and the Croat police set up a gendarmerie brigade.

The Cetniks currently numbered about 30,000, but Mihailovich could only control those he could physically reach. At his headquarters he had German and British advisers!

The Serbs had expanded their Volunteer Corps and police to over 30,000, and the Russian immigrants had increased their defence force to 15,000.

In the face of all this in November Tito had the gall to capture Bihac and set up a government.

Atrocities continued unabated. The German SS Security Police, who had worked to death 15,000 Jews, asked the Croats to hand over their Jews. The ustaci could only find 9,000. They had murdered the others. The Hungarians had massacred 3,309 Serbs and Jews in retaliation for the deaths of seventeen Hungarian soldiers. At Skopje the Bulgarians executed 288 innocents in retaliation for the killing of 32 soldiers. Near Sandjak Cetniks murdered 9,200 Moslems.

On 16 January 1943 the axis partners launched their final offensive to destroy Tito. At once Tito's main force shuffled their frozen feet through deep snow and chilling winds towards the Neretva River. A rearguard at Kordun used captured artillery to stop German tanks. After two weeks of retreat Tito estimated he had 20,000 partisans left, of which 4,500 were on stretchers.

At Prozor when an Italian battalion stopped the column, the partisans massacred the Italians when they ran out of ammunition.

Chasing the partisans for thirty days cost the Devil's Division 335 killed, 101 missing and several hundred wounded. Croat army and ustaci units lost 700 casualties. They had killed 8,500 partisans and taken 2,010.

In a three-day battle a German division beat the Titoists at Ivan Sedloe, thereby outflanking a Titoist rearguard that was blocking the Italian VIth Corps. Though an Italian battalion was destroyed at Jablanica, the Italians were able to advance.

Tito blew up a bridge, only to realise this act cut off one of his columns. He spent the rest of his life lying about his error. One of his rearguards at Vilica Guvno held up Cetniks, a German division, the Devil's Division and an ustaci brigade from 2 to 7 March, thus enabling Tito's main force to escape once again.

On the opposite bank of the Neretva the resting partisans were suddenly attacked by Cetnik infantry and cavalry, waving gigantic flags as usual. The manoeuvre failed and the Cetniks died in heaps.

Two weeks later the Titoists broke through a Cetnik/Italian force on the Drina River, took Foca and escaped into Montenegro, where they captured Podgoritza and Javorak.

Mihailovich was down to 9,000 men in his main force. They licked their wounds and congratulated Milhailovich when they heard the British had recognised him as Yugoslavia's Minister of War! However, this worried the Germans and in May fearing a British invasion they began to disarm the Cetniks by ruses. Mihailovich and some diehards hid.

In mid-May the axis partners launched their final offensive to kill off Tito. However, almost at once an Italian unit was defeated at Bioce. From the north over the Drina Tito was attacked by the Devil's Division; from the east by the Croat 1st Mountain Division, a Bulgarian regiment and an Italian division; from the south-west came two Italian divisions and the SS Prinz Eugen Division; from the north-west a German division. This trapped Tito on Mount Durmitor and in the Lim and Tara valleys.

Incredibly, the Titoists broke out, heading for the Zelengora River. By 12 June they were across and on the 18th they 'disappeared'.

During the summer the Germans brought in reinforcements: a Danish SS regiment and a Dutch SS brigade.

On 8 September Italy broke apart in civil war, which took everyone by surprise. A lightly armed Cetnik band came to an agreement with the Italians in Priboj, whereby the Cetniks were armed with Italian weapons. At Split the Italian Bergamo Division armed local Titoists. Anti-fascist Italians also released 18,000 Titoist prisoners. Moreover, Tito announced he would accept Italian volunteers: fully 30,000 joined him, bringing their artillery, tanks and supplies with them!

However, any Italians who tried to join the Cetniks were handed over to fascist Italians for execution. By such methods the Cetniks were soon in German favour again.

The Germans and fascist Italians rushed in troops to attack the anti-fascist Italians: the SS Prinz Eugen Division had a rough time defeating the surrounded Bergamo Division, but eventually the Italians ran out of ammunition. The Yugoslavian Volksdeutsch executed all the Italian officers. It was mid-October before all the anti-fascist Italians were killed or captured, but for those who had joined Tito. The Italian-sponsored militias now accepted German sponsorship.

Counting new recruits, released prisoners and his Italian volunteers, Tito now had about 90,000 partisans and was receiving some British supplies by sea. He faced an impressive array of axis forces: 55,000 Cetniks; 600,000 Germans and locally-raised troops and police in German uniform; 70,000 Bulgarians; 30,000 Hungarians; a few thousand fascist Italians; 30,000 Serbs; and 240,000 Croats (90,000 army, 20,000 police and 130,000 ustaci). Currently the German SS was raising a division of Bosnian Moslems and was conscripting Volksdeutsch aged from 17 to 45 into the Horst Wessel division.

In November the axis partners launched their final offensive to destroy Tito with the German Second Panzer Army of three German, the Devil's and the SS Prinz Eugen Divisions, but they only succeeded in driving Tito into western Bosnia. Wisely, the German generals ordered a shut down for the winter. Meanwhile the Germans raised a second Moslem SS division.

Tito was happy, come spring. With British supplies and even British planes on call now and again, he was able to recruit thousands of men and women into his army, while he set up his headquarters on the island of Vis.

Mihailovich was not happy. The British had withdrawn their support and he was now well and truly in the German camp whether he liked it or not.

In May 1944 the axis partners launched their seventh final offensive to destroy Tito with the Croat army and ustaci and a German division. German paratroopers jumped onto Tito's headquarters on Vis: they managed to capture his new uniform, but it was empty. Otherwise the offensive failed.

In July Tito launched his own offensive from the Bosnian coast towards Serbia, pushing aside Croats, Germans and Bulgarians. A German counter-offensive in August by a mountain division, the SS Prinz Eugen Division and a Moslem SS division attacking out of Montenegro against Tito's flank failed to impress the Titoists. The Titoists did not rest until they were just south of Belgrade. Tito had lost 5,394 partisans on the march, but had inflicted 936 killed, 1,235 wounded and 255 missing on the German-controlled forces.

In September German forces entered Serbia in force, but they were not attacking: rather, they were retreating out of Romania in the face of a Soviet offensive. Tito, who as a communist had always been in touch with Stalin, now began to plan a joint offensive with the Soviets.

By the end of the month a Romanian army and nine Bulgarian divisions were actively fighting alongside two Soviet armies against the Germans in eastern Serbia. The Germans responded by sending as many troops into the front line as possible, including the Russian immigrant self-defence force, Serbian Volunteer Corps and the Cetniks. Some Cetniks turned against the Germans.

Tito formed his partisans into four regular armies with a significant amount of equipment including a small air force.

When the allied forces approached Belgrade in October the Serbian Volunteer Corps, frontier guard, factory guards and police fled, leaving actual Germans to defend their capital. The Titoists joined the attack from the south. On 19 October the Titoists, Bulgarians and Soviets entered Belgrade. The offensive had cost the Titoists alone 2,953 killed. At Nish the SS Prinz Eugen Division was defeated by Soviets, but along the Drava River German-sponsored Cossacks repelled the Soviets.

By November the Titoists were holding a solid front line from just north of Belgrade south to Montenegro thence west to the sea. To hold their Yugoslav front the axis partners were using three German army divisions of Croats (including the Devil's), a corps of Cossacks, a Ukrainian SS division, the SS Prinz Eugen Division, eleven divisions of Croat army and ustaci, several brigades of Cetniks, the Serbian Volunteer Corps and ten divisions of actual Germans. In December Cetniks and Serbs attacked Tuszla on the part of the front held by Titoists. They failed miserably.

North of the front line German, Croat and Serb police and the whites were still battling Titoist partisans.

Mihailovich was at Sarajevo establishing a joint force of Cetniks, Montenegran militia and Serbs with the intention of creating a large enough army for self-protection. Old animosities would have to be put on hold.

In February 1945 at Mostar the Devil's Division was badly hurt on the front line by a Titoist attack. In March a Cetnik force on the front at Doboj was forced to withdraw slightly by a Titoist attack. A full offensive by Tito's Third Army on the Drava River was repulsed by German troops.

However, in late March axis units began to retreat against orders, especially Serbs, Croats, Montenegrans and Russians. Even at this stage some ustaci couldn't resist massacring retreating Serbs! The Serbs including the Cetniks were only safe when they reached Slovenia where the whites and blues had formed an alliance.

On 3 April the entire front collapsed under a Titoist, Bulgarian and Soviet offensive. On the 17th the Croat government ordered the police to the front, but there was no front line any longer. Everyone in the axis forces was retreating. On the 24th Titoists entered Italy.

In early May British forces in Italy and Austria counted among their prisoners 11,000 Slovenian whites and 25,000 Serbs. Among their hundreds of thousands of prisoners in German uniform were scores of thousands of Yugoslavians.

On 6 May Titoists entered Austria and attacked Slovenian whites at Forlach. Two days later Tito captured Zagreb, the Croat capital. The following day the Germans in northern Croatia surrendered 150,000 troops.

On 11 May Titoists attacked a Cetnik camp at Klagenfurt in Austria. Nearby British troops tried to bring a halt to the fighting.

Meanwhile, Milhailovich was heading in the opposite direction, south to wage guerrilla war. On the 18th he and his remaining Cetniks were caught at Sutjeska. The Titoists killed or captured 9,235 Cetniks. With less than 3,000 followers Milhailovich fled.

The British appeased the Titoists by handing over 40,000 axis Yugoslavs, including women and children. Officially all such Yugoslavs were to be screened as to their degree of 'guilt'. In reality the Titoists went on the rampage massacring thousands. The British also handed many of the Russian immigrants to the Soviets, though most had never been Soviet citizens and some had never seen Russia.

Not until 1946 did the Titoists run Milhailovich and followers to ground.

During the war 276,000 Yugoslavs wore Croat uniform and 246,000 wore German uniform. At least another 120,000 wore only Italian, Bulgarian, Hungarian, Serb, Cetnik or 'blue' uniform. How many of these 642,000 died in action is unknown. Fascists claim that the Titoists murdered 260,000 people in 1945, but this is a gross exaggeration: 150,000 may be too high.

A figure of 150,000 Titoists killed, not counting their Italian volunteers, is probably a good starting point.

Civilian losses were astonishingly high from massacres, air raids, cross-fire, disease and starvation: 90% of the Gypsies died as combatants or were murdered; 85% of the Jews died in like manner.

The conservative estimate of Yugoslavs who died as a result of the war is 800,000. The liberal estimate is 1,700,000.

For Yugoslavia more than any other nation the war was a civil war. Tito had a daunting job ahead of him: to build a nation out of the British-French Frankenstein creation that was Yugoslavia following such a genocidal conflict. It is to his credit that he managed to do so, fending off Western and Soviet influence alike, and kept the peace, though in a police state, for almost half a century, including a decade after his death.

However, there were those who would never forget and they simply waited for the day they could renew old hatreds.
See Index

SUMMARY

If ever there was a hypocritical war, this was it. The allies won and therefore are recognised as the good guys, but their destruction and murder of innocents was almost as monumental as that of the axis nations. Remember that Stalin, who murdered approximately thirty million people, was an allied leader.

Seen exclusively on their own merits and out of context, the British bombing of German civilians and the deportation of hundreds of thousands of refugees from communism into the hands of the NKVD appear monstrous. Seen in the same light the American air raids on Japan culminating in the use of atomic weapons appear equally bestial. Yet within context they seem logical.

Western Europeans who volunteered to fight communists in 1939 and 1950 are today seen as heroes in their native land, but those who volunteered to fight communists in 1941 are seen as traitors.

The Japanese are only now repentant for their sins, but then again they have never been asked to before, but Germans born after the war are expected to carry the burden of the holocaust just as Christian babies are supposedly born with original sin.

The British had in part entered the war because Poland was invaded in September 1939. At the end of the war one of the armies that had invaded Poland then, the Red Army, was back in Poland. Yet the British called this victory!

This was because the British had changed horses in midstream, choosing to fight for the American goal. The British had not declared war to save the world for democracy. After all they delayed true democracy to a third of the world, but, once it became clear the Americans would only support them if they espoused the cause of democracy, the British government overnight became a champion of freedom. Thus the war was won for democracy. Yet the allied victory reduced the number of democratic states, rather than increased them.

The British people had no need to justify their war on Germany, because they had suffered in the Blitz, but as the war caused the Blitz, the Blitz did not cause the war, this does seem a very unusual way of looking at things.

The Americans, themselves, were hypocritical, for while they were liberating decrepit wretches from concentration camps, they consistently denied basic human rights to millions of their own people on racial grounds.

The Americans had no need of speeches to justify their war on Japan. The surprise attack on Pearl Harbor said more than any politician could. However, seeing the inadequate result of Roosevelt's war in Europe, the American press seized upon the Holocaust as justification: for after all, had the Nazis not turned upon the Jews and had there been no concentration camps, the European war's outcome would have had a very hollow ring to it for the Americans.

American politicians also wanted to create something of their own to sit on the mantelpiece to signify the American victory and the sacrifice of 400,000 of her sons and daughters, thereby differing this victory from the victory in World War I. Thus was born the United Nations, the most expensive trophy ever made.

The hypocrisy continued after the war as each nation rewrote bits of history to suit itself, e.g. the post war communist Romanian government omitted Romania's war on the USSR from the school books and only introduced the conflict with Romania's declaration of war on Germany. Anglo-American historians ignore allied Italian units, not even placing them in the index of their books. American historians continue to write about the American liberation of the Philippines without mentioning the essential part played by the Army of the Philippines. Retired generals and politicians wishing to whitewash their careers have added to the confusion.

Napoleon said morality was on the side of the big battalions, meaning battalions of infantry. Had he lived in the latter half of the 20th century he would have meant battalions of authors.

World War I created democracies and hope. World War II created police states, despair, disgust with humanity, Cold War mistrust and fear of 'the Bomb'.

After this exposé at how the war affected the various nations of the world, it is almost deflating to note that some nations sailed past World War II without ever putting in to the port of battle. To the South American states the war was never closer than a newspaper headline. In effect, apart from Brazil's contribution, a whole continent missed the war.

For those who did participate, the war was something extraordinary, even for those whose experience was mild. They knew something profound was going on. While engaged in it, which 99% of the time was tedious inglorious training or ration juggling or 'war work', the people knew in their subconscious that they were involved in something greater than had ever happened before. For most belligerents the war was terrible, and for some it was hell on earth. This variation in degrees becomes clearer, when one looks at the casualties: not so much the numbers, but as a percentage of population.

As befits their size as the two largest nations on earth, China and the USSR suffered the most casualties, almost two thirds of the total, but neither suffered the highest as a percentage of their population.

It is also worth noting that of the sixty-eight million (minimum) who died as a result of the war less than a third were engaged on military operations at the time, the rest being prisoners of war or civilians.

Among axis nations the ten that lost the largest number of personnel while engaged on military operations were:

Germany	1,700,000
Japan	1,630,000
Austria	300,000
Romania	245,000
Hungary	147,000
Italy	120,000
Czecho-Slovakia	100,000
Finland	80,000
Lithuania	80,000
Poland	70,000

However, if one looks at population size the list looks like this:

Austria	1 person in 23
Lithuania	1 person in 30
Germany	1 person in 39
Japan	1 person in 45
Finland	1 person in 50
Hungary	1 person in 54
Latvia	1 person in 60
Romania	1 person in 71
Luxembourg	1 person in 73
Estonia	1 person in 94

Among allied nations the ten that lost the largest number of personnel while engaged on military operations were:

USSR	10,000,000
China	1,400,000
USA	400,000
UK	258,000
Yugoslavia	150,000
Poland	145,000
France	125,000
Italy	80,000
Romania	60,000
Canada	38,000

However, if one looks at population size the list looks like this:

USSR	1 person in 19	Greece	1 person in 14.5
Yugoslavia	1 person in 100	Germany	1 person in 15
New Zealand	1 person in 130	Romania	1 person in 17.5
Albania	1 person in 150		
UK	1 person in 178		
Poland	1 person in 236		
Greece	1 person in 276		
Romania	1 person in 290		
Canada	1 person in 303		
China	1 person in 320		

If one looks at the indigenous central ethnic groups of the above states, i.e. excluding Jews and other minorities (USSR would read Russians) the percentages do change, but these nations would still remain within the largest ten, e.g. ethnic Poles lost 1 person in 8.

The nations with the greatest human loss were:

To look at English-speaking nations one would have to go much further down the list:

USSR	28,848,000
China	13,500,000
Poland	5,780,000
Germany	4,400,000
Netherlands East Indies	4,000,000
Japan	2,670,000
India	1,500,000
Indo-China	1,000,000
Romania	1,000,000
Yugoslavia	800,000

UK	1 person in 127
New Zealand	1 person in 130
Australia	1 person in 247
Canada	1 person in 283
USA	1 person in 320

However, if one looks at population size the list looks like this:

Poland	1 person in 5.9
USSR	1 person in 6.6
Lithuania	1 person in 8
Latvia	1 person in 9
Hungary	1 person in 12.3
Austria	1 person in 12.7
Estonia	1 person in 14

Statistics can be played with, but the above gives an idea of the extreme hardship within some nations compared to others. To put it bluntly, while many civilian Americans remembered the war in terms of not getting enough gasoline for their Sunday outings, and Britons remembered strict rationing and the inconvenience of the blackout, Germans remembered the horrific bombing and loss of loved ones at the front, Russians remembered the constant fear of being occupied by the SS and of being liberated by the NKVD, while the surviving Jews of Eastern Europe remembered losing every member of their extended family.

SOURCES

Documents

von Bosse, Colonel Alexander. *The Cossack Corps*, MS P-064 US Army.

Dorsch, Xaver. *Organisation Todt in France and Germany*, MS B-670, US Army.

Erfurth, General Dr. W. *Volunteers in the Finnish Army*, MS P-063, US Army.

Felmy, General Helmut. *German Exploitation of Arab Nationalist Movements in World War Two*, MS P-207 US Army.

Gaisser, Police Colonel Karl and Lieutenant General Hubert Lanz. *German Anti-Guerilla Operations in the Balkans*, MS DA-20-243, Office of the Chief of Military History, Department of the Army, Washington DC.

von Geitner, Major-General Curt. *German Military Government in the Balkans*, MS P-033, US Army.

Hierl, Reichsarbeitsfuehrer Konstantin. *RAD Reich Labor Service*, MS D-256, US Army.

Kesselring, Field Marshal Albert. *Guerilla Warfare in Italy*, MS C-032 Office of the Chief of Military History, Department of the Army, Washington DC.

Koestring, General Ernst, and Major Hans Seraphim, and Lieut-General Ralph von Heygendorf. *Eastern Nationals as Volunteers in the German Army*, MS P-122 and MS C-043, Office of the Chief of Military History, Department of the Army, Washington DC.

O.K.W. War Diary, MS C020 USAREUR.

Operations of Encircled Forces: German Experiences in Russia, MS 20-234 Office of the Chief of Military History, Department of the Army, Washington DC.

Rauss, General Erhard. *The Pomeranian Battle*, MS D-189 US Army.

Reinhardt, General Hellmuth. *Voluntary Service in the German Army and in the Armies Allied with Germany in World War Two*, MS 23 A6 US Army.

Rear Area Security in Russia, MS 20-240 US Army.

Edited Works

Arrow Cross Men: National Socialists 1933–44, E. Pamlenyi, Akademiai Kiado, Budapest, 1969

The Black Book: the German New Order in Poland. Polish Ministry of Information, London, 1941.

Danmarks Historie. Bind 14, Politikens Forlag, Kobenhaven, 1966.

Das Diensttagebuch des Deutschen General Gouveneurs in Polen 1939–45, Deutsche Verlags – Anstalt, Stuttgart.

Dokumentation der Vertriebung der Deutschen aus Ost- und Mitteleuropa, Band 3. Bonn, 1957.

Enciclopedia Italiana, Rome

European Fascism, S. J. Woolf, Random House, New York, 1968.

Finito – Po Valley Campaign, Milan: 15th Allied Army Group Military History Section, 1945.

Hansard Parliamentary Debates.(UK) Fifth Series, Vol. 413–418.

Historia del Franquisme Origines y Configuracion 1939–45, Editorial Planeta, Barcelona.

History of the Romanian People, Andrei Otetea, Scientific Publishing House, Bucharest, 1970.

Hitler's War Directives 1939–45, H. R. Trevor-Roper, Pan Books Ltd., London, 1966.

L'Italia e la Seconda Guerra Mondiale, E. Faldella, Capelli, 1960.

L'Italia Nell' Europa Danubiana durante la Seconda Guerra Mondiale, Istituto Nazionale per la Storia del Movimento di Liberazione, 1966.

Lloyd's War Losses, London, 1991.

Luxembourg Grey Book, Luxembourg Government, London, 1943.

The Official History of the Indian Armed Forces in the Second World War, Bisheshwar Prasad, Combined Interservices Historical Section of India and Pakistan, Bombay: Orient Longman's, 1956.

Official History of New Zealand in the Second World War, Wellington.

Okinawa: Victory in the Pacific, Nicholas and Shaw, US Marine Corps Historic Branch.

Pages from the History of the Romanian Army, Edditura Academii Republicii Socialiste, Bucharest, 1975.

The Rommel Papers, Basil H. Liddell-Hart, Collins, London, 1953.

The Russian Front: Germany's War in the East 1941–45, James F. Dunnigan, Arms and Armour Press, London 1978.

Scandinavia during the Second World War, Henrik S. Nissen, Universitets Forlaget, Oslo, 1983.

A Short History of Yugoslavia, Cambridge University Press, 1966.

The Truth About Oberlander, Committee for German Unity, Berlin (east) 1959.

Ukraine Concise Encyclopaedia, Volodmyr Kubijovyc, University of Toronto, 1963.

The Violations of Human Rights in Soviet Occupied Lithuania, The Lithuanian Association of Great Britain, 1982.

War in the Aegean, Smith and Walker, William Kimber, London, 1974.

Whitaker's Almanac: 1940, London.

Who Were the Fascists? Universitets Forlaget, Oslo, 1980

Der Zweite Weltkrieg, Hans-Adolf Jacobsen und Hans Dollinger, Verlag Kurt Desch, München, 1962.

Books

Abbot, Peter and Nigel Thomas. *Partisan Warfare 1941–45*, London: Osprey, 1983.

Absolon, Rudolf. *Die Wehrmacht im Dritten Reich*, Schriften des Bundesarchivs, Boppard am Rhein: Harald Boldt Verlag, 1975.

Adams, Henry. *Italy at War*, Alexandria, Va, Time-Life Books, 1982.

Adelman, Robert H. and George Walton. *Rome Fell Today*, Boston: Little, Brown, 1968.

d'Aragon, Charles. *La Resistance sans Heroisme*, Paris Editions du Seuil, 1977.

Armstrong, John A. *Ukrainian Nationalism*, New York: Columbia University. 1963.

Ash, William. *Pickaxe and Rifle: the Story of the Albanian People*, London: Howard Baker, 1974.

Auty, Phyllis. *Tito*, New York: Balantine, 1972.

Barclay, Glen. *The Rise and Fall of the New Roman Empire*, London: Sidgwick and Jackson, 1973.

Barker, A. J. *Eritrea*, London: Faber and Faber, 1966.

Barker, Elisabeth. *British Policy in South East Europe in the Second World War*, London: MacMillan, 1976.

Barker, Thomas M. *The Slovenes of Carinthia*, New York: Studia Slovenica, 1960.

Becker, Rolf O. *Niederschlesien 1945: Die Flucht – Die Besetzung*, Bad Nauheim: Podzun Verlag, 1965.

Bennett, Ralph. *Ultra and Mediterranean Strategy*, London: Hamish Hamilton, 1989.

Bethel, Nicholas. *The Last Secret: Forcible Repatriation to Russia 1945-47*, London : Andre Deutsch, 1974.

Bidwell, Shelford. *The Chindit War*, London: Hodder & Stoughton, 1979.

Bierman, John. *Righteous Gentile: the Story of Raoul Wallenberg*, London Allen Lane, 1981.

Blaxland, Gregory. *Destination Dunkirk*, London: William Kimber, 1973.

— *The Plain Cook and the Great Showman; the First and the Eighth Armies in North Africa*, London: William Kimber, 1977.

Borets, Yuriy. *In the Whirlpool of Combat*, München Ukrainisches Institut fur Bildungspolitik, 1974.

Bose, Mihir. *The Lost Hero: Subhas Bose*, London: Quartet Books, 1982.

Bradley, Omar N. *A Soldier's Story*, London: Eyre and Spottiswoode, 1951.

Brockdorf, Werner. *Kollaboration oder Widerstand*, München Verlag Welsermühl, 1968.

Bruce, George. *The Warsaw Uprising*, London: Rupert Hart-Davis, 1972.

Caccia-Dominioni, Paolo. *Alamein: An Italian Story*, London Allen and Unwin, 1966.

Cannistraro, Philip V. *Historical Dictionary of Fascist Italy*, Westport, Conn.: Greenwood Press, 1982.

Carell, P. *Hitler's War on Russia*, London: Harrap, 1964.

Carsten, F. L. *Fascist Movements in Austria*, Beverly Hills Sage Publications, 1977.

Cervi, Mario. *The Hollow Legions: Mussolini's Blunder in Greece 1940-41*, London: Chatto and Windus, 1972.

Chalfont, Alun. *Montgomery of Alamein*, London: Weidenfeld and Nicolson, 1976.

Chapman, Guy. *Why France Collapsed*, London: Cassell, 1968.

Cobb, Richard. *French and Germans: Germans and French*, University of Vermont, 1983.

Condon, Richard W. *The Winter War: Russia Against Finland*, New York Ballantine, 1972.

Conot, Robert E. *Justice at Nuremburg[Nuremberg?]*, London: Weidenfeld and Nicolson, 1983.

Conquest, Robert. *The Nation Killers: The Soviet Deportation of Nationalities*, New York: MacMillan, 1970.

Costello, John. *The Pacific War*, London: Collins, 1981.

van Crefeld, Martin. *Fighting Power: German and US Army Performance 1939-45*, London: Arms and Armour Press, 1983.

Crosskill, W. E. *The 2000 Mile War*, London: Hale, 1980.

Dallin, Alexander. *German Rule in Russia 1941-45*, London MacMillan, 1957.

Dank, Milton. *The French Against the French*, London Cassell, 1978.

Davis, Melton S. *Who Defends Rome?* London: Allen & Unwin, 1972.

Dawidowicz, Lucy S. *The War Against the Jews*, New York Holt, Rinehart and Winston, 1975.

Deakin, F.W.D. *The Embattled Mountain*, Oxford University Press, 1971.

Degrelle, Leon. *Front de l'Est*, Paris: La Table Rond, 1969.

Deschner, Gunther. *Warsaw Uprising*, New York: Ballantine, 1972.

Djilas, Milovan. *Wartime*, London: Harcourt Brace Jovanovitch, 1977.

Dower, John. *War Without Mercy: Race and Power in the Pacific War*, Boston: Faber and Faber, 1986.

Ehrlich, Blake. *The French Resistance*, London: Chapman and Hall, 1966.

Elliot, Mark R. *Pawns of Yalta*, Chicago: University of Illinois, 1982.

Ellis, John. *Brute Force: Allied Strategy and Tactics in the Second World War*, New York, Viking, 1990.

Ellis, John. *World War II Data Book*, London: Aurum Press, 1994

Ellis, L.F. *History of the Second World War*, UK Military series, HMSO 1962.

Erickson, John. *The Road to Berlin*, London: Weidenfeld and Nicolson, 1983.

d'Este, Carlo. *Bitter Victory*, London, Collins, 1988.

Evans, Stanley G. *A Short History of Bulgaria*, London Lawrence and Wishart, 1960.

Falk, Stanley. *Liberation of the Philippines*, New York Ballantine, 1970

Falk, Stanley. *70 Days to Singapore*, London: Hale, 1975

Farago, Ladislas. *Patton: Ordeal and Triumph*, London: Arthur Barker, 1966

Fenyo, Mario D. *Hitler, Horthy and Hungary*, Yale University, 1972.

Fischer, George. *Soviet Opposition to Stalin: A Case Study in World War Two*, Harvard University. 1952.

Foot, M.R.D. *Resistance*, London: Granada Publishing, 1978.

Forty, George. *The First Victory: O'Connor's Desert Triumph*, Tunbridge Wells: Nutshell, 1990.

Fricke, Gert. *Kroatien 1941-44*, Freiburg: Verlag Rombach, 1972.

Fuller, J. F. C. *Military History of the Western World*, New York Minerva, 1956.

de Gaulle, Charles. *War Memoirs*, London: Weidenfeld and Nicolson, 1960.

George, Margaret. *The Warped Vision: British Foreign Policy 1933-39*, University of Pittsburgh, 1965.

Gilbert, Martin. *The Final Journey: The Fate of the Jews in Nazi Europe*, Boston: Allen and Unwin, 1979.

— *Second World War*, London: Weidenfeld and Nicolson, 1989.

Gjelsvik, Tore. *Norwegian Resistance*, London: C. Hurts, 1979.

Glow, Michael. *The Improvised War: the Abyssinian Campaign*, London: Leo Cooper, 1987.

Glubb, John Bagot. *The Story of the Arab*

Legion, London Hodder & Stoughton, 1948.

Goerlitz, Walter. *Paulus and Stalingrad*, London: Methuen, 1960.

Goldschmidt, Arthur, Jr. *A Concise History of the Middle East*, Boulder, Col.: Westview Press, 1979.

Gordon, Bertram M. *Collaborationism in France during the Second World War*, Ithaca, NY: Cornell University, 1980.

Gosztony, Peter. *Endkampf an der Donau 1944-45*, Vienna Verlag Fritz Molden, 1969.

Grant Duff, Sheila. *A German Protectorate: The Czechs under Nazi Rule*, London: Frank Cass, 1970.

Gross, Jan Thomasz. *Polish Society under German Occupation*, Princeton University, 1979.

Gutman ,Yisrael. *The Jews of Warsaw 1939-43*, Brighton Harvester Press, 1982.

Hammond, Nicholas. *Venture into Greece*, London: William Kimber, 1983.

Hanson, Joanna K. M. *The Civilian Population and the Warsaw Uprising of 1944*, Cambridge University, 1982.

Harvey, J. M. Lee. *The D-Day Dodgers*, London: William Kimber, 1979.

Hastings, Max. *Das Reich: Resistance and the March of the 2nd SS Panzer Division Through France*, London: Michael Joseph, 1981.

Hausser, Paul. *Waffen SS in Einsatz*, Göttingen: Plesse Verlag, 1953.

Hawes, Stephen and Ralph White. *Resistance in Europe*, London: Allen Lane, 1975.

Heckmann, Wolf. *Rommel's War in Africa*, London: Granada Publishing, 1981.

Hehn, Paul N. *The German Struggle Against Yugoslavian Guerillas in World War Two*, New York: Columbia University, 1979.

Heike, Wolf-Dietrich. *Sie Wolten Die Freiheit: Der Geschichte der Ukrainischen Division*, Dorheim: Podzun Verlag, 1970.

Hesse, Erich. *Der Sowjetrussische Partisanenkrieg*, Göttingen Musterschmidt Verlag, 1969.

Hoehne, Heinz. *The Order of the Death's Head*, New York Coward, McCann and Geoghegan, 1970.

Hogan, George. *Malta: the Triumphant Years*, London: Hale, 1978

Holmes, Richard and Anthony Kemp. *The Bitter End: The Fall of Singapore*, Strettington: Bird.

Holmes, Richard. *Bir Hakim: Desert Citadel*, New York Ballantine, 1971.

Horrocks, Brian. *A Full Life*, London: Leo Cooper, 1974.

Hoxha, Enver. *History of the Party of Labour in Albania*, Tirana: Naim Frasheri, 1971.

Hoyt, Edwin P. *To the Marianas*, New York: Van Nostrand Reinholdt, 1980

Irving, David. *The Trail of the Fox: The Life of Field Marshal Erwin Rommel*, London: Weidenfeld and Nicolson, 1977.

— *The War Between the Generals*, London, Penguin, 1981.

Jackson, W. G. F. *The Battle for Italy*, London: B. T. Batsford, 1967.

— *Overlord: Normandy 1944*, London: Davis Poynter, 1978.

John, H. E. Pomersche Passion, Preetz, Holstein: Ernst Gerdes Verlag, 1964.

Kallay, Nicholas. *Hungarian Premier: A Personal Account*, New York Columbia University, 1954.

Kamenetsky, Ihor. *Hitler's Occupation of Ukraine*, Milwaukee Marquette University, 1956.

Kedward, H. R. *Fascism in Western Europe 1900-45*, Glasgow Blackie, 1969.

Keegan, John. *Waffen SS: The Asphalt Soldiers*, New York Ballantine, 1970.

Khrushchev, Nikita. *Khrushchev Remembers: The Last Testament*, London Andre Deutsch, 1974.

Klein, Harry. *Springboks in Armour*, South African National War Museum, MacMillan.

Klingamann, William K. *1941*, London, Harper and Row, 1988.

Knight, Freda. *The French Resistance*, London: Lawrence and Wishart, 1975.

Kohlhammer, W. *Geschichte der Polnischen Nation*, Stuttgart Gmb H, 1961.

Kolko, Gabriel. *The Politics of War: Allied Dilpomacy and the World Crisis 1943-45*, London: Weidenfeld and Nicolson, 1968.

Komjathy, Anthony and Rebecca Stockwell. *German Minorities and the Third Reich*, New York: Holmes and Meier, 1980.

Krejci, Jaroslav and Viteslav Velimsky. *Ethnic and Political Nations in Europe*, London: Croom Helm, 1981.

Lampe, David. *The Savage Canary*, London: Cassell, 1957.

Lass, Edgar Guenther. *Die Flucht: Ostpreussen 1944-45*, Bad Nauheim Podzun Verlag, 1964.

Lazzaro, Ricciotti. *Le SS Italiane*, Milan: Rizzoli Editore, 1982.

Lee, Ulysses. *Employment of Negro Troops*, Washington DC, Office of the Chief of Military History, 1966

Lenzi, Loris. *Dal Dnieper al Don: La 63a Legione C. C. N. N. Tagliamento Nella Campagna di Russia*, Rome: Volpe, 1972.

Levytsky, Boris. *The Uses of Terror: The Soviet Secret Service 1917-70*, London: Sidgwick and Jackson, 1971.

Lewin, Ronald. *Slim: the Standardbearer*, London: Leo Cooper, 1976.

Lindsay, Oliver. *At the Going Down of the Sun: Hong Kong and South East Asia*, London: Hamish Hamilton, 1981.

Littlejohn, David. *The Patriotic Traitors: A History of Collaborationism in German-Occupied Europe 1940-45*, London William Heinemann, 1972.

Long, Gavin. *MacArthur as Military Commander*, London: B. T. Batsford, 1969.

Longworth, Philip. *The Cossacks*, London: Constable, 1969.

Lucas, James. *War on the Eastern Front*, London: Janes, 1979.

Lucas, P. B. *Malta: the Thorn in Rommel's Side*, London, Stanley and Paul, 1992.

Lucas Phillips, C. E. *Alamein*, London: William Heinemann, 1973.

Maas, Walter B. *The Netherlands at War*, London: Abelard Schuman, 1970.

Macintyre, Donald. *The Battle for the Mediterranean*, London B. T. Batsford, 1964.

Macksay, Kenneth. *The Crucible of Power: The Fight for Tunisia*, London Hutchinson, 1969.

McKee, Alexander. *The Race for the Rhine Bridges*, London Pan Books, 1974.

Majdalany, Fred. *The Battle of Cassino*, London: Longman's Green, 1957.

Martin, David. *Patriot or Traitor? The Case of General Milhailovich*, Stanford University, 1978.

Mastny, Vojtech. *The Czechs Under Nazi Rule*, New York Columbia University, 1971.

Matley, Ian M. *Rumania: A Profile*, London: Pall Mall Press, 1970.

von Mellenthin, F. *Panzer Battles*, Norman: University of Oklahoma, 1956.

Messe, Giovanni. *Come fini la Guerra in Africa*, Milan Rizzoli, 1946.

Messe, Giovanni. *La Guerra al Fronte Russo*, Milan: Rizzoli, 1947.

Messenger, Charles. *The Tunisian Campaign*, London: Ian Allen, 1982.

Mikus, Joseph A. *Slovakia: A Political History*, Milwaukee Marquette University, 1963.

Milazzo, Matteo J. *The Cetnik Movement and the Yugoslavian Resistance*, Baltimore: Johns Hopkins University, 1975,

Miller, Marshal Lee. *Bulgaria during the Second World War*, Stanford University, 1975.

Mockler, Anthony. *Haile Selassie's War*, Oxford University, 1984.

Moller, Herbert: *Population Movements in Modern European History*, New York: MacMillan, 1964.

Mollo, Andrew. *The Armed Forces of World War Two*, London Orbis, 1981.

Montanari, Mario. *Le Operazione in Africa Settentionale*, Ufficio Storico SME, 1984.

Moorehead, Alan. *An African Trilogy*, London: Hamish Hamilton, 1944.

Moraes, J. *Brazil Exercito*, Washington DC: Department of Military History, 1966.

Morison, Samuel. *Battle of the Atlantic*, Boston: Little, Brown, 1947.

Morison, Samuel. *History of US Naval Operations in World War Two*, Boston: Little, Brown, 1957.

Morison, Samuel. *The Oxford History of the American People*, Oxford University, 1965.

Mountfield, David. *The Partisans: Secret Armies of World War Two*, London: Hamlyn, 1979.

Nekrich, Aleksandr M. *The Punished Peoples: The Deportation and Fate of Soviet Minorities at the End of the Second World War*, New York Norton, 1978.

Neumann, William L. *After Victory: Churchill, Roosevelt and Stalin and the Making of the Peace*, New York: Harper and Row, 1967.

O'Ballance, Edgar. *Greek Civil War*, London: Faber and Faber, 1968.

Oram, John. *The Giant Killers: The Story of the Danish Resistance*, London: Michael Joseph, 1975.

Petrow, Richard. *The Bitter Years: The Invasion and Occupation of Denmark and Norway*, London: Hodder & Stoughton, 1974.

Pitt, Barrie. *Churchill and the Generals*, London: Sidgwick and Jackson, 1981.

Pollo, Stefanaq and Arlsen Puto. *The History of Albania*, London Routledge and Kegan Paul, 1981.

Polonsky, Antony. *The Little Dictators*, London: Routledge and Kegan Paul, 1975.

Rhodes-Wood, E. H. *A War History of the Pioneer Corps*, Aldershot: Gale & Polden, 1960

Roberts, Walter R. *Tito, Milhailovich and the Allies*, New Brunswick, NJ: Rutgers University, 1973.

Robertson, John. *Australia at War*, Melbourne: William Heinemann, 1981

Rosignoli, Guido. *The Allied Forces in Italy*, Newton Abbot, Devon: David and Charles, 1989.

Roskill, S. W. *The War at Sea 1939-45*, London: HMSO 1961.

Schwarz, Urs. *The Eye of the Hurricane: Switzerland in World War Two*, Boulder, Col.: Westview, 1980

Scurr, John. *Germany's Spanish Volunteers*, London: Osprey, 1980.

Seaton, Albert. *The German Army 1933-45*, London: Weidenfeld and Nicolson, 1982.

Seaton, Albert. *The Russo-German War*, London: Arthur Barker, 1971.

von Senger und Etterlin, Fridolin. *Neither Fear, Nor Hope*, London MacDonald, 1963.

Serafis, Stefanos: *ELAS: Greek Partisan Army*, London Merlin, 1980.

Seton-Watson, Hugh. *The East European Revolution*, London Methuen, 1950.

Solzhenitsyn, Alexander. *The Gulag Archipelago*, London William Collins, 1974.

Steenbeek, Wilhelmina. *Rotterdam: Invasion of Holland*, New York Ballantine, 1973.

Stephan, John J. *The Russian Fascists*, London: Hamish Hamilton, 1978.

Strik-Strikfeldt, Wilfried. *Against Stalin and Hitler*, London MacMillan, 1970.

Swettenham, J. A. *The Tragedy of the Baltic States*, London Hollis and Carter, 1952.

Thomas, David A. *Japan's War at Sea*, London: Andre Deutsch, 1978.

Thomas, Hugh. *Armed Truce: the Beginnings of the Cold War*, London Hamish Hamilton, 1986.

Toland, John. *The Last One Hundred Days*, London: Arthur Barker, 1966.

Tolstoy, Nikolai. *Stalin's Secret War*, London: Johnathan Cape, 1981.

— *Victim's of Yalta*, London: Hodder & Stoughton, 1977.

Tulloch, Derek. *Wingate in Peace and War*, London: MacDonald, 1972.

Tys-Krokhmaliuk, Yuriy. *UPA Warfare in Ukraine*, New York Society of Veterans of the Ukrainian Insurgent Army, 1972.

Upton, Anthony F. *Finland 1939-40*, London: Davis-Poynter, 1974.

Vader, John. *New Guinea: the Tide is Stemmed*, New York Ballantine, 1971

Vakar, Nicholas P. *Belorussia: the Making of a Nation*, Harvard University, 1950.

Vardis, V. Stanley. *Lithuania Under the Soviets*, New York Lithuanian Association, 1965.

Vardis, V. Stanley and Romauld J. Misiunias. *The Baltic States in Peace and War*, Pennsylvania State University, 1978.

Villari, Luigi. *The Liberation of Italy*, Appleton, Wis.: C. C. Nelson, 1950.

Warner, Geoffrey. *Iraq and Syria 1941*, London Davis-Poynter, 1974.

Warner, Oliver. *Marshal Mannerheim and the Finns*, London Weidenfeld and Nicolson, 1960.

Willmott, H.P. *The Great Crusade*, London: Michael Joseph, 1989.

Windrow, Michael. *Waffen SS*, London: Orbis, 1982.

Woodhouse, C. M. *The Struggle for Greece 1941-49*, London Hart-Davis, McGibbon, 1976.

INDEX